T0214410

Communications
in Computer and Information Science 909

Commenced Publication in 2007
Founding and Former Series Editors:
Phoebe Chen, Alfredo Cuzzocrea, Xiaoyong Du, Orhun Kara, Ting Liu,
Dominik Ślęzak, and Xiaokang Yang

More information about this series at http://www.springer.com/series/7899

András Benczúr · Bernhard Thalheim
Tomáš Horváth · Silvia Chiusano
Tania Cerquitelli · Csaba Sidló
Peter Z. Revesz (Eds.)

New Trends in Databases and Information Systems

ADBIS 2018 Short Papers and Workshops
AI*QA, BIGPMED, CSACDB, M2U, BigDataMAPS, ISTREND, DC
Budapest, Hungary, September, 2–5, 2018
Proceedings

 Springer

Editors
András Benczúr [ID]
Eötvös Loránd University
Budapest
Hungary

Bernhard Thalheim
Abt. Informatik
Universität Kiel
Kiel
Germany

Tomáš Horváth
Eötvös Loránd University
Budapest
Hungary

Silvia Chiusano
Politecnico di Torino
Turin
Italy

Tania Cerquitelli
Polytechnic University of Turin
Turin
Italy

Csaba Sidló
Hungarian Academy of Sciences
Budapest
Hungary

Peter Z. Revesz
University of Nebraska–Lincoln
Lincoln, NE
USA

ISSN 1865-0929   ISSN 1865-0937 (electronic)
Communications in Computer and Information Science
ISBN 978-3-030-00062-2   ISBN 978-3-030-00063-9 (eBook)
https://doi.org/10.1007/978-3-030-00063-9

Library of Congress Control Number: 2018952648

This Springer imprint is published by the registered company Springer Nature Switzerland AG
The registered company address is: Gewerbestrasse 11, 6330 Cham, Switzerland

Leonid Andreevich Kalinichenko

10 June 1937 – 17 July 2018

One of the pioneers of the theory of databases passed away. The name of Leonid Andreevich is rightly associated with the development of promising directions in databases, the founding of an influential scientific school, the creation of two regularly held international scientific conferences. Leonid Andreevich Kalinichenko received his Ph.D. degree from the Institute of Cybernetics, Kiev, Ukraine, in 1968 and his degree of Doctor of Sciences from the Moscow State University in 1985. Both degrees in Computer Science.

He served as Head of the Laboratory for Compositional Information Systems Development Methods at the Institute of Informatics Problems of the Russian Academy of Science, Moscow. As Professor, he taught at the Moscow State University (Computer Science department) courses on distributed object technologies and object-oriented databases. His research interests included: interoperable heterogeneous information resource mediation, heterogeneous information resource integration, semantic interoperability, compositional development of information systems, middleware architectures, digital libraries.

His pioneering work on database model transformation (VLDB 1978) and fundamental book on data integration "Methods and tools for heterogeneous database integration" (Moscow, 1983) were ahead of time. His theoretical studies of semantic interoperability attracted attention of the international community in the 90s, when interoperability became a hot topic. He is also a co-author of the four books: "SLANG - programming system for discrete event system simulation" (Kiev, 1969), "Computers with advanced interpretation systems" (Kiev, 1970), "Computer networks" (Moscow, 1977), "Database and knowledge base machines" (Moscow, 1990). He had a number of papers in journals and conference proceedings and served as PC member for numerous international conferences.

During the last few years his activities and work were devoted to problems in data intensive domains. In 2013–2016 he initiated several research projects aiming at conceptual modeling and data integration within distributed computational infrastructures. He also launched a Master program "Big data: infrastructures and methods for problem solving" at Lomonosov Moscow State University.

In addition to his own research, Leonid spent significant energy on integration of database research communities in different countries. He had a key role in the organization of a series of East-West workshops (Klagenfurt and Moscow), as well as of the ADBIS series of international workshops held in Moscow in 1993–1996. This series of workshops was transformed into ADBIS (Advances in Data Bases and Information Systems) conference series. He also established the "Russian Conference on Digital Libraries" (RCDL) in 1999, transformed into "Data Analytics and Management in Data Intensive Domains" conference (DAMDID/RCDL) in 2015. Finally, he launched the Moscow Chapter of ACM SIGMOD in 1992. Monthly seminars of this chapter play significant role in shaping local research and professional communities in Russia.

L.A. Kalinichenko was a member of the ACM, the Chair of the Moscow ACM SIGMOD Chapter, the Chair of the Steering Committee of the European Conference "Advances in Databases and Information Systems" (ADBIS), the Chair of the Steering Committee of the Russian Conference on Digital Libraries (RCDL), a Member of the Editorial Board of the International Journal "Distributed and Parallel Databases", Kluwer Academic Publishers. All of us will remember him for what he did to build a wider community in Europe overcoming the divisions that had existed for decades. We, the members of the Steering Committee, remember him as a very generous person and an excellent scientist.

Paolo Atzeni
Ladjel Bellatreche
Andras Benczur
Maria Bielikova
Albertas Caplinskas
Barbara Catania
Johann Eder
Janis Grundspenkis
Hele-Mai Haav
Theo Haerder
Mirjana Ivanovic
Hannu Jaakkola
Marite Kirikova
Mikhail Kogalovsky
Margita Kon-Popovska
Yannis Manolopoulos

Rainer Manthey
Manuk Manukyan
Joris Mihaeli
Tadeusz Morzy
Pavol Navrat
Mykola Nikitchenko
Boris Novikov
Jaroslav Pokorny
Boris Rachev
Bernhard Thalheim
Gottfried Vossen
Tatjana Welzer
Viacheslav Wolfengagen
Robert Wrembel
Ester Zumpano

Preface

The 22nd East-European Conference on Advances in Databases and Information Systems (ADBIS 2018) took place in Budapest, Hungary, during September 2–5, 2018. The ADBIS series of conferences aims at providing a forum for the dissemination of research accomplishments and at promoting interaction and collaboration between the database and information systems research communities from Central and East European countries and the rest of the world. The ADBIS conferences provide an international platform for the presentation of research on database theory, development of advanced DBMS technologies, and their advanced applications. As such, ADBIS has created a tradition with editions held in St. Petersburg (1997), Poznań (1998), Maribor (1999), Prague (2000), Vilnius (2001), Bratislava (2002), Dresden (2003), Budapest (2004), Tallinn (2005), Thessaloniki (2006), Varna (2007), Pori (2008), Riga (2009), Novi Sad (2010), Vienna (2011), Poznań (2012), Genova (2013), Ohrid (2014), Poitiers (2015), Prague (2016), and Nicosia (2017). The conferences are initiated and supervised by an international Steering Committee consisting of representatives from Armenia, Austria, Bulgaria, Czech Republic, Cyprus, Estonia, Finland, France, Germany, Greece, Hungary, Israel, Italy, Latvia, Lithuania, FYR Macedonia, Poland, Russia, Serbia, Slovakia, Slovenia, and the Ukraine.

The program of ADBIS 2018 included keynotes, research papers, thematic workshops, and a doctoral consortium. The conference attracted 69 paper submissions from 46 countries from all continents. After rigorous reviewing by the Program Committee (102 reviewers and 14 subreviewers from 28 countries in the PC), the 17 papers included in the LNCS proceedings volume LNCS 11019 were accepted as full contributions, making an acceptance rate of 25 % for full papers and 41% in common. As a token of our appreciation of the longstanding, successful cooperation with ADBIS, Springer sponsored for ADBIS 2018 a best paper award. Furthermore, the Program Committee selected 11 more papers as short contributions.

This volume CCIS 909 contains short research papers, workshop papers, and doctoral consortium papers presented at ADBIS 2018.

The authors of the ADBIS papers are from 19 countries. The 6 workshop organizations acted on their own and accepted 24 papers for the BigDataMAPS, M2U, AI*QA, BIGPMED, and Current Trends in contemporary Information Systems and their Architectures (less than 50% acceptance rate of each workshop) workshops and 3 from the doctoral consortium. All papers were evaluated by at least three reviewers. A summary of the content of these workshops is included in this volume.

The selected short papers span a wide spectrum of topics in databases and related technologies, tackling challenging problems and presenting inventive and efficient solutions. These papers are organized according to the six workshops and the doctoral consortium: (1) Short Papers ADBIS 2018, (2) First International Workshop on Advances on Big Data Management, Analytics, Data Privacy and Security (BigDataMAPS 2018), (3) First International Workshop on New Frontiers on

Meta-data Management and Usage, M2U, (4) First Citizen Science Applications and Citizen Databases Workshop, CSADB, (5) First International Workshop on Artificial Intelligence for Question Answering, AI*QA, (6) First International Workshop on BIG Data Storage, Processing and Mining for Personalized MEDicine, BIGPMED, (7) First Workshop on Current Trends in Contemporary Information Systems and Their Architectures, ISTREND, and (8) Doctoral Consortium.

The ADBIS Doctoral Consortium (DC) 2018 was a forum where PhD students had a chance to present their research ideas to the database research community, receive inspiration from their peers and feedback from senior researchers, and tie cooperation bounds. DC papers are single-authored and aim at describing the current status of thesis research. Out of six submissions, the DC Committee selected three papers that were presented at the DC, giving an acceptance rate of 50%. Various topics were addressed, i.e., similarity queries, payload-based packet classification, and consistency mainte-nance. The DC chairs would like to thank the DC Program Committee members for their dedicated work.

The best papers of the main conference and workshops were invited to be submitted to special issues of the following journals: *Information Systems* and *Informatica*.

We would like to express our gratitude to every individual who contributed to the success of ADBIS 2018. Firstly, we thank all authors for submitting their research paper to the conference. However, we are also indebted to the members of the com-munity who offered their precious time and expertise in performing various roles ranging from organizational to reviewing roles—their efforts, energy, and degree of professionalism deserve the highest commendations. Special thanks goes to the Pro-gram Committee members and the external reviewers for their support in evaluating the papers submitted to ADBIS 2018 and the workshops, whereby ensuring the quality of the scientific program. Thanks also to all the colleagues, secretaries, and engineers involved in the conference and workshops organization, particularly Altagra Business Services and Travel Agency Ltd. for the endless help and support. A special thank you goes to the members of the Steering Committee, and in particular, its chair, Leonid Kalinichenko, and his co-chair, Yannis Manolopoulos, for all their help and guidance. Finally, we thank Springer for publishing the proceedings containing the research papers in the CCIS series. The Program Committee work relied on EasyChair, and we thank its development team for creating and maintaining the platform; it offered great support throughout the different phases of the reviewing process. The conference would not have been possible without our supporters and sponsors: Faculty of

Informatics of the Eötvös Loránd University, Pázmány-Eötvös Foundation, and ACM Hungarian Chapter.

July 2018

András Benczúr
Tomáš Horváth
Bernhard Thalheim
Silvia Chiusiano
Csaba Sidló
Tania Cerquitelli
Peter Revesz

Organization

Program Committee

Bernd Amann	Sorbonne University, France
Birger Andersson	Royal Institute of Technology, Sweden
Andreas Behrend	University of Bonn, Germany
Ladjel Bellatreche	LIAS/ENSMA, France
András Benczúr	Eötvös Loránd University, Hungary
András A. Benczúr	Institute for Computer Science and Control Hungarian Academy of Sciences (MTA SZTAKI), Hungary
Maria Bielikova	Slovak University of Technology in Bratislava, Slovakia
Zoran Bosnic	University of Ljubljana, Slovenia
Doulkifli Boukraa	Université de Jijel, Algeria
Drazen Brdjanin	University of Banja Luka, Bosnia and Herzegovina
Albertas Caplinskas	Vilnius University, Lithuania
Barbara Catania	DIBRIS University of Genova, Italy
Ajantha Dahanayake	Lappeenranta University of Technology, Finland
Christos Doulkeridis	University of Piraeus, Greece
Antje Düsterhöft-Raab	Hochschule Wismar, University of Applied Science, Germany
Johann Eder	Alpen Adria Universität Klagenfurt, Austria
Erki Eessaar	Tallinn University of Technology, Estonia
Markus Endres	University of Augsburg, Germany
Werner Esswein	TU Dresden, Germany
Georgios Evangelidis	University of Macedonia, Thessaloniki, Greece
Flavio Ferrarotti	Software Competence Centre Hagenberg, Austria
Peter Forbrig	University of Rostock, Germany
Flavius Frasincar	Erasmus University Rotterdam, The Netherlands
Jan Genci	Technical University of Kosice, Slovakia
Jānis Grabis	Riga Technical University, Latvia
Gunter Graefe	HTW Dresden, Germany
Francesco Guerra	Università di Modena e Reggio Emilia, Italy
Giancarlo Guizzardi	Federal University of Espirito Santo, Brazil
Peter Gursky	P. J. Safarik University, Slovakia
Hele-Mai Haav	Seniour Researcher, Institute of Cybernetics at Tallinn University of Technology, Estonia
Theo Härder	TU Kaiserslautern, Germany
Tomáš Horváth	Eötvös Loránd University, Hungary
Ekaterini Ioannou	Technical University of Crete, Greece
Márton Ispány	University of Debrecen, Hungary
Mirjana Ivanovic	University of Novi Sad, Serbia

Heri Ramampiaro	Norwegian University of Science and Technology, Norway
Karel Richta	Czech Technical University, Prague, Czech Republic
Stefano Rizzi	University of Bologna, Italy
Peter Ruppel	Technische Universität Berlin, Germany
Gunter Saake	University of Magdeburg, Germany
Petr Saloun	VSB-TU Ostrava, Czech Republic
Shiori Sasaki	Keio University, Japan
Kai-Uwe Sattler	TU Ilmenau, Germany
Milos Savic	Faculty of Science, University of Novi Sad, Serbia
Ingo Schmitt	Technical University of Cottbus, Germany
Timos Sellis	Swinburne University of Technology, Australia
Maxim Shishaev	IIMM, Kola Science Center RAS, Russia
Bela Stantic	Griffith University, Australia
Kostas Stefanidis	University of Tampere, Finland
Claudia Steinberger	Universität Klagenfurt, Austria
Sergey Stupnikov	Russian Academy of Sciences, Russia
James Terwilliger	Microsoft, USA
Bernhard Thalheim	Christian-Albrechts University, Kiel, Germany
Raquel Trillo-Lado	Universidad de Zaragoza, Spain
Olegas Vasilecas	Vilnius Gediminas Technical University, Lithuania
Goran Velinov	UKIM, Skopje, FYR Macedonia
Peter Vojtas	Charles University Prague, Czech Republic
Isabelle Wattiau	ESSEC and CNAM, France
Robert Wrembel	Poznan University of Technology, Poland
Weihai Yu	The Arctic University of Norway, Norway
Jaroslav Zendulka	Brno University of Technology, Czech Republic

Additional Reviewers

Irina Astrova, Estonia	Christos Mettouris, Cyprus
Dominik Bork, Austria	Patrick Schäfer, Germany
Antonio Corral, Spain	Jiří Šebek, Czech Republic
Senén González, Argentine	Jozef Tvarozek, Slovakia
Selma Khouri, Algeria	Theodoros Tzouramanis, Greece
Vimal Kunnummel, Austria	Goran Velinov, FYR Macedonia
Jevgeni Marenkov, Estonia	Alexandros Yeratziotis, Cyprus

Steering Committee

Chair

Leonid Kalinichenko   Russian Academy of Science, Russia

Co-chair

Yannis Manolopoulos   Aristotle University of Thessaloniki, Greece

Members

Paolo Atzeni   Università Roma Tre, Italy
Ladjel Bellatreche   LIAS/ENSMA, France
András Benczúr   Eötvös Loránd University, Hungary
Maria Bielikova   Slovak University of Technology in Bratislava, Slovakia
Albertas Caplinskas   Vilnius University, Lithuania
Barbara Catania   DIBRIS University of Genova, Italy
Johann Eder   Alpen Adria Universität Klagenfurt, Austria
Janis Grundspenkis   Riga Technical University, Latvia
Hele-Mai Haav   Tallinn University of Technology, Estonia
Theo Haerder   TU Kaiserslautern, Germany
Mirjana Ivanovic   University of Novi Sad, Serbia
Hannu Jaakkola   Tampere University of Technology, Finland
Leonid Kalinichenko   Institute of Informatics Problems of the Russian
                              Academy of Science, Russia
Marite Kirikova   Riga Technical University, Latvia
Mikhail Kogalovsky   Market Economy Institute of the Russian Academy
                              of Sciences, Russia

Margita Kon-Popovska   SS. Cyril and Methodius University Skopje, Macedonia
Yannis Manopoulos   Aristotle University of Thessaloniki, Greece
Rainer Manthey   University of Bonn, Germany
Manuk Manukyan   Yerevan State University, Armenia
Joris Mihaeli   Israel
Tadeusz Morzy   Poznan University of Technology, Poland
Pavol Navrat   Slovak University of Technology, Slovakia
Boris Novikov   St. Petersburg University, Russia
Mykola Nikitchenko   Kyiv National Taras Shevchenko University, Ukraine
Jaroslav Pokorny   Charles University in Prague, Czech Republic
Boris Rachev   Technical University of Varna, Bulgaria
Bernhard Thalheim   Christian Albrechts University, Kiel, Germany
Gottfried Vossen   University of Münster, Germany
Tatjana Welzer   University of Maribor, Slovenia
Viacheslav Wolfengangen   Russia
Robert Wrembel   Poznan University of Technology, Poland
Ester Zumpano   University of Calabria, Italy

General Chair

András Benczúr   Eötvös Loránd University, Budapest, Hungary

Program Chairs

Tomáš Horváth   Eötvös Loránd University, Budapest, Hungary
Bernhard Thalheim   University of Kiel, Germany

Proceedings Chair

Bálint Molnár   Eötvös Loránd University, Budapest, Hungary

Workshops Chairs

Silvia Chiusiano   Politecnico di Torino, Italy
Csaba Sildó   SZTAKI (Institute for Computer Science and Control,
                             Hungarian Academy of Sciences), Budapest, Hungary
Tania Cerquitelli   Politecnico di Torino, Italy

Doctoral Consortium Chairs

Michal Kopman   Slovak University of Technology in Bratislava, Slovakia
Peter Z. Revesz   University of Nebraska-Lincoln, USA
Sándor Laki   Eötvös Loránd University, Budapest, Hungary

Organizing Committee

András Benczúr   Eötvös Loránd University, Budapest, Hungary
Tomáš Horváth   Eötvös Loránd University, Budapest, Hungary
Bálint Molnár   Eötvös Loránd University, Budapest, Hungary
Anikó Csizmazia   Eötvös Loránd University, Budapest, Hungary
Renáta Fóris   Eötvös Loránd University, Budapest, Hungary
Ágnes Kerek   Eötvös Loránd University, Budapest, Hungary
Gusztáv Hencsey   Hungarian Academy of Sciences, Institute for Computer
                             Science and Control, Budapest, Hungary
Klára Biszkupné-Nánási   Altagra Business Services and Travel Agency Ltd.,
                             Gödöllő, Hungary
Miklós Biszkup   Altagra Business Services and Travel Agency Ltd.,
                             Gödöllő, Hungary
Judit Juhász   Altagra Business Services and Travel Agency Ltd.,
                             Gödöllő, Hungary

Workshops

First International Workshop on Advances on Big Data Management, Analytics, Data Privacy and Security, BigDataMAPS

Program Chairs

Jérôme Darmont — Université de Lyon, France
Nadia Kabachi — Université de Lyon, France
Ilaria Matteucci — Istituto di Informatica e Telematica, Consiglio Nazionale delle Ricerche, Italy
Marinella Petrocchi — Istituto di Informatica e Telematica, Consiglio Nazionale delle Ricerche, Italy
Angelo Spognardi — Sapienza Universitá di Roma, Italy

First International Workshop on New Frontiers on Metadata Management and Usage, M2U

Program Chairs

Claudia Diamantini — Università Politecnica delle Marche, Italy
Domenico Ursino — Università Politecnica delle Marche, Italy
Sham Navathe — Georgia Institute of Technology, USA

First Citizen Science Applications and Citizen Databases Workshop, CSADB

Program Chairs

Ajantha Dahanayake — Lappeenranta University of Technology, Finland
Bernhard Thalheim — Christian-Albrechts University zu Kiel, Germany

First International Workshop on Artificial Intelligence for Question Answering, AI*QA 2018

Program Chairs

Ermelinda Oro   National Research Council, Italy
Massimo Ruffolo   National Research Council, Italy
Eduardo Fermè   University of Madeira, Portugal

First International Workshop on BIG Data Storage, Processing and Mining for Personalized MEDicine, BIGPMED

Program Chairs

Fabio Fassetti   University of Calabria, Italy
Simona E. Rombo   University of Palermo, Italy

First Workshop on Current Trends in Contemporary Information Systems and Their Architectures, ISTREND

Program Chairs

Bálint Molnár   Eötvös Loránd University, Hungary
Udo Bub   Eötvös Loránd University, Hungary

Contents

Short Papers ADBIS 2018

Extracting Format Transformation Examples from Manual Data Corrections . . .   3
  Nurzety A. Azuan, Suzanne M. Embury, and Norman W. Paton

Towards Service Orchestration in XML Filtering Overlays   12
  Kirill Belyaev and Indrakshi Ray

Real-Time Skyline Computation on Data Streams   20
  Lena Rudenko and Markus Endres

Statistical Data Generation Using Sample Data   29
  Bálint Fazekas and Attila Kiss

EthernityDB – Integrating Database Functionality into a Blockchain   37
  Sven Helmer, Matteo Roggia, Nabil El Ioini, and Claus Pahl

LOD Query-Logs as an Asset for Multidimensional Modeling   45
  Selma Khouri and Ladjel Bellatreche

Parallelization of XPath Queries Using Modern XQuery Processors   54
  Shigeyuki Sato, Wei Hao, and Kiminori Matsuzaki

Towards Detection of Usability Issues by Measuring Emotions   63
  Elena Stefancova, Robert Moro, and Maria Bielikova

Personal Names Popularity Estimation and Its Application
to Record Linkage   71
  Ksenia Zhagorina, Pavel Braslavski, and Vladimir Gusev

Streaming FDR Calculation for Protein Identification   80
  Roman Zoun, Kay Schallert, Atin Janki, Rohith Ravindran,
  Gabriel Campero Durand, Wolfram Fenske, David Broneske,
  Robert Heyer, Dirk Benndorf, and Gunter Saake

ADBIS 2018 Workshops

Contributions from ADBIS 2018 Workshops   91
  Udo Bub, Ajantha Dahanayake, Jérôme Darmont, Claudia Diamantini,
  Fabio Fassetti, Eduardo Fermé, Nadia Kabachi, Ilaria Matteucci,
  Bálint Molnár, Sham Navathe, Ermelinda Oro, Marinella Petrocchi,
  Simona E. Rombo, Massimo Ruffolo, Angelo Spognardi,
  Bernhard Thalheim, and Domenico Ursino

First International Workshop on Advances on Big Data Management, Analytics, Data Privacy and Security, BigDataMAPS 2018

Online Testing of User Profile Resilience Against Inference Attacks
in Social Networks   105
    Younes Abid, Abdessamad Imine, and Michaël Rusinowitch

Towards Personal Data Identification and Anonymization
Using Machine Learning Techniques   118
    Francesco Di Cerbo and Slim Trabelsi

Personalised Privacy Policies   127
    Harshvardhan Jitendra Pandit, Declan O'Sullivan, and Dave Lewis

Black-Box Model Explained Through an Assessment
of Its Interpretable Features   138
    Francesco Ventura, Tania Cerquitelli, and Francesco Giacalone

First International Workshop on New Frontiers on Metadata Management and Usage, M2U

How Metadata Can Support the Study of Neurological Disorders:
An Application to the Alzheimer's Disease   153
    Francesco Cauteruccio and Giorgio Terracina

A New Metadata Model to Uniformly Handle Heterogeneous Data
Lake Sources   165
    Claudia Diamantini, Paolo Lo Giudice, Lorenzo Musarella,
    Domenico Potena, Emanuele Storti, and Domenico Ursino

Comparing SLAs for Cloud Services: A Model for Reasoning   178
    Antonella Longo, Domenico Potena, Emanuele Storti, Marco Zappatore,
    and Andrea De Matteis

Automatic Extraction of Affective Metadata from Videos Through Emotion
Recognition Algorithms   191
    Alex Mircoli and Giampiero Cimini

Citizen Science Applications and Citizen Databases Workshop, CSADB

Characterizing Air-Quality Data Through Unsupervised Analytics Methods   205
    Elena Daraio, Evelina Di Corso, Tania Cerquitelli, and Silvia Chiusano

Missing Data Analysis in Emotion Recognition for Smart Applications   218
    Andrei Gorbulin, Ajantha Dahanayake, and Tatiana Zudilova

Overview of Data Storing Techniques in Citizen Science Applications.   231
    Jiri Musto and Ajantha Dahanayake

Data Provenance in Citizen Science Databases   242
    Nikita Tiufiakov, Ajantha Dahanayake, and Tatiana Zudilova

Internet of Things: Trends, Challenges and Opportunities.   254
    Marina Tropmann-Frick

First International Workshop on Artificial Intelligence for
Question Answering, AI*QA

Analysis of Why-Type Questions for the Question Answering System.   265
    Manvi Breja and Sanjay Kumar Jain

Towards Multilingual Neural Question Answering.   274
    Ekaterina Loginova, Stalin Varanasi, and Günter Neumann

Knowledge Base Relation Detection via Multi-View Matching   286
    Yang Yu, Kazi Saidul Hasan, Mo Yu, Wei Zhang, and Zhiguo Wang

First International Workshop on BIG Data Storage,
Processing and Mining for Personalized MEDicine, BIGPMED

Software Tools for Medical Imaging Extended Abstract.   297
    Luciano Caroprese, Pietro Lucio Cascini, Pietro Cinaglia,
    Francesco Dattola, Pasquale Franco, Pasquale Iaquinta, Miriam Iusi,
    Giuseppe Tradigo, Pierangelo Veltri, and Ester Zumpano

Humanity Is Overrated. or Not. Automatic Diagnostic Suggestions
by Greg, ML (Extended Abstract).   305
    Paola Lapadula, Giansalvatore Mecca, Donatello Santoro,
    Luisa Solimando, and Enzo Veltri

Variable Ranking Feature Selection for the Identification of Nucleosome
Related Sequences.   314
    Giosué Lo Bosco, Riccardo Rizzo, Antonino Fiannaca,
    Massimo La Rosa, and Alfonso Urso

First Workshop on Current Trends in Contemporary
Information Systems and Their Architectures, ISTREND 2018

Towards an Integrated Method for the Engineering of Digital Innovation
and Design Science Research   327
    Udo Bub

A Data-Driven Framework for Business Analytics in the Context
of Big Data 339
   Jing Lu

An Industrial Application Using Process Mining to Reduce the Number
of Faulty Products. 352
   Zsuzsanna Nagy, Ágnes Werner-Stark, and Tibor Dulai

Towards a Hypergraph-Based Formalism for Enterprise Architecture
Representation to Lead Digital Transformation 364
   Bálint Molnár and Dóra Őri

EAM Based Approach to Support IT Planning for Digital Transformation
in Public Organizations 377
   Dóra Őri and Zoltán Szabó

Doctoral Consortium

Similarity Queries on Script Image Databases. 391
   Shruti Daggumati

Payload-Based Packet Classification and Its Applications
in Packet Forwarding Pipeline 402
   Mohammed Fekhreddine Seridi

Consistency Maintenance in Distributed Analytical Stream Processing 413
   Artem Trofimov

Author Index 423

Short Papers ADBIS 2018

Extracting Format Transformation Examples from Manual Data Corrections

Nurzety A. Azuan(✉), Suzanne M. Embury, and Norman W. Paton

School of Computer Science, University of Manchester, M13 9PL, Manchester, UK
{nurzetybintiahmadazuan,suzanne.embury,norman.paton}@manchester.ac.uk

Abstract. One of the challenges in data analysis is the substantial cost of human involvement. Before any analysis can take place, data from heterogeneous sources must be cleaned, integrated and transformed into a uniform format. These tasks often require both technical skill *and* domain expertise. Current tools support data scientists by allowing them to define rules to carry out the preparation work, but the problem of the manual work needed to create such rules remains. We propose an approach that observes the updates made by data scientists when manually correcting errors in query results, and uses them to derive format transformation rules that can be applied to this and future query results.

Keywords: Data wrangling · Format transformation
Data integration · User feedback · Implicit feedback

1 Introduction

In data wrangling, data scientists take a data set needed for some analysis task, and spend substantial amounts of time diagnosing, tweaking and manually configuring the data into the form required [1,2]. A common data wrangling task is *format transformation*, which causes values to have consistent representations across columns or data types. For example, our software may expect names in the form *initial, dot, surname* (as in *B. Obama*), but the data supplied may have values in other forms *Barack Obama* and *Barack Hussein Obama*.

Recent research has proposed tools to support format transformation. These tools aim to automate some part of the manual work involved in the writing of data transformation rules. For instance, FlashFill [3], a data transformation technique available in Microsoft Excel, uses programming-by-example to transform data automatically once the data scientist has supplied several example of before-and-after value pairs representing the format transformations required. Another example is the Wrangler tool [4], a visual programming system that combines data visualization with inference of candidate transformations.

Tools like these reduce the cost of transforming data to their required format, but don't completely remove the need for iterative manual work. However, consider the case when a data scientist is under pressure to produce good quality

© Springer Nature Switzerland AG 2018
A. Benczúr et al. (Eds.): ADBIS 2018, CCIS 909, pp. 3–11, 2018.
https://doi.org/10.1007/978-3-030-00063-9_1

data for a deadline. In such circumstances, data scientists are likely to do what users of data have always done: they will take the best data the tools can provide them with, copy them into some convenient tool (such as Excel), and manually fix the remaining problems they can see. This gets the job done, but is also a missed opportunity since much of this manual work will need to be repeated the next time a similar dataset is encountered by this or another user. This means that the learning opportunity for the wrangling tool is lost. The manual corrections performed by the data scientist are a valuable form of feedback, which can be used to incrementally increase automation of the wrangling process.

This paper explores the possibility of extracting format transformation rules from examples derived from manual corrections, building on our earlier work on inferring true and false positive feedback on tuples within a result set from manual corrections [5]. The aim is not to reduce the work for data scientists on their first encounter with a data set or data type, but to gather information from that work that can be used to reduce the manual effort needed for future analysis tasks. The question we set out to answer in this paper is: *can format transformation examples suitable for learning useful transformation rules be extracted from manual data corrections?* Specifically, we wanted to see if we could use manual corrections as a source of training examples for FlashFill [3], instead of requiring the user to provide examples explicitly.

The paper is organized as follows: Sect. 2 describes existing work on examples for format transformation and on user feedback for data cleaning. An overview of the proposed approach is given in Sect. 3, while Sect. 4 describes how examples are derived from manual data corrections. The evaluation of the work is presented in Sect. 5, followed by conclusions in Sect. 6.

2   Related Work

Surveys have established that data scientists typically spend up to 80% of their time on data preparation[1]. In this section, we review proposals for supporting this data cleaning process, focusing primarily on user involvement in data transformation. An important body of work in this respect involves Potter's Wheel [6] and its successor Wrangler [4]. Potter's Wheel is a menu-based system that allows users to construct sequences of data transformation operations on a subset of data, which can then be applied to the rest of the data or to future data. Building on the transformation language of Potter's Wheel, Wrangler is an interactive data cleaning system that can suggest candidate transformations to the user through an automatic inference mechanism. Wrangler seeks to reduce the time taken to specify data transformation rules using a learning-based approach and predictive model [7]. A similar tool is OpenRefine [8], which allows a user to state their intended result graphically, although most of the user's intention still needs to be expressed through a command language.

---

[1] https://www.forbes.com/sites/gilpress/2016/03/23/data-preparation-most-time-consuming-least-enjoyable-data-science-task-survey-says/#33d344256f63.

Another approach to data transformation builds on programming-by-example (PBE), as in the case of FlashFill [3], which learns syntactic string transformation programs from input-output example pairs provided by the user. Because FlashFill operates only on the given examples, they must cover the space of relevant cases to obtain a good result. Various extensions to FlashFill have been developed, for example to allow it to use supplementary data as well as data examples [9], and to support a wider range of structure transformations [10]. Wu *et al.* showed how to obtain strong conditional statements for data transformations by requiring users to examine incorrect as well as correct records, thus obtaining both positive and negative examples [11].

Another approach that seeks to reduce the cost of data format transformation is proposed by Bogatu *et al.* [12]. In this approach, FlashFill is used for transformation rule synthesis, but examples are obtained from existing data sets. Although the approach requires no user involvement, and thus is in contrast with our work, the goal is the same: to reduce the time and effort spent by the data scientist during the data transformation process.

Proposals for the use of feedback to support data repair (rather than format transformation) include KATARA [13], an end-to-end data cleaning system that uses crowd-sourcing to collect user feedback, and Guided Data Repair [14], a system based on active learning that acquires user feedback through an iterative process. Both KATARA and Guided Data Repair involve explicit feedback collection, and thus require valuable human effort.

3   Learning Transformations from Data Corrections

We propose to extract examples for learning format transformation rules implicitly from corrections made by data scientists on data sets. The system we have built is called *ManED* (short for "manual edits to data"). Our working scenario involves a data scientist is working on a data set to prepare it for use in some analysis task. She first uses a tool to extract the data set resulting from her query. She examines the query results using some preferred editor and fixes errors where she sees them. This might involve changing the format of some of the values, to bring them into line with the formats used by other data sets involved in the analysis, for example. Other rows she leaves unchanged (even though they may not be in the desired format). At this point, she submits the two versions of the data set (the original and the corrected ones) to ManED.

Figure 1 shows the architecture of the tool: a pipeline of 3 components. The first component examines the two versions of the data and generates a set of before-and-after examples pairs for each column. These examples are passed to an implementation of the Flashfill algorithm.[2] It learns a transformation rule from the generated examples for each column, and passes them all to the Rule Validator component. Because, in general, the Example Generator component will only been able to guess at a suitable set of examples, the rules learnt by

---

[2] We use the implementation by Wu and Knoblock [11].

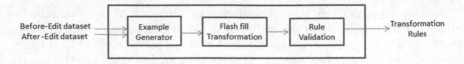

Fig. 1. Basic framework of manual correction transformation (ManEd)

the Flashfill component may be incorrect. This final component has the task of checking that the rules seem sensible. Only rules that pass the checks are output.

The rules learnt in this way can be applied to the entire data set, to correct the format of rows the data scientist has not explicitly corrected herself. Or they can be passed to a data integration tool, to be stored for use on later data sets.

4   Generating Format Transformation Examples

Although it may seem trivial to generate examples from data corrections, in general the situation can be complicated. Data sets may be large and the data scientist may only be able to correct a sample of the rows. She may also need to correct errors in the data that are unrelated to the format or add missing elements. It is even possible that errors may be introduced during manual editing, or that inconsistent formats may be used for different parts of the data. All these factors complicate the task of example generation in ManED.

4.1   Example Pair Generation Strategies

We propose three example pair generation strategies: null filtering, edited value filtering and augmented edited value filtering. Each takes a list of the full before/after value pairs from the data set versions supplied by the user and outputs a set of example pairs to be used in learning format transformation rules. We assume that the data set has a set of key columns that can allow us to find corresponding rows in the before-edit and after-edit versions, even if the after-edit version has been reordered before saving. To simplify the presentation, we assume that we are working with the contents of a single non-key column.

Null Filtering (Baseline). The first and simplest strategy is proposed only as a baseline case, for assessing the performance of the other strategies. In it, we use all before/after pairs as examples, whether they were edited or not. This increases the chance that our set of example pairs includes at least one of each representative case of the format transformation desired - a property that is known to be important if Flashfill is to produce reliable rules. For example, when transforming name data, we would need examples of the before and after versions for names with double-barrelled surnames or prefixes. Of course, this strategy also has the serious disadvantage that it will likely include incorrectly formatted values as well, making it difficult to learn an accurate rule.

The following table shows (in the Example Pair column) the pairs that would be sent to the Flashfill Rule Learner component by ManEd using this strategy.

In this case, the user has only corrected a sample of the rows (all rows except 3 and 6), but all are used to create an example pair to pass to the rule learner.

Row	Before-edit value	After-edit value	Example pair	Transformed result
1	Ben Kenyon	B. Kenyon	Ben Kenyon, B. Kenyon	
2	Gina O'Connor	G. O'Connor	Gina O'Connor, G. O'Connor	
3	Branwen Hywel	Branwen Hywel	Branwen Hywel, Branwen Hywel	Branwen Hywel
4	A K Perks	A. Perks	A K Perks, A. Perks	A. Perks
5	E Davidson	E. Davidson	E Davidson, E. Davidson	

The final column (labelled Transformed Result) shows what result we get if we allow Flashfill to learn a transformation rule from these examples, and then apply the rule to the values in the version of the data set that has been manually corrected. We can see that the learnt rule manages to transform only Row 4 correctly Row 3 (unsurprisingly) retains its original incorrectly formatted value, while rows 1, 2 and 5 were transformed to an empty string. Generally, Flashfill returns an empty string because the learnt rule does not cover all allowable cases.

Edited Value Filtering. In this strategy, we lean on the domain expertise of the data scientist, and assume that all values that have been edited by the user are now correctly formatted. Thus, we create example pairs only from rows where there is a difference in the value before editing and after. The table below illustrates how this strategy works on our running example:

Rows	Before-edit value	After-edit value	Example pair	Transformed result
1	Ben Kenyon	B. Kenyon	Ben Kenyon, B. Kenyon	
2	Gina O'Connor	G. O'Connor	Gina O'Connor, G. O'Connor	
3	Branwen Hywel	Branwen Hywel		B. Hywel
4	A K Perks	A. Perks	A K Perks, A. Perk	
5	E Davidson	E. Davidson	E Davidson, E. Davidson	

This strategy produces fewer examples than the previous one. This means that fewer incorrect example are used for learning the rules but, where data sets are large and only a sample of rows can be corrected, we will have the disadvantage that some representative cases may not be included. We can see from this small example (where most of the rows have been edited) that the rule learnt from by this strategy can correct the formatting of the unedited row (row 3).

Augmented Edited Value Filtering. Early trials of Edited Value Filtering revealed an interesting feature of the learnt rules. They performed well on incorrectly formatted results but performed poorly when asked to transform correctly formatted values (converting them to empty strings). We hypothesise that this was because we were not providing Flashfill with examples showing that correctly formatted values needed to retain their formatting. To address this, we propose a third strategy that extends Edited Value Filtering. It creates two examples from every edited row in the data set: one example contains the before and after values, while the second pair consists of the after value being transformed to the after value. This means that the Rule Learner is given examples of how to correct the formatting of incorrect examples and of how to retain the formatting of examples that are already correct.

The table below shows the example pairs generated when this strategy is used on our running example. We can see that the learnt rule behaves much better than the others (on this small example, at least).

Rows	Before-edit	After-edit	Example pair	Transformed result
1	Ben Kenyon	B. Kenyon	Ben Kenyon, B.Kenyon B. Kenyon, B. Kenyon	B. Kenyon
2	Gina O'Connor	G. O'Connor	Gina O'Connor, G. O'Connor G. O'Connor, G. O'Connor	G. O'Connor
3	Branwen Hywel	Branwen Hywel	Branwen Hywel	B. Hywel
4	A K Perks	A. Perks	A K Perks, A. Perks A. Perks, A. Perks	A. Perks
5	E Davidson	E. Davidson	E Davidson, E. Davidson E. Davidson, E. Davidson	E. Davidson

5   Evaluation of the Strategies

5.1   Experimental Harness

We wanted to learn whether our strategies for inferring examples from manually corrected data lead to accurate transformation rules being learnt by Flashfill, and how they performed with respect to one other. We therefore created an experimental harness that allowed us to assess the accuracy of the learnt rules with respect to "ground truth" format rules. Our harness achieves this by mimicking some of the actions that would be taken by a data scientist using ManED. It requires a seed data set containing format inconsistencies to be provided, along with a version of the same data with consistent formats (manually created by the harness user). We refer to this latter version as the *formatted seed data set*. Both data set versions are loaded into a PostgresSQL database, for easy access.

Next, the harness uses the seed data to create the data sets that will be given as input to ManED: the original version of the data that the data scientist sees, and the version with corrections to selected rows. The harness user can set: the size of the *before data set* (in rows, up to the size of the *seed data set*); the proportion of rows in this set that will be modified in the *after data set*, and the proportion of modifications that match the ground truth. The harness creates the *before-edit* data set by taking a sample of rows from the *seed data set*. It then creates the *after-edit* data set by selecting at random the rows that will be modified correctly and those that will be modified incorrectly. For the former, values are taken from the equivalent rows in the *formatted seed data set*, while for the latter, values are created by changing characters at random in the original seed data. Both the generated *before-edit* and the *after-edit* datasets are then passed on to ManED, which attempts to learn a format transformation rule from the corrections injected by the experimental harness.

Finally, the harness needs to determine how closely rules learnt by ManED matche the ground truth. Because Flashfill rules are highly procedural in form, it would be challenging to compare them statically. Instead, we opt for the conceptually simpler approach of assessing how correctly they transform a second data set, selected by the harness at random from the *seed data set*. The harness applies the learnt rule to the column on interest in this new data set, and then compares the result in each row with the same column value in the corresponding row of the *formatted seed data set*. We count up the number of correctly and incorrectly transformed values, to give precision and recall scores for the rule.

5.2 Experimental Setup

Our aim was to assess the relative performance of our three example generation strategies in inferring examples for use by Flashfill. We predicted that the *augmented edited value filtering* strategy would perform best, with the *null filtering* strategy performing worst. We based our experiment around a scenario in which primary school performance around the United Kingdom is analysed based on publicly available data, and in which there is a need to integrate headteacher information from different sources. We used school information from an open government dataset[3] to seed the experimental harness.

The data set we are using contains names in a wide variety of formats. We manually created a consistently formatted version of the data set, using an *initial, full stop, space, capitalised surname* format. We set the harness to work with two sizes of data set: 20 rows and 40 rows. The harness created 5 data sets of each size, cumulatively increasing the proportion of correctly formatted values by 5% and the proportion of manually corrected rows by 10%. The generated data set versions are then passed to ManED, which generates a transformation rule. The harness calculates the average score for each rule from the 10 runs of the experiment for each set of parameters.

5.3 Results

The results are shown in Fig. 2. We found that Edited Value Filtering performs surprisingly poorly across all data sets and actually decreases in performance as the proportion of corrected rows increases. This is because, when the transformation rule produced is applied to the *after-edit* dataset, a significant proportion of the edited values were transformed to the empty string. More edited rows means more wrongly transformed values. However, the *Augmented Edited Value*

---

[3] https://data.gov.uk.

Filtering strategy shows much better results, across all the data sets, including an improved transformation result with increasing manual corrections.

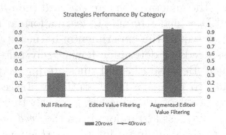

Fig. 2. Results by individual strategy and dataset category

6   Conclusion

We have presented an approach to extracting example pairs for learning format transformations from manual correction to data. The approach generates pairs of before/after values from the corrections made to the data by the data scientist, using three different strategies. It then uses an implementation of the Flashfill algorithm to learn transformation rules from the examples. We found that the *augmented edited value filtering* strategy gave the best results. For future work, we aim to understand how this approach can be applied across multiple columns, taking account of corrections made by data scientists over multiple interactions with the data set and will look at combining corrections from multiple data scientists working on the same type of data.

References

1. Kandel, S., et al.: Research directions in data wrangling: visualizations and transformations for usable and credible data. Inf. Vis. **10**(4), 271–288 (2011)
2. Chessell, M., Scheepers, F., Nguyen, N., van Kessel, R., van der Starre, R.: Governing and managing big data for analytics and decision makers. IBM Redguides for Business Leaders (2014)
3. Gulwani, S.: Automating string processing in spreadsheets using input-output examples. In: Proceedings of 38th Annual ACM SIGPLAN-SIGACT Symposium on Principles of Programming Languages, POPL 2011, pp. 317–330. ACM (2011)
4. Kandel, S., Paepcke, A., Hellerstein, J., Heer, J.: Wrangler: interactive visual specification of data transformation scripts. In: Proceedings of the SIGCHI Conference on Human Factors in Computing Systems, CHI 2011, pp. 3363–3372. ACM (2011)
5. Azuan, N.A., Embury, S.M., Paton, N.W.: Observing the data scientist: using manual corrections as implicit feedback. In: Proceedings of 2nd Workshop on Human-in-the-Loop Data Analytics, HILDA 2017, pp. 13:1–13:6. ACM (2017)
6. Raman, V., Hellerstein, J.M.: Potter's wheel: an interactive data cleaning system. VLDB **1**, 381–390 (2001)

7. Heer, J., Hellerstein, J.M., Kandel, S.: Predictive interaction for data transformation. In: CIDR (2015)
8. Verborgh, R., De Wilde, M.: Using OpenRefine. Packt Publishing Ltd (2013)
9. Singh, R., Gulwani, S.: Transforming spreadsheet data types using examples. In: Proceedings of 43rd Annual ACM SIGPLAN-SIGACT Symposium on Principles of Programming Languages, St. Petersburg, FL, USA, pp. 343–356 (2016)
10. Harris, W.R., Gulwani, S.: Spreadsheet table transformations from examples. In: Proceedings of 32nd ACM SIGPLAN Conference on Programming Language Design and Implementation, San Jose, CA, USA, pp. 317–328, June 2011
11. Wu, B., Knoblock, C.A.: Maximizing correctness with minimal user effort to learn data transformations. In: Proceedings of 21st International Conference on Intelligent User Interfaces, IUI 2016, pp. 375–384. ACM (2016)
12. Bogatu, A., Paton, N.W., Fernandes, A.A.A.: Towards automatic data format transformations: data wrangling at scale. In: Calì, A., Wood, P., Martin, N., Poulovassilis, A. (eds.) BICOD 2017. LNCS, vol. 10365, pp. 36–48. Springer, Cham (2017). https://doi.org/10.1007/978-3-319-60795-5_4
13. Chu, X., et al.: KATARA: reliable data cleaning with knowledge bases and crowdsourcing. Proc. VLDB Endowment 8(12), 1952–1955 (2015)
14. Yakout, M., Elmagarmid, A.K., Neville, J., Ouzzani, M., Ilyas, I.F.: Guided data repair. Proc. VLDB Endowment 4(5), 279–289 (2011)

Towards Service Orchestration in XML Filtering Overlays

Kirill Belyaev[✉] and Indrakshi Ray

Computer Science Department, Colorado State University, Fort Collins, USA
kirill.belyaev@outlook.com,Indrakshi.Ray@colostate.edu

Abstract. Various types of applications and services generate vast amounts of XML data feeds that may be streamed in near real time to different subscribing endpoints in order to take actions in a timely manner. In an earlier work we proposed an XML overlay network comprised of brokers that can be configured for efficient XML message filtering and replication with concurrent subscribers. The selective filtering reduces the bandwidth consumption of the network and also provides applications with data on a need-to-know basis. In our current work we propose the improvement upon original architecture through addition of service orchestration features to individual broker nodes. The filtering overlay network can be orchestrated to update service properties on individual filtering nodes. We provide a preliminary implementation to demonstrate the feasibility of our approach.

Keywords: XML overlays · Content-based publish/subscribe · Service orchestration

1 Introduction

Various types of applications and services generate vast amounts of unstructured data feeds that may be streamed in near real time to different subscribing endpoints [2,3]. Some services generate data in XML so that it can be easily distributed to other applications by operational runtime environments [2,9]. Unstructured data transport using JSON or XML remains a convenient communication exchange format [2,7,11] in spite of its heavy network bandwidth utilization. XML-based data dissemination networks are starting to become a reality [9]. Therefore, data represented in XML format may be disseminated and filtered prior to consumption by the subscribing applications and services. Some applications focus on processing of relatively small XML messages, where they only require specific elements to be extracted from individual document message [6,12]. Other applications and services may require the contents of entire XML document [2,3,9]. Such XML messages may be arriving rapidly and have to be delivered to large number of interested subscribers. Individual XML messages must be filtered based on content and delivered to end-point applications which get only the relevant messages.

© Springer Nature Switzerland AG 2018
A. Benczúr et al. (Eds.): ADBIS 2018, CCIS 909, pp. 12–19, 2018.
https://doi.org/10.1007/978-3-030-00063-9_2

Towards this end, we introduced the TeleScope XML filtering broker to carry out the selective dissemination of complete XML messages to consuming end-points via content filtering [2]. The brokers can be connected into a filtering overlay network that comprises a set of TeleScope nodes organized in the form of a partial mesh for selective dissemination to the end-points. The filtering capabilities are provided by a simple domain specific language that supports Boolean logic operators but does not require knowledge of complex and structure-oriented XPath/XQuery [4] expressions [2,3,10].

Although individual TeleScope XML filtering broker has a number of desirable features, we lack the mechanism to orchestrate the filtering service across the nodes of our filtering overlay. Specifically, filtering queries on individual nodes currently have to be changed and reset manually. TeleScope nodes are also not able to perform alternative routing subscription in the event of upstream fault. In such cases, it is important for every broker node to have knowledge about several upstream brokers in order to re-establish the publication flows. In other words, we require support for reconfigurable transportation facility for XML dissemination. In this paper, we address these shortcomings.

In this paper, we introduce and discuss the basic support for orchestrating the filtering service in XML transport overlays. The actual XML stream that is transmitted across the individual TeleScope nodes may have two types of XML messages. Data messages are the ones that need to be filtered on content and are of interest to subscribers. Control messages are used to regulate the flow of data messages. The control messages contain information about upstream brokers and filtering queries that must be executed on the individual nodes. The individual nodes are also equipped with capabilities to automatically choose alternative upstream broker in the event that an initial upstream broker shuts down. We also provide details of proposed bootstrap protocol that permits the configuration of filtering overlay without manual intervention during initial deployment phase. We provide the implementation details of our vision and outline the overall architecture to demonstrate the feasibility of our approach.

The rest of the paper is organized as follows. Section 2 provides details on support for basic service orchestration in TeleScope XML overlays. Section 3 provides discussion on feasibility of our approach by describing the preliminary experience with orchestrating our filtering service. Section 4 lists some relevant literature on the subject. Section 5 concludes the paper.

2   Service Orchestration

In one of our previous works on the subject, we proposed XML content filtering [2] architecture for efficient dissemination of XML streams to the end-points. The filtering overlay in Fig. 1 operates on semi-structured data stream of a stock exchange. Here, the stocks stream, comprised of individual XML documents is filtered at child brokers according to the specific company symbols, originating stock exchange points and other filtering conditions such as sales price and bidding information.

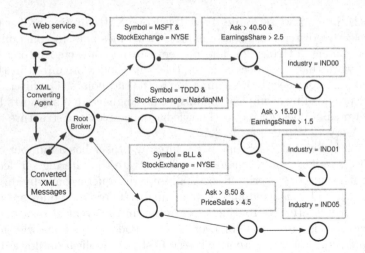

Fig. 1. Architecture of a filtering overlay

In order to address reconfigurability issues, we make two major modifications to TeleScope. We alter the capabilities of a TeleScope node that will allow it to connect with a different upstream broker should the original one go down. The second is a need for update mechanism to filtering queries and upstream metadata on individual broker nodes that permits the management of service properties across a filtering overlay. These two are outlined in the following sections.

2.1 Support for Upstream Brokers List

The addition of enhanced subscription capabilities to individual broker nodes in the XML overlay network will allow them to subscribe to alternative upstream brokers in the event of parent broker failures. Each broker node is now equipped with a list of upstream brokers – Upstream Brokers List (UBL) that the child node can subscribe to in the event that original parent broker is unavailable. The file consists of a list of prioritized records, each of which gives the details of an upstream broker who has the potential to be a parent of the child node. Note, that in the original TeleScope architecture [2], individual broker was limited to information about a single upstream subscription. Therefore, such a limitation did not provide any form of routing resiliency.

The structure of each record in this prioritized list consists of the following entries.

1. *IP address:* IP address of the upstream (potential parent) broker,
2. *Port:* port number of the upstream broker,
3. *NameID:* name of the upstream broker, and
4. *Priority:* priority is an integer from 0 to 100 with 0 being the lowest priority and 100 being the highest one.

A child broker is now capable of switching to an alternative upstream broker in the event of original parent broker failure. If several potential upstream brokers have identical priority values, the subscription choice is given to the next one in the list. Note that the storage and maintenance of individual UBLs do not incur significant overheads for individual broker nodes in small to medium sized overlays. For instance, 512 entries in the UBL (considered to be a relatively large XML dissemination overlay) occupies only several kilobytes of storage. Consequently, the list updates in our predominantly static overlay configuration are infrequent and do not incur performance penalties.

2.2 Update Mechanism

The second major change that we need to make to the architecture of our filtering service is the support for automated mechanism that will allow the updates to filtering queries and UBLs on individual broker nodes without a need of manual intervention. Such a mechanism will allow to regulate the flow of XML data messages.

One possible solution to such a problem is through injection of service updates in the form of XML control messages into the publication stream of root broker node that disseminates control messages to the broker nodes in the overlay. Such an approach offers the advantage of interleaving control and data flows within a single message transmission mechanism that permits the propagation of service updates to all the nodes without a reliance on alternative solutions such as service management via a centralized controller node. Such a centralized controller node may be a single point of failure that requires a design and deployment of sophisticated fault-tolerant mechanisms. It also has to connect to all individual brokers in the overlay to update service metadata. Aside from implementation complexity, controller has to maintain state of every broker it needs to reconfigure. Therefore, a more simple approach is preferred in our settings.

XML data and control messages are distinguished via the corresponding root element of every XML document that is received. Every data message is denoted by the 'XML_MESSAGE' root element. Every control message is denoted by the 'CRL_MESSAGE' root element. Propagation of control messages to all brokers in the service overlay is ensured by the downstream-only property of message flow. Moreover, every broker should possess the necessary logic that has to inject a received control message in its publication stream at all times to ensure the dissemination to child brokers. Note, that such injection will happen only to control messages that are not destined for the current broker and have to be forwarded to appropriate child nodes. Therefore, every control message that is received by the broker is subject to such a verification.

The proposed update mechanism may be effectively applied to the orchestration of filtering service depicted in Fig. 1. The control messages are added into the XML store on the filesystem that in turn are subsequently injected into a publication stream of the root broker. We can easily regulate the content flow of XML data messages by instructing individual child brokers in the service overlay on what filtering queries to perform on the incoming stream. We can also control the potential publication flow in the event of arbitrary upstream failures through UBL metadata if necessary. Note that in the event of a change to current service requirements, new service updates can be easily propagated to targeted child broker or a set of them via injection of new control messages to the root broker.

2.3   Bootstrap Protocol

One of the main deficiencies of original overlay architecture was a need to manually configure individual brokers with information about the corresponding upstream broker during the initial phase of forming such a filtering overlay. Specifically, we have to address the problem of automatic propagation of initial service update to all nodes in the overlay. In this section we propose a simple bootstrap protocol that permits the initial formation of an overlay without manual intervention. The protocol preserves a downstream-only property of message flow and therefore does not require bidirectional control flows between parent and child brokers. This retains initial simplicity of service orchestration mechanism and keeps modifications to broker implementation at minimum.

The protocol consists of three phases and relies on adding support for pre-configured metadata about IP address and service port of a root broker (essentially its ID) at child nodes. Such metadata can be hardwired into individual broker. For the purpose of this discussion the IP of a root broker is set at '192.168.100.1' and its service port at 50000 which can be adjusted at compile time of broker's executable. Therefore, ID of a root broker may be easily adjusted for deployment in any network where its IP address is dependent upon the size of network and design of its topology.

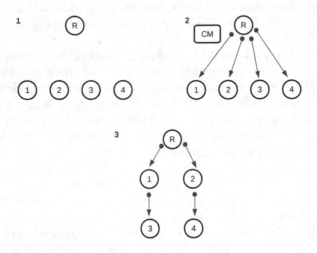

Fig. 2. Bootstrap protocol

The phases of a protocol for initial formation of a sample filtering overlay are depicted in Fig. 2. The overlay consists of a single root broker (labeled R) and four child brokers.

1. Phase 1 – initially we assume that a root broker accepts subscribers and a set of downstream brokers are aware of its location via pre-configured service metadata without reliance on dynamic service discovery mechanisms. We also assume that initial control messages are properly generated and injected into the publication stream of a root broker.
2. Phase 2 – during this phase brokers subscribe to root broker and obtain initial service update via control messages (labeled CM). Individual control message contains initial UBL and filtering query (if any) specific to the subscribing broker.
3. Phase 3 – during this phase each broker subscribes to the upstream broker that has the highest priority in initial UBL. In Fig. 2 brokers labeled 1 and 2 keep original subscription to the root broker while brokers labeled 3 and 4 subscribe to them instead. Thus, initial filtering overlay is formed at the end of protocol execution without manual intervention.

After execution of such a simple bootstrap protocol and the establishment of initial overlay, subsequent changes to upstream subscriptions and filtering queries will be propagated via proposed update mechanism that is described in this section (Sect. 2).

3   Discussion on Service Deployment and Evaluation

The enhanced prototype of TeleScope is available at its respective GitHub repository [1]. Due to the properties of our filtering architecture the transport of XML messages is organized via the hierarchical acyclic overlay that is formed as a partial mesh. In such a mesh, only a single downstream path exists between two given brokers and flow of XML data messages is hierarchically unidirectional – from a publisher down to a subscriber.

The sample overlay in the form of publication tree is depicted in Fig. 3. It shows a basic XML overlay that consists of 5 nodes with the root publishing broker labeled R. The UBL created at node 4 is depicted in Table 1 for the sake of completeness. Node onion in this table corresponds to node 1 in Fig. 3 and node oranges corresponds to node R, a root broker. Terminal node labeled 4 has a UBL that has records for the root broker and its three child broker nodes. Brokers have corresponding subscription priority values assigned to them in succession with root broker given the least priority of 85, as shown in Table 1. Therefore, node 4 will try to subscribe to root broker only in the event if all three of its child brokers have failed. Node 4 is subscribed to node 1 by default with subscription priority of 100. Therefore, node 1 is the immediate upstream broker for node 4. TCP port in UBL record instructs the subscriber of the subscription port where XML transport takes place at the upstream broker.

Note, that only updates related to UBL and filtering query are extracted from corresponding XML elements of XML control message.

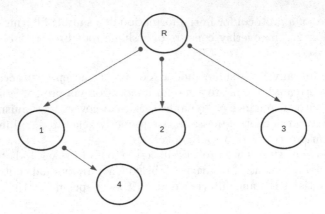

Fig. 3. Sample overlay

Table 1. Sample UBL

IP address	TCP port	Hostname	Subscr-n priority
129.82.47.230	50000	Onion	100
129.82.47.247	50000	Wasabi	95
129.82.47.234	50000	Pepper	90
129.82.45.208	50000	Oranges	85

4   Related Work

The problems of XML dissemination and XML message processing in the context of content-based pub/sub paradigm have been extensively studied in the past [8]. In our original work on XML content filtering broker code-named TeleScope [2], we have addressed the problem of content filtering of individual XML messages arriving at high rates with the necessity for dissemination to a potentially large number of concurrent subscribers. In our current work we propose to extend the functionality with support for orchestration of TeleScope XML filtering overlays.

Other researchers have also worked on content-based XML stream processing [5,6,12]. However, their approaches do XML filtering using XPath expressions. Documents, emitted from a data publisher at one point in the network are matched against XPath queries and delivered to the interested subscribers located anywhere throughout the network [9]. However, in our approach it is possible to express filtering queries without prior knowledge of XML schema. We do not consider our nodes to be full-fledged content routers but rather transport brokers with a capability for a single filtering transaction. Also, our work targets applications in which the subscribing data sinks need the entire contents of the messages [9].

5 Conclusion and Future Work

Many services generate streaming data at various sources that must be selectively distributed and processed in near real-time by consuming endpoints. Towards this end, we proposed the orchestration mechanism for the previously introduced content filtering service architecture. We enhanced the existing TeleScope broker so that it can support subscription in the event of a failure to a list of alternative upstream brokers and performed experiments to demonstrate the feasibility of our approach. We have also implemented a separate message processor that is responsible for processing XML control messages that are required for service orchestration. Our experience with the enhanced prototype suggests that the proposed approach may potentially be applied to orchestration of similar service architectures where information in the form of complete XML messages needs to be selectively disseminated.

Our future work includes the investigation into security aspects of control message dissemination. Specifically, various nodes of the filtering service may have different levels of trustworthiness. We plan to design validation protocols to ensure the authenticity of control flow between root broker and the child nodes in the filtering overlay.

Acknowledgement. This work was supported in part by grant from NIST Award Number 60NANB16D250 and a grant from NSF Award Number CNS 1650573 and support from AFRL, CableLabs, Furuno Electric Company, and SecureNok.

References

1. Belyaev, K.: TeleScope - XML data stream broker/replicator (2016). https://github.com/kirillbelyaev/telescope/tree/telescope2. Accessed 17 May 2017
2. Belyaev, K., Ray, I.: Towards efficient dissemination and filtering of XML data streams. In: Proceedings of IEEE DASC, pp. 1870–1877. IEEE (2015)
3. Belyaev, K., Ray, I.: Enhancing applications with filtering of XML message streams. In: Proceedings of IDEAS, pp. 322–327. ACM (2016)
4. Berglund, A., et al.: XML path language (XPATH). W3C (2003)
5. Diao, Y., Franklin, M.: Query processing for high-volume XML message brokering. In: Proceedings of VLDB, vol. 29, pp. 261–272. VLDB Endowment (2003)
6. Diao, Y., Rizvi, S., Franklin, M.J.: Towards an internet-scale XML dissemination service. In: Proceedings of VLDB, vol. 30, pp. 612–623. VLDB Endowment (2004)
7. Fenner, W., et al.: XTreeNet: scalable overlay networks for XML content dissemination and querying. In: WCW Workshop, pp. 41–46. IEEE (2005)
8. Josifovski, V., Fontoura, M., Barta, A.: Querying XML streams. VLDB J. **14**(2), 197–210 (2005)
9. Li, G., Hou, S., Jacobsen, H.-A.: Routing of XML and XPath queries in data dissemination networks. In: Proceedings of ICDCS, pp. 627–638. IEEE (2008)
10. Li, G., Feng, J., Wang, J., Zhou, L.: KEMB: a keyword-based XML message broker. IEEE TKDE **23**(7), 1035–1049 (2011)
11. Miliaraki, I., Koubarakis, M.: FoXtrot: distributed structural and value XML filtering. ACM TWEB **6**(3), 12 (2012)
12. Snoeren, A.C., Conley, K., Gifford, D.K.: Mesh-based content routing using XML. ACM SIGOPS **35**(5), 160–173 (2001)

Real-Time Skyline Computation on Data Streams

Lena Rudenko[✉] and Markus Endres

University of Augsburg, 86135 Augsburg, Germany
{lena.rudenko, markus.endres}@informatik.uni-augsburg.de

Abstract. Skyline processing has received considerable attention in the last decade, in particular when filtering the most preferred objects from a multi-dimensional set on contradictory criteria. Nowadays, an enormous number of applications require the analysis of time evolving data and therefore the study of continuous query processing has recently attracted the interest of researchers all over the world. In this paper, we propose a novel algorithm called SLS for evaluating Skyline queries with low-cardinality domains on data streams, and empirically demonstrate the advantage of this algorithm on artificial and real data.

Keywords: Streams · Skyline · Preferences · Realtime

1 Introduction

Today, data processed by humans as well as computers is very large, rapidly increasing and often in form of data streams. Users want to analyze this data to extract personalized and customized information [1,2]. Many modern applications such as financial analysis, infrastructure manufacturing, meteorological observations, or social networks require query processing over data streams [1,3]. Therefore stream data processing is a highly relevant topic nowadays.

A stream is a continuous unbounded flow of data objects made available over time. It needs to be processed sequentially and incrementally. However, queries on streams run continuously over a period of time and return different results as new data arrive. Hence, analyzing streams can be considered as a difficult and complex task. Many scientists all over the world try to process and analyze streams in order to extract important information from such continuous data.

On the other hand, preference queries [2] have received considerable attention in the past, especially when the filtering criteria are contradictory. In particular, *Skyline queries* [4], also known as *Pareto preference queries*, select those objects from a dataset D that are not dominated by any others. An object p having d attributes (dimensions) dominates an object q, if p is better than q in at least one dimension and not worse than q in all other dimensions. This dominance criterion defines a partial order and therefore transitivity holds. Without loss of generality, the Skyline with the *min* function for all attributes is used in this paper.

© Springer Nature Switzerland AG 2018
A. Benczúr et al. (Eds.): ADBIS 2018, CCIS 909, pp. 20–28, 2018.
https://doi.org/10.1007/978-3-030-00063-9_3

Example 1. Fig. 1 presents the Skyline of some tweets[1]. Each tweet is represented as a point in the 2-dim space of user *activity status* and *hashtag*. The first dimension is represented by the status values {active, non-active, unknown} which are mapped to the scores 0, 1, and 2. The second dimension is an element of {#pyeongchang2018, #olympics, #olympia2018, #teamgermany, #others} and is represented with the values $0, \ldots, 4$.

The objective is to find all Pareto optimal tweets w.r.t. the activity status and the hashtag, since we assume that *very active users* using the hashtag *#pyeongchang2018* post the most interesting information on the Olympic winter games 2018. Of course, there are also less active users using the same hashtag, or users using, e.g., *#olympia2018* for their tweets.

Of interest are all tweets that are not worse than any other tweet in both dimensions w.r.t. to our search preference. Tweet t_4 is dominated by the tweets t_1 and t_2, t_5 by t_1, t_2 and t_3. The tweets t_1, t_2 and t_3 are not dominated by any other tweet and build the *Skyline*.

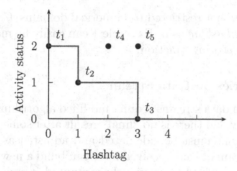

Fig. 1. Skyline on Twitter data.

Algorithms proposed for traditional database Skyline computation [4] are not appropriate for continuous data and therefore new techniques should be developed to fulfill the requirements posed by the data stream model [1]: (1) fast response time, (2) incremental evaluation, (3) limited number of data access, and (4) in memory storage to avoid expensive disk accesses.

In this paper we present the SLS algorithm for *real-time Skyline processing on data streams*. The proposed algorithm is based on the lattice structure representing the better-than relationships that must be built only once for efficient Skyline computation on continuous data. Our algorithm satisfies all four requirements on stream-oriented algorithms as mentioned before.

The remainder of this paper is organized as follows: Sect. 2 recapitulates essential concepts of Skyline queries. In Sect. 3, we introduce the *Stream Lattice Skyline* algorithm. Our results on comprehensive experiments are shown in Sect. 4. Section 5 contains a summary and outlook.

---

[1] Twitter: https://twitter.com/.

2   Background

2.1   Skyline Queries

The aim of a Skyline query or Pareto preference [2,4] is to find *the best objects* in a dataset D, denoted by *Sky(D)*. More formally:

Definition 1 (Dominance). *Assume a set of vectors $D \subseteq \mathbb{R}^d$. Given $p = (p_1, ..., p_n), q = (q_1, ..., q_d) \in D$, p dominates q on D, denotes as $p \prec q$, if the following holds:*

$$p \prec q \Leftrightarrow \forall i \in \{1, ..., d\} : p_i \leq q_i \wedge \exists j \in \{1, ..., d\} : p_j < q_j \tag{1}$$

Definition 2 (Skyline Sky(D)). *The Skyline Sky(D) of D is defined by the maxima in D according to the ordering $\prec$, or explicitly by the set*

$$Sky(D) := \{p \in D \mid \nexists q \in D : q \prec p\} \tag{2}$$

In this sense, the minimal values in each domain are preferred and we write $p \prec q$ if p is better than q.

Note that Skylines are not restricted to numerical domains: Categorical domains like *activity status* or *hashtag* as in Example 1 can easily be mapped to a numerical domain by some scoring function.

2.2   Skyline Queries on Data Streams

Skyline processing on data streams require modified algorithms, since a stream is a continuous dataflow and there is no "final" result after some data of the stream is processed. The result must be calculated and adjusted as soon as new data arrive, since new stream objects received later can build a new Skyline compared to objects already recognized in previously computed (temporary) Skylines. To the best of our knowledge, only *Block-Nested-Loop* (BNL) style algorithms [4–6] can be adapted to Skyline evaluation on continuous data. These algorithms follow an *object-to-object* comparison approach, an expensive operation with a worst-case runtime of $O(n^2)$, where n is the number of objects.

For analyzing a data stream, it is necessary to divide it into a series of (non-overlapping) chunks $c_1, c_2, \ldots$. A BNL-style algorithm would evaluate the Skyline on the first chunk, i.e., $Sky(c_1)$, cp. Definition 2. Since c_2 could contain better objects w.r.t. the dominance criterion in Definition 1, one also has to compare the new objects from c_2 to the current Skyline, i.e., compute $Sky(Sky(c_1) \cup c_2)$ and so on. However, this leads to a computational overhead if c_2 is large.

3   The Stream Lattice Skyline Algorithm

Our *Stream Lattice Skyline* (SLS) algorithm was developed for efficient real-time Skyline computation on unbounded streams. It depends on the lattice structure constructed by a Skyline query over low-cardinality domains. For a low-cardinality domain and $s_i \in \mathbb{R}$, a one-to-one mapping function $f : dom(\mathbb{R}) \rightarrow \mathbb{N}_0$, $f(s_i) = i - 1$, can be defined to get discrete values as required in our algorithm.

3.1   The Idea of SLS

Our SLS algorithm is based on *Hexagon* [7] and *Lattice Skyline* [8]. A Skyline
query over discrete domains constructs a *lattice* [7,9]. Visualization of such lat-
tices is often done using *Better-Than-Graphs* (BTG). An example of a BTG is
shown in Fig. 2. The nodes in the BTG represent *equivalence classes*. The idea
is to map objects from the stream to these equivalence classes using some kind
of scoring function. All values in the same class are considered *substitutable*.

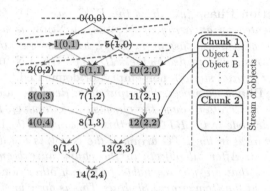

Fig. 2. Stream processing with SLS. (Color figure online)

We write [2,4] to describe a two-dimensional domain as well as the maximal
possible values of the score vector representing objects. For example, the BTG
in Fig. 2 could present a Skyline on the *activity status* and the *hashtag* (cp.
Example 1). The arrows in the BTG show dominance relationships between
nodes. The node $(0,0)$ presents the *best node*, whereas $(2,4)$ is the *worst node*.
The bold numbers next to each node are *unique identifiers* (ID) for each node in
the BTG. Nodes having the same level are *indifferent*. That means for example,
that neither the objects in the node $(0,4)$ are better than the objects in $(2,2)$
nor vice versa. All gray nodes are occupied with an element of the data and
therefore *non-empty*, white nodes are *empty*.

The elements of the Skyline are those in the BTG that have *no path leading
to them from another non-empty node*. In Fig. 2 these are the nodes $(0,1)$ and
$(2,0)$. All other nodes have direct or transitive edges from these both nodes, and
therefore are dominated.

Our approach in general works as follows: After constructing the BTG, all
objects of a chunk are mapped to the corresponding nodes, e.g., object A is
mapped to $(2,0)$, object B to $(2,2)$, and so on. Afterwards, a *breadth-first
traversal* (BFT) runs to find the non-empty nodes (blue dashed line in Fig. 2).
For the first non-empty node (here $(0,1)$) we start a *depth-first traversal* (DFT)
(red arrows) to mark all transitive dominated nodes as *dominated*. If the DFT
reaches the bottom node $(2,4)$ (or an already dominated node) it will recursively
follow all other edges. Thereafter, the BFT continues with node $(1,0)$, which is

empty. The next non-empty node is $(1,1)$, but dominated. Continue with $(2,0)$. Since all other nodes are marked as dominated, the remaining nodes, $(0,1)$ and $(2,0)$, present the Skyline.

3.2   The SLS Algorithm

In this section we describe our SLS algorithm. More details and a pseudo code can be found in [10]. SLS is based on a series of finite chunks as described in Sect. 2.2. We divide SLS into three phases:

1. The **Construction Phase** *initializes the BTG (see [7,11] for details). The BTG is represented by an array of* NODES. *A* NODE *is a data structure representing an equivalence class in the BTG, which may contain objects from the stream.* NODES *are identified by their IDs (cp. [7]). A* NODE *also contains its status* empty *(initial status),* non-empty, *or* dominated.
2. In the **Adding Phase** *we process the input data: Read the next chunk c_i from the data stream S. Iterate through the objects o_j of chunk c_i. Each object will be mapped to one node in the BTG. For this, we compute the ID of the current object o_j and store it in the BTG array, if the* NODE *is not dominated.*
3. **Removal Phase**: *After all objects in the chunk have been processed, the* non-empty *nodes that are not reachable from any other* non-empty *node of the BTG represent the (temporary) Skyline. This is done by a combination of* breadth-first traversal (BFT) *and* depth-first traversal *(DFT).*
   We start a BFT at the top of BTG and search for the first non-empty *node. From this node on, we start a DFT recursively. When processing objects from the next chunk, we do not need to add objects to already dominated nodes. After processing all nodes in the DFT, we continue with the BFT until all nodes are visited. The remaining nodes contain the temporary Skyline set.*

The Skyline computation in Phase 3 can be done after an arbitrary number of processed chunks or after a pre-defined time. Therefore, our algorithm can be used for real-time Skyline evaluation.

Since SLS follows the idea of Hexagon and Lattice Skyline, the linear runtime complexity of $\mathcal{O}(dn + dV)$ remains for our algorithm. Thereby, n is the number of input objects, d number of dimensions, and V the size of the lattice, i.e., the product of the cardinalities of the d low-cardinality domains from which the attributes are drawn.

4   Experiments

For our experiments we generated artificial data streams as described in [12]. For real data, we used Twitter records. We used Apache Flink[2] for stream processing to divide the data streams into a series of chunks. Our algorithms have been implemented using Java 8. All experiments are performed on a single node (Intel Xeon 2.53 GHz) running Debian Linux 7.1. For more details and benchmarks we refer to [10,13].

---

[2] https://flink.apache.org/.

4.1   Influence of the Chunk Size

In our first experiment we varied the chunk size to find out the optimal number of objects per chunk. We also compared BNL to SLS w.r.t. their runtime on anti-correlated data. For a more reliable result we considered different domains: [1,2,2,3] (Fig. 3a) and [2,3,7,8,4,10] (Fig. 3b).

SLS performs significantly better than BNL independent of the chunk size. A closer look spawns that SLS itself is slower for small chunks (up to 200 objects) than for chunks with more than 200 objects (cp. [10]). This can be explained by the frequent repeating of the BFT and DFT. For the chunk size over $20K$ objects, the runtime of SLS increases again, because the adding of new objects to the BTG in SLS is more expensive. In summary, we claim that the optimal chunk size for the best runtime of SLS is between 200 and $20K$ objects.

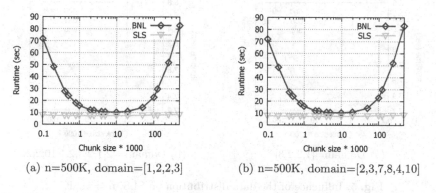

(a) n=500K, domain=[1,2,2,3]   (b) n=500K, domain=[2,3,7,8,4,10]

Fig. 3. Influence of the chunk size. SLS vs BNL, anti-correlated data distribution.

4.2   Influence of Different Domains

In Fig. 4a we varied the number of attributes, while the domain values remain within the low-cardinality range. The runtime behavior is similar for all domains, because low-cardinality domains produce *flat* BTGs. In Fig. 4b we varied the number of distinct values for each attribute domain. In these cases, we produce *deeper* BTGs in the sense of the *height*, but observe a similar behaviour as in Fig. 4a. In summary, the runtimes of SLS are nearly independent from the number of attributes and the size of the (low-cardinality) domain.

4.3   Influence of the Data Distribution

In this experiment we used independent (ind), correlated (cor), and anti-correlated (anti) data and varied the domains. SLS does not depend on any object-to-object comparisons. Therefore, we expected that the runtime of SLS is nearly the same for any kind of data distribution. Figure 5 confirms our assumption. It also shows that the best runtime is for chunks within $[200; 20K]$ objects.

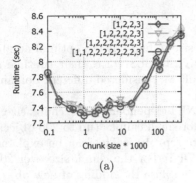 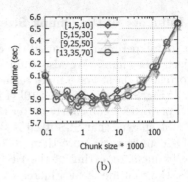

Fig. 4. Influence of different domains, n = 500K, anti-correlated data distribution.

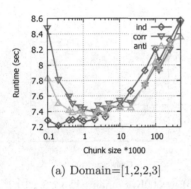 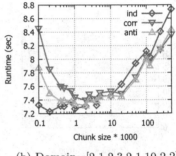

(a) Domain=[1,2,2,3]   (b) Domain=[2,1,2,3,2,1,10,2,2]

Fig. 5. Influence of the data distribution on SLS, n = 500K.

4.4   Real-World Data

For real data experiments we used tweets collected from Twitter. We considered dataset with $100K$ (Fig. 6a) and $500K$ (Fig. 6b) objects. BNL becomes better

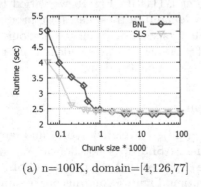 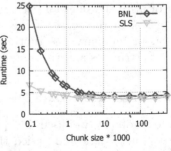

(a) n=100K, domain=[4,126,77]   (b) n=500K, domain=[4,126,77]

Fig. 6. Performance of SLS on real Twitter data.

for larger chunks. We assume that there are some *killer objects*, which can be accessed earlier by BNL through the larger chunk sizes and speed-ups performance. Nevertheless, SLS is still better than BNL. In addition, we see that also for real data chunk sizes between 200 and $20K$ objects are a good choice.

5   Conclusion

In this paper, we presented our novel algorithm SLS to find the Skyline on a data stream. Exploiting the lattice, SLS does not rely on object-to-object comparisons like BNL-style approaches, is independent of any data partitioning, and has a linear runtime complexity. In addition, SLS fulfills all requirements on modern stream algorithms: (1) fast runtime as seen in our experiments, (2) incremental evaluation since new chunks can easily be added to the BTG, (3) limited number of data access, because only non-dominated objects are added to the BTG, and (4) in-memory storage since the BTG is hold in RAM.

References

1. Kontaki, M., Papadopoulos, A.N., Manolopoulos, Y.: Continuous processing of preference queries in data streams. In: van Leeuwen, J., Muscholl, A., Peleg, D., Pokorný, J., Rumpe, B. (eds.) SOFSEM 2010. LNCS, vol. 5901, pp. 47–60. Springer, Heidelberg (2010). https://doi.org/10.1007/978-3-642-11266-9_4
2. Kießling, W., Endres, M., Wenzel, F.: The preference SQL system - an overview. In: Bulletin of the Technical Commitee on Data Engineering, vol. 34(2). IEEE CS (2011)
3. Chen, J., DeWitt, D.J., Tian, F., Wang, Y.: NiagaraCQ: a scalable continuous query system for internet databases. In: Proceedings of SIGMOD 2000, pp. 379–390. ACM, New York (2000)
4. Chomicki, J., Ciaccia, P., Meneghetti, N.: Skyline Queries, Front and Back. SIGMOD **42**(3), 6–18 (2013)
5. Xuemin, L., Yidong, Y., Wei, W., Hongjun, L.: Stabbing the sky: efficient skyline computation over sliding windows. In: Proceedings of ICDE 2005, pp. 502–513. IEEE Computer Society, Washington (2005)
6. Junchang, X., Zhiqiong, W., Mei, B., Guoren, W.: Reverse Skyline Computation over Sliding Windows. Mathematical Problems in Engineering (2015)
7. Preisinger, T., Kießling, W.: The hexagon algorithm for pareto preference queries. In: Proceedings of the 3rd Multidisciplinary Workshop on Advances in Preference Handling in conjunction with VLDB 2007, Vienna, Austria (2007)
8. Morse, M., Patel, J.M., Jagadish, H.V.: Efficient skyline computation over low-cardinality domains. In: Proceedings of VLDB 2007, pp. 267–278 (2007)
9. Endres, M., Kießling, W.: Parallel skyline computation exploiting the lattice structure. JDM J. Database Manage. **26**(4), 18–43 (2016)
10. Rudenko, L., Endres, M.: Real-Time Skyline Computation on Data Streams with SLS - Implementation and Experiences. Technical Report 2018–01, University of Augsburg (2018)

11. Endres, M., Kießling, W.: High parallel skyline computation over low-cardinality domains. In: Manolopoulos, Y., Trajcevski, G., Kon-Popovska, M. (eds.) ADBIS 2014. LNCS, vol. 8716, pp. 97–111. Springer, Cham (2014). https://doi.org/10.1007/978-3-319-10933-6_8
12. Börzsönyi, S., Kossmann, D., Stocker, K.: The skyline operator. In: Proceedings of ICDE 2001, pp. 421–430. IEEE Computer Society, Washington (2001)
13. Rudenko, L., Endres, M., Roocks, P., Kießling, W.: A preference-based stream analyzer. In: Proceedings of STREAMEVOLV 2016, Riva del Garda, Italy (2016)

Statistical Data Generation Using Sample Data

Bálint Fazekas[✉] and Attila Kiss

Faculty of Informatics Department of Information System,
ELTE Eötvös Loránd University, Budapest, Hungary
bfazekas@inf.elte.hu, kissae@ujs.sk

Abstract. Due to the ever increasing data stored in databases, it is important to develop software which can generate large numbers of test data that reflect the properties of a given sample. By generating such data, database algorithms can be stress-tested and evaluated by their performance. If the generated data is much greater in number than the given sample, then the process is called *data augmentation* or *synthetic data generation*. Data augmentation can also be very useful in Big Data benchmarking tests. The scope of this paper is to describe a method for statistical data generation based on a given sample, where the generated result attempts to reflect the statistical properties of the sample as much as possible. Throughout the paper we explain how any given data can be represented numerically, and hence clustered using the DBSCAN and K-means algorithms. We introduce a *hybrid* clustering method, which combines both of the previously mentioned algorithms. The *hybrid* algorithm focuses on unifying the strengths of both clustering algorithms. After the data is clustered, the individual sub-clusters are statistically analyzed, and based on the analytical results pseudo-random data are generated. The results of the hybrid clustering algorithm show that such artificial data can be created, which reflect the statistical properties of any given sample.

Keywords: Clustering · Database · Data generation

1 Introduction

Creating artificial data can be a very powerful and useful approach for testing software and databases. With the generated data, a given software can be effectively tested for its liability, effectiveness, and overall performance.

However, not any *random* data is sufficient for testing intricate software, or special, specifically written database algorithms – hence, the generation of artificial, but *truthful* datasets is neither a trivial task.

Once our data structure is defined, we need to extract, or manually define a sample of data. This sample of data will give the base for the artificially recreated dataset.

Dr. Kiss was also with J. Selye University, Komárno, Slovakia.

© Springer Nature Switzerland AG 2018
A. Benczúr et al. (Eds.): ADBIS 2018, CCIS 909, pp. 29–36, 2018.
https://doi.org/10.1007/978-3-030-00063-9_4

Using clustering algorithms on the selected sample, we can identify *groups*, or *patterns* in our dataset. Since the defined data structure could contain any $n \in \mathbb{N}^+$ number of information – including non–numeric types – the groups created by clustering may not be obvious. The clusterization, however, recognizes these patterns, and with the help of statistical analysis on the properties of these patterns, we are able to generate a similar, or even a much bigger dataset that matches these patterns.

This artificially generated dataset therefore can be used for simulating inflated databases, where the dataset – rather than being purely randomly generated – reflects the statistical properties of a desired database.

1.1 Clustering Methods

In this paper, we consider using both a density based and a spatial clustering method, namely the DBSCAN (*density-based spatial clustering of applications with noise*) and the *k–means* algorithms. By combining the DBSCAN and the k–means algorithms to create a *Hybrid* clustering algorithm, we attempt to eliminate the weaknesses and exploit the strengths of both algorithms.

2 Related Works

Storing, processing, loading and moving great amounts of data is called Big Data. Due to the increasing information stored in online services, Big Data benchmarking grew to be a real aspect to be considered. However, "current benchmarks related to big data only focus on isolated aspects", such as "the processing, storage and loading aspects" [1]. In the benchmarking process, we might not have access to a testing database, therefore it is required to create data via synthetic data generation. This allows for "knowledge about the actual or anticipated usage profile of the system under test for estimating system reliability" [2], meaning that "the generated data satisfy any logical validity constraints as the actual data", which then can be used to "evaluate and compare the performance of these" data [2,3,9]. Another aim "is to limit the risk of disclosure of survey respondents' identities or sensitive attributes, but simultaneously retain enough detail in the synthetic data to preserve the inferential conclusions drawn on the target population, in potential future legitimate statistical analyses" [6].

Hjoukær et al. introduces a "DBMS independent, and highly extensible data generation tool", that "uses a graph model to direct the data generation" which "makes it very simple to generate data even for large database schema with complex inter- and intra table relationships" [4]. Gray et al. describes a number of techniques for synthetic data generation, namely "parallelism", "congruential generators to get dense unique uniform distributions", "Special-case discrete logarithms to generate indices concurrent to the base table generation", and "Modification of [congruential method] to get exponential, normal, and self-similar distributions" [5]. Rabl et al. outlines a technique which involves "the high degree of parallelism that allows linear scaling for arbitrary numbers of nodes" [8].

Ming et al. "develop a tool, called Big Data Generator Suite (BDGS), to efficiently generate scalable big data while employing data models derived from real data to preserve data veracity" [10].

In this paper, describe a method of data augmentation that considers the density, and n dimensional spatial shape of a dataset in the promise of reliable clusterization. The clustered data is then statistically analyzed for number of points, centroid (or average in other words), and normal distribution values. We can use the acquired data to augment the original dataset. This method is similar to the one discussed by Pei et al. [7].

3 Data Representation

3.1 Data Structure Set

As it was outlined in the introduction of this paper, we interpret data structure as an array that can store any type of information within. A dataset is composed of many occurrences of such arrays, where the only restriction is that all arrays must represent the same type of data. Since we are talking about a set, it is assumed that each pair in the set are different – meaning that they must differ in at least one attribute from one another.

3.2 Numerical Representation of Textual Data

Keeping in mind that the purpose of this paper is generate artificial data which reflects (or approximates) the properties of the original dataset, the length of the texts were considered for their numerical representation. Based on the length of each textual data, we could generate new data that matches the length of the text, but is not the exact same information as the original one.

We now have all information in the dataset copied into a sequence of array of real numbers. This conversion allows for comparison between each member, and statistical analysis of the entire dataset.

4 Clustering Methods and Algorithms

4.1 K–Means Algorithm

The first algorithm this paper considers as a powerful clustering method, is the so called *k–means* algorithm. This algorithm is a spatial-temporal clustering method, which means that it attempts to split the dataset into k equal parts.

This algorithm requires two parameters: the first is the original dataset, the second is the k, the number of clusters we would want for the algorithm to create.

Steps. In the first step, the algorithm analyses the dataset, and estimates a uniform probability of position where most of the data points could possibly occur. This position is the initial marker of the entire dataset.

Starting with the initial marker, the algorithm additionally iterates $k - 1$ more times, further partitioning the 2–dimensional plane in each iteration.

With each new iteration, a new random point is chosen within the range of the data points and added to the list of markers. The newly chosen points are always different from the previously ones. It can be said that the markers of the k–clusters are defined in a set (where no repetition of a member is allowed). Then, the distances of all points are measured from all the markers, and reallocate their correspondences to the closest marker.

The iteration stops when the plane is divided into k partitions, and all the data points are corresponded to a cluster marker.

The next step in the algorithm is to fine–adjust the created clusters, which is done by the following method:

Since there are a finite number of points in the dataset, the algorithm is expected to stop the fine–adjustment phase after a few iterations.

The *Elbow Method*. Similarly to the idea of checking the difference of magnitude between two markers, the elbow method measures the average distance of all the points in a given cluster to the marker to that cluster. In the beginning, it is expected the difference to be high, but converge to a small value throughout the iterations. Comparing the average distances, we can set a threshold that is "good enough", and stop the algorithm.

In this paper, the (*corrected stop until unchanged means*) method is used to terminate the fine–adjustment of the k–means algorithm, however the *Elbow method* is considered to be a much better choice.

After the termination of the k–means algorithm, a group of k sub–clusters should have been created.

4.2   DBSCAN Algorithm

DBSCAN stands for *density-based spatial clustering of applications with noise*. In this algorithm, the Euclidean distance between each data points are considered to be the main aspect of cluster creation, rather than spatial partitioning. This allows us to identify concave–shaped clusters, without coinciding its neighboring clusters.

This algorithm thoroughly explained in the book called *Data & Knowledge Engineering* by *Birant et al.* [11].

Steps of the Algorithm. The DBSCAN algorithm requires three parameters to work. The first is the entire dataset. The second parameter is an $\epsilon \in \mathbb{R}$, ($\epsilon > 0$) number, which determines how close the data points should be to each other in order to consider them as one single cluster. The third indicates the minimum number of points that is needed for a set of data points to be considered as a cluster.

The first step of the algorithm is the arbitrarily choose a point from the dataset. The DBSCAN algorithm is a deterministic algorithm, therefore the choice of the starting point is irrelevant to the result of the clustering.

After a starting point has been chosen, the algorithm checks the neighborhood of ϵ radius of the point, and attaches those points to the starting point. If the thus created net of points contains as many data points as the minimum required, then a cluster is defined. If not, then the points are considered as outliers, and will not be a member of any cluster.

The DBSCAN algorithm will definitely terminate, given a finite dataset, since it either classifies a data point as a member of a cluster, or as noise. The algorithm terminates once all the data points have been classified.

4.3 Exploiting the Strengths of both Algorithms

As mentioned above, both the DBSCAN and K–means algorithms use the Euclidean distance to cluster the given dataset. The distance function can be extended up to any $k \in \mathbb{N}^+$ number of dimensions, therefore both algorithms can handle any k dimensional data.

By performing the DBSCAN algorithm first on our initial, numeric dataset, we can identify those clusters, which "intuitively" belong together.

However, the thus created clusters might be of any shape, which would still cause problems for performing valid statistical analysis on them. Therefore, for each cluster we run the k–means algorithm as well. The k–means algorithm will result in sub–clusters, where the points of each sub–cluster embrace their k dimensional centroid.

With all the identified sub–clusters created by the combination of using the DBSCAN and the k–means algorithms, we now have statistically analyzable data.

5 Statistical Analysis

In this paper, we are examining three very simple properties of the clusters.

First, we are looking at the number of points each cluster holds (n for further reference). This number helps us explicitly define the number of data we will generate – let it be the same, or a much larger number. To generate a much bigger dataset from our sample, we can apply a multiplier to n value, which we pass to the generator algorithm. The second property we need to extract is the centroid of the points in the cluster. We can get this value by simply calculating an average.

The final property we want to find out is the distribution of the data within a cluster. By extracting the normal distribution in all dimensions of the dataset, we can tell the scope of each cluster.

6 Synthetic Data Generation

6.1 Using Normal Distribution

Using the previously acquired pieces of information about each cluster, we can assemble an algorithm that will generate artificial data for each cluster.

For each identified cluster, we calculate the centroids and the normal distributions, and generate n number of datapoint with a multivariate normal distribution random value generator. To increase the number of data generated, we can simple multiply n by a positive $m \in \mathbb{R}$ number. In this case, we can talk about data augmentation. (If $0 < m < 1$, then the number of generated points will be less than what is present in the sample dataset.)

6.2 Using Uniform Distribution

In the previous section, we explained how the normal distribution of each sub–cluster can be used for the synthetic data generation. The problem with using strictly only the normal distribution for generating data is that the regenerated clusters might appear to be smaller "blobs" of clusters.

We can encapsulate each cluster by its extremal values, and use them to generate clusters with uniform distribution.

7 Results

Based on the results of the synthetic data generation using both distributions, we can state that indeed, the hybrid method is adequate for the task. However, in some cases – where the clusters could not be approximated correctly – the generation with the uniform distribution seems to generate ambiguous clusters (Fig. 1).

Fig. 1. On the triplet of images above, we can see the original dataset on the *left*, the synthetically generated dataset using the normal distribution on the *middle*, and the synthetically generated dataset using the uniform distribution of the *right*.

7.1   Speed of the Hybrid Algorithm

The following diagrams show the speed of the hybrid algorithm on different datasets.

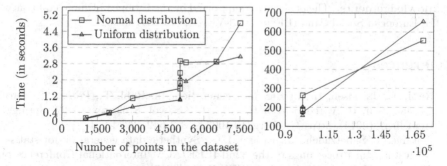

Dim.	Number of clusters	Largest difference in distributions of a corresponding cluster in every dimensions
2	11	2.375773, 2.740710 2.185325, 2.278970
3	12	32.206703, 40.238171, 37.005211 32.355637, 31.006762, 34.254261
5	11	50.881187, 53.762848, 61.116722, 67.602982, 57.316814 52.398487, 50.678226, 47.839535, 53.783073, 50.094315
9	8	57.362629, 62.505939, 59.682968, 55.935524, 61.643772, 70.316696, 63.057480, 65.735901, 61.742653 60.590473, 58.573429, 53.545685, 57.154350, 57.458927, 58.119232, 55.449238, 59.794643, 55.689960
12	13	66.344612, 53.064713, 56.163540, 55.857380, 67.622047, 63.862854, 61.600574, 62.900955, 62.944111, 66.601341, 62.751911, 63.505623 70.387451, 61.990356, 68.966225, 65.002014, 66.271294, 65.187050, 68.951828, 65.793198, 61.893456, 64.270515, 63.222546, 69.350632

The table above compares the distributions of all dimensions of some sample data. The leftmost column tells the number of dimensions of the dataset. The rightmost column compares the distributions of the identified clusters, and the regenerated clusters, chosen the distributions that fall furthers from its corresponding values. The distribution arrays are written below each other. We can see, that the difference is less than 20% in 12, and smaller in lower dimensions.

8   Conclusion

In this paper, we proposed a method for synthetic data generation and data augmentation. We used two clustering methods, and combined them to get much more precise sub–clusters of the original dataset. By examining the statistical properties of the identified sub–clusters, we described how these extracted pieces of information can be used to synthetically generate a dataset. Based on the results, we concluded that the Hybrid clustering algorithm is able to correctly identify sub–clusters in a given dataset, and thus so, we were able to use its results to create synthetic datasets that show high similarity with the original dataset.

Acknowledgements. The project was supported by the European Union, co-financed by the European Social Fund (EFOP-3.6.3-VEKOP-16-2017-00002).

References

1. Rabl, T., Jacobsen, H.-A.: Big data generation. In: Rabl, T., Poess, M., Baru, C., Jacobsen, H.-A. (eds.) WBDB -2012. LNCS, vol. 8163, pp. 20–27. Springer, Heidelberg (2014). https://doi.org/10.1007/978-3-642-53974-9_3
2. Soltana, G., Sabetzadeh, M., Briand, L.C.: Synthetic data generation for statistical testing. In: Proceedings of the 32nd IEEE/ACM International Conference on Automated Software Engineering. IEEE Press (2017)
3. Nowok, B., Raab, G.M., Dibben, C.: synthpop: Bespoke creation of synthetic data in R. J. Stat. Softw. **74**(11), 1–26 (2016)
4. Houkjær, K., Torp, K., Wind, R.: Simple and realistic data generation. In: Proceedings of the 32nd International Conference on Very Large Data Bases. VLDB Endowment (2006)
5. Gray, J., et al.: Quickly generating billion-record synthetic databases. ACM Sigmod Rec. **23**(2) (1994)
6. Loong, B.W.L.: Topics and applications in synthetic data. Harvard University, Dissertation (2012)
7. Pei, Y., Zaïane, O.: A synthetic data generator for clustering and outlier analysis. Computing Science Department, University of Alberta, Edmonton, Canada T6G 2E8
8. Rabl, T., Frank, M., Sergieh, H.M., Kosch, H.: A data generator for cloud-scale benchmarking. In: Nambiar, R., Poess, M. (eds.) TPCTC 2010. LNCS, vol. 6417, pp. 41–56. Springer, Heidelberg (2011). https://doi.org/10.1007/978-3-642-18206-8_4
9. Ghazal, A., et al.: BigBench: towards an industry standard benchmark for big data analytics. In: Proceedings of the 2013 ACM SIGMOD International Conference on Management of Data. ACM (2013)
10. Ming, Z., et al.: BDGS: a scalable big data generator suite in big data benchmarking. In: Rabl, T., Jacobsen, H.-A., Raghunath, N., Poess, M., Bhandarkar, M., Baru, C. (eds.) WBDB 2013. LNCS, vol. 8585, pp. 138–154. Springer, Cham (2014). https://doi.org/10.1007/978-3-319-10596-3_11
11. Birant, D., Kut, A.: ST-DBSCAN: an algorithm for clustering spatial-temporal data. Data Know. Eng. **60**(1), 208–221 (2007)

EthernityDB – Integrating Database Functionality into a Blockchain

Sven Helmer[✉], Matteo Roggia, Nabil El Ioini, and Claus Pahl

Free University of Bozen-Bolzano, Piazza Domenicani 3, 39100 Bolzano, Italy
{shelmer,nelioini,claus.pahl}@unibz.it, matteo.roggia@gmail.com

Abstract. We develop EthernityDB, a system that integrates database functionality into an Ethereum blockchain. In contrast to other systems, in our approach all the data is kept on the chain, giving us all the guarantees of a blockchain in terms of consistency, immutability, and security. Mapping the database functionality onto Ethereum's smart contracts is not a straightforward process: by modularizing the code in certain ways, we can bring down the transaction cost considerably. In a experimental evaluation we illustrate various trade-offs, measuring these transaction costs, and also discuss building blockchain-based data storage in a more general context.

Keywords: Blockchain · Decentralized databases · Smart contracts

1 Introduction

The cost of storage space has been in free fall for the last couple of decades, for instance the cost per GByte for hard drives came down from over $100,000 in the early 1980s to less than a dime in 2010 [8]. This now makes it possible to build append-only databases that keep a complete history of all the updates. Rather than changing the data in place for updates or deletions, we make the changes by adding new entries. Pat Helland argues that managing immutable data sets makes a lot of sense for many applications such as accounting and other financial services, digital archives, and data provenance, and that this is actually becoming affordable [7]. However, as he also notes, data is more and more dispersed, making it harder to coordinate between the different locations to keep the data consistent.

Nevertheless, buying hardware is usually just a fraction of the cost for running and maintaining a database. We investigate the usefulness of blockchain technology as a platform for running and maintaining fully decentralized databases in a peer-to-peer network context (which means we cannot necessarily trust all of the participating nodes). In particular, we are interested in storage capabilities that go beyond storing simple (financial) transaction data, as we want to explore the limits of implementing a database completely inside of a blockchain, i.e., all the data and all the components of the database management system are part of the

© Springer Nature Switzerland AG 2018
A. Benczúr et al. (Eds.): ADBIS 2018, CCIS 909, pp. 37–44, 2018.
https://doi.org/10.1007/978-3-030-00063-9_5

blockchain data structure. While there are some projects combining blockchains with databases, for instance BigChainDB [11], the actual data resides outside of the blockchain, i.e., the blockchain only stores a link and a cryptographic hash of the referenced data to verify its validity. The main reasons for this are the low throughput of blockchain transactions and that adding data to blockchains costs real money.

While databases are able to store payload data safely and durably off the chain, we have to trust that they actually do so. Faulty or malicious resource managers can join the peer-to-peer network, meaning that we may lose resistance against data loss. Consequently, we have to introduce mechanisms that replicate data in a tamper-proof way. Exactly this mechanism is provided by a blockchain, meaning that our data is protected by moving it on-chain. The underlying assumption is that the majority of the total computational power is controlled by honest nodes. However, blockchains have not been developed with database-like query processing in mind and are lacking user-friendly query language interfaces.

Our goal is to investigate how far we can push existing blockchain technology to support decentralized databases running in an untrusted environment. We implement basic database functionality inside the Ethereum blockchain [18], demonstrating that running a database inside a blockchain is indeed possible. On the other hand, we also show that the existing blockchain technology is not a perfect match when it comes to implementing and running database systems. In summary, we make the following contributions:

– We give an overview of the architecture of our system, called EthernityDB.
– We illustrate how Ethereum's smart contracts can be leveraged to integrate database functionality into a blockchain and how to optimize the contracts to bring down the costs and make the system more flexible.
– An experimental evaluation shows what running a database inside a blockchain means in terms of financial costs.

2 Related Work

Early blockchain systems, such as the one used for Bitcoin [13], were used exclusively for financial transactions and payment schemes or simple public ledgers to record ownership of digital assets, as they only provided limited capabilities for other more general applications. With newer systems, such as Ethereum [18], in addition to offering more (auxiliary) storage space, there is now the possibility of integrating code into the blockchain [10], allowing more sophisticated applications to be built.

As can be widely seen, applications have gone beyond pure financial transactions and public ledgers. For instance, Safecast is an open source sensor network in Japan for measuring radiation levels [15]. In order to be able to provide trustworthy data and to keep the whole operation sustainable, this project employs a blockchain schema. Factom was hailed as the world's first blockchain operating system [4] and Permacoin is an interesting approach trying to repurpose the proof-of-work principle for useful tasks by replacing it with a proof-of-retrievability and making memory and storage resources of local hosts available for archival purposes [12].

Compared to the previously mentioned approaches for utilizing blockchains, we believe that databases and blockchains are a more natural fit and there are already attempts to use blockchain technology as an infrastructure for database systems, such as BigChainDB [11], or to add a query layer on top of a blockchain system, called EtherQL [9]. For an overall view and a taxonomy of block-chain-based systems, Xu et al. offer an excellent survey, highlighting the advantages and disadvantages of different design decisions [19].

We modeled the database part of EthernityDB on MongoDB, a popular and well-known document store [3]. Apart from offering the flexibility of a document store, the command line interface of MongoDB uses JavaScript for formulating queries, which makes it easier to integrate this query interface into Ethereum's Solidity language.

3   Blockchains and Smart Contracts

A blockchain is a distributed storage mechanism that maintains a continuously growing list of records, grouped into structures called blocks. Each block of the blockchain contains records of transactions, the hash of the previous block, and a timestamp. This chain of hash values ensures the immutability of the records, as changing a block either invalidates the chain or the entire chain from that point on must be recomputed.

The system is maintained by a peer-to-peer network, each node of which collects transactions, joins them in a new block, and validates this block. The block validation is implemented with the help of a proof-of-work (or other) scheme that ensures that the validation is not done by a small number of nodes but spread around the peer-to-peer network. A node that successfully validates a block receives a reward, e.g. currency tokens usable in the blockchain. As long as most of the computational power is in the hands of honest nodes, invalid extensions and fraud attempts will be detected by the peer-to-peer network and rejected.

A smart contract is a function, represented by a piece of code, that resides on the blockchain and can be executed by the nodes of the peer-to-peer network. The distributed consensus protocol enforces the correct execution of the code: each node runs the function locally and checks that it gets the same results as the other nodes before validating it. For instance, a smart contract could check that certain conditions are met before going ahead with a monetary transfer, basically acting as an escrow service. The expressiveness of smart contracts depends on the employed language, Ethereum uses Solidity, a programming language based on JavaScript [6]. Functions written in Solidity are compiled into byte code and executed on the Ethereum Virtual Machine (EVM).

The smart contracts in Ethereum are identified by a 160-bit address and are called by sending a transaction to this address. Additionally, contracts are stateful, i.e., they have a private storage area for variable values, and can hold digital coins. When invoking a contract, a user usually supplies some payment (a node has to be paid to run code on their EVM) and input parameters. On top of that, a smart contract has access to the current state of the blockchain.

4   EthernityDB

4.1   Requirements

Unlike database systems, blockchains are typically not known for providing easy access to the data they store. Our goal is to integrate a lightweight database system with an API inspired by MongoDB into an Ethereum blockchain. Ideally, users should be able to create databases, query them, and insert data in a way they are used to from other database systems. We also want to use an easy-to-parse, easy-to-query data format that is well-known, in order not only to simplify the storing of data, but also the answering of future queries without using any external interpreters.

Working in an environment in which every single CPU operation has a monetary cost, confronts us with some unique design constraints. Consequently, we need to encode the data in a compact format to keep the storage overhead to a minimum. Additionally, every call of a smart contract also incurs costs depending on the length of the code that is run: the more code, the more has to be paid. Thus, we want to keep our codebase as small as possible.[1]

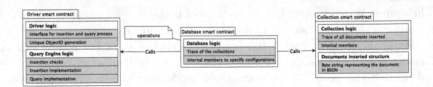

Fig. 1. Architectural overview of the smart contracts

4.2   Design

Figure 1 gives an architectural overview of EthernityDB, outlining the responsibilities of the different smart contracts. It was clear from the beginning that the different aspects of the database system had to be implemented using a set of smart contracts, as there is a maximum amount of gas spendable on each block.[2]

---

[1] The code itself is available here: https://github.com/Luscha/EthernityDB.

[2] Gas is a unit of measure defining how much computational power is needed to execute a transaction. In order to determine the cost of a transaction, this is multiplied by the gas price.

Consequently, this limits the size of a contract in terms of the compiled bytecode. It was not so clear how to divide up the functionality among different contracts and we went through a few iterations before settling on the architecture in Fig. 1. We discuss some of the design decisions as we go along.

The *driver* is the most important (and also largest and most expensive) module in the system. For this reason, we designed our system in such a way that this contract only has to be deployed once. Every new database contract references the current driver instance. In case the driver needs to be updated, every database owner simply has to point to the new instance. The driver is responsible for the query processing: validating insertions, parsing queries, accessing the data stored in the document contracts, and producing query results. Basically, it acts as the query engine of EthernityDB. In an earlier version, some of the query logic was embedded into a document smart contract, which in turn became larger and costlier to deploy (this document contract had to be deployed every time a new document was created).

The *database* contract is deployed only once for each database instance when it is created and acts as the entry point for all operations on that database. It contains some configuration parameters for the database and indexes the collections managed by this database instance. In an earlier version we had combined the database and collection logic into a single contract, which meant that every time we created a new collection or made changes in the way collections are handled, a new database contract had to be deployed. It would be even worse to integrate the document handling into the database contract, as creating a new document would trigger the redeployment of this contract.

The final contract deals with *collections* and *documents*. It would have been possible to create two separate contracts, one for collections and one for documents, but then for the insertion of a document we would have had to deploy an additional document contract, resulting in higher costs. We used a little trick here, embedding the documents in the storage space of the collection contract. Every contract in Ethereum is associated with a key-value store, storing 32 bytes per value, with 2^{256} different possible keys to address it. As a consequence, the insertion costs of a document now only depend on the length of the document and do not incur any additional costs. All querying of documents is done locally and, as it does not introduce any changes to the blockchain, does not incur any financial costs.

4.3   Data Representation and Storage

For the database storage facility we opted for a document store loosely based on MongoDB [3], which means that every document is represented in JSON format. For efficiency reasons we use binary JSON, or BSON, to store documents in EthernityDB, as BSON allows faster traversal of documents, speeding up encoding and decoding, and a more compact representation. It also supports some additional types not available in JSON. In an earlier version with a separate document contract we had also underutilized the storage capacity of documents, making it more expensive to insert new documents. In our current storage configuration, we split each document into chunks of 32 bytes, which are re-assembled when retrieving the document. Nevertheless, seen from the outside, the document enters and leaves the collection contract as a single byte string.

5   Evaluation

Figure 2 shows the results of an experimental evaluation focusing on the (monetary) costs for inserting documents in EthernityDB. The full modular structure system refers to an earlier architecture in which we had four separate smart contracts for databases, collections, documents, and the driver logic; the hybrid system follows the architecture shown in Fig. 1. *Verbose* means that we fully validate the inserted documents, i.e., only well-formed BSON documents with no unsupported data types are accepted. In the non-verbose case we do not do any checks and just insert a document. The numbers on the x-axis indicate the number of nested levels in an inserted document (zero standing for a flat document with no nesting).[3] The unit of measurement on the y-axis is the cost of the insertion operations in gas, which is measuring the computational power needed to execute the operations. In terms of the size of a document we pay 1,800 gas per byte plus 100,000 gas for the function call (in the non-validated case).

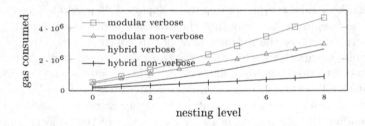

Fig. 2. Cost of inserting documents

As can be clearly seen in Fig. 2, the validation of the inserted BSON documents incurs an overhead, since we have to execute additional smart contract code to do it. More importantly, though, by redesigning the overall architecture of the system we can bring down the execution costs significantly. For the validated case, the costs are approximately halved, for the non-validated case they are even lower.

As we are operating on a test chain, it is not easy to get realistic measurements in terms of the confirmation delay or lookup time. From the previous experiment we know that the cost for data insertion is 1,800 gas per byte and 100,000 for the function call. Currently, the block gas limit of the Ethereum blockchain is 7.7 million gas, which means that each block can potentially store

---

[3] The starting document has one key and one value with a total size of 34 bytes. On each level we nest the document of the previous level inside the original one.

4,222 bytes. Given an average rate of 15 s per block, this would give us a through-put of 281 bytes per second for insertions. The querying is done locally, so it depends on the computational power of the local machine. It can be sped up by building an index, which does not have to reside on the blockchain.

Assuming a gas price of 0.02 microether and a price of US$ 300 for 1 Ether (which were the prices at the time of writing), operations with a cost of 1,000,000 gas, e.g. inserting a document with a nesting depth of four, would cost us $6, which is fairly expensive compared to a (traditional) database system. However, we have to consider the fact that this document is now stored on a blockchain and will be kept there as long as the blockchain is in existence. Running a database system and its infrastructure or paying a cloud provider for storage space over years or even decades is also not for free. There are a lot of parameters to consider here: lifetime of systems, costs of running and maintaining systems, changes and improvements in technology affecting the costs, replication factor of the data, and inflation (just to name a few). Omaar has tried to come up with a model to calculate the costs of storing data indefinitely[4] in a blockchain to be able to compare it to the costs of storing the data with a cloud provider [14]. The result of these calculations is a price of $100 per Gigabyte for a sustainable business model. The comparable number for Ethereum in [14] is around $4.6 million, for Bitcoin it is even higher at around $22 million.

6   Conclusion and Outlook

Looking at the costs seems discouraging and currently building a database that keeps the data on-chain in an Ethereum-based system is probably not a viable option. In general, storing and replicating the content of a large database on every node of a peer-to-peer network wastes a lot of space. ForkBase [16] and Chainspace [1] are two approaches trying to remedy this situation. ForkBase splits large data objects into chunks, assuming that usually only small parts of these objects change. This schema can also reduce the redundant storage of duplicate chunks. Chainspace reduces the storage overhead by partitioning the data into shards. However, to compensate for f faulty nodes, a shard must have a size of at least $3f + 1$ nodes. Also, Ethereum has a couple of disadvantages that does not make it an ideal platform for our needs. Other people speculating with a currency that will determine the storage costs is far from optimal, it would be better to create an environment with a different set of incentives to decouple the storage costs from a speculative currency. For instance, a participant in the schema could also pay via the provision of storage space for the blockchain [17]. Also, currently Ethereum uses a proof-of-work consensus mechanism, which is a costly and computationally intensive way of reaching a consensus. There are currently plans to switch to a proof-of-stake mechanism called Casper [5]. (For an overview of blockchain consensus protocols, see [2].)

In summary, building EthernityDB gave us a lot of insights into the mat-ter. We were confronted with a completely different way of building a database

---

[4] The calculations are actually done for 50 years.

system, optimizing the code according to the constraints set by the blockchain environment. We also realized that Solidity, even though a general-purpose programming language, is not an ideal language for building systems, we would have preferred a more powerful virtual machine. Nevertheless, our experience can be used as a basis for formulating the requirements and designing a blockchain that would meet our needs.

References

1. Al-Bassam, M., Sonnino, A., Bano, S., Hrycyszyn, D., Danezis, G.: Chainspace: a sharded smart contracts platform. In: NDSS 2018 (2018)
2. Bano, S., et al.: Consensus in the age of blockchains. CoRR abs/1711.03936 (2017)
3. Chodorow, K.: MongoDB: The Definitive Guide. O'Reilly, Sebastopol (2013)
4. Code, K.: Use case for factom: the world's first blockchain operating system (2015). http://kencode.de/projects/ePlug/Factom-Linux-Whitepaper.pdf. Accessed Feb 2015
5. CoinDesk: Ethereum's big switch: The new roadmap to proof-of-stake (2017). https://www.coindesk.com/ethereums-big-switch-the-new-roadmap-to-proof-of-stake/. Accessed Oct 2017
6. Dannen, C.: Solidity programming. In: Introducing Ethereum and Solidity, pp. 69–88. Springer, Berkeley (2017). https://doi.org/10.1007/978-1-4842-2535-6_4
7. Helland, P.: Immutability changes everything. In: CIDR 2015. Asilomar, California, January 2015
8. Komorowski, M.: A history of storage cost. http://www.mkomo.com/cost-per-gigabyte (2009). Accessed Aug 2017
9. Li, Y., Zheng, K., Yan, Y., Liu, Q., Zhou, X.: EtherQL: a query layer for blockchain system. In: Candan, S., Chen, L., Pedersen, T.B., Chang, L., Hua, W. (eds.) DASFAA 2017. LNCS, vol. 10178, pp. 556–567. Springer, Cham (2017). https://doi.org/10.1007/978-3-319-55699-4_34
10. Luu, L., Chu, D.H., Olickel, H., Saxena, P., Hobor, A.: Making smart contracts smarter. In: CCS 2016, pp. 254–269. ACM (2016)
11. McConaghy, T., et al.: BigchainDB: a scalable blockchain database. white paper, BigChainDB (2016)
12. Miller, A., Juels, A., Shi, E., Parno, B., Katz, J.: Permacoin: repurposing bitcoin work for data preservation. In: SP 2014, pp. 475–490. IEEE (2014)
13. Nakamoto, S.: Bitcoin: a peer-to-peer electronic cash system (2008)
14. Omaar, J.: Forever isn't free: the cost of storage on a blockchain database (2017). https://medium.com/ipdb-blog/forever-isnt-free-the-cost-of-storage-on-a-blockchain-database-59003f63e01. Accessed Oct 2017
15. Tech, R., Neumann, K., Michel, W.: Blockchain technology and open source sensor networks. In: 1. Interdisziplinäre Konferenz zur Zukunft der Wertschöpfung. pp. 125–134. Hamburg (2016)
16. Wang, S., et al.: Forkbase: an efficient storage engine for blockchain and forkable applications. CoRR abs/1802.04949 (2018)
17. Wilkinson, S., Boshevski, T., Brandoff, J., Buterin, V.: Storj a peer-to-peer cloud storage network (2014)
18. Wood, G.: Ethereum: a secure decentralised generalised transaction ledger. Ethereum Project Yellow Paper 151 (2014)
19. Xu, X., et al.: A taxonomy of blockchain-based systems for architecture design. In: ICSA 2017, pp. 243–252. IEEE (2017)

LOD Query-Logs as an Asset
for Multidimensional Modeling

Selma Khouri[1,2](✉) and Ladjel Bellatreche[2]

[1] Ecole Nationale Supérieure d'Informatique, Algiers, Algeria
s_khouri@esi.dz
[2] LIAS/ISAE-ENSMA - Poitiers University, Futuroscope, France
bellatreche@ensma.fr

Abstract. The spectacular development of Web-databases and intensive-query applications such as data warehouses ($\mathcal{DW}$) contributes to the vulgarization of query-logs. The main particularity of these logs is that they are exploited internally by the owners of these $\mathcal{DW}$s. Recently, external resources such as Linked Open Data ($\mathcal{LOD}$) bring two main elements: valuable data and stored Sparql query-logs of end users. This situation brings a dual fact: $\mathcal{DW}$ query-logs are located at the operational $\mathcal{DW}$, whereas the $\mathcal{LOD}$ logs are located at a source level. If they are curated and analyzed efficiently, the $\mathcal{LOD}$ logs may represent an interesting asset for the $\mathcal{DW}$ design, to build new multidimensional knowledge. In this paper, we propose a $\mathcal{LOD}$ logs-driven approach for $\mathcal{DW}$ multidimensional modeling. To show the effectiveness of our approach, we instantiate it using DBpedia query-logs.

Keywords: Multidimensional modeling · $\mathcal{LOD}$ · Query-logs

1 Introduction

The database as a research discipline has been strongly associated all along its evolution to *Logs*. Logs may be used inside and outside DBMS hosting databases. More precisely, logs are associated to the four main components of database environment that includes: the DBMS, its hosted databases, their design life-cycle and the end user accesses. Each evolution of the database technology raises new logs and additional usages. To illustrate this point, let us consider the data warehouse ($\mathcal{DW}$) technology that brings three main novelties compared to traditional databases which are: *(i)* multidimensional ($\mathcal{MD}$) modelling based on the fact/dimension dichotomy. The fact is placed at the center of the multidimensional space and dimension concepts define analytical perspectives. The attributes of facts are called measures, used for aggregating data. A dimension consists of a hierarchy of levels of detail representing different granularities (e.g. Day-Month-Year), levels contain attributes. *(ii)* ETL (Extract, Transform, Load) phase which covers a process of how the data of traditional sources are integrated into the $\mathcal{DW}$ store. *(iii)* Amplification of the interest of physical design phase due

© Springer Nature Switzerland AG 2018
A. Benczúr et al. (Eds.): ADBIS 2018, CCIS 909, pp. 45–53, 2018.
https://doi.org/10.1007/978-3-030-00063-9_6

to the complexity brought by OLAP queries and decision makers requirements in terms of QoS (Quality of Service). This amplification has pushed DBMS editors to propose advisors that suggest, based on query-logs, optimization features such as indexes to administrators. The ETL and physical design logs are mainly used respectively for ETL quality [4] and QoS of the target $\mathcal{DW}$ [12]. An active research direction has been launched during the last 10 years related to the analysis of query-logs of decision makers by recommender systems [2]. The $\mathcal{DW}$ technology has also evolved from many perspectives. This paper is not the venue for discussing all facets of this evolution, but we focus on one evolution which is in the line of our discussion. This evolution concerns the externalization of data sources feeding the $\mathcal{DW}$ [6], for adding more value to decision makers. The Linked Open Data ($\mathcal{LOD}$) are an example of representative external sources. They are a set of design principles for sharing machine-readable data on the Web for public administrations, business and citizens usages[1]. They use Semantic Web standards like RDF and Sparql query languages. DBpedia[2] is one of the most popular $\mathcal{LOD}$ used for its diversity of themes.

The above mentioned database environment can be easily reproduced to the $\mathcal{LOD}$. To illustrate this point, Dbpedia $\mathcal{LOD}$ uses OpenLink Virtuoso[3] DBMS, it contains the knowledge bases (KBs) corresponding to the different themes, which are constructed following a specific design cycle and accessed by different end users through Dbpedia Sparql endpoint[4]. Interestingly, the $\mathcal{LOD}$ environment includes also its own logs of Sparql queries. Query-logs are gathered and published through initiatives like USEWOD[5] or the Linked SPARQL Queries Dataset (LSQ) [6]. The main characteristic of these logs concerns their provenance, i.e., they are issued from various users with different profiles and skills (simple user, expert users, analyst users, etc.). Therefore, the pool of these logs may contain a variety of queries including naive queries used for the exploratory purpose, as well as complex queries[7], requiring several combinations of KBs. By deeply exploring existing studies incorporating $\mathcal{LOD}$ in $\mathcal{DW}$ design, we figure out that they mainly use the second component of the $\mathcal{LOD}$ environment representing the KB [1,3,8] and *ignore Sparql query-logs*. Our study conforms to existing studies that pursue the goal of adding value to $\mathcal{DW}$ design, and follow the *schema-on-read* approach in which the $\mathcal{DW}$ schema can be extended during exploitation phase of the $\mathcal{DW}$, by opposition to the traditional *schema-on-load* approach, requiring designers to propose a 'static' schema upfront before exploiting the $\mathcal{DW}$ [13]. In this paper, the main issue is related to the inclusion of query-logs of the $\mathcal{LOD}$ in $\mathcal{DW}$ design. The direct impact of this inclusion is the

---

[1] https://www.w3.org/DesignIssues/LinkedData.html.
[2] http://wiki.dbpedia.org/.
[3] http://wiki.dbpedia.org/OnlineAccess.
[4] A SPARQL endpoint is a conformant SPARQL protocol service that enables users to query a KB via the SPARQL language eg. http://dbpedia.org/sparql.
[5]   http://usewod.org/.
[6] http://aksw.github.io/LSQ/.
[7]   http://wp.sigmod.org/?p=2277.

multidimensional modeling of the $\mathcal{DW}$ following the *schema-on-read* approach. By doing this, the obtained multidimensional schema can be complementary to the one obtained from internal and/or external sources. Answering the question of query-logs inclusion is not an easy task, requiring substantial analysis (cleaning, transforming, etc.). The paper is organized as follows: Sect. 2 presents the related works addressing $\mathcal{DW}$ design in internal context and in $\mathcal{LOD}$ context. Section 3 provides the background defining theoretical concepts. Section 4 presents the proposed approach for exploring query-logs. Section 5 illustrates the impact of incorporating query-logs of DBpedia using a set of experiments. Finally, Sect. 6 draws the conclusions.

2 Related Work

Different studies have been proposed for $\mathcal{MD}$ modeling in traditional approaches [9]. Most studies define $\mathcal{MD}$ patterns from relational datasets using to-one relationships between facts and their related dimensions. $\mathcal{DW}$ design approaches using a set of requirements define heuristics to identify $\mathcal{MD}$ patterns from the input structure of requirements. Our goal in this study is not to identify a new approach for $\mathcal{MD}$ design (new heuristics). Knowing that our approach should not disturb usual practices of designers but reproduce them, we adapt existing $\mathcal{MD}$ constraints on this new source (query-logs). Existing studies propose traditional approaches in these sense they consider a set of *internal* sources. Motivated by the possibility of discovering new insights from external data sources, different studies proposed $\mathcal{DW}$ design methods from open semantic spaces published as $\mathcal{LOD}$ [1]. Most of these studies focus on integration issues of $\mathcal{LOD}$ datasets extracted to cover some given requirements [3], merging OLAP cubes and RDF cubes from $\mathcal{LOD}$ fragments, or translation of OLAP queries into Sparql queries applicable to $\mathcal{LOD}$ [7]. Some studies like [8] focus on identifying the $\mathcal{MD}$ knowledge from $\mathcal{LOD}$ datasets. In realistic scenarios, requirements are not always well identified and exploring huge resources of $\mathcal{LOD}$ is a hard task. Our study overcomes these limitations by helping designers to explore $\mathcal{MD}$ knowledge from query-logs without prior knowledge on $\mathcal{LOD}$ or on specific analytical requirements. Note that query-logs of $\mathcal{LOD}$ have been subject of analysis in some studies [5] that provide data-driven statistics like the number of patterns used, the execution time, number of joins, etc.

3 Formalization

In what follows, we provide a formalization of Sparql[8] queries provided in $\mathcal{LOD}$ logs. The $\mathcal{LOD}$ resources are based on a knowledge base ($\mathcal{KB}$) definitions. At deployment level, $\mathcal{LOD}$ dataset is published as a set of triples or statements, following the standard Resource Description Framework (RDF[9]). Each statement in RDF takes the form <s, p, o, g> such that in the graph label g, subject s has

---

[8] Standard query language of the Semantic Web.
[9] https://www.w3.org/RDF/.

the predicate p, and the value of that property is the object o. Valid statements take the following form: $s \in (I \cup B)$, $p \in (I)$, $o \in (I \cup B \cup L)$ such as I, B, L are disjoint sets of IRIs, blank nodes (non-distinguished variables), and literals. Based on [5], a SPARQL query Q is a 3-tuple of the form <query-type, Graph Pattern P, Solution-modifier>. The query describes patterns that are matched onto the RDF data. The result of the query is a multiset of mappings $\mathbf{L}$ that match the pattern to the data.

- Query-type: four types of queries are identified: Select, Ask, Construct and Describe.
- Graph Pattern: is the central element of the query. It is defined based on RDF language, as follows: Let V = ?x, ?y, ?z,... be a set of variables, disjoint from the sets I, B, and L. A triple pattern is an element of $(I \cup B \cup V) \times (I \cup V) \times (I \cup B \cup L \cup V)$. A graph pattern P is an expression that can be generated by the following grammar: P:: = t | P_1 And P_2 | P_1 Union P_2 | P_1 Opt P_2 | P Filter R | graph i P | Graph ?x P, Where: t ranges over triple patterns, i ranges over IRIs in I, and ?x ranges over variables in V. R ranges over Sparql filter constraints.
- Solution-modifier: used for the aggregation, sorting, grouping removal and returning a specific subset of the mappings obtained from the pattern matching.

4   Proposed Approach for Exploring Query-Logs

The proposed approach illustrated in Fig. 1, explores the query-logs and analyses each input query to explore $\mathcal{MD}$ patterns which are then consolidated to form star schemas. "Exploring $\mathcal{MD}$ patterns" means analyzing the query and checking if it retrieves data that can be analyzed from a $\mathcal{MD}$ perspective [10]. The problem is formalized as follows: Given a set of queries <query-type, Pattern P, Solution-modifier>, the method annotates ontological resources (concepts and properties of the KB) identified in patterns P with $\mathcal{MD}$ labels: *Fact, Dimension, Level, Measure, FactAttribute* or *DimensionAttribute*. This $\mathcal{MD}$ knowledge forms a model of facts related to their dimensions <F, D_1, ..., D_n >.

Our approach considers the set of queries incrementally for identifying valid $\mathcal{MD}$ patterns from the structure of queries. Because there is no standard $\mathcal{MD}$ algebra, our analysis is based on study [10] that identified four mandatory constraints to be guaranteed to represent a combination of $\mathcal{MD}$ operators that we adapted to our context. These constraints are: *(C1) Multidimensional compliance*: the query must be a valid query template. Query-logs contain thousands of queries proposed by expert and non-expert users, many queries can be syntactically incorrect. A cleaning procedure is required at this step to identify correct queries. *(C2) Star-schema*: facts are related to levels by to-one relationships. *(C3) Uniqueness*: Every two different data instances retrieved by the query must be placed in different points of the $\mathcal{MD}$ space (either facts or dimensions). *(C4) Orthogonality*: The set of concepts that produce the

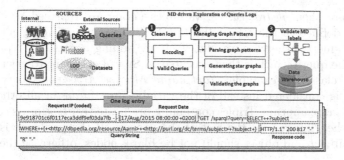

Fig. 1. Proposed approach for $\mathcal{MD}$ exploration of query-logs

$\mathcal{MD}$ space must be orthogonal. This constraint is used to determine that two different levels of one single hierarchy cannot be related to the same fact. In order to meet these constraints, we defined a process composed of three steps: (1) cleaning the logs, (2) managing graph patterns according to the constraints cited above. (3) Validating $\mathcal{MD}$ labels. Due to lack of space, the algorithm that formalizes the main steps of our approach is published in the following link: https://drive. google.com/file/d/12Gow_QKRjyyewIzY0VxmK-2oyjkHwNm4/view.

(1) Cleaning the Logs. This process aims to meet constraint *C1*. Given the logs have textual format (see Fig. 1) containing the Sparql queries and additional information like IP addresses that have been set to "0.0.0.0" for anonymisation, the country code, hash of the IP, etc., we wrote prototype in *Java* language to decode log format, to normalize the logs and to extract queries from the log. A second cleaning step is to identify Select queries or sub-queries. The other types of queries (Ask, Describe) describe the contents of $\mathcal{LOD}$ and do not reflect retrieval of data for analytical requirements. The third step parses queries, using Apache Jena 3 and Dbpedia Sparql endpoint, in order to identify valid Sparql queries, and eliminate duplicate queries.

(2) Managing Graph Patterns of Queries. This step relies on the core part of the query: the graph patterns. In order to meet constraint (*C2: facts are related to levels by to-one relationships*), this process relies on identifying graph patterns that are joined. The intuitive idea is to identify the queries where the user expresses a $\mathcal{MD}$ requirement by joining facts according to different dimensions. Managing graph patterns is achieved in three steps:

(i) Parsing graph patterns. Using Jena API, the triple algebra <subject (s), predicate (p), object (o)> of each pattern is generated. For instance, the triple algebra of a DBpedia Query (Q1) is parsed as follows:

```
query parser (distinct  (bgp
    (triple ?art_name rdf:type <http://dbpedia.org/ontology/artist>)
    (triple ?alb_name <http://dbpedia.org/property/artist> ?art_name)
    (triple ?alb_name <http://dbpedia.org/property/name> ?alb)
    (triple ?alb_name <http://dbpedia.org/ontology/genre> ?genre)   ))
```

Triples are then *abstracted*, i.e. variables (?var) are replaced by their real resource as defined in the $\mathcal{KB}$ of the $\mathcal{LOD}$. This resource can be indicated in the original query, otherwise we identify it by adding a pattern (*?var rdf:type ?class*) to the query which is then executed in Sparql endpoint to get the result of variable ?class. For example: (*?art_name rdf:type Artist*) in Query Q1, the class *Artist* is considered instead of the variable *?art_name* in all other triples where *?art_name* appears. Triples containing predicate (*rdf:type* or its equivalent *dbo:a*) are then ignored for the rest of the process. If the predicate is a blank node, the subject and object should not be blank nodes, otherwise the triple is not considered.

(ii) Generating Star graphs. According to how joins connect triple patterns, study [11] identified four types of graphs: Star, Path, Hybrid and Sink. We consider the Star join graph which corresponds to the join structure of constraint C2 (i.e. facts are joined to their dimesnions). Star graphs are constructed from the set of triples as follows. A graph vertex is generated for each new subject of a triple. Graphs sharing the same subject are consolidated incrementally to form a single graph. The predicate of the triple is then analyzed. If the predicate is a real node, its type is analyzed (relationship or datatype property) using ASK query. If the predicate is a data type property, it is added as additional information in the vertex. If the predicate is of type ObjectProperty, the multiplicity of the predicate is then analyzed to check if it is to-one relationship (constraint (C2)). A node defining the object of the triple and an edge (predicate name) from the vertex to this node are created. If the predicate is a blank node, the triple is retained. Later, the designer can decide if an adequate relationship can be assigned. The set of graphs formed by triples are directed acyclic graph (DAG) as illustrated in Fig. 2.

(iii) $\mathcal{MD}$ labeling of the graphs. Before labeling the graphs obtained, two cases allow rejecting some graphs: (1) Graphs containing only one node are either rejected or presented to the designer. (2) Facts that have not any numerical property (can not be aggregated) are considered but require the validation of the designer. The $\mathcal{MD}$ patterns are identified in the consolidated graphs. The structure of the star graph identifies intuitively the central node as a fact and the outgoing nodes as potential dimensions or attributes. For example, from query Q1, the classes <MusicGenres> and <Artist> are identified as dimensions of the fact <Album> which has *name* as an attribute.

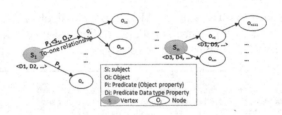

Fig. 2. Graph construction

(3) Validating $\mathcal{MD}$ Labels. Once the labeling is done, the validation of the graphs checks special cases: (1) If a node is identified as a fact in graph S1 and as a dimension in graph S2, constraint C3 is not respected. In this case, we give priority to the fact concept in S1 and we reject the dimension in S2. (2) If a node is identified as a base dimension in one graph (in path P1) and as a level dimension in the same graph (in path P2), constraint C4 is not respected. In this case, and because P2 includes P1, path P1 is rejected and P2 is retained.

5   Results

The experiments we conducted analyze the logs obtained from USEWOD 2016 Research Dataset[10] containing queries formulated against dbpedia-3.9 (file of *49,4* Gigabyte containing *45.639.521* queries). The experiments were performed on a machine OS Ubuntu server 16.04 LTS, 8 Go of RAM, Processor Intel(R) Xeon(R) CPU E5-2630 v3 @ 2.40GHz. Table 1 resumes the results obtained. Because Dbpedia is a generalist $\mathcal{KB}$ (not related to a specific domain), each column of the table represents a given concept used to filter the queries. The table illustrates the results according to criteria related to the main steps of our approach (cleaning logs, managing graph patterns, $\mathcal{MD}$ labelling). Note that the third criterion refers to the number of intermediate graphs, i.e. star graphs considered before the consolidation. These results show that for each concept, a considerable set of queries are valid, i.e. they can be analyzed for identifying $\mathcal{MD}$ patterns. The script we implemented for the process generates important number of graphs incrementally. From the valid graphs, the number of identified $\mathcal{MD}$ patterns vary according to the concept entered. For example, the concept *University* shows the highest $\mathcal{MD}$ patterns, and *Publication* shows the lowest number of $\mathcal{MD}$ patterns. When analyzing the contents of these $\mathcal{MD}$ patterns, we have noticed that some concepts do not have the same meaning of the intended concept (for example, for concept Game, some queries refer to Game of Thrones TV show). These mismatch concepts are present with an average rate of 6%. What is reported in the table is the number of facts validated by a $\mathcal{DW}$ designer, i.e. star schema that are valid semantically. We notice that an important rate of fact and dimension concepts are identified by the process, but the number of attributes is low. This is explained by the low rate of attributes in the formulation of queries comparing to concepts. The number of levels is also low, which indicates that the relevant queries are constructed by users as star schemas and not according to different levels of analysis. However, once the fact or dimension is identified by our process, the designer can easily find their corresponding attributes on Dbpedia $\mathcal{KB}$. These results show the added-value of query-logs in terms of $\mathcal{MD}$ knowledge that the designer can incorporate to the $\mathcal{DW}$, at the schema level and at the instance level (last line of the table).

---

[10] M. Luczak-Roesch, Z. A. Saud, B. Berendt, and L. Hollink. Usewod 2016 research dataset, 2016.

Table 1. Results obtained from logs analysis

Results	Book	University	Publication	Media	Software	Album	Movie	Game	Hotel	Airport
Valid queries	7222	4262	2876	349	6114	2451	1208	55	979	673
Non valid Qr	3433	1746	2009	2193	1359	2263	646	126	186	722
Inter. graphs	8030	14647	12167	496	33666	13489	3603	105	4481	1354
Nb facts	20	10	9	22	3	1	19	2	5	4
Nb measures	2	1	6	1	2	2	17	1	1	1
Nb dim	25	19	13	29	4	2	12	2	14	7
Nb dim Att	11	5	2	1	1	2	3	1	1	1
Nb levels	1	0	0	1	1	1	1	0	0	0
Nb triples	52143	31091	54961	40155	20327	40254	20435	20034	20200	27329

6   Conclusion

The challenge of data management systems in a world facing the $\mathcal{LOD}$ is to rip the relevant information from these important amounts of data. In $\mathcal{DW}$ design context, $\mathcal{MD}$ knowledge represents the valuable information that designers use to enrich the $\mathcal{DW}$ system. We propose in this study to exploit a component of $\mathcal{LOD}$ ecosystem that has not been exploited yet in $\mathcal{DW}$ design: the query-logs. We propose a process for analyzing the logs and incrementally identifying $\mathcal{MD}$ patterns respecting four constraints defined for retrieving data from a $\mathcal{MD}$ perspective. Query-logs of Dbpedia are used to evaluate the process. As perspectives, this study can be extended by: (i) the evaluation of the quality of $\mathcal{MD}$ patterns in a real world scenario, (ii) the consideration of advanced $\mathcal{MD}$ patterns (like multiple hierarchies) and (iii) the evaluation of the provenance and more generally the quality of $\mathcal{LOD}$ fragments identified.

Acknowledgments. This research work is carried out thanks to the support of the European Union through the PLAIBDE (Plateforme Intégrée Big-Data pour les Données Entreprise) project of the Program FEDER-FSE (http://www.europe-en-poitou-charentes.eu/Les-projets-soutenus-en-Poitou-Charentes/Travaux-de-recherche-pour-la-creation-d-une-Plateforme-integree-Big-Data-pour-les-donnees-entreprise-PLAIBDE-PC470) of Nouvelle Aquitaine region. The FEDER-PLAIBDE project is directed by the lead manager of aYaline (https://www.ayaline.com/) company, and the laboratories partners: L3i (http://l3i.univ-larochelle.fr/) laboratory of La Rochelle University (France) and LIAS laboratory of ENSMA (France).

References

1. Abelló, A.: Using semantic web technologies for exploratory OLAP: a survey. IEEE Trans. Knowl. Data Eng. **27**(2), 571–588 (2015)
2. Aligon, J., Gallinucci, E., Golfarelli, M., Marcel, P., Rizzi, S.: A collaborative filtering approach for recommending olap sessions. Decis. Support. Syst. J. **69**, 20–30 (2015)

3. Baldacci, L., Golfarelli, M., Graziani, S., Rizzi, S.: QETL: an approach to on-demand etl from non-owned data sources. DKE **112**, 17–37 (2017)
4. Belo, O., Dias, N., Ferreira, C., Pinto, F.: A process mining approach for discovering ETL black points. In: Rocha, Á., Correia, A.M., Adeli, H., Reis, L.P., Costanzo, S. (eds.) WorldCIST 2017. AISC, vol. 570, pp. 426–435. Springer, Cham (2017). https://doi.org/10.1007/978-3-319-56538-5_43
5. Bonifati, A., Martens, W., Timm, T.: An analytical study of large SPARQL query logs. Proc. VLDB Endow. **11**(2), 149–161 (2017)
6. Chaudhuri, S., Dayal, U., Narasayya, V.: An overview of business intelligence technology. Commun. ACM **54**(8), 88–98 (2011)
7. Etcheverry, L., Vaisman, A., Zimányi, E.: Modeling and querying data warehouses on the semantic web using QB4OLAP. In: Bellatreche, L., Mohania, M.K. (eds.) DaWaK 2014. LNCS, vol. 8646, pp. 45–56. Springer, Cham (2014). https://doi.org/10.1007/978-3-319-10160-6_5
8. Gamazo, A., et al.: Towards exploratory OLAP on linked data. In: SEBD, pp. 86–93 (2016)
9. Rizzi, S., Abelló, A., Lechtenbörger, J., Trujillo, J.: Research in data warehouse modeling and design: dead or alive? In: DOLAP, pp. 3–10. ACM (2006)
10. Romero, O., Abelló, A.: Automatic validation of requirements to support multidimensional design. Data Knowl. Eng. **69**(9), 917–942 (2010)
11. Saleem, M., Ali, M.I., Hogan, A., Mehmood, Q., Ngomo, A.-C.N.: LSQ: the linked SPARQL queries dataset. In: Arenas, M., et al. (eds.) ISWC 2015. LNCS, vol. 9367, pp. 261–269. Springer, Cham (2015). https://doi.org/10.1007/978-3-319-25010-6_15
12. Sapia, C.: PROMISE: predicting query behavior to enable predictive caching strategies for OLAP systems. In: Kambayashi, Y., Mohania, M., Tjoa, A.M. (eds.) DaWaK 2000. LNCS, vol. 1874, pp. 224–233. Springer, Heidelberg (2000). https://doi.org/10.1007/3-540-44466-1_22
13. Spoth, W., Arab, B.S., et al.: Adaptive schema databases. In: CIDR (2017)

Parallelization of XPath Queries Using Modern XQuery Processors

Shigeyuki Sato[✉], Wei Hao, and Kiminori Matsuzaki

Kochi University of Technology, 185 Miyanokuchi, Tosayamada, Kami, Kochi
782–8502, Japan
{sato.shigeyuki,matsuzaki.kiminori}@kochi-tech.ac.jp,
188004h@gs.kochi-tech.ac.jp

Abstract. A practical and promising approach to parallelizing XPath
queries was proposed by Bordawekar et al. in 2009, which enables parallelization on top of existing XML database engines. Although they
experimentally demonstrated the speedup by their approach, their practice has already been out of date because the software environment has
largely changed with the capability of XQuery processing. In this work,
we implement their approach in two ways on top of a state-of-the-art
XML database engine and experimentally demonstrate that our implementations can bring significant speedup on a commodity server.

1 Introduction

Parallelization of XPath queries has been studied but still far from practical
use. Most of the existing studies [4,8,9] were based on divide-and-conquer algorithms on a given XML document. Although these approaches are algorithmi-
cally sophisticated, they are, unfortunately, impractical in terms of engineering
because they confine input queries to small subsets of XPath and necessitate
implementing dedicated XML database engines. In contrast, Bordawekar et al.
[3] presented an ad hoc yet practical approach that allows us to use off-the-shelf
XML database engines for parallelization on shared-memory computers; it was
based on cheap query split. In this work, we focus on the latter approach from
a practical perspective.

Although Bordawekar et al.'s approach itself is promising in terms of engineering, their work has already been out of date in this day and age, particularly in terms of software environment. A big difference exists in sophistication
of XML database engines. They used an XSLT processor (Xalan-C++ version
1.10) released in 2004, when a matter of the highest priority would have been
standards conformance. Now, industrial-grade XML database engines such as
BaseX[1] are freely available and we thus can enjoy high-performance queries of
high expressiveness. We therefore should implement parallelization with serious consideration of underlying XML database engines, in analogy with existing

---

[1] http://basex.org/.

A. Benczúr et al. (Eds.): ADBIS 2018, CCIS 909, pp. 54–62, 2018.
https://doi.org/10.1007/978-3-030-00063-9_7

studies [1,5] on efficient XPath query processing on relational database management systems. In summary, the following is our research question: *How should we implement query-split parallelization on state-of-the-art XML database engines?*

To answer this question, in this work, we have developed two implementations of query-split parallelization on top of BaseX, which implements XQuery and extensions efficiently [7] and involves a powerful query optimizer [12]. We have evaluated our implementations experimentally with non-trivial queries according to prior work [3] over gigabyte-scale datasets and achieved significant speedup on a modern server. Through this practice, we have discovered a simple way of accommodating query-split parallelization to the query optimization in BaseX. Our main contributions are summarized as follows.

- We have developed two implementations of query-split parallelization [3] on top of BaseX (Sect. 3). One is a simple revival of prior work [3] on BaseX; the other takes advantage of rich features of BaseX.
- We have discovered a simple remedy for a problem on integrating query-split parallelization with the query optimization of BaseX (Sect. 4).
- We have experimentally demonstrated that our implementations were able to achieve up to 4.86x speedup on a 12-core commodity server for non-trivial queries over gigabyte-scale datasets (Sect. 5).

2   Query-Split Parallelization

In this section, we describe Bordawekar et al.'s approach [3] to parallel XPath query processing. We assume readers' familiarity with XPath.

Bordawekar et al. presented a cheap approach to parallel evaluation of a single XPath query. Their approach is to split a given query into subqueries in an ad hoc manner and to evaluate them in parallel. Although they basically proposed several strategies, in this paper, we deal with one of them, data partitioning, because it is easier to apply without the knowledge on target XML data and generally outperformed the other strategies in their experimental comparison [3].

Data partitioning is to split a given query into a prefix query and a suffix query, e.g., from q_1/q_2 to prefix q_1 and suffix q_2, and to run the suffix query in parallel on each node in the result of the prefix query. To construct final results, we have only to concatenate results in order.

In this paper, we use the same set of queries over XMark [11] datasets and the DBLP dataset as [3] except for DB3, which is a little modified from the original one for experiments (see Sect. 5). See the full version [10] for the details.

3   Implementing Data Partitioning with BaseX

We describe our two implementations called of data partitioning on top of BaseX. We call them the client-side implementation and the server-side implementation because of the difference in the way of managing the results of prefix queries.

Our implementations involve worker threads of simple BaseX clients that hold independent connections to the BaseX server. After the master thread issues a prefix query, each worker thread issues a suffix query.

In the rest of this section, we describe our implementations by using XM3(a) as a running example, assuming the input database to be named 'xmark'. Let P be the number of threads. We assume reders' familiarity with the XQuery APIs of BaseX. See the full version [10] for detailed discussions on BaseX's features.

Client-Side Implementation. The client-side implementation is a simple implementation of data partitioning with database operations on BaseX. It sends the server a prefix query that returns the PRE values of hit nodes as follows.

```
for $x in db:open('xmark')/site//open_auction
  return db:node-pre($x)
```

Let this prefix query return sequence (2, 5, 42, 81, 109, 203) through a network. Letting $P = 3$, it is block-partitioned to (2, 5), (42, 81), and (109, 203), each of which is assigned to a worker thread. To avoid repetitive ping-pong between the client(s) and the server, we use the following suffix query template:

```
for $x in ⟨⟨sequence of PRE⟩⟩
  return db:open-pre('xmark', $x)/bidder[last()] ,
```

where ⟨⟨sequence of PRE⟩⟩ is a placeholder to be replaced with a concrete partition, e.g., (42, 81). Each thread instantiates this template with its own partition and sends the server the instantiated query.

Server-Side Implementation. A necessary task on the results of a prefix query is to block-partition them. The client-side implementation does it simply on the client side. In fact, we can also implement it efficiently on the server side by utilizing BaseX's features.

First, we prepare an in-memory XML database named 'tmp' initialized with <root> </root>, which is a temporary database for storing the results of a prefix query. The prefix query is implemented as follows:

```
let $P := ⟨⟨number of partitions⟩⟩
let $s := db:open('xmark')/site//open_auction ! db:node-pre(.)
for $i in 1 to $P
  return insert node element part { $blk_part($i, $P, $s) }
         as last into db:open('tmp')/root ,
```

where ⟨⟨number of partitions⟩⟩ denotes a placeholder to be replaced with a concrete value of P and $blk_part($i, $P, $s) denotes the $ith one of $P partitions of $s implemented in logarithmic time with sequence operations.

In the example case used earlier, 'tmp' database results in the following:

```
1<root>
  2<part>32 5</part>4<part>542 81</part>6<part>7109 203</part>
  </root> ,
```

where a left superscript denotes a PRE value. Note that its document structure determines the PRE value of ith partition to be $2i + 1$.

A suffix query is implemented with deserialization of a partition as follows:

```
for $x in ft:tokenize(db:open-pre('tmp', ⟨⟨PRE of partition⟩⟩))
  return db:open-pre('xmark', xs:integer($x))/bidder[last()]) ,
```

where ⟨⟨PRE of partition⟩⟩ denotes a placeholder to be replaced with the PRE value of a target partition and the care of empty partitions is omitted for brevity.

The server-side implementation is more efficient because transferred data between clients and a server except for output are in a constant size.

4 Integration with Query Optimization

BaseX is equipped with a powerful query optimizer. For example, BaseX optimizes XM3 to /site/open_auctions/open_auction/bidder[last()] on the basis of the path index, which brings knowledge that open_auction exists only immediately below open_auctions and open_auctions exists only immediately below site. The search space of this optimized query has significantly reduced because an expensive step of descendant-or-self axis is replaced with two cheap steps of child axes. It is worth noting that a more drastic result is observed in XM2, where the attribute index is exploited through function db:attribute.

Data partitioning converts a given query to two separate ones and therefore affects the capability of BaseX in query optimization. In fact, the suffix query of XM3(b) is not optimized to the corresponding part of optimized XM3 because BaseX does not utilize indices for optimizing queries starting from nodes specified with PRE values even if possible in principle.

A simple way of resolving this discord is to apply data partitioning after BaseX's query optimization. Data partitioning is applicable to any multi-step XPath query in principle. Even if an optimized query is thoroughly different from its original query as in XM2, it is entirely adequate to apply data partitioning to the optimized query, forgetting the original. In fact, XM2–4(c) are instances of such data partitioning after optimization. This coordination is so simple that we are still able to implement data partitioning only by using BaseX's dumps of optimized queries without any modification on BaseX. This is a big benefit.

5 Experiments

5.1 Experimental Setting

We have conducted several experiments to evaluate the performance of the two implementations of parallel XPath queries. All the experiments were conducted on a computer that equipped with two Intel Xeon E5-2620 v3 CPUs (2×6 cores, 2.4 GHz, Hyper-Threading off) and 32-GB memory (DDR4-1866). The software environment we used was Java OpenJDK 64-Bit Server VM (ver. 9-internal,

`9~b114-0ubuntu1` in Ubuntu 16.04 LTS) and BaseX ver. 9.0.1 (`3a8b2ad6`) with minor modifications to enable TCP_NODELAY.

We used two datasets: XMark and DBLP. We generated an XMark dataset with XMLgen[2] giving `-f 10`, which was of 1.1 GB and had 16 million nodes. The root of the XMark tree has six children `regions`, `people`, `open_auctions`, `closed_auctions`, `catgraph`, and `categories`, which have 6, 255000, 120000, 97500, 10000, and 10000 children, respectively. Refer to [11] for more details of the XMark dataset. The DBLP dataset was the latest one downloaded from the DBLP website[3], where the date of the downloaded file was August 29, 2017 and the dataset was of 2.2 GB and had 53 million nodes. The DBLP tree was flat; the root element has 6 million children.

We used the XPath queries are the same as those used in [3] except for DB3. We modified DB3 to alleviate the computational cost because the original one costs quadratic time, which was too costly to run over the latest DBLP dataset. The suffixes (a)–(c) mean variations of data partitioning. We measured execution time until the client received all the results of suffix queries into byte streams. We executed both the client-side implementation and the server-side one for each parallel XPath query. The execution time does not include the loading time, that is, the input dataset was loaded into memory before the execution of queries. We measured the execution time of 25 runs after a warm-up run and picked up their median.

5.2   Total Execution Time

Table 1 summarizes the execution time of the queries. The "orig t_o" column shows the time for executing original queries XM1–XM6 and DB1–DB3 with BaseX's `xquery` command. The "seq t_s" columns show the time for executing the prefix query and the suffix query with one thread. The "par t_p" columns show the time for executing the prefix query with one thread and the suffix query with 12 threads. The table also includes for reference the speedup of parallel queries with respect to original queries and the size of results of the prefix queries and the whole queries.

By using the pair of the prefix and suffix queries split at an appropriate step, we achieved speedups by factor about 2.0 for XM1 and XM3, and by factor of more than 3.7 for XM4 and XM6. The execution time of XM2 was very short because BaseX executed an optimized query that utilized the attribute index as mentioned in Sect. 4. By designing the parallel query XM2(c) based on that optimized query, the execution time of parallel query was just longer than that of original query by 2 ms. Comparing the two implementations, we observed that the server-side implementation ran faster for most queries.

Although some of parallel queries did not reached the performance of their original queries, these were reasonable. XM2(a)–(b) were due to index-based optimizations; XM2(c) was too cheap to benefit from parallel evaluation. XM4(a)

---

[2] https://projects.cwi.nl/xmark/downloads.html.
[3] https://dblp.uni-trier.de/xml/.

Table 1. Summary of execution time.

Key	orig t_o	Client-side			Server-side			Result size	
		seq t_s	par t_p	(t_o/t_p)	seq t_s	par t_p	(t_o/t_p)	Prefix	Final
XM1(a)	37263	44443	18058	(2.06)	40084	16137	(2.31)	54 B	994 MB
XM2(a)	2	2856	1055	(0.00)	1075	808	(0.00)	6.62 MB	1.55 KB
XM2(b)		1029	937	(0.00)	1049	902	(0.00)	54 B	
XM2(c)		3	4	(0.50)	3	4	(0.50)	671 B	
XM3(a)	639	1180	304	(2.10)	848	302	(2.12)	1.08 MB	14.5 MB
XM3(b)		1816	1663	(0.38)	1857	1490	(0.43)	54 B	
XM3(c)		1154	305	(2.10)	850	321	(1.99)	1.08 MB	
XM4(a)	1148	1595	1595	(0.72)	1647	1084	(1.06)	49 B	26.4 MB
XM4(b)		1858	545	(2.11)	1402	493	(2.33)	1.75 MB	
XM4(c)		1121	245	(4.69)	1232	236	(4.86)	106 KB	
XM5(a)	715	2535	828	(0.86)	1288	651	(1.10)	5.38 MB	15.9 MB
XM5(b)		1209	462	(1.55)	955	432	(1.66)	1.08 MB	
XM6(a)	820	954	929	(0.88)	970	933	(0.88)	49 B	22.2 MB
XM6(b)		1004	219	(3.74)	1084	207	(3.96)	183 KB	
DB1(a)	6759	12498	4185	(1.62)	8451	2730	(2.48)	15.8 MB	176 MB
DB2(a)	15641	34729	8555	(1.83)	19191	6082	(2.57)	56.9 MB	423 MB
DB2(b)		34713	8564	(1.83)	19105	6405	(2.44)	56.9 MB	
DB3(a)	888	1115	1092	(0.81)	1043	953	(0.93)	139 KB	1.9 MB

and XM6(a) were due to load imbalance derived from data skewness. XM5(a) and DB3(a) were due to the cheapness of the suffix queries compared to the prefix ones; their suffix queries visited few nodes from a starting one and merely filtered the results of their prefix queries.

See the full version [10] for the performance breakdown of parallel queries.

5.3   Scalability Analysis

When we analyze the speedup of parallel execution, the ratio of sequential execution part to the whole computation is important because it limits the possible speedup by Amdahl's law. In the two implementations, most of the sequential execution part consists in the prefix query. The ratio of the sequential execution part was small in general: more specifically, the client-side implementation had smaller ratio (e.g. 12.6% for DB1(a)) than the server-side implementation had (e.g. 16.6% for DB1(a)). In our implementations, the suffix queries were independently executed in parallel through individual connections to the BaseX server. The speedups we observed for the suffix queries were, however, smaller than we had expected. We also noticed that in some cases the execution time was longer with more threads (for example, XM3(c) P = 12 with the server-side implementation).

Table 2. Load balance and increase of work of server-side implementation (load-balance/increase-of-work)

	$P=2$	$P=3$	$P=6$	$P=12$
XM1(a)	1.51/1.02	1.59/1.04	2.83/1.15	2.87/1.15
XM3(c)	1.95/1.12	2.84/1.18	5.38/1.46	9.01/2.84
XM4(c)	1.97/1.19	2.82/1.27	2.59/3.55	10.25/1.84
XM5(b)	1.91/1.19	2.79/1.31	3.97/3.13	11.31/4.57
XM6(b)	1.94/1.15	2.76/1.25	5.40/1.30	10.35/1.82
DB1(a)	1.95/1.12	2.86/1.13	5.69/1.24	10.79/2.27
DB2(a)	1.58/1.07	2.38/1.12	4.68/1.25	9.80/2.22
DB3(a)	1.16/0.97	1.24/1.06	1.45/1.15	1.83/1.52

To understand the reason why the speedups of the suffix queries were small, we made two more analyses (Table 2). The degree of load balance in processing suffix queries was calculated as the cumulative execution time divided the maximum execution time: $\sum t_i^p / \max t_i^p$, where t_i^p denotes the execution time of the ith suffix query in parallel with p threads. The increase of work of the suffix queries was calculated by the cumulative execution time divided by the single-thread execution time: $\sum t_i^p / t_1^1$.

From Table 2, we can observe the reasons of the small speedups in the suffix queries. Obvious load imbalances were incurred in XM1(a) and DB3(a) for different reasons. For XM1(a), the hit nodes by the prefix query were very few and less than the number of cores. For DB3(a), the computational cost of each suffix query was quite different because of data skewness. For the other cases, we achieved good load balance, and the degrees of load balance were more than 75% even with 12 threads, which means that load imbalance was not the main cause of small speedups for those queries. The increase of work was significant for XM5(b) and XM3(c), and it was the main cause that the queries XM5(b) and XM3(c) had small speedups. For the other queries, we observed very small increase of work until 6 threads, but the work increased when 12 threads. Such an increase of work is often caused by contention to memory access, and it is inevitable in shared-memory multicore computers.

6   Concluding Remarks

In this paper, we have reassesed data-partitioning parallelization of XPath queries proposed by Bordawekar et al. [3] on top of BaseX. We have developed two implementations on the basis of BaseX's features. The server-side implementation, which particularly exploits rich features of BaseX, achieved roughly better experimental speedup because of lower overhead in querying.

Surprisingly, Bordawekar et al.'s approach [3] has not been well studied regardless of its great virtue in engineering. They studied by themselves on the sophistication of the query split strategies based on the statistics of a given document [2]. Since that, follow-up studies had not been seen for a long time, but most recently, Karsin et al. [6] has studied on the scheduling of suffix query tasks. They investigated three kinds of task generation and showed experimentally their trade-off between overhead and load imbalance. However, they did not focus on the great advantage in engineering and used their own sequential query engine for pursuing experimental performance predictability. In contrast, our work focuses on how to integrate Bordawekar et al.'s approach into state-of-the-art XML database engines from a practical perspective.

Acknowledgements. We would like to thank Christian Grün of the BaseX team for his technical comments and feedback on BaseX.

References

1. Boncz, P., Grust, T., van Keulen, M., Manegold, S., Rittinger, J., Teubner, J.: MonetDB/XQuery: a fast XQuery processor powered by a relational engine. In: Proceedings of the 2006 ACM SIGMOD International Conference on Management of Data (SIGMOD 2006), pp. 479–490. ACM (2006)
2. Bordawekar, R., Lim, L., Kementsietsidis, A., Kok, B.W.L.: Statistics-based parallelization of XPath queries in shared memory systems. In: Proceedings of the 13th International Conference on Extending Database Technology (EDBT 2010), pp. 159–170. ACM (2010)
3. Bordawekar, R., Lim, L., Shmueli, O.: Parallelization of XPath queries using multicore processors: challenges and experiences. In: Proceedings of the 12th International Conference on Extending Database Technology (EDBT 2009), pp. 180–191. ACM (2009)
4. Cong, G., Fan, W., Kementsietsidis, A., Li, J., Liu, X.: Partial evaluation for distributed XPath query processing and beyond. ACM Trans. Database Syst. **37**(4), 32:1–32:43 (2012)
5. Grust, T., Rittinger, J., Teubner, J.: Why off-the-shelf RDBMSs are better at XPath than you might expect. In: Proceedings of the 2007 ACM SIGMOD International Conference on Management of Data (SIGMOD 2007), pp. 949–958. ACM (2007)
6. Karsin, B., Casanova, H., Lim, L.: Low-latency XPath query evaluation on multicore processors. In: Proceedings of the 50th Hawaii International Conference on System Sciences (HICSS 2017), pp. 6222–6231 (2017)
7. Kircher, L., Grossniklaus, M., Grün, C., Scholl, M.H.: Efficient structural bulk updates on the pre/dist/size XML encoding. In: Proceedings of the 31st IEEE International Conference on Data Engineering (ICDE 2015), pp. 447–458. IEEE (2015)
8. Kling, P., Özsu, M.T., Daudjee, K.: Scaling XML query processing: distribution, localization and pruning. Distrib. Parallel Databases **29**(5–6), 445–490 (2011)
9. Ogden, P., Thomas, D., Pietzuch, P.: Scalable XML query processing using parallel pushdown transducers. PVLDB **6**(14), 1738–1749 (2013)
10. Sato, S., Hao, W., Matsuzaki, K.: Parallelization of xpath queries using modern xquery processors. CoRR abs/1806.07728 (2018). https://arxiv.org/abs/1806. 07728

11. Schmidt, A., Waas, F., Kersten, M., Carey, M.J., Manolescu, I., Busse, R.: XMark: a benchmark for XML data management. In: Proceedings of the 28th International Conference on Very Large Data Bases (VLDB 2002), pp. 974–985. VLDB Endowment (2002)
12. Wörteler, L., Grossniklaus, M., Grün, C., Scholl, M.H.: Function inlining in XQuery 3.0 optimization. In: Proceedings of the 15th Symposium on Database Programming Languages (DBPL 2015), pp. 45–48. ACM (2015)

Towards Detection of Usability Issues
by Measuring Emotions

Elena Stefancova, Robert Moro[✉][iD], and Maria Bielikova[iD]

Faculty of Informatics and Information Technologies, Slovak University of Technology
in Bratislava, Ilkovicova 2, 842 16 Bratislava, Slovak Republic
{xstefancovae,robert.moro,maria.bielikova}@stuba.sk

Abstract. User Experience is one of the most important criteria when
designing and testing user interfaces with emotions as its essential element. To assess, how emotions could be used for automatic detection of
usability issues, we carried out a user study with a website which included
intentionally inserted usability issues. We classified valence of emotions,
i.e., negative vs. positive ones based on data from electroencephalography
(EEG) and facial expressions recognition. The study results confirmed
that usability issues cause negative emotional response of the user and
that presence of a negative emotion is a good predictor of a usability
issue presence. When detecting negative and positive emotional states
from the acquired dataset, we achieved the accuracy of 94% for samples
with seconds granularity and 70% for the task granularity.

Keywords: Usability · Emotions · EEG · Facial expressions
Data analysis

1 Introduction and Related Work

User experience (UX) according to ISO-9241-210 is "a person's perceptions and
responses that result from the use or anticipated use of a product, system or
service". One of its factors is usability [9] which is "extent to which a product
can be used by specific users to achieve specific goals with effectiveness, efficiency
and satisfaction in a specified context of use" (ISO/TS 20282-2:2013). Usability
of a website can be measured by how easily and effectively the user can browse
and perform specific tasks on the website.

One of the components of UX are *emotions*, which can be measured by
questionnaires or by various sensors [7,9]. They are commonly represented by
Ekman's model of six basic emotions (joy, fear, sadness, disgust, anger, and surprise) [3] or a dimensional approach [11], which distinguishes two main dimensions, namely *valence* (how positive the emotion is) and *arousal* (the strength of
an emotion). When using sensors, emotions can be detected from many physio-
logical responses, such as changes in blood pressure, skin conductance (GSR), or
the character of brain waves (EEG) [5]. An interesting approach is to recognize
emotions from facial expressions, since it does not require a special equipment

© Springer Nature Switzerland AG 2018
A. Benczúr et al. (Eds.): ADBIS 2018, CCIS 909, pp. 63–70, 2018.
https://doi.org/10.1007/978-3-030-00063-9_8

(a normal webcam is usually sufficient). The accuracy of facial expression recognition can near 90% [13], but the participant usually has to stay still during the measurement, otherwise the recording can be damaged [4]. In [7], Matlovic et al. showed that the accuracy for seven classes of emotions measured by EEG using EMOTIV Epoc device was 58%, while it was only 19% in case of facial expressions recognition software Noldus FaceReader. The problem with FaceReader probably was that they took into account only the dominant emotion.

The researchers have not found a connection between significantly positive emotions and a level of usability yet, but it seems that a bad usability level can result into negative ones [9], especially when the user performs a task with a specific goal. This field of study is still to be explored, because the majority of papers on detection of emotions are concerned with affective corpora, such as watching videos or other multimedia content [7], instead of the impact of a user interface. The interface gives to a user more freedom in interaction, thus resulting into more challenges in emotions detection.

One work that did focus on emotion detection in context of usability, was the work of Aggarwal et al. They used a combination of EEG data and facial expression recognition [1] and designed two websites with the same functionality, but the first one with good and the other one with poor level of usability, established according to Shneiderman's eight golden rules of interface design [12]. The results of their exploratory study showed that user experience indeed influences emotions; in this case, it was excitement and frustration. The frustration occurred mostly during interaction with the worse website.

In our paper, we aim to verify these findings on a larger user sample. Moreover, our primary hypothesis is that a low level of usability not only causes emotional response, but that negative emotional response of a user can help to automatically expose usability issues (no automatic classification was performed in the aforementioned work [1]). This is significant during development and testing of user interfaces. A reliable method of usability issues detection would be useful mainly in such UX testing setups, where it is possible to work with more participants at once and, thus, save significant amount of (recording as well as data analysis) time or for remote testing setups.

We proposed a method of binary emotions classification using a combination of features extracted from EEG and facial expressions analysis. For the evaluation of our proposed method, we used data from sensors and self-report surveys collected during a user study, in which participants had to fulfill tasks on a website, the interface of which was modified by adding usability issues.

2 Study Methodology

Our main aim was to find out, how usability can influence emotional state of a user and if emotional response is strong enough to detect issues of usability. We used EEG and facial expressions as data sources for emotions classification. The study was conducted in the User Experience and Interaction Research Centre at the Slovak University of Technology in Bratislava[1].

For gaining EEG data we used Emotiv Epoc[2]. It is a wearable device, commonly used for interaction with applications. For analysis of facial expressions, we employed Noldus FaceReader[3], which provides basic emotion features (valence, arousal) for every frame and can recognize neutral, contempt, happy, sad, angry, surprised, scared, and disgusted facial expressions. It uses a common web camera as its input. Tobii Studio[4] was used for orchestration of our study.

2.1 Test Scenario

The participants performed eight tasks on a groupon-like website Zlava Dna[5], half of which contained an artificially added issue. The order of the tasks was counterbalanced (using *Wiliams Design*[6]). The issues were inserted by a web browser extension Greasemonkey[7]. It allowed us to customize display and behaviour of a web page by using JavaScript scripts, which could be de/actvivated during the usage of a website. We designed the issues as a violation of the commonly used heuristics of usability by Nielsen [8] and Schneiderman [12]. Some of the tasks were essentially the same, e.g., *product search*, but they differed in the product that was searched for and also in the presence or absence of an issue. There were four tasks without usability issues; the participants were asked to:

- *Find the cheapest ticket to a water park.*
- *Find, what the number of offers for a specific meal is.*
- *Find three offers for a sauna.*
- *Find a contact email on the website.*

There were four tasks with usability issues; the participants were asked to:

- *Find a specific product* – in this task, the search button was disabled unless the user clicked on it three times in a row.
- *Find five specific products on the map* – we added an issue causing problems with loading the map.
- *Find a specific product and buy three pieces of it* – the button for increasing the number of products in the basket was disabled, so the participants had to write the number manually.
- *Register* – we modified the registration so that it was necessary to enter password longer than 20 characters, but there was no error message notifying the participants of this constraint.

---

[1] http://uxi.sk.
[2] https://www.emotiv.com/epoc.
[3] http://www.noldus.com/human-behavior-research/products/facereader.
[4] http://www.tobiipro.com/product-listing/tobii-pro-studio.
[5] https://www.zlavadna.sk.
[6] http://statpages.info/latinsq.html.
[7] https://addons.mozilla.org/firefox/addon/greasemonkey.

After every task, the participants had to answer three questions: (i) How *intensive* were the emotions that you felt?, (ii) How *positive* were the emotions that you felt?, and (iii) What was the *strongest* emotion you felt? They answered on a 5-point Likert scale for the first two questions (options ranging from non-intensive to intensive for the first one and from negative to positive for the second one) and selected one of the seven options (joy, fear, sadness, disgust, anger, surprise, neutral) for the last one.

2.2   Collected Dataset

We collected data from 21 participants (18 men and 4 women with ages ranging from 18 to 30 years, all being students). We excluded recordings of insufficient quality, i.e., when FaceReader was able to analyze less than 70% of the video (this happened, e.g., when participants obstructed the view of their face with their hands). In the rest of the videos, we filled the missing data by linear interpolation. We also excluded tasks where participants gave contradictory answers, i.e., when:

– participants labeled their emotion on a negative scale in the answer to the second post-study question, but then selected a positive emotion, such as joy as their strongest emotion or vice versa,
– the participants' answer to one of the questions was "neutral", since we were interested in binary classification of emotions (positive vs. negative); however, they were left for the first part of the analysis (see Fig. 1).

Tasks were labeled *positive* or *negative* based on the emotion a participant felt during solving of the task. The total number of labeled solved tasks was 147 for EEG and 35 for both EEG and facial expressions, out of which 47% were labeled negative and 53% as positive. We worked with the collected data at seconds precision; we labeled each second as positive or negative based on the recording label. The final dataset consisted of 13 336 s of EEG (70.33% labeled negative) and 3 564 s of both EEG and facial expressions (74.76% labeled negative). Each second in the dataset was described by raw EEG features, participant's emotional state self-reported at the end of a task, and valence and arousal from analysis of facial expressions.

3   Method of Emotion Detection

Since we hypothesize that usability issues cause negative emotions and these in turn indicate a usability issue, we formulate the task of emotion detection as a binary classification problem. We extract features from raw EEG data and from facial expressions; we aim to evaluate these two data sources individually as well as their combination. We process the EEG data as follows:

1. The patterns captured by EEG are divided by frequency [6]. For this purpose, we employ Discrete wavelet transform (DWT) similarly as in [7]. To measure emotions, the most important are the *alpha* (8–13 Hz) and *beta* (14–30 Hz) waves and we must also take into account the intensity of these waves, given their localization in areas of the brain [2].

2. For arousal, high values of beta waves in the frontal lobe are typical [10]. We compute the arousal using following formula [2]:

$$Arousal = \frac{\alpha(AF3 + AF4 + F3 + F4)}{\beta(AF3 + AF4 + F3 + F4)} \tag{1}$$

where α and β are the strength of the waves and a letter with a number is a label of the electrode, on which the waves are measured. The layout and naming of electrodes for measuring EEG is standardized.

3. The most important electrodes for valence are $F3$ and $F4$ [2], which are placed also near the frontal lobe [10]. Activity of the lobe indicates positive emotions. The valence is computed as follows [2]:

$$Valence = \frac{\alpha(F4)}{\beta(F4)} - \frac{\alpha(F3)}{\beta(F3)} \tag{2}$$

Similarly, we extract valence and arousal using facial expressions analysis on videos of participants; this is provided by the Noldus FaceReader. The resulting features are normalized using *z-score normalization*[8]. From normalized data we can derive the rest of the features. To smooth the normalized valence and arousal values, we use the so-called rolling time windows, which take into account 5 s before and 5 s after the current one (the shortest tasks duration are about 10 s). After applying the smoothing, we get a new set of features including window mean, maximum, minimum, maximum deviation from the mean and difference of the current second from the mean. All of these together with the normalized and raw data are used as input to the emotion classifier. We also use features unrelated with valence and arousal, namely order of the current second to the whole duration of the task, and how the previous task was labeled (i.e., the initial emotional state of a participant).

For classification, we use a decision tree, which is commonly used to detect emotions. We divide data into training set (90%) and test set (10%) following a standard division and aiming to maximize the amount of data used for training. For feature selection, we use logistic regression with regularization L1 (LASSO). In order to find the optimal hyperparameters of the used machine learning algorithm, we perform 5-fold cross-validation on the training set; the results reported in the paper are from the application of the trained model on the test set.

4   Results

Firstly, we analyzed whether usability issues do in fact cause significantly negative emotions as suggests the distribution of participants' answers for different tasks with or without usability issues (see Fig. 1). To determine whether the observed difference is significant, we used a *paired t-test* comparing the mean self-reported values of valence for tasks with added usability issues and

---

[8] http://www.statisticshowto.com/probability-and-statistics/z-score.

without them for each participant. We found the difference to be significant $(T(83) = -9.77, p < 0.0001)$, thus confirming our hypothesis. In addition, if we considered solely the reported negative emotion as indicative of a usability issue, such a classifier would have 80.95% accuracy (82.5% precision, 78.57% recall). These results are very promising and suggest the potential of using emotions for automatic usability issues detection.

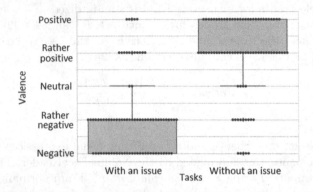

Fig. 1. Distribution of valence values for tasks self-reported by participants.

However, we first need to be able to reliably distinguish positive emotions from negative ones. Therefore, we explored the usefulness of features described in the previous section for this task; we performed automatic feature selection using logistic regression with L1 regularization on the training set. The best feature turned out to be mean value of arousal for the 10s window as measured by EEG, followed by features derived from normalized value of valence (based both on EEG and facial expressions). We explain the usefulness of arousal feature by the fact that if participants felt positive emotions, these were usually mild, while with the negative ones (caused by a usability issue) they were more aroused.

We classified emotions using our proposed method on the collected dataset (using every second of tasks as samples). We report the results for each data source (EEG and facial expressions) as well as their combination in Table 1. The combination of EEG and facial expressions outperformed the individual classifiers. These results were achieved by optimized versions of the decision tree $(criterion = \text{"gini"}, max\_depth = 9, min\_samples\_in\_leaf = 1)$. We used grid search with 5-fold cross-validation on the training set to find the optimal values the classifier hyperparameters.

Next, we wanted to evaluate the capability of our approach to generalize for unseen task or user. We created a new training set, where the ratio of the negative second samples was the same as the positive ones, and all three sets of extracted features (EEG, facial expression, and their combination) were trained on this training set. Leave-one-out cross-validation was used, i.e., we used seconds of one task of one user, which were not included in the training, as validation set in

Table 1. The results of emotion classification using EEG, facial expressions, and their combination.

	Accuracy	Precision	Recall	F1
EEG	85.6%	85.0%	76.4%	79.3%
Facial expressions	89.6%	89.4%	83.0%	85.4%
Combination	94.4%	94.6%	90.6%	92.4%

each iteration. This was done for every solved task and the results were averaged. All three classifiers achieved much lower accuracy around 55%, which is above random, but suggests problems with over-fitting.

To overcome this problem, we tried to apply our proposed method on the data averaged for the whole tasks. Since we had 147 observation of task solving for EEG data, but only 35 for combination of EEG and facial expressions, we carried out this part of evaluation only for EEG data. The trained decision tree classifier had accuracy of about 70% (on approximately balanced data). The best features in this case were maximal and minimal values of arousal and maximal deviation of valence from its mean (computed based on the whole task duration).

5 Conclusions and Future Work

We demonstrated the potential of using emotions to automatically detect usability issues during usability testing. The results of our study suggest that usability has a strong connection to emotions—mainly negative ones—and the detected negative emotion is a good indicator of a usability issue. We also proposed a method of emotions detection or more precisely, their valence that combines features from EEG device and facial expressions recognized with a basic webcam. The achieved classification results are promising.

Nevertheless, the presented evaluation had several limitations. First, the usability issues were added into the tested webpage intentionally, which might have lowered their ecological validity. An experiment with natural usability issues is needed in the future. Further experiments are also needed to determine, how the severity of the usability issues affects the emotions, i.e., what level of severity is a borderline to illicit an emotion and thus for issues to be recognized by our proposed method. Additionally, the participant sample was quite homogeneous in our study. It remains an open question, how other factors (age, gender, computer literacy, etc.) can impact the emotional effects of the usability issues.

Second, although we worked with the data at seconds precision, they were labeled for the whole task; a more fine-grained labelling of changing emotional states might lead to better results. Lastly, we did not test, how the trained model generalizes for a different tested interface, i.e., whether it would be possible to train the model during testing of one interface and apply it (with sufficient accuracy) to a new one. This remains a future work as well.

Acknowledgement. This work was partially supported by grants No. APVV-15-0508, VG 1/0646/15 and VG 1/0667/18 and it was created with the support of the Ministry of Education, Science, Research and Sport of the Slovak Republic within the Research and Development Operational Programme for the project "University Science Park of STU Bratislava", ITMS 26240220084, co-funded by the ERDF.

References

1. Aggarwal, A., Niezen, G., Thimbleby, H.: User experience evaluation through the brain's electrical activity. In: Proceedings of the 8th Nordic Conference on Human-Computer Interaction Fun, Fast, Foundational - NordiCHI 2014, pp. 491–500. ACM Press, New York, USA (2014). https://doi.org/10.1145/2639189.2639236
2. Blaiech, H., Neji, M., Wali, A., Alimi, A.M.: Emotion recognition by analysis of EEG signals. In: 13th International Conference on Hybrid Intelligent Systems (HIS 2013), pp. 312–318. IEEE (2013). https://doi.org/10.1109/HIS.2013.6920451
3. Ekman, P.E., Davidson, R.J.: The Nature of Emotion: Fundamental Questions. Oxford University Press, New York (1994)
4. Landowska, A.: Towards emotion acquisition in IT usability evaluation context. In: Proceedings of the Mulitimedia, Interaction, Design and Innnovation, pp. 1–9 (2015). https://doi.org/10.1145/2814464.2814470
5. Levenson, R.W.: Autonomic nervous system differences among emotions. Psychol. Sci. **3**(1), 23–27 (1992). https://doi.org/10.1111/j.1467-9280.1992.tb00251.x
6. Lin, Y.P., Wang, C.H., Wu, T.L., Jeng, S.K., Chen, J.H.: EEG-based emotion recognition in music listening: a comparison of schemes for multiclass support vector machine. In: 2009 IEEE International Conference on Acoustics, Speech and Signal Processing, pp. 489–492 (2009). https://doi.org/10.1109/ICASSP.2009.4959627
7. Matlovic, T., Gaspar, P., Moro, R., Simko, J., Bielikova, M.: Emotions detection using facial expressions recognition and EEG. In: Proceedings of 11th International Workshop on Semantic and Social Media Adaptation and Personalization (SMAP 2016), pp. 18–23. IEEE (2016). https://doi.org/10.1109/SMAP.2016.7753378
8. Nielsen, J.: Enhancing the explanatory power of usability heuristics. In: Proceedings of the SIGCHI Conference on Human Factors in Computing Systems, CHI 1994, pp. 152–158. ACM, New York (1994). https://doi.org/10.1145/191666.191729
9. Raita, E., Oulasvirta, A.: Mixed feelings?: the relationship between perceived usability and user experience in the wild. In: Proceedings of the 8th Nordic Conference on Human-Computer Interaction: Fun, Fast, Foundational, NordiCHI 2014, pp. 1–10. ACM, New York (2014). https://doi.org/10.1145/2639189.2639207
10. Russell, J.A.: A circumplex model of affect. J. Pers. Soc. Psychol. **39**, 1161–1178 (1980)
11. Scherer, K.R.: What are emotions? And how can they be measured? Soc. Sci. Inf. **44**(4), 695–729 (2005). https://doi.org/10.1177/0539018405058216
12. Shneiderman, B.: Designing the User Interface: Strategies for Effective Human-computer Interaction. Addison-Wesley Longman Publ. Co. Inc., Boston (1986)
13. Takahashi, K.: Remarks on emotion recognition from multi-modal bio-potential signals. In: 2004 IEEE International Conference on Industrial Technology, ICIT 2004, vol. 3, pp. 186–191. IEEE (2004). https://doi.org/10.1109/ICIT.2004.1490720

Personal Names Popularity Estimation and Its Application to Record Linkage

Ksenia Zhagorina[1], Pavel Braslavski[2,3]([⊠]), and Vladimir Gusev[2]

[1] Yandex, Yekaterinburg, Russia
Ksenia.Zhagorina@yandex.ru
[2] Ural Federal University, Yekaterinburg, Russia
{Pavel.Braslavsky,Vladimir.Gusev}@urfu.ru
[3] JetBrains Research, Saint Petersburg, Russia

Abstract. In this study, we investigate several statistical techniques for personal name popularity estimation and perform a record linkage experiment guided by name popularity estimates. The results show that name popularity can leverage personal name matching in databases and be of interest for many other domains.

Keywords: Personal name matching · Record linkage
Name distribution

1 Introduction

Record linkage – the task of matching records referring to the same real-world entity – is a well-studied field within database technology. The task arises when several databases are merged or one is interested in linking duplicate records within a single database. Records referring to people are the most common objects of linkage task. Our study is motivated by an applied record linkage task in a large database, where occurrences of personal names are accompanied with no or only scarce additional information. Under these circumstances, name popularity estimates serve as the main signal for record matching.

Knowing an estimate of people bearing a particular name is beneficial not only for record linkage, but also for social network analysis, people search, information security, and information extraction. Unfortunately, accurate name popularity estimation based on limited number of observations is a hard task. Even very large collections contain many unique names – names are a good example of *large number of rare events (LNRE)* distributions. Therefore, maximum likelihood estimates based even on large name samples are poor predictors, since

---

The work was carried out while authors were at Kontur Labs, the research department of SKB Kontur, https://kontur.ru/eng/. The authors benefit from the Russian Ministry of Education and Science, project no. 1.3253.2017, and the Competitiveness Enhancement Program of Ural Federal University.

© Springer Nature Switzerland AG 2018
A. Benczúr et al. (Eds.): ADBIS 2018, CCIS 909, pp. 71–79, 2018.
https://doi.org/10.1007/978-3-030-00063-9_9

there are always many unseen names. To address this issue we employ several smoothing techniques that redistribute probability mass from already seen names towards yet unseen ones. Moreover, we use LNRE models to estimate the number of unique names and use this estimate as a smoothing parameter.

In our study we used a large dataset of open government data. We conducted two experiments: (1) name popularity estimation and (2) record linkage guided solely by the name popularity estimates. We performed evaluation both for name triples (first, middle, and last) and doubles (first and last). Our results suggest that theoretically informed approaches outperform simple heuristics. The main contribution of our study is a thorough comparative evaluation of several statistical techniques applied to the name popularity estimation task on a sizable dataset. The study provides guidance for choosing the most appropriate model depending on available data, task, and performance requirements.

Related Work. Our study is close to personal name matching [6], a special case of *record linkage* – the task of matching records referring to the same real-world person in the presence of errors, spelling variants, omissions, abbreviation, etc. Most name matching method rely on pre-defined or machine-learned similarity measures for field values and tuples, see [7]. The main difference of our study is that we deal with *identical* names and no additional fields. Moreover, we do not adjust our methods to a particular database; we rather aim at modeling name popularity at a global scale. As such, name popularity models can deliver additional evidence for record linkage tasks applied to different databases and in case of scarce additional information. The advent and proliferation of online social networks had a powerful impact on quantitative research on names, as name is often the only available information about the user. There is a series of studies that derive ethnicity [4,16] and gender [2] from names in social network profiles. Perito et al. [17] and Liu et al. [15] introduce the problem of linking user profiles belonging to the same physical person between online social networks based solely on the uniqueness of usernames.

Smoothing techniques we employ in the study have been actively developed within statistical language modeling [5,12]. Khmaladze [14] introduced the notion of *LNRE* distributions and studied their statistical properties. Baayen [1] and Evert [8] elaborated the models for a better fitting of frequency distributions of words in large corpora, with special attention to *hapax legomena* (words with frequency 1). We use LNRE models for a more accurate choice of smoothing parameters in several evaluated methods.

2   Data

In our study we experiment with a dataset that originates from the *Russian registry of legal entities*[1]. There is a many-to-many relationship between persons and companies: each legal entity is associated with one or more persons – managers and/or founders; each real-word person can be associated with several companies. The registry contains about 32 million name mentions. Full names in

---

[1] http://egrul.nalog.ru/.

Russian official documents are triples comprising of first, middle (patronymic), and last names, for example, *Alexander Sergeyevich Pushkin*.

A subset of records contains persons' taxpayer identification numbers (TINs) that can be used as a key. In the rest of the paper we focus on about 20.6 million records containing both TIN and full name that refer to about 13.4 million real persons, which constitutes about one tenth of the entire Russian population.

First, middle, and last names taken separately or as full names are a good example of *LNRE* regime: the majority of names occur only once, while a small number of combinations are relatively common. Expectedly, last names tend to be more rare than first names and patronymics (the latter are derivatives from male first names). Figure 1 shows proportions of unique name combinations in random samples of different sizes. For example, in a random population of 100,000 a combination of first, middle and last name is an almost perfect identifier (about 96% people bear a unique name), while name pairs (first, last) reliably distinguish less then 75% of people in the same sample.

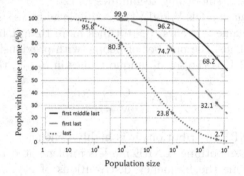

Fig. 1. Share of unique names depending on population size.

3   Methods

Name Popularity Prediction. In this section, we informally describe name popularity prediction models evaluated within the study. In what follows, $C(x)$ is the number of people with a name x in a training set S_{train}, where x can be either a full name or its constituents; f stands for first name, m and ℓ – for middle and last names, respectively; N_r is the number of names that occur exactly r times in S_{train} and N is the total number of persons in S_{train}.

We start with a naïve estimate assuming all people have unique names (model I). So, the number of people with the name x is equal to 1 in the population of any size. Then, we proceed with straightforward maximum likelihood estimates (MLE) for full names (II):

$$P_{MLE}(fm\ell) = \frac{C(fm\ell)}{N} \tag{1}$$

Model II assigns zero probabilities to names unseen in S_{train}. To partially mitigate the problem we can assume independence of name constituents and approximate the probability of a full name as follows, which defines model III:

$$P_{ind}(fm\ell) = P_{MLE}(f)P_{MLE}(m)P_{MLE}(\ell) = \frac{C(f)}{N} \cdot \frac{C(m)}{N} \cdot \frac{C(\ell)}{N} \qquad (2)$$

This model assigns a zero probability to a name if one of its components is new in the test set.

Some combinations of first, middle, and last names occur together more frequently than others. To capture these dependencies we use conditional probabilities. In the case of names triples we apply Markov assumption, in other words – we account only for dependencies between pairs of constituents leading to model IV:

$$P(fm\ell) = P(f)P(m|f)P(\ell|f,m) \approx P(f)P(m|f)P(\ell|m) \qquad (3)$$

Further, to mitigate the problem of zero probabilities of unseen name components, we use several smoothing techniques [5, 12].

Laplace smoothing (models V and VI) is a simple additive smoothing method: pretend that every name x occurs $\alpha > 0$ times more than it has been observed in the training set. Thus, the number of people with previously unseen name is estimated to be α. If V is the set of unique names in S_{train}, then

$$P_L(x) = \frac{C(x) + \alpha}{N + \alpha|V|} \qquad (4)$$

In the case of LNRE distributions it is highly beneficial to have an estimate of unseen events for smoothing. LNRE models implemented in *zipfR* [10] allow us, starting with name the frequency distributions of S_{train}, to estimate the number of different names in a set of larger size and consequently the number of names not appearing in S_{train}. As Table 1 shows, the *Generalized Inverse Gauss-Poisson (GIGP)* model implemented in *zipfR* performs very well.

Table 1. Prediction of the number of unique names (the third column contains country-wide estimates for reference).

Name	$GIGP$ estimates	Actual counts in S	Country-wide $GIGP$ estimates
f	111,538	111,287	405,154
m	155,635	155,726	462,738
ℓ	461,343	463,613	729,218
$f\,\ell$	4,383,342	4,391,157	20,330,441
$f\,m\,\ell$	9,088,527	9,087,716	65,867,708

Good-Turing smoothing [11] is a more gentle smoothing approach widely employed in language modeling (VII). The general idea behind the approach is to estimate the probability of all unseen names roughly equal to the total probability of names that appear only once in S_{train}, i.e. $\frac{N_1}{N}$. The counts of all other names are discounted as $C^*(x) = (C(x) + 1)N_{C(x)+1}/N_{C(x)}$. The Good-Turing probability estimates are given by:

$$P_{GT}(x) = \begin{cases} \frac{C^*(x)}{N}, & \text{if } C(x) > 0 \\ \frac{N_1}{N} \cdot \frac{1}{E}, & \text{if } C(x) = 0 \end{cases}, \tag{5}$$

where E is a *GIGP* estimate of hapaxes in S based on S_{train}. Note that it implies we know the size of the test set S beforehand.

One of the drawbacks of the Good-Turing smoothing is that it discounts probabilities uniformly in different frequency ranges. It leads often to severely distorted probabilities for high-frequency items. *Katz smoothing* [13] uses MLE for high-frequency names ($C(x) > 3$ in our experiment) and Good-Turing smoothing for low-frequency ones (model VIII).

Aiming at combining the simplicity of Laplace smoothing and the selectivity of Katz smoothing, we introduce *pseudo-Laplace smoothing* with a small $\alpha > 0$ (model IX):

$$P^*_{PL}(x) = \begin{cases} \frac{C(x)}{N+\alpha}, & \text{if } C(x) > 0 \\ \frac{\alpha}{N+\alpha}, & \text{if } C(x) = 0 \end{cases} \tag{6}$$

The idea is quite simple: names present in the training set obtain probability close to the MLE, while unseen names get reasonable non-zero probabilities. In a strict mathematical sense, these are not probabilities, since they do not sum up to unity (and that is why we denote it P^*). Such probability-like scores are widely used in many practical applications, see for example "stupid back-off" introduced in [3].

Name Popularity Evaluation. The first experiment is estimation of name popularity, i.e. estimation of the number of people bearing each name. Evaluation of models on samples with a large number of unique events is not an easy task. Evaluation results may diverge significantly on different test samples and depend on the size of test sample, particularly in low frequencies ranges. For example, LNRE models are traditionally evaluated by looking at how well expected values generated by them fit empirical counts extracted from the same dataset used for parameter estimation [1,8]. In this experiment we follow extrapolation setting for evaluation described in [9]: the parameters of the model are estimated on a subset of the data used subsequently for testing. The whole data set S is a list of 13.4 million real-world persons represented by TINs and corresponding names. We randomly sampled a training set S_{train} of 6.7 million persons, which is 50% of S. We employ *root-mean-square error* (RMSE) between the estimates and actual counts averaged over all names as evaluation measure. RMSE of a model $\mathcal{M}$ on the test set of people S over the set of unique full names V is defined as follows:[2]

$$\sigma = \sqrt[2]{\frac{\sum_{x \in V}(|S| \cdot P_{\mathcal{M}}(x) - C(x))^2}{|V|}} \tag{7}$$

In order to have a better understanding of models' behavior and their applicability to different tasks and data volumes, we calculate σ for the following name frequency buckets: 1 (hapaxes), $2 - 5$, $6 - 20$, $21 - 100$, and > 100.

Record Linkage. For the second task we calculate the probability that there is a single person with a given name x in the population of size $|S|$ using estimates by different models $\mathcal{M}$. If the probability surpasses the threshold t, we link records with identical names. Note that all identical names are linked at once, whereby q records with a given name trigger $\frac{q(q-1)}{2}$ linkages. The evaluation measure for the task are standard classification measures: *precision* – the fraction of linked records pairs that are correct, i.e. both refer to the same real-world person, and *recall* – the fraction of correct links identified. There are about 63.2 million pairs of identical names among 20.6 million occurrences, i.e. potential links between same-person records; 32% of them are correct according to TINs. Taking into account these figures, linking all possible pairs results in *precision* = 32% and *recall* = 100%.

In contrast to the first experiment that presumably reflects a global distribution of names, the second experiment deals with a concrete database and its particular characteristics, e.g. the number of companies associated with a person.

Table 2. Name models performance for full name triples

Model	Description	σ_1	σ_{2-5}	σ_{6-20}	σ_{20-100}	$\sigma_{>100}$
I	Always 1	0.000	1.833	9.163	38.279	163.327
II	$P_{MLE}(fml)$	1.000	1.611	**3.061**	**5.949**	**12.627**
III	$P_{MLE}(f)P_{MLE}(m)P_{MLE}(\ell)$	0.940	1.842	4.633	14.573	56.297
IV	$P_{MLE}(f|m)P_{MLE}(m|\ell)P_{MLE}(\ell)$	0.897	**1.608**	3.165	6.639	16.925
V	$P_L(f|m)P_L(m|\ell)P_L(\ell) \quad \alpha = 1$	0.999	2.720	9.779	36.277	137.747
VI	$P_L(f|m)P_L(m|\ell)P_L(\ell) \quad \alpha = \frac{1}{|S_{train}|}$	0.897	**1.608**	3.165	6.639	16.925
VII	$P_{GT}(f|m)P_{GT}(m|\ell)P_{GT}(\ell)$	0.900	1.622	3.171	6.644	16.931
VIII	$P_K(f|m)P_K(m|\ell)P_K(\ell)$	0.901	1.614	3.165	6.639	16.925
IX	$P^*_{PL}(f|m)P^*_{PL}(m|\ell)P^*_{PL}(\ell) \quad \alpha = 1$	**0.885**	**1.608**	3.165	6.639	16.925

---

[2] Note, that in this case $C(x)$ corresponds to the number of persons bearing name x in S (not in S_{train} as in equations above).

4   Results

Table 2 summarizes evaluation results for nine name popularity prediction models.[3] The first model (I) is a naïve "always 1" baseline that assumes all names are unique. Obviously, the model performs ideally on hapaxes. MLE model for full name triples (II) demonstrates the best prediction results in higher frequency ranges. The product of individual probabilities for first, middle and last names (III) performs slightly better on hapaxes, but substantially underestimates the probability of more frequent names. We investigated different dependencies between full name constituents, and combination in the model IV performed best. As one can see, conditional probabilities considerably improve over model III that assumes independence of name constituents. The next five models incorporate smoothing. Add-1 smoothing (V) is too aggressive in case of LNRE distributions and model with independent name components (III) has too many zeros probabilities in case of one of name component is unseen. All other models perform slightly worse then MLE model, but comparably to each other models with smoothing. Our method (IX) performs best in the low-frequency range and equally well as models IV and VI in higher-frequency areas.

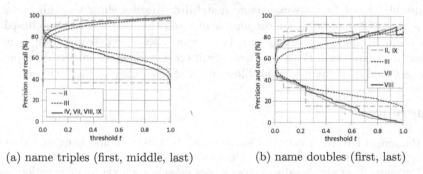

(a) name triples (first, middle, last)   (b) name doubles (first, last)

Fig. 2. Record linkage evaluation results: precision (upper curves) and recall (lower curves) of various name count prediction methods depending on the threshold value t

Results of the record linkage experiment are presented in Figs. 2a (name triples) and 2b (name doubles). The threshold t governs the linkage process: the higher the threshold the less name mentions are linked. One can imagine the process of gradual data linkage going from right to left, from higher to lower t values. Stepped curves of the MLE models are due to the fact that at some t values a large number of links is established at a time. In the case of full name triples (Fig. 2a) all 'advanced' methods deliver almost identical results. The simplest MLE method for full names works well when we favor precision over recall. Threshold $t = 0.2$ delivers precision of about 90% and recall above

---

[3] We also performed an experiment with first-last name doubles that showed similar behavior of the models. We do not cite the results here due to limited space.

70%. In the case of first and last name doubles, the task of record linkage in such a sizable dataset based solely on name popularity estimates is much less effective (see Fig. 2b).

5   Conclusion

In our experiments we make use of a large name dataset with unique identifiers that contains names of approximately one tenth of the Russian population. We conducted a series of experiments with different name popularity prediction models built upon the name dataset. We thoroughly evaluated several models, including well-known smoothing approaches and proposed a new simple yet effective method for adjusting probability estimates accounting for unseen events. Results show that the considered methods behave differently depending on the frequency range of names to be estimated, the name structure (full name triples vs. first and last name doubles), and the population size for which the prediction is made. These experimental results can serve as guidelines for choosing the most suitable method for a specific task and available data.

We conducted a record linkage experiment in a database based solely on name popularity estimates. The outcomes suggest that name popularity estimates are a valuable signal for personal name matching. Results show that all methods using smoothing perform almost identically and the simplest method based on maximum likelihood estimates can be a good choice, when precision is more important than recall. However, these results reflect the peculiarities of a specific database and serve merely as an illustration of feasibility of the approach.

References

1. Baayen, H.: Word Frequency Distributions. Text, Speech and Language Technology. Kluwer Academic Publishers, Dordrecht (2001)
2. Bergsma, S., et al.: Broadly improving user classification via communication-based name and location clustering on Twitter. In: NAACL-HLT, pp. 1010–1019 (2013)
3. Brants, T., Popat, A.C., Xu, P., Och, F.J., Dean, J.: Large language models in machine translation. In: EMNLP-CoNLL, pp. 858–867 (2007)
4. Chang, J., Rosenn, I., Backstrom, L., Marlow, C.: ePluribus: ethnicity on social networks. In: ICWSM, pp. 18–25 (2010)
5. Chen, S.F., Goodman, J.: An empirical study of smoothing techniques for language modeling. Comput. Speech Lang. 13(4), 359–393 (1999)
6. Christen, P.: A comparison of personal name matching: techniques and practical issues. Technical report. TR-CS-06-02, Australian National University, September 2006
7. Christen, P.: Data Matching: Concepts and Techniques for Record Linkage, Entity Resolution, and Duplicate Detection. Springer, Heidelberg (2012). https://doi.org/10.1007/978-3-642-31164-2
8. Evert, S.: A simple LNRE model for random character sequences. In: JADT, pp. 411–422 (2004)
9. Evert, S., Baroni, M.: Testing the extrapolation quality of word frequency models. In: Corpus Linguistics Conference Series, vol. 1 (2005)

10. Evert, S., Baroni, M.: zipfR: word frequency distributions in R. In: Proceedings of ACL, pp. 29–32 (2007)
11. Good, I.J.: The population frequencies of species and the estimation of population parameters. Biometrika **40**(3/4), 237–264 (1953)
12. Goodman, J.T.: A bit of progress in language modeling. Comput. Speech Lang. **15**(4), 403–434 (2001)
13. Katz, S.M.: Estimation of probabilities from sparse data for the language model component of a speech recognizer. IEEE Trans. Acoust. Speech Sig. Process. **35**(3), 400–401 (1987)
14. Khmaladze, E.V.: The statistical analysis of a large number of rare events. Technical report MS-R8804, CWI (1988)
15. Liu, J., et al.: What's in a name? An unsupervised approach to link users across communities. In: WSDM, pp. 495–504 (2013)
16. Mislove, A., Lehmann, S., Ahn, Y.Y., Onnela, J.P., Rosenquist, J.: Understanding the demographics of Twitter users. In: ICWSM (2011)
17. Perito, D., Castelluccia, C., Kaafar, M.A., Manils, P.: How unique and traceable are usernames? In: Fischer-Hübner, S., Hopper, N. (eds.) PETS 2011. LNCS, vol. 6794, pp. 1–17. Springer, Heidelberg (2011). https://doi.org/10.1007/978-3-642-22263-4_1

Streaming FDR Calculation for Protein Identification

Roman Zoun[1]([✉]), Kay Schallert[2], Atin Janki[1], Rohith Ravindran[1],
Gabriel Campero Durand[1], Wolfram Fenske[1], David Broneske[1],
Robert Heyer[2], Dirk Benndorf[2], and Gunter Saake[1]

[1] Working Group Databases and Software Engineering,
University of Magdeburg, Magdeburg, Germany
[2] Chair of Bioprocess Engineering, University of Magdeburg,
Magdeburg, Germany
{roman.zoun,kay.schallert,atin.janki,rohith.ravindran,
gabriel.campero,wolfram.fenske,david.broneske,
robert.heyer,dirk.benndorf,gunter.saake}@ovgu.de

Abstract. Identification of proteins is a key step of metaproteomics research. This protein identification task should be migrated to a fast data streaming architecture to increase horizontal scalability and performance. A protein database search involves two steps: the pairwise matching of experimental spectra against protein sequences creating peptide-spectrum-matches (PSM) and the statistical validation of PSMs. The peptide-spectrum-matching is inherently parallelizable since each match is independent. However, false positive matches are inherent to this method due to measurement errors and artifacts, thus requiring statistical validation. State of the art validation is achieved using the target-decoy method, which estimates the false discovery rate (FDR) by searching against a shuffled version of the original protein database. In contrast to the protein database search, validation by target-decoy is not parallelizable, because the FDR approximation requires all experimental data at once. In short, when using a fast data architecture for the workflow, the target-decoy approach is no longer feasible. Hence a novel approach is required to avoid false discovery of PSM on streaming single-pass experimental data. To this end, the recently proposed nokoi classifier seems promising to solve the aforementioned problems. In this paper, we present a general nokoi pipeline to create such a decoy-free classifier, that reach over 95% accuracy for general metaproteomics data.

Keywords: Metaproteomics · Fast data · Decoy-free
Stream · Machine learning

Supported by de.NBI.

A. Benczúr et al. (Eds.): ADBIS 2018, CCIS 909, pp. 80–87, 2018.
https://doi.org/10.1007/978-3-030-00063-9_10

1   Introduction

Metaproteomics is the biological research of all proteins of microbial communities. The main task of metaproteomics is to analyze the taxonomic composition and metabolic functionality of these communities, such as the ones present in biogas plants or the human gut and extract bio markers for certain parameters, diseases or process disturbances [9,10,12,16,20]. In the metaproteomics workflow, the prepared biological sample is measured using a mass spectrometer [1,14].

Analysis of the data can be done with so called protein identification engines [2,6,17]. Protein identification is a pairwise comparison and statistically it contains false positive peptide-spectrum-matches (PSM) due to measurement errors and artifacts. A common approach to remove the false positive matches is the target-decoy approach [5]. In this approach, a complete search runs twice, on target data and on decoy data [5]. A collection of these two search results is used to approximate the false discovery rate (FDR) for the experiment under the assumption that all hits of the decoy search are false positives.

Protein identification using the target-decoy FDR approximation is inflexible and hardly parallelizable, because the workflow needs the whole experiment data as input and incurs two searches. Since the mass spectrometer device produces experiment data continuously, a fast data streaming architecture seems promising for the metaproteomics use case. On a fast data environment involving a huge amount of independent streaming experiment data, a target-decoy approach is no longer feasible. So we need an approach without decoy search that is still able to identify false positive matches.

Gonnelli et al. show a possible usage of logistic regression on specific proteomics (only a single species) data using ranked PSMs of the Mascot search engine for the training [8]. However, the question arises whether similar accuracies are possible for metaproteomics data, which contains multiple species. Addressing this question we create a pipeline with four components for the nokoi approach. Using our nokoi pipeline we developed a general classifier for metaproteomicsthat takes as input data from any arbitrary protein identification engine.

In our work we implemented a feature detector for X!Tandem results. We used the X!Tandem results as training sets for our nokoi classifier, which can be produced using the target-decoy method or ranked method. Furthermore, we evaluate the streaming nokoi on different metaproteomics data. Additionally, we evaluate the process using ranked PSMs training and the target-decoy training method. We show that our approach can reach over 95% accuracy for general metaproteomics while raising the horizontal scalability and effectively doubling the processing speed, since no decoy search is needed after the trained classifier.

2   Background

From the biological area, it is important to understand protein identification and how to the false discovery rates are calculated. Furthermore, we present the components of the fast data architecture.

2.1   State of the Art Protein Identification

The input of protein identification is, on the one hand, the experimental spectral data from a biological sample, and on the other hand the protein database that contains information of already known proteins.

Experimental Spectrum: is a mass of fragmented ions represented as an intensity to mass-to-charge-ratio plot. With the help of those measurements, the mass of the ions can be calculated [3,13].

Protein Database: is a collection of proteins, that are represented as a text. A Protein is a sequence of peptides and a peptide is a sequence of amino acids. One amino acid is represented by a specific character. A theoretical spectrum can be calculated for each peptide. This theoretical spectrum has only perfect values without any measurement artifacts or noise. The list of proteins in the file serves as a protein database. Typically, a FASTA format is used for the textual representation of proteins [15].

The protein identification process is a pairwise comparison. For each experimental spectrum, all proteins from the database in the FASTA file get transformed into a theoretical spectrum. The theoretical spectrum and the experimental spectrum from the bio-sample are compared using a similarity function. The best similarity score is stored as a match. In this way, one experimental spectrum is identified [14].

In our work we focus on X!Tandem, since it is an open source library, that is recommended by biologists [5].

2.2   False Discovery Rate for Matches

After the identification the peptide-spectrum-matches need a validation. Accurate and precise methods for estimating incorrect peptide and protein identifications are crucial for effective large-scale metaproteomics analyses by mass spectrometry. The target-decoy FDR Approximation strategy has emerged as an effective tool for estimating the false discovery rates of peptide identifications [4,5]. This strategy is based on the premise that obvious, necessarily incorrect decoy sequences added to the search space will correspond with incorrect search results that might otherwise be deemed correct. The target-decoy search strategy requires to search the mass-spectrometry data twice. Once with correct (target) protein sequences and once with incorrect (decoy) sequences. The sorted list of target and decoy matches by the similarity scores is used to estimate the FDR. Until the FDR is not reached, the last element of the list with the lowest similarity score is removed. The removing of elements stops, when the FDR has reached the desired value.

2.3   State of the Art Fast Data

The workflow of protein identification of metaproteomics includes huge amounts of data processing, therefore Big Data technologies should be used. Big Data systems work batch oriented on distributed data for analysis or processing. Nowadays big data systems evolve to stream oriented systems, where data is processed in mini-batches as it arrives into the system. These so called fast data applications process the data continuously, considering possibly infinite data streams [19]. Fast data focuses on real-time production of data using streaming messaging [11]. The idea of incoming data changes some analytical behavior. The streaming data should be independent, since only a specific time window of the data is available.

Using the fast data architecture for a protein identification application, the target-decoy FDR approximation is not feasible, due to the need of streamed input data. Hence, the nokoi approach seems to be a reasonable substitution.

3 The Requirement of Streaming Protein Identification

Since protein identification needs a pairwise comparison and already uses the streaming implementation patterns, such as batch-wise processing, a fast data architecture seems promising, which promises real time analysis of sensor data [7, 11,18]. For the case of metaproteomics, the mass spectrometer device produces the sensor data and streams it to the cloud system. The identification of the incoming spectra data produces peptide-spectrum-matches (PSMs). The system must decide if the match is below the false discovery rate or not. The goal of this work is to create a general classifier to decide whether the PSM is a true or a false positive for metaproteomics data.

Unfortunately, the common target-decoy FDR calculation needs the whole experiment data and makes the protein search as a streaming application infeasible. Hence, A decoy-free FDR estimation is necessary. Furthermore, the decoy-free approach should work generally for all metaproteomics data and with all protein search engines. To this end, we introduce four components of our nokoi systems.

The first component is the feature extractor, which extracts the numeric features of the matches from the results of a protein search engine. The next part of the system is the trainer. The input for the trainer component is a labeled feature list in CSV format and results in a trained model. The last component is the classifier, that takes the feature data and predicts whether the match is true positive or false positive according to the trained model. The architecture with the four components is shown in Fig. 1.

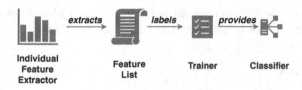

Fig. 1. General nokoi approach with the provided four components.

Individual Feature Extractor and the Feature List: The goal of these two components is to read the features that describe one peptide-spectrum-match and transform them into our defined format. The chosen features are from the nokoi approach [8].

The Trainer: The third component uses the labeled PSM feature list to train a classifier. We implement two different ways for the training. The first way is the ranked PSM training. The first match is labeled as TRUE and the second rank is labeled as FALSE (see Fig. 2). The second way is the target-decoy training. For the target-decoy training, we need to extract features from the target result and from the decoy result. Using these feature lists a target-decoy approach decides if a PSM of the target result is TRUE or FALSE (see Fig. 3).

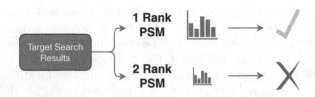

Fig. 2. The method ranked labeling method.

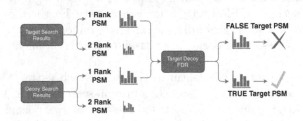

Fig. 3. The method ranked labeling method.

The Classifier: The last component is the classifier, which relies on a trained logistic regression model to estimate the quality of the PSM.

4   Evaluation

Evaluation of the nokoi streaming pipeline was done using two different sets of training data and a modified version of the search engine X!Tandem. The training steps are only done once resulting in a classifier. Only the classifier is part of the production system, with negligible influence on overall performance. Therefore, a performance evaluation is not needed and we focus on the accuracy evaluation.

To evaluate the nokoi approach for the streaming metaproteomics workflow, we generated data from different experimental datasets using X!Tandem. We used three experiment datasets of a biogas plant[1] and three experiment datasets from a human gut[2]. In our evaluation, we tested the accuracy of the nokoi approach on metaproteomics data. We evaluate our two training methods: the ranked PSM method and the target-decoy PSM method. In the evaluation, we test the accuracy and compare the two training methods to find the best nokoi classifier for metaproteomics data. The accuracy reported corresponds to the average value of 50 runs. We combined the data to evaluate the metaproteomics use case for the general purpose. To this end, we trained the classifier using only biogas or human gut data and additionally, we mixed the datasets to show different training scenarios.

The best accuracy is 96% and the worst result is 93%. The average accuracy using the ranked training method is 95%.

The best accuracy is 95% and the worst is 93%. The average accuracy using the target-decoy training method is 94%.

Our evaluation shows, both training methods bring good accuracy results to explore the experimental data. The accuracy of 95% can be considered good, because it matches the statistical uncertainty typical for metaproteomics experiments. For general purposes the target-decoy training is realizable for each protein identification engine while the ranked approach has to be implemented in the software itself. Using our general pipeline we created a general metaproteomics classifier that is highly parallelizable and suitable for a streaming architecture. Since the accuracy in all scenarios is comparable, we propose to use the target-decoy method for training data generation as it is the easiest to apply to other search engines.

5   Related Work

The work done by Elias et al. on target-decoy search strategy for providing a reasonable estimation of false discovery rate in the peptide-to-spectrum matches is a widely used approach in metaproteomics [5]. Another model was proposed by Gonnelli et al. for the Mascot Search Engine, which allows fast yet reliable decoy-free separation of correct from incorrect peptide-to-spectrum matches (PSMs) when compared to the traditional decoy database paradigm, using a binary classification algorithm [8].

In our work, we created a generalized pipeline to create a nokoi classifier for metaproteomics data on all protein search engines. Furthermore, we used a stream processing library Apache Spark that is required for an integration in a fast data system. To the end, we implemented a X!Tandem connector to our

---

[1] Data sizes: BIOGAS1 (5984 PSMs) BIOGAS2 (8367 PSMs) BIOGAS3 (8921 PSMs).
[2] Data sizes: GUT1 (4819 PSMs) GUT2 (2317 PSMs) GUT3 (2685 PSMs).

pipeline and evaluate the classifier using two training methods on the complex metaproteomics use case.

6   Conclusion and Future Work

The identification is a required step in the metaproteomics workflow, that needs a validation of the results. To improve the performance, a fast data streaming architecture seems promising but the currently used target-decoy validation is not parallelizable because it needs all the experiment data at once. In this paper, we show that a decoy-free approach is feasible for general, multi-species metaproteomics data with over 95% of accuracy, which can be considered as good, because it matches the statistical uncertainty typical for metaproteomics data. Our approach propose an individual entry point that relies on the chosen protein search engine. We implemented one feature extractor for X!Tandem, a popular protein search software. The final result is a classifier that removes false positive peptide-spectrum-matches (PSM) from measured metaproteomics data. The classification can be made on only one PSM, which is important for the feasibility on streaming systems.

In the future, we plan several quality improvements on the input data and on the system itself. Some of the attributes of one peptide-spectrum-match (PSM), are calculated using another features. Therefore we plan to research different weights and combination of the PSM features. This can result in a higher accuracy or in reduction of the input data. Furthermore, we will realize feature extractors for different protein search engines such as mascot and OMSSA. Additionally, we will investigate whether a new classifier or a deep learning approach is feasible and brings better results to the validation of metaproteomics data.

Acknowledgment. The authors sincerely thank Xiao Chen, Sebastian Krieter, Andreas Meister and Marcus Pinnecke for their support and advice. This work is partly funded by the de.NBI Network (031L0103), the European Regional Development Fund (grant no.: 11.000sz00.00.0 17 114347 0), the DFG (grant no.: SA 465/50-1), by the German Federal Ministry of Food and Agriculture (grants no.: 22404015) and dedicated to the memory of Mikhail Zoun.

References

1. Aebersold, R., Mann, M.: Mass spectrometry-based proteomics. Nature **422**(6928), 198 (2003)
2. Cottrell, J.S., London, U.: Probability-based protein identification by searching sequence databases using mass spectrometry data. Electrophoresis **20**(18), 3551–3567 (1999)
3. Deutsch, E.W.: File formats commonly used in mass spectrometry proteomics. Mol. Cell. Proteomics **11**(12), 1612–1621 (2012)
4. Eisenacher, M., Kohl, M., Turewicz, M., Koch, M., Uszkoreit, J., Stephan, C.: Search and decoy: the automatic identification of mass spectra. Methods Mol. Biol. (2012). https://doi.org/10.1007/978-1-61779-885-6_28

5. Elias, J., Gygi, S.: Target-decoy search strategy for mass spectrometry-based proteomics. Methods Mol. Biol. **604**, 55–71 (2010). https://doi.org/10.1007/978-1-60761-444-9_5
6. Eng, J.K., McCormack, A.L., Yates, J.R.: An approach to correlate tandem mass spectral data of peptides with amino acid sequences in a protein database. J. Am. Soc. Mass Spectrom. **5**(11), 976–989 (1994)
7. Estrada, R.: Fast Data Processing Systems with SMACK Stack. Packt Publishing, Birmingham (2016)
8. Gonnelli, G.: A decoy-free approach to the identification of peptides. J. Proteome Res. **14**(4), 1792–1798 (2015)
9. Heyer, R., Kohrs, F., Reichl, U., Benndorf, D.: Metaproteomics of complex microbial communities in biogas plants. Microb. Technol. **8** (2015). https://doi.org/10.1111/1751-7915.12276
10. Heyer, R., Schallert, K., Zoun, R., Becher, B., Saake, G., Benndorf, D.: Challenges and perspectives of metaproteomic data analysis. J. Biotechnol. **261**(Supplement C), 24–36 (2017). https://doi.org/10.1016/j.jbiotec.2017.06.1201. Bioinformatics Solutions for Big Data Analysis in Life Sciences presented by the German Network for Bioinformatics Infrastructure
11. Kipf, A., Pandey, V., Boettcher, J., Braun, L., Neumann, T., Kemper, A.: Analytics on fast data: main-memory database systems versus modern streaming systems (2017)
12. Maron, P.A., Ranjard, L., Mougel, C., Lemanceau, P.: Metaproteomics: a new approach for studying functional microbial ecology. Microb. Ecol. **53**, 486–493 (2007)
13. Matrix Science: Data File Format (2016). http://www.matrixscience.com/help/data_file_help.html
14. Millioni, R., Franchin, C., Tessari, P., Polati, R., Cecconi, D., Arrigoni, G.: Pros and cons of peptide isolectric focusing in shotgun proteomics. J. Chromatogr. A **1293**, 1–9 (2013). https://doi.org/10.1016/j.chroma.2013.03.073
15. National Center for Biotechnology Information: Fasta Format, November 2002. https://blast.ncbi.nlm.nih.gov
16. Petriz, B.A., Franco, O.L.: Metaproteomics as a complementary approach to gut microbiota in health and disease. Front. Chem. (2017). https://doi.org/10.3389/fchem.2017.00004
17. Robertson, C., Ronald, C.B.: A method for reducing the time required to match protein sequences with tandem mass spectra. Rapid Commun. Mass Spectrom. **17**(20), 2310–2316 (2003)
18. Wampler, D.: Fast data: big data evolved. White Paper (2015)
19. Wampler, D.: Fast Data Architectures for Streaming Applications, 1st edn. OReilly Media, Sebastopol (2016)
20. Zhang, J., Liang, Y., Yau, P., Pandey, R., Harpalani, S.: A metaproteomic approach for identifying proteins in anaerobic bioreactors converting coal to methane. Int. J. Coal Geol. **146**, 91–103 (2015)

ADBIS 2018 Workshops

Contributions from ADBIS 2018 Workshops

Udo Bub[1], Ajantha Dahanayake[2](✉), Jérôme Darmont[3], Claudia Diamantini[4],
Fabio Fassetti[5], Eduardo Fermé[6], Nadia Kabachi[7], Ilaria Matteucci[8],
Bálint Molnár[1], Sham Navathe[9], Ermelinda Oro[10], Marinella Petrocchi[8],
Simona E. Rombo[11], Massimo Ruffolo[10], Angelo Spognardi[12],
Bernhard Thalheim[13], and Domenico Ursino[4]

[1] Eötvös Loránd University, ELTE, Pázmány Péter Sétány 1/C, Budapest, Hungary
[2] Lappeenranta University of Technology, Lappeenranta, Finland
ajantha.dahanayake@lut.fi
[3] Université de Lyon, Lyon 2, ERIC EA3083, Lyon, France
[4] Università Politecnica delle Marche, Ancona, Italy
[5] University of Calabria, Rende, Italy
[6] University of Madeira, Funchal, Portugal
[7] Université de Lyon, Lyon 1, ERIC EA3083, Lyon, France
[8] Istituto di Informatica e Telematica, Consiglio Nazionale delle Ricerche, Pisa, Italy
[9] Georgia Institute Of Technology, Atlanta, USA
[10] National Research Council, Rende, CS, Italy
[11] University of Palermo, Palermo, Italy
[12] Sapienza Universitá di Roma, Roma, Italy
[13] Christian-Albrechts University Zu Kiel, Kiel, Germany

1 Introduction

The ADBIS conferences provide an international forum for the presentation of research on database theory, development of advanced DBMS technologies, and their applications. The 22nd edition of ADBIS, held on September 2–5, 2018, in Budapest, Hungary, includes six thematic workshops collecting contributions from various domains representing new trends in the broad research areas of databases and information systems.

The aim of this paper is to present and overview of such events, their motivations and topics of interest, as well as briefly outline their programs and the papers selected for presentations. The selected papers have been included in this volume. Specifically, the following workshop events have been organized in ADBIS 2018:

- International Workshop on Advances on Big Data Management, Analytics, Data Privacy and Security (BigDataMAPS)
- 1st International Workshop on New Frontiers on Metadata Management and Usage (M2U)
- Citizen Science Applications and Citizen Databases (CSADB) Workshop
- Artificial Intelligence for Question Answering (AI*QA)

© Springer Nature Switzerland AG 2018
A. Benczúr et al. (Eds.): ADBIS 2018, CCIS 909, pp. 91–102, 2018.
https://doi.org/10.1007/978-3-030-00063-9_11

- International Workshop on BIG data storage, processing and mining for Personalized MEDicine (BIGPMED)
- Current Trends in contemporary Information Systems and their Architectures (ISTREND)

In the following, for each workshop, a brief introduction of its main motivations and topics of interest is presented, as well as its program including interesting keynotes, invited papers and the selected papers for presentations. Each workshop had its own international program committee, whose members served as the reviewers of papers included in the rest of this volume. Some acknowledgments from the workshop organizers to program committee members are also provided.

2   International Workshop on Advances on Big Data Management, Analytics, Data Privacy and Security (BigDataMAPS)

Introduction. The International Workshop on Advances on Big Data Management, Analytics, Data Privacy and Security (BigDataMAPS) has been organized by Jérôme Darmont (Université de Lyon, Lyon 2, ERIC EA3083, France), Nadia Kabachi (Université de Lyon, Lyon 1, ERIC EA3083, France), Ilaria Matteucci (Istituto di Informatica e Telematica, Consiglio Nazionale delle Ricerche, Pisa Italy), Marinella Petrocchi (Istituto di Informatica e Telematica, Consiglio Nazionale delle Ricerche, Pisa Italy) and Angelo Spognardi (Sapienza Universitá di Roma, Roma, Italy).

BigDataMAPS seeks to promote novel contributions in the field of big data processing and management, big data analytics and big data privacy and security. The aim of this workshop is to become a regular, interdisciplinary exchange forum for researchers and practitioners interested in big data as a research object. By exchanging research results, experiences, and products, the ultimate goal is to conceive new trends and ideas on designing, implementing and evaluating solutions for efficient, safe, reliable and compliant information sharing, with an eye to the cross-relations between ICT and regulatory aspects of data management.

Information sharing is essential for today's business and societal transactions. Nevertheless, such a sharing should not violate the security and privacy requirements either dictated by Law to protect data subjects or by internal regulations, which can be provided both at the organization and at the individual level. An effectual, rapid, and unfailing electronic data sharing among different parties, while protecting legitimate rights on these data, is a key issue with several shades. Among them, how to translate the high-level law obligations, business constraints, and users' requirements into system-level security and privacy policies, and how to engineer efficient and practical technical solutions for policy definition and enforcement.

Topics of interest for this workshop include but are not limited to the following, and should not be limited to an IT perspective: big data management and analytics, crowd-sourcing and collaborative analyses, meta-data management, data security in the cloud, smart cloud, energy-efficient computing. Moreover, applications may lie in the fields of digital humanities, health care, smart cities, environment, management, social media, Internet of things, etc.

Keynote Presentation. Oscar Romero: *Big Data Variety: On-Demand Data Integration.* As big data systems get more complex, the data variety challenge has become the driving factor in current big data projects. In this talk, the current state-of-the-art of the data variety challenge is addressed and recent solutions to manage the problem are presented.

Oscar Romero is a tenure-track lecturer at the Universitat Politècnica de Catalunya, Barcelona. His research interests lie in business intelligence, big data and the semantic Web. More specifically, he has been working on data ware-housing, NoSQL (and any technology beyond relational databases), bridging big data management and analytics, open data platforms (mostly at the database level), recommendation systems and semantic-aware systems (based or exploiting semantic formalisms such as ontology languages or RDF). He is also interested in agile methodologies and formalisms to incorporate non-technical people in the design, maintenance and evolution of database systems.

Program. Harshvardhan Jitendra Pandit, Declan O'Sullivan and Dave Lewis: *Personalised Privacy Policies.* The authors of the paper propose a remodeling of the privacy policy (General Data Protection Regulation -GDPR-) based on provision of relevant information regarding personal data specific to the user. The discussion is supported with an example use-case of a GDPR-based privacy policy adopted from online services.

Younes Abid, Abdessamad Imine and Michael Rusinowitch: *Online testing of user profile resilience against inference attacks in social networks.* The authors have designed a tool, SONSAI, for Facebook users to audit their own profiles. SONSAI predicts values of sensitive attributes by machine learning and identifies user public attributes that have guided the learning algorithm towards these sensitive attribute values.

Francesco Di Cerbo and Slim Trabelsi: *Personal Data Identification and Anonymization using Machine Learning techniques.* The author proposes a solution based on a supervised machine learning system that identifies personal information in large datasets. Once the different parts of personal information are identified and tagged (also in real time), an anonymization technique is applied as example of processing. A proof-of-concept implementation is presented and evaluated.

Francesco Ventura, Tania Cerquitelli and Francesco Giacalone: *Black-box model explained through an assessment of its interpretable features.* Nowadays, greater algorithm transparency is indispensable to provide more credible and reliable services. EBANO is a new engine able to produce prediction-local explanations for a black-box model exploiting interpretable feature perturbations. It is tested on a set of heterogeneous images. Results highlight its effectiveness in explaining a CNN classification through the evaluation of interpretable features influence.

Acknowledgments. The workshop chairs would like to acknowledge all PC members for their reviews. The alphabetically ordered list of PC members follows: Alberto Abello, Abdelkader Adla, Varunya Attasena, Antonio Badia, Nadjia Benblidia, Fatma Bouali, Kamel Boukhalfa, Arnaud Castelltort, Gianpiero Costantino, Vittoria Cozza, Karen Davis, Francesco Di Cerbo, Ioanna Dionysiou, Nicola Dragoni, Carmen Fernandez Gago, Matteo Golfarelli, Anastasios Gounaris, Le Gruenwald, Abdelkader Hameurlain, Sorren Hanvey, Jens Jensen, Hedi Karray, Okba Kazar, Daniel Lemire, Gabriele Lenzini, Flavio Lombardi, Erisa Karafili, Mirko Manea, Patrick Marcel, Aaron Massey, Jose-Norberto Mazon, Kevin McGillivray, Franck Ravat, Abdelmounaam Rezgui, Prasan Kumar Sahoo, Andrea Saracino, Daniele Sgandurra, Alkis Simitsis, Jatinder Singh, Somayeh Sobati Moghadam, Claudio Soriente, Debora Stella, Won-Kyung Sung, Slim Trabelsi, Panos Vassiliadis, Robert Wrembel, Mahdi Zargayouna.

3   1st International Workshop on New Frontiers on Metadata Management and Usage (M2U)

Introduction. The 1st International Workshop on New Frontiers on Metadata Management and Usage (M2U) has been organized by Claudia Diamantini (Università Politecnica delle Marche, Ancona, Italy), Domenico Ursino (Università Politecnica delle Marche, Ancona, Italy) and Sham Navathe (Georgia Institute Of Technology, USA).

Metadata is traditionally defined as "data about data". Metadata can provide information about data schemes (i.e. data structure, relationships, etc.) or about content, the latter being especially relevant to unstructured data like images or text. Metadata can also describe low level characteristics of the storage like e.g. the naming of files and items, encoding, position, format, organization, and so forth. While metadata has been the subject of research for a long time, there are still unexplored research issues and opportunities raised by the advent of large scale distributed data management systems or Big Data. Large scale systems and Big Data make integration approaches all the more challenging, with the resurgence of virtual and dynamic approaches based on rich metadata and semantics (think, for instance, of Data Lakes). Also, discovery of relevant sources, sharing and reuse, and data quality and auditability strongly rely on metadata. Furthermore, data exploration, description, explanation, and summarization are becoming a key facility to make sense of a huge amount of data and let users learn from them. This applies to both unstructured, semi-structured and structured data. For unstructured datasets, which are commonly estimated to make up roughly 80% of data currently generated, the challenge is to find scalable and semi-automated methods for generating the metadata required for data indexing, retrieving and analysis. This workshop aims at providing a forum to discuss recent advancements on new forms of meta-data representation, management and use, and exchange ideas and share experiences.

Program. The workshop features one keynote speaker, one invited speaker and four technical papers. The keynote is entitled *Integrative Bioinformatics: Metadata, Ontologies and Dictionaries for Data Analysis in the Biological and Biomedical Domains* and is given by Simona Rombo from Università di Palermo. It focuses on the role of meta-data and semantic technologies in dealing with complex bioinformatics tasks, like functional network data integration and epigenomics k-mer dictionaries for the study of nucleosome positioning. The invited talk is given by Rihan Hai from RWTH Aachen University. It provides an overview of key challenges in Data Lakes, like meta-data extraction, schema summary and schema mapping over heterogeneous data, and presents the design of a Data Lake system under development at RWTH Aachen University and the Fraunhofer-Institute for Applied Information Technology.

As for the technical program, the paper *A new meta-data model to uniformly handle heterogeneous data lake sources* develops further on the Data Lake topic, proposing a new metadata model and methods to partially structure unstructured sources and to extract thematic views from heterogeneous sources.

The paper entitled *How meta-data can support the study of neurological disorders: an application to the Alzheimer's disease* discusses potential of meta-data in the medical domain, in particular to analyze neurological disorders. It shows how computer-based analysis of meta-data associated with clinical observations may help physicians in understanding clinical stages and hypothetical course of the disease.

Modeling is the topic of paper *Comparing SLAs for cloud services: a model for reasoning*. A conceptualization of Service Level Agreements (SLAs) is presented, including the explicit modeling of formulas for Service Level Indicators. It also discusses the open, reusable ontological representation of this model, which enables the definition of operators for analysis and comparison of SLAs.

Finally, a contribution to automatic meta-data generation is provided by the paper entitled *Automatic extraction of affective meta-data from videos through emotion recognition algorithms*. It introduces a model for emotional video meta-data, capturing the fact that emotions in videos vary over time, and proposes a methodology for the automatic generation of such meta-data, which is particularly suitable for Big Data sources where manual video analysis is challenging and cost-ineffective.

Acknowledgments. The M2U workshop chairs would like to acknowledge all PC members for their reviews. The alphabetically ordered list of PC members contains: Sonia Bergamaschi, Philip Bernstein, Chiara Eva Catalano, Isabelle Comyn-Wattiau, Valeria De Antonellis, Laura Genga, Giancarlo Guizzardi, Stuart E. Middleton, Paolo Missier, Stefano Modafferi, John Mylopoulos, Luigi Palopoli, Thorsten Papenbrock, Oscar Pastor, Domenico Potena, Christoph Quix, Erhard Rahm, Karina Rodriguez Echavarria, Emanuele Storti, Panos Vassiliadis, Nicola Zannone.

4   Citizen Science Applications and Citizen Databases (CSADB) Workshop

Introduction. The first workshop of Citizen Science Applications and Citizen Databases (CSADB) has been organized by Ajantha Dahanayake (Lappeenranta University of Technology, Finland) and Bernhard Thalheim (Christian-Albrechts University Zu Kiel, Germany).

CSADB is sought with the aim to provide a platform for exchanging empirical and theoretical research results about CSADB problems and solutions and to bring together researchers and practitioners working in the relatively new field of Citizen Science. The goal is to exchange experiences and view-points in building state of the art solutions from realizations, challenges, and reuse, to adapting solutions that have been proposed in other domains.

Citizens Science field of study is in the constant development. Despite its young age, it has already proved that Citizen Science can be beneficial as much as Classical Science. There are varied sectors such as scientific research, science literacy improvement, community services, ecological knowledge, environmental education, technology and many more are created for citizen science programs. The main objective is to contributing data, helping researchers to find solution, and monitoring the problems and providing solutions. Nevertheless, it has particular problem: every Citizens Science project uses databases, which are in turn typically disjunct, disparate, incomplete, and outdated. However, the monitoring and building comprehensive up-to-date database is one of the main challenges for citizen science database. In addition, the lack of user participation, funding, flexible database design and user-friendly applications are also other challenges. Volunteer-based participation of citizens is one of the main solutions for monitoring databases and collecting data. Similarly, designing the flexible approaches for collecting data, providing services to use gathered data in various sectors of science, designing user friendly design approach for user involvement are possible solutions considered in citizen science database programs.

Program. *Characterizing air-quality data through unsupervised analytics methods* (Daraio, et al.) introduces how several cities have built on-the-ground air quality monitoring stations to measure daily concentration of air pollutants. This paper presents a two-level methodology based on unsupervised analytics methods, named PANDA, to discover interesting insights from air quality-related data. As a case study, PANDA has been validated on real pollutant measurements collected in a major Italian city.

Missing Data Analysis in Emotion Recognition for Smart Applications. (Gorbulin, et al.) presents missing data as a widespread fundamental problem that cannot be ignored. It distorts the data, sometimes even to the point where it is impossible to analyze data at all. In this article EEG (electroencephalography) data is used to test which missing data techniques are more efficient and reliable in emotion recognition. The article concludes with techniques useful for missing data analysis, and applicable in emotion recognition applications.

Overview of Data Storing Techniques in Citizen Science Applications. (Musto, et al.) provides an overview on interest in citizen science and the number of related projects that are found during the last decade. Citizen science revolves around gathering data and using it. Many researches focus on the citizen side, while the data side is often left out. This study aims to fill the gap by trying to find the current data storing practices in the field of citizen science.

Data Provenance in Citizens Science Databases. (Tiufiakov et al.) looks into scientific groups and the development of citizen science applications. One of the major challenges citizen science face is the data quality assurance. It uses several techniques to verify the data quality based on expert evaluation, voting systems, etc. Data provenance by itself has many types such as "Why provenance", "When provenance", and "What provenance". The purpose of this work is to build a prototype of a database with built-in data provenance.

Internet of Things: Trends, Challenges, and Opportunities. (Tropmann-Frick) discusses the rapid evolving technology and the availability of more and more cheaper and smaller devices. This paper gives an overview of the trends, challenges and opportunities in the field of IoT and serves as a starting point for research in this field focusing on integration of IoT and Cloud computing, especially the extension of classic Cloud towards Fog and Edge computing.

Acknowledgments. The CSADB workshop chairs would like to acknowledge all PC members for their reviews. The alphabetically ordered list of PC members contains: Ajantha Dahanayake, Markus Endres, Margita Kon-Popovska, Elio Masciari, Heinrich C. Mayr, Jari Porras, Henk Sol, Bernhard Thalheim, Marina Tropmann-Frick, Isabella Watteau, Naofumi Yoshida.

5   1st International Workshop on Artificial Intelligence for Question Answering (AI*QA 2018)

Introduction. The 1st Workshop on Artificial Intelligence for Question Answering (AI*QA 2018) has been organized by Ermelinda Oro and Massimo Ruffolo (National Research Council, Italy), and Eduardo Fermè (University of Madeira, Funchal, Portugal).

Artificial Intelligence (AI) is attracting much attention. It will be a major driver for technology changes that will deeply impact how we live and work. Question Answering (QA), which has the goal to automatically provide pertinent answers to natural language questions, is a complex task that requires contextual natural language understanding (NLU), and reasoning abilities. Almost all Natural Language Processing (NLP) tasks can be seen as a QA problem (e.g. entity extraction, sentiment analysis, machine translation). Recently, QA based on novel AI techniques has seen scientific and commercial popularity that attracted media attention, but effective QA is a challenging task for machines that try to simulate the human behavior. Some solutions are based on Information Retrieval (IR) techniques, other on Information Extraction (IE) processes that enable to create Knowledge Bases (KBs), so logic-based query languages are used to infer answers from KBs. Novel approaches for QA over documents are based on Deep Neural Networks that encode the documents and the questions to determine the answers. A lot of research has focused on learning from fixed training sets of labeled data, but other try to learn through on-line interaction (dialog) with humans or other agents.

The purpose of the AI*QA workshop is to bring together researchers, engineers, and practitioners interested in the theory and applications related to QA problems by using AI techniques. Topics of interest include the following categories: theoretical models for answering questions, algorithms and methods, databases and knowledge representations, tools and solutions, evaluation of results, application to domains.

Keynote presentation. This year, a keynote presentation were offered at AI*QA. The talk was provided by Prof. Giuseppe Riccardi, founder and director of the Signals and Interactive Systems Lab at University of Trento, Italy. His current research interests are natural language modeling and understanding, spoken/multi-modal dialog, affective computing, machine learning and social computing. His presentation at AI*QA is about Talking to Machines: A Conversational Journey. Talking to machines is not evoking science fiction scenes as it used to be in the sixties or even the nineties, any more. In the last fifty years we have explored the space of human-computer communications via speech, text, touch and multi-modal input and output. We now have computers in various forms sitting in our living room ready to take on new social roles. Wearable computers may interject in our daily routine and persuade us to healthy behavior. In his talk, Giuseppe reviews what is the current state-of-the-art in modeling the human-machine conversational dialog and the many challenges ahead.

Program. The 1st Workshop on Artificial Intelligence for Question Answering received 8 submissions, out of which 3 were accepted. Thus, the acceptance rate for the workshops is 37%. The three selected papers address different interesting research challenges and issues related to the use of artificial intelligence models, approaches, and analysis for answering questions. They are listed below:

- Yang Yu, Kazi Saidul Hasan, Mo Yu, Wei Zhang, and Zhiguo Wang, *Knowledge Base Relation Detection via Multi-View Matching*.
- Ekaterina Loginova, Stalin Varanasi, and Güunter Neumann, *Towards Multilingual Neural Question Answering*.
- Manvi Breja and Sanjay Kumar Jain, *Analysis of Why-type Questions for the Question Answering System*.

Acknowledgments. The AI*QA workshop chairs would like to acknowledge all PC members for their reviews. The alphabetically ordered list of PC members contains: Muhammad Arif, Alexandra Balahur, Ioannis Hatzilygeroudis, Ivan Jureta, Joohyung Lee, Marco Leo, Yuan-Fang Li, Olga Kalimullina, Thomas Meyer, Guenter Neumann, Rafael Pealoza, David Schlangen, Koichi Takeda, Wei Zhang.

6 International Workshop on BIG Data Storage, Processing and Mining for Personalized MEDicine (BIGPMED)

Introduction. The International Workshop on BIG data storage, processing and mining for Personalized MEDicine (BIGPMED) has been organized by Fabio Fassetti (University of Calabria, Italy) and Simona E. Rombo (University of Palermo, Italy).

In the last few years we have witnessed an exponential growth of biological and medical data, coming from the always more advanced sequencing technologies, clinical and imaging data, electronic health records, etc. The resulting data are complex in contents, heterogeneous in formats and order of Tera-bytes in amount. These "big data" in the biological and medical domain provide unprecedented opportunities to work on exciting problems, but also raise many new challenges for data storage, process and mining. A very challenging scenario is that of Personalized (or Precision) Medicine, according to which medical decisions, treatments, practices, or products should be tailored to the individual patient. In this respect, the selection of appropriate and optimal therapies can be based on the context of a patient's genetic content or other molecular or cellular analysis. To this aim, heterogeneous data collected from different sources, such as genetic heritage, lifestyle and environmental context, may be combined in order to advance disease understanding, diagnosis and treatment, and ensure delivery of appropriate therapies. This Workshop aims to provide the opportunity of introducing and discussing new methods, theoretical approaches, algorithms, tools, and platforms that are relevant for the database community in the domain of Personalized Medicine. This will hopefully imply also the definition of new problems raised in managing complex data, and the dissemination of novel ideas on the application of "big data" methodologies in the biological and medical domain. The main topics of the workshop include:

- Integration of biomedical databases and sources.
- High Performance Computing architectures, applications for omics data.
- Parallel Machine Learning approaches for personalized medicine.
- Next-Generation Sequencing data analysis and interpretation.
- NoSQL databases in healthcare.
- Big data analytics for omics data.
- Data privacy and security in healthcare.
- Clinical decision support systems, Healthcare Systems.
- Models for clinic and genetic data.

Keynote Presentation. BIGPMED 2018 includes also a keynote presentation on *A "big data oriented" and "complex network based" model supporting the uniform investigation of heterogeneous personalized medicine data*, provided by Domenico Ursino, Full Professor in Computer Engineering at DII (Polytechnic University of Marche). Professor Ursino works on the usage of Network Analysis in several application contexts such as Biomedical Engineering, Data Lakes,

Innovation Management and Internet of Things. He published more than 180 papers on Data Integration, Multi-Agents and Recommendation Systems, Folksonomies and Network Analysis. In these fields he coordinated several research projects. The talk is on the proposal of a complex network based model and a set of associated parameters, applied to investigate three neurological disorders, namely Alzheimer's Disease, Childhood Absence Epilepsy and Creutzfeldt-Jacob Disease.

Program. The accepted papers for this workshop focus on automatic diagnostic suggestions, epigenomics and medical imaging. They are listed below:

1. *Humanity is Overrated. Or not. Automatic Diagnostic Suggestions by Greg, ML*, Paola Lapadula, Giansalvatore Mecca, Donatello Santoro, Luisa Solimando and Enzo Veltri.
2. *Variable Ranking Feature Selection for the Identification of Nucleosome Related Sequences*, Giosue' Lo Bosco, Riccardo Rizzo, Antonio Fiannaca, Massimo La Rosa and Alfonso Urso.
3. *Software Tools for Medical Imaging*, Luciano Caroprese, Giuseppe Lucio Cascini, Pietro Cinaglia, Francesco Dattola, Pasquale Franco, Psquale Iaquinta, Miriam Iusi, Giuseppe Tradigo, Pierangelo Veltri and Ester Zumpano.

Acknowledgments. The BIGPMED workshop chairs would like to acknowledge all PC members for their reviewes. The alphabetically ordered list of PC members contains: Fabio Cunial, Umberto Ferraro Petrillo, Valeria Fionda, Angelo Furfaro, Pietro Hiram Guzzi, Giosué Lo Bosco, Cinzia Pizzi, Blerina Sinaimeri, Filippo Utro, Cesare Valenti.

7   Current Trends in Contemporary Information Systems and Their Architectures (ISTREND)

Introduction. The Current Trends in contemporary Information Systems and their Architectures workshop (ISTREND) has been organized by Bálint Molnár (Eötvös Loránd University, ELTE, Pázmány Péter Sétány 1/C, Budapest, Hungary) and Udo Bub (Eötvös Loránd University, ELTE, Pázmány Péter Sétány 1/C, Budapest, Hungary).

The goal of the workshop is to provide a forum to present and discuss finished and on-going work in Informations Systems research and its applications. A special focus is given to current trends in conjunction with modeling. The workshop expects contributions that leverage the use of Information Systems for Digital Innovation and the Digital Transformation by modeling and architecture-center approaches considering the trend of Industrial Internet (Industry 4.0).

The various models and description and design approaches for architecture of information systems can be investigated; those approaches that reflect the different facets of an operating environment in a socio-technological ecosystem that includes components as human resources, business processes, processes of data and information, applications, IoT, mobile equipment etc. Their relationships to each other and to the environment, furthermore the principles for guiding its design and evolution could be analyzed. The scientific methods for the examination of such a complex environment is the Design Science Research and Case Study Paradigm. The experiences of using the before-mentioned scientific paradigms as meta-methodologies can be summarized as well and the experience can yield insights into the successful results.

Program. Zsuzsanna Nagy, Ágnes Werner-Stark and Tibor Dula, *An industrial application using process mining to reduce the number of faulty products.* The paper discusses the use of process mining in an industrial case study. The authors analyze the adequate approaches to the specific application and develop a suitable method for the particular task and data collection. The manufacturing environment was an automated coil production and the related assembly line. The article presents a contemporary IT solutions to leverage digital transformation in manufacturing and offers the opportunity for further improvement.

Jing Lu, *A Data-Driven Framework for Business Analytics in the Context of Big Data.* The proposed framework exploit the Data Science approaches in unified methodology that combines data preprocessing, data modeling, integration at data level, and business intelligence. The use of the proposed framework and the related tool set is illustrated by some cases in health informatics and marketing. The author expounds the application of contemporary data analysis methods as statistics, machine learning and visualization as one of the way for the Digital Transformation of businesses.

Dóra Őri and Bálint Molnár, *Towards a Hypergraph-based Formalism for Enterprise Architecture Representation to Lead Digital Transformation.* The paper explicates mathematics-based, formal descriptions of semi-formal Enterprise Architecture models that yield an opportunity for automated processing to explore discrepancies, gaps, and provide chances for alignment of the business goals and information system services. The article elucidates how the introduction of formal models may help the Digital Transformation of enterprises that use disciplined architecture modeling.

Dóra Őri and Zoltán Szabó, *EAM Based Approach to Support IT Planning for Digital Transformation in Public Organizations.* The article, in fact, is a case study at an organization providing public cervices for citizens. As the services are typically combinations of IT services, IT products, human services and other manufactures products the Digital Transformation is unavoidable even in state-funded public organization. The IT governance in tandem with Enterprise Architecture plays a significant role to make manageable the whole transformation process. The article analyzes the opportunities for Digital Transformation through exploiting the proposed framework. The article shows the chances for harmonization of business and IT services by the assistance of Enterprise Architecture.

Udo Bub, *Towards an Integrated Method for the Engineering of Digital Innovation and Design Science Research.* The innovation and Digital Transformation are intimately coupled recently as e.g. service innovation may happen through the assistance of IT. There are methods that give guidelines for company how organize the business process of innovation and the related project. The article proposes a disciplined, systematic, grounded in science and engineering methodology for governing the digital innovation that involves a dedicated business process model as well. The viability and feasibility of the proposed framework is illustrated by a case that implementation was studied in an innovation labor that was created by a university-industry partnership.

Acknowledgments. The ISTREND workshop chairs would like to acknowledge all PC members for their reviewes. The alphabetically ordered list of PC member by their last name contains: Witold Abramowicz, Udo Bub, Peter Dobay, Anna Medve, Bálint Molnár, Robert Mueller-Toeroek, Tamás Orosz, Mária Raffai, Márta Seebauer, Viorica Varga.

8   Conclusions

ADBIS 2018 workshop organizers would like to express their thanks to everyone who contributed to the success of their events and to this volume content. Specifically, they would like to thank the authors, who submitted papers to the workshops, as well as the Program Committee members, who provided comprehensive, critical, and constructive comments on submitted papers. This evaluation process ensured the quality of the scientific program and of this volume. We all hope you will find the volume content a useful contribution to promote novel ideas for further research and developments in the areas of databases and information systems.

First International Workshop on Advances on Big Data Management, Analytics, Data Privacy and Security, BigDataMAPS 2018

Online Testing of User Profile Resilience Against Inference Attacks in Social Networks

Younes Abid, Abdessamad Imine, and Michaël Rusinowitch[✉]

Lorraine University, Cnrs, Inria, 54000 Nancy, France
{younes.abid,abdessamad.imine,michael.rusinowitch}@loria.fr

Abstract. To increase awareness about privacy threats, we have designed a tool, SONSAI, for Facebook users to audit their own profiles. SONSAI predicts values of sensitive attributes by machine learning and identifies user public attributes that have guided the learning algorithm towards these sensitive attribute values. Here, we present new aspects of the system such as the automatic combination of link disclosure attacks and attribute prediction. We explain how we defined sensitive subjects from a survey. We also show how the extended tool is fully interfaced with Facebook along different scenarios. In each case a dataset was built from real profiles collected in the user neighbourhood network. The whole analysis process is performed online, mostly automatically and with accuracy of 0.79 in AUC when inferring the political orientation.

Keywords: Online Social Network (OSN) · Inference attacks
Privacy · Link disclosure

1 Introduction

Personal information if revealed may have serious consequences on social network users. This information can be exploited to carry out personalized spam attacks [7], identity theft attacks [4], cloning attacks [12], Sybil attacks [11], etc. They might cause serious damages to companies such as degradation of reputation, copyright infringement, loss of intellectual property, etc.

Social networks provide several solutions in order to safeguard the privacy of users. However, their main deficiencies are related to complicated, non-uniform, periodically updated and unintelligible privacy policies, long and ambiguous user charters, and non-ergonomic privacy management interfaces. Although most social networks offer similar services (creating profiles, pages and groups, establishing links and interactions), their visibility management and the definition of links (symmetrical, non-symmetrical) are different. These design differences may be confusing for users of multiple social networks that are careless with checking each network settings. Moreover the default parameters promotes public dissemination but increases the risk of sensitive information leakage.

© Springer Nature Switzerland AG 2018
A. Benczúr et al. (Eds.): ADBIS 2018, CCIS 909, pp. 105–117, 2018.
https://doi.org/10.1007/978-3-030-00063-9_12

Most importantly, social networks do not provide protection against inference of implicit information. Derived by correlating different public attributes or different public profiles, as in collaborative recommendation, this information is actually the main profit source of social networks' business model as they can be exploited for targeted advertising. Therefore, knowledge accumulated in social networks about users goes beyond what is published and can be a threat to their privacy. In [13], Winter Mason has mined the cultural similarities between American Facebook users and their political view (Democrats or Republicans). He sampled Facebook users' profiles who liked the campaign pages of some Democrat or Republican politicians. Then, he collected their lists of liked pages. Finally, he statistically identified the page types that are most disproportionately liked by the supporters of one political view versus the other. The results of his work show that politics is highly correlated to musicians, landmarks, authors, books and TV shows.

Contributions. In order to combat privacy leakage, it is important to define which personal information is sensitive. Some researchers consider that all the unpublished values of attributes (masked or not specified) by a given user are sensitive for him [15,16]. While others select a few attributes and consider them to be sensitive such as sexual orientation [10], political affiliation [6,10] and age [14]. It is also possible to rely on the definition of sensitive information given by law. However, social networks are evolving faster than legislation. For instance, health data were not considered sensitive by the French law of January 6, 1978[1] related to computers, files and freedoms. It was considered sensitive much later. It is also possible to rely on a definition of sensitive subject given by social media themselves. But can we trust social networks in defining what is sensitive or not as they make most of their profit using personal information for targeted advertising?

Hence, we have first conducted a questionnaire survey to define sensitive subjects based on the behaviour of french Net-surfers. This method has the advantage of being fast, objective, accurate and up-datable. The most sensitive subjects according to Facebook french users who have participated in our survey are *Religion, Money, Politics, Dating, Shopping* and *Health*.

Then, we present SONSAI, our application to help Facebook users to protect their privacy. To that end, SONSAI tests a user profile against privacy attacks and tracks their origin. This approach allows one to delimit the perimeter of threats and to design effective countermeasures. Concretely, SONSAI performs online inference attacks on the world largest social network, Facebook. The attacks have been tested by several real volunteer profiles. SONSAI allows users to identify public attributes that are correlated with sensitive attributes and therefore to prevent these attacks by modifying these public attributes. In the context of *General Data Protection Regulation* (GDPR)[2], promulgated recently by the European Union, to stress on users' control over their personal data, our

---

[1] Loi n° 78-17 du 6 janvier 1978 relative á l'informatique, aux fichiers et aux libertés.
[2] https://www.eugdpr.org/.

tool may contribute to increase user awareness as for the risks related to personal data processing.

Outline. In Sect. 2 we discuss the problems. In Sect. 3 we recall some related works. In Sect. 4 we present the result of a survey conducted to identify sensitive subjects. In Sect. 5 we overview the architecture and component functionalities of SONSAI, a tool for users to test their profile against inference attacks. In Sect. 6 we describe experiments on real data. Finally we discuss accuracy of SONSAI attacks in Sect. 7, countermeasures in Sect. 8, and conclude in Sect. 9.

2   Discussion

Let us discuss briefly the problems that had to be solved in order to design SON-SAI. In order to effectively track privacy leakage, it is important to combine link prediction and attribute prediction. For instance, an adversary can perform link prediction attacks in order to disclose the local network of his target (friends and group members). Then, he can perform more accurate attribute prediction attacks with extra information provided by the discovered local network. Online attribute prediction attacks encompasses two steps: (i) data collection and (ii) data analysis. Data collection must be fast, selective, passive and unnoticed. Since social networks are highly dynamic and contain a huge amount of data, random collection may result in useless data. On the other hand, massive collection is time wasting. A fast and selective sampling algorithm must be used in order to guide the collector toward most relevant data and speed up the process. Moreover, the adversary must limit his interaction with his target. He must perform his attack in a passive way in order to go unnoticed by the target to him. The adversary should only send legal requests to collect data and should not exceed some threshold to remain unnoticed by the social network. Data analysis should be fast, accurate and deal with sparsity. We recall that the system (collection and analysis) is meant to help users safeguard their privacy against real attacks. Hence, data analysis must not exceed a few minutes in order to rapidly put the hand on the origins of threats and quickly put countermeasures into action. Analysis results should be accurate in order to reduce false positive alerts and cover all threats. As the collector only samples a few data from an ocean of them, the analyser should deal with the fact that collected data may be sparse and incomplete.

3   Related Works

In [5] the authors propose to combat attribute prediction attacks in social network by creating new links between users in order to reduce the difference of the distribution of attribute values in the user local network and in the global one. In [10], the authors propose a content&link-based classifier that outperforms both content-based classifiers and link-based classifiers when predicting the political views and the sexual orientation of Facebook users. In addition, they explore the effectiveness of sanitization techniques to prevent such attacks. In contrast to [5], sanitization solutions in [10] consist of removing contents and links. However, selecting the right contents and links to remove or to add without altering the utility of the social network is a challenging task. In our present work we aim to help users to identify the critical attributes that are correlated to sensitive subjects in their communities and that lead to the undesirable inference. It is then up to users to intervene by adding links in order to alter the accuracy of inference due to data disagreement or by deleting links in order to disrupt inferences by lack of data. In [6], the authors design a classifier to predict the political alignment of Twitter users based on the tweet contents and the retweet network. They show that such classifiers widely outperform classifiers that are based only on content. Our first tests [3] show that some attributes such as political alignment are correlated to the network structure (e.g., friendship links). However, this is not the case for other ones such as gender and relationship status (e.g., married, . . .). In [18], the authors introduce an information re-association attack in order to predict the values of sensitive attributes of users. This attack consists in combining web search with information extraction and data mining techniques. This study shows that the attack is more successful when including information about the target university networks. In addition, it shows that Facebook graduated users from top schools are more vulnerable under this attack than random users. In our work, we quantify the correlation between attributes. SONSAI generates inference rules that depends on the behaviours of users in the target neighborhood. For instance, SONSAI can automatically decide whether the university networks around the target is an important factor for inference success or not. In [15] the authors show that an adversary can infer sensitive attribute values of a target based only on the target local network (1-hop friendship network) and the public attribute within it. The proposed predictor takes into consideration the network structure by quantifying the importance of friendship relations. Then, it measures the power of each attribute value according to the importance of the target friend that publishes it. In [9], the authors extend the attribute-augmented social network model that is introduced in [17]. In the initial model, attribute values are represented by nodes. The users that publishes a particular value of an attribute are linked to its representing node in the model. The extended model adds negative links between users and their hidden attribute values and mutex links between mutually exclusive values of the same attribute such as male and female. This model is used with both supervised and unsupervised methods to predict links between users as well as links between users and attribute values. In [16], the authors design a classifier to predict the missing attribute values of a Google+ user. The classifier only takes into consideration users that are one hop distant from the target. In addition to attributes, the designed classifier exploit the direction of links (follower or followings), the type of links (acquaintance, family, friend . . .) and the tie-strength of the links. In [8], the authors extend the attribute-augmented social network model [17] by adding behaviours nodes to the framework. Then, they design a vote distribution attack to predict attribute values. They show that by taking into account social friendship, attributes and behaviours, the accuracy of attacks is considerably increased.

In our work, we analyse the local friendship network of the target (direct friends). When the target hides friends we first perform link disclosure attack with certainty to disclose his local network. This combination of link disclosure (with certainty) and attribute inference coordinated within the same system (fully interfaced with Facebook) seems to be unique. Each attribute is represented by a bipartite graph where edges connect users to the attribute values they like. The system also relies on our previous works: specific graph comparison techniques to measure attribute correlations [3], a clustering algorithm to group similar sensitive attribute values (for instance similar politicians) and a shallow neural network to infer semantic proximity between public values and sensitive ones [2].

4   Definition of Sensitive Subjects

We have conducted a questionnaire survey to define sensitive subjects according to the behaviours of french net-surfer. We have analysed the behaviours of 232 users of social media aged between 20 and 78 years that live in 21 different French regions. We have classified the subjects discussed on social media according to four criteria: rate of discussion on social networks, rate of discussion on forums and websites, rate of anonymous publications and avoided subjects. Based on those criteria, we have proposed a definition of sensitive subjects.

Table 1. Statistics related to the sensitive subjects.

Category	Discussion on social networks (in %)	Discussion on forums and websites (in %)	Anonymous publications (in %)	Avoided subjects (in %)
Money	0.94	54.42	25	10.14
Religion	5.63	26.05	14.28	33.33
Shopping	1.88	66.05	9.09	0
Dating	5.16	24.19	0	21.74
Health	17.37	66.05	9.09	5.8
Politics	25.82	54.42	25	50.72

Sensitive Subjects. Let V be the set of avoided subjects, N the set of subjects whose rate of anonymous publications on forums and websites is above average and D the set of subjects whose discussion rate on the forums/websites **or**[3] social networks are below the mean of all discussions minus the standard deviation on that media. A discussed subject on social media is **sensitive**, if and only if, it belongs to at least two sets from the defined sets (V, N and D). The most sensitive subjects according to french Facebook users that participate in our survey are *Religion, Money, Politics, Dating, Shopping* and *Health*. Table 1 details the

---

[3] Or indicates an inclusive disjunction.

statistics related to the defined sensitive subjects with regard to the analysed criteria. Additionally, the analysis of the participants behaviours results in the following privacy attack vector statistics:

- 52.05% use the same e-mails and 65.75% use the same user-names on different social networks.
- 90% have the same friends over different networks.
- 72.16% do not cleanly delete their profiles when leaving social networks.
- 15.96% publish photos without asking the consent of people appearing in these photos.
- 8.45 % add strangers to their friend lists only because they have common friends.
- In a test, 6.10 % are not able to recognize a person added randomly to their friend lists.

5   SOcial Networks Sensitive Attribute Inference

In this section we present the *SOcial Networks Sensitive Attribute Inference* system (SONSAI). Algorithm 1 summarizes the flow of tasks performed by SONSAI in order to detect privacy threats. SONSAI first collects the 1-hop friendship network around the user u and their attributes (lines 1–6). If the user u hides his friend list then SONSAI performs link disclosure attacks as detailed in [1] in order to disclose with certainty some of his friends. The attacker model is passive as the attack does not require interaction with users. The preparation of the link disclosure attack consists of sampling users that have high probability to be friend with u and that publish their friend list. To that end, SONSAI explores the group network at distance 2 from u. Then, it performs friendship and mutual friend disclosure attacks by taking advantages of queries provided by the social networks APIs. A friendship attack consists of disclosing links between u and members of the explored groups. A mutual friend attack consists of disclosing links between u and the friends of members of the explored groups. The results of our previous work [1] show that about half of Facebook users are exposed to friendship disclosure through their membership to groups of less than 50 members.

In Sect. 4 we have identified the most sensitive subjects for french users. Assume User u wants to check with SONSAI whether a sensitive subject information can be inferred from his profile. He first selects through a Combobox an attribute correlated to these sensitive subjects (line 7). For instance he can select politicians or political parties for *Politics* subject. Correlation of attributes is quantified by comparing their bipartite graph representation (see [3]).

The sensitive attribute is selected from a displayed list of attributes discovered in the user local social network. To simulate an inference attack on the selected sensitive attribute, the user is asked to provide two pieces of information: (i) *top_n*, the percentage of attributes to be selected for learning and (ii) whether the sensitive attribute values have to be clustered by similarity to reduce the search space (lines 9–11).

SONSAI uses random walks (line 12) and Word2Vec algorithm (line 13) in order to infer the sensitive values of the target based on his preferred values for the selected attributes for learning. The results of the inference attack help the users understand the source of information leakage. SONSAI ranks the list of selected attribute for learning according to their correlation to the sensitive attributes (line 14).

Finally, SONSAI interacts with User u in order to check inference accuracy (i.e., whether the infered values are correct) and to assess the privacy leakage risk (line 15). The risk evaluation returned by SONSAI depends solely on the collected data around User u. This verdict is given as a score quantifying the risk of inferring correct values for a given sensitive attribute. The score is obtained by comparing the ranking of sensitive values to the values that are really liked by user u. We use the *Area Under the Curve* to compute this score. The risk of disclosing values of a sensitive attribute is considered to be high when the score is higher than 65%, moderate when the score is between 50% and 65% and low when the score is less than 50%.

Data: *target* ▷ target profile (user input)
    top_n ▷ learning attributes ratio to be selected (user input)
    cluster_b ▷ boolean for clustering option (user input)
    sensitive_att ▷ sensitive attribute (user input)
Result: *correlated_attributes* ▷ attribute ranking
    ranked_values ▷ sensitive value ranking
    risk_level ▷ sensitive value disclosing risk

```
1  if masked_friend_list(target) then
2  |   friend_list ← friend_disclosure_attack(target);
3  else
4  |   friend_list ← get_public_friend_list(target);
5  end
6  attributes ← crawl(friend_list);          ▷ attributes are stored as bipartite graphs
7  correlated_atts ← graph_comparison(sensitive_att, attributes);
8  selected_atts ← select_atts(top_n, correlated_atts);
9  if cluster_b then
10 |   cluster_values(sensitive_att);
11 end
12 walks_text_files ← random_walk(sensitive_att, selected_data);
13 embeddings ← word2vec(walks_text_files);
14 ranked_values ← ranks(embeddings, target, sensitive_att.values);
15 risk_levels ← compare_ranks(ranked_values, user_real_values);
```

Algorithm 1. SONSAI crawling and analysis steps.

6 Inference Scenarios

In the following we detail two scenarios of inferring the pages of politicians liked by two real Facebook users u_1 and u_2. Table 2 gives a sample of values of the

Table 2. Some attribute values of targets u_1 and u_2.

Targets	Musicians/Bands	News/Media websites	Communities
u_1	Clean Bandit	Spi0n	Pour le retrait du timbre Femen
	Dillon Francis	BuzzFilGeek	Bordel De Droit
	Monsieur Monsieur	My Little Paris	Soigner Dans la Dignité
	Max Vangeli	confidentielles.com	ADDM - Respect it Enjoy it
	DJ Fresh	Boiler Room	Entourage - Réseau Civique
	Cazzette	MY Secret NY	Soutien au bijoutier de Nice
	Charlotte de Witte	Street FX Motorsport & Graphics	Valls Dégage
	RL Grime	Hitek	Banamak
	Bassjackers	Le Figaro	Fab Bike
	Tritonal	PIX GEEKS	Pour la démission de Hollande
u_2	Justice	TED	Keep Calm & Be Real
	The Prodigy	InfopresseJobs	Es-tu game?
	Queen	Too Close To Call	Nos casseroles contre la loi spéciale
	Crystal Castles	Radio-Canada Information	The Voyage North
	Le husky	Isarta - Emplois	Arcade MTL
	Daniela Andrade	NowThis	Nous sommes les 68%
	Boys Noize	Infos Insolites	Larping.org
	Gunther	Faits et Causes	Pierre Céré
	Heroik	Progrès Villeray - Parc-Extension	Commodore 64
	Les Poignards		Astuces de Mac Gyver

pages of *Musicians/Bands, News/Media Websites and Communities* that are liked by u_1 and u_2. Target u_1 is a french user. He publishes his friend list on Facebook. Target u_2 is a canadian user that hides his friend list. SONSAI first performs link disclosure attack in order to disclose the friends of u_2. Then, SONSAI crawls the revealed friendship network and collects the values of attributes liked by u_2 direct friends.

The analysis phase generates a first table that summarizes the list of the most correlated attributes to the sensitive one. The correlations are quantified in percentage. A second table presenting sorted values of the sensitive attribute according to the probability they are liked by the user is displayed too. Values in the second table are grouped in clusters in a way that maximizes the similarity between values inside a cluster and minimizes it between values from different clusters. The size of clusters is controlled so that any of them never gets twice larger than any other one. The similarity inside a cluster is the mean of all similarity indexes of its elements. It is computed by Eq. 1:

$$similarity(c) = 2 \frac{\sum_{(v,v') \in c \times c} similarity\_index(v,v')}{|c|(|c|-1)} \tag{1}$$

$|c|$ is the number of values in Cluster c. The similarity index computes the similarity between two values. In order to select an adequate similarity index to be implemented in SONSAI, we have first tested four well-known indexes. These indexes are defined in Table 3. $\Gamma(v)$ is the set of users that like value v.

Table 3. Similarity indexes

Jaccard	$\frac{|\Gamma(v)\cap\Gamma(v')|}{|\Gamma(v)\cup\Gamma(v')|}$
Adamic adar	$\sum_{z\in\Gamma(v)\cap\Gamma(v')}\frac{1}{\log|\Gamma(z)|}$
Common neighbours	$|\Gamma(v)\cap\Gamma(v')|$
Preferential attachment	$\frac{|\Gamma(v)|\times|\Gamma(v')|}{|\Gamma(v)|+|\Gamma(v')|}$

SONSAI implements the algorithm detailed in [2] to define clusters. The clustering algorithm is greedy. It defines one cluster at a time. At each step, it adds the most similar value from the set of non clustered values to the last created cluster. When size conditions are met and when adding any non clustered values will only decrease the average similarity of the cluster values, a new cluster is initialized that contains the most liked non clustered value. Overall, the algorithm computes the $n(n-1)/2$ similarities between all couples of values.

Figure 1 gives the similarity variations with respect to the sizes of clusters. The algorithm clusters 4 589 politician pages. The x-axis represents the minimal sizes of clusters. The y-axis represents the similarities inside clusters computed using the corresponding similarity index. We notice that Adamic Adar, Common Neighbours and Preferential Attachment based clustering methods are very sensitive to the size of clusters: when the size of cluster increases the similarities dramatically decreases. On the other hand, Jaccard based clustering method maintains high similarities inside clusters even when the size of cluster is $\sqrt{n}$, with n the total number of values. Four volunteers have manually checked the similarities of clusters based on their political backgrounds. They confirmed that

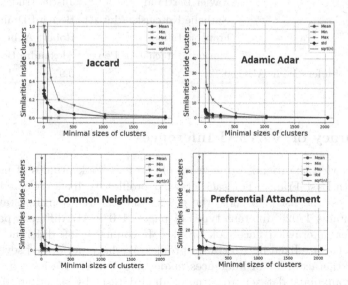

Fig. 1. Variations of similarities with respect to the size of clusters.

Jaccard based clustering method generates better clusters than Adamic Adar, Common Neighbours and Preferential Attachment based clustering method. Hence, SONSAI implements Jaccard index to measure the similarity between sensitive attribute values. Moreover, the mean Jaccard index, MJ, between the values of a cluster C can be interpreted as follows: if a user likes a particular value from the cluster C then he tends to like $MJ \times 100\%$ of values of the rest of values from the same cluster C.

SONSAI allows users to open any cluster displayed on the table and click on any value to open its corresponding Facebook page. The user can specify the number of values he really likes in any cluster. Then SONSAI algorithm measures the accuracy of its proposed ranking using the Area Under the Curve (AUC). Table 4 summarizes the politicians that are liked by u_1 and u_2. Target u_1 is a politically right-oriented french user. The inference accuracy for the politician pages he likes is 0.72. Target u_2 is a canadian user of left political orientation. The inference accuracy for the politician pages he likes is 0.97.

Table 4. Politicians liked by targets u_1 and u_2.

Targets	u_1	u_2
Liked politicians	Marine Le Pen	Simon Marcill
	Jean-François Copé	Martine Ouellet
	Laurent Wauquiez	Amir Khadir
	Bruno Le Maire	Jack Layton
	Jean-Marie Le Pen	Jocelyn Beaudoin
	Nicolas Dupont-Aignan	Alain Therrien
	Xavier Bertrand	Justin Trudea
	Nathalie Kosciusko Morizet	Bernard Drainville
	Francois Fillon	Robert Aubi
	Marion Maréchal-Le Pen	Alexandre Boulerice
Accuracy of inference in AUC	0.72	0.97

7   Accuracy of SONSAI Inferences

We have crawled the friendship network of 100 Facebook profiles of users that live in North-East France. For each crawled profiles we have collected the list of liked pages, the list of friends, the gender and the relationship status. The dataset contains 1 926 different types of pages, 1 022 847 different pages and 15 012 different crawled Facebook profiles. It counts 4 589 different pages of politicians that are liked by 2 554 user profiles. We have performed several tests to evaluate the accuracy of inferences made by SONSAI. We have first generated a new auxiliary dataset from the original dataset by selecting 10% of the users that publish their liked pages of politicians. Then we have removed all their preferences concerning politicians. The experiments have consisted then in inferring back the deleted preferences by analysing the remaining dataset. When the analyser selects 23 attributes that are the most correlated to the attribute pages of politicians, the inference accuracy is 0.79 in AUC. In other words, in average, the set of pages of politicians inferred by the analyser is 79% similar to the ones that are really liked by the target. However, inference accuracy is only 41% when the 23 attributes are selected randomly.

8   Toward Efficient Countermeasures

SONSAI discloses friendship networks, quantifies the correlation between attributes and analyses the behaviours of users in order to infer the values of a target sensitive attribute. It helps users to safeguard their privacy by identifying attributes that are correlated to the sensitive one. Users should then act on these correlated attributes to prevent these revealing correlations. However, SONSAI is not fine-grained enough to identify which attribute values must be modified to hinder a sensitive value inference. First, to derive effective countermeasures one has to somewhat trade network utility for privacy by hiding some information. Second, a collaboration has to be established between users since their respective private data are interrelated. Figure 2 depicts an example of social network where music is correlated to politics. It is easy to correlate the Beatles music to Democrats and George Strait music to Republicans. Consequently, it is easy to infer that the target is probably democrat-oriented as he likes the Beatles. One solution to hinder this inference is to delete the link between the target and the Beatles. However, the target will remain connected to Beatles through Lady Gaga that is in its turn correlated to Beatles. David and the target need to collaborate and delete their preference for Beatles in order to keep private their political orientation. It is obvious that any decision taken by David or the target can affect their mutual privacy. This example shows that deriving a general solution is a challenging problem.

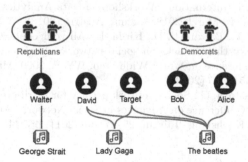

Fig. 2. Musics and politics.

9   Conclusion

We have presented a first prototype for self-auditing Facebook profile resilience against inference attacks. As it will probably take time before legal enforcement of privacy is fully implemented by social networks, SONSAI may contribute in the period to user awareness against privacy threats. E-reputation awareness raising has already motivated the recent development of tools to analyse how a person or a brand is perceived on social medias. "Soyez net sur le net"[4] and "mes datas et moi"[5] are such platforms oriented toward teenagers. These tools are based on explicit content processing. However many companies and their recruiters are nowadays equipped with AI systems that are also able to extract latent information by machine learning. Our proposed approach is to defeat or at least degrade the performance of these systems by letting basic users, and also entities or companies, anticipate the leakage of their information. Hence our results may contribute too to a new generation of E-reputation management applications.

Acknowledgements. This work is supported by MAIF Foundation (www.fondation-maif.fr/).

References

1. Abid, Y., Imine, A., Napoli, A., Raïssi, C., Rusinowitch, M.: Online link disclosure strategies for social networks. In: Cuppens, F., Cuppens, N., Lanet, J.-L., Legay, A. (eds.) CRiSIS 2016. LNCS, vol. 10158, pp. 153–168. Springer, Cham (2017). https://doi.org/10.1007/978-3-319-54876-0_13
2. Abid, Y., Imine, A., Napoli, A., Raïssi, C., Rusinowitch, M.: Two-phase preference disclosure in attributed social networks. In: Benslimane, D., Damiani, E., Grosky, W.I., Hameurlain, A., Sheth, A., Wagner, R.R. (eds.) DEXA 2017. LNCS, vol. 10438, pp. 249–263. Springer, Cham (2017). https://doi.org/10.1007/978-3-319-64468-4_19
3. Abid, Y., Imine, A., Rusinowitch, M.: Sensitive attribute prediction for social networks users. In: 2nd International Workshop on Data Analytics Solutions for Real-LIfe APplications, 26 March 2018, Vienna, Austria (2018)
4. Bilge, L., Strufe, T., Balzarotti, D., Kirda, E.: All your contacts are belong to us: automated identity theft attacks on social networks. In: Proceedings of the 18th International Conference on World Wide Web, WWW 2009, Madrid, Spain, 20–24 April 2009, pp. 551–560 (2009)
5. Chester, S., Srivastava, G.: Social network privacy for attribute disclosure attacks. In: International Conference on Advances in Social Networks Analysis and Mining, ASONAM 2011, Kaohsiung, Taiwan, 25–27 July 2011, pp. 445–449 (2011)

---

[4] http://www.ereputation.paris.fr/.
[5] https://www.mesdatasetmoi.fr/.

6. Conover, M., Gonçalves, B., Ratkiewicz, J., Flammini, A., Menczer, F.: Predicting the political alignment of twitter users. In: 2011 IEEE Third International Conference on PASSAT/SocialCom 2011, Privacy, Security, Risk and Trust (PASSAT) and 2011 IEEE Third International Conference on Social Computing (SocialCom), Boston, MA, USA, 9–11 October 2011, pp. 192–199 (2011)
7. Garrett Brown, M.I.A.P., Howe, T., Borders, K.: Social networks and context-aware spam. In: ACM Conference on Computer Supported Collaborative, no. 10 (2008)
8. Gong, N.Z., Liu, B.: Attribute inference attacks in online social networks. ACM Trans. Priv. Secur. **21**(1), 3:1–3:30 (2018)
9. Gong, N.Z., et al.: Joint link prediction and attribute inference using a social-attribute network. ACM TIST **5**(2), 27:1–27:20 (2014)
10. Heatherly, R., Kantarcioglu, M., Thuraisingham, B.M.: Preventing private information inference attacks on social networks. IEEE Trans. Knowl. Data Eng. **25**(8), 1849–1862 (2013)
11. Kayes, I., Iamnitchi, A.: A survey on privacy and security in online social networks. CoRR, abs/1504.03342 (2015)
12. Kontaxis, G., Polakis, I., Ioannidis, S., Markatos, E.P.: Detecting social network profile cloning. In: Ninth Annual IEEE International Conference on Pervasive Computing and Communications, PerCom 2011, Workshop Proceedings, 21–25 March 2011, Seattle, WA, USA, pp. 295–300 (2011)
13. Mason, W.: Politics and culture on Facebook in the 2014 midterm elections (2014)
14. Perozzi, B., Skiena, S.: Exact age prediction in social networks. In: Proceedings of the 24th International Conference on World Wide Web Companion, WWW 2015, Florence, Italy, 18–22 May 2015 - Companion Volume, pp. 91–92 (2015)
15. Ryu, E., Rong, Y., Li, J., Machanavajjhala, A.: Curso: protect yourself from curse of attribute inference: a social network privacy-analyzer. In: Proceedings of the 3rd ACM SIGMOD Workshop on Databases and Social Networks, DBSocial 2013, New York, NY, USA, 23 June 2013, pp. 13–18 (2013)
16. Vidyalakshmi, B.S., Wong, R.K., Chi, C.: User attribute inference in directed social networks as a service. In: IEEE International Conference on Services Computing, SCC 2016, San Francisco, CA, USA, June 27–July 2 2016, pp. 9–16 (2016)
17. Yin, Z., Gupta, M., Weninger, T., Han, J.: A unified framework for link recommendation using random walks. In: International Conference on Advances in Social Networks Analysis and Mining, ASONAM 2010, Odense, Denmark, 9–11 August 2010, pp. 152–159 (2010)
18. Zhang, L., Zhang, W.: An information extraction attack against on-line social networks. In: 2012 International Conference on Social Informatics (SocialInformatics), Washington, D.C., USA, 14–16 December 2012, pp. 49–55 (2012)

Towards Personal Data Identification and Anonymization Using Machine Learning Techniques

Francesco Di Cerbo[(⊠)] and Slim Trabelsi

Security Research, SAP Labs France, 805, Av. du Docteur Maurice Donat,
06250 Mougins, France
{francesco.di.cerbo,slim.trabelsi}@sap.com

Abstract. The requirements imposed by the new European personal
Data Protection Regulation (GDPR) are applicable for all European
citizens data processed anywhere in the world. The GDPR requires companies to identify, protect and make compliant their processing of personal data collected from European citizens. Identifying personal data
in a non- structured set of big data can be a painful and cost-ineffective
operation. In a static search or in a big data streaming mode, this kind
of operation requires a huge human effort and/or computing resources,
if done manually. The strain becomes event harder when after detection,
one has to pseudo- or anonymize some pieces of information according
to their category (name, address, age, etc.). The current approaches to
identify personal data to anonymize are mainly based on text identification executed via regular expression scripts that are not dynamic enough
to identify different formats of personal information.

In this paper, we propose a solution based on a supervised machine
learning system that identifies personal information in large datasets.
Once the different parts of personal information are identified and tagged
(also in real time), a pseudo- or anonymization technique is applied as
example of processing. A preliminary proof-of-concept implementation
is presented.

Keywords: Personal data protection · Privacy · Machine learning

1 GDPR Requirements

The advent of the new European General Data Privacy Regulation (GDPR Regulation (EU) 2016/679) [3], entered in force in May 2018, changed the legal
framework and the requirements for data processing of European citizens. Such
changes are applicable for all entities that process EU citizens personal data
anywhere in the world. This imposes to all such entities modifications in their
processes and in their software to be compliant with the new regulation.

The GDPR definition of personal data identifies them as "information relating to an identified or identifiable natural person *data subject*". Whenever such

A. Benczúr et al. (Eds.): ADBIS 2018, CCIS 909, pp. 118–126, 2018.
https://doi.org/10.1007/978-3-030-00063-9_13

pieces of information are processed (if they belong to European citizens), GDPR provisions must be applied. It is worth noting that the word "identifiable" comprises the applicability of GDPR to documents or datasets that do not contain direct data subject attributes such as name and surname or social security number, but combinations of attributes that may lead to the identification of an individual [6].

Therefore, the determination of the applicability of the GDPR for a piece of data may not be as simple as checking for the presence of names and surnames or email addresses. The GDPR (in Recital 26) forces to consider such situations, compelling data controllers (the custodians of personal information, like companies) to consider re-identification risks and whether they are "reasonably likely to be used, such as singling out, either by the controller or by another person to identify the natural person directly or indirectly."

With respect to personal data identification as prerequisite of processing, limiting the scope of this analysis to technical aspects and omitting all organisational aspects, data controllers can be asked to:

R1 conduct a risk analysis on the information schema in databases/datasets /documents to understand what parts fall under GDPR

R2 classify each piece of information deemed GDPR-sensitive as personal information

R3 process personal information in accordance to GDPR

To simplify a data controller's obligation and at the same time, to reinforce the protection for personal information in processing, the GDPR recommends the use of pseudonymization, privileged over anonymization.

Pseudonymization deals with the suppression or obfuscation of direct identifiers but also of indirect identifiers as defined before. The removed or manipulated values are stored in a separate data store but linked to the original record where they come from, by means of a key (or pseudonym). This technique is useful to process information in datasets, limiting however the disclosure to the bare minimum (see also GDPR Article 5 and 25 on *data minimisation*). The effectiveness of pseudonymization must be carefully addressed by the data controller, however GDPR (in Recital 26) states that one has to take into account "of all the objective factors, such as the costs of and the amount of time required for identification, taking into consideration the available technology at the time of the processing and technological developments". So, an re-identification risk analysis can accept risks that are assessed as too costly or too complex considering the current technologies and those upcoming in the near future. This makes pseudonymization a very effective technique when information is to be retained for a long time.

In other scenarios, anonymization may be preferred. Anonymization is similar to pseudonymization in that it eliminates or obfuscates direct or indirect identifiers in a dataset. However, the manipulated values are destroyed and not retained anymore by the data controller. Re-identification risk analysis must still be conducted. Only at these conditions, an anonymized dataset or document is no more subject to GDPR prescriptions. Anonymization may result helpful when, for example, the retention period for retaining a personal information expires. The data controller may decide to anonymize the GDPR-sensitive part of a data record but not the others, leaving untouched for instance the financial trans-actions, order records and so on. This would allow to use freely the remaining information.

We may indicate the adoption of pseudo- or anonymization techniques as **R2a**, for consistency with the previous requirements, however noting that such adoption is only recommended.

2   The Problem

In the previous section, we highlighted 4 required operations for data controllers, **R1, R2, R2a, R3**. This paper deals specifically with **R2 and R2a**. In fact, the identification of personal data and the application of corresponding sanitization techniques is not a trivial operation, especially when guiding an organization transition towards GDPR compliance.

About **R2**, we observe that personal data may be expressed in many differ-ent formats. Some of them depend on the country where the data are collected (e.g. numbers, street addresses), some on the language used to express them. Especially considering big data architecture, information may be captured in semi-structured or unstructured forms, thus making information schema anal-ysis very difficult if not impossible. Let us consider for example information collected from social media or in general obtained through search engines, espe-cially with respect to the magnitude and variety of results. If an automatic or semi-automatic identification of personal data becomes complicated, we deem an automatic or semi-automatic application of **R2a** techniques to be at least sim-ilarly complicated; a meaningful application of pseudonymization for indirect identifiers becomes impossible without human intervention, exactly for identify-ing the relevant pieces of information and the sensitive data combinations to be sanitized.

3   Our Vision

The vision we present in this paper consists of:

- the adoption of ML techniques to detect personal data (according to GDPR definition), in Sect. 3.1.
- the proposition of an algorithm to integrate ML techniques with pseudonymization or even anonymization solutions, to ease the processing of personal information in an organization, in Sect. 3.2.
- an architecture to materialize the proposed algorithm, in Section 3.4.

3.1   Machine Learning Algorithms for Personal Data Identification

We claim that the results brought by the recent developments of ML techniques can be positively adopted for the identification of personal information in documents. The advantage they bring in comparison with the usage of regular expressions or more in general, to deterministic approaches can be summarized as follows:

- increased flexibility: a single ML model can be used to detect multiple personal data categories, without the need to provide specific parameters for their identification but only adequate training datasets, letting the machine to determine which parameters to consider.
- increased robustness: a ML model can detect a class of information even if typos or format inconsistencies are detected, in contrast to deterministic approaches like regular expression. This characteristic is particularly valuable for human-produced artefacts.
- simplified maintenance: changes or new categories of data can be detected by training or re-training existing models, instead of having to modify complex regular expressions.

More precisely, our proposal aims at combining the benefits of deterministic approaches to those brought by ML techniques. For certain well-formed pieces of information (e.g. an IPv4/v6 address), deterministic approaches outperform ML in that, for example, they do not require any training to become effective. We foresee the possibility to choose one of the two approaches according to the classes of information to be classified, or better, to have a per-information class configuration. Naturally, the results computed by each of the approaches Therefore, an approach as shown in Sect. 3.4 allows to achieve the benefits of both approaches for classifying different classes of information, at the cost of (limited) additional computation resources.

3.2   An Algorithm for Personal Data Detection and Manipulation

We propose the adoption of machine learning (ML) techniques in order to address the problems connected to **R2**, personal data identification. The ML approach would allow to identify personal data categories (e.g. name, surname, email, addresses and so on), thus enabling the application of specific pseudo- or anonymization techniques (**R2a**). As mentioned, the approach is to be used in conjunction with deterministic approaches, for the classes of information that do not cope well with the ML characteristics. However, the adoption of ML makes possible to overcome the problems brought by the various formats and country- or language-dependency, provided that sufficiently complete training set are made available. This flow is illustrated in the following Algorithm 1 and described as follows.

In a first stage (phase *initialization*), supervised machine learning systems are trained to identify the occurrence of certain textual patterns that are recurrent in a large dataset. They are based on probabilistic models that can identify the content of a data flow according to the occurrence of certain textual patterns. Subsequently (phase *execution*), we propose to use the machine learning systems to identify the occurrence of personal information contained in big data set independently from the structure and the format in which this data is written. Once this information identified we use different anonymization techniques (according to the privacy requirements) in order to anonymize personal information on real time.

Algorithm 1. Process

Data: A generic *input_text*, in any format
Result: An *output_text* with *input_text* contents but anonymized personal
    information
begin initialization:
⎮   train a machine learning algorithm with personal data training sets;
end
begin execution:
⎮   // step R2
⎮   evaluate *input_text* against the machine learning algorithm previously
⎮   trained to identify personal information;
⎮   // step R2a
⎮   pseudo- or anonymize personal information;
⎮   create *output_text* from *input_text* inserting anonymized personal
⎮   information;
⎮   return *output_text*;
end

Listing 1.1. Regular Expression to match US Addresses.

```
^(?n:(?<address1>(\d{1,5}(\ 1\/[234])?(\x20[A-Z]([a-z])+)+ )|(P\.0
↪ \.\ Box\ \d{1,5}))\s{1,2}(?i:(?<address2>(((APT|B LDG|DEPT|
↪ FL|HNGR|LOT|PIER|RM|S(LIP|PC|T(E|OP))|TRLR|UNIT)\x20\w
↪ {1,5})|(BSMT|FRNT|LBBY|LOWR|OFC|PH|REAR|SIDE|UPPR)\.?)\s
↪ {1,2})?)(?<city>[A-Z]([a-z])+(\.?)(\x20[A-Z]([a-z])+){0,2})
↪ \, \x20(?<state>A[LKSZRAP]|C[AOT]|D[EC]|F[LM]|G[AU]|HI|I[
↪ ADL N]|K[SY]|LA|M[ADEHINOPST]|N[CDEHJMVY]|O[HKR]|P[ARW]|RI|
↪ S[CD] |T[NX]|UT|V[AIT]|W[AIVY])\x20(?<zipcode>(?!0{5})\d
↪ {5}(-\d {4})?))$
```

3.3 Use Case Example

Let's assume that the company ACME is maintaining a huge data set containing their customer personal information written and structured in different formats (databases, text documents, data structures, etc.). ACME is a European company that must comply with the GDPR and identify all the sorted personal data to be able to delete it or presented to the data owners (customers) at any time. In order to identify all this spread and non-structured personal information, the ACME Data Protection Officer (DPO) decided to put in-place regular expression scripts querying all the datasets with the objective to identify personal information. The regular expression to identify a postal address (only for US) was written as for Listing 1.1..

This regular expression captures US street address in a text. As natural for regular expressions, an address can be extracted if its constituents match the foreseen format, as stated in the regular expression structure. In this case, the matched address format is: *##### Street 2ndunit City, ST zip+4 address1*, meaning that it must have street number and proper case street name. It must not cater for punctuation or P.O Box *####*, while punctuation is mandatory for P.O. address2. As exemplification, it can match with *123 Park Ave Apt 123 New York City, NY 10002* but it would not match *C/O John Paul, POBox 456, Motown, CA 96090*.

With a Naive Bayes machine learning algorithm for example, if we train the algorithm with a set of addresses in an heterogeneous format, the probabilistic model will identify the occurrence of certain keywords contained in the addresses without any specific order then it will compute the probability for this data to be labelled as address. For the string *123 Park Ave Apt 123 New York City, NY 10002*, the elements {Park, Ave, Apt, New York city, NY 10002} are identified as address key words than the probability for a document, containing this keyword, to be an address would be very close to 1. The same for *John Paul, POBox 456, Motown, CA 96090*, where {POBox, Motown, CA 96090} will be identified as address key words. The ACME's DPO will then train the machine to recognize personal data information from publicly available databases and will execute the evaluation on his company's data to identify on the fly different formats and combinations of personal data.

Naive Bayes is a general-purpose algorithm that can be applied for different classes of problems. Another option is to use specific ML algorithms for Named Entity Recognition (NER) in the family of Natural Language Processing (NLP). Conditional Random Fields (CRF) or Deep Learning techniques like Convolutional Neural Networks (CNN) can be used to recognize data classes in a text, respectively using a set of features computed on the word under analysis and some of the previous words (CRF), or comparing a word chunck against a set of reference word patterns.

The availability of multiple options for the detection of personal information, each with strong points and weaknesses, leads to a simple consideration: a solution able to integrate different options at the same time would give the overall best results. We used this consideration for the proposition of an architecture for the implementation of our vision, described in the following section.

3.4   Architecture

An architecture implementing our vision must be able to integrate multiple techniques for the detection of pieces of personal information, classify them in a consistent taxonomy and thus permitting the execution of pseudonymization or anonymization techniques. Such architecture is depicted in Fig. 1.

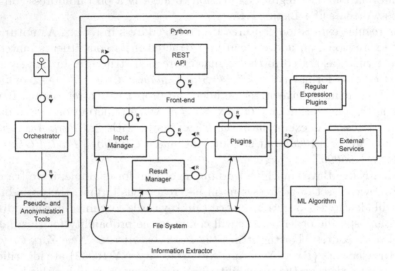

Fig. 1. Architecture.

It is composed of the following parts:

- an actor submitting a text to analyse. It can be an human actor, as in the figure, or a software (e.g. the streaming branch of a big data architecture)
- an *Information Extractor* component, in charge of classifying the pieces of information of interest in the input text
- a set of *pseudonymization or anonymization tools*, working specifically on a class of pieces of information, and
- an *Orchestrator* to coordinate all architecture components, exposing an interface able to receive a text and return as output the input contents, appropriately anonymized or pseudonymized.

The core of the architecture is a component called *Information Extractor*. It is composed by a number of subcomponents, namely for input manipulation (the *Input Manager*, necessary for operations like text tokenization, chunking etc.) or result management (the *Result Manager*, used to determine the output format and any necessary conversion routines). The Information Extractor integrates with a number of *Plugins*: notably, the ML algorithms, but also external services and regular expression plugins. The latter are still useful for well-formed information classes, like for example IPv4/v6/MAC addresses, MD5/SHA1 hashes etc.:

in such cases, deterministic approaches normally outperforms statistical methods. The Information Extractor defines an internal taxonomy for the consistent classification of the recognized pieces of information. In this way, the Orchestrator can successfully trigger the operations of the pseudonymization/anonymization modules on the respective information classes. For example, anonymization methods like differential privacy normally work on a set of values, simpler approaches like information suppression only require to know which elements to delete from the input text. Orchestrator can be configure to apply a method or another for different information classes on the returned pieces of information.

4   State of the Art

In data mining, machine learning algorithms are used extensively, for pattern recognition, classification or regression. In those cases, it is assumed that those algorithms are applied on specific data classes; for example, to observe the variance of salaries of a company's employees according to their gender, or record linkage [2,9], a technique to understand whether parts of two datasets overlap. In our proposal, however, ML is used to recognize elements of specific data classes, the personal data. With this respect, a closer similarity can be found in a branch of Natural Language Processing, called Named Entity Recognition(NER). It consists of the problem of locating and categorizing important nouns and proper nouns in a text [5]. Different approaches can be followed for implementing NER. Conditional Random Fields [8] and their implementations (for example, [4]) or deep learning, for exemple, using Convolutional Neural Networks [1]. As similar applications, Penti and Rani B [7] proposed to use data mining techniques based on word matching in order to identify confidential data within a company in order to calculate a confidentiality level and prevent data leakage. This solution is documents-centric and thus more coarse-grained, if compared to our approach; the application of the work of Penti and Rani B in our context would seem to fail to identify the relevant pieces of information for GDPR compliance within a company's data, plus it would introduce a certain amount of false negatives in the classification process, that is not acceptable in our use case.

5   Conclusion

GDPR demands to data controllers and in particular to companies active in the European market, specific measures for protecting the personal information of European citizens. The role of pseudonymization is relevant to implement a Privacy by Design approach as well as the data minimisation principle: its adoption permits to limit the amount of pieces of personal data used in a business process, lowering the impact of data breaches and thus their consequences. However, the application of GDPR prescriptions may not be simple, starting from the identification of pieces of personal data in the heterogeneous data repositories that companies normally store and process. For this reason, after having observed the limitation of deterministic approaches (like regular expressions), we propose the usage of ML algorithms to identify the presence and the nature of personal information, especially for semi-structured or non-structured data repositories or documents. Their application following a classification taxonomy allows for applying specific pseudonymization or anonymization tools on the different information classes.

The current results to produce an implementation of the proposed algorithm and architecture are promising. We adopted Naive Bayes and CNN for Named Entity Recognition, together with simple anonymization approaches for the processing of data collected from social media and the Internet. In the future, we plan to report about the effectiveness of the approach, especially with respect to the different ML approaches used to classify personal information and their performances.

Acknowledgements. This work was partly supported by EU-funded H2020 project C3ISP [grand no. 700294].

References

1. Spacy, industrial-strength natural language processing. https://spacy.io. Accessed 12 May 2018
2. Bilenko, M., Basil, S., Sahami, M.: Adaptive product normalization: using online learning for record linkage in comparison shopping. In: Fifth IEEE International Conference on Data Mining, p. 8. IEEE (2005)
3. European Parliament and Council: Regulation (EU) 2016/679 of the European Parliament and of the Council - On the protection of natural persons with regard to the processing of personal data and on the free movement of such data, and repealing Directive 95/46/EC (General Data Protection Regulation) (2016). http://goo.gl/LfwxGe. Accessed 27 Apr 2016
4. Finkel, J.R., Grenager, T., Manning, C.: Incorporating non-local information into information extraction systems by GIBBS sampling. In: Proceedings of the 43rd Annual Meeting on Association for Computational Linguistics, Association for Computational Linguistics, pp. 363–370 (2005)
5. McCallum, A., Li, W.: Early results for named entity recognition with conditional random fields, feature induction and web-enhanced lexicons. In: Proceedings of the Seventh Conference on Natural Language Learning at HLT-NAACL 2003-vol. 4, Association for Computational Linguistics, pp. 188–191 (2003)
6. Ohm, P.: Broken promises of privacy: responding to the surprising failure of anonymization. Ucla. L. Rev. **57**, 1701 (2009)
7. Peneti, S., Rani, B.P.: Confidential data identification using data mining techniques in data leakage prevention system. Int. J. Data Min. Knowl. Manage. Process. **5**(5), 65–73 (2015)
8. Sutton, C., McCallum, A.: An introduction to conditional random fields. Found. Trends® Mach. Learn. **4**(4), 267–373 (2012)
9. Winkler, W.E.: Methods for record linkage and bayesian networks. Technical report, Statistical Research Division, US Census Bureau, Washington, DC (2002)

Personalised Privacy Policies

Harshvardhan Jitendra Pandit[(✉)], Declan O'Sullivan, and Dave Lewis

ADAPT Centre, Trinity College Dublin, Dublin, Ireland
{harshvardhan.pandit,declan.osullivan,dave.lewis}@adaptcentre.ie

Abstract. Internet services have become an important part of the daily life for a large number of people, and often deal with varying amounts of personal information. A privacy policy is a legal document governed by territorial laws that outlines the collection, usage, storage, and sharing of personal data. A known problem with such documents is its ambiguity and difficulty in comprehension for end users. The General Data Protection Regulation (GDPR) requires transparency regarding the provision of such information to the data subject through its various obligations and rights. We propose a remodelling of the privacy policy based on provision of relevant information regarding personal data specific to the user. Such a policy will dynamically reflect the state of activities over personal data using a legal and comprehensive document, and can be used as a tool for the provision of rights and requests from data subjects. We support our discussion with an example use-case of a GDPR-based privacy policy adopted from online services. We present our analysis on identifying changes and our approach towards the representation and creation of such dynamic policies.

Keywords: Privacy policy · Personalisation · GDPR · Metadata

1 Introduction

The internet has become an ubiquitous part of modern daily life by providing a plethora of services and content through more than a billion websites[1]. The use of personal data on such websites and services is governed by legal obligations and must adhere to their compliance. Privacy policies act as a form of legal agreement between the service providers and their users [15], and provide information on the collection, usage, storage, and sharing of personal information. A privacy policy is expected to change or update with changes in the underlying activities and their use of personal data. Therefore, it can be considered to be a dynamic document based on changes to the underlying system which it reflects.

The problem of privacy policies being difficult to read and comprehend is well known [6,8], and has seen several efforts to remedy this [2,9,13,14]. Additionally, a privacy policy is a common document for all users of the service, and therefore contains ambiguous legal language that is broad enough to capture all

---

[1] http://www.internetlivestats.com/total-number-of-websites/.

© Springer Nature Switzerland AG 2018
A. Benczúr et al. (Eds.): ADBIS 2018, CCIS 909, pp. 127–137, 2018.
https://doi.org/10.1007/978-3-030-00063-9_14

possible uses of the service. It does not contain any specifics and reflects only the possibility of some action over data. For example, the sentence *"we may collect your email..."* informs about the action (collect) over data (email) but does not specify whether this *will happen* or has happened already.

Under the General Data Protection Regulation (GDPR) [1], data subjects are provided the right to information about their personal data. Service providers (*Controllers*) are required to provide this information to the users (*Data Subjects*) upon request, which necessitates some technical implementation capable of recording and providing the required information. Such an implementation must be capable of distinguishing individual requests from each data subject and providing only the required information pertaining to that particular individual.

We propose to remodel the privacy policy into a personalised document for providing information specific to the data subject. Such a privacy policy would be specific to the user, and would contain information about activities and data only for a particular data subject. The information provided can be used as part of provision of GDPR rights or Subject Access Requests, or combined with a more general privacy policy to better inform users about the use of their personal data.

In this paper, we present our discussion on the creation of personalised privacy policies. We start by discussing the relevant work in Sect. 2. The identification and representation of dynamic metadata specific to data subjects is presented in Sect. 3, with the creation of a personalised privacy policy discussed in Sect. 4. Potential applications are discussed in Sect. 5. The conclusion and future work are presented in Sect. 6.

2   Related Work

The related work is presented in two sections. The first, Sect. 2.1, presents work related to the systematic studies and categorisation of privacy policies. This work is relevant towards understanding the composition of information in privacy policies, and how it can be extracted and represented. The second, Sect. 2.2, presents work relevant to the visualisation of information associated with GDPR rights. This work is relevant towards understanding what information is required to be presented to the user and the various approaches associated with it.

2.1   Study of Privacy Policies

There have been several studies of privacy policies across a wide range of topics from readability to summarising. Automatic categorisation of privacy policies using machine learning [2,7,9] has been shown to be effective in annotating privacy policies with context. The UsablePrivacy Project[2] has used this method to categorise sentences in a privacy policy which can be queried and used in more

---

[2] https://usableprivacy.org/.

complex systems for better representation of information [9,15]. PrivacyGuide [13,14] is a similar approach that uses machine learning to summarise privacy policies. It uses a risk-based approach based on GDPR to identify relevant information, and presents it in the visual form of a dashboard.

The work described above highlights the difficulty in human comprehension of privacy policies and the applicability of machine-based techniques to convert information into a more suitable format for end-users. The work also highlights the limitations of information that can currently be extracted automatically. Both the UsablePrivacy and PrivacyGuide projects can currently identify the context of a sentence, but do not work on extracting relevant metadata from it. This is in part due to the complex nature of such sentences as well as the ambiguity in the language (see example in Sect. 1). More information about data purpose and its specificity [3] is required for privacy policies to better inform users. A privacy policy personalised to the data subject would ideally contain lesser ambiguity and more specitivity, which can help such efforts (both manual and automated) to better extract the relevant information.

2.2 Visualising Information for GDPR Rights

Considering that the privacy policy exists as a mechanism to provide information about personal data to users, other approaches with similar aims will also use the same information. One such approach describes a visualisation of the privacy policy and consent forms as a decision tree [12] with the aim to provide better information about choices made by users. PrivacyGuide [13,14] provides a dashboard that contains a visual summary of privacy policy. Other approaches exist that use icons [5] or information flow diagrams [4,7] as graphical representations of privacy policies. The UsablePrivacy project shows a visual representation of categorisation of annotations using colours [9,15].

3   Dynamic Metadata in Privacy Policies

We focus on change in information describing personal data collection, storage, usage, sharing, and deletion. At the time of writing this paper, GDPR has not yet entered into force, and few organisations have public policies related to the provision of various rights. We discuss our work and approach using privacy policies publicly provided by Airbnb Ireland[3] and Twitter[4], with archived copies made available[5] in case of changes to the policy in future. We selected these examples due to their prominence as known commercial enterprises and their suitability for purposes of this research.

---

[3] https://www.airbnb.ie/terms/privacy_policy.

[4] https://twitter.com/en/privacy.

[5] https://opengogs.adaptcentre.ie/harsh/privacy-policy-dashboard/.

3.1 Structure of Information

The analysis of these policies requires identification of what information may change or is ambiguous and could be resolved using information provided from resolution of GDPR rights. For this purpose, the selected examples of privacy policies have a suitable structure which is ordered into contextual sections. Such organisation of information not only helps the reader better understand and navigate information, it also helps in categorising the different types of information represented within the policy. We primarily discuss this structure in relation to the policy provided by Airbnb Ireland, though the discussion is also applicable to the policy from Twitter.

The policy follows a very structured approach towards presenting information to the user. The broad sections of the policy provide information about data collection, usage, sharing, and rights. These are further classified based on the context of activity. We focus on the first section which deals with data collection (termed "Information we collect" in the policy). The policy provides two sources of data - collected directly from the data source (section 1.1 and 1.2) and obtained from third parties (section 1.3). The information collected from the data subject is further categorised based on whether it is necessary (section 1.1.1 and 1.1.3) or opt-in (section 1.1.2). Information about the nature of the data collection mechanism is also provided, whereby some of it is collected via automated systems (section 1.2). This structure is presented visually in Fig. 1.

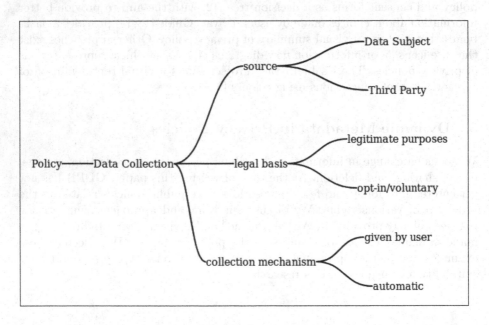

Fig. 1. Structuring of information related to data collection in policy

While the above information reflects the structure of the policy, the contents within each section provide information about the personal data involved. For example, the information in section 1.1.1 describes the categories of data involved. Each category is further described with the specific types of data that fall under it. For example, *Account Information* is the first category within the section, which contains information about data types such as *first name, last name, email address*, and *date of birth*. Additionally, the sentence also mentions the specific process (*account sign-up*) used to collect this information.

This information is distinct from the earlier structuring of information in that it can change (is dynamic) based on the operation and provision of services. For example, it is possible that additional information such as nationality may be added as essential account information in the future. In such a case, it will be listed along with the other data types under the *"Account Information"* data category. Similarly, the mechanism for data collection may change as well to some other new or existing process or step.

3.2   Annotation Metadata

We distinguish between metadata representing the 'structure' of information and the representation of the underlying system. While the former will be common to all services and policies, the latter reflects information specific to organisation or service (and to the data subject). From the example, all privacy policies will have a section for describing the data categories, but the specific categories mentioned within the policy are unique and associated with the organisation and service it provides, and is updated based on changes to the system and operations. We term such information as 'dynamic metadata' to reflect this.

Based on this definition, we annotated the example privacy policy to visualise the different types of metadata, as presented in Fig. 2. The annotations are highlighted with different colours based on the context of the metadata, as shown in the legend in the picture. The figure reflects only a part of the annotated policy, which is available online[6]. The colours serve to visually represent the dynamic metadata, and help in understanding the different types of information and their context throughout the policy. This visual distinction of information is presented to view the different contexts within the privacy policy identified in our analysis. This follow a similar approach from the UsablePrivacy project [9] which use different colours to visually highlight the different types of information.

4   Implementation Approach

In this section we describe our approach towards the implementation of a personalised privacy policy using the dynamic metadata. The approach provides a general overview of how such policies can be implemented, and can be adopted to any set of technologies in practice. The first section, Sect. 4.1, describes a

---

[6] https://openscience.adaptcentre.ie/projects/privacy-policy/personalise/.

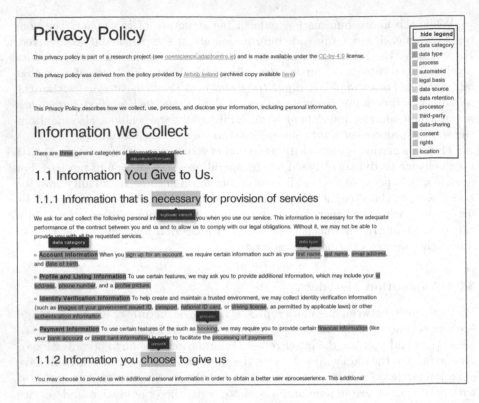

Fig. 2. Visualising annotations for dynamic metadata in privacy policy

common template for a privacy policy which is then personalised using dynamic metadata specific to the user. The second section, Sect. 4.2, presents our approach towards representation and generation of dynamic metadata in policies.

4.1 Privacy Policy Template

The privacy policy itself can be represented as a template with information that is common to all policies being considered as static text, and that which is specific to the underlying processes or the data subject being considered as dynamic text. Based on this template, the information for the data subject or user is then used to populate and present a personalised privacy policy to the user. This approach allows reusing a common privacy policy layout and some part of the overall text for all users. In addition, it also allows personalisation of information specific to certain user-cases such as in case of minors or information pertaining to exercised rights.

Existing privacy policies (including the specified example) are monolithic documents composed primarily of text. They do not have any metadata that can describe the content or its context. We take this opportunity for remodelling the privacy policy to also annotate its contents with metadata that can assist in its interpretation and use in other tools and services.

Providing contextual information about the dynamic metadata can assist other systems and tools to interpret the results in order to assist the user, or for research purposes. Since the privacy policy is inevitably served as a web-based document, the metadata too must be served in a compatible format such as Microdata[7] or RDFa[8] along with a suitable vocabulary such as schema.org[9]. Such formats and vocabularies must essentially be open in nature to foster inter-operability.

The underlying contextual information about the dynamic metadata is largely abstracted by the displayed privacy policy as the user does not see or interact with it. However, it is of consequence to the organisation as they are required to maintain and provide it. It is therefore beneficial to store this infor-mation along with the relevant metadata in a form that assists in the creation of dynamic privacy policy. Such information is also required and is useful for compliance purposes as well as the provision of various rights. All of these can benefit from a structured method for representation of associated information along with the involved metadata. The ability of the underlying technology for expressing queries provides a means to efficiently retrieve information in a struc-tured and relevant format.

4.2   Storage and Representation of Metadata

For our work, we focus on the use of semantic web technologies due to their open and extensible nature. For representing the metadata related to processes and the data they use, we use the GDPRov ontology [11] which extends PROV-O[10] and P-Plan[11]. PROV-O is a W3C recommendation, which provides interoper-ability of provenance information. P-Plan is an extension of PROV-O that allows representation of abstract workflows. For annotating information with concepts and terms from the GDPR, we use the GDPRtEXT resource [10].

Representing metadata using structured vocabularies such as GDPRov and GDPRtEXT allows querying for required information as well as annotating the policy with relevant metadata. We present our preliminary work towards using these to annotate privacy polices using RDFa. An example of this is presented in Listing 1, which shows the possible RDFa annotation of a personalised privacy policy continued from the previous example. The policy is provided as a HTML page and describes the data type *"first-name"* within the *"AccountInformation"* data category. *AccountInformation* is a defined as a subclass of *PersonalData* declared in GDPRov, and *first-name* is an instance of this class. This information stands to informs the data subject that their *first name* is being collected as part

---

[7] https://www.w3.org/TR/microdata/.
[8] https://www.w3.org/TR/rdfa-primer/.
[9] http://schema.org/.
[10] http://www.w3.org/TR/prov-o/.
[11] http://purl.org/net/p-plan.

of the *Account Information*. The data category as well as data type is an example of dynamic metadata used to personalise the privacy policy for the data subject.

We describe here a more detailed technical description of the implementation of this system to demonstrate the particular use-case.

```
1   <body
2       vocab="http://example.com/use-case"
3       prefix="gdprov:
4           http://purl.org/adaptcentre/openscience/ontologies/gdprov#
5           rdfs: http://www.w3.org/2000/01/rdf-schema#">
6       <p resource="#AccountInfo">
7           <span property="rdfs:label">Account Information</span></p>
8       <ul>
9           <li><label
10              resource="#first-name"
11              typeof="gdprov:PersonalData #AccountInfo">
12              <span property="rdfs:label">First Name</span>
13          </label></li>
14      </ul>
15  </body>
```

1. The model of the system is defined using GDPRov and GDPRtEXT to represent activities and how they interact with personal data. This is stored as RDF data in a triple store.
2. This is followed by the creation of a privacy policy template using a templating engine such as Jinja[12] that allows programmatically populating it with dynamic metadata.
3. As data subjects or users use and interact with the system, relevant metadata is stored using GDPRov in the triple store as RDF data.
4. When data subjects request to view a personalised privacy policy or exercise their right to retrieve information, the relevant data is retrieved using queries modelled using SPARQL[13].
5. The results are then used to populate the policy template to create a personalised privacy policy or information report that is annotated with RDFa.

5   Potential Applications

The work described in this paper has broader applications apart from personalising privacy policies such as addressing various rights and access requests (such as for GDPR) and to automate other similarly structured documents.

Address GDPR Rights and SARs

GDPR provides the data subjects with several rights through which an organisation is required to provide information about their activities over personal data.

---

[12] http://jinja.pocoo.org/.
[13] https://www.w3.org/TR/sparql11-query/.

This can necessitate the creation of new technical measures to handle requests and to provide this information in a legally acceptable way. The use of a personalised privacy policy document can aid in the provision of this information as it uses legally relevant language and outlines the use of personal data in a structured way. Similarly, a Subject Access Report (SAR) can be created from the same mechanism used to implement the personalised privacy policy, as it largely operates on the same information.

Automate Reports and Documentation

Documentation related to compliance and other processes is often structured and refers to information in a specific way. A similar approach as the one described in this paper where stored metadata is used to dynamically populate a structured document can be used to automate this process. This can be used for generating reports that describe the various processes and how they relate with personal data based on the underlying model of the system. It can also be extended to create various technical reports regarding the use of internal processes.

6 Conclusion and Future Work

Through this paper, we presented our work on a personalised privacy policy that provides specific information about a data subject's personal data. We presented our analysis of existing real-world policies where we identified the structure of information and the dynamic metadata based on changes to the underlying system as well as the specific data subject. We presented our approach towards the representation of this metadata using a common and open format, and described our work towards creating such personalised policies using semantic web technologies. We also discussed how this work can be used as a tool for the provision of rights and requests from data subjects, with potential applications in similarly structured documents.

The primary future work is the implementation of such a personalised policy using the approaches and technologies described in this paper. With the advent of GDPR, we expect to see more examples of similarly structured privacy policies, which will need to be analysed to identify relevant metadata. This also presents an opportunity to assess the information provided by various organisations as part of the various rights and SARs; and to modify this work to better reflect real-world use-cases.

While the work presented in this paper presents the motivation for a personalised privacy policy, the generic privacy policy that is shown to all users must also be preserved to be displayed before any data or processes have been executed. Therefore, in effect, the organisation will have two privacy policies - one generic and the other personalised, that will contain largely similar structures and metadata regarding the processes and data used. More work needs to be undertaken to distinguish the similarities between the two to take advantage of the similar structure and to also possibly generate such generic privacy policies in an automated manner.

Acknowledgements. This work is supported by the ADAPT Centre for Digital Content Technology which is funded under the SFI Research Centres Programme (Grant 13/RC/2106) and is co-funded under the European Regional Development Fund.

References

1. Regulation (EU) 2016/679 of the European Parliament and of the Council of 27 April 2016 on the protection of natural persons with regard to the processing of personal data and on the free movement of such data, and repealing Directive 95/46/EC (General Data Protection Regulation). Official Journal of the European Union L119, 1–88, May 2016. http://eur-lex.europa.eu/legal-content/EN/TXT/?uri=OJ:L:2016:119:TOC
2. Ammar, W., Wilson, S., Sadeh, N., Smith, N.A.: Automatic categorization of privacy policies: a pilot study (2012). http://repository.cmu.edu/lti/199/
3. Bhatia, J., Breaux, T.D.: A data purpose case study of privacy policies. In: 2017 IEEE 25th International Requirements Engineering Conference (RE), pp. 394–399. IEEE (2017)
4. Bier, C., Kühne, K., Beyerer, J.: PrivacyInsight: the next generation privacy dashboard. In: Schiffner, S., Serna, J., Ikonomou, D., Rannenberg, K. (eds.) APF 2016. LNCS, vol. 9857, pp. 135–152. Springer, Cham (2016). https://doi.org/10.1007/978-3-319-44760-5_9
5. Esayas, S., Mahler, T., McGillivray, K.: Is a picture worth a thousand terms? Visualising contract terms and data protection requirements for cloud computing users. In: Casteleyn, S., Dolog, P., Pautasso, C. (eds.) ICWE 2016. LNCS, vol. 9881, pp. 39–56. Springer, Cham (2016). https://doi.org/10.1007/978-3-319-46963-8_4
6. Fabian, B., Ermakova, T., Lentz, T.: Large-scale readability analysis of privacy policies. In: Proceedings of the International Conference on Web Intelligence, WI 2017, pp. 18–25. ACM, New York (2017). https://doi.org/10.1145/3106426.3106427
7. Fawaz, H.H.K., Schaub, R.L.F., Karl, K.G.S.: Polisis: automated analysis and presentation of privacy policies using deep learning. Technical report, EPFL (2017). https://pribot.org/files/Polisis_Technical_Report.pdf
8. Jensen, C., Potts, C.: Privacy policies as decision-making tools: an evaluation of online privacy notices. In: Proceedings of the SIGCHI Conference on Human Factors in Computing Systems, CHI 2004, pp. 471–478. ACM, New York (2004). https://doi.org/10.1145/985692.985752
9. Oltramari, A., et al.: PrivOnto: a semantic framework for the analysis of privacy policies. Semant. Web **9**(2), 185–203 (2018). https://doi.org/10.3233/SW-170283
10. Pandit, H.J., Fatema, K., O'Sullivan, D., Lewis, D.: GDPRtEXT - GDPR as a linked data resource. ESWC 2018. LNCS, vol. 10843, pp. 481–495. Springer, Cham (2018). https://doi.org/10.1007/978-3-319-93417-4_31
11. Pandit, H.J., Lewis, D.: Modelling provenance for GDPR compliance using linked open data vocabularies. In: Proceedings of the 5th Workshop on Society, Privacy and the Semantic Web - Policy and Technology (PrivOn2017) (PrivOn) (2017). http://ceur-ws.org/Vol-1951/#paper-06
12. Rossi, A., Palmirani, M.: A visualization approach for adaptive consent in the european data protection framework. In: 2017 Conference for E-Democracy and Open Government (CeDEM), pp. 159–170, May 2017. https://doi.org/10.1109/CeDEM.2017.23

13. Tesfay, W.B., Hofmann, P., Nakamura, T., Kiyomoto, S., Serna, J.: I read but don't agree: privacy policy benchmarking using machine learning and the EU GDPR. In: WWW 2018 Companion Proceedings of the Web Conference 2018, pp. 163–166. International World Wide Web Conferences Steering Committee, Republic and Canton of Geneva, Switzerland (2018). https://doi.org/10.1145/3184558.3186969
14. Tesfay, W.B., Hofmann, P., Nakamura, T., Kiyomoto, S., Serna, J.: PrivacyGuide: towards an implementation of the EU GDPR on internet privacy policy evaluation. In: Proceedings of the Fourth ACM International Workshop on Security and Privacy Analytics, IWSPA 2018, pp. 15–21. ACM, New York (2018). https://doi.org/10.1145/3180445.3180447
15. Wilson, S., et al.: The creation and analysis of a website privacy policy corpus. In: Proceedings of the 54th Annual Meeting of the Association for Computational Linguistics (Volume 1: Long Papers), pp. 1330–1340. Association for Computational Linguistics, Berlin, Germany, August 2016. http://www.aclweb.org/anthology/P16-1126

Black-Box Model Explained Through an Assessment of Its Interpretable Features

Francesco Ventura[✉], Tania Cerquitelli[✉], and Francesco Giacalone[✉]

Politecnico di Torino, Corso Duca degli Abruzzi, 24, 10129 Torino, Italy
{francesco.ventura,tania.cerquitelli}@polito.it,
francesco.giacalone@studenti.polito.it

Abstract. Algorithms are powerful and necessary tools behind a large part of the information we use every day. However, they may introduce new sources of bias, discrimination and other unfair practices that affect people who are unaware of it. Greater algorithm transparency is indispensable to provide more credible and reliable services. Moreover, requiring developers to design transparent algorithm-driven applications allows them to keep the model accessible and human understandable, increasing the trust of end users. In this paper we present EBAnO, a new engine able to produce prediction-local explanations for a black-box model exploiting interpretable feature perturbations. EBAnO exploits the hypercolumns representation together with the cluster analysis to identify a set of interpretable features of images. Furthermore two indices have been proposed to measure the influence of input features on the final prediction made by a CNN model. EBAnO has been preliminary tested on a set of heterogeneous images. The results highlight the effectiveness of EBAnO in explaining the CNN classification through the evaluation of interpretable features influence.

Keywords: Transparent mining · Neural networks · Image processing

1 Introduction

Transparent data solutions is an emerging area of data management and analytics with a considerable impact on society. This is an important subject of debate in both engineering and law, involving scientists as well as activists and the press, because of the profound societal effects of such discrimination and biases.

In the last few years algorithms have been widely exploited in many practical use cases, thus they increasingly support and influence various aspects of our life. With little transparency in the sense that it is very difficult to ascertain why and how they produce a certain output, wrongdoing is possible. For example, algorithms can promote healthy habits by recommending activities that minimize risks only for a subset of the population because of biased training data. Whether these effects are intentional or not, they are increasingly difficult to

© Springer Nature Switzerland AG 2018
A. Benczúr et al. (Eds.): ADBIS 2018, CCIS 909, pp. 138–149, 2018.
https://doi.org/10.1007/978-3-030-00063-9_15

spot due the opaque nature of machine learning and data mining. Since algorithms affect us, transparent and better algorithms are indispensable by making accessible not only the results of the data management and analysis but also the processes and models used.

Today, the most efficient machine learning algorithms - such as deep neural networks - operate essentially as black boxes. Specifically, deep learning algorithms have an increasing impact on our everyday life: complex models obtained with deep neural network architectures represent the new state-of-the-art in many domains [1] concerning image and video processing [2], natural language processing [3] and speech recognition [4]. However, neural network architectures present a natural propensity to opacity in terms of understanding data processing and prediction [5,6]. This overall opacity leads to black-box systems where the user remains completely unaware of the process that models inputs over output predictions. Thus, with the introduction of complex, black-box systems, in the real world decision-making process, the need for algorithmic transparency becomes even more prominent.

This paper presents a new engine, named EBAnO (Explaining BlAck-box mOdel) to explain the main relationships between the inputs and outputs of a given prediction made by a black-box algorithm. As a first attempt EBAnO explains predictions made by a convolutional neural network (CNN) [7] on image classification. To this aim, the main contributions of this work are threefold:

- Definition of a set of *interpretable features* (input) characterizing the images through hypercolumn representation [8]. Hypercolums, representing pixels of a given image through all CNN layers, are clustered through K-means [9] to identify groups of correlated pixels. Each group models a given portion of the image representing an interpretable feature used to explain the black-box model.
- Definition of two indices to explain the behavior of the black-box model. The first, IR , measures the *local influence of input feature with respect to the real class* of the image, while the second, IRP , measures the *inter-class feature influence for each feature* of an image. Through these indices EBAnO provides more insights on how a black-box model works.
- Definition of an iterative process of perturbation (based on blur) and classification to analyze the real impact/influence of a given interpretable feature over the local classification.

A preliminary experimental validation of EBAnO performed on 85 images demonstrate the effectiveness of EBAnO in providing interesting relationships between a set of interpretable features characterizing the images and the class label selected through the CNN black-box model.

The paper is organized as follows. Section 2 provides a general overview of the EBAnOengine providing process details in Sects. 2.1 and 2.2, while in Sect. 3 some of the more interesting preliminary results are discussed with a detailed explanation of the meaning of the IR and IRP indexes. Lastly, Sect. 4 provides a general discussion about other related works and some final considerations.

2   The EBANO Engine

EBANO (Explaining BlAck-box mOdel) is a new data analytics engine to open up black-box algorithms by increasing their transparency. Its ultimate aim is to put existing, effective, and efficient algorithms to practical use cases. The EBANO engine explains the inner functioning of algorithms by providing explanations about the outcome produced through a deep convolutional neural network. EBANO analyzes the impact of each input feature on the final outcome (classification) through an iterative process based on input perturbation and classification and it has been tailored to the image processing and classification.

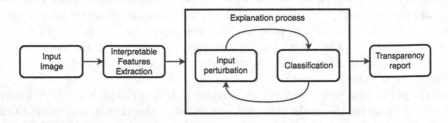

Fig. 1. Process

A convolutional network (CNN) [7] is a deep, feed-forward artificial neural network composed of many specialized hidden layers i.e. convolutional layers, pooling layers, fully connected layers and normalization layers. They have had great success in large-scale image and video recognition, achieving state-of-the-art accuracy on classification and localisation tasks, also thanks to very deep convolutional networks [10]. The main limitation of CNNs exploitation in many practical use cases is due to their opacity, i.e., their inner functioning is unclear. EBANO helps CNNs to be more transparent.

When given a pre-trained classification model, obtained through a black-box system (e.g., CNNs), EBANO identifies an interpretable explanation over a local classification. Figure 1 shows the main building blocks of the EBANO architecture. Given an image, the *Interpretable Features Extraction* step is performed through the hypercolumns extracted from the target convolutional model to identify a set of interpretable features (input) characterizing the images. An iterative perturbation of image features is then applied. At every iteration the system performs the classification on the perturbed image and produces a transparency report to provide details about how the algorithm made the prediction. To this aim, two innovative indices have been proposed. The following sections describe the interpretable feature extraction process, and then address the generation of the transparency report.

2.1   Interpretable Feature Extraction

The first step towards the human-oriented analytics process is the definition of a set of interpretable features to correctly explain the forecasting/classification of a black-box model. The identification of this set of features when dealing with unstructured data, such as images and textual data, requires ad-hoc strategies to correctly ascertain why and how a given black-box classifier produces a certain output.

Interpretable features should be neither too specific nor too general to effectively explain the classification outcome. In image processing, a single pixel of an image is both totally trifling and completely opaque in explaining how a black-box classifier produces a given output, whereas portions of image defined by a set of correlated pixels should be intuitively more effective.

To identify portions of image to be used as interpretable features EBANO performs a Simultaneous Detection and Segmentation (SDS) analysis [11] based on hypercolumns [8] and cluster analysis via the K-Means algorithm [9]. The SDS process is particularly suitable for this task because of its ability to segment the image in multiple portions, identifying the presence of multiple instances of the same object in an image. Figure 3d shows a clear example of multiple instance identification with the 5 highlighted items belonging to the same group of objects (in the specific case, 5 pizzas).

Algorithms based on CNNs use the output of the last network layer to model the analyzed features. However, this layer usually produces a very coarse, not easily interpretable output, that cannot be used to explain the classification outcome. At the opposite side, earlier layers (hidden layers) are characterized by too many details, losing their semantic expressiveness. We believe that all the information contained in different CNN layers should be exploited to correctly explain the prediction outcome. Thus, hypercolumns provides an exhaustive behavioral description of the pixels through all the layers of the CNN.

Hypercolumns have been widely exploited in the SDS pipeline [8] yielding new state-of-the-art accuracy values in object detection and image segmentation. However in this work we use them with a different purpose and a slight variant in the implementation. In EBANO hypercolumns are used to identify correlated portions of the image instead of well defined objects, so the segmentation step is simpler (based on the K-means [9]) than the one described in [8].

Given a black box CNN model composed of many layers and a labeled image belonging to a specific class, we compute the hypercolumns for each pixel of the image, as described in [8]. Specifically, given an image, we process it with a CNN and get only its representation through the most representative layers. A matrix of vectors is generated where each column in the matrix represents an input pixel through the relevant CNN layers.

Hypercolumns are then clustered exploiting the k-means algorithm to identify groups of pixels representing interpretable portions of the image with similar behavior through the most representative layers of the CNN model. The output of the cluster analysis produces k groups of correlated pixels corresponding to k interpretable features. Figure 2 shows an example of interpretable feature extraction through hypercolumns and cluster analysis. It is noticeable how this strategy is able to identify homogeneous and highly interpretable portions of an image.

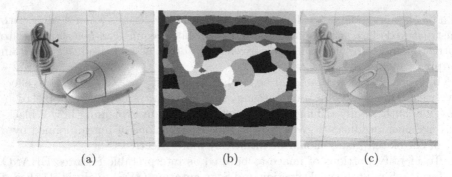

(a)   (b)   (c)

Fig. 2. Interpretable feature extraction example with $K = 10$. (a) represents the original image. (b) shows the image after the segmentation through hypercolumns clustering. (c) shows the visual report produced by EBAnO (Color figure online)

2.2 Influence Analysis

When given a set of interpretable features for a specific labeled image, EBAnO performs an iterative process of input perturbation (based on blur) and classification to analyze the impact of input over the classifier output. First, EBANOexploits the black-box model to identify, for the original image, the set of probability values for each membership class. Then, for each interpretable feature, EBAnO performs a blur perturbation of the original image in correspondence with a given feature and it uses the black-box model to predict the set of probability values for each membership class of the perturbed image.

Since our aim is to explain how the model works rather than assess how far the classification is accurate, we suppose that we know the label (membership class) of the original image. EBAnO computes two indices to explain the black-box model behaviour:

- The IR index (Influence Relation) measures the *local influence of the input feature with respect to the real class* of the image.
- The IRP index (Influence Relation Precision) measures the *inter-class influence of input features*.

The IR index is calculated for each perturbed image as the ratio between the probability of belonging to the real class of the original image and the corresponding probability of the perturbed image. It ranges in $[0, \text{inf})$. When there are no features able to give the correct label to the image, IR is equal to 0. On the other hand, there is no upper limit to the IR value. Specifically, IR assumes a very high value if the probability of belonging to the real class of the original image is very high and the probability of the perturbed version of the image has a value close to 0. Both values are rare enough to be considered exceptions that never affect this kind of analysis. In general IR values higher then 1 represent a positive influence of the feature, while values lower then 1 show a negative influence over the prediction of the real class. To measure the influence of each input feature in the whole set of classes the IRP index is proposed. IRP is computed as the ratio between the IR value for the target class and the weighted average of IR for whole set of predicted classes, where the weights correspond to the probabilities of the predicted membership class for the original image.

IRP represents the ability of an input feature to uniquely represent the class of the original image. For IRP values lower than 1 the input feature not only has an impact on the predicted class but also on all the others. Instead, if the IRP value is higher than 1, the importance of the input feature for the real class is significant with respect to the whole set of predicted classes. Obviously, perturbations with IRP values close to 1 can be considered neutral in the prediction process.

EBANO produces a report as output for each image classification/prediction. In the original image it highlights each feature's influence (Fig. 2c) and it provides details about the perturbation process along with the probability to belong to the real class and both IR and IRP values.

3   Preliminary Results

Some of the preliminary results obtained through the EBANO system are discussed here below.

Preliminary Development and Experimental Settings. EBANO is implemented in python and it exploits the features of Keras [12], a high-level neural network library, running on top of TensorFlow [13]. We exploit the K-means algorithm implemented in the scikit-learn python library [14] with the K-means++ initialization strategy. The convolutional model selected for this preliminary work is the VGG-16 [10] developed by the VGG team from Oxford for the ImageNet competition ILSVRC-2014. It is a black-box model composed of 16 layers (convolutional and fully connected layers) and it is able to predict, for each image, a membership class probability label from a predefined set of 1000 classes. To identify the set of interpretable features for each image we consider the hypercolumns for the last 10 layers of the CNN model. These layers correspond to the most representative ones. Moreover, we experimentally define the k parameter for the K-means to 10.

Preliminary results were obtained on a set of 85 images of which 75 belong to as many categories and 10 belong to the same category *pizza*.

Preliminary experiments address the evaluation of interpretable feature influence to explain block-box model. Figure 2 shows the original version of a sample image belonging to class *mouse*, the analysis of 10 interpretable features and the visual report of feature influence produced by EBANO. The black-box model alone is not able to predict the *mouse* class for the original image within the top 5 predictions as shown in Table 1. Indeed, the *mouse* label is predicted just with 5.10% of probability conversely to the wrong prediction of *hand_blower* with a probability of 26.20% (see Table 1). EBANO explores the impact of each interpretable feature to understand what the reason behind the misleading prediction is. In Table 2 the analysis of 4 interpretable features (i.e., 2 relevant/positive impact, 1 neutral and 1 irrelevant/negative impact features on the final prediction) of the mouse in Fig. 2 is reported and analyzed. The first feature (row 1 in Table 2) describes the contour of the mouse. When we perturbed this portion of the picture the probability of the image belonging to class of *mouse* decreases. Therefore, the impact of the contours of the mouse has a positive impact on the prediction of the *mouse* class and this is highlighted by the IR value equal to 5.10. The third interpretable feature (row 3 in Table 2) models top and right edges of the image and it can be considered neutral to the prediction. In fact the prediction of the *mouse* class is slightly affected by the perturbation of this feature and this is reflected by the value of IR close to 1. The last interpretable feature reported in row 4 of Table 2 clearly highlights the line between floor tiles. By perturbing this feature, an increment for the *mouse* class probability is obtained. Thus, the original model based its prediction on this feature. It is highlighted by the low IR value of 0.68, suggesting that the black-box model mainly uses this feature to make the prediction. Moreover, the IRP coefficient confirms the relevance, positive or negative, of each feature showing the same decreasing trend between IRP and IR.

EBANO summarizes the knowledge gained by IR through a visual report (Fig. 2c). Each interpretable feature is colored according to the influence that it has on the prediction of the target class. Figure 2c is characterized by three different colors with different intensity: red describes a feature with a negative impact on the prediction of the target class, yellow represents a neutral feature for the class of the image and green shows a feature with a positive impact on the prediction of the correct class: the higher the intensity of the color, the higher the positive or negative influence.

Table 1. The top 5 predicted classes for the original image in Fig. 2a. The real label of the image with the corresponding prediction is highlighted in bold.

Class	P(C)%
hand_blower	26.20
washbasin	13.93
soap_dispenser	11.90
toilet_seat	8.77
toilet_tissue	7.35
mouse	**5.10**

Through IR and IRP EBANO makes it possible to distinguish between really useful features and misleading ones. Moreover, EBANO provides useful knowledge for understanding whether a feature with a positive or negative impact on the prediction uniquely identifies the target class with respect to the other predicted classes. Figure 3 shows the report for two images belonging to the same class *pizza* (Figs. 3a and b) along with the selection of one of the most

Table 2. Features perturbation impact evaluation.

Features	Pertubations	P(c) %	IR	IRP
		0.99	5.10	2,96
		1.17	2.87	2,00
		4.67	1.09	1,09
		7.49	0.68	0,36

significant features analyzed by the model shown in Fig. 3c and d respectively. For Fig. 3a the model is not able to distinguish between the relevant features and the misleading ones with a predicted probability of belonging to class *pizza* of 3.71%. Moreover, the visual report in Fig. 3a shows a positive impact for all the extracted features. To understand the reason behind this behavior the IRP values for each feature should be analyzed. Figures 4a and c show respectively the trend of the IR and the corresponding IRP value for each of 10 interpretable features. The feature in Fig. 3c corresponds to the second most positively influencing feature (9th bar in figure 4a) with IR = 3.02. However, the misleading knowledge contained in the feature is highlighted by the IRP bar chart shown in Fig. 4c. The IRP value for this feature is largely lower than 1, with a value of 0.09, meaning that this portion of the picture has a great influence not only on the target class but also on a multitude of classes. Thus, in this case the model produces a wrong prediction because of the presence of features that positively influence many different classes. On the opposite side, the second report (Fig. 3b) clearly shows how EBANO correctly understands the feature that positively influences the class *pizza*. In this case there is a very influential feature (Fig. 3d) that has a positive effect that is noticeable in Fig. 4b. Moreover, the IRP value of 6.49 confirms the positive influence of this feature, represented by the last bar in Fig. 4d.

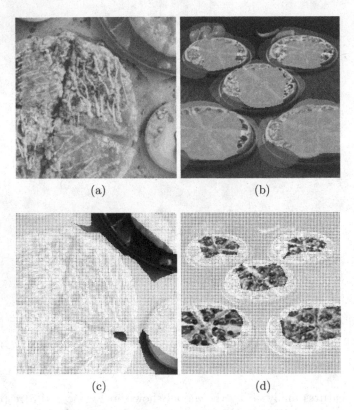

(a)   (b)

(c)   (d)

Fig. 3. IRP evaluation

4   Discussion

The importance of algorithmic transparency and accountability is becoming even more relevant in our daily life [15,16]. The quantity of data collected and analyzed with very complex algorithms in many different contexts is increasingly changing our lives. However, as algorithmic complexity increases, so the risk of misleading results increases as well: the more complex is the model, the more difficult it is to assert the reliability and fairness of the algorithmic decision-making process [17], thus also compromising the user's trust in the classification model even if outcomes are very accurate [18].

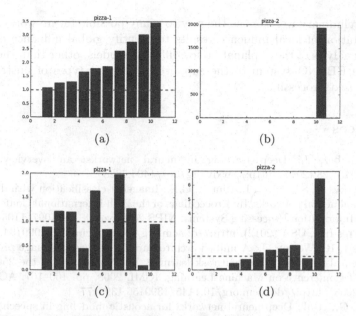

Fig. 4. Relation between IR values (top) and IRP values (bottom) for the features of two images belonging to class *pizza*.

In the last few years some research efforts have been devoted to explaining the behavior of complex black-box models in different fields [17–20] and by presenting different metrics to evaluate the impact of input features on the final outcomes. The proposed techniques have been tailored to unstructured (e.g., image and text processing) [6,18,21,22] or structured data [17]. Focusing on unstructured data, some works have put forward metrics for evaluating the impact of inputs on the classification outcomes [18], while others have exploited image segmentation [21], visualization methods [22], or self-explaining techniques [6].

In this paper we have proposed EBAnO, a new engine for black-box prediction-local explanation tailored to images. EBAnO shows the explanation through visual reports and through the evaluations of two new indices: IR and IRP. Similarly to [18] we analyzed the impact of a set of correlated pixels on the final classifier outcomes and we exploit a blur-perturbation approach as in [21]. However we used a different technique based on hypercolumns representation jointly with cluster analysis to identify interpretable portions of correlated pixels exploiting the information contained in the black-box model, increasing the expressiveness of the explanation. Moreover, we introduce different indices to study the local influence of input features with respect to the real class of an image and the inter-class feature influence for each interpretable feature of an image. In particular, unlike other works [17,18,21], we take advantage of the architecture of the classification model to detect the real behavior of the algorithm, extracting an interpretable set of features that are significant and functional to the explanation of the classification.

This preliminary work opens the way to many possible future works such as the exploitation of local influence results to identify global influence explanations, the analysis of the explanation for different models, other than the extension of the EBANO system to the support of different types of unstructured data (e.g., text processing).

References

1. Schmidhuber, J.: Deep learning in neural networks: an overview. CoRR abs/1404.7828 (2014). http://arxiv.org/abs/1404.7828
2. Krizhevsky, A., Sutskever, I., Hinton, G.E.: Imagenet classification with deep convolutional neural networks. In: Proceedings of the 25th International Conference on Neural Information Processing Systems, NIPS 2012, vol. 1, pp. 1097–1105. Curran Associates Inc., USA (2012). http://dl.acm.org/citation.cfm?id=2999134.2999257
3. Collobert, R., Weston, J.: A unified architecture for natural language processing: deep neural networks with multitask learning. In: Proceedings of the 25th International Conference on Machine Learning, ICML 2008, pp. 160–167. ACM, New York (2008). http://doi.acm.org/10.1145/1390156.1390177
4. Hinton, G., et al.: Deep neural networks for acoustic modeling in speech recognition: the shared views of four research groups. IEEE Signal Process. Mag. **29**(6), 82–97 (2012)
5. Strannegård, C., Häggström, O., Wessberg, J., Balkenius, C.: Transparent neural networks. In: Bach, J., Goertzel, B., Iklé, M. (eds.) AGI 2012. LNCS (LNAI), vol. 7716, pp. 302–311. Springer, Heidelberg (2012). https://doi.org/10.1007/978-3-642-35506-6_31
6. Zhang, Q., Wu, Y.N., Zhu, S.: Interpretable convolutional neural networks. CoRR abs/1710.00935 (2017). http://arxiv.org/abs/1710.00935
7. Lecun, Y., Bottou, L., Bengio, Y., Haffner, P.: Gradient-based learning applied to document recognition. Proc. IEEE **86**(11), 2278–2324 (1998)
8. Hariharan, B., Arbeláez, P.A., Girshick, R.B., Malik, J.: Hypercolumns for object segmentation and fine-grained localization. CoRR abs/1411.5752 (2014). http://arxiv.org/abs/1411.5752
9. Juang, B.H., Rabiner, L.R.: The segmental k-means algorithm for estimating parameters of hidden Markov models. IEEE Trans. Acoust. Speech Signal Process. **38**(9), 1639–1641 (1990)
10. Simonyan, K., Zisserman, A.: Very deep convolutional networks for large-scale image recognition. CoRR abs/1409.1556 (2014). http://arxiv.org/abs/1409.1556
11. Hariharan, B., Arbelaez, P., Girshick, R.B., Malik, J.: Simultaneous detection and segmentation. CoRR abs/1407.1808 (2014). http://arxiv.org/abs/1407.1808
12. Chollet, F., et al.: Keras (2015). https://github.com/fchollet/keras
13. Abadi, M., et al.: TensorFlow: large-scale machine learning on heterogeneous systems (2015). https://www.tensorflow.org/
14. Pedregosa, F., et al.: Scikit-learn: machine learning in Python. J. Mach. Learn. Res. **12**, 2825–2830 (2011)
15. Lepri, B., Staiano, J., Sangokoya, D., Letouzé, E., Oliver, N.: The tyranny of data? The bright and dark sides of data-driven decision-making for social good. CoRR abs/1612.00323 (2016). http://arxiv.org/abs/1612.00323

16. Diakopoulos, N.: Enabling accountability of algorithmic media: transparency as a constructive and critical lens. In: Cerquitelli, T., Quercia, D., Pasquale, F. (eds.) Transparent Data Mining for Big and Small Data. SBD, vol. 11, pp. 25–43. Springer, Cham (2017). https://doi.org/10.1007/978-3-319-54024-5_2

17. Datta, A., Sen, S., Zick, Y.: Algorithmic transparency via quantitative input influence: theory and experiments with learning systems. In: 2016 IEEE Symposium on Security and Privacy (SP), pp. 598–617, May 2016

18. Ribeiro, M.T., Singh, S., Guestrin, C.: "Why should I trust you?": explaining the predictions of any classifier. CoRR abs/1602.04938 (2016). http://arxiv.org/abs/1602.04938

19. Alufaisan, Y., Kantarcioglu, M., Zhou, Y.: Detecting discrimination in a black-box classifier (2016)

20. Adler, P., et al.: Auditing black-box models for indirect influence. Knowl. Inf. Syst. 54, 1–28 (2017)

21. Fong, R., Vedaldi, A.: Interpretable explanations of black boxes by meaningful perturbation. CoRR abs/1704.03296 (2017). http://arxiv.org/abs/1704.03296

22. Simonyan, K., Vedaldi, A., Zisserman, A.: Deep inside convolutional networks: visualising image classification models and saliency maps. CoRR abs/1312.6034 (2013). http://arxiv.org/abs/1312.6034

First International Workshop on New Frontiers on Metadata Management and Usage, M2U

How Metadata Can Support the Study of Neurological Disorders: An Application to the Alzheimer's Disease

Francesco Cauteruccio[(✉)] and Giorgio Terracina

DEMACS, University of Calabria, Rende, Italy
{cauteruccio,terracina}@mat.unical.it

Abstract. This paper deals with the analysis of neurological disorders. In particular we focus on the potentialities of metadata to support the analysis process. We focus on the analysis of the Alzheimer disease and we show how computer-based analysis of metadata associated with clinical observations may help doctors in understanding clinical stages of a patient. We also introduce a general framework than can help in understanding the hypothetical course of the disease by simulating degeneration of the patient by metadata alteration.

Keywords: Neurological disorders · Network-based analysis · Metadata · Simulation

1 Introduction

Nowadays, neurological disorders have a huge impact in the daily living. People around the globe suffer from neurological disorders, specially elder ones. Thanks to the effort of the academic community, the possibility for domain experts, such as neurologists, to use various computational tools to support analysis of neurological disorder gained a deserved attention. In particular, there is a large interest in retrieving and organizing data acquired by different medical analysis and using them in support of different analysis and e-Health services [9]. As an example, suppose there exits a computational tool for studying the course of a disease by exploiting related data to the disease itself. Such a tool could support the analysis of a domain expert by allowing different processes of planning and decisioning. Tools supporting neurologists are becoming more complex and sophisticated, as well as the data acquired by them. Due to the high variety of possibly acquired data, the "fine-grained" data analysis has become a hard task. Thus, to acquire a broader view of the analysis context, it could be useful to define and study the *metadata* of a particular neurological disorder. There is no a general metadata such that any neurological disorder can be defined by, thus the definition of metadata for a neurological disorder should strictly depend on it. In this work, we define a metadata for supporting the study of the Alzheimer's disease. In particular, we define a metadata based on data acquired

A. Benczúr et al. (Eds.): ADBIS 2018, CCIS 909, pp. 153–164, 2018.
https://doi.org/10.1007/978-3-030-00063-9_16

by electroencephalograms (EEG). The metadata is based on an innovative representation of the EEG as a network, thus the main feature of the metadata is the network itself. The analysis of this metadata, via a novel indicator for the (dis)connection degree of the network, is first used for analyzing the stage of the patient in the Alzheimer's course. Then, a general framework is introduced in which the metadata and its possible variations are used to study the potential evolution of the disease.

The structure of the paper is as follows. In Sect. 2 we give the appropriate background on the Alzheimer's disease and we explain the context, in which we present the definition of the metadata and its expressiveness. In Sect. 3 the defined metadata is used for analyzing the disorder and few experiments are discussed. Then, in Sect. 4 we introduce the general framework and illustrate the key role of metadata in simulating the evolution of the disease. Finally, in Sect. 5 we draw some conclusions.

2   Context and Metadata Definition

2.1   Alzheimer's Disease

Nowadays, Alzheimer's disease (AD) represents the most common neurodegenerative disorder characterized by cognitive and intellectual deficits [6]. In particular, it is the main cause of dementia in elder people, affecting approximately 30 million individuals worldwide and, due to the aging of the older population in developed nations, the high incidence of AD is expected to triple over the next 50 years [11]. In recent years, the efforts to design approaches which could be useful in the early diagnosis of AD are becoming more intense [5,11]. However, it is worth noting that its early diagnosis still represents a hard and complex task, although the task itself became challenging from the academic point of view.

One of the issues that makes the diagnosis on these patients very difficult is represented by the fact that, due to the nature of their disease, they are not particularly suited for examinations like Magnetic Resonance Imaging, which essentially "force" them to stay still and motionless for a long period of time. Functional imaging modalities, including Single Photon Emission Computer Tomography (SPECT) and positron emission tomography (PET) are often involved in the process of achieving early diagnosis, too. However, the evaluation of these analysis often relies on operator-dependant tasks, such as visual reading of tomographic slices and semiquantitative analysis of certain regions of interest [11]. These steps are obviously subjective to the operator and time consuming, thus prone to error.

A non invasive and well tolerated examination for patients undergoing AD is represented by EEG. In [6,7], the EEG is indicated as a tool used for diagnosing AD and it has been already used for several decades. In particular, the EEGs of patients with AD highlight some hallmarks, namely slowing, reduced complexity and perturbations in synchrony, which are thought to be associated with functional disconnections among cortical areas. The disconnections should result in the death of cortical neurons, cholinergic deficits, axonal pathology, etc. [6].

It is worth pointing out that Mild Cognitive Impairment (MCI) can be pro-dromal for AD [10]. MCI is the most frequently utilized term to define a tran-sitional phase between normal aging and dementia [4]. Indeed, it is indicated that patients witch MCI tend to convert to AD with a rate of about 10–15% annually [3]. Therefore, a variety of approaches have been proposed in the past literature, where the aim is that of characterizing both MCI and AD. Indeed, a discrete number of these approaches are based on the analysis of EEG, taking in account that in AD progression and in MCI progression towards AD, the loss of connectivity among cortical areas plays a crucial role. Thus, in this context, our approach can support the experts in evaluating whether a certain patient is probably suffering from MCI or from AD and, in particular and more interest-ing, in evaluating whether an individual with MCI is converting to AD or not. It is important to recall that a clinical diagnosis of AD is currently very difficult, especially at the early stages of the disease.

2.2   Metadata and Colored Network

The metadata definition for the context of studying both MCI and AD patients relies on a set S of EEGs, that are the results of the examination on a single patient. For each EEG, all the necessary pre-processing steps to eliminate pos-sible artifacts have been carried out. In our contest, each EEG is discretized to obtain strings from the analog data. In particular, the discretization step repre-sents an important process, due to the fact that some amount of discretization error can always be present. Thus, it is important to apply a discretization step capable to reduce this error as much as possible while representing the data with a good level of detail. Various discretization techniques have been presented in the literature [2, 8, 13]. In the proposed study, we employ the well known SAX (Symbolic Aggregate approXimation) algorithm presented in [8], which presents two important features: *(i)* a fast computation of discretized data, *(ii)* the dimen-sionality reduction of the analog signal into a string. In its process, it requires two main parameters, which are the length d of the output string, and the number σ of symbols to be considered for the alphabet whom output string is defined on. SAX transforms an input data series with n measurements points into a string.

We define the metadata associated to an EEG as a network. In particular, a network $\mathcal{N} = \langle V, E \rangle$ is the network associated to an EEG $\mathcal{E} \in S$, where each node $v_i \in V$ represents an electrode of the EEG and each arc $e_{i,j} \in E$ connecting the nodes v_i and v_j can be represented as $e_{i,j} = (v_i, v_j, w_{i,j})$.

In our approach, the weight $w_{i,j}$ measures the degree of connectivity distance between the two nodes v_i and v_j; in particular, it quantifies the disconnection level between the points of the brain sensed by electrodes v_i and v_j. Generally speaking, this weight can be computed with different measures of similarity. Since in our approach we exploit string-based representations of signals, we resort to an extended version of the Semi-Blind Edit Distance (SBED) [12], called cMPED. SBED has been designed to compare pairs of strings, possibly defined over independent alphabets. cMPED is able to compare a set of strings. In particular, cMPED is used to compare all the signals included in $\mathcal{E}$ and single out the disconnection level of each pair of electrodes. The detailed description of cMPED is out of the scope of this paper.

It is worth noting that, by definition, the network $\mathcal{N}$ is totally connected. Thus, in order to evaluate connection level of sub-networks, it is important to discriminate between strong connections from weak ones. Therefore, we define the metadata as a new, more expressive, model derived from $\mathcal{N}$ as follows. We first define a new network, namely $\mathcal{N}_\pi$ and we call it the *colored network of* $\mathcal{N}$, by performing a "projection" of $\mathcal{N}$ with the specific objective of removing the weakest arcs from it and by coloring the other ones on the basis of their weights. The kind of projection and its details depend on the neurological disorder to analyze; indeed, here we present the context of AD but different neurological disorders could be approached with the same principle, such as Epilepsy. In this paper, in the definition of the projection, we use three colors, namely blue, red and green. Blue arcs indicate strong connections, i.e., small weights, red arcs indicate intermediate ones and green arcs indicate weak connections. Formally, $\mathcal{N}_\pi$ can be represented as $\mathcal{N}_\pi = \langle V, E_\pi \rangle$. Note how the projection is defined only on the set of edges E of the original network, whereas the set of nodes remains unchanged. The set of arcs E_π is defined by using the distribution of the weights of the arcs of N. In particular, let max_E (resp., min_E) be the maximum (resp., minimum) weight of an arc in E. We define $d^k(E), 0 \leq k \leq 9$, as the number of arcs of E with weights belonging to the interval between $min_E + k \cdot \frac{max_E - min_E}{10}$ and $min_E + (k+1) \cdot \frac{max_E - min_E}{10}$.

E_π consists of all the edges of E belonging to $d^k(E)$.

The edges of E_π are colored according to the color scheme aforementioned. More in detail, $E_\pi = E_\pi^b \cup E_\pi^r \cup E_\pi^g$. Essentially, E_π^b (resp., E_π^r, E_π^g) represents the set of edges colored as blue (resp., red and green), where:

- $E_\pi^b = \{e_{ij} \in E \mid e_{ij} \in \bigcup_{t_{min} \leq k \leq t_{br}} d^k(E)\}$,
- $E_\pi^r = \{e_{ij} \in E \mid e_{ij} \in \bigcup_{t_{br} < k \leq t_{rg}} d^k(E)\}$,
- $E_\pi^g = \{e_{ij} \in E \mid e_{ij} \in \bigcup_{t_{rg} < k \leq t_{max}} d^k(E)\}$.

In particular, $t_{min}, t_{br}, t_{rg}, t_{max}$ are threshold values belonging to the integer interval $(0..9)$, suitably selected for the neurological disorder and can be determined experimentally.

2.3 Expressiveness of Colored Networks

The intuition behind the expressiveness of a colored network N_π indicates that, with such a model, it is possible to discriminate stronger connections from the weaker ones. In Fig. 1 we show the colored networks of a control subject, a patient with MCI and a patient with AD, respectively, where the thresholds for the colored network are $t_{min} = 0, t_{br} = 1, t_{rg} = 4$ and $t_{max} = 6$. The network resembles the 10–20 system used for the EEG. Note that, for a better presentation, the nodes are rotated $90°$ clockwise. Here, the control subject presents a weight distribution more biased on blue edges than the patient with the MCI, where the distribution is more biased on red edges than the patient with the AD.

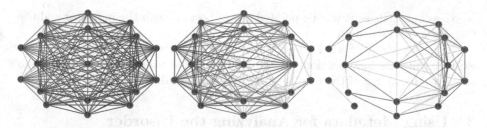

Fig. 1. Representation of colored network (from left to right) for a control subject, a patient with MCI and a patient with AD.

In other words, the colored network of the patient with AD presents lesser and weaker edges than the colored network of the patient with MCI, which preserves the same behaviour with respect to the colored network of the control subject.

The metadata defined by the colored network N_π allows to *(i)* discriminate strong connections from the weak ones, *(ii)* to represent connections in an easy-to-understand and expressive way; *(iii)* to make the adoption of different metrics, such as the connection coefficient, possible.

2.4   An Indicator for Network Analysis

As we pointed out in the Introduction, in the context of studying and analyzing diverse neurological disorders, a key role is played by the interconnections of the nodes present in the network. In particular, an important information is given by the (dis)connection degree of the network nodes, which does not represent a novel concept; it is widely known in the literature that several parameters to measure such a property are already defined and used. For example, the simplest one is the so called network density, while the most common one is represented by the clustering coefficient. Here we exploit a novel coefficient, called *connection coefficient*, which stems from the more classic concept of clique. We start by considering the set Q_d of the cliques of dimension d in $\mathcal{N}$, with $|Q_d|$ indicating the number of cliques in Q_d. Then, we define the connection coefficient $C_\mathcal{N}$ as

$$C_\mathcal{N} = \sum_{d=1}^{|V|} |Q_d| \cdot 2^d.$$

The given definition of connection coefficient is based on the fact that both the dimension, and the number of cliques, represent important connectivity indicators. Moreover, with respect to the classic clustering coefficient, which is based on triads, the aim of the connection coefficient is to capture different subnetworks of the general network. In fact, a clique of n nodes represents a subnetwork of nodes totally connected such that it cannot be further extended to $n+1$ nodes.

We use the connection coefficient as an indicator for the proposed approach, combined with the metadata represented by the colored network. It is important to stress out that, as it will be pointed out in Sect. 4, both the indicator and the metadata can be generic.

In particular, in Sect. 4 we show how the approach can be generalized to exploit synthetic modifications on the metadata and user-defined properties to simulate the course of the disease under different conditions.

3   Using Metadata for Analyzing the Disorder

In this section, we apply an approach based on the metadata introduced in the previous section, to study the Alzheimer Disease, and we present some preliminary experimental results supporting our hypothesis of their effectiveness. In particular, we combine the metadata defined in Sect. 2.2 and the connection coefficient presented in Sect. 2.4 to support the analysis of AD and for determining the stage of the a patient.

The only preliminary requisite of the proposed approach is that of having a set S of the EEGs of interest, which can be first built by performing electroencephalograms of the subjects to analyze, and to preprocess each obtained EEG to remove artifacts. Then, the approach can be summarized as follows:

1. For each EEG $\mathcal{E} \in \mathcal{S}$:
   (a) Compute cMPED for the set of electrodes in $\mathcal{E}$,
   (b) Compute a basic graph $\mathcal{N}$ where arc weights are the cMPED values,
   (c) Build the colored network(s) metadata $\mathcal{N}_\pi$,
   (d) Compute the connection coefficient $C_{\mathcal{N}_\pi}$ for each colored network,
   (e) Analyze the results.

After all the EEGs of S have been analyzed and the corresponding connection coefficient has been computed, several analysis can be performed on the results, to extract useful and supportive information. These analyses straightly depend on the neurological disorder to investigate and can be performed by an expert. Indeed, here the metadata and the indicators play a key role by allowing specific analysis. In our context using colored networks, we decided to encompass the information regarding the connectivity level of the networks as indicator. To give an idea of this analysis, we next present some experimental results.

3.1   Preliminary Experiments

In the context of supporting the analysis of AD, we considered the EEG of a patient P acquired at two different time instants t_0 and t_1, where t_1 is some months ahead of t_0. From both the EEGs, we constructed the colored networks $\mathcal{N}_{0_\pi} = \langle V, E_{0_\pi} \rangle$ and $\mathcal{N}_{1_\pi} = \langle V, E_{1_\pi} \rangle$ representing the metadata. The arc sets $E_{0_\pi} = E_{0_\pi}^b \cup E_{0_\pi}^r \cup E_{0_\pi}^g$ and $E_{1_\pi} = E_{1_\pi}^b \cup E_{1_\pi}^r \cup E_{1_\pi}^g$ have been computed by applying the definitions introduced in Sect. 2.2. Note that, in the computation of E_{1_π}, the reference interval $[min_E, max_E]$ for the arc weight distribution is the same of the edges of E_{0_π}. This is necessary for making the comparison of the course of the neurological situation from t_0 to t_1 possible.

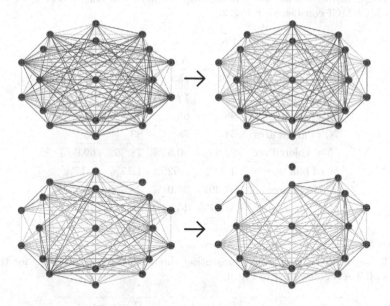

Fig. 2. The networks $\mathcal{N}_{0_\pi}$ and $\mathcal{N}_{1_\pi}$ for two patients with MCI at both t_0 and t_1

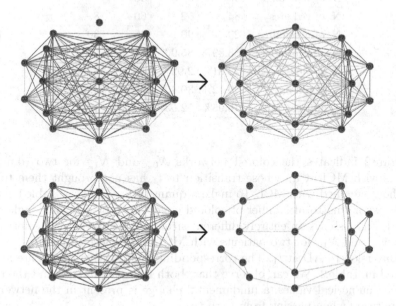

Fig. 3. The networks $\mathcal{N}_{0_\pi}$ and $\mathcal{N}_{1_\pi}$ for two patients with MCI at t_0, who converted to AD at t_1

Table 1. Quantitative measures representing the networks $\mathcal{N}_{0_\pi}$ and $\mathcal{N}_{1_\pi}$ for the two patients MCI-MCI considered in Fig. 2.

	I patient		II patient	
	$\mathcal{N}_{0_\pi}$	$\mathcal{N}_{1_\pi}$	$\mathcal{N}_{0_\pi}$	$\mathcal{N}_{0_\pi}$
N. of colored arcs	159	155	134	118
N. of blue arcs	7	12	2	2
N. of red arcs	98	65	49	31
N. of green arcs	54	78	83	85
% of colored arc	92.98%	90.64%	78.36%	69.00%
% of blue arc	4.09%	7.02%	1.17%	1.17%
% of red arc	57.30%	38.01%	28.65%	18.13%
% of green arcs	31.57%	45.61%	48.54%	49.71%

Table 2. Quantitative measures representing the networks $\mathcal{N}_{0_\pi}$ and $\mathcal{N}_{1_\pi}$ for the two patients MCI-AD considered in Fig. 3.

	I patient		II patient	
	$\mathcal{N}_{0_\pi}$	$\mathcal{N}_{1_\pi}$	$\mathcal{N}_{0_\pi}$	$\mathcal{N}_{0_\pi}$
N. of colored arcs	152	147	139	39
N. of blue arcs	39	5	33	1
N. of red arcs	84	52	60	8
N. of green arcs	29	90	46	30
% of colored arc	88.89%	85.96%	81.28%	22.80%
% of blue arc	22.81%	2.92%	19.29%	0.58%
% of red arc	49.12%	30.40%	35.08%	4.68%
% of green arcs	16.95%	52.63%	26.90%	17.54%

Figure 2 indicates the colored networks $\mathcal{N}_{0_\pi}$ and $\mathcal{N}_{1_\pi}$ for two (different) patients with MCI at t_0, whose transition to t_1 has not brought them to AD, e.g., they remained with MCI. To make a quantitative analysis, Table 1 reports the corresponding total number of colored edges, both overall and single color. Instead, Fig. 3 shows an entirely different situation, displaying the colored networks $\mathcal{N}_{0_\pi}$ and $\mathcal{N}_{1_\pi}$ for two patients with MCI at t_0 whose transitions resulted in a conversion to AD at t_1. The corresponding quantitative results are instead reported in Table 2. We can observe that, both from the images and the corresponding numerical values, a fundamental change is present in the networks of these patients when passing from t_0 to t_1.

Having this data, let us compute and review the connection coefficient by considering its variation when passing from t_0 to t_1. More in detail, we compute the variation as $\frac{C_{\mathcal{N}_{1\pi}}-C_{\mathcal{N}_{0\pi}}}{C_{\mathcal{N}_{0\pi}}}$. It is interesting to analyze the variation: for the two patients in Fig. 2, this variation is equal to -25.00% for the first patient and -4.96% for the second one, while for the two patients in Fig. 3, this variation is respectively equal to -89.06% and -99.41%. These results indicate that the proposed approach, combining metadata and connection coefficient, can really help experts to evaluate a possible conversion of a subject from MCI to AD. In comparison, let us consider both the variation of network density and clustering coefficient, respectively computed as $\frac{D_{\mathcal{N}_{1\pi}}-D_{\mathcal{N}_{0\pi}}}{D_{\mathcal{N}_{0\pi}}}$ and $\frac{CL_{\mathcal{N}_{1\pi}}-CL_{\mathcal{N}_{0\pi}}}{CL_{\mathcal{N}_{0\pi}}}$. We recall that $D_{\mathcal{N}}$ is the density of the (undirected) network $\mathcal{N}$, classically defined as $D_{\mathcal{N}} = \frac{|E|}{\frac{|V|(|V|-1)}{2}}$ and $CL_{\mathcal{N}}$ is the clustering coefficient, defined as $CL_{\mathcal{N}} = \frac{\text{number of closed triangle}}{\text{total number of triangle}}$, s where a triangle is a subnetwork consisting of three nodes, where in turn these nodes could be totally disconnected, partially connected or totally connected (also defines as a closed triangle).

Thus, the numerical value obtained for the variation of the network density are equal to -2.51% and -11.19% for the patients in MCI-MCI and to -3.29% and -71.94% for the two MCI-AD patients, while the results obtained for the clustering coefficient are equal to -1.61% and -3.19% for the two MCI-MIC patients and to -5.48% and -39.89% for the patients in MCI-AD. Finally, these results indicate that, in this context, the connection coefficient together with the metadata represented by the colored network is better than the classical network density and the clustering coefficient in discriminating the transition between MCI and AD.

4   Generalizing the Framework for Studying the Disease Course Based on Selective Metadata Alteration

In Sects. 2 and 3 we introduced a method for exploiting metadata to support the study of neurological disorders, and in particular to determine the profile of a patient possibly affected by AD.

Beyond the identification of the current clinical profile of a patient, predicting a patient's evolution and response to a therapy based on clinical, biological and imaging markers still represents a challenge for neurologists. In particular, it would be highly interesting to simulate the course of the disease by simulating brain connections degradation, in order to understand which kind of modifications might mostly determine an evolution of the disease into a worst state, or which recovery processes might induce a remission state, whenever possible.

Unfortunately, this process represents a not trivial challenge due to various reasons, including the fact that the mechanisms guiding the evolution of the pathology are still unknown. One possible solution would be to simulate the progress of the pathology by means of a set of custom-defined rules for modeling the disruption of the brain structure, which may involve a certain background knowledge. However, this is still not enough as, since the mechanism is unknown, it is not possible to validate a hypothetical evaluation model. Hence, an approach able to explore and discover this underlying mechanism is needed.

From this point of view, two important ingredients would be extremely useful: *(i)* some automatic mechanism to *classify* the profile of a patient, *(ii)* some automatic and easily customizable way of simulating brain damages.

In this context, quite an effective "weapon" could consist of the use of an integrated environment which would allow the application of a set of rules, possibly based on constraints, that identify minimal alterations of brain connections possibly inducing a change of state in the disease; the possible change of state can be in turn detected exploring latent relations expressed by the metadata. These last can be either detected exploring fixed properties, like the connection coefficient introduced in Sect. 2, or by more general tools based on neural networks.

In the following paragraphs we define a modular framework which can be easily extended and enhanced, paving the way to a fully integrated environment that combines various artificial intelligence tools to support doctors in the study of clinical courses.

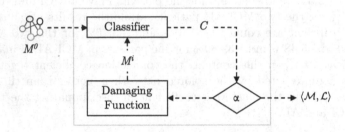

Fig. 4. Architecture of the proposed framework.

The general workflow is presented in Fig. 4. Intuitively, it takes a metadata representing the brain as input, classifies the current stage of the disease, and then simulates the disease course by "damaging the brain". The newly obtained brain representation is then classified, and used for the next steps. These steps are iterated until some condition holds. The representation of the brain of a patient can be, for example, obtained as described in Sect. 2.2. Recall that this is expressed as a weighted network $\mathcal{N}^0 = (V, E_0)$ representing the brain connections of the patient as detected by the ECG. In principle, other kind of representations could be exploited, such as brain connectoma built from MRI, which can be useful in the analysis of other diseases.

The brain metadata are then processed by a *classifier* which outputs an evaluation of the current status of the patient. This evaluation can be carried out with the approach described in Sect. 3 or with some neural network-based approach, which can also analyze different pathologies. Some more metadata of this analysis is the output of the classifier, which is passed on to the next steps. The metadata is then processed by the *Damaging Function* module, which takes as input a network $\mathcal{N}^i$ and first determines a set of edges $E' \in E$ that should be altered. Here, different ways of altering $\mathcal{N}^i$ can be adopted. Logic programs

```
e(X,Y,W) :- edge(X,Y,W), clique(X), clique(Y).
{ clique(X) } :- node(X).
activeEdge(X,Y) :- edge(X,Y,W), W!=0.
:- clique(X), clique(Y), X < Y, not activeEdge(X,Y).
:~ node(X), not clique(X). [1@1,X]
```

Fig. 5. An ASP encoding for the *Clique* problem.

and rules supported by datalog-based systems [1] can be used to easily define particular kind of structures of the brain connections that one wishes to study; rules allow to easily specify and identify even complex structures in a network. Just to show how easy is the identification of complex properties using logic programs, Fig. 5 reports the code for idendifying the maximal clique in a network. Output consists of the set of edges $e(X, Y, W)$ to modify. Obviously, other kinds of properties can be easily checked simply by changing the logic program. An altering function $f : (\mathcal{N}^i, E') \rightarrow \mathcal{N}^{i+1}$ is then applied to the selected edges. Any modification useful for the analysis can be applied. As an example, an altering function can be intended to simulate the disrupting process of the disease on the portion of brain identified by the chosen property; hence, it may act as a degradation function on the weights of selected edges, thus simulating a degradation in the connection. In particular, given the initial graph $\mathcal{N}^0$ a *degradation coefficient* is computed for each edge (x, y, w_{xy}) in $\mathcal{N}^0$ as $d_{xy} = w_{xy} \times p$, where p is a percentage of degradation set as a parameter. Once the module singles out the set of edges E' in $\mathcal{N}^i$ to modify, each edge (x, y, w_{xy}) in E' is changed to $(x, y, max\{w_{xy} - d_{xy}, 0\})$. Here, a weight set to 0 may mean a deletion of the edge from the resulting graph, and consequently a complete distruption of the corresponding connection; in this case, the subsequent iteration and the corresponding logic program will no longer consider this edge as belonging to the network.

The newly obtained network $\mathcal{N}^{i+1}$ is then given as input to the *Classifier*, and possibly used as input of the next iteration. The process is reiterated until a certain condition α is satisfied. Eventually, when the process stops, the result of the framework is represented by a pair $\langle \mathcal{M}, \mathcal{L} \rangle$ where $\mathcal{M}$ is the set of the altered metadata and $\mathcal{L}$ is the set of corresponding results computed by the Classifier for each $M \in \mathcal{M}$.

5   Conclusion

In this paper we proposed the usage of metadata as an aid to support the study of neurological disorders, focusing on the Alzheimer's disease. In particular, the metadata is built from an EEG and i represented by a colored network. We have shown how it is capable to highlight strong and weak connections between different areas and how these properties are related to the evolution of the disease. Finally, we introduced a general framework that can be adopted to study the course of the disease. The framework is general enough to accommodate different kind of analysis for different neurological disorders. We plan for our future work to implement such a framework for different kind of neurological disorders.

Acknowledgement. This work was partially supported by the Italian Ministry for Economic Development (MISE) under the project "Smarter Solutions in the Big Data World", funded within the call "HORIZON2020" PON I&C 2014–2020.

References

1. Alviano, M., Faber, W., Leone, N., Perri, S., Pfeifer, G., Terracina, G.: The disjunctive datalog system DLV. In: de Moor, O., Gottlob, G., Furche, T., Sellers, A. (eds.) Datalog 2.0 2010. LNCS, vol. 6702, pp. 282–301. Springer, Heidelberg (2011). https://doi.org/10.1007/978-3-642-24206-9_17
2. Chan, K., Fu, A.W.: Efficient time series matching by wavelets. In: Proceedings of the 15th IEEE International Conference on Data Engineering (ICDE 1999), Sydney, Australia, pp. 126–133. IEEE Computer Society Press (1999)
3. Davatzikos, C., Bhatt, P., Shaw, L.M., Batmanghelich, K.N., Trojanowski, J.O.: Prediction of MCI to AD conversion, via MRI, CSF biomarkers, and pattern classification. Neurobiol. Aging **32**(12), 2322-e19–2322-e27 (2011d)
4. Fernndez, A., Hornero, R., Mayo, A., Poza, J., Gil-Gregorio, P., Ortiz, T.: Meg spectral profile in Alzheimer's disease and mild cognitive impairment. Clin. Neurophysiol. **117**(2), 306–314 (2006)
5. Hebert, L., Weuve, J., Scherr, P., Evans, D.: Alzheimer disease in the United States (2010–2050) estimated using the 2010 census. Neurology **80**(19), 1778–1783 (2013)
6. Hornero, R., Abásolo, D., Escudero, J., Gómez, C.: Nonlinear analysis of electroencephalogram and magnetoencephalogram recordings in patients with Alzheimer's disease. Philos. Trans. R. Soc. Lond. A Math. Phys. Eng. Sci. **367**(1887), 317–336 (2009)
7. Jeong, J.: EEG dynamics in patients with Alzheimer's disease. Clin. Neurophysiol. **115**(7), 1490–1505 (2004)
8. Keogh, E.J., Chakrabarti, K., Pazzani, M.J., Mehrotra, S.: Dimensionality reduction for fast similarity search in large time series databases. J. Knowl. Inf. Syst. **3**(3), 263–286 (2001)
9. De Meo, P., Quattrone, G., Ursino, D.: Integration of the HL7 standard in a multiagent system to support personalized access to e-health services. IEEE Trans. Knowl. Data Eng. **23**(8), 1244–1260 (2011)
10. Petersen, R.: Mild cognitive impairment as a diagnostic entity. J. Intern. Med. **256**(3), 183–194 (2004)
11. Ramirez, J.: Computer-aided diagnosis of Alzheimer's type dementia combining support vector machines and discriminant set of features. Inf. Sci. **237**, 59–72 (2013)
12. Stamile, C., Cauteruccio, F., Terracina, G., Ursino, D., Kocevar, G., Sappey-Marinier, D.: A model-guided string-based approach to white matter fiber-bundles extraction. In: Guo, Y., Friston, K., Aldo, F., Hill, S., Peng, H. (eds.) BIH 2015. LNCS (LNAI), vol. 9250, pp. 135–144. Springer, Cham (2015). https://doi.org/10.1007/978-3-319-23344-4_14
13. Yi, B.K., Faloutos, C.: Fast time sequence indexing for arbitrary Lp norms. In: Proceedings of the 26th International Conference on Very Large Databases, Cairo, Egypt, pp. 385–394 (2000)

A New Metadata Model to Uniformly Handle Heterogeneous Data Lake Sources

Claudia Diamantini[1], Paolo Lo Giudice[2], Lorenzo Musarella[2],
Domenico Potena[1], Emanuele Storti[1], and Domenico Ursino[1(✉)]

[1] DII, Polytechnic University of Marche, Ancona, Italy
d.ursino@univpm.it
[2] DIIES, University "Mediterranea" of Reggio Calabria, Reggio Calabria, Italy

Abstract. Metadata have always played a key role in favoring the cooperation of heterogeneous data sources. This role has become much more crucial with the advent of data lakes, in which case metadata represent the only possibility to guarantee an effective and efficient management of data source interoperability. For this reason, the necessity to define new models and paradigms for metadata representation and management appears crucial in the data lake scenario. In this paper, we aim at addressing this issue by proposing a new metadata model well suited for data lakes. Furthermore, to give an idea of its capabilities, we present an approach that leverages it to "structure" unstructured sources and to extract thematic views from heterogeneous data lake sources.

1 Introduction

Metadata have always played a key role in favoring the cooperation of heterogeneous data sources [3,6,19,20]. This role was already relevant in the past architectures (e.g., Cooperative Information Systems and Data Warehouses) but has become much more crucial with the advent of data lakes [8]. Indeed, in this new architecture, metadata represent the only possibility to guarantee an effective and efficient management of data source interoperability. As a proof of this, the main data lake companies are performing several efforts in this direction (see, for instance, the metadata organization proposed by Zaloni, one of the market leaders in the data lake field [18]). For this reason, the definition of new models and paradigms for metadata representation and management represents an open problem in the data lake research field.

In this paper, we aim at providing a contribution in this setting and we propose a new metadata model well suited for data lakes. Our model starts from the considerations and the ideas proposed by data lake companies (in particular, it starts from the general metadata classification also used by Zaloni [18]). However, it complements them with new ideas and, in particular, with the power guaranteed by a network-based and semantics-driven representation of metadata. Thanks to this choice, our model can benefit from all the results already found

A. Benczúr et al. (Eds.): ADBIS 2018, CCIS 909, pp. 165–177, 2018.
https://doi.org/10.1007/978-3-030-00063-9_17

in network theory and semantics-driven approaches. As a consequence, it can allow a large variety of sophisticated tasks that the metadata models currently adopted do not guarantee. For instance, it allows the definition of a structure for unstructured data, which currently represent more than 80% of available data sources. Furthermore, it allows the extraction of thematic views from data sources [2], i.e., the construction of views concerning one or more topics of interest for the user, obtained by extracting and merging data coming from different sources. This problem has been largely investigated in the past for structured and semi-structured data sources stored in a data warehouse, and this witnesses its extreme relevance. These are only two of the tasks that can benefit from our model and, in this paper, we illustrate them. Actually, many other ones could be thought and investigated, and they will represent the subject of our future research efforts.

This paper is structured as follows: Sect. 2 illustrates related literature. In Sect. 3, we propose our metadata model. Section 4 presents the application of this model to the problems of structuring unstructured data and of extracting thematic views from heterogeneous data lake sources. In Sect. 5, we present our example case, whereas, in Sect. 6, we draw our conclusions and discuss future work.

2   Related Literature

In the literature, several metadata classifications have been proposed in the past. For instance, the authors of [4] propose a tree-based classification. They split metadata into several categories, propose a conceptual schema of the metadata repository and use RDF for metadata modeling. The strength of this model is undoubtedly its richness, whereas its weakness is its complexity that cannot guarantee a fast processing of the corresponding data.

A metadata model well suited for data lakes in proposed in [18]. This is also the model adopted by Zaloni. It divides metadata based on their generation time or on the meaning and information they bring. In this latter case, metadata can be divided in three categories, namely operational, technical and business metadata. As will be clear in the following, our metadata model starts from this, but it goes much further. In particular, it assumes that the three classes are not independent from each other because there are several intersections of them. Some of these intersections are particularly expressive and important; for them, it provides a network-based representation rich enough to allow several interesting tasks, but, at the same time, not excessively complex in such a way as to prevent a slow processing.

Several metadata models and frameworks are widely adopted by the Linked Data community (e.g., DCMI Metadata Terms and VoID). DCMI Metadata Terms [13] is a set of metadata vocabularies and technical specifications maintained by the Dublin Core Metadata Initiative. It includes generic metadata, represented as RDF properties, on dataset creation, access, data provenance, structure and format. A subset was also published as ANSI/NISO and ISO standards and as IETC RFC. The Vocabulary of Interlinked Datasets (VoID) [14] is an RDF Schema vocabulary that provides terms and patterns for describing RDF datasets. It is intended as a bridge between the publishers and the users of RDF data. It focuses on: *(i)* *general metadata*, following the Dublin Core model; *(ii)* *access metadata*, describing how RDF data can be accessed by means of several protocols; *(iii)* *structural metadata*, describing the structure and the schema of datasets, mostly used for supporting querying and data integration.

As for the applications of our metadata model proposed in this paper (i.e., structuring of unstructured data and thematic view extraction), most approaches proposed in the literature to carry out this task do not completely fit the data lake paradigm. Two surveys on this issue can be found in [1,11].

Another family of approaches leverages materialized views to perform tree pattern querying [22] and graph pattern queries [7]. Unfortunately, all these approaches are well-suited for structured and semi-structured data, whereas they are not scalable and lightweight enough to be used in a dynamic context or with unstructured data. Interesting advances in this area can be found in [2,5,21].

Finally, semantic-based approaches have long been used to drive data integration in databases and data warehouses. More recently, in the context of big data, formal semantics has been specifically exploited to address issues concerning data variety/heterogeneity, data inconsistency and data quality in such a way as to increase understandability [12]. In the data lake scenario, semantic techniques have been successfully applied to more efficiently integrate and handle both structured and unstructured data sources by aligning data silos and better managing evolving data model (see, for instance, [9,10]). Similarly to what happens in our approach, knowledge graphs in RDF are used to drive integration. To reach their objectives, these techniques usually rely on tools assisting users in linking metadata to uniform vocabularies (e.g., ontologies or knowledge repositories, such as DBpedia).

3   A Unifying Model for Representing the Metadata of Data Lake Sources

In this section, we illustrate our network-based model to represent and handle the metadata of a data lake, which we will use in the rest of this paper.

Our model represents a data lake DL as a set of m data sources: $DL = \{D_1, D_2, \cdots, D_m\}$. A data source $D_k \in DL$ is provided with a rich set $\mathcal{M}_k$ of metadata. We denote with $\mathcal{M}_{DL}$ the repository of the metadata of all the data sources of DL: $\mathcal{M}_{DL} = \{\mathcal{M}_1, \mathcal{M}_2, \ldots, \mathcal{M}_m\}$.

3.1   Typologies of Metadata

Following what it is said in [18], metadata can be divided into three categories, namely: *(i)* *Business metadata*, which include business rules (e.g., the upper and lower limit of a particular field, integrity constraints, etc.); *(ii)* *Operational metadata*, which include information generated automatically during data processing (e.g., data quality, data provenance, executed jobs); *(iii)* *Technical metadata*, which include information about data format and schema. Based on this reasoning, $\mathcal{M}_k$ can be represented as the union of three sets $\mathcal{M}_k^B \cup \mathcal{M}_k^O \cup \mathcal{M}_k^T$.

As an advancement of the model of [18], we observe that these three subsets are intersected with each other (as shown in Fig. 1). For instance, since business metadata contain all business rules and information allowing to better understand data fields, and since the data schema is included in the technical metadata, we can conclude that data fields represent the perfect intersection between these two subsets. Analogously, technical metadata contain the data type and length, the possibility that a field can be NULL or auto-incrementing, the number of records, the data format and some dump information. These last three things are in common with operational metadata, which contain information like sources and target location and the file size as well. Finally, the intersection between operational and business metadata represents information about the dataset license, the hosting server and so forth (e.g. see the DCMI Metadata Terms).

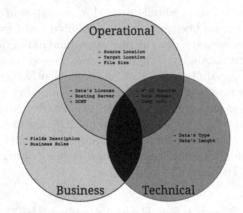

Fig. 1. The three kinds of metadata proposed by our model.

In this paper, we focus on business metadata and on the intersection between them and the technical ones. This intersection contains the data fields, both domain description and technical details. For instance, in a structured database, this intersection contains the attributes of the tables. Instead, in a semi-structured one, it consists of the names of the (complex or simple) elements and attributes of the schema. Finally, in an unstructured source, it could consist of a set of keywords generally adopted to give an idea of the source content.

3.2   A Network-Based Model for Business and Technical Metadata

As already mentioned, in this paper we focus especially on the business and technical metadata and on their intersection. Indeed, they denote, at the intensional level, the information content stored in the data lake sources and are those of interest for supporting most tasks, including the ones described in this paper.

We indicate by $\mathcal{M}_k^{BT}$ the intersection between $\mathcal{M}_k^B$ and $\mathcal{M}_k^T$. We denote by Obj_k the set of all the objects stored in $\mathcal{M}_k^{BT}$. The concept of "object" depends on data source typology. For instance, in a relational database, objects denote its tables and their attributes. In an XML document or in a JSON one, objects include complex/simple elements and their attributes.

In order to represent $\mathcal{M}_k^{BT}$, our model relies on a suitable directed graph $G_k^{BT} = \langle N_k, A_k \rangle$. For each object $o_{k_j} \in Obj_k$ there exists a node $n_{k_j} \in N_k$. As there is a one-to-one correspondence between a node of N_k and an object of Obj_k, in the following, we will use the two terms interchangeably.

On the other hand, each $a_{k_i} = \langle (n_s, n_t), l_{k_i} \rangle \in A_k$ is an arc; here, n_s is the source node, n_t is the target one, whereas l_{k_i} is a label representing the kind of relationhip between n_s and n_t. Some possible relationships are: *(i) Structural relationship*: it is represented by the label "contains" and is used to represent the relationhip between a relational table and its attributes, a complex object and its simple ones, or between a simple object and its attributes. *(ii) Similarity relationship*: it is represented by the label "similarTo" and denotes a form of similarity between two objects. We will see an example of its semantics and usage in Sect. 4.1. *(iii) Lemma relationship*: it is represented by the label "lemma" and denotes that the target node is a lemma of the source one. Again, its usage will be clear in Sect. 4.1.

Our model enables a scalable and flexible approach in the representation and management of metadata of heterogeneous data lake sources. Indeed, adding a new data source only requires the extraction of its metadata and their conversion to our model. Furthermore, the integration of metadata regarding different data sources can be simply performed by adding suitable arcs between the nodes for which there exists some relationship.

Similarly, G_k^{BT} can be extended with external knowledge graphs (e.g., DBpedia[1]). In the following, we refer to an extension of G_k^{BT} as G_k^{Ext}. It consists of $G_k^{Ext} = G_k^{BT} \cup G^E$, where G^E is an external knowledge graph. An arc from a node of G_k^{BT} and its corresponding node in G^E will be labeled as "externalSource_X", where X is the name of the external knowledge graph at hand.

4 Examples of Applications of Our Metadata Model

As pointed out in the Introduction, in order to give an idea of the expressiveness and the power of our data model, in this section, we will exploit it in two application tasks, namely "structuring" unstructured data sources and extracting thematic views from heterogeneous data lake sources.

4.1 Defining a Structure for Unstructured Sources

Based on a generic graph representation, our model is perfectly fitted for representing and managing both structured and semi-structured data sources. The

---

[1] http://wiki.dbpedia.org.

highest difficulty regards unstructured data because it is worth avoiding a flat representation, consisting of a simple element for each keyword provided to denote the source content. As a matter of fact, this kind of representation would make the reconciliation, and the next integration, of an unstructured source with the other (semi-structured and structured) ones of the data lake very difficult. Therefore, it is necessary to (at least partially) "structure" unstructured data. Our approach to addressing this issue consists of four phases.

During the first phase, it creates a node representing the source as a whole and a node for each keyword. Then, it links the former to the latter through arcs with label "contains". During the second phase, it adds an arc with label "lemma" from the node n_{k_1}, corresponding to the keyword k_1, to the node n_{k_2}, corresponding to the keyword k_2, if k_2 is registered as a lemma[2] of k_1 in a suitable thesaurus (we adopted BabelNet [17] for this purpose). During the third phase, our approach derives lexical similarities. In particular, it states that there exists a similarity between the nodes n_{k_1}, corresponding to the keyword k_1, and n_{k_2}, corresponding to the keyword k_2, if k_1 and k_2 have at least one common lemma in a suitable thesaurus. Also in this case, we have adopted BabelNet. After having found lexical similarities, it derives string similarities and states that there exists a similarity between n_{k_1} and n_{k_2} if the string similarity degree $kd(k_1, k_2)$, computed by applying a suitable string metric on k_1 and k_2, is higher than a suitable threshold th_k. After several experiments, we have chosen N-Grams [15] as string similarity metric. In both these cases, if there exist a similarity between n_{k_1} and n_{k_2}, our approach adds an arc with label "similarTo" from n_{k_1} to n_{k_2}, and vice versa. During the fourth phase, if there exists a pair of arcs with label "similarTo" between two nodes n_{k_i} and n_{k_j}, our approach merges them into one node $n_{k_{ij}}$, which inherits all the incoming and outgoing edges of n_{k_i} and n_{k_j}. Finally, if there exist two or more arcs from a node n_{k_i} to a node n_{k_j} with the same label, our approach merges them into one node[3].

4.2   An Approach to Extracting Thematic Views

Our approach to extracting thematic views operates on a data lake DL whose data sources are represented by means of the model described in Sect. 3. It consists of two steps, the former mainly based on the structure of the sources at hand, the latter mainly focusing on the corresponding semantics.

Step 1 of our approach receives a data lake DL, a set of topics $T = \{T_1, T_2, \cdots, T_l\}$, representing the themes of interest for the user, and a dictionary Syn of synonymies involving the objects stored in the sources of DL. This dictionary could be a generic thesaurus, such as BabelNet [17], a domain-specific thesaurus, or a dictionary obtained by taking into account the structure

---

[2] In this paper, we use the term "lemma" according to the meaning it has in Babel-Net [17]. Here, given a term, its lemmas are other objects (terms, emoticons, etc.) contributing to specify its meaning.

[3] Please note that Phases 3 and 4 could be merged in a unique one, avoiding to define arcs with label "similarTo". Here, we maintain these arcs and both phases to keep the information about similarity between nodes for future use.

and the semantics of the sources, which the corresponding objects refer to (such as the dictionaries produced by XIKE [6], MOMIS [3] or Cupid [16]). Let T_i be a topic of T. Let $Obj_i = \{o_{i_1}, o_{i_2}, \cdots, o_{i_q}\}$ be the set of the objects synonymous of T_i in DL. Let $N_i = \{n_{i_1}, n_{i_2}, \cdots, n_{i_q}\}$ be the corresponding nodes. First, our approach constructs the ego networks $E_{i_1}, E_{i_2}, \cdots, E_{i_q}$ having $n_{i_1}, n_{i_2}, \cdots, n_{i_q}$ as the corresponding egos. Then, it merges all the egos into a unique node n_i. In this way, it obtains a unique ego network E_i from $E_{i_1}, E_{i_2}, \cdots, E_{i_q}$. If a synonymy exists between two alters belonging to different ego networks, then these are merged into a unique node and the corresponding arcs linking them to the ego n_i are merged into a unique arc. At the end of this task, we have a unique ego network E_i corresponding to T_i. After having performed the previous task for each topic of T, we have a set $E = \{E_1, E_2, \cdots, E_l\}$ of l ego networks. At this point, Step 1 finds all the synonymies of Syn involving objects of the ego networks of E and merges the corresponding nodes. After all the possible synonymies involving objects of the ego network of E have been considered and the corresponding nodes have been merged, a set $V = \{V_1, \cdots, V_g\}, 1 \leq g \leq l$, of networks representing potential views is obtained. If $g = 1$, then there exists a unique thematic view comprising all the topics required by the user. Otherwise, there exist more views each comprising some (but not all) of the topics of interest for the user.

Step 2 starts by constructing the graph G_k^{Ext} obtained by extending G_k^{BT} with an external knowledge graph G^E (in this work, we rely on DBpedia). For this purpose, first it links each node n_{i_j} of V_i to the corresponding entry $n_{e_{ij}} \in G^E$ through an arc with label "externalSource_DBpedia". In our scenario, such a DBpedia node $n_{e_{ij}}$ is already specified in the BabelNet entry corresponding to n_{i_j} (or to any of its synonyms in Syn)[4]. Then, for each $n_{e_{ij}}$ considered above, all the related concepts are retrieved. In DBpedia, knowledge is structured according to the Linked Data principles, i.e. as an RDF graph built by triples. Each triple $\langle s(ubject), p(roperty), o(bject)\rangle$ states that a subject s has a property p, whose value is an object o. Therefore, retrieving the related concepts for a given element x implies finding all the triples where x is either the subject or the object. For each view $V_i \in V$, the procedure to extend it consists of the following three substeps: (1) Mapping: for each node $n_{i_j} \in V_i$, its corresponding DBpedia entry $n_{e_{ij}}$ is found. (2) Triple extraction: all the related triples $\langle n_{e_{ij}}, p, o\rangle$ and $\langle s, p, n_{e_{ij}}\rangle$, i.e., all the triples in which $n_{e_{ij}}$ is either the subject or the object, are retrieved. (3) View extension: for each retrieved triple $\langle n_{e_{ij}}, p, o\rangle$ (resp., $\langle s, p, n_{e_{ij}}\rangle$), V_i is extended by defining a node for the object o (resp., s), if not already existing, linked to n_{i_j} through an edge labeled as p. Substeps 2 and 3 are recursively repeated for each new added node. The procedure stops after a given number of iterations, limiting the length of external incoming and outcoming paths of nodes in V_i. The longer the path, the weaker the semantic link between nodes.

---

[4] Whenever this does not happen, the mapping can be automatically provided by the DBpedia Lookup Service (http://wiki.dbpedia.org/projects/dbpedia-lookup).

The enrichment procedure is performed for all the views of V. It is particularly important if $|V| > 1$ because the new derived relationships could help to merge the thematic views that was not possible to merge during the Step 1. In particular, let $V_i \in V$ and $V_l \in V$ be two views of V, and let V_i' and V_l' be the extended views corresponding to them. If there exist two nodes $n_{i_h} \in V_i'$ ad $n_{l_k} \in V_l'$ such that $n_{i_h} = n_{l_k}$[5], then they can be merged in one node; in this way, V_i' and V_l' become connected. After all equal nodes of the views of V have been merged, all the views of V could be either merged in one view or not. In the former case, the process terminates with success. Otherwise, it is possible to conclude that no thematic views comprising all the topics specified by the user can be found. In this last case, our approach still returns the enriched views of V and leaves the user the choice to accept of reject them.

5   An Example Case

In this section, we present an example case aiming at illustrating the various tasks of our approach. Here, we consider: *(i)* a structured source, called *Weather Conditions* (W, in short), whose corresponding E/R schema is not reported for space limitations; *(ii)* two semi-structured sources, called *Climate* (C, in short) and *Environment* (E, in short), whose corresponding XML Schemas are not reported for space limitations; *(iii)* an unstructured source, called *Environment Video* (V, in short), consisting of a YouTube video and whose corresponding keywords are: *garden, flower, rain, save, earth, tips, recycle, aurora, planet, garbage, pollution, region, life, plastic, metropolis, environment, nature, wave, eco, weather, simple, fineparticle, climate, ocean, environmentawareness, educational, reduce, power, bike.*

By applying the approach mentioned in Sect. 4.2, we obtain the corresponding representations in our network-based model, shown in Fig. 2[6].

Assume, now, that a user specifies the following set T of topics of her interest: $T = \{Ocean, Area\}$. First, our approach determines the terms (and, then, the objects) in the five sources that are synonyms of *Ocean* and *Area*. As for *Ocean*, the only synonym present in the sources is *Sea*; as a consequence, Obj_1 comprises the node *Ocean* of the source V ($V.Ocean$[7]) and the node *Sea* of the source C ($C.Sea$). An analogous activity is performed for *Area*. At the end of this task we have that $Obj_1 = \{V.Ocean, C.Sea\}$ and $Obj_2 = \{W.Place, C.Place, V.Region, E.Location\}$.

Step 1 of our approach proceeds by constructing the ego networks corresponding to the objects of Obj_1 and Obj_2. They are reported in Fig. 3[8].

---

[5] Here, two nodes are equal if the corresponding name coincide.

[6] In this figure, we do not show the arc labels for the sources C, W and E because all of them are "contains" and their presence would have complicated the layout unnecessarily.

[7] Hereafter, we use the notation $S.o$ to indicate the object o of the source S.

[8] In this figure, for layout reasons, we do not show the arc labels because they are the same as the corresponding arcs of Fig. 2.

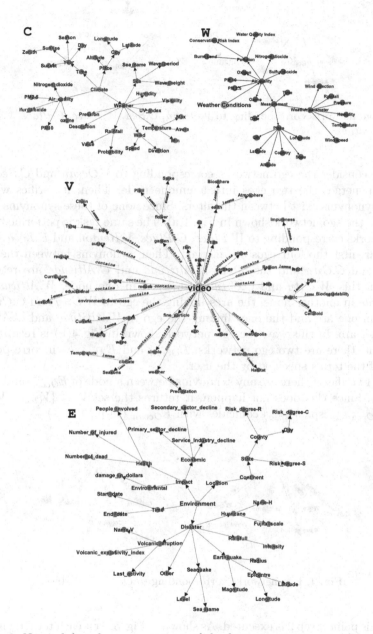

Fig. 2. Network-based representations of the four sources into consideration.

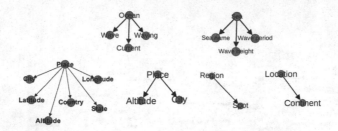

Fig. 3. Ego networks corresponding to *V.Ocean*, *C.Sea*, *W.Place*, *C.Place*, *V.Region* and *E.Location*.

Now, consider the ego networks corresponding to *V.Ocean* and *C.Sea*. Our approach merges the two egos into a unique node. Then, it verifies whether further synonyms exist between the alters. Since none of these synonyms exists, it returns the ego network shown in Fig. 4(a). The same task is performed to the ego networks corresponding to *W.Place*, *C.Place*, *V.Region* and *E.Location*. In particular, first the four egos are merged. Then, synonyms between the alters *W.City* and *C.City* and the alters *W.Altitude* and *C.Altitude* are retrieved. Based on this, *W.City* and *C.City* are merged in one node, *W.Altitude* and *C.Altitude* in another node, the arcs linking the ego to *W.City* and *C.City* are merged in one arc and the ones linking the ego to *W.Altitude* and *C.Altitude* in another arc. In this way, the ego network shown in Fig. 4(b) is returned. At this point, there are two ego networks, E_{Ocean} and E_{Area}, each corresponding to one of the terms specified by the user.

Step 1 verifies if there are any synonyms between a node of E_{Ocean} and a node of E_{Area}. Since this does not happen, it returns the set $V = \{V_{Ocean}, V_{Area}\}$, where V_{Ocean} (resp., V_{Area}) coincides with E_{Ocean} (resp., E_{Area}).

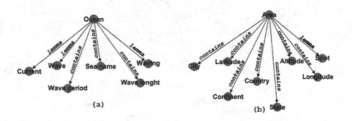

Fig. 4. Ego networks corresponding to *Ocean* and *Area*.

At this point, Step 2 is executed. As shown in Fig. 5, first each term (synonyms included) is semantically aligned to the corresponding DBpedia entry (e.g., *Ocean* is linked to *dbo:Sea*, *Area* is linked to *dbo:Location* and *dbo:Place*, while *Country* to *dbo:Country*[9], respectively). After a single iteration, the following triples are retrieved: ⟨*dbo:sea rdfs:range dbo:Sea*⟩ and ⟨*dbo:sea rdfs:domain dbo:Place*⟩. Other connections can be found by moving to specific instances of the mentioned resources. Indeed, the following triples are retrieved: ⟨*instance rdf:type dbo:Sea*⟩, ⟨*instance rdf:type dbo:Location*⟩, ⟨*instance rdf:type dbo:Place*⟩. Furthermore, a triple ⟨*instance dbo:country dbo:Country*⟩ can be retrieved. As a result, Step 2 succeeded in merging the two views that were separated after Step 1.

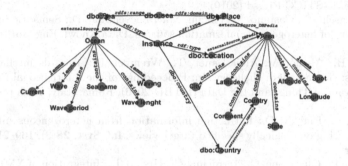

Fig. 5. The integrated thematic view.

6   Conclusion

In this paper, we have proposed a new metadata model well suited for representing and handling data lake sources. We have seen that our model starts from the ones generally used by data lake companies (in particolar, it starts from the model of Zaloni), but complements them with new ideas and, in particular, with the power guaranteed by a network-based and semantics-driven representation of available data. We have also seen that our model can allow a large variety of sophisticated tasks that the current metadata models cannot guarantee. This paper is not to be intended as an ending point. Actually, it could be the starting point of a new family of approaches that leverage our metadata model to address several open issues in data lake research; think, for instance, of approaches to supporting a flexible and lightweight querying of the sources of a data lake, as well as of approaches to schema matching, schema mapping, data reconciliation and integration strongly oriented to data lakes based mainly on unstructured data sources.

---

[9] Prefixes *dbo* and *dbr* stand for http://dbpedia.org/ontology/ and http://dbpedia.org/resource/.

References

1. Abiteboul, S., Duschka, O.M.: Complexity of answering queries using materialized views. In: Proceedings of the International Symposium on Principles of Database Systems (SIGMOD/PODS 1998), Seattle, WA, USA, 1998, pp. 254–263. ACM (1998)
2. Aversano, L., Intonti, R., Quattrocchi, C., Tortorella, M.: Building a virtual view of heterogeneous data source views. In: Proceedings of the International Conference on Software and Data Technologies (ICSOFT 2010), Athens, Greece, 2010, pp. 266–275. INSTICC Pressd (2010)
3. Bergamaschi, S., Castano, S., Vincini, M., Beneventano, D.: Semantic integration and query of heterogeneous information sources. Data Knowl. Eng. **36**(3), 215–249 (2001)
4. Bilalli, B., Abelló, A., Aluja-Banet, T., Wrembel, R.: Towards intelligent data analysis: the metadata challenge. In: Proceedings of the International Conference on Internet of Things and Big Data (IoTBD 2016), Roma, Italy, 2016, pp. 331–338 (2016)
5. Biskup, J., Embley, D.: Extracting information from heterogeneous information sources using ontologically specified target views. Inf. Syst. **28**(3), 169–212 (2003). Elsevier
6. De Meo, P., Quattrone, G., Terracina, G., Ursino, D.: Integration of XML schemas at various "severity" levels. Inf. Syst. **31**(6), 397–434 (2006)
7. Fan, W., Wang, X., Wu, Y.: Answering pattern queries using views. IEEE Trans. Knowl. Data Eng. **28**(2), 326–341 (2016). IEEE
8. Fang, H.: Managing data lakes in big data era: what's a data lake and why has it became popular in data management ecosystem. In: Proceedings of the International Conference on Cyber Technology in Automation (CYBER 2015), Shenyang, China, 2015, pp. 820–824. IEEE (2015)
9. Farid, M., Roatis, A., Ilyas, I.F., Hoffmann, H., Chu, X.: CLAMS: bringing quality to Data Lakes. In: Proceedings of the International Conference on Management of Data (SIGMOD/PODS 2016), San Francisco, CA, USA, 2016, pp. 2089–2092. ACM (2016)
10. Hai, R., Geisler, S., Quix C.: Constance: an intelligent data lake system. In: Proceedings of the International Conference on Management of Data (SIGMOD/PODS 2016), San Francisco, CA, USA, 2016, pp. 2097–2100. ACM (2016)
11. Halevy, A.: Answering queries using views: a survey. VLDB J. **10**(4), 270–294 (2001). Springer
12. Hitzler, P., Janowicz, K.: Linked data, big data, and the 4th paradigm. Semant. Web **4**(3), 233–235 (2013)
13. Dublin Core Metadata Initiative. DCMI metadata terms. Technical report (2012)
14. Keith, A., Cyganiak, R., Hausenblas, M., Zhao, J.: Describing linked datasets with the void vocabulary. Technical report (2011)
15. Kondrak, G.: N-gram similarity and distance. In: Consens, M., Navarro, G. (eds.) SPIRE 2005. LNCS, vol. 3772, pp. 115–126. Springer, Heidelberg (2005). https://doi.org/10.1007/11575832_13
16. Madhavan, J., Bernstein, P.A., Rahm, E.: Generic schema matching with Cupid. In: Proceedings of the International Conference on Very Large Data Bases (VLDB 2001), Rome, Italy, 2001, pp. 49–58. Morgan Kaufmann (2001)
17. Navigli, R., Ponzetto, S.P.: BabelNet: the automatic construction, evaluation and application of a wide-coverage multilingual semantic network. Artif. Intell. **193**, 217–250 (2012). Elsevier

18. Oram, A.: Managing the Data Lake. O'Reilly, Sebastopol (2015)
19. Palopoli, L., Pontieri, L., Terracina, G., Ursino, D.: Intensional and extensional integration and abstraction of heterogeneous databases. Data Knowl. Eng. **35**(3), 201–237 (2000)
20. Rahm, E., Bernstein, P.A.: A survey of approaches to automatic schema matching. VLDB J. **10**(4), 334–350 (2001)
21. Singh, K., Singh, V.: Answering graph pattern query using incremental views. In: Proceedings of the International Conference on Computing (ICCCA 2016), Greater Noida, India, 2016, pp. 54–59. IEEE (2016)
22. Wang, J., Li, J., Yu, J.X.: Answering tree pattern queries using views: a revisit. In: Proceedings of the International Conference on Extending Database Technology (EDBT/ICDT 2011), Uppsala, Sweden, 2011, pp. 153–164. ACM (2011)

Comparing SLAs for Cloud Services: A Model for Reasoning

Antonella Longo[1], Domenico Potena[2], Emanuele Storti[2(✉)], Marco Zappatore[1], and Andrea De Matteis[3]

[1] SET-LAB, Department of Engineering for Innovation, University of Salento, via Monteroni, 73100 Lecce, Italy
{antonella.longo,marcosalvatore.zappatore}@unisalento.it
[2] DII, Department of Information Engineering, Marche Polytechnic University, via Brecce Bianche, 60131 Ancona, Italy
{e.storti,d.potena}@univpm.it
[3] RoboLab, University of Pavia, via Ferrata 5, 27100 Pavia, Italy
andrea.dematteis01@universitadipavia.it

Abstract. Nowadays cloud services are gaining their momentum. A Service Level Agreement (SLA) represents an agreement between a service provider and a customer for a particular service provision. Cloud providers and services are often selected more dynamically than in traditional IT services. Hence, services need to be compared according both to technical aspects and the promised SLAs, but no widely accepted model, standard or best practice, that would lead to a more rigorous SLA comparison, are currently available. In this paper, we present a conceptualization of SLAs including the explicit modeling of formulas for service level indicators, and its corresponding open, reusable ontological representation. On its top, we provide operators for analysis and comparison of SLAs, relying on a reasoning framework in Logic Programming capable to manipulate indicator formulas and other SLA features. We provide an evaluation by considering a cloud scenario where several SLAs have to be compared.

Keywords: Service level agreement · Cloud service governance
Semantic interoperability · OWL · Prolog

1 Managing Cloud Service Governance with SLAs

Cloud computing technology empowers a scalable and flexible paradigm where infrastructures, platforms and software are offered to customers as (bundle of) services via brokers [1] and virtual marketplaces [2]. For instance, a Platform-as-a-Service (PaaS) e-commerce application might use proprietary persistence services and manage IDs and payments via different 3rd-party cloud services. In addition, cloud microservices technologies and Business Process Outsourcing (BPO) services [3] discloses even more dynamic scenarios where service owners must rely on the quality commitments of external service vendors through

© Springer Nature Switzerland AG 2018
A. Benczúr et al. (Eds.): ADBIS 2018, CCIS 909, pp. 178–190, 2018.
https://doi.org/10.1007/978-3-030-00063-9_18

SLAs (i.e., Service Level Agreements formalizing commitments and claims of providers and customers over an agreed service offer) and their effective comparison. SLAs enable negotiation on quality and technical goals (Service Levels, SLs) depending on obligations on agreed metrics (Service Level Indicators, SLIs). These metrics allow to evaluate providers' liabilities by comparing quantitative thresholds (Service Level Objectives, SLOs) within specific time windows, such as: contract validity interval (e.g., *1 Jan. 2017–31 Dec. 2020*); guarantee calendar for SLA conditions (e.g., *working days, 8am–6pm*); SLA observation calendar (e.g., *monthly*); SLA measurement period (e.g., *10 s*); reporting calendar for SLA enforcement (e.g., *first day of month*). Even if the dynamicity of cloud services demands for service (and SLAs) comparison and interoperability, the available SLA modelling languages do not offer formal description of services, specifications of customer guarantees, normalization of service semantic heterogeneity (for instance: when the same service capability belongs to two bundles with same SLI, different parameters, overlapping guarantee calendars, different validity intervals). Instead, these languages show limited effectiveness and poor service discovery and brokering [4], as they only allow *syntactic* (automatic, if SLIs and units are the same) or *semantic* (semi-automatic) comparisons. Several under-definition standards for SLAs [5,6] should ease SLA comparison [7] but this aim is still far to be reached. Formal SLA comparison can add collaborative governance and effective distribution models to cloud services: therefore, we present a conceptualization of SLAs focused on the explicit modeling of SLA terms and its corresponding open, reusable and formal representation in OWL. On top of this model, we provide a set of logic operators for SLA analysis and comparison, which rely on a reasoning framework in Logic Programming for manipulating SLA features. The operators are evaluated in a real scenario (which exploits our experience as tenderers involved in designing a cloud service broker for public administrations in the Cloud for Europe (C4E) research project [1]) to show the effectiveness and correctness of the broker-managed comparison of cloud services, w.r.t. a subset of the most significant SLA technical aspects. The broker [5] manages SLAs and suggests to customers the services closest to their requests after automatic service comparison. We have considered three self-contained services differing for numerical parameters and time-validity constraints (Table 1). These services have the same SLI (i.e., service availability) with different SLOs, time windows and metrics. For service#1 availability is computed as $1 - \frac{DownTime}{TotalPossibleAvailableTime}$, for service#2 is computed as $TotalPossibleAvailableTime - TotalDowntime$ while for service#3 is computed as $\frac{NumCorrectlyProcessedRequests}{NumSubmittedRequests}$. We consider the following set requirements: (R1) determine whether two SLAs have compatible guarantee and validity intervals (i.e., they refer to services operating in the same timeframes); (R2) calculate the right sub-timeframe when such windows are overlapping (e.g., when the two SLA are valid at the same time); (R3) understand if, and to what extent, the SLIs are mathematically equivalent, in order to check among alternatives with the same guarantees.

Table 1. SLA specifications for the use case.

Service	SLI	SLO	Unit of measurement	Guarantee	Validity	Observation	Measurement	Reporting
service#1	Service availability	>99.9	%	8:30-13:30 14:30-18:30	01/01/2017 31/12/2017	yearly	30s	By the 15th of the following Measurement interval
service#2	Service uptime	>98	%	24x7	01/01/2017 30/06/2017	monthly	30s	By the 15th of the following Measurement interval
service#3	Service availability	>98	%	8:30-13:30 14:30-18:30	01/01/2017 30/06/2017	monthly	30s	By the 15th of the following Measurement interval

The paper is structured as it follows: Sect. 2 surveys relevant related works. The proposed model is detailed in Sect. 3 while Sect. 4 describes the Prolog-based reasoning framework. In Sect. 5, the SLA analysis and comparison operators are discussed and applied to the use case, while Sect. 6 ends the paper.

2   Related Work

SLA languages are crucial in cloud service lifecycle management [8,9]: the most significant ones are XML-based (e.g., WSOL [10], WSLA [11], WS-Agreement [12], SLA* [13], CSLA [14], SLAC [15]) or based on domain-specific languages (e.g., rSLA [16]). By extending the work presented in [8], we have compared (Table 2) such languages and our proposed model against these analysis criteria, in order to show the improvements.

- Cloud Domain: language devised specifically (or not) for the cloud domain.
- Cloud Delivery Models: fully supported when a language covers IaaS, PaaS and SaaS; partially supported when only one of these models is covered.
- Multi-party: fully (or partially) supported when the language supports all (or at least two) of the following features: (1) all roles defined, (2) multiple parties with the same role, (3) multiple roles for the same party.
- Broker support: fully (or partially) achieved by specifying all (or at least two) of these features: (1) involved parties, (2) service offers/requests, (3) broker's role, (4) actions/metrics needed for assessing responsibilities and liabilities.
- Time Windows: fully (or partially) supported when all (or at least two) of these quantities are expressed: (1) validity interval, (2) guarantee calendar, (3) observation calendar, (4) measurement period, (5) reporting calendar.
- SLI formulations: it allows managing different formulations for the same SLI.
- Ease of Us: fully (or partially) supported when the language is domain-ready and (respectively, or) it is easy to understand, also for human actors.
- Business Metrics and Actions: fully (or partially) supported when it is possible to define business-related metrics and (respectively, or) to define actions describing common business behaviors (e.g., payment of penalties).
- Formal Syntax: supported only when a formal definition of the syntax is available.

- Formal Semantics: fully supported if a formal (e.g., operational) definition of the SLA evaluation is available; partially supported if ambiguous tools are used.
- Formal Verification: fully supported when the formal verification of agreement exists before execution time; partially supported if only the syntax is verified;
- Evaluation Tools: fully supported if a tool evaluates SLAs against services monitoring information; partially supported If only design time verification is available.
- Open source: the model is based upon open source modelling standards.

Many of these languages lack of effective semantics modelling (and verification capabilities) and were devised for neither the cloud computing scenario nor a cloud service brokering context, so that some features that would result crucial in comparing this kind of SLAs are not fully supported. In order to improve the semantic expressivity, several research studies are approaching ontologies for cloud services, as it has been reviewed in [17], where a platform for building smart cloud solutions grounded on cloud computing ontology is also presented. However, cloud service metric benchmarks are still not available, thus creating a gap between the level of details in cloud service offerings and the available methodologies for classifying and comparing SLAs and metrics: our proposed model addresses those limitations.

Table 2. Comparison of existing SLA models with the proposed approach (rightmost column). Analysis criteria are grouped into General (G), Business-related (B), Formal (F) and Tools-related (T), while •, o and − symbols stand for a feature totally, partially or not covered, respectively.

	Analysis criterion	WSOL	SLAng	WSLA	WS-Agr.	SLA*	CSLA	SLAC	rSLA	Proposed
G	Cloud domain	−	−	−	−	o	•	•	•	•
	Cloud service models	−	−	−	−	o	•	o	•	•
	Multi-party	−	−	−	−	−	•	•	−	•
	Broker support	−	−	−	−	−	o	•	−	•
	Time windows	−	−	−	−	−	−	−	−	•
	SLI formulations	−	−	−	o	−	−	o	−	•
	Ease of use	o	o	−	o	o	•	o	o	o
B	Business metrics	o	o	o	o	o	•	•	•	•
F	Syntax	•	•	•	•	•	•	•	•	•
	Semantics	−	o	−	−	−	•	•	•	•
	Verification	−	o	−	−	−	•	•	•	•
T	Evaluation	•	•	•	•	•	•	•	•	•
	Open-source	•	•	−	•	•	•	•	•	•

3 A Model for SLA

When dealing with cloud services and how their provisioning and consuming are agreed upon via proper service contracts, it is fundamental to know several formal, technical and legal aspects. In particular, it is necessary to know in details the agreement terms composing a cloud service contract as well as how many of them refer to an SLA. In the same way, SLAs have to be examined in terms of availability of SLs, corresponding SLIs, proper SL measurement metric and techniques, availability of standardized SLIs, targeted SLOs and related penalties. Moreover, once dealing with cloud services, several additional elements must be considered, such as the specification of validity, guarantee, observation, measurement, reporting and maintenance time intervals and the ways they are enforced. In this context, we are going to consider cloud services (and the corresponding contracts) having at least one SLA specified for each service in order to determine how to manage, measure and assess SLAs as well as to compare them with specifically required (or proposed) SL thresholds.

As depicted in Fig. 1, we designed a UML class diagram, in order to clearly define the associations existing amongst the elements characterizing a SLA specification. This approach also paves the way for a more rigorous, shared and formalized representation of the model in OWL2 RL[1], which is the profile of OWL2 used also by external vocabularies that are here reused (e.g. KPIOnto [18]). Whenever not specified, it is assumed that all the UML classes are implemented as an `owl:Class`, associations are represented as an `owl:ObjectProperty` and attributes as a `owl:DataProperty`. In Fig. 2 we show a fragment of the instantiation of the model for service#1.

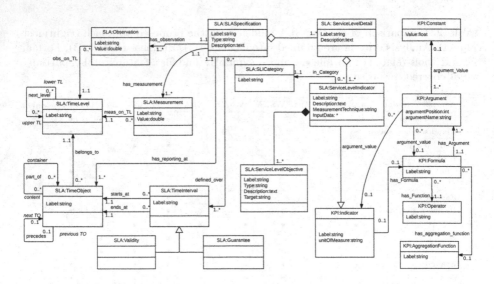

Fig. 1. UML model for SLA

We propose to consider a SLA specification as the aggregation of a set of SL details (i.e., class `ServiceLevelDetail`), aimed at defining all the measurable and controllable aspects of the cloud service the SLA specification refers to.

---

[1] https://www.w3.org/TR/owl2-profiles/.

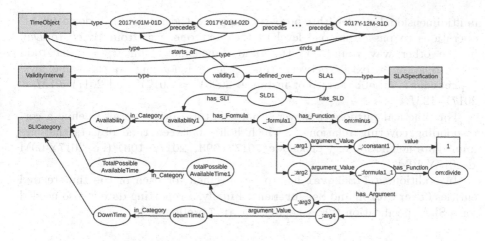

Fig. 2. A fragment of the instantiation of the model for service#1.

Similarly, each SL detail is simply an aggregation of SLIs (class `ServiceLevel-Indicator`), which specify how to measure SLs (via a set of proper calculation metrics) and how to compare them against predefined SLOs (class `Service-LevelObjective`, i.e. SL thresholds that have to be considered when specific events occur). Since SLOs exist only in connection with the specific SLIs they refer to, we can consider each SLI as a composition of SLOs rather than an aggregation, from a modelling perspective.

3.1 Modeling of Time Windows and Entities

A SLA Specification specifies one or more time intervals (∃`specifies.TimeInterval`), which may be either a `ValidityInterval` or a `GuaranteeInterval`.

An interval is temporally defined through a time window characterized by a start and an end event, each represented as an instance of the TimeObject class (∃`start_at.TimeObject`and ∃`ends_at.TimeObject`) at a certain granularity level (∃`in_Level. TimeLevel`). For instance, year 2017 is represented by the time object '2017Y', which is in level *Year*, while time object '2017Y-12M', used for december 2017, is in level *Month*. Indeed, we rely on a representation of the time granularities of the time objects according to the multidimensional model, through a hierarchy of TimeLevels (e.g. *Year, Semester, Month, Week, Day*), represented through the partial order relation next_Level (∀`next_Level.TimeLevel`), e.g. `next_Level(Month, Semester)`. Please note that this definitions allows for multiple hierarchies, for instance `next_Level(Day, Week)`, `next_Level(Day,Month)`.

Given two levels L1 and L2, with `next_Level(L1,L2)`, a part-of relation (∀`part_Of. TimeObject`) maps an object belonging to L1 to an object belonging to L2. For instance, given *Day* and *Month*, a specific day is part of a specific month, and therefore: `part_Of(2017Y-09M-23D, 2017Y-09M)`. As in the multidimensional model, this property supports the roll-up/drill-down OLAP operations to pass from one level to the next one, e.g. from $Week$ to Day or the other way round. As the time dimension is linear, a strict total order relation $<$ exists between time objects belonging to the same level ($\forall precedesT.TimeObject$). For instance, $2000Y < 2017Y$ and $2017Y\text{-}01M < 2017Y\text{-}12M$.

For practical purpose, however, from this total order we also define a corresponding covering relation $\lessdot$, which holds between time objects that are immediate neighbors, e.g. `precedes(2017Y-09M, 2017Y-10M)` (i.e. $2017Y\text{-}09M \lessdot 2017Y\text{-}10M$).

In addition, a `TimeLevel` has to be specified for each of the time-related entities `Observation` and `Measurement`. Finally, a reporting date is also needed for a SLA specification ($\forall has\_reporting\_at.TimeObject$).

3.2 Modeling of a SLI

A SLI is a quantitative measurement of a certain phenomenon. Indicators have long been adopted in several domains, for monitoring purposes, and several frameworks have been defined in the Cloud service domain. Each SLI is here considered as the specific instance of a more generic indicator category ($\exists in\_Category.\ SLICategory$). For instance, with reference to the use case, the SLIs for the three services refer to $Availability$ as $SLICategory$. For modeling indicators and their formulas, in this work we take the approach of KPIOnto, a vocabulary firstly developed in the FP7 project BIVEE [18] and devised to formally model indicators and their calculation formulas[2]. Indeed, the `ServiceLevelIndicator` class is here defined as subclass of the KPIOnto `kpi:Indicator` class. In KPIOnto an indicator can be either atomic or compound, built by combining other indicators. Dependencies of a compound indicator ind on its building elements are defined through an expression $f(ind_1, \ldots, ind_n)$, i.e. a formula stating how to calculate the indicator in terms of ind_i, which may be in turn indicators, constants or other formulas ($\forall hasFormula.Formula$).

In KPIOnto, a `kpi:Formula` is represented as the application of an `kpi:Operator` to one or more `kpi:Argument`. Operators are represented as defined by OpenMath [19], an extensible XML-based standard for representing the semantics of mathematical objects. An argument specifies its name and its position as properties (in order to distinguish, for instance, between a dividend from the divisor for a ratio) and a value. This last can be either another SLI, a numeric `kpi:Constant` or, recursively, a `kpi:Formula`. For instance, the formula $A + (B * 100)$ is represented as the application of the operator '$+$' (i.e., 'http://www.openmath.org/cd/arith1/plus') to the two summands 'A' (a SLI) and '$B * 100$' (a formula). Further properties include unit of measurement and the aggregation function ($\forall has\_aggregation\_function.Aggregati\text{-}onFunction$), which represents how to summarise a set of values of the indicator

---

[2] Classes with namespace 'KPI' belong to the KPIOnto data model.

into a single value. According to widely accepted models (e.g. [20]), aggregation functions can be categorized into the following types: distributive (e.g., sum, min, max), algebraic (e.g., average), holistic (e.g., median). We refer the interested reader to [21] for a discussion on these functions.

With reference to the use case, we define three formulas for the corresponding SLIs:

- service#1: $Availability_1 = 1 - \frac{TotalPossibleAvailableTime_1}{DownTime_1}$
- service#2: $Uptime_1 = TotalPossibleAvailableTime_1 - DownTime_1$
- service#3: $Availability_2 = \frac{NumCorrectlyProcessedRequests_1}{NumSubmittedRequests_1}$

As a convention, we represent a specific SLI by a name followed by a number (e.g., $Availability_1$), in order to avoid duplication of names. When a new SLA descriptor is created, the user should always refer to already defined SLIs to use them as components of the SLI formula (e.g., in order to define the formula for $Availability_1$, the SLIs $DownTime_1$ and $TotalPossibleAvailableTime_1$ must have been defined earlier). If this is not the case, firstly the missing SLIs should be added to the ontology in order to define the formula.

4 Reasoning Framework

Specific reasoning functions must be defined on the top of the model to implement comparison functionalities by exploiting the formal representation of time windows and formulas. To this end, we refer to a reasoning framework in Logic Programming, specifically Prolog, as logic-based language for its capability to manipulate both (properly translated) OWL2 axioms and mathematical equations.

Reasoning on time windows may be conceived as reasoning on sets of time objects. Firstly, `part_of` properties are translated as facts $part\_of$ (t_1, t_2), where $t_1 \in L_1$, $t_2 \in L_2$ and $L_1 < L_2$. Similarly, property `in_Level` or property `precedes` are represented as facts. As such, a Prolog goal like `part_of(X, '2017-M3')` allows to retrieve all the components `X=['2017Y-M3-D1', ..., '2017Y-M3-D31']` of the given time object. Specific Prolog predicates have been defined in order to support the higher-level operators discussed in next Section, e.g. to check the validity of a time interval (i.e. if its start and end time objects belong to the same level and start<end) and to derive all the time objects included in a given interval.

Mathematical formulas are here represented as Prolog facts by referring to an infix notation, e.g. $SLI_A = SLI_B + SLI_C$ is represented as `formula('SLI`$_A$`', 'SLI`$_B$`'+ 'SLI`$_C$`')`. Manipulation of mathematical expressions is performed by predicates from PRESS (PRolog Equation Solving System) [22], which is a formalisation of algebra in Logic Programming for solving symbolic, transcendental and non-differential equations.

Basic functionalities enable manipulation of mathematical formulas, resolution of equations by applying mathematical properties (e.g., commutativity, factorisation), and properties of equality. For instance, the equation $A = \frac{(B*C+B*D)}{B}$ can be rewritten by factorisation of B as $A = \frac{B*(C+D)}{B}$ and then as $A = C + D$. Finally, it can be solved with respect to C, with solution $A - D$. More advanced functions for supporting analysis and comparison of SLAs are based on those basic functionalities (see also [21]):

- `get_formulas(SLI,X)`, which retrieves in X all alternative formulas for SLI, by performing manipulation and rewriting of all the formulas for all the defined SLIs. Even if the SLI at hand is not provided with a formula, the predicate can derive a formula from other already defined formulas, e.g. if $SLI_A = SLI_B * SLI_C$, then $SLI_B = \frac{SLI_A}{SLI_C}$. A variant of this predicate allows to derive all alternative formulas for a SLI-Category, e.g. `get_formulas('Availability', X)` will produce the list $X = \{1 - \frac{downTime_1}{totalPossibleAvailableTime_1}, totalPossibleAvailableTime_1 - downTime_1, \frac{totalPossibleAvailableTime_1 - downTime_1}{totalPossibleAvailableTime_1}, \frac{uptime_1}{totalPossibleAvailableTime_1}, \frac{numCorrectlyProcessedRequests_1}{numSubmittedRequests_1}\}$.

- `equivalence(SLI,X)`, which returns in X all the formulas mathematically equivalent to that of SLI.

- `equivalentTo(SLI_A,SLI_B)`, which determines whether the two indicators are mathematically equivalent by executing `equivalence` on both input indicators, and intersecting the corresponding outputs.

- `get_common_measures(SLI_A, SLI_B, X)`, which returns in X the components in common, for any rewriting of the two indicators such that they share at least one component. For instance, if formulas $SLI_A = SLI_B + SLI_C$, $SLI_B = SLI_D * SLI_E$ and $SLI_F = SLI_E/SLI_D$ are defined, then SLI_A can be rewritten as $SLI_A = SLI_D * SLI_E + SLI_C$. Hence, `get_common_measures` (SLI_A, SLI_F) returns $\{SLI_D, SLI_E\}$. This reasoning functionality is useful to determine common dependencies and similarities between formulas, as shown in the next Section.

5   Analysis and Comparison of SLAs

In this Section we discuss the high-level operators that, relying on the model and the reasoning functions, are devised to support those functionalities listed in Sect. 1 as requirements for a service broker. In particular, requirements R1 and R2 refer to comparison of SLA time windows, while requirement R3 is related to comparison of SLI formulas. Given SLA_1 and SLA_2 with corresponding validity/guarantee time windows, SLIs and calculation metrics, the problem is hence to verify whether their validity time windows are comparable, i.e. mutually temporally consistent by (at least partially) referring to the same time periods and their calculation metrics are compatible. These properties are verified by checking if and to what extent (1) their time windows are overlapping and (2) their SLIs are mathematically equivalent, as detailed below.

5.1 Comparison of Time Windows

The notion of *compatibility* is hereby used to specify under which conditions two time windows are comparable. Then, we describe a procedure for its assessment, which is a necessary step for their comparison and for service composition. Hereafter, we specifically refer to validity and guarantee time windows, as they respectively refer to the time periods during which the SLA must be operating and must be guaranteed. As the other intervals define operative details of the measurement procedure, there is no need to further constrain the evaluation of compatibility by their comparison.

Definition 1. *Full compatibility of time windows. Given two SLAs with validity windows v_1, v_2 and guarantee windows g_1, g_2, they have a full time compatibility iif:*

$$(g_1 \subseteq g_2 \wedge v_1 \subseteq v_2) \vee (g_2 \subseteq g_1 \wedge v_2 \subseteq v_1)$$

Note that this holds when intervals are identical or one is included in the other. As discussed in Sect. 3, we rely on a representation of time granularities according to the multidimensional model, through a hierarchy of levels. Hence, given two SLAs with different time windows, compatibility is assessed through the following procedure: (1) if they refer to different levels of the time dimension, drill-down is used to make the granularity levels uniform; (2) having obtained two comparable sets, their intersection allows to determine the common validity window, i.e. the overlap when the two SLAs are compatible from the time perspective.

To make an example related to the case study discussed in Sect. 1, let us consider service#1 and service#2, with time windows v_1 = {⟨'2017Y-01M-01D', '2017Y-12M-31D'⟩} and v_2 = {⟨'2017Y-01M', '2017Y-06M'⟩}. Let us consider a guarantee windows for service#2 equal to the whole semester of validity, namely g_2 = {⟨'2017Y-01M-01D', '2017Y-06M-30D'⟩}, and a window for service#1 given as the set of all the guarantee intervals specified in Table 1, for the whole year, i.e. g_1 = {⟨'2017Y-01M-01D-08H-30M', '2017Y-01M-01D-13H-30M',⟩,..., ⟨'2017Y-06M-30D-14H-30M', '2017Y-06M-30D-18H-30M'⟩}.

The procedure firstly detects the corresponding levels of the intervals (e.g., l_1 = *Day* and l_2 = *Month*). Secondly, it computed the sets T_1 including all the 365 days in the year, and T_2 including the 6 months in the interval. Given that *Day* < *Month*, the interval T_2 is translated from month to day level, in order to make it comparable with T_1. Finally, the converted set T_2 is intersected with T_1. In this case, the result is that $T_2 \subset T_1$.

The comparison of g_1 and g_2 follows a similar procedure and the result of the intersection shows that $T_2 \not\subseteq T_1$, but $T_1 \cap T_2 \neq \emptyset$. In particular, the intersection corresponds to the interval between 8:30–13:30 and 14:30–18:30 for the first six months of the year. As a conclusion, the two services do not have fully compatible time windows according to Definition 1.

5.2 Comparison of SLIs

Given two SLIs, the question of whether they are compatible or not is crucial in order to properly perform analysis and also in the perspective of service composition. SLIs belonging to the same SLICategory, indeed, may have different calculation formulas. On the other hand, SLIs with different names may be actually equivalent. Given that only a proper formal comparison between formulas can guarantee the comparability of the corresponding services, we firstly provide the definition for compatible SLIs.

Definition 2. *Compatibility of SLIs. Given two SLIs with formulas f_1 and f_2, with unit of measurement m_1 and m_2, they are compatible iif: (f_1 and f_2 are mathematically equivalent) $\land$ ($m_1 = m_2$).*

In order to evaluate equivalence between formulas, predicate `equivalentTo` is executed. As an example from the use case, for service#1 availability is measured as $availability_1 = 1 - \frac{downTime_1}{totalPossibleAvailableTime_1}$, while for service#2 $uptime_2 = totalPossibleAvailableTime_1 - downtime_1$. By comparing these definitions through predicate `equivalence`, the reasoner would conclude that $availability_1$ is equal to $\frac{uptime_1}{totalPossibleAvailableTime_1}$. As such, the two formulas are not equivalent.

In case the two formulas are found to be non-equivalent, other operators can support users in determining how and to what extent they are similar. Firstly, two formulas can be compared through the predicate `get_common_measures(SLI`$_1$`, SLI`$_2$`, X)` in order to retrieve their common set of related SLIs. As for the use case, by executing `get_common_measures('Availability`$_1$`', 'Uptime`$_1$`',X)`, we would obtain X = $\{totalPossibleAvailableTime_1, downTime_1\}$ as result, meaning that the two formulas are actually composed by refering to the same operands. Furthermore, a formula for a SLI can be checked against all the other SLIs in order to find those that share the same operands with it. This can be achieved by executing the predicate `get_formulas(SLI`$_1$`,X)` and by using `get_common_measures(SLI`$_1$`,SLI`$_i$`,Y)` for any SLI$_i \in X$, obtaining in Y a list of common measures.

6 Conclusion

In this paper we have proposed to model the pivotal SLA elements in order to support their analysis and comparison. To this aim, an ontological representation of SLAs with respect to their indicators and technical parameters has been introduced by exploiting OWL2-RL. Although the work is not focused on a comparative analysis between the relevant ontologies in the Literature modeling SLAs, here we refer to a set of generally accepted criteria [23]: *clarity* is guaranteed by the reference to a formal representation language; the ontological model is *coherent* as it has been formally evaluated by using a reasoner; being implemented in OWL2, the model is *extensible* and, in turn, it already extends the external vocabulary KPIOnto. Finally, the terms included in the model are among those that are widely agreed upon most of the available SLA models. This allows a minimal *ontological commitment*. We also introduced a set of logic operators supporting analysis/comparison of SLIs and time windows, that represent the first challenge to be tackled when comparing different SLAs. In order to ascertain the effectiveness and formal rigorousness of our solution, a concrete use case, mimicking real cloud service SLAs, has been used for testing the model expressivity with respect to the comparison of SLA time windows and SLIs. We have achieved a satisfactory usage of formal reasoning on the structure of mathematical formulas that can be extended to the evaluation of other SLA terms, thus paving the way to thorough SLA comparison in the next future. For most practical cases, the level of expressivity enabled by PRESS is enough for performing comparison and analysis of SLAs, as many frameworks of indicators comprising formulas with only arithmetic operators. However, in some cases that are left out of the present discussion, SLIs are defined through more complex algorithms, that cannot be expressed as a unique formula. These may include computation procedures or indicators expressed as queries (or views) over a database, e.g., 'availability in the last week' which embeds a temporal reference to the query time. Moreover, although the use case deals with cloud services, the model is devised to capture the most frequent concepts for generic services and scenarios, that will be considered for a more comprehensive future evaluation.

References

1. Longo, A., Zappatore, M., Bochicchio, M.A., Livieri, B., Guarino, N., Napoleone, D.: Cloud for Europe: the experience of a tenderer. In: 2016 30th International Conference on Advanced Information Networking and Applications Workshops (WAINA), pp. 153–158. IEEE (2016)
2. Pudasaini, D., Ding, C.: Service selection in a cloud marketplace: a multi-perspective solution. In: 2017 IEEE 10th International Conference on Cloud Computing (CLOUD), pp. 576–583, June 2017
3. del–Río–Ortega, A., Gutiérrez, A.M., Durán, A., Resinas, M., Ruiz–Cortés, A.: Modelling service level agreements for business process outsourcing services. In: Zdravkovic, J., Kirikova, M., Johannesson, P. (eds.) CAiSE 2015. LNCS, vol. 9097, pp. 485–500. Springer, Cham (2015). https://doi.org/10.1007/978-3-319-19069-3_30
4. Alkandari, F., Paige, R.F.: Modelling and comparing cloud computing service level agreements. In: Proceedings of the 1st International Workshop on Model-Driven Engineering for High Performance and CLoud Computing, MDHPCL 2012, pp. 3:1–3:6. ACM, New York (2012)
5. Liu, F., et al.: NIST Cloud Computing Reference Architecture: Recommendations of the National Institute of Standards and Technology (Special Publication 500-292). CreateSpace, USA (2012)
6. Van der Wees, A., Catteddu, D., Luna, J., Edwards, M., Schifano, N., Scoca, L.M.: Cloud service level agreement standardisation guidelines. Technical report, C-Sig Sla (2014)
7. Kecskemeti, G., Kertesz, A., Nemeth, Z. (eds.): Developing Interoperable and Federated Cloud. IGI-Global, Hershey (2016)

8. Maarouf, A., Marzouk, A., Haqiq, A.: A review of SLA specification languages in the cloud computing. In: 2015 10th International Conference on Intelligent Systems: Theories and Applications (SITA), pp. 1–6, October 2015
9. Mubeen, S., Asadollah, S.A., Papadopoulos, A.V., Ashjaei, M., Pei-Breivold, H., Behnam, M.: Management of service level agreements for cloud services in IoT: a systematic mapping study. IEEE Access **99**, 1 (2017)
10. Tosic, V., Patel, K., Pagurek, B.: WSOL — web service offerings language. In: Bussler, C., Hull, R., McIlraith, S., Orlowska, M.E., Pernici, B., Yang, J. (eds.) WES 2002. LNCS, vol. 2512, pp. 57–67. Springer, Heidelberg (2002). https://doi.org/10.1007/3-540-36189-8_5
11. Ludwig, H., Keller, A., Dan, A., King, R.P., Franck, R.: Web Service Level Agreement (WSLA) Language Specification, v1.0, January 2003
12. Heiko, L., Dan, A., Kearney, R.: Cremona: an architecture and library for creation and monitoring of WS-agreements. In: 2nd International Conference on Service Oriented Computing (ICSOC 04), pp. 65–74. ACM (2004)
13. Kearney, K.T., Torelli, F., Kotsokalis, C.: SLA⋆: an abstract syntax for service level agreements. In: 2010 11th IEEE/ACM International Conference on Grid Computing, pp. 217–224, October 2010
14. Kouki, Y., de Oliveira, F.A., Dupont, S., Ledoux, T.: A language support for cloud elasticity management. In: 2014 14th IEEE/ACM International Symposium on Cluster, Cloud and Grid Computing, pp. 206–215, May 2014
15. Uriarte, R.B., Tiezzi, F., Nicola, R.D.: SLAC: a formal service-level-agreement language for cloud computing. In: 2014 IEEE/ACM 7th International Conference on Utility and Cloud Computing, pp. 419–426, December 2014
16. Tata, S., Mohamed, M., Sakairi, T., Mandagere, N., Anya, O., Ludwig, H.: rSLA: a service level agreement language for cloud services. In: 2016 IEEE 9th International Conference on Cloud Computing (CLOUD), pp. 415–422, June 2016
17. Bellini, P., Bruno, I., Cenni, D., Nesi, P.: Managing cloud via smart cloud engine and knowledge base. Future Gener. Comput. Syst. **78**(Part 1), 142–154 (2016)
18. Diamantini, C., Potena, D., Storti, E.: SemPI: a semantic framework for the collaborative construction and maintenance of a shared dictionary of performance indicators. Future Gener. Comput. Syst. **54**, 352–365 (2015)
19. Buswell, S., Caprotti, O., Carlisle, D.P., Dewar, M.C., Gaetano, M., Kohlhase, M.: The open math standard. Technical report, version 2.0, The Open Math Society (2004). http://www.openmath.org/standard/om20
20. Gray, J., et al.: Data cube: a relational aggregation operator generalizing group-by, cross-tab, and sub-totals. Data Min. Knowl. Discov. **1**(1), 29–53 (1997)
21. Diamantini, C., Potena, D., Storti, E.: Extended drill-down operator: digging into the structure of performance indicators. Concurrency Comput. Pract. Exp. **28**(15), 3948–3968 (2016)
22. Sterling, L., Bundy, A., Byrd, L., O'Keefe, R., Silver, B.: Solving symbolic equations with PRESS. J. Symb. Comput. **7**(1), 71–84 (1989)
23. Gruber, T.R.: Toward principles for the design of ontologies used for knowledge sharing? Int. J. Hum.-Comput. Stud. **43**(5), 907–928 (1995)

Automatic Extraction of Affective Metadata from Videos Through Emotion Recognition Algorithms

Alex Mircoli[✉] and Giampiero Cimini

Dipartimento di Ingegneria dell'Informazione,
Università Politecnica delle Marche, Via Brecce Bianche, 60131 Ancona, Italy
{a.mircoli,g.cimini}@univpm.it

Abstract. In recent years, the diffusion of social networks has made available large amounts of user-generated data containing people's opinions and feelings. Such data are mostly unstructured and hence need to be enriched with a large set of metadata to allow for efficient data indexing and querying. In this work we focus on videos and we extend traditional metadata extraction techniques by taking into account emotional metadata, in order to enable data analysis from an affective perspective. To this purpose, we present a 3-phase methodology for the automatic extraction of emotional metadata from videos through facial expression recognition algorithms. We also propose a simple but versatile model for metadata that takes into account variations in emotions among video chunks. Experiments on a real-world video dataset show that our non-linear classifier reaches a remarkable 72% classification accuracy in facial expression recognition.

1 Introduction

In recent times, the large-scale diffusion of social networks and video sharing platforms (e.g., Youtube) has made available a huge amount of User-Generated Content (UGC), mostly in the form of unstructured data (e.g., texts, pictures and videos), which contain people's opinions and feelings about a large variety of topics. This phenomenon represents a great opportunity for marketers and business analysts, since thoughts and emotions expressed by users while they spontaneously talk about a product or a service provide genuine hints about customer satisfaction. Therefore, their exploitation can help analysts in monitoring the impact of marketing campaigns and evaluate how the introduction of a new product feature has been perceived by consumers.

The indexing and analysis of such huge amounts of unstructured data require the generation of a rich set of metadata. Traditional metadata extraction techniques (e.g., [6,14]) are focused on factual aspects, like the presence of certain entities in a text or objects in a scene, but usually ignore emotional aspects which could enable meaningful and valuable analysis. Therefore, there is the need for automated procedures for the extraction of such emotional metadata from UGC.

© Springer Nature Switzerland AG 2018
A. Benczúr et al. (Eds.): ADBIS 2018, CCIS 909, pp. 191–202, 2018.
https://doi.org/10.1007/978-3-030-00063-9_19

Several works have focused on sentiment analysis techniques for text [3,5] or on emotion detection algorithms for images [15], while few research has been made on emotional analysis of videos. For this reason, in the present work we propose a methodology for the automatic generation of emotional metadata for videos through emotion recognition algorithms, in order to enable video indexing and querying from an emotional perspective. Even if there have been some attempts to detect emotions from text or audio (e.g., [12]), the majority of works are focused on facial expression recognition, since it is generally acknowledged that the most expressive way humans display emotions is through their faces [2]. In order to use a general framework for emotion representation, in the paper we adopt Ekman's theory of archetypal emotions [4], which states that every emotion can be described as a linear combination of six basic emotions.

The analysis of facial expressions in real-world videos poses several challenges, since there are many factors that can affect the recognition of people's face in a scene. For instance, frames without people, as well as frames containing actors not facing the camera, cannot be analyzed due to the lack of correctly recognizable faces. For this reason, we also discuss some video preprocessing techniques to filter out noisy and irrelevant (with respect to facial expression analysis) frames.

The main contributions of our work are: (i) the discussion of a simple but versatile model for emotional video metadata, based on the assumption that emotions in videos vary over time, and (ii) the definition and experimental evaluation of a methodology for the automatic generation of emotional metadata for videos. Such methodology is particularly suitable for Big Data sources, where the manual video analysis is usually challenging and cost-ineffective. The rest of the paper is organized as follows: in Sect. 2 we discuss some related work on emotion analysis through facial expression recognition. In Sect. 3 we present the methodological framework for the automatic extraction of emotional metadata while in Sect. 4 we show the results of an experimental evaluation of the emotion recognition algorithm. Finally, in Sect. 5 we draw conclusions and discuss future work.

2   Related Work

The theory of archetypal emotions proposed by the psychologist Paul Ekman [4] is one of the first attempts to systematically describe and analyze facial expressions. It defines a framework of six universal basic emotions, from which every emotion is derived through linear composition: anger, disgust, fear, happiness, sadness and surprise. Such theory is based on the Facial Action Coding System (FACS), which is an anatomical system for describing any observable facial expression. As stated in [8], the use of FACS offers many advantages, since they are language- and domain-independent and hence facial expression analysis can be carried out for every language and scope of application. Ekman's theory has been widely used in image-based facial expression recognition (e.g., [1,11]), even if many works only consider a subset of universal emotions [10]. A comprehensive survey on facial expression recognition can be found in [13].

Only few authors have focused on the creation of annotated datasets for facial expressions recognition. Among them, Sun et al. [17] used an hidden camera to build a database of authentic facial expressions where the test subjects are showing the natural facial expressions based upon their emotional state. They also use such database to evaluate the performance of several machine learning techniques in facial expression recognition. However, each video in their dataset has a unique emotion by design and hence their approach is not suitable for real-world videos, where people express a large variety of emotions; moreover, the released dataset is relatively small. An attempt to solve the problem of scarcity of annotated data is presented in [16], where the authors use a computer graphics program to synthetize more than 100,000 faces expressing emotions.

Mo et al. [9] propose a set of features for emotion recognition in videos that are based on the Hilbert-Huang Transform (HHT), which is able to capture the time-varying characteristics of visual signals. A different approach is used in [7], where, instead of manually engineering facial features, the authors combine Linear Regression Classification model (LRC) and Principal Component Analysis (PCA) in order to automatically select features.

Cohen et al. [2] propose Hidden Markov Models (HMMs) for automatically segmenting and recognizing facial expressions from video sequences. Our video preprocessing phase is similar to [19] in the use of face detection but we also consider some other aspects, such as face orientation. Poria et al. [10] propose to perform facial expression recognition through Open-face and SVM classifiers; however, there are many differences between their work and ours, including that we use both Action Units and point distances as features and we evaluate the technique on a real-world video dataset.

3 Methodology

3.1 Design Methodology

In this Section we describe the methodology for the automatic generation of emotional metadata for videos. As depicted in Fig. 1, it consists of three steps: first, videos are split into smaller parts with the purpose of obtaining video chunks with constant emotional content (step 1). Then, noisy and irrelevant frames are filtered out through video preprocessing techniques (step 2) and finally emotional metadata are extracted from video chunks through facial expression recognition algorithms (step 3). We consider as emotional metadata a set of basic emotions (in accordance to Ekman's theory) expressed by people in the video.

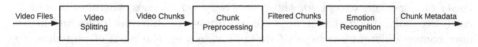

Fig. 1. The proposed methodology for automatic extraction of emotional metadata from videos.

A detailed description of each methodology step is presented in the following subsections, along with the discussion of the main issues of each phase.

3.2   Video Splitting

Video-level metadata are unable to represent variations in emotions among frames. For this reason, it is reasonable to consider a video as the composition of smaller video chunks. Such approach allows for fine-grained analysis of emotions: for instance, it permits to detect the dominant emotion (i.e., the emotion that occurs in the largest number of chunks) or the emotion expressed by a person while he/she talks about a specific product feature.

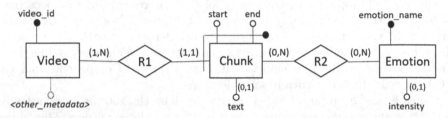

Fig. 2. Conceptual representation of the proposed model for emotional metadata. Video-level metadata are omitted.

To this purpose, we propose a simple conceptual model for emotional metadata (see Fig. 2), which is centered on video chunks. The *text* and *intensity* attributes are optional, since they respectively depend on the availability of subtitles and the output (i.e., numeric or categorical) of the chosen emotion classifier. Videos can be split into chunks following different strategies, on the basis of the desired granularity of the analysis. Generally speaking, short chunks (e.g., 2–3 s) allow for a better evaluation of emotions, since in such case the latter are usually constant.

A simple strategy consists in the use of temporal windows of fixed length. The approach is fast, as it does not require video and/or text preprocessing, but it does not offer any guarantee about the presence of a unique emotion in the chunk. Moreover, video chunks are created (and hence unnecessarily analyzed by the face analyzer) even in case of scenes without people, which represents a waste of time and computational resources. Consequently, it is preferable to adopt different strategies in order to create video chunks where there is a high probability of having people which may express emotions. For instance, the analysis could be limited to subtitled videos, since they can be split on the basis of sentences. This approach offers two advantages: first, a subtitle implies the presence of (at least) one speaker, except for those relatively rare scenes where voice-over is used. Secondly, different sentences are usually about different topics and hence may convey different emotions: if we split videos on the basis of sentences we have higher probability of obtaining video chunk with uniform emotions. The approach can be further refined by taking into account syntactical aspects: for instance the presence of adversative conjunctions (e.g., "The battery is excellent but the user interface is really confusing") in a subtitle may indicate a variation in the emotional content of the sentence and, probably, in the facial expression of the speaker. Moreover, the presence of emotion-bearing words, such as "excited" or "boring", may suggest that the speaker is subjectively talking about a topic and hence there is likely that his/her face is expressing an emotion.

3.3   Chunk Preprocessing

The accuracy of the following facial expression recognition phase strongly depends on the number of recognized key facial points in frames. Since there are many factors that can negatively impact on the process, we use some preprocessing techniques to evaluate frame quality with respect to emotion recognition and hence filter out noisy or irrelevant frames. A non-exhaustive list of factors that may affect facial expression recognition includes:

1. lateral position of face and consequent non-recognizability of an eye.
2. presence of many people in a frame, since it requires the use of more sophisticated face recognition techniques to track emotional variations of each person in the chunk.
3. phonatory movements that may alter mouth opening (e.g., the pronunciation of phonems like /ee/ or /ow/).
4. bearded men or people with glasses/hats that can mask facial points.
5. old white people, since white eyebrows are similar to skin color and are hardly detected by face detection algorithms.

In particular, in this work we focus on the first two factors and hence we analyze the presence (and number) of faces, their orientation and the recognizability of eyes and mouth in each frame. To this purpose, we use the Viola-Jones face detector [18] implemented in OpenCV 3.0, which is based on Haar features. Such classifier is often inaccurate in detecting mouth: in fact, in preliminary experiments we found that it detects several mouths in the upper part of face. Hence, we improved the technique by defining boundaries for the upper and lower part of face (see Fig. 3) and by discarding detected mouths and eyes whose coordinates were out of respective areas. In particular, we divided the face rectangle into two smaller rectangles with width equal to original width and height respectively equal to 55% (top rectangle) and 45% (bottom rectangle) of original height.

On the basis of the above-mentioned analysis, we assign a score between 0 and 10 to each frame (see Table 1) and we filter out frames with score below a certain threshold γ. Faces where less than two eyes are detected are strongly penalized, since the area around eyes contains relevant markers for the following phase of facial expression recognition. In preliminary experiments we found that $\gamma \geq 8$ offers accurate facial expression recognition.

3.4   Emotion Recognition

The goal of this step is to extract emotional metadata from video chunks produced in previous step, in which irrelevant and noisy frames have been removed.

Fig. 3. Example of mouth detection before (a) and after (b) the definition of boundaries for the upper and lower part of face. Detected mouth and eyes are discarded if their coordinates are out of respective areas.

Table 1. Classification of frame quality on the basis of recognizable faces, eyes and mouths

Score	10	9	8	7	6	5	4	3	2	1	0
Faces	1	1	1	1	1	1	1	1	2	>2	0
Eyes	2	2	2	2	1	1	0	0	0	0	0
Mouths	1	2	0	$\geq$2	1	0,>1	1	0,>1	0	0	0

To this end, relevant features are extracted and then aggregated to be fed to a facial expression classifier. The entire process is depicted in Fig. 4.

To extract facial features we use the Open-Face library[1], a tool intended for facial landmarks detection and Action Unit (AU) recognition. The Open-face software allows for the extraction of 68 characteristic facial points from each frame. The 2-D landmarks point distribution is shown in Fig. 5. Facial points are used to construct facial features for each frame. We manually define a set of 19 features, calculated as distances in pixels between some characteristic points. Note that Open-face provides both 2-D and 3-D location estimations of the 68 landmarks, but we only consider the 2-D coordinates in pixels, since the 3-D representation is intrinsically noisier because it is based on an estimation of the camera position in world space. The chosen distances between points are: {(17,33), (18,33), (19,33), (20,33), (21,33), (22,33), (23,33), (24,33), (25,33), (26,33), (38,40), (37,41), (44,46), (43,47), (51,57), (48,54), (50,58), (52,56)}.

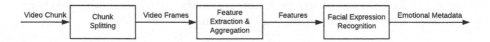

Fig. 4. The emotion recognition process.

---

[1] https://cmusatyalab.github.io/openface/.

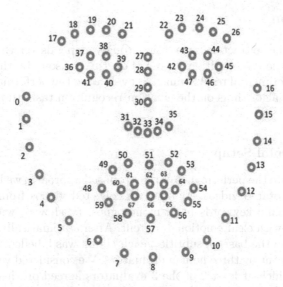

Fig. 5. The 2-D landmarks point distribution .

These distances are then normalized through division by the distance (29,30); such distance is expected to remain constant over frames as it is not affected by any facial muscle contraction. Along with the above distances we also consider AUs, since they are related to the expression of basic emotions. Open-face detects 17 AUs and assigns them a level of intensity between 0 and 5. Moreover, the presence of the "Orbicularis Oris" action unit, commonly known as "lip suck" gesture, is reported as a 0/1 value. We therefore construct a vector of 37 facial features (18 action units and 19 distances) for each frame. Since we have one feature vector for each frame, from the analysis of each chunk we obtain a feature matrix.

The subsequent step is feature aggregation among frames belonging to the same chunk: this is performed by averaging the values of each feature over the frames in the chunk. This operation has the effect of reducing the distortion introduced by phonatory movements, such as the natural mouth opening for the pronunciation of the phoneme /ee/, that could be interpreted as happiness. A problem in averaging the feature vectors related to a chunk is that, in case of video chunks containing people expressing two or more emotions that are in contrast, the aggregated feature vector will be likely classified as neutral. This issue outlines the importance of creating video chunks with homogeneous emotions.

The final step is the assignment of emotional metadata to each video chunk. To this purpose, the aggregated feature vector of a chunk is classified through supervised learning techniques. For an empirical comparison of the performance of several algorithms on a real-world video dataset see Sect. 4.

4   Evaluation

The quality of the extracted metadata strongly depends on the accuracy of the facial expression recognition model. For this reason, in this section we present some experimental results aimed at evaluating the performance of several machine learning algorithms on the emotion recognition task using a real-world video dataset.

4.1   Experimental Setup

In order to evaluate the performance of the proposed approach, we built a dataset of real-world annotated videos. At first, we collected videos from YouTube by searching for specific keywords (e.g., monologues, tv shows), with the aim of obtaining results with clear emotional content. After automatically dividing each video in chunks on the basis of subtitles, each chunk was labelled with regard to its emotional content by three human evaluators. We considered valid only those annotations in which at least 2 of the 3 evaluators agreed on the presence of a specific emotion. Similarly to [10], we limited our analysis to the following emotions: anger, happiness, neutral and sadness. Among the annotated video chunks, we randomly selected 200 chunks in order to have a balanced dataset. The class distribution is shown in Table 2: In addition to the classification accuracy, we also considered the execution time of the entire emotion recognition phase (i.e., feature extraction, aggregation and classification of facial expressions) as a key metric of the system, in order to evaluate if the proposed technique is suitable for the analysis of large amounts of videos.

Table 2. Class distribution for the considered dataset

Emotion	Number of occurrences
Anger	50
Happiness	50
Neutral	50
Sadness	50

In order to improve the quality of emotion recognition, we chose to extract features only from those frames where the confidence level of the Open-face software in detecting human faces was higher than a threshold value. We empirically verified that considering only frames with confidence above 0.95 ensures a high level of accuracy in landmark detection.

We trained several traditional classification algorithms on our features, namely Support Vector Machines (SVM), k-Nearest Neighbors (k-NN), Decision Tree (DT) and Random Forests (RF). In order to thoroughly evaluate the performance of the selected classifiers, we performed a 10-fold cross validation.

For what concerns the SVM classifier, the internal parameters were estimated through a preliminary phase of parameter optimization. We chose a C-SVC Support Vector Machine with a radial basis function (rbf) kernel and the following values for the internal parameters: $\gamma = 0.166$, $C = 0.979$ and $\epsilon = 0.049$. The SVM was trained with a 1-vs-all configuration in order to perform multiclass classification.

4.2   Results

The total execution time of the emotion recognition phase for our dataset of 200 videos (2.86 GB) is about 12 min on an laptop with an Intel i7-2670QM CPU and 8 GB RAM, which means that the system processes videos at 3.89 MB/s. Such performance allows for the analysis of large amounts of videos in reasonable times. It is also important to notice that execution time can be further reduced by considering higher sampling rates.

The experimental results for the selected classifiers are summarized in Table 3. The table clearly shows that the SVM classifier outperforms the other models, with a remarkable +13.5% improvement in accuracy with respect to k-NN. The experiments suggest that data are not linearly separable, since using a non-linear classifier (i.e., SVM with rbf kernel) results in higher classification accuracy.

The confusion matrix for the SVM classifier and the results in terms of precision and recall are reported in Table 4.

The model has recall = 0.72 and precision = 0.73, while F_1-score is $F_1 = 2 \cdot \frac{precision \cdot recall}{precision + recall} = 0.725$. The confusion matrix shows that the model has

Table 3. Accuracy of the considered algorithms estimated with 10-fold cross validation.

Algorithm	Accuracy
SVM	72%
k-NN	58.5%
DT	48%
RF	50%

Table 4. Confusion matrix for the SVM classifier

	Actual neutral	Actual happiness	Actual anger	Actual sadness
Predicted neutral	36	1	5	4
Predicted happiness	8	44	5	11
Predicted anger	2	3	35	6
Predicted sadness	4	2	5	29
Recall	**72.00%**	**88.00%**	**70.00%**	**58.00%**
Precision	**78.26%**	**64.71%**	**76.09%**	**72.50%**

high recall for happiness, anger and neutral emotions; neutral and anger classes also have the highest precision. The last column suggests that the model is less accurate in the classification of sadness, since there are many misclassifications: it indicates that our model would benefit from the introduction of more sadness-related features, i.e. point distances whose variations are strongly related to sadness.

5 Conclusion

The goal of this work was the definition of a methodology for the automatic extraction of affective metadata from videos, in order to allow for data description and analysis from an emotional perspective. To this purpose, we defined an ad-hoc emotional metadata model for videos, which is centered on the concept of video chunk. Moreover, we combined several video preprocessing techniques to filter out irrelevant frames and, hence, to speed up the subsequent metadata extraction. In order to perform emotion detection through the analysis of people's facial expressions, we also introduced a novel set of visual features for facial expression recognition.

Finally, we performed some experiments on a manually-annotated video dataset using several supervised classifiers, as to evaluate the quality of the extracted emotional metadata in terms of classification accuracy. The experimental results showed that the coupled use of action unit and point distances as features for the SVM classifier leads to state-of-the-art accuracy.

In future work, we plan to investigate further techniques to split videos, in order to create chunks with higher chances of containing strong and unambiguous emotional content. In this respect, a preliminary evaluation of techniques based on the semantic analysis of speech have demonstrated to be promising and they will need further experimentation. Another open issue is the determination of a sampling rate for frames which may represent a good compromise between accurate classification of emotions and speed of analysis. The problem is particularly relevant in presence of Big Data sources, where there is necessary to minimize execution time in order to guarantee the feasibility of the analysis. To address such problem we plan both to study the time required for a variation of emotions among consecutive frames, in order not to analyze similar frames with redundant information, and to evaluate the information loss (in terms of emotions) in case of high sampling rates. We also plan to extend the evaluation of classification algorithms for facial expression recognition by taking into account commercial tools, such as IBM Watson[2] or Microsoft Cognitive Services[3]. Another extension of this work consists on the evaluation of deep learning algorithms for facial expression recognition, which are demonstrated to obtain high accuracy in presence of large training sets. To this purpose, due to the scarcity of emotionally-annotated video datasets in literature, the creation of

---

[2] https://www.ibm.com/watson/.
[3] https://azure.microsoft.com/it-it/services/cognitive-services/emotion/.

a large manually-annotated dataset of YouTube videos for emotion recognition represents a future direction of research.

References

1. Benitez-Garcia, G., Nakamura, T., Kaneko, M.: Multicultural facial expression recognition based on differences of western-caucasian and east-asian facial expressions of emotions. IEEE Trans. Inf. Syst. **5**, 1317–1324 (2018)
2. Cohen, I., Sebe, N., Garg, A., Chen, L.S., Huang, T.S.: Facial expression recognition from video sequences: temporal and static modeling. Comput. Vis. Image Underst. **91**, 160–187 (2003)
3. Diamantini, C., Mircoli, A., Potena, D., Storti, E.: Semantic disambiguation in a social information discovery system. In: Proceedings of the 2015 International Conference on Collaboration Technologies and Systems (CTS), pp. 326–333 (2015)
4. Ekman, P.: An argument for basic emotions. Cogn. Emotion **6**, 169–200 (1992)
5. Felbo, B., Mislove, A., Sgaard, A., Rahwan, I., Lehmann, S.: Using millions of Emoji occurrences to learn any-domain representations for detecting sentiment, emotion and sarcasm. In: Proceedings of the 2017 Conference on Empirical Methods in Natural Language Processing (EMNLP), pp. 1616–1626 (2017)
6. Fourati, M., Jedidi, A., Gargouri, F.: Generic descriptions for movie document: an experimental study. In: Proceedings of IEEE/ACS International Conference on Computer Systems and Applications, AICCSA 2017, pp. 766–773, October 2018
7. Huang, J., Yuan, C.: Weighted-PCANet for face recognition. In: Arik, S., Huang, T., Lai, W.K., Liu, Q. (eds.) ICONIP 2015. LNCS, vol. 9492, pp. 246–254. Springer, Cham (2015). https://doi.org/10.1007/978-3-319-26561-2_30
8. Mircoli, A., Cucchiarelli, A., Diamantini, C., Potena, D.: Automatic emotional text annotation using facial expression analysis. In: Proceedings of CEUR Workshop 1848, pp. 188–196 (2017)
9. Mo, S., Niu, J., Su, Y., Das, S.K.: A novel feature set for video emotion recognition. Neurocomputing **291**, 11–20 (2018)
10. Poria, S., Peng, H., Hussain, A., Howard, N., Cambria, E.: Ensemble application of convolutional neural networks and multiple kernel learning for multimodal sentiment analysis. Neurocomputing **261**, 217–230 (2017)
11. Pramerdofer, C., Kampel, M.: Facial expression recognition using convolutional neural networks: state of the art. arXiv preprint arXiv:1612.02903 (2016)
12. Sailunaz, K., Dhaliwal, M., Rokne, J., Alhajj, R.: Emotion detection from text and speech: a survey. Soc. Netw. Anal. Min. **8**(1) (2018)
13. Sariyanidi, E., Gunes, H., Cavallaro, A.: Automatic analysis of facial affect: a survey of registration, representation and recognition. IEEE Trans. Patt. Anal. Mach. Intell. **37**, 1113–1133 (2015)
14. Sikos, L.F., Powers, D.M.W.: Knowledge-driven video information retrieval with LOD: Lrom semi-structured to structured video metadata. In: Proceedings of the 2015 Workshop on Exploiting Semantic Annotations in Information Retrieval (ESAIR), pp. 35–37 (2015)
15. Soltani, M., Zarzour, H., Babahenini, M.C.: Facial emotion detection in massive open online courses. In: Rocha, Á., Adeli, H., Reis, L.P., Costanzo, S. (eds.) WorldCIST'18 2018. AISC, vol. 745, pp. 277–286. Springer, Cham (2018). https://doi.org/10.1007/978-3-319-77703-0_28

16. Sun, W., Zhao, H., Jin, Z.: A complementary facial representation extracting method based on deep learning. Neurocomputing **306**, 246–259 (2018)

17. Sun, Y., Sebe, N., Lew, M.S., Gevers, T.: Authentic emotion detection in real-time video. In: Sebe, N., Lew, M., Huang, T.S. (eds.) CVHCI 2004. LNCS, vol. 3058, pp. 94–104. Springer, Heidelberg (2004). https://doi.org/10.1007/978-3-540-24837-8_10

18. Viola, P., Jones, M.: Robust real-time object detection. Int. J. Comput. Vis., 137–154 (2001)

19. Yu, Z., Zhang, C.: Image based static facial expression recognition with multiple deep network learning. In: Proceedings of the 2015 International Conference on Multimodal Interaction (ICMI), pp. 435–442 (2015)

Citizen Science Applications and Citizen Databases Workshop, CSADB

Characterizing Air-Quality Data Through Unsupervised Analytics Methods

Elena Daraio[1]([⊠]), Evelina Di Corso[1], Tania Cerquitelli[1], and Silvia Chiusano[2]

[1] Dipartimento di Automatica e Informatica, Politecnico di Torino, Turin, Italy
{elena.daraio,evelina.corso,tania.cerquitelli}@polito.it
[2] Dipartimento Interateneo di Scienze, Progetto e Politiche del Territorio,
Politecnico di Torino, Turin, Italy
silvia.chiusano@polito.it

Abstract. Several cities have built on-the-ground air quality monitoring stations to measure daily concentration of air pollutants, like PM_{10} and NO_2. The identification of the causalities for air pollution will help governments' decision-making on mitigating air pollution and on prioritizing recommendations. This paper presents a two-level methodology based on unsupervised analytics methods, named PANDA, to discover interesting insights from air quality-related data. First, PANDA discovers groups of pollutants that have occurred with similar concentrations. Then, each cluster is locally characterized through three forms of human-readable knowledge to provide interesting correlations between air pollution and meteorological conditions at different abstraction level. As a case study, PANDA has been validated on real pollutant measurements collected in a major Italian city. Preliminary experimental results show that PANDA is effective in discovering cohesive and well-separated groups of similar concentrations of pollutants along with different forms of interpretable correlations among air pollution and weather data.

Keywords: Data mining · Data exploration · Pollutant data
Meteorological data · Sensor data

1 Introduction

Several cities have built on-the-ground air quality monitoring stations to measure daily concentration of air pollutants, like PM_{10} and NO_2. The health effects of air pollutants are miscellaneous: from the less serious, like irritation of the eyes and of airways, up to the most severe, like respiratory deficiencies, cardiovascular illness and cancer development. For these reasons, it is important to raise awareness on daily actions that have an impact on the air quality. Understanding the premises of air pollution will help governments' decision-making on mitigating it and on prioritizing recommendations [20].

In urban areas, the most widespread pollutants are a result of human activity that increases their presence in the atmosphere by burning fossil fuels, building

© Springer Nature Switzerland AG 2018
A. Benczúr et al. (Eds.): ADBIS 2018, CCIS 909, pp. 205–217, 2018.
https://doi.org/10.1007/978-3-030-00063-9_20

plant stations and using cars. Once in the air, pollutants react and change their nature in terms of dangerousness for health and environmental damaging [20]. These reactions are also correlated with weather conditions because chemical processes vary depending on temperature, pressure and element concentrations [14]. Many research efforts have been devoted to address different and orthogonal issues in the area of urban computing that mainly affect air pollution in urban settings. Research contributions can be classified based on the addressed issues such as: (i) improving urban planning and easing traffic congestion [15], (ii) reducing energy consumption [3,8], and (iii) reducing air pollution [20]. Parallel research efforts have been instead carried out to address more specific issues related to the analysis of pollutant concentrations in urban settings, like: (i) discovering cause-and-effect relations among air pollutant concentrations and spatio-temporal space or meteorology [21], (ii) characterizing the environmental noise pollution in urban area [19], and (iii) discovering high-utility itemsets [7] and generalized rules [6] to characterize pollutant concentrations in urban environments.

This paper presents an exploratory data mining engine, named PANDA (PollutANt Data Analysis), whose target is to analyze air quality-related data through a two-level unsupervised methodology. Different from [6,7], PANDA analyzes pollutant concentrations along with meteorological data through a joint approach based on cluster analysis and pattern discovery. The clustering analysis allows the discovery of groups of pollutants that have occurred with similar concentrations. Each cluster is then locally characterized through three forms of human-readable knowledge to provide interesting insights easily validated by a domain expert. Specifically, each cluster, enriched with weather data, is locally characterized with (i) statistics-based indicators, (ii) heatmap representation, and (iii) correlation analysis based on association rules. As a case study, PANDA has been validated on real pollutants measurements collected during three years in a major Italian city. Preliminary experimental results show that the proposed approach is effective in discovering (a) cohesive and well-separated groups of similar concentrations of pollutants and (b) different forms of human-readable correlations among air pollution and weather data. The discovered knowledge can be easily exploited by government bodies to adopt targeted strategies to enhance air quality on urban settings. Specifically, the discovered knowledge could be used together with the weather forecast to adopt targeted strategies and actions, such as traffic block or restriction on precise areas, in order to mitigate vehicle pollution. This knowledge could also increase people's awareness through interactive dynamic dashboards where representative colors from green to red could ease the understanding of current air quality with respect to time and space dimensions.

The paper is organized as follow, Sect. 2 introduces the PANDA system and describes its main components. Section 3 discusses the preliminary experimental results obtained on real data, and Sect. 4 draws conclusions and presents the future development of this work.

2   The PANDA System

The PANDA (PollutANt Data Analysis) system adopts a two-level method-ology exploiting unsupervised machine learning techniques to analyze air pollutant-related data. The main PANDA components and their interactions are depicted in Fig. 1. PANDA focuses on air pollutant-related data in urban environments like air pollutant concentrations and weather conditions. Collected data are prepared for the subsequent analytics task exploiting cluster analy-sis along with different strategies to discover interesting correlations among air pollutant-related data. The ultimate goal of PANDA is to extract useful infor-mation by highlighting cause-and-effect relations between human behavior and environmental impact.

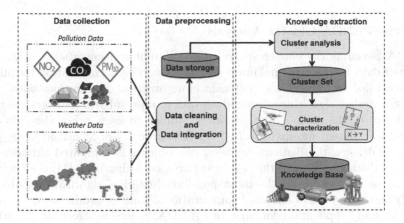

Fig. 1. The PANDA system architecture.

Specifically, PANDA includes three main components, named *Data collec-tion*, *Data preprocessing* and *Knowledge extraction*. First, the *Data collection* component collects two different measurements in the urban environment: (i) the concentration levels of the main air pollutants and (ii) weather data. Air Pollutant concentrations include the most damaging pollutants such as particu-late matters PM_{10} and $PM_{2.5}$, carbon monoxide CO, ozone O_3, nitrogen dioxide NO_2, nitric oxide NO, benzene C_6H_6, and black carbon BC. Weather conditions considered in PANDA are temperature [C], relative humidity [%], precipitation [mm], wind speed [Km/h] and atmospheric pressure [Pa].

The *data preprocessing* performs a data cleaning process to provide high-quality data for the subsequent analytics step. Pollutant concentrations and whether conditions are first cleaned separately to remove missing values and incorrect readings. Then, they are integrated with meteorological data. Since the goal is to characterize pollutant concentrations, PANDA only considers data records with values of pollutant concentrations are in the expected range of values reported in [1].

The collected measurements may adopt a different time-line in sampling pollutant concentrations and weather conditions. Thus, PANDA integrates measurements by considering a common time granularity. Since some pollutants are monitored once per day (e.g., PM_{10}), PANDA considers daily time granularity. In detail, measurements are collected from several sensors deployed a major Italian city, they are aggregated for each hour and then averaged on a daily-time period. The data produced as output of the data preprocessing are stored together in a common data repository.

Lastly, the *Knowledge extraction* component includes a two-level data analytics approach. Specifically, PANDA performs the cluster analysis on pollutant concentrations to identify groups of data with similar pollutant distributions. Each cluster is then locally characterized through different forms of correlations among pollutant concentrations and meteorological conditions.

2.1 The PANDA Cluster Analysis

PANDA performs the cluster analysis on pollutant concentrations to identify groups of data with similar pollutant distribution. The normalization technique [0,1] is applied to uniform the pollutant concentration distributions with each other. Clustering algorithms divide data into groups/subsets (clusters) so that objects within the same group are more similar to each other than objects assigned to different groups [16]. In PANDA, groups are identified using pollutants as drivers, the distance between two objects is computed through the Euclidean distance [16], and the K-means partitional algorithm [11] is exploited.

K-means [11] is one of the most popular clustering algorithm capable to identify the cluster set in a limited computational time by producing quite good results in many application domains. In PANDA, K-means algorithm partitions the pollutant concentrations into K groups, where K is defined by the user and each object is assigned to a single cluster. Each group is represented by its centroid computed as the average of all the objects in the cluster. The algorithm iteratively assigns points to the closest centroid, and then recalculate the set of centroids for the subsequent iteration.

One of the biggest drawbacks of K-means is that it requires the number of clusters to be a-priori specified. PANDA integrates a combined approach based on the analysis of (i) Sum of Squared Errors index (SSE) [16] and (ii) weighted Silhouette index [10] to automatically evaluate the quality of different configurations, to rank them accordingly, and select the best configuration for k. Specifically, the *SSE index* measures the cluster quality in terms of cluster cohesion. The total SSE is computed for all objects in the dataset, where for each object the error is computed as the squared Euclidean distance from the closest centroid. The Silhouette index [18] measures both intra-cluster cohesion and inter-cluster separation. The *weighted Silhouette index* (assuming values in [0; 1]) represents the percentage of measurements in each positive bin properly weighted with an integer value $w \in [1; 10]$ (the highest weight is associated with the first bin [1-0.9] and so on) and normalized within the sum of all the weights. The higher the weighted silhouette index, the better the identified partition.

PANDA selects as possible good values of K the coordinates where the marginal decrease in the SSE curve is maximized – the Elbow zone [16]. For these values, the weighted Silhouette index is computed and K corresponds to the highest weighted silhouette among the configurations selected through the Elbow zone.

2.2 The Cluster Characterization Phase

Clusters are anonymous groups of pollutants occurred in similar concentration levels, but more human-readable insights can be discovered and easily validated by a domain expert. To this aim, PANDA enriches the cluster set found by the K-means algorithm with temporal and meteorological information to provide three forms of human-readable knowledge: (i) statistics-based cluster characterization, (ii) heatmap representation, and (iii) correlation analysis based on association rules. While (i) focuses on the analysis of the pollutant concentrations, (ii) and (iii) highlight the correlations between air pollution and meteorological conditions for each cluster at different abstraction levels. Specifically, (ii) analyses separately the correlation between pollutants and each *single* meteorological condition and (iii) extracts interesting correlations between *sets* of pollutants and *sets* of weather attributes.

Statistics-Based Cluster Characterization. PANDA characterizes the cluster set through different methods to highlight the quality of the identified partitions in terms of well-separated and cohesive groups of pollutant concentrations. Specifically, the following methods are adopted. The (a) *singular value decomposition* (SVD) [17] is exploited to visualize the cluster set in a graphical and user-friendly way, using the first three components. Instead, (b) the boxplot distribution [17] is used to characterize each cluster content in terms of pollutant concentrations. A boxplot (whiskers plot) is a standardized way of displaying the distribution of data through their quartiles. In PANDA the boxplot is exploited to graphically verify if the pollutant level partitions are well separated for each cluster.

Heatmap Representation. Data visualization aims to ease the extraction of useful information from the data mining phase. In PANDA the heatmaps [17] are carried out to better visualize the knowledge characterizing each cluster. A heatmap is a graphical representation of data where the individual values contained in a two-dimensional matrix are represented as colors. Larger values were represented by dark colors and smaller values by lighter ones. In PANDA, heatmaps are used to provide an immediate visual summary of interesting correlations in each cluster between pollutants and a single meteorological phenomenon at a time.

Correlation Analysis Based on Association Rules. PANDA discovers interesting correlations from the cluster set in the form of association rules [4].

In PANDA rules model the correlations between sets of pollutant concentrations and sets of weather conditions. Since a transactional dataset of categorical attributes is required for the association rules extraction, PANDA applies a discretization step to convert continuously-valued measurements into categorical bins. A transactional dataset is a set of transactions in which each one is a set of items (also defined itemset). An item is represented in the form *attribute = value*. In our work, each attribute describes pollutant concentrations (e.g., PM_{10} or $PM_{2.5}$) or meteorological features (e.g., wind direction). An association rule is expressed in the form $X \rightarrow Y$, where X and Y are disjoint and non-empty itemsets. X is also called *rule antecedent* or *rule body* and Y *rule consequent* or *rule head*. PANDA includes four traditional metrics to evaluate the goodness of the extracted rules, which are *support (s)*, *confidence (c)*, *lift* and *conviction*. The *rule support* is the percentage of transactions that contain both X and Y. The *rule confidence*, instead, is the conditional probability that the consequent Y is true under the condition of the antecedent X. Lift index [16] measures the symmetric correlation between rule body and rule head of the extracted rules. Lift values above 1 (below 1) show a positive (negative) correlation between itemsets X and Y. When a rule reaches a lift equal to one, X and Y are independent and there is no correlation between rule body and rule head. Conviction [5] tackles some of the weaknesses of previous metrics and measures the degree of implication of a rule. It compares the probability that X appears without Y if they were dependent with the actual frequency of the appearance of X without Y. It is infinite for logical implications (confidence = 1), while values around 1 imply that X and Y are independent.

In PANDA rules are filtered based on their support and confidence values using the *minsup* and *minconf* thresholds. Then, selected rules are ranked according to their lift and conviction values to focus on the subset of most positively correlated and informative rules. Furthermore, the PANDA's aim is to characterize pollutant levels with respect to weather condition. Thus, association rules are locally extracted from each cluster content and each rule should satisfy the following pattern: {*pollutant level*} $\rightarrow$ {*weather condition*}.

3   Experimental Results

We carried out a preliminary validation of PANDA on a real data collection, that includes pollutant measurements collected through several sensors by the ARPA Lombardia in the central area of Milan (Italy). These data are then integrated with meteorological measurements collected from the open data source Weather Underground web service [9]. Experimental validation has been designed to address two main issues related to the effectiveness of PANDA in: (i) identifying well-separated and cohesive groups of pollutant concentrations, and (ii) discovering interesting set of patterns in order to compactly characterize each group of pollutant concentrations.

PANDA has been developed using the open source RapidMiner toolkit [2] for the cluster analysis and association rule extraction. The MATLAB toolkit

[12] has been used to analyze data distribution and to draw the heatmap representation. The cluster analysis and the boxplot characterization are performed by considering three years (from 2015 to 2017). For the association rules and heatmap representation, we gather on a single year (i.e., 2015) to better focus the characterization task. All experiments were performed on a 2.66-GHz Intel(R) Core(TM) 2 Quad PC with 8 GBytes of main memory.

3.1 Cluster Analysis

PANDA leverages the cluster analysis through K-Means to identify groups of pollutants that occurred in similar concentrations. To set the desired number of clusters K, PANDA firstly analyzes the SSE trend, then it computes the weighted silhouette to select the best configuration. Many K-means runs have been performed by varying K between 2 and 15. Figure 2 shows the SSE trend against the K parameter. Its value tends to decrease when K increases. The elbow area (circled in red in Fig. 2) includes values of K between 3 and 5. To identify a good trade-off between the number of clusters and their significance, we locally analyzed the weighted silhouette impact for the K values belonging to the elbow zone, as reported in Table 1. Based on these results, $K = 3$ is selected as good value since it corresponds to the maximization of the weighted silhouette. The cardinality of the cluster set is Cluster_1 = 146, Cluster_2 = 337 and Cluster_3 = 517.

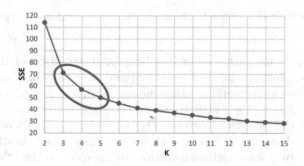

Fig. 2. SSE trend against K

Table 1. Weighted silhouette trend

K	Weighted silhouette
3	**0.404**
4	0.307
5	0.259

3.2   Cluster Characterization

Since clusters represent anonymous groups of measurements with similar pollutant concentrations, a more human-readable representation should be presented.
PANDA characterizes the cluster set through: (i) *statistics-based cluster characterization*, (ii) *heatmap representation* and (iii) *correlation analysis based on
association rules*.

Statistics-Based Cluster Characterization. Once the cluster set has been
computed, PANDA plots the *Singular Value Decomposition (SVD)* to visualize
the results in a graphical and user-friendly way, as shown in Fig. 3. Since all
clusters in Fig. 3 are well separated, K-means is able to identify a good partition
for the dataset under analysis.

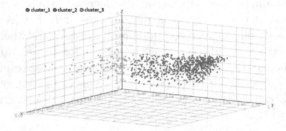

Fig. 3. Characterization of the K-Means cluster set through SVD representation.

Figure 4 shows, for each cluster, the boxplot distribution of the eight pollutants. The boxplots should be jointly analyzed. K-means has partitioned the
dataset into three well-separated and cohesive groups of homogeneous concentrations. In all clusters the distributions for the eight pollutants are quite symmetric. For all the pollutants (except O_3) *Cluster_1* is characterized by the
lowest median values, while *Cluster_3* shows a reversed trend. Lastly, *Cluster_2*
is characterized by a intermediate behavior with respect to the other clusters.

Heatmap Representation. PANDA includes the heatmap visualization to
ease the understanding of correlation between pollutant concentrations and
meteorological conditions. Figure 5 shows the heatmap analysis for two significant meteorological attributes, temperature and humidity. The two heatmaps
show how many records contain a particular attribute level for each cluster
through the color scale. All values are normalized with respect to the cluster
cardinality. Precisely, Fig. 5 (left) shows that *cluster_1* is characterized by *warm
temperature* and *cluster_3* by *cold temperature*, while *cluster_2* contains records
with *mild temperature*. This representation shows that the temperature attribute
is highly explicative for the cluster characterization. As regard Fig. 5 (right), we
observe that *high humidity* level occurs in all the clusters. This means that

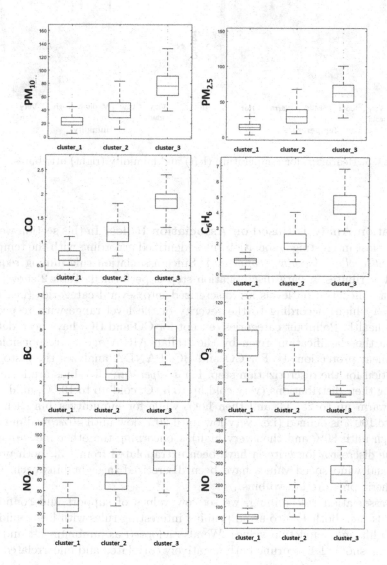

Fig. 4. Pollutant concentration distribution for K = 3

humidity and temperature are weather conditions that characterize pretty well the whole cluster set.

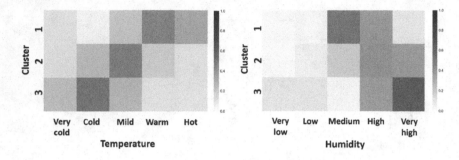

Fig. 5. Heatmaps for temperature (left) and humidity (right) attributes.

Correlation Analysis Based on Association Rules. In this section we discuss the most interesting association rules identified according with the template {*pollutant level*} → {*weather condition*}. Since association rule mining requires nominal attributes, a data discretization step is performed. Table 2 shows how pollutant concentration levels are discretized into several categories (i.e., from low to very high) according to the severity of the level range with respect to citizen's health. Pollutant categories (except for CO and BC) have been defined based on the classification given by the Italian ARPA agency responsible for environment protection [1]. For CO and BC, PANDA analyzes the histogram distribution for the discretization step. For *temperature*, five bins are identified analyzing their distributions (very cold up to 5 °C, cold up to 10 °C, mild up to 18 °C, warm up to 25 °C, and then hot), while for humidity a bin each 20% from 0 to 100% is defined (i.e., very low until 20%, low until 40%, medium until 60%, high until 80% and then very high). Concerning the other *meteorological data*, the discretization criteria have been extrapolated from [13]: both precipitation and wind speed values have been discretized in eight bins each, while atmospheric pressure in two bins.

For association rule mining, we set low values of support and confidence thresholds (i.e., both 1%) to avoid pruning interesting rules with low confidence but high lift and conviction values. We also adopted as minimum lift and conviction thresholds 1.1 to prune both negatively correlated and uncorrelated item patterns.

Table 3 shows a subset of extracted rules from Cluster_1. All of them show a positive correlation between low values of pollutant concentrations and relatively good weather conditions. When the pollutant levels are likely to be non-critical, the temperature is warm or hot, the humidity is medium, and the wind flows slowly, as described in rules R_4 and R_5. R_2 described a similar rule body characterization but the weather conditions are characterized by moderate rain and

Table 2. Pollutant concentration levels of discretization

Pollutants	Low	Medium	High	Very high
BC	0−1.5	1.5−2.5	2.5−3.5	3.5+
C6H6	0−2	2−3.5	3.5−5	5+
CO	0−1.5	1.5−2.5	2.5−3.5	3.5+
NO	0−40	40−80	80−120	120+
NO2	0−40	40−80	80−120	120+
O3	0−40	40−80	80−120	120+
PM10	0−25	25−50	50−100	150+
PM2.5	0−30	30−60	60−90	90+

low pressure. Rain can reduce pollution washing it out of the air. Rain makes the ground wet, and that makes it harder for dust to get kicked up into the air again. On a dry day, particles that have settled on tree leaves will get kicked up when the wind blows. But on a wet day, those particles will be less easy to kick up. Conversely, rules in Table 4 are extracted from Cluster_3. An inverse trend is defined. In fact, when the temperature is quite cold and the precipitations are too weak to disperse the pollutants in the air, the concentrations of the aforesaid pollutants are likely to be fairly critical. Cold temperatures and stagnant air have a way of creating a build-up of these substances near the ground, particularly

Table 3. Subset of interesting rules extracted in Cluster_1 according to the proposed template

Rid	Rule	Supp %	Conf %	Lift	Conv
R_1	{BC = low, C6H6 = low, NO = low, CO = low} → {precip = no rain, humidity = medium, temperature = warm}	4	87	7.58	7.8
R_2	{C6H6 = low, PM2.5 = low, NO = low, O3 = medium, PM10 = low, NO2 = low} → {wind speed = light air, pressure = low, precip = drizzling}	1	100	7.43	Inf
R_3	{O3 = high, BC = medium, PM10 = medium, CO = low, C6H6 = low, PM2.5 = low, NO = medium} → {precipitations = no rain, pressure = high, temperature = hot, humidity = medium}	12	80	3.80	15.00
R_4	{CO = low, PM2.5 = low, NO = medium, NO2 = medium, BC = medium, PM10 = medium, C6H6 = low, O3 = high} → {pressure = high, wind_speed = light air, humidity = medium, temperature = warm}	12	80	3.53	14.61
R_5	{O3 = high} → {temperature = hot, humidity = medium}	23	95	2.44	3.36
R_6	{PM2.5 = low, NO = medium, O3 = high} → {temperature = hot}	22	80	2.18	3.17

Table 4. Subset of interesting rules extracted in Cluster_3 according to the proposed template

Rid	Rule	Supp %	Conf %	Lift	Conv
R_7	NO = medium, PM10 = high, O3 = low, BC = very high, PM2.5 = high, CO = medium, NO2 = medium} → {pressure = high, wind speed = light breeze, precipitation = no rain, humidity = very high, temperature = cold}	15	100	2.07	Inf
R_8	{NO = very high, PM10 = high, O3 = low, BC = very high, PM2.5 = high} → {pressure = high, wind speed = light breeze, precipitation = no rain, humidity = high, temperature = cold}	17	91	1.95	5.88
R_9	{O3 = low, C6H6 = high, PM2.5 = high} → {pressure = high, temperature = cold}	24	86	1.71	2.93
R_{10}	{NO = very high, C6H6 = high, PM2.5 = high} → {temperature = cold, pressure = high}	24	82	1.71	2.93
R_{11}	{pressure = high, C6H6 = high, O3 = low, BC = very high, PM2.5 = high} → {temperature = cold}	24	82	1.71	2.93
R_{12}	{BC = very high, C6H6 = high, NO2 = medium, PM2.5 = high, PM10 = high } → {humidity = very high, temperature = cold}	20	80	1.55	2.41

during a weather phenomenon called temperature inversion. During a temperature inversion, smoke cannot rise and carbon monoxide can reach unhealthy levels, as described by rule R_7 and R_8. Moreover, air pollution caused by traffic has a more difficult time dissipating into the atmosphere (high pollutant concentration values in the rule bodies) which co-occurred during cold spells. The air pollution tends to get stuck nearer the ground.

4   Conclusion and Future Works

In this paper we presented PANDA a two-level methodology able to extract groups of pollutants that have occurred with similar concentrations together with different forms of interpretable correlations between pollutant concentrations and meteorological features. As future work, we plan to extend the PANDA engine with prediction abilities to forecast pollutant concentrations.

References

1. Regional Agency for the Protection of the Environment. http://www.arpa.piemonte.it/english-version. Accessed May 2018
2. The Rapid Miner Project. http://rapid-i.com/. Accessed May 2018
3. Acquaviva, A., et al.: Energy signature analysis: knowledge at your fingertips. In: 2015 IEEE International Congress on Big Data, New York City, NY, USA, June 27–July 2 2015 (2015)

4. Agrawal, R., Imielinski, T., Swami, A.: Mining association rules between sets of items in large databases. In: ACM SIGMOD 1993, pp. 207–216 (1993)
5. Brin, S., Motwani, R., Ullman, J.D., Tsur, S.: Dynamic itemset counting and implication rules for market basket data. ACM SIGMOD Rec. **26**(2), 255–264 (1997)
6. Cagliero, L., Cerquitelli, T., Chiusano, S., Garza, P., Ricupero, G., Xiao, X.: Modeling correlations among air pollution-related data through generalized association rules. In: IEEE International Conference on Smart Computing, 18–20 May 2016 (2016)
7. Cagliero, L., Chiusano, S., Garza, P., Ricupero, G.: Discovering high-utility itemsets at multiple abstraction levels. In: Kirikova, M., et al. (eds.) ADBIS 2017. CCIS, vol. 767, pp. 224–234. Springer, Cham (2017). https://doi.org/10.1007/978-3-319-67162-8_22
8. Cerquitelli, T., Di Corso, E.: Characterizing thermal energy consumption through exploratory data mining algorithms. In: Proceedings of the Workshops of the EDBT/ICDT 2016 Joint Conference, Bordeaux, France, 15 March 2016 (2016)
9. Data, W.U.: http://www.wunderground.com/. Accessed May 2018
10. Di Corso, E., Cerquitelli, T., Ventura, F.: Self-tuning techniques for large scale cluster analysis on textual data collections. In: Proceedings of the 32nd Annual ACM Symposium on Applied Computing, Marrakesh, Morocco, 3rd–7th April 2017 (2017)
11. Juang, B.H., Rabiner, L.: The segmental k-means algorithm for estimating parameters of hidden markov models. IEEE Trans. Acoust. Speech Sig. Process. **9**, 1639–1641 (1990)
12. MathWorks: www.mathworks.com. Accessed May 2018
13. Meteo: en.wikipedia.org/wiki/Rain en.wikipedia.org/wiki/Wind http://www.en.wikipedia.org/wiki/Atmospheric_pressure. Accessed May 2018
14. Namieśnik, J., Rabajczyk, A.: The speciation and physico-chemical forms of metals in surface waters and sediments. Chem. Speciat. Bioavailab. **22**(1), 1–24 (2010)
15. Newman, P.W., Kenworthy, J.R.: The transport energy trade-off: fuel-efficient traffic versus fuel-efficient cities. Transp. Res. Part A Gen. **22**, 163–174 (1988)
16. Pang-Ning, T., Steinbach, M., Kumar, V.: Introduction to Data Mining. Addison-Wesley, Boston (2006)
17. Ross, S.M.: Introduction to Probability and Statistics for Engineers and Scientists, 2nd edn. Academic Press, New York (2000)
18. Rousseeuw, P.J.: Silhouettes: a graphical aid to the interpretation and validation of cluster analysis. J. Comput. Appl. Math. **20**, 53–65 (1987)
19. Santini, S., Ostermaier, B., Vitaletti, A.: First experiences using wireless sensor networks for noise pollution monitoring. In: Proceedings of the Workshop on Real-World Wireless Sensor Networks, pp. 61–65. ACM (2008)
20. Zheng, Y., Capra, L., Wolfson, O., Yang, H.: Urban computing: concepts, methodologies, and applications. ACM Trans. Intell. Syst. Technol. **5**, 1–55 (2014)
21. Zhu, J.Y., Zheng, Y., Yi, X., Li, V.O.: A Gaussian Bayesian model to identify spatio-temporal causalities for air pollution based on urban big data. In: 2016 IEEE Conference on Computer Communications Workshops (2016)

Missing Data Analysis in Emotion Recognition for Smart Applications

Andrei Gorbulin[1,2], Ajantha Dahanayake[1(✉)], and Tatiana Zudilova[2]

[1] Lappeenranta University of Technology,
P.O. Box 20, 53851 Lappeenranta, Finland
Andrei.Gorbulin@student.lut.fi,
Ajantha.Dahanayake@lut.fi
[2] St Petersburg National Research University of Information Technologies,
Mechanics, and Optics (ITMO University), St Petersburg, Russian Federation
zudilova@ifmo.spb.ru

Abstract. Missing data is a widespread fundamental problem that cannot be ignored. It distorts the data, sometimes even to the point where it is impossible to analyze data at all. In emotion recognition, it is discovered that one of the best approaches to identify human emotions is by analyzing EEG (electroencephalography) results combined with peripheral signals. In this article EEG data is used to test which missing data techniques are more efficient and reliable in emotion recognition. During the research, created software is used for testing all the methods. The article concludes with techniques useful for missing data analysis, and applicable in emotion recognition applications.

Keywords: Missing data · Emotion recognition · EEG · Listwise deletion
Hot deck imputation · Linear regression analysis

1 Introduction

People use emotions to communicate with each other on a daily basis. Moreover, even a simple conversation between two people involves emotions to convey the message. This mechanism allows people to understand each other better and behave according to the situation, because the same sentence can be treated differently depending on the emotions person displays. Due to emotions being so important in human to human interaction, it is essential that interaction between human and machine is also based on emotions [1]. Furthermore, it has been proven that humans would feel more comfortably engaging with machines that can react to their emotions [2].

First an introduction of essential terms to avoid ambiguity: (1) Emotion recognition is a technique that allows machines to detect and correctly recognize human emotions; (2) A facial expression is a visible manifestation of the affective state, cognitive activity, intention, personality, and psychopathology of a person [3].

Emotions can be expressed both verbally and non-verbally. It has been discovered that it is better to use non-verbal methods, because they yield more reliable information [1]. Using non-verbal methods, information can be collected differently: by analyzing gestures, facial expressions or even using electroencephalography or magnetoencephalography [4]. An electroencephalography (EEG) is a test that detects electrical

© Springer Nature Switzerland AG 2018
A. Benczúr et al. (Eds.): ADBIS 2018, CCIS 909, pp. 218–230, 2018.
https://doi.org/10.1007/978-3-030-00063-9_21

activity in brain using small, flat metal discs (electrodes) attached to scalp [5]. Magnetoencephalography (MEG) is a noninvasive technique that detects and records the magnetic field associated with electrical activity in the brain [6].

By being able to recognize emotions correctly we can make existing technologies more human-friendly as well as when creating new ones. For example, by using emotion recognition, nursing robots can have smooth user interaction, which is especially important in this area [7]. Smart cities can also use this technology in order to have information about its inhabitants' behavior. This will reduce crime rates and prevent several mental problems people might have by notifying respective specialists in time. Additionally, this feature can be used in Virtual Reality teaching [8]: by understanding what students can feel during the lecture, teacher will have some feedback about his work, which will give him an opportunity to improve.

Despite its usefulness, emotion recognition has some major challenges and problems. In this research, we will focus on missing data.

Missing data are observations which are planned and are missing [9]. This is a fundamental problem that can be stumbled upon during any experiments or surveys. Furthermore, any kind of data acquisition is always in danger of getting results with missing values. This is by no means exception to emotion recognition. Actually, getting missing data results is one of the main problems in recognizing emotions [10], particularly in face recognition.

For example, during data acquisition process in EEG, some data is inevitably missed due to power line interference, motion artifacts, electrode contact noise, and sensor device failure [1]. Consequently, missing data distorts the results, which may lead to incorrect conclusions regarding the emotion that is displayed. Nevertheless, this problem is completely ignored for decades and only recently getting attention [10].

If emotion recognition techniques will be used in the future, it is extremely important that human emotions are recognized correctly. For nursing robots, recognized emotions are deciding factor in how they would approach interaction with a person. In emotion recognition, handling missing data correctly will give researchers working on this technology more precise data, which will increase the percentage of correctly recognized emotions.

Considering the research problem, there are three research questions:

RQ1. What are the techniques that can be used to deal with missing data?
RQ2. What are the most suitable techniques for detecting missing data in emotion recognition?
RQ3. When is each of those suitable techniques can be used?

First and foremost, in "Definition of missing data" section, classification of missing data and key concepts are explained. In the next section techniques that can be used to deal with missing data are described. After that, we introduce the methods that have been used in the past in emotion recognition. "Findings" section contains description of software that is made during research as well as the results of the tests that are conducted on methods. Finally, we conclude with the research outcomes and further research directions.

2 Definition of Missing Data

In the field of emotion recognition the missing data problem occurs quite often [1, 10]. This problem is widespread and occurs not only in this particular field, but also in sociology, political science, psychology, education and communication. Traditionally, reasons that lead to partial absence of data are impossibility of obtaining or by processing data, distortion or intentional hiding of information. Consequently, incomplete data is thrown into programs that analyze data.

Above is an example of missing data. Complete data about average temperature in Saint Petersburg [11] is shown in Fig. 1. Now, let's assume that during April and October measurement equipment is broken and we couldn't measure temperature during these periods of time. This means now we have to deal with missing values in the middle of our measurement. An example is illustrated in Fig. 2. While the measurement is conducted, data for April and October went missing and we still have to use this data with analytic software, which leads to a problem.

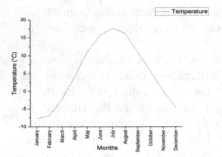 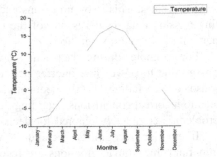

Fig. 1. Average temperature in Saint Petersburg throughout the year

Fig. 2. An example of missing data while measuring temperature

3 Techniques for Dealing with Missing Data

There are lots of techniques that can be used to deal with missing data. However, for this particular study, the easiest methods to implement and test are chosen. They are: (1) Listwise deletion; (2) Mean substitution; (3) Cold deck imputation; (4) Hot deck imputation; (5) Linear regression analysis.

3.1 Listwise Deletion

Listwise deletion (also known as complete case analysis) [12] is a method that comes to mind first when thinking about missing data problems. This method removes from the data set all the results that have missing values. It does not require any restoration of data, only conducting the following analysis without incomplete objects. Consider a hypothetical data set that has X as complete variable and Y as incomplete variable. It is

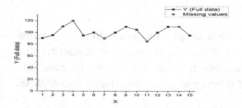 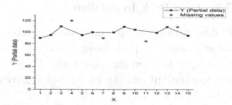

Fig. 3. Full data before listwise deletion (Color figure online)

Fig. 4. Data set after listwise deletion (Color figure online)

easy to see how this method will affect data from illustrations in Figs. 3 and 4: graph of full data and graph of data that remains after listwise deletion. Black dots represent complete data and red dots represent objects that have missing information about Y variable.

This method is used by default [13], although in reality it is "a method known to be one of the worst available". According to [13], this method should be given up in favor of hot-deck imputation method (see Sect. 3.3).

3.2 Mean Substitution

Mean substitution [12] is a wide-spread technique used by many researchers [14]. The core idea is that you simply replace missing values with mean of the values observed. In Fig. 5 an example of mean substitution on hypothetical data is presented. Black dots represent observed values; red dots represent missing values that have been replaced with mean.

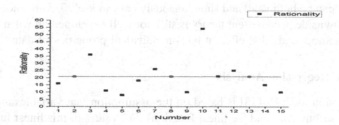

Fig. 5. Mean substitution technique (hypothetical data). Mean value is around 21. (Color figure online)

This technique has many problems. First of all, if there is a lot of missing values, it would be incorrect to replace them with mean value: it would lower the dispersion significantly [13]. Considering the fact that quite often missing values can be much lower (or higher) than mean value, this approach should only been used in some specific cases and shouldn't be go-to strategy for handling missing values [15].

3.3   Cold Deck Imputation

In this method, missing data found in input data is simply imputed with static external value (usually 0) [16]. Quite often, this value is based on the previous researches that have been done on the same topic. There is not much to be said: it provides false data just to get rid of missing values, but usually it is better to just use available data analysis methods in this case.

3.4   Hot Deck Imputation

Main idea of this method is to substitute missing value with value of another observation that is the closest to this one [13]. The thinking process is as follows: if observation is close to another observation, then it should take all the similar parameters. In the example shown in Table 1, we have two observations: observation i and observation j. When we encounter observation k, that has Z variable missing we compare k to both i and j using X and Y. In this example, k is much closer to i than to j, which means that Z should be taken from there, making it 67.

Table 1. Hot deck imputation example (hypothetical data)

Variable	Observation i	Observation j	Observation k	Observation k (restored)
X	53	25	45	45
Y	85	76	84	84
Z	67	23	?	67

Some researchers seriously advise to use this method instead of listwise and pairwise deletions as well as mean substitution [13]. This is mainly due to the fact that this method "can be both valid and simultaneously easy to use". This method also has a significant downside: a consistent theory is still not well developed on when and where to use this method, and what effect it has on statistical properties of data [17].

3.5   Linear Regression Analysis

Linear regression analysis [18] is based on the assumption that variables are collinear (somehow distributed around the linear function). So, values of this linear function can be used to substitute the missing values. As Draper mentioned [18], if you consider data lying on the linear function, then this function can be calculated as follows (for 2 variables case):

$$y(x) = a + bx.$$

The coefficients a and b can be acquired using following formulas:

$$b = \frac{n * \sum_{i=1}^{n} x_i y_i - \sum_{i=1}^{n} x_i * \sum_{i=1}^{n} y_i}{n * \sum_{i=1}^{n} x_i^2 - \left(\sum_{i=1}^{n} x_i\right)^2} \text{ and}$$

$$a = \frac{\sum_{i=1}^{n} y_i - b \sum_{i=1}^{n} x_i}{n},$$

where n is amount of observed data values.

The example of this method is in Fig. 6. As all missing values have been substituted with values that are lying on the line, which is determined with above formulas.

The main advantage of this method is that theory is well developed, however method also has a major downside. In order to use this method, have to prove that variables are collinear, and in some areas collinearity problem has been recognized as a serious problem [18].

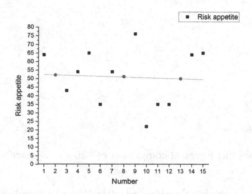

Fig. 6. Substitution of missing values using linear regression method (hypothetical data).

4 Missing Data in Emotion Recognition

Modern emotion recognition researches are based on circumplex model proposed by Russel in 1970 [19]. Particularly, this model suggests that all human emotions can be found in two-dimensional space. The successor to this model is Arousal-valence model (see Fig. 7). That is, to determine person's emotion it is enough to know his arousal and valence. And this is exactly what modern researchers do [1, 10, 20].

As mentioned in the introduction, missing data problem in emotion recognition is completely ignored until 2011 [10]. In his study, Wagner uses several methods to deal with missing data, such as: listwise deletion and cold deck imputation. Since then, only 2 studies have addressed missing data problem in emotion recognition. One of these studies [1] use restricted Boltzmann machine, which is a maximum likelihood algorithm. This is one of the methods that are not included in this study (see Sect. 3).

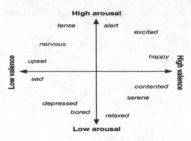

Fig. 7. Arousal-valence model [21]

As this study shows, their approach has much better results than methods used in previous study [10] (see Fig. 8).

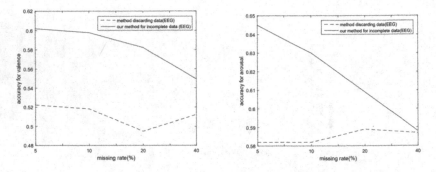

Fig. 8. Graphs that represent comparison of Shu and Wagner's studies [1]

Second study [20], which us conducted after Wagner, involved use of EM algorithm, which is also a maximum likelihood algorithm. Afterwards, restored data set is used in Bayesian network to make a decision.

5 Findings

Based on the research, software that can cope missing data problem is created. All the methods discussed in this article are implemented (see Sect. 3).

The software is created using C# language due to its simplicity and flexibility. Necessary debugging and performance measurement are conducted using standard debugging tools provided with Visual Studio. An example of working software is shown in Fig. 9. Full source code of an application is available online [22].

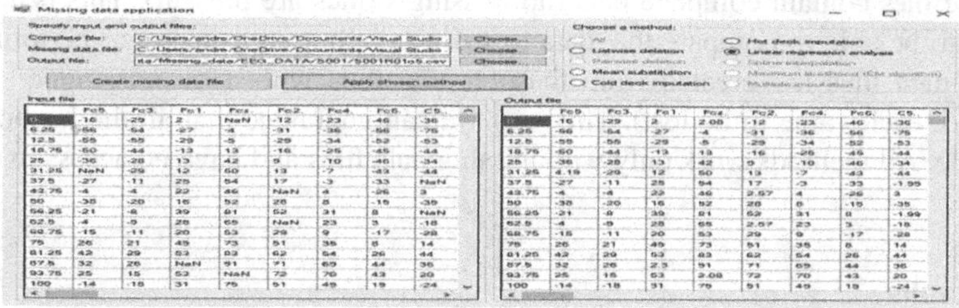

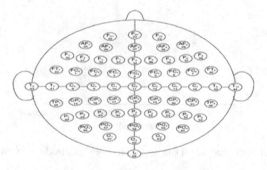

Fig. 9. Software at work. In this example, linear regression analysis is used to restore the values.

5.1 Data Description

Data that is used to conduct the experiment comes from [23]. The data itself is an EEG of 109 participants who are asked to do 14 different tasks. Each task takes about 1–2 min to complete. Recordings of each of these tasks for each participant is located in a separate EDF file. Each of these files contain information about measurements of 64 electrodes located as shown in Fig. 10.

Fig. 10. Location of electrodes [23]

Using EEGLAB software [24], these EDF files are converted into tab-delimited CSV files. This way, it is much easier to process them. Simplified structure of CSV files is shown in Table 2.

Table 2. Simplified structure of CSV files

Time (ms)	Electrode 1	Electrode 2	...	Electrode 64
0	–16	–29	...	25
6.25	–56	–54	...	36
...	...	...	...	...

These files contain complete data (no missing values are present). This is done on purpose to be able to compare this data to software's output to measure performance. Missing data files are created from these source files with 10% missingness (10% chance for each value to be lost). This way we can guarantee that all the methods are applicable. All methods work only with missing data files and have no access to source files.

5.2   Results

After the data has been processed, results are analyzed. Listwise deletion has the worst result among all methods. As in Fig. 11, pretty much all the data is deleted while using this method. From original 9760 entries, we only have 14 left. This happened due to the relatively high missingness in files.

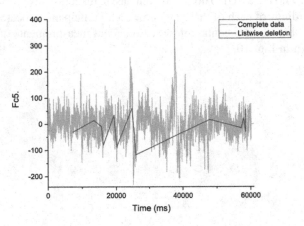

Fig. 11. Listwise deletion analysis. Data is taken from electrode Fc5 for first task by first participant.

With 10% missingness every line only has 0.9^{64} chance to make it to output, which leaves with 11.5 lines on average for every EDF file, which originally has 9760 lines. Even with only 1% missingness in files, almost 50% of data would be lost anyways. Obviously, these results cannot be treated seriously and this method should never be used if there is any risk to get more than 1% of missing data.

Imputation methods are much more promising. For imputation methods, least squares method is used to determine the best method. Main idea of least squares method is that sum

$$S = \sum_{i=1}^{n} (y_m - y_0)^2$$

should be minimized. Here y_m is value that has been imputed, y_0 is value that is actually acquired during the experiment, n is the amount of missing values. The results are shown in Fig. 12.

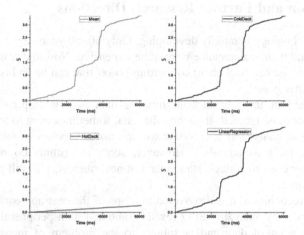

Fig. 12. Analysis of imputation methods. Data is taken from electrode Fc5 for first task by first participant.

Interestingly, three methods show very similar results. It can be explained that mean substitution, cold deck imputation and linear regression analysis are essentially doing the same thing. Due to the nature of EEG, all the values are centered around 0, which means that: (1) Mean value was 0; (2) Cold deck imputed 0; (3) Linear regression function is very similar to X axis.

This way, all of these three methods are imputing close to 0 values all the time. On the other hand, hot deck imputation method works differently; this is why its graph looks different comparing to others.

5.3   Performance Measurements

During algorithm testing, performance of all implemented algorithms are also measured using debugging tools provided by Visual Studio. The conducted results are shown in Table 3.

Table 3. Performance measurements

	Listwise deletion	Mean substitution	Cold deck imputation	Hot deck imputation	Linear regression
Time (ms)	70	24	10	144048	33

Four of these methods are quick (less than a second), while hot deck imputation is rather slow (around 2 min).

6 Conclusion and Further Research Directions

The world of technology is rapidly developing. Only 50–60 years ago computers were size of a barn and their maintenance were quite expensive. Nowadays, we have insane (compare to what we had back then) computing power that can be and is used to make life of a researcher easier.

As mentioned in the introduction, missing data is a widespread fundamental problem that cannot be ignored. It distorts the data, sometimes even to the point where it is impossible to analyze at all. Today, we can use computers to take care of that problem for us (at least partially). However, some algorithms do require serious computing power even by today's standards; but nevertheless, it is still possible to use them in near future.

In emotion recognition, it is discovered that one of the best approaches to identify human emotions is by analyzing EEG results combined with peripheral signals. EEG generates quite a lot of data and is subject to the problem of missing data. It is extremely important to find out the methods to cope with missing data that would be applicable and efficient.

We have shown that there is no clear answer. But: the listwise deletion method, which is so widely used and still is go-to strategy for most researchers, should never be used. Not only it removes huge chunks of data once missingness goes up, it makes it impossible for data to be analyzed anyhow, it is not even cost-effective. It takes much less time to use other methods instead.

Three other methods (mean substitution, cold deck imputation and linear regression analysis) have shown almost identical results. It is, however, related specifically to the way EEG works. Therefore, specifically for EEG, it is a good idea to use cold deck imputation, because of its low demand on computer resources and decent results.

Finally, hot deck imputation method prove to be the best of all tested methods. However, it is also the most demanding of them. This means that you need a good computer, or your amount of data is relatively short so speed would not be an issue, then this method is the best choice.

It is worth noting that not all available methods are tested during this research. Other methods, such as pairwise deletion, spline interpolation, EM algorithm and multiple imputation methods should all be tested. It might be one of them that is more suitable, than what we have now. Moreover, these methods should be tested under high pressure as well. Using large amounts of data to process might also change behavior of these methods. So it is definitely something that should be done in future.

Considering the level of technology that we have now, there is no real reason not to handle missing data. At very least, every researcher who is working with any kind of data acquisition, should know the basic ways to handle it. It will allow reducing the amount of mistakes that are made because of incorrect data analysis and thus make the researches more consistent and reliable. Works similar to this one should be done in every field of science to determine the best suitable techniques for researchers to use.

This way, we can build a solid basis which will help future scientists to conduct their researches more reliably.

References

1. Shu, Y., Wang, S.: Emotion recognition through integrating EEG and peripheral signals. In: 2017 IEEE International Conference on Acoustics, Speech and Signal Processing (ICASSP), pp. 2871–2875 (2017)
2. Lakin, J.L., Chartrand, T.L.: Using nonconscious behavioral mimicry to create affiliation and rapport. Psychol. Sci. **14**, 334–339 (2003)
3. Chibelushi, C.C., Bourel, F.: Facial expression recognition: a brief tutorial overview. In: CVonline: On-Line Compendium of Computer Vision, vol. 9 (2003)
4. D'mello, S.K., Kory, J.: A review and meta-analysis of multimodal affect detection systems. ACM Comput. Surv. (CSUR) **47**, 43 (2015)
5. Mayo Clinic (2018). EEG. https://www.mayoclinic.org/tests-procedures/eeg/about/pac-20393875
6. Merriam-Webster (2018). Magnetoencephalography. www.merriam-webster.com/dictionary/magnetoencephalography
7. Roy, N., Baltus, G., Fox, D., Gemperle, F., Goetz, J., Hirsch, T., et al.: Towards personal service robots for the elderly. In: Workshop on Interactive Robots and Entertainment (WIRE 2000), p. 184 (2000)
8. Farsi, M., Munro, M., Al-Thobaiti, A.: The effects of teaching primary school children the Islamic prayer in a virtual environment. In: 2015 Science and Information Conference (SAI), pp. 765–769 (2015)
9. OECD, 19 December 2005. OECD Glossary of Statistical Terms - Missing data definition. https://stats.oecd.org/glossary/detail.asp?ID=6131
10. Wagner, J., Andre, E., Lingenfelser, F., Kim, J.: Exploring fusion methods for multimodal emotion recognition with missing data. IEEE Trans. Affect. Comput. **2**, 206–218 (2011)
11. Pogodaiklimat (2018). Climate in Saint Petersburg (in Russian). http://www.pogodaiklimat.ru/climate/26063.htm
12. Graham, J.W.: Missing data analysis: making it work in the real world. Annu. Rev. Psychol. **60**, 549–576 (2009)
13. Myers, T.A.: Goodbye, listwise deletion: presenting hot deck imputation as an easy and effective tool for handling missing data. Commun. Methods Measures **5**, 297–310 (2011)
14. Acock, A.C.: Working with missing values. J. Marriage Family **67**, 1012–1028 (2005)
15. Little, R.J.: Regression with missing X's: a review. J. Am. Stat. Assoc. **87**, 1227–1237 (1992)
16. Bennett, D.A.: How can I deal with missing data in my study? Aust. New Zealand J. Publ. Health **25**, 464–469 (2001)
17. Andridge, R.R., Little, R.J.: A review of hot deck imputation for survey non-response. Int. Stat. Rev. **78**, 40–64 (2010)
18. Draper, N.R., Smith, H.: Applied Regression Analysis, vol. 326. Wiley, New York (2014)
19. Russell, J.A.: A circumplex model of affect. J. Pers. Soc. Psychol. **39**, 1161 (1980)
20. Cohen, I., Sebe, N., Gozman, F., Cirelo, M.C., Huang, T.S.: Learning Bayesian network classifiers for facial expression recognition both labeled and unlabeled data. In: 2003 IEEE Computer Society Conference on Computer Vision and Pattern Recognition, Proceedings, p. I (2003)

21. Graziotin, D., Wang, X., Abrahamsson, P.: Understanding the affect of developers: theoretical background and guidelines for psychoempirical software engineering. In: Proceedings of the 7th International Workshop on Social Software Engineering, pp. 25–32 (2015)
22. Gorbulin, A.: Missing data (2018). https://github.com/host-ru/Missing-data
23. Physionet (2009). EEG Motor Movement/Imagery Dataset. https://www.physionet.org/pn4/eegmmidb/
24. Delorme, A., Makeig, S.: EEGLAB: an open source toolbox for analysis of single-trial EEG dynamics including independent component analysis. J. Neurosci. Methods **134**, 9–21 (2004)

Overview of Data Storing Techniques in Citizen Science Applications

Jiri Musto$^{(\boxtimes)}$ and Ajantha Dahanayake

Lappeenranta University of Technology, 53850 Lappeenranta, Finland
{Jiri.Musto,Ajantha.Dahanayake}@lut.fi

Abstract. Interest in citizen science and the number of related projects have increased considerably during the last decade. Citizen science revolves around gathering data and using it. This means, that data storing is a vital part of any citizen science project and can affect the success or failure. Many researches focus on the citizen side, while the data side is often left out. This study aims to fill the gap by trying to find the current data storing practices in the field of citizen science. A systematic literature review was conducted and multiple similarities in data storing and management techniques were identified between different citizen science projects. Results show that most projects used a traditional relational database to store data, a separate web interface to add, use, modify, and access the data, and data validation was left to users by having them vote on existing data. Data models always considered the data provider (citizen) but left out the end user in their design. In the future, the results will be compared to ongoing citizen science project and see if it is possible to improve the efficiency and overall quality of citizen science databases.

Keywords: Citizen science · Data storing · Data management

1 Introduction

Citizen science has had different definitions over the years [1]. Oxford dictionary defines citizen science as "The collection and analysis of data relating to the natural world by members of the general public, typically as part of a collaborative project with professional scientists" [2].

In this research, citizen science is defined as a field where citizens participate in collecting, analyzing or reporting data for some purpose. The purpose can be scientific research, to provide information for other citizens, or to provide data for government. The citizens can be the end users but not always. The following terms have been associated with or used as synonyms to citizen science: crowdsourcing, community-based monitoring, public participation, volunteer monitoring, volunteered geographic information (VGI) [1, 3–5].

The concept of citizen science is not particularly new as it has been around for decades. However, it did not come into a wider usage until the first web based citizen science project eBird launched in 2002 by the Cornell Lab of Ornithology in New Zealand [6, 7]. Other projects can be easily found for example from SciStarter [8] to Zooniverse [9].

© Springer Nature Switzerland AG 2018
A. Benczúr et al. (Eds.): ADBIS 2018, CCIS 909, pp. 231–241, 2018.
https://doi.org/10.1007/978-3-030-00063-9_22

Table 1 gives a collection on different projects and most are found through websites. The interaction type is classified into one of the three possibilities depending on the primary end user of data: citizen-citizen, citizen-government, and citizen-researcher. These projects collect data and involve citizens in different ways, not just by going out and gathering data with sensors.

Table 1. Citizen science projects

Project	Observation	Interaction type
Galaxy Zoo	Citizens observe and identify objects in space	Citizen – Researcher
Fossil Finder	Citizens observe fossils in Kenya	Citizen – Researcher
ISEEChange	Citizens observe weather sightings	Citizen – Researcher
Globe at Night	Citizens observe constellations	Citizen – Citizen
iNaturalist	Citizens observe nature	Citizen – Citizen
WildPaths	Citizens observe wildlife road crossing	Citizen – Government
FixMyStreet [10]	Citizens observe roads	Citizen – Government
OpenStreetMap [11]	World Map	Citizen – Citizen

Data gathering and storing are a vital part of citizen science, which makes databases, database management systems (DBMS), data models and data structures important for citizen science projects.

The purpose of this literature review is to find out what are the current data models, data structures, databases, and DBMS used in different fields of citizen science.

The main research question is "What type of data storing techniques and technologies are used in citizen science applications?" This question can be answered by answering the following sub-questions:

- What type of databases are common in citizen science applications?
- What are the varieties of data models and structures in citizen science applications?

A systematic literature review is conducted on citizen science applications in order to answer the questions above.

2   Literature Review on Citizen Science Data Models

This research used the systematic literature review method to find relevant articles related to citizen science databases, data models, or data structures. Six different queries are used to narrow down the possible results. The search results are from 2008 onwards as the area of citizen science had not been largely researched before it. A single query for finding out different data models or data structures is created. As mentioned in the introduction, citizen science has multiple terms associated with it and the terms used are given in the Table 2 below.

Table 2. Queries to databases – Springer format.

Query
"citizen science" AND ("data model" OR "data struct*")
"community-based monitoring" AND ("data model" OR "data struct*")
"public participation" AND ("data model" OR "data struct*")
"volunteer monitoring" AND ("data model" OR "data struct*")
"volunteered geographic information" AND ("data model" OR "data struct*")
"participatory sensing" AND ("data model" OR "data struct*")

Systematic literature review is conducted in following scientific databases: ACM, IEEE, Scopus, Springer, and Web of Knowledge. Figure 1 shows the number of papers in each phase.

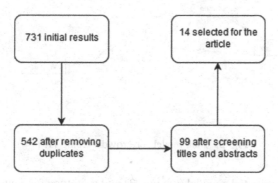

Fig. 1. Systematic literature review results

3 Results

For this article, we decided to use 14 articles that provide diverse information regarding the state of citizen science data models, architectures, databases and how they are applied in applications.

Veen et al. [12] present an object-oriented relational data model for citizen science observation. Their approach was compared to Darwin Core, Access to Biological Collection Data (ABCD), and R2000. The model was found to have an improved integration and ease-of-use, but it imposed more constraints on data and data provider.

Lukyanenko et al. [13] proposed an attribute-based model to replace an instance-based structure. This model was meant to increase participation in citizen science projects. The benefit of this model is that the users are not required to have exact knowledge on the things surveyed as they can use attributes to describe what they have seen so more amateurs can join the project and contribute information. The limitation in this model is that not all things can be expressed through attributes, such as general categories like animals or vehicles. In a later research, Lukyanenko et al. [14] noted that an attribute or instance -based data structure can potentially be better than class-based data structures as they can lead to higher quality, accuracy and flexibility. The attribute-based design can have challenges like having too many attributes to cover.

Cuong et al. [15] created a generic data model for crowdsourcing (see Fig. 2) to cope with data uncertainty. This model was applied to an emergency response setting, where citizens can inform about possible emergencies. The model has citizens to vote on reports to measure their validity. While the model itself could be applied to a variety of situations, there is no detailed design. The application of the data model and a detailed design is left to the user of the model as specific attributes are outside of the data model.

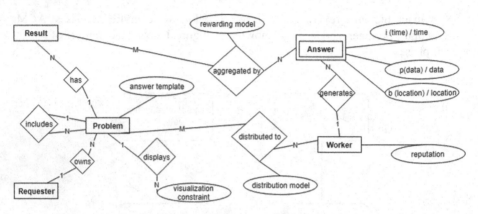

Fig. 2. Data model for crowdsourcing [15]

Zhao et al. [16] created a model (see Fig. 3) and prototype for a citizen VGI system, which was implemented on a PostgreSQL database. The model considers the user's reputation and trustworthiness to assess the reliability and quality of the data that user feeds to the system. However, it does not necessarily mean that the information given by the most trustworthy person is always the best. Another problem is that the system needs an initial reputation model to be accurate and this initial model is based on registration information of the user, which can lead to privacy issues.

Sheppard et al. [17] tackled the challenges of provenance in citizen science. They created a review and rating system for each data report users gave. Other users could contribute to the original submission by adding new information such as pictures and multiple historical versions on the same event can be stored in the database for other uses. The researchers argued that while their model creates more difficulties to new users and possible performance issues, their model's flexibility and provenance capabilities are worth the additional complexity as most of the performance issues can be managed through various technical means.

Sofos et al. [18] created a new framework for VGI to be used with collaborative network-based concepts. These concepts include a reference network and the usage of networked devices. The concepts were added to reduce errors in measurements for increased data quality and credibility. For example, if multiple participants gathered data on the same location from different viewpoints, the measurement results could be

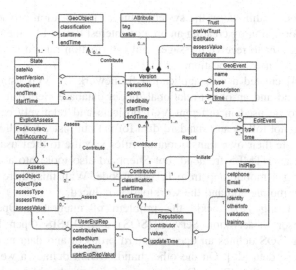

Fig. 3. UML representation of a data model for volunteered geographical information with trust-related information [16]

compared against each other and corrected appropriately. The test design was composed of a web application and a database using MySQL. Their results show that the networking reduced the amount of errors by a considerable amount and additionally reduces the number of collected data points to achieve same results.

Bröring et al. [19] designed a platform for mapping car-sensor data. Their design uses a NoSQL database and the data model was inspired by the Observations & Measurements standard of the Sensor Web Enablement initiative at the Open Geospatial Consortium. The backend was created as a separate entity from the frontend so that the data could be accessed with Representational state transfer (REST) APIs [20]. These work with HTTP protocol using POST or GET requests to return a JSON formatted data from the backend to the frontend. The key contribution was the design of the system that can be reused in collecting sensor data from cars [19].

Kotsev et al. [21] created an architecture for a service-enabled sensing platform. They tested different hardware and software in their research. Most notably, they compared three different relational databases (SQLite, H2 and PostgreSQL) and nothing outside of relational databases.

In 2011, Rees et al. [22] created a web application for monitoring rabies. Their design split the system into an SQL Server with a relational DBMS and a web API for a frontend. The design included the ability to monitor citizen participation regionally. With this, the system owners can design incentives to encourage more people to participate in the areas where citizen participation is decreasing. The data integration and storage architecture are used for the development of similar databases.

Havlik et al. [23] designed a new framework for citizen science. In their design, a NoSQL database CouchDB with a document-oriented database was employed. They found out that this design increased flexibility in the data model and as the database was easy to replicate on frontend and backend, it increased the system's usability on unstable networks. Additionally, the system handles the location privacy issue when trying to find information by creating an area of interest defined by the user. This area of interest allows user to receive messages and information related to that area and it eliminates the need of exact location.

Sheppard [24] created a web application framework for VGI using Django and Python for backend and an object-relational model database GeoDjango. The framework is meant to be used in different VGI projects and relatively easy to use and configure. It does not follow any standard data format but instead, it allows the system developers to create their own transformation rules specific to their usage. The application employed an HTML5 frontend, but Sheppard also took into account the possibility of creating a mobile app from HTML5 code. With this, there is no need to design a separate mobile app and the workload is reduced.

Huang and Liang [25] tackle the problem of integrating Open Geospatial Consortium Sensor Observation Service (SOS) and OASIS Open Data Protocol (OData) together. SOS defines an open standard protocol and data model for sensor devices and sensor data [26]. On the other hand, OData defines a web protocol for querying and updating data [27]. OData is meant for general public and SOS is meant for used with sensors only. Having different data models and structures make it difficult to use and export data to other sources, so it was necessary to create an adapter between two different models.

Soranno et al. [28] designed a database to handle a massive amount of data centred around lakes in the US. The data was collected from multiple different sources and integrated into one relational database. Lakes are the core identifier in their relational database model and other information such as data originator, climate, topography, and road density around the lake area are connected to the core identifier. The design has to handle data for 50 000 different lakes. While the study is not directly related to citizen science but rather data re-use, it provided good insights. The researchers found out that a long or vertical data matrix format is more flexible for storage and manipulation. Their conclusion is that when integrating datasets from different sources, numerous steps are required from experts. The data can be in different formats and have different data structures across the datasets so that they first need to be transformed into one generalized structure to effectively upload them into one database. Another step is to automate this process, if the amount of datasets surpass the amount researchers can manually process.

In Table 3, a collection of the reviewed articles, their respective database, frontend design, application of provenance, and the observation usage is presented. The observations-column shows that the designs and applications have been used in a variety of different fields but all of them revolve around spatial data. Six of the reviewed articles do not apply the designed data model in an actual application, and one of the models is a data integration model for two different data models.

Most projects employed their frontend with HTML and JavaScript. Some only mentioned employing a web interface without any specific programming language but it can be assumed, that HTML and JavaScript were used. One project used the ArcGIS engine as the user interface for testing but did not create an actual frontend. With web technology it is easier to reach multiple users and upkeep the frontend compared to a traditional desktop application or even a mobile application.

Table 3. Database and frontend implementations from the reviewed articles.

Article	Database and DBMS	Frontend	Provenance	Observations
Veen et al. [12]	Relational	–	Yes	Species
Huang and Liang [25]	–	–	–	–
Zhao et al. [16]	Relational, PostgreSQL	ArcGIS	Yes	Geographical information
Rees et al. [22]	Relational, RageDB	Web interface	Yes	Rabies
Sofos et al. [18]	Relational, MySQL	HTML/JavaScript/PHP	Yes	Land
Kotsev et al. [21]	Relational, PostgreSQL	Web interface	Yes	Soil moisture
Soranno et al. [28]	Relational, PostgreSQL	–	Yes	Lakes
Sheppard et al. [17]	–	Web interface	Yes	Weather example
Lukyanenko et al. [13]	Relational	–	Yes	Flora and fauna
Cuong et al. [15]	–	–	Yes	Emergency example
Bröring et al. [19]	NoSQL, MongoDB	Web interface	Yes	Car data
Havlik et al. [23]	NoSQL, CouchDB	HTML5/JavaScript	Yes	Trees and pollen
Lukyanenko et al. [14]	Relational	–	–	–
Sheppard [24]	Relational, GeoDjango	HTML5/JavaScript	–	Geographical information

In Table 4 are four additional projects listed from Brovelli's [29] for comparison with the reviewed articles. It shows similar results to the reviewed articles. Many other DBMSs are not found in citizen science usage but could be considered as viable solutions such as SQLite, Apache Cassandra, HBase, Scalaris, and OrientDB among others.

Figures 2 and 3 show examples of data models used for citizen science applications from their respective articles. Figure 2 has a general entity-relationship model without more detailed attributes and Fig. 3 has a UML representation of the data model.

There are similarities in both models such as the Worker in Fig. 2 and Contributor in Fig. 3. These have their own reputation, which is shown to other users and they are linked to reputation or a report (GeoEvent, Answer). The rewarding model in Fig. 2 is similar to Assess in Fig. 3. In those places, the other citizens vote for the validity and accuracy of the report.

Table 4. Project examples from Brovelli's [29]

Article	Database and DBMS	Frontend	Provenance	Observations
Land cover validation game	Relational, MySQL	Angular.js/Web interface	–	Land
Osaka bike parking report	Relational, PostgreSQL	JavaScript/Web interface	–	Bike parks
Via Regina	NoSQL, CouchDB	Cross platform	–	Buildings
PoliCrowd 2.0	Relational, PostgreSQL	Cross platform	–	Participatory platform

Aside from similarities, there are some glaring differences as well. In Fig. 2, there is an answer template mentioned in the model, which would be useful to get more accurate data. Additionally, in Fig. 2 the end user is taken into account as the Requester of data while in Fig. 3, there is no mentioning of the probable end user.

4   Implications and Discussion

This literature review demonstrated recurring themes in citizen science applications. First, most applications employ a relational database for their design. This can be explained with the fact, that alternative ways are not common knowledge until recently and most people are taught to use relational databases. Some of the relational database models implement an object-oriented relational model but they are still relational databases [13, 16, 18, 21, 22, 24, 28]. Havlik et al. [23] used a NoSQL database for their design and found it better than a relational database. On the other hand, Kotsev et al. [21] tested three different relational databases for their own work and disregarded NoSQL options entirely. This shows that not all database options have been evaluated properly and most database models are designed solely on relational databases. The relational models can be transformed into NoSQL models, but they might not be as effective if they are not optimized.

In one article outside the literature review, a citizen science project is constructed using SQL Server. The project observed mammals, birds, reptiles and amphibians. The project used mobile app and excel spreadsheet for data uploading. While the original version used SQL server, the researches decided to change to MongoDB in the future to allow easier data processing and integration from multiple sources and faster content delivery to users [30].

Another recurring design in newer publications is that the database and backend are separate from the frontend and the data is accessed through REST APIs or some remote interface. This improves the usability of most designs as the backend is not tied down to a frontend and can then be used in multiple different scenarios. However, it does impose some challenges if the remote interface is not following any standards or there is not enough documentation on how it works [19, 21–24].

Most papers described a system where other users can rate or improve pre-existing data. The voting system can be combined to a reputation model that shows which users are trustworthy and provide more data that is accurate. This improves the data quality and accuracy as long as most users behave correctly and do not abuse the rating system for their own benefit. When correcting the data, it can be modifiable or require a new submission. A new submission is easier for the database but can be confusing for users, so it can be easier if the existing data can be modified by the owner or by other users. This can lead to issues on access and misuse, as other users need to have access to the data to be able to modify [12, 15–19, 21, 23].

Finally, many models and applications consider or implement provenance in their design. Provenance is important because knowing the origin of data increases the possibility of validating the data. This increases data quality and accuracy, which will reflect on the usage of the data. The models and applications handle provenance either explicitly or directly by design. Most models record the location and time information for each data. When that data is combined to specific users, the provenance of data is fulfilled [12, 13, 15–19, 21–23, 28].

5 Conclusions

In this article, we present a systematic literature review on citizen science databases, data models and data structures.

Citizen science covers a variety of research fields, which means that the data needed for each project change. The most common database for citizen science applications is a relational database, most notably PostgreSQL. An object-oriented relational model is employed in few cases, but the dominant option is a traditional relational data model. In two cases, a NoSQL solution is used.

All data structures and models had some common ground. Data provenance is taken into account in most data models. Most had location and time data included in their data model and in all cases, the spatial data had some information about the originator. Most papers included some type of voting system for data validation. Other users could rate and give scores depending on how accurate that data is. This does raise some issues with misuse and harassment.

In newer papers, the backend and frontend are separated from each other to create simplicity and modularity. This also adds flexibility to modifications and reuse of either the front or the backend.

From these points, we can conclude that relational databases are the most common databases in citizen science applications and almost every data model have data provenance, separate backend and frontend, and a rating system to have participants rate each other's data.

In most cases, the end user of the data is not actually taken into account in the design of the data model or data structure and only the participant is considered. This is a limited view of the whole database design if the other end of the spectrum is not considered. The designed database might be easy for participants to add new data into but the end users who use that data might have difficulties. These end users can vary from software designers, to scientists or normal citizens. In the worst case, the end users have to be experts to be able to use the collected data. There should be a relatively easy way to use the collected data to get more benefits from the citizen science project.

There are few limitations to this research. Although the starting sample is quite big, the reduction to only 14 papers gives limitations to the generalisability of this research. Another limitation is that some papers might have been lost during the citation export from scientific database to a referencing software.

In the future, ongoing citizen science projects will be selected for closer inspection to see if they have these similarities implemented in their systems and if others arise. These common features will be closely inspected to see how they are designed and if they could be enhanced or redesigned to improve efficiency and overall quality in citizen science databases. Additionally, data quality is often a major issue in citizen science databases and it is be affected by the data model and the chosen technology. With correct techniques and technologies, the quality of data can also be improved which then leads to more efficient citizen science projects and better results.

References

1. See, L., Mooney, P., Foody, G., Bastin, L., Comber, A., Estima, J., et al.: Crowdsourcing, citizen science or volunteered geographic information? The current state of crowdsourced geographic information. ISPRS Int. J. Geo-Inf. **5**(5), 55 (2016)
2. Definition of citizen science in English by Oxford Dictionaries. https://en.oxforddictionaries. com/definition/citizen_science. Accessed 26 Jan 2018
3. United States Environmental Protection Agency Office of Water. Starting Out in Volunteer Monitoring (2012). https://www.epa.gov/sites/production/files/2015-10/documents/2009_06_12_monitoring_volunteer_startmon.pdf
4. Conrad, C., Hilchey, K.: A review of citizen science and community-based environmental monitoring: issues and opportunities. Environ. Monit. Assess. **176**, 273–291 (2011)
5. SciStarter - What is citizen science. https://scistarter.com/. Accessed 25 Apr 2018
6. New Zealand eBird. http://ebird.org/content/newzealand/. Accessed 26 Jan 2018
7. Wikipedia eBird. https://en.wikipedia.org/EBird/. Accessed 26 Jan 2018
8. SciStarter. https://scistarter.com/. Accessed 20 Apr 2018
9. Zooniverse. https://www.zooniverse.org/. Accessed 20 Apr 2018
10. FixMyStreet. https://www.fixmystreet.com/. Accessed 26 Apr 2018
11. OpenStreetMap. https://www.openstreetmap.org/. Accessed 26 Apr 2018
12. Veen, L., Van Reenen, G., Sluiter, F., Van Loon, E., Bouten, W.: A semantically integrated, user-friendly data model for species observation data. Ecol. Inf. **8**, 1–9 (2012)
13. Lukyanenko, R., Parsons, J., Wiersma, Y.: Citizen science 2.0: data management principles to harness the power of the crowd. In: Jain, H., Sinha, A.P., Vitharana, P. (eds.) DESRIST 2011. LNCS, vol. 6629, pp. 465–473. Springer, Heidelberg (2011). https://doi.org/10.1007/978-3-642-20633-7_34
14. Lukyanenko, R., Parsons, J., Wiersma, Y.: The IQ of the crowd: Understanding and improving information quality in structured user-generated content. Inf. Syst. Res. **25**, 669–689 (2014)
15. Cuong, T.T., Mehta, P., Voisard, A.: DOOR: a data model for crowdsourcing with application to emergency response. In: Giaffreda, R., Cagáňová, D., Li, Y., Riggio, R., Voisard, A. (eds.) IoT360 2014. LNICST, vol. 151, pp. 265–270. Springer, Cham (2015). https://doi.org/10.1007/978-3-319-19743-2_37

16. Zhao, Y., Zhou, X., Li, G., Xing, H.: A spatio-temporal VGI model considering trust-related information. ISPRS Int. J. Geo-Inf. **5**, 10 (2016)
17. Sheppard, S., Wiggins, A., Terveen, L.: Capturing quality: retaining provenance for curated volunteer monitoring data. In: Proceedings of the 17th ACM Conference on Computer Supported Cooperative Work and Social Computing, ACM, New York (2014)
18. Sofos, I., Vescoukis, V., Tsakiri, M.: Applications of volunteered geographic information in surveying engineering: a first approach. In: Bação, F., Santos, M.Y., Painho, M. (eds.) AGILE 2015. LNGC, pp. 53–72. Springer, Cham (2015). https://doi.org/10.1007/978-3-319-16787-9_4
19. Bröring, A., Remke, A., Stasch, C., Autermann, C., Rieke, M., Möllers, J.: enviroCar: a citizen science platform for analyzing and mapping crowd-sourced car sensor data. Trans. GIS **19**, 362–376 (2015)
20. Fielding, R., Taylor, R.: Architectural styles and the design of network-based software architectures. University of California, Irvine Doctoral dissertation (2000)
21. Kotsev, A., Pantisano, F., Schade, S., Jirka, S.: Architecture of a service-enabled sensing platform for the environment. Sensors **15**, 4470–4495 (2015)
22. Rees, E., Gendron, B., Lelièvre, F., Coté, N., Bélanger, D.: Advancements in web-database applications for rabies surveillance. Int. J. Health Geograph. **10**, 48 (2011)
23. Havlik, D., Egly, M., Huber, H., Kutschera, P., Falgenhauer, M., Cizek, M.: Robust and trusted crowd-sourcing and crowd-tasking in the future Internet. In: Hřebíček, J., Schimak, G., Kubásek, M., Rizzoli, Andrea E. (eds.) ISESS 2013. IAICT, vol. 413, pp. 164–176. Springer, Heidelberg (2013). https://doi.org/10.1007/978-3-642-41151-9_16
24. Sheppard, S.: wq: A modular framework for collecting, storing, and utilizing experiential VGI. In: Proceedings of the 1st ACM SIGSPATIAL International Workshop on Crowdsourced and Volunteered Geographic Information. ACM, California (2012)
25. Huang, C.-Y., Liang, S.: A sensor data mediator bridging the OGC Sensor Observation Service (SOS) and the OASIS Open Data Protocol (OData). Ann. GIS **20**, 279–293 (2014)
26. OGC - Sensor Observation Service. http://www.opengeospatial.org/standards/sos. Accessed 19 Apr 2018
27. OData - the Best Way to REST. http://www.odata.org/. Accessed 20 Apr 2018
28. Soranno, P., Bissell, E., Cheruvelil, K., Christel, S., Collins, S., Fergus, C., et al.: Building a multi-scaled geospatial temporal ecology database from disparate data sources: fostering open science and data reuse. GigaScience **4**, 28 (2015)
29. Brovelli, M.: Citizen Generated Content and FOS participative platforms VGI, Lecture Notes (2016). https://earth.esa.int/documents/973910/2642313/MB3.pdf
30. Bonacic, C., Neyem, A., Vasquez, A.: Live ANDES: mobile-cloud shared workspace for citizen science and wildlife conservation. In: IEEE 11th International Conference on e-Science 2015, pp. 215–223. IEEE, Germany (2015)

Data Provenance in Citizen Science Databases

Nikita Tiufiakov[1,2], Ajantha Dahanayake[1(✉)], and Tatiana Zudilova[2]

[1] Lappeenranta University of Technology,
P.O. Box 20, 52851 Lappeenranta, Finland
Tyfyakov@gmail.com, Ajantha.Dahanayake@lut.fi
[2] ITMO University, St. Petersburg, Russian Federation
zudilova@ifmo.spb.ru

Abstract. Today, more and more scientific groups are developing citizen science applications. Citizen science is a relatively new domain of science that has already proved to be as beneficial as classical science. One of the major challenges citizen science face is the data quality assurance. It uses several techniques to verify the data quality based on expert evaluation, voting systems, etc. Data provenance is used in many scientific systems and provides reliable mechanism for tracking data history. It includes history of origin, changes, and all interactions between different parts of data. Data provenance by itself has many types such as "Why provenance", "When provenance", and "What provenance". The purpose of this work is to build a prototype of a database with built-in data provenance. Several databases systems and models such as Relational databases, NoSQL databases are taken into consideration. Experiments are been conducted to test limitations of proposed prototype.

Keywords: Citizen science · Databases · Probabilistic databases
Deterministic databases · Data provenance
Scientific workflow management system

1 Introduction

Citizen Science is a relatively new platform for voluntary participation of amateur scientists in scientific endeavors; it has proved its relevance and value on the same level as classical science [1]. Its main objective is to contribute data, monitor the problem and help find the solution. The example of citizen science is a reporting application. It collects data from volunteers, and further used by the scientists. For instance, citizens may want to report about water pollution in the local lake or to report about fires in the forest. Citizen science allows to expand research capacity while providing stimulating opportunities for participants, engaging volunteers directly in conservation science and management, and improving science and environmental literacy.

During the recent years, this field of science has grown rapidly [2]. There are many societies of citizen science established around the world. Universities, international and national organizations with the government agencies have recognized its potential and use citizen science for their work. Moreover, many of new formed organizations devoted to the citizen science have very strong goals [2]. Although citizen science creates huge amount of data with the potential for scientific progress facilitation, data

A. Benczúr et al. (Eds.): ADBIS 2018, CCIS 909, pp. 242–253, 2018.
https://doi.org/10.1007/978-3-030-00063-9_23

quality verification is still one of the issues due to limitations of existing database structures [3]. Data validation is important for checking its usefulness and relevance by establishing the quality. In citizen science applications with such domains as biology and ecology, data without validation or species without proper recognition are considered having limited value [4].

Today there are a lot of citizen science databases. However, data validation is still a huge issue. The idea of the article is to study provenance structure in terms of citizen science using a particular case study considering several provenance techniques for database models and to evaluate its influence.

Based on these considerations the following research questions have been formulated:

- What is the provenance data and what applications use it and what kind of applications benefit from it?
- What are the benefits of provenance in databases?
- How provenance structure may be applied to citizen science application databases?

Several database systems have been considered during an implementation phase, and NoSQL has been chosen. The research approach is qualitative and uses systematic literature review.

2 Literature Review

A systematic literature review [19] is conducted on scientific databases ACM, IEEE, Springer, Science direct, and Web of science using the key words "Citizen Science", "Citizen Science Databases", "Citizen Science database design", "data provenance", "data quality verification", "citizen science provenance". The publications are searched between 2010 and 2017, and includes several books [1, 5, 6].

2.1 Citizen's Science

Since technologies and Internet are evolving, it brings more and more ways for problem solving and citizen science is one of them. It is a relatively new domain of science that allows people to participate in the scientific process by contributing data. In this case, citizens are volunteers who are making observations, collecting data, making measurements and finally interpreting data without any scientific knowledge. By doing so, citizens are able to improve science by making such observations around the world in a way that would not be possible earlier [7]. The Internet has enabled the existence of citizen science projects that can be accomplished online, making it possible to attach media files such as videos, photos, and audios.

Citizen science also has been powered by statistical tools and computational techniques for complex data analysis. Existence of mobile phones and wearable devices have made participation possible for social groups that are not served enough by citizen science before [8]. Despite its young age, citizen science has already proved relevance and ability to be as beneficial as classical science [1]. Moreover, during the 2013 US government recognized the value of this domain and White House's Office of

Science and Technology hosted the Citizen Science Champions of Change event for honoring the scientists whose works have been based on crowdsourcing or citizen science [7].

Typically, citizen science applications are used in astronomy, ecology and biology. One of the greatest examples of citizen science is eBird. This application absorbs all the data about birds' population. There are over 5 million observation every month about birds across the world that are done by this app. All observations are queried to the central database where they can be collected, analyzed and documented [8]. Besides eBird, there are huge variety of existing citizen science applications. Table 1 represents survey results of science initiatives that have contributed case studies including start date, scope, observation domain, number of participants, and number of records [9].

Table 1. Citizen science applications statistics

Title	Start date	Scope	Observations	Participants	Records
Big Garden Bird Watch	1979	UK	Birds	592475	100000000
eBird	2002	Global	Birds	25000	100000000
Galaxy Zoo	2007	Global	Galaxy classification	300000	200000000
Weather Observations Website	2011	Global	Weather	2000	38000000
Old Weather	2010	Global	Weather	16400	1600000

As shown in Fig. 1, the architecture of citizen science application is always the same - mobile or Web client, PHP server and underlying MySQL database [10]. Basically, underpinning the entire website is a spatially enabled MySQL database, which stores all elements of the data that appear on the site. To ensure that the level of response remains high, videos and photos may be stored externally and links are made from the database to the resource. Typically, the server-side code is written in PHP. This code allows connection to the database and retrieval or update of data together with login. The client application or web code is written in JavaScript, making extensive use of the Google Maps API to provide mapping functionality. Client-side design and layout is powered by HTML and CSS. Communications between the client and the PHP on the server are made using AJAX – which allows part of a web page to be refreshed without changing another part using HTML DIVS to divide the page into sub components. AJAX also allows the illusion of a permanent 'session' on the web page.

As one of the examples, Marine Debris Tracker application [10] has been developed to report and gather information about litter and debris in lakes, rivers, and especially at ocean coast. As demonstrated in Fig. 2, there are several screens - authorization screen, report screen, and finally confirmation screen.

Despite all the pros of citizen science there are few cons such as disjunction, incompleteness, and outdatedness of databases [10]. Quality of data and improper

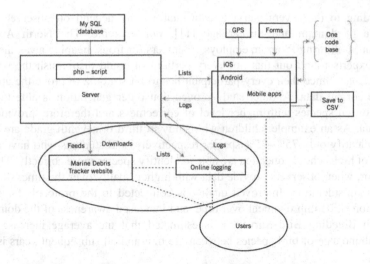

Fig. 1. Architecture of citizen science application (Source: [10])

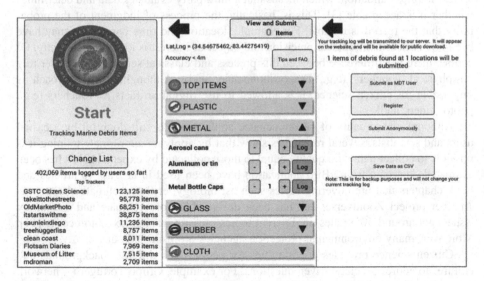

Fig. 2. Screens of MDT (Marine Debris Tracker) mobile application (Source: [8])

analysis approach are two more issues. For example, the declines of neotropical migrants, have been considered to be conservation biology for around 50 years. Initially declines are caused by tropical deforestation, according to BBS (North American Breeding Bird Survey) data. Subsequent analysis, on the contrary, suggested that declines are a statistical artifact and they are real, only caused by brown-headed cowbird parasitism [11]. This example demonstrates that different approaches applied to the same data set may result in absolutely opposite conclusions.

According to the several surveys data quality may depend on observer's basic knowledge of domain and his/her age [11]. For example, The North American Amphibian Monitoring Program employs volunteers for frogs' heaping away the roads. Program experts found out that not every participant could distinguish the sound of particular frogs. Since then every participant has to pass a quiz to prove the ability to contribute correct data. Another study proved that older generation is able to differentiate between species with higher level of correctness and therefore, provide more correct data. As an example, children who study in third or seventh grade are able to correctly identify only 75%–95% species respectively, and students who have at least two years of high school education are able to identify species more correctly. The 'first year' factor, when observers provide data with higher quality over the time, should be taken into consideration. Improved quality is connected to the protocols familiarity, identification skills improvement over time, and increased awareness of the domain. In the French Breeding Bird Survey, it is estimated that the average increase in the detected abundance of bird species between the first and all subsequent years is about 4.3% [11].

Another way to ensure data quality is expert reviews. Quality control via expert review implies validation, which means that a third party evaluates data and determines whether it is acceptable [3]. This is, basically, the process of judgment of the probability that the record is reliable. For example, location and time parameters may have been reported with acceptable precision and object of interest is identified correctly. Of course, there is a difference between this process and classical science, since latter rely on physical vouchers (e.g., Deoxyribonucleic acid). Although, such approach is impossible for citizen science, it is allowed to use digital artifacts as vouchers (e.g., photo, video, audio).

Although data quality of citizen science applications is still doubtful by a casual users and scientists, several researches show that by applying appropriate training it is possible to collect data with quality equal to those collected by experts [12]. It has been estimated, that data from eBird application have been used in at least 90 articles and book chapters that are covering topics such as: biology, ecology, climate change etc. Another project Zooniverse, that has been designed to solve climate and astronomy issues, got around 50 articles on different topics ranging from galaxies to oceans [11]. Moreover, many environmental protection agencies are using this data.

Citizen science provides opportunities for people with different backgrounds and cultures to address society-driven questions. For example, Grupo Tortugero – network for monitoring turtles, supports scientific work [11]. Collaboration of citizens and scientist in this project have helped to establish protected sea areas for turtles. Another example – The West Oakland Environmental Indicators Project encouraged citizens who live in financially dysfunctional neighborhoods to collect data and report about air quality [11].

To sum up, considering the conservatism of classical scientific communities with respect to quality of data and diversity of participants' experience and knowledge, the citizen science data quality issue requires tracking of data creation processes along with validation and modification processes. That is where provenance and scientific workflows are coming into play.

2.2 Data Provenance

Nowadays the tracking of data provenance is crucially important and few methods are proposed so far. Data provenance or sometimes lineage is used intensively in such fields as: audit trail, replication recipes, data citation etc. [12]. The goal of data provenance in citizen science applications is to verify the quality of contributed data.

Two major approaches for provenance recording exist – the first one is coarse-grain, which records complete history of the data derivation. This approach tracks not only interaction between programs, but data from external devices and sensors (e.g. cameras).

The second approach is fine–grain that is focused on representation of the derivation of only a part of the resulting data set [12]. If for example researcher deals with relational database the fine–grained provenance for a tuple of database is a tuple or data element in the source. There are few reasons to use fine–grain approach:

- The whole workflow is complicated for simple derivation of component of interest
- Workflow may not be available at that moment as a whole
- Workflow may be characterized as a log of actions on particular element of database

The fine–grain approach, in turn, can be divided into where- and why-provenance. Where – provenance represents identification of elements of a source where the data is copied from [12]. Why – provenance keeps also justification for the element of output. There is one more type of provenance – How – provenance which is pretty similar to Why – provenance but does not require the identification process that contributed data.

The concept of data provenance has been proposed by Wang and Madnick in early 2000 [13, 14]. Initially they proposed algebra and polygen model that includes not only queries and their results but also source attributions in each column and tuple [12]. Woodruff and Stonebraker later proposed the theory of building fine-grained provenance based on database management systems [15]. The idea is to give permission to programmers to define weak inverses for the functions in code. When a weak inverse is applied to elements, the function returns approximation to the provenance, which is associated with this function. Proposed solution also includes a verification phase that verifies information returned by weak inverse.

3 Proposed Solution

Considering all the challenges and problems of modern citizen science databases and data provenance tracking, a solution has been proposed. The proposed solution is a combination of NoSQL database with a framework to track provenance.

3.1 Database Requirements

Current section describes NoSQL structure, that is used for the experiment, and the process of capturing "How" and "Why" provenance. Additionally, this section includes the description of an experimental application and results of the experiment.

First, it is necessary to describe an application that implements the database; it has been decided to build a database for reporting water pollution that may represent a citizen science application.

Since this article focuses on building a prototype only, two example types of entities are designed – User and Report. For Report model type it is required to create a predicated list of pollution types similar to one that is used in Marine Debris Tracker (MDT) application [8]. This list includes following types: Plastic, Metal, Glass, Rubber, and Cloth.

It is also required to track the timestamp of the report to distinguish the old ones from the new ones. One more obligatory data field is for location. Since we want to know the exact location of a water pollution, the database may receive this data from an application due to the fact that today's web or mobile applications can get an access to the user location easily.

User model type includes all the information about the person who contributed data to the system. There are also different roles for users such as authorities' representatives, casual users, experts, or administrators. An additional field is used to reflect an approximate level of user qualification.

3.2   Database System Selection

For an implementation part NoSQL database has been chosen. NoSQL stands for "Not only SQL" and allows to store huge volumes of unstructured data. NoSQL databases provide simple data models but weak security. Nonetheless, their strongest quality is dynamic schema which allows storing in one collection or rather tables of different types of data that is unstructured. These databases store data in the form of objects like JSON or XML instead of relational models, which is a good option if data do not conform to a strictly relational database. It allows to store different types of data such as video, photo, audio, etc. which is very important for citizen science applications since participants want to send not only raw text but also may want to upload additional content. Being JSON – oriented, NoSQL database provides lower parse overhead and support of binary data [17]. NoSQL queries are JavaScript – based and have syntax similar to SQL.

Another reason is that the NoSQL databases are designed with log systems for replication of changes to ensure transparent scalability and partition across different servers. Today's NoSQL databases support only CRUD operations.

For implementation part NoSQL database MongoDB has been chosen. This system has several advantages among analogous ones, such as Cassandra and HBase. Since MongoDB supports only CRUD operations, additional built-in MapReduce framework is required for complex analytic querying. Moreover, MongoDB understands geospatial coordinates and natively supports geo-spatial indexing which is crucial for citizen science applications. Last but not the least is the fact that MongoDB in conjunction with third party frameworks provide even more than just data storage. This system is commonly used in the development and that is why there is a lot of information and articles about it, which is also one of the determining factors.

The implementation part is separated into two steps – first is an implementation of "How Provenance" which is stored in MongoDB and the second "Why Provenance" which is powered by MapReduce framework. Combination of both these types of provenance give enough information for the tuples in the resulting databases. Third "Where Provenance" approach is not applied to the system since it handles data contributed only by users and does not interact with other external systems or databases. For this reason, provenance representing a source where the data was copied from is not needed for the proposed prototype.

3.3 "How Provenance"

In order to capture "How - provenance" the system has to handle all the operations that final tuple came through. Resources that require provenance may be listed as "resource expressions". It can be written for particular document collection (which is similar to table in relational databases): <Database/Collection/Id>, or for the whole collection: <Database/Collection>, which means that all documents in the current collection will be tracked with provenance.

MongoDB implements built-in capped collection Oplog for tracking all operations that occur in the database. Capped collections are fixed size collections in which documents are retrieved in order of insertion [18]. When a collection is running out of memory the first records are erased so that new data could be written.

Oplog collections in MongoDB include unique id, time, name of the operation, namespace with the information of the database, and document affected by the operation with its new state. Primary Oplog system tracks all operations that are used in the primary node. The secondary ones copy and execute these operations in an asynchronous process. To sum up, although Oplog provides information for "How - provenance", additional data about users or systems executing the action have to be captured.

"How provenance" is handled by Oplog script in parallel to MongoDB process. When new entry comes to Oplog, the system checks whether this data is required for provenance. If this is the case, Oplog converts a timestamp to ISO date format, and operation is stored in separate provenance collection.

An example of "How provenance" capture of a document in citizen science application is as follows: a database that is called "mydb" stores information about three main types of entities such as Users, Reports, and Garbage. If it is required to track provenance for the particular user, for example by using his Id, the expression is specified as follows: <mydb/Users/userID>.

Figure 3 demonstrates results of "How provenance". For example, administrator wants to get all provenance data about the user with id "5aac35ceb9c93378bcff47fe". Since all data stored in NoSQL is JSON, results of "How provenance" are also represented in the same format. Provenance data is retrieved by "Provenance" key. The "OP_Type" key stores type of the operation – input or update. Every operation has its own timestamp represented in ISO date format.

3.4 "Why Provenance"

The provenance is called "Why provenance" because it provides reason/witness for why the particular output is obtained. A new model for that type of provenance is

```
{
"_id"  :  "myBD.Users.5aac35ceb9c93378bcff47fe",
"Provenance"  :  [
{       "Op_Type"  :  "i"
        "Operation"  :  "{  "firstName"  :  "Emma",  "secondName"
:  "Alley",  "age"  :  "24",  "memberSince"  :  "Fri  Mar  16  2018
23:23:26  GMT+0200  (EET)"
}",
        "Time"  :  ISODate("2018-03-16T23:23:26"),
        "user"  :  "admin",
},
{       "Op_Type"  :  "u"
"Operation"  :  "{"$set":{"firstName":"Liam"}}",
"Time"  :  ISODate("2018-04-16T23:23:26")
        "user"  :  "admin",
},
{       "Op_Type"  :  "u"
"Operation"  :  "{"$set":{"age":"28"}}",
"Time"  :  ISODate("2018-04-22T23:23:26")
        "user"  :  "admin",
},
]
}
```

Fig. 3. Results of "How provenance"

proposed in [6]. It is powered by MapReduce framework and called RAMP (Reduce and Map Provenance). The wrapper-based approach is used in this framework to store provenance by wrappers for different components such as: Record Reader, Mapper, Reader, and etc. Because MapReduce computations by itself deliver computational overhead and delays, a lazy approach is used. Mapper and writer are writing data into two separate files that represent provenance for precise operation. The document writer writes pairs in the result collection that is contained in file2. After the provenance is collected, system uses script that takes file1 and file2 and maps it to get the output results by key. As the result, final output is a list of all documents that contributed to the final result.

The following example describes the application of "Why provenance". In proposed citizen science prototype, the status of different users' reports at different times are tracked in the database. For example, user Emma Alley initially creates new report about plastic garbage in the water, and due to the absence of information, it is considered as incorrect by the user John Jonson. Month later the same user updates data complaining about metal in water and attach a photo. User Madison Nerd analyses this report and finds it correct. At that moment, this post has one negative and one positive vote. One more month later Alley updates report once again and uploads audio record. Finally, user Nikita checks complete report and verify the contributed data.

By combining «Why provenance» and «How provenance» it is possible to get following schema represented in Fig. 4. It is possible to keep track of every report in the system. Resulting provenance table will represent keys and provenance hash values that are linked to the particular portions of information in the database. In case of our application, it is crucial to track the value of "correct" field since the major point of having provenance in citizen science is to ensure the correctness of data that is collected by volunteers.

Social network interaction between volunteers is applied to the citizen science applications. In this case, every portion of data contributed by the user should be

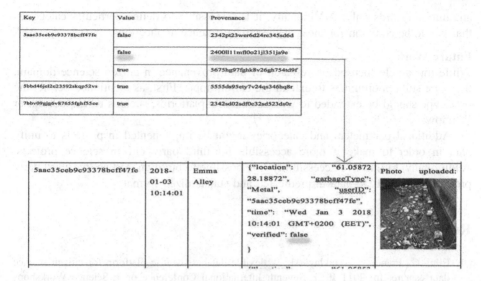

Key	Value	Provenance
5aac35ceb9c93378bcff47fe	false	2342pt23wer6d24re345sd6d
	false	2400lI11mfl0o21jl351ja9e
	true	5675hg97fghk8v26gh754td9f
5bbd46jel2e23592skqp52vs	true	5555ds95ety7v24qs346hq8r
7bbv09gjg6v87655fghf55ee	true	2342sd02sdf0c32sd523ds0r

| 5aac35ceb9c93378bcff47fe | 2018-01-03 10:14:01 | Emma Alley | {"location":   "61.05872 28.18872",   "garbageType": "Metal",   "userID": "5aac35ceb9c93378bcff47fe", "time": "Wed Jan 3 2018 10:14:01 GMT+0200 (EET)", "verified": false } | Photo   uploaded: |

Fig. 4. Resulting provenance for reports

verified by other users. According to this requirement, Report model contains counter "correct" which is analogous to likes counter in any social networks. Researches shows that general correctness of the data might be gained by user reviews [3].

4 Conclusion and Further Research Directions

In general, data provenance is a structure that describes the steps that a particular data went through to get to the final result. It allows to verify correctness and quality of data. There are few ways to describe provenance, such as coarse–grain and fine–grain. Also, there are types of provenance implementations, such as How – provenance, Why provenance, and Where provenance.

An overview of requirements for citizen science applications and existing NoSQL databases has been presented and taken into consideration. In general, data provenance provides security due to the fact that it might be used for audits. It allows to verify the data quality and authenticity.

Nevertheless, experiments show that the storage of provenance is necessary, it also requires a lot of memory and depends on the complexity of database structure. Furthermore, despite the fact that parallel processes are used provenance storage lead to time overheads.

In the prototype database built during the experiment stage shows that the entity parameters of the database are reflecting interaction between users and helps to track history of changes.

Limitations
Although the research has reached its aims, there are several limitations. Due to the fact that only test dataset is used in this project, the system has been tested for particular

amount of records only. Additionally, it is impossible to define particular categories that would be common for most of the citizen science applications.

Future Work

While this article focused on research of data provenance in citizen science domain, there are still opportunities to extend the current topic. First, as mentioned before, the prototype should be extended to web and mobile platforms, such as iOS, Android, or Windows.

Additional parameters and categories might be implemented in projects to unify data in order to make it more accessible for third party citizen science projects. Additionally, to improve accessibility it is possible to build an API so that third party projects could get the data in predicated and standardized format.

References

1. Ellul, C., Francis, L., Haklay, M.: A flexible database-centric platform for citizen science data capture. In: 2011 IEEE Seventh International Conference on E-Science Workshops (eScienceW) (2011)
2. McKinley, D.C., et al.: Citizen science can improve conservation science, natural resource management, and environmental protection. Biol. Conserv. **208**, 15–28 (2017)
3. Wiggins, A., He, Y.: Community-based data validation practices in citizen science. In: CSCW (2016)
4. Sheppard, S.A., Wiggins, A., Terveen, L.: Capturing quality: retaining provenance for curated volunteer monitoring data. In: Proceedings of the 17th ACM Conference on Computer Supported Cooperative Work and Social Computing (2014)
5. Memarsadeghi, N.: Citizen science [Guest editors' introduction]. Comput. Sci. Eng. **17**(4), 8–10 (2015)
6. Bonney, R., et al.: Next steps for citizen science. Science **343**(6178), 1436–1437 (2014)
7. Understanding Citizen Science and Environmental Monitoring. Final Report. https://www.ceh.ac.uk/sites/default/files/citizensciencereview.pdf
8. Jambeck, J.R., Johnsen, K.: Citizen-based litter and marine debris data collection and mapping. Comput. Sci. Eng. **17**(4), 20–26 (2015)
9. Dickinson, J.L., Zuckerberg, B., Bonter, D.N.: Citizen Science as an ecological research tool: challenges and benefits. Ann. Rev. Ecol. Evol. Syst. **41**, 149–172 (2010)
10. Danielsen, F., et al.: A multicountry assessment of tropical resource monitoring by local communities. Bioscience **64**(3), 236–251 (2014)
11. Smith, A., Lynn, S., Lintott, C.J.: Human Computation and Crowdsourcing: Works in Progress and Demonstrations (2013)
12. Buneman, P., Khanna, S., Wang-Chiew, T.: Why and where: a characterization of data provenance. In: Van den Bussche, J., Vianu, V. (eds.) ICDT 2001. LNCS, vol. 1973, pp. 316–330. Springer, Heidelberg (2001). https://doi.org/10.1007/3-540-44503-X_20
13. Wang, Y.R., Madnick, S.E.: A polygen model for heterogeneous database systems: the source tagging perspective (1990)
14. Woodruff, A., Stonebraker, M.: Supporting fine-grained data lineage in a database visualization environment. In: 1997 Proceedings of the 13th International Conference on Data Engineering (1997)
15. Ioannou, E., Garofalakis, M.: Query analytics over probabilistic databases with unmerged duplicates. IEEE Trans. Knowled. Data Eng. **27**(8), 2245–2260 (2015)

16. Ioannou, E., Garofalakis, M.: Query analytics over probabilistic databases with unmerged duplicates. IEEE Trans. Knowl. Data Eng. **27**(8), 2245–2260 (2015)
17. Stonebraker, M.: SQL databases v. NoSQL databases. Commun. ACM **53**(4), 10–11 (2010)
18. Kulkarni, D.: A fine-grained access control model for key-value systems. In: Proceedings of the Third ACM Conference on Data and Application Security and Privacy (2013)
19. Kitchenham, B., et al.: Systematic literature reviews in software engineering – a tertiary study. Inf. Softw. Technol. **52**, 792–805 (2010)

Internet of Things: Trends, Challenges and Opportunities

Marina Tropmann-Frick[✉]

Hamburg University of Applied Sciences, Berliner Tor 7, 20099 Hamburg, Germany
`Marina.Tropmann-Frick@haw-hamburg.de`

Abstract. The technology around us evolves rapidly. More and more cheaper and smaller devices become available. These devices vary in many aspects, e.g., in size, computational power or operating mode and are connected to some kind of a network for communication and data transmission. We refer to such devices as smart objects, e.g., smart car, smart home, smart city, etc. Combined they form a complex infrastructure, known as Internet of Things (IoT). Huge amounts of data produced in the IoT provide significant challenges for processing and analysis.

This paper gives an overview over the trends, challenges and opportunities in the field of IoT and serves as a starting point for our research in this field. We focus hereby on integration of IoT and Cloud computing, especially the extension of classic Cloud towards Fog and Edge computing.

1 Introduction

We live in a world of data-driven analytics and process-oriented explorations. We use high-performance computing technologies in our daily life and are interested in more powerful, more effective and more comfortable applications. We call them smart or intelligent. Many of those applications are by now so complex that only some people can understand and control them fully. And, nonetheless, we don't want to miss the comfort and integrate the applications in many devices and everyday objects around us.

In this way we get numerous sensors, devices and services that are producing, collecting and transporting huge amounts of data. Some of them are connected to each other, e.g., smart car - or smart home - systems. However, most of them are connected to the Internet. This scenario is known as the Internet of Things (IoT). In [1] the IoT is defined as a global infrastructure for the information society, enabling advanced services by interconnecting (physical and virtual) things based on existing and evolving interoperable information and communication technologies.

In comparison to traditional communication networks the IoT is a large scale, geographically distributed and *heterogeneous* network. The demands on IoT and user requirements on the functionality of the underlying technology are also different from the common network requirements. Additionally, such issues as monitoring, controlling and securing IoT devices are also very important.

© Springer Nature Switzerland AG 2018
A. Benczúr et al. (Eds.): ADBIS 2018, CCIS 909, pp. 254–261, 2018.
https://doi.org/10.1007/978-3-030-00063-9_24

In this paper we won't discuss the advantages and drawbacks of smart devices or applications. And we don't want to comment the latest events and affairs in this area.

Our goal for this work is to give an overview of existing technologies and to indicate the trends of this field in the future.

Since beginning of research and development in the area of the IoT we observe unstoppable growth of devices becoming wirelessly connected to the Internet. With the emergence of next generation of cheaper and smaller compute and networking units various additional *smart things* appear in this field.

According to [2] around 29 billion connected devices are forecast by 2022 of which around 18 billion will be related to the IoT. Furthermore, in this year mobile phones are expected to be surpassed in numbers by IoT devices, which include connected cars, machines, measuring instruments, wearables, RFID tags and other consumer devices. In 2022 the compound annual growth rate of IoT devices is expected to increase by 21 percent compared to 2016.

Other sources come up with other figures. For instance, it is estimated in [3] that the amount of IoT devices in 2020 would be about 50 billion. Huawei [4] forecasts in 2016 even 100 billion physical connections for 2025 and an exceedance of 1 trillion virtual connections. The company declared the IoT as one of its strategic priorities.

Meanwhile the estimations are not so high, but the trend keeps on increasing. All those devices generate an enormous amount of data that would be falling within the category of *big data*. This involves among other characteristics the volume, variety, velocity, veracity, validity and viability of data combined with such challenges as heterogenety, performance, scalability, reliability, security and privacy. This list does not aim to be complete. But it indicates very well the direction towards cloud computing regarding data storage and data processing.

The main idea behind cloud computing is not new. Nonetheless, the concepts of a cloud became important with the development of Google, Amazon and Microsoft. The principles of cloud computing are described in the definition provided by the *National Institute of Standard and Technologies* (NIST) [6]: "Cloud computing is a model for enabling ubiquitous, convenient, on-demand network access to a shared pool of configurable computing resources (e.g., networks, servers, storage, applications, and services) that can be rapidly provisioned and released with minimal management effort or service provider interaction."

Large companies quickly adopted this paradigm for delivering or leasing virtualized (nearly unlimited) resources over the Internet. Cloud architecture combines four main layers [7]: datacenter (storage, hardware), infrastructure, platform and application. Each layer is available as a service for the layer above and behave as a consumer for the layer below. Cloud essentially offers three levels of abstraction: Infrastructure as a Service (IaaS), Platform as a Service (PaaS) and Software as a Service (SaaS). SaaS provides access to applications running on Cloud environments mostly through a thin client or a web browser. PaaS presents the platform-layer services (e.g., operating system support, software development frameworks, etc.) for developing and/or running own applications.

IaaS provides access to underlying resources (e.g., storage, processing units, network, etc.). Meanwhile there are even more XaaS, whereby X stands for instance for Business Process (BPaaS) or Security (SaaS).

The combination of the two paradigms, IoT and Cloud, resulted in many new integration scenarios. Ranging from the *Internet of Everything* (IoE) [8, 9] to *Things as a Service* [10–12]. The ideas behind result mainly from the convictions that either Cloud fills some gaps of IoT (e.g. the limited storage) or IoT fills gaps of Cloud.

The authors in [5] describe the integration of the paradigms as CloudIoT and give a summarized overview of some of existing approaches, shown in Table 1.

Table 1. New paradigms enabled by CloudIoT: everything as a service [5]

XaaS (Acronym)	X (Expansion)	Description
	Things as a service [10–12]	Aggregating and abstracting heterogeneous resources according to tailored thing-like semantics
SaaS [13–15] S²aaS [16–18]	Sensing as a service	Providing ubiquitous access to sensor data
SAaaS [14]	Sensing and Actuation as a service	Enabling automatic control logics implemented in the Cloud
SEaaS [13, 14]	Sensor Event as a service	Dispatching messaging services triggered by sensor events
SenaaS [15]	Sensor as a service	Enabling ubiquitous management of remote sensors
DBaaS [15]	DataBase as a service	Enabling ubiquitous database management
DaaS [15]	Data as a service	Providing ubiquitous access to any kind of data
EaaS [15]	Ethernet as a service	Providing ubiquitous layer-2 connectivity to remote devices
IPMaaS [15]	Identity and Policy Management as a service	Enabling ubiquitous access to policy and identity management functionalities
VSaaS [19]	Video Surveillance as a service	Providing ubiquitous access to recorded video and implementing complex analyses in the Cloud

Closely related to this topic are another two concepts: *Fog Computing* and *Edge Computing*. We take a closer look on these concepts in the following.

2   Concepts of IoT

Due to the advancement in microelectronics, telecommunication networks and the use of RFID tags, devices are capable of communicating with the physical world and making decisions based on data analytics. IoT devices are capable of sensing, collecting, inferring, processing, receiving, transmitting and storing data.

Todays IoT deployments are fundamentally heterogeneous, because they often evolve from the integration of already independently deployed IoT sub-networks that are characterized by very heterogeneous devices and connectivity capabilities [20].

Use cases in the IoT vary from home safety and management system, smart electricity monitoring in electricity grids, in-car system from road traffic to health monitoring and disaster management. Due to the large number of use cases and their individual requirements the entire IoT domain cannot be converged on a single reference model, however a generalized architecture of the IoT is presented by [21].

Generalized IoT Architecture

The concepts of IoT Architecture are broadly discussed in literature. The information for the following summary originated mostly from [21].

Many IoT architecture models follow a four-layer approach. They are comprised of a *perception, network, middleware* and *application* layer.

- The perception layer consists of the actual physical objects, e.g., RFID tags, sensors or mobile devices. Data collected from the environment gets transmitted to a gateway or receiver.
- The network layer is responsible for transmitting the collected data. This layer uses different technologies for transmission, e.g., 6LoWPAN [22], ZigBee [23] or Bluetooth Low Energy (BLE) [24]. The diversity of the transmission technologies contributes to the heterogeneity of IoT.
- The middleware layer abstracts the complexities of the underlying system and is associated with service management, addressing and naming the requested service.
- The application layer deals with the applications and services. It manipulates the information collected from the perception layer and processed in the processing system.

Obviously, there are more components (e.g., information gathering, processing, controlling) with an important role for IoT. Some of them are categorized by [21] as follows:

- *Edge services* are responsible for transporting information through the Internet, e.g., Domain Name Services (DNS), Content Delivery Networks (CDN), firewalls or load balancer.

- *Analytics services* guide and automate the process of data analysis, discovery and visualization.
- *Process management services* help in managing the workflow of the information processing and connects devices with their respective services.
- *Authentication services* enable authentication of a registered user with the associated service.

3   Fog Computing for IoT

Though it is convenient, the integration of Cloud and IoT is not a simple task. For the accomplishment of such integration Cloud has to meet the requirements of IoT and, moreover, of IoT users and consumers. Some important challenges are presented below.

Performance and Quality of Service (QoS). Performance and QoS are crucial issues for the acceptance of IoT [25]. There is no guarantee for the fulfilment of these requirements. Internet is an unreliable transfer medium especially regarding the connection quality.

Real-Time Capability and Low Latency. Real-time and low latency requirements have significant impact on the direction of IoT development. This becomes more clear in the context of industrial facilities and smart cities environment.

Network Bandwidth. The capacity of the communication network for data transmission is crucial for handling the increasing amount of data exchanged between the participants of the IoT environment. Lack of resources can lead to the collapse of the whole system.

Data Handling. The increasing amount of IoT devices leads to enormous data growth. This data has to be somehow stored and processed. The challenges here correspond to the characteristics of big data involving volume, variety, velocity, veracity, validity and viability of data.

Identification and Mobility. In a fast growing IoT infrastructure we certainly need to provide means to reliably identify all the participants. Moreover, this have to be done for mobile devices over the physical boundaries of local mobile networks.

Resource Limitation. Most of the IoT devices are limited in their resources: disk space and memory, processing and communication capabilities. Many devices are operating unplugged and have therefore to take care of their power consumption.

Availability and Maintenance. Especially in the environment of smart cities, smart homes, smart cars etc. there is a high demand for availability and maintenance of the productive systems.

Security and Privacy. Security and privacy become even more important in the context of IoT systems. Such systems handle and transfer sensitive data. Many IoT devices have capabilities to interact with physical environment and can cause great harm in case of malfunction.

Cloud is able to meet many of the IoT requirements, but some of them are not feasible and there some that are not reasonable regarding Cloud characteristics. For instance, it is not absolutely necessary to store all data from every sensor in the cloud. It is more appropriate to preprocess the data and to store only meaningful or important parts.

Such considerations created room for the two approaches Fog computing [27,28] and Edge computing [26]. Both strategies are very similar. Both replace processing capabilities closer to the data sources (to the edge of the network). The resources, such as network, storage or processing units belong to both the Cloud and the Fog (or Edge). Nonetheless, Fog and Edge are able to ensure location awareness implying low latency. Often there is a very large number of nodes in contrast to centralized Cloud and support for mobility through wireless access.

The main difference between Fog computing and Edge computing lies in the location of processing resources. Fog computing is mainly operating in the local area network, processing data in a fog node or IoT gateway. Edge computing place resources directly into devices like programmable automation controllers (PACs). In this way it is possible to process more data directly on the sensor.

In [29] the authors analyze the process of building Fog computing projects and shows the challenging tasks regarding this context. Various specific algorithms and methodologies are required, which can handle issues concerning reliability of the networks of smart devices and specific fault tolerant techniques.

4   Conclusion

We discussed in this work some trends and research challenges in the area of the IoT and opportunities concerning combination of IoT requirements and Cloud technology. The extension of classic Cloud computing towards Fog and Edge computing is a promising strategy, which we aim to pursue.

This survey is based mainly on the analysis and a comparison of many scientific publications in this area. The number of existing papers in this field goes far beyond the list of references stated below. We intend to pursue the scientific and technical development here in order to be able to develop well-founded and comparable solutions.

Our research activities relate to such open issues in this area as standardization, security and privacy. While most people are already concerned about privacy and security in IoT and in Cloud-based applications, there is still more effort required.

References

1. International Telecommunication Union: Series Y: Global Information Infrastructure, Internet Protocol Aspects and Next-Generation Networks. Next Generation Networks Frameworks and functional architecture models. Overview of the Internet of Things (Y.2060) (2012). https://www.itu.int/ITU-T/recommendations/rec. aspx?rec=11559&lang=en. Accessed 27 Apr 2018
2. Kreutz, D., Ramos, F.M., Verissimo, P.E., Rothenberg, C.E., Azodolmolky, S., Uhlig, S.: Software-defined networking: a comprehensive survey. Proc. IEEE **103**(1), 14–76 (2015)
3. Gerhardt, B., Griffin, K., Klemann, R.: Unlocking value in the fragmented world of big data analytics. Cisco Internet Business Solutions Group (2012)
4. Huawei Technologies Co., Ltd.: Huawei's Heavy Investment in Five IoT Solutions Leads to Impressive Breakthroughs (2016). http://www.huawei.com/en/news/2016/4/wuda-IoT-jiejue-fangan. Accessed 27 Apr 2018
5. Botta, A., De Donato, W., Persico, V., Pescape, A.: Integration of cloud computing and internet of things: a survey. Future Gener. Comput. Syst. **56**, 684–700 (2015)
6. Mell, P., Grance, T.: The NIST definition of cloud computing. Natl. Inst. Stand. Technol. **53**(6) (2009)
7. Zhang, Q., Cheng, L., Boutaba, R.: Cloud computing: state-of-the-art and research challenges. J. Internet Serv. Appl. **1**(1), 7–18 (2010)
8. Evans, D.: The internet of everything: how more relevant and valuable connections will change the world. Cisco IBSG, pp. 1–9 (2012)
9. Abdelwahab, S., Hamdaoui, B., Guizani, M., Rayes, A.: Enabling smart cloud services through remote sensing: an internet of everything enabler. IEEE Internet Things J. **1**(3), 276–288 (2014)
10. Christophe, B., Boussard, M., Lu, M., Pastor, A., Toubiana, V.: The web of things vision: things as a service and interaction patterns. Bell Lab. Technol. J. **16**(1), 55–61 (2011)
11. Mitton, N., Papavassiliou, S., Puliafito, A., Trivedi, K.S.: Combining cloud and sensors in a smart city environment. EURASIP J. Wirel. Commun. Netw. **2012**(1), 1–10 (2012)
12. Distefano, S., Merlino, G., Puliafito, A.: Enabling the cloud of things. In: 2012 Sixth International Conference on Innovative Mobile and Internet Services in Ubiquitous Computing (IMIS), pp. 858–863. IEEE (2012)
13. Dash, S.K., Mohapatra, S., Pattnaik, P.K.: A survey on application of wireless sensor network using cloud computing. Int. J. Comput. Sci. Eng. Technol. **1**(4), 50–55 (2010)
14. Rao, B.P., Saluia, P., Sharma, N., Mittal, A., Sharma, S.V.: Cloud computing for Internet of Things & sensing based applications. In: 2012 Sixth International Conference on Sensing Technology (ICST), pp. 374–380. IEEE (2012)
15. Zaslavsky, A., Perera, C., Georgakopoulos, D.: Sensing as a service and big data. ArXiv Preprint arXiv:1301.0159 (2013)
16. Perera, C., Zaslavsky, A., Christen, P., Georgakopoulos, D.: Sensing as a service model for smart cities supported by Internet of Things. Trans. Emerg. Telecommun. Technol. **25**(1), 81–93 (2014)
17. Kantarci, B., Mouftah, H.T.: Mobility-aware trustworthy crowdsourcing in cloud-centric Internet of Things. In: 2014 IEEE Symposium on Computers and Communication (ISCC), pp. 1–6. IEEE (2014)

18. Kantarci, B., Moufta, H.: Trustworthy sensing for public safety in cloud-centric Internet of Things. IEEE Internet Things J. **1**(4), 360–368 (2014)
19. Prati, A., Vezzani, R., Fornaciari, M., Cucchiara, R.: Intelligent video surveillance as a service. In: Atrey, P.K., Kankanhalli, M.S., Cavallaro, A. (eds.) Intelligent Multimedia Surveillance: Current Trends and Research, pp. 1–16. Springer, Heidelberg (2013). https://doi.org/10.1007/978-3-642-41512-8_1
20. Qin, Z., Denker, G., Giannelli, C., Bellavista, P., Venkatasubramanian, N.: A software defined networking architecture for the Internet-of-Things. In: Network Operations and Management Symposium (NOMS), pp. 1–9. IEEE (2014)
21. Tayyaba, S.K., Shah, M.A., Khan, N.S.A., Asim, Y., Naeem, W., Kamran, M.: Software-Defined Networks (SDNs) and Internet of Things (IoTs): a qualitative prediction for 2020. Network **7**(11) (2016)
22. Montenegro, G., Kushalnagar, N., Hui, J., Culler, D.: Transmission of IPv6 Packets over IEEE 802.15.4 Networks. RFC 4944, September 2007
23. Zigbee Alliance: Zigbee. http://www.zigbee.org. Accessed 27 Apr 2018
24. Bluetooth SIG Working Groups: Specification of the Bluetooth System: Covered Core Package version **5** (2016)
25. Cavalcante, E., Pereira, J., Alves, M.P., Maia, P., Moura, R., Batista, T., Delicato, F.C., Pires, P.F.: On the interplay of Internet of Things and cloud computing: a systematic mapping study. Comput. Commun. **89**, 17–33 (2016)
26. Garcia Lopez, P., Montresor, A., Epema, D., Datta, A., Higashino, T., Iamnitchi, A., Barcellos, M., Felber, P., Riviere, E.: Edge-centric computing: vision and challenges. SIGCOMM Comput. Commun. Rev. **45**(5), 37–42 (2015)
27. Bonomi, F., Milito, R., Zhu, J., Addepalli, S.: Fog computing and its role in the Internet of Things. In: Proceedings of the First Edition of the MCC Workshop on Mobile Cloud Computing, pp. 13–16. ACM (2012)
28. Byers, C.C.: Architectural imperatives for fog computing: use cases, requirements, and architectural techniques for fog-enabled iot networks. IEEE Commun. Mag. **55**(8), 14–20 (2017)
29. Madsen, H., Albeanu, G., Burtschy, B., Popentiu-Vladicescu, F.: Reliability in the utility computing ERA: towards reliable fog computing. In: 20th International Conference Systems, Signals and Image Processing (IWSSIP), pp. 43–46 (2013)

First International Workshop on Artificial Intelligence for Question Answering, AI*QA

Analysis of Why-Type Questions for the Question Answering System

Manvi Breja[⊠] and Sanjay Kumar Jain

National Institute of Technology, Kurukshetra, Haryana, India
manvi.breja@gmail.com

Abstract. Question Answering Systems (QASs) form an exciting research area as it helps provide the user with the most accurate answer to the input question. For the accuracy of QAS, interpreting the information need of the user is quite pivotal. Thus, question classification forms an imperative module in question answering systems, which will help determine the type of question and its corresponding type of answer. The paper delivers a distinct classification of why-type questions and their corresponding answer types to yield a robust QAS.

Keywords: Question Answering System · Why-questions
Question classification · Answer types

1 Introduction

Question Answering Systems (QASs) employ the approach of Natural language Processing, Information Retrieval, and Machine Learning that help the user, get precise answers to his query. There are two general classification of questions viz. factoid questions beginning with what, when, who and where [9] that are answered in a single phrase or sentence, and non-factoid questions starting with why and how whose answers range from one sentence to a full document. The research on non-factoid QAS has seen limited success in the past. This paper is aimed to contribute positively towards the development of Why-type QAS. The general functioning of QAS is handled by four modules, namely question processing, passage retrieval, answer extraction and answer ranker as illustrated in Fig. 1. A very significant component of QAS is question analysis module that analyzes a users input to extract useful information according to user's need. It tries to unearth the type of question, to generate appropriate answers. We classify why-type questions into four classes by understanding the questioner's intent. To enable the automatic detection of these four types of questions by a parser, we discuss the lexical features that helps to recognize them. We also propose the expected answer-types of why-questions on the basis of RST theory.

The organization of the paper is as follows: Sect. 2 discusses the importance and our motivation for carrying out research in why-QA. Section 3 reviews the related work. Section 4 explores the research objectives. Section 5 describes the

© Springer Nature Switzerland AG 2018
A. Benczúr et al. (Eds.): ADBIS 2018, CCIS 909, pp. 265–273, 2018.
https://doi.org/10.1007/978-3-030-00063-9_25

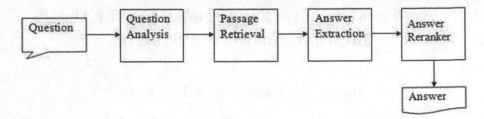

Fig. 1. Architecture of Question Answering System

methodology and the procedure of data collection to carry out research, Sect. 6 gives an account of the proposed classification of why-questions and their distinguished feature analysis. Section 7 explores the procedure used by parser to automatically assign a class to a why-question. Section 8 explains the proposed answer types. Section 9 throws light on the properties of questions that help to determine answer types. Finally, Sect. 10 concludes our work with future plans.

2 Importance of Question Classification and Motivation for Carrying Out Research in Why-Questions

Understanding the classification of a question forms the bedrock of question answering system. Moldovan [6] points out that the accuracy of QAS is strongly dependent on accurate question classification. Lot of research has been done on classification of What-type questions [7,30], questions on social networking sites [5,10,31], questions asked in Community QAS [12,24,27,32], etc., but work on why-type questions is limited [8,13,16,19–22,28,29]. Through our research, we aim to expand the work on question classification of Why-type questions that will help select an appropriate source to search answers.

3 Related Work

Till now many researchers have focused on classification of questions in different domains. Research by Lili Aunimo [1] aimed at developing a typology of questions based on features like lemmatized words, punctuation marks, part-of-speech (POS) tags, semantic and target tags. Li et al. [16] used head nouns tag to classify what-type questions. Huang et al. [11] utilized question wh-word, head word, WordNet semantic features (hypernym), word grams, and word shape features to classify questions. Li et al. [14] matched the topic and answer type of question with the candidate answers to determine correct answer. Harper et al. [7] classified open domain questions into conversational and informational. In [14] Yahoo! Answers served as a source to classify questions into informational, suggestion, opinion, and other. Chen et al. [3] who classified the questions asked on community QAS as subjective, objective, and social. [15] tried to determine the subjectivity orientation of questions by exploring supervised machine learning algorithms with features like char 3-grams, word, word+char 3grams, word-n-gram, and word POS n-gram. Moving to research in Why-type questions, Moldovan et al. [6] declared answer type of all why-questions 'reason' type. Ferret et al. [4] proposed a syntactic categorization of factoid questions. Verberne [13,16,19,23] used Ferrets approach for syntactically categorizing the why-questions and determining their expected answer type. The syntactic categorization of question was chosen by applying hand-written rules on the parse tree [17] generated by a parser and were defined as (1) action questions (2) process questions (3) intensive complementation questions (4) monotransitive have questions (5) existential there questions and (6) declarative layer questions. Their answer types were subdivided as cause, motivation, circumstance, and purpose based on the classification of adverbial clauses given by Quirk [11]. However, the system failed the following cases, (1) in action questions, subject was incorrectly not marked as agentive (2) questions having non-agentive subject and action verb as main verb (3) passive questions and (4) no formula set for monotransitive have questions.

4 Research Objectives

Mentioned below are the key research objectives of our work:

1. Presenting a classification of why-questions to understand the questioners need, and extract an appropriate correct answer [25].
2. Exploring lexical features of why-question.
3. Classifying why-questions using hand written rules.
4. Proposing answer types corresponding to various types of why-questions.

5 Research Methodology and Data Collection

We are carrying out an exploratory research [15] to explore the best research design, collate data and gain future insights in the domain of why-QA. Qualitative research [18] under the broad head of exploratory research, is used to understand reasoning and opinions about a given problem. We gathered a data set of why-type questions and their answers from various question answering sites such as Yahoo! Answers, Quora, Twitter [1]. We have also incorporated questions and their answers from the research by Verberne [2]. Post this data collection, we had a dataset of 1000 why-questions.

6 Proposed Taxonomy of Why-Questions

Why-questions are categorized into four categories [25] to better understand user's intent and the context in which it is to be answered. These are (1) Informational why-questions, (2) Historical why-questions, (3) Situational why-questions and (4) opinionated why-questions. Informational why-questions need reasoning or explanation of the facts in their answers. There is less ambiguity to their answers as they are quite well defined. For example, questions like Why sun rises in the east? Historical why-questions relate to an actions/events happened in the past that require justification. Example is Why did World War II happen? Situational why-questions have reference to events that occurred at a particular time. Their answers are ambiguous, varying with time and answerer. For example, Why do the clouds darken when it rains?. Last class of questions are opinionated questions which need reasoning related to a person or product which vary with the person's experience. Example is, Why do you prefer iPhone instead of Samsung phones?

7   Algorithm of the Parser to Assign a Class to a Why-Question

An exploratory study of lexical features is done to formulate handcrafted rules used to categorize why-questions. The parser takes a why-question as input, and uses rule based approach as shown in Fig. 2 to assign a class to a question.

Assumption: If none of the rules apply, label the question as informational why-question. Sometimes, algorithm might assign two labels to a why-question for which a priority rule is followed to resolve such ambiguity, i.e. opinionated >situational >historical >informational, which assigns higher priority label to a why-question.

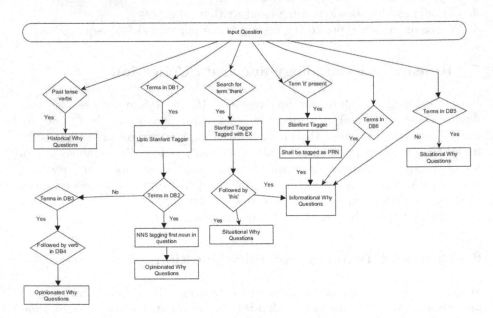

Fig. 2. Question classification algorithm

Appendix to the algorithm: DB1: contains personal pronouns, common noun pointing to a person, and concrete nouns referring to a person like we, you, I, my, your, he, she, man, woman, boy, girl, female, male, they, people, DB2: contains personal pronouns, people, human, DB3: noun pointing to a person, and concrete nouns referring to a person, DB4: action verbs like sit, move, eat, look, wander, DB5: comparative conjunctions like when, if, while, though, after, before, during, and longer, turn, this, that, those, and DB6: named, called as, referring to, referred as, considered as.

8   Proposed Answer Types of Why-Questions

This section explores different answer types possible for Why-type questions, on the basis of RST relations between text segments. Rhetorical Structure Theory (RST) [26] is used to understand the structure of text by finding the relations between different text fragments. The categorizations are (1) comparative answer which contains the reasoning behind the comparison of one or more facts, (2) motivated answer which contains reasoning for someone to have an interest or enthusiasm for something. The why-question contains shall/should/must as modal auxiliary verb, (3) conditional answer which contains reasoning for doing something under a given situation or context of time, (4) justified answer which contains the reasoning of the facts, inventions to be proved by some evidence or theory, (5) unconditional answer which is not restricted by any condition or circumstance. The why-questions involve cause of something, which are answered by explaining the effect of that cause, and (6) interpreted answer which contains logical reasoning for the facts. The questions are related to the domains of mathematics, logic, and statistics.

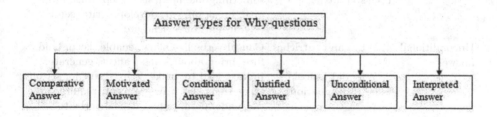

Fig. 3. Answer types

9   Properties of Questions that Help to Determine Answer Types

This section discusses the properties of questions which are used to determine their answer types as mentioned in Table 1. In some cases, the above rules don't

Table 1. Examples of questions with their properties having particular answer types

Answer types	Example of questions	Lexical features in questions
Comparative answer	1. Why does the sun lighten our hair but darken our skin? 2. Why is hollow steel pipe stronger than solid steel pipe	Conjunctions like but, over, even, though, like, likewise, than, and, similar to/similarly/similar with/similar in, though, besides, while, as, except, apart from, in contrast/contrasts to, yet, unlike, equal, different from/different than, different to etc.
Motivated answer	1. Why are accounting standards necessary? 2. Why internet is important for your life?	Helpful, famous, popular, important, significant, necessary, need, interest, desire, wish, conservative, admire, adore, dignity, fulfill, fascinate, heroism, inspire, incredible, marvelous, optimistic, renowned, special, unique, useful, valuable, viable, worthy, conserved, beneficial etc.
Conditional answer	1. Why are sea otters nearly extinct? 2. Why does the moon turn orange?	Near, Yearly, Keep growing/decreasing, during, everywhere, lastly, nowhere, towards, today, immediately, presently, daily, instantly, finally, longer, regularly, after, before, interval, turn, increasing, becoming(as a verb), months, days, time, when, even though, less, then, if, decrease with, overtime, particularly, smaller in, more in, nearly, turning, increasingly etc.
Justified answer	1. Why sun rises in the east? 2. Why do athletes take steroids?	Etymology questions using keywords like called, known as, considered as etc., keywords depicting reason for doing something like need, use, keep, take, grant, give, break off, eat, develop, write, send, buy, invent, offer, lend etc.
Unconditional answer	1. Why can't ostriches fly? 2. Why did Lincoln issue Proclamation?	Causal verbs like allow, enable, keep, hold, fore, bring about, cause, affect, generate, induce, lead to, make, help, result in, set off, trigger, get, let, have, prevent, require, persuade, permit etc. , lexical verbs to attain a target like issue, encourage, beneficial, accomplish, achieve, acquire, approve, appraise, deliver, serve, permit, inspire, advance, excel, reach, succeed, transcend, progress, volunteer etc.
Interpreted answer	1. why does $1 - 5 + 5 - 7 + \cdots$ converge to $\pi/4$, rather than some other real number? 2. Why P implies (not P) is true?	Questions related to the domains of medical, logic, statistics.

suffice to decide one answer type to a why-question. Such ambiguity is resolved by applying following rules. (1) If the adjectives like smaller, bigger, more, less etc. are used with conjunction "than" in why-question, then it expects comparative answer. Whereas, if these adjectives are used with preposition "in" then the questions have conditional answer. (2) If the question has "Need to + some lexical verb", then it has motivated answer. Whereas, the question has "Need of/Needed/Need for + Subject", then it has Justified answer. (3) When the term "and" is used as a coordinating conjunction, they expect comparative answer. (4) If the term "popular" is used as a noun, it expects unconditional answer. Whereas, if it is used as an adjective, it has motivated answer. (5) When the term "similar" is used as an adjective, the question expects unconditional answer. Whereas, if the similar is used with prepositions, then the question has comparative answer. (6) When the term "different" is used as an adjective, then the question expects comparative answer, Whereas, when it is used alone in a question like Why do people speak different languages?, then the question expects unconditional answer. (7) Lastly, Comparative and conditional answer types are always preferred over other answer types.

10   Conclusions and Future Work

The paper has addressed the issue of question classification through exploratory analysis of why-questions and their answers. This paper provides a first attempt to address why-question classification and we believe, our continued work will help us achieve promising results. In the future, we also plan to design a parser on the proposed classification and perform an experimental analysis to gauge the accuracy of parser.

References

1. Yahoo! Answers. https://in.answers.yahoo.com/, Quora. https://www.quora.com/, Twitter. https://twitter.com/search
2. Suzan webpage. http://liacs.leidenuniv.nl/~verbernes/
3. Chen, L., Zhang, D. Mark, L.: Understanding user intent in community question answering. In: Proceedings of the 21st International Conference on World Wide Web. ACM (2012)
4. Ferret, O., et al.: Finding an answer based on the recognition of the question focus. In: TREC (2001)
5. Harper, F.M., Moy, D., Konstan, J.A.: Facts or friends?: distinguishing informational and conversational questions in social Q and A sites. In: Proceedings of the SIGCHI Conference on Human Factors in Computing Systems. ACM (2009)
6. Moldovan, D., et al.: The structure and performance of an open-domain question answering system. In: Proceedings of the 38th Annual Meeting on Association for Computational Linguistics. Association for Computational Linguistics (2000)
7. Li, F., et al.: Classifying what-type questions by head noun tagging. In: Proceedings of the 22nd International Conference on Computational Linguistics-Volume 1. Association for Computational Linguistics (2008)

8. Verberne, S.: Developing an approach for why-question answering. In:: Proceedings of the Eleventh Conference of the European Chapter of the Association for Computational Linguistics: Student Research Workshop. Association for Computational Linguistics (2006)
9. Jurafsky, D.. Martin, J.H.: Speech and Language Processing: An Introduction to Natural Language Processing, Computational Linguistics and Speech Recognition. Prentice-Hall, Englewood Cliffs (2015)
10. Kim, S., Oh, J.S., Oh, S.: Best-answer selection criteria in a social Q and A site from the user-oriented relevance perspective. In: Proceedings of the Association for Information Science and Technology (2007)
11. Leech, G., Randolph, Q., Greenbaum, S., Svartvik, J.: A Comprehensive Grammar of the English Language. Longman, London and New York (1985)
12. Li, B., et al.: Exploring question subjectivity prediction in community QA. In: Proceedings of the 31st Annual International ACM SIGIR Conference on Research and Development in Information Retrieval. ACM (2008)
13. Verberne, S.: In Search of the Why: Developing a System for Answering Why-Questions. [Sl: sn] (2010)
14. Mizuno, J., et al.: Non-factoid question answering experiments at NTCIR-6: towards answer type detection for realworld questions. In: NTCIR (2007)
15. https://research-methodology.net/research-methodology/research-design/exploratory-research/
16. Verberne, S, et al.: Discourse-based answering of why-questions (2007)
17. Oostdijk, N.: Using the TOSCA analysis system to analyse a software manual corpus. Ind. Parsing Software Manuals **17**, 179 (1996)
18. http://nursing.utah.edu/research/qualitative-research/what-is-qualitative-research.php
19. Verberne, S., et al.: Using syntactic information for improving why-question answering. In: Proceedings of the 22nd International Conference on Computational Linguistics-Volume 1. Association for Computational Linguistics (2008)
20. Liu, Z., Jansen, B.J.: Identifying and predicting the desire to help in social question and answering. Inf. Process. Manag. **53**, 490–504 (2017)
21. Brill, E.: Discovering the lexical features of a language. In: Proceedings of the 29th Annual Meeting on Association for Computational Linguistics. Association for Computational Linguistics (1991)
22. Oh, J.-H., et al.: Multi-column convolutional neural networks with causality-attention for why-question answering. In: Proceedings of the Tenth ACM International Conference on Web Search and Data Mining. ACM (2017)
23. Verberne, S., Boves, L.W.J., Oostdijk, N.H.J., Coppen, P.A.J.M.: Discourse-based answering of why-questions (2007)
24. Xiang, Y., et al.: Answer selection in community question answering via attentive neural networks. IEEE Sig. Process. Lett. **24**(4), 505–509 (2017)
25. Breja, M., Jain, S.K.: Why-type question classification in question answering system. Forum for Information Retrieval Evaluation (2017)
26. Mann, W.C., Thompson, S.A.: Rhetorical structure theory: description and construction of text structures. In: Kempen, G. (ed.) Natural Language Generation. NATO ASI Series (Series E: Applied Sciences), vol. 135, pp. 85–95. Springer, Dordrecht (1987). https://doi.org/10.1007/978-94-009-3645-4_7
27. Guy, I., et al.: Identifying informational vs. conversational questions on community question answering archives (2018)
28. Pearl, J., Mackenzie, D.: The Book of Why: The New Science of Cause and Effect. Penguin, UK (2018)

29. Kruengkrai, C., et al.: Improving event causality recognition with multiple background knowledge sources using multi-column convolutional neural networks. In: AAAI (2017)
30. Mohasseb, A., Bader-El-Den, M., Cocea, M.: Question categorization and classification using grammar based approach. Inf. Process. Manag. (2018)
31. Oh, S.: Social Q&A. In: Brusilovsky, P., He, D. (eds.) Social Information Access. LNCS, vol. 10100, pp. 75–107. Springer, Cham (2018). https://doi.org/10.1007/978-3-319-90092-6_3
32. Zhou, X., et al.: Recurrent convolutional neural network for answer selection in community question answering. Neurocomputing **274**, 8–18 (2018)

Towards Multilingual Neural Question Answering

Ekaterina Loginova[(✉)], Stalin Varanasi, and Günter Neumann

DFKI, Saarbrücken, Germany
{ekaterina.loginova,stalin.varanasi,neumann}@dfki.de
https://www.dfki.de

Abstract. Cross-lingual and multilingual question answering is a critical part of a successful and accessible natural language interface. However, many current solutions are unsatisfactory. We believe that recent developments in deep learning approaches are likely to be efficient for question answering tasks spanning several languages. This work aims to discuss current achievements and remaining challenges. We outline requirements and suggestions for practical parallel data collection and describe existing methods and datasets. We also demonstrate that a simple translation of texts can be inadequate in case of Arabic, English and German languages (on InsuranceQA and SemEval datasets), and thus more sophisticated models are required. We hope that our findings will ignite interest in neural approaches to multilingual question answering.

Keywords: Question answering
Multilingual natural language processing
Neural natural language processing · Deep learning

1 Introduction

The focus in natural language processing has always been on the English language. Nonetheless, other languages (such as Spanish, Hindi and Chinese) have equal or larger number of native speakers, so cross and multilingual language technologies have great potential in the field of intelligent assistance, information retrieval and question answering (QA). Cross-lingual (essentially, bilingual) techniques are concerned with the retrieval of information in a language different from that of a query, while multilingual work with information sources in several languages simultaneously. With the development of deep learning approaches, which do not require manual feature engineering, we strongly feel it is time to revisit the research area and broaden the language coverage.

In this work, we focus on QA task and provide an overview of the current state of the field for multilingual (MLQA) and cross-lingual (CLQA) subtasks. We also include a preliminary attempt to analyse the performance of a simple deep learning model in multiple language setting. Our research question is how

© Springer Nature Switzerland AG 2018
A. Benczúr et al. (Eds.): ADBIS 2018, CCIS 909, pp. 274–285, 2018.
https://doi.org/10.1007/978-3-030-00063-9_26

well does the same model perform on original Arabic (English) texts and their English (German) translations, and if there is a difference, then why.

This paper is divided into five sections. The first section provides a brief overview of existing datasets for cross-lingual and multilingual QA and discusses the collection and analysis of such linguistic resources. The second section examines approaches to the problem and reports state-of-the-art results on several shared tasks. In the third section, a case study is presented for which we compare the performance of a deep learning model before and after translating a corpus of non-factoid questions and answers. Possible directions for future research are outlined in the fourth section. Our conclusions are drawn in the final section.

2 Datasets

2.1 Existing Datasets

Parallel. Cross-Language Evaluation Forum (CLEF) provided the following multilingual datasets: Multisix corpus [24], (200 questions, 6 languages), the DISEQuA corpus [23] (450 questions, 4 languages), the Multieight-04 corpus [25] (700 questions, 7 languages), and the Multi9-05 [37] (900 questions, 9 languages). Some corpora also include question type in their annotation [4]. A small parallel corpus for Japanese and English was constructed by the NTCIR organisers [32].

Lack of resources (such as parallel corpora or sufficiently large dictionaries) for many languages is a significant problem. Not only does it hinder the employment of machine translation methods, but also the generation of cross-lingual embeddings, effectively leaving little choice in approaches. At the time of publication, to the best of our knowledge, there are no parallel corpora for QA sufficiently large to take advantage of deep learning techniques fully.

Code-Mixed. Code-mixing or code-switching is a linguistic phenomenon frequently occurring in multilingual communities. It results in texts where words of two languages are used simultaneously within a single sentence. Code-mixing is particularly noticeable in India, where native speakers of Telugu, Hindi and Tamil are often using English words without translating them. As an example, consider the following Hinglish (Hindi + English) sentence: "Bhurj Khalifa kaha located he?" ("Where is Burj Khalifa located?"). Due to the morphological richness and non-latin alphabets of many languages, it can be even more complicated. For instance, a sentence can include combinations of transliterated English stems with native affixes or switching alphabets (cross-script).

Despite extensive use of code-mixing in informal conversations, there are not many datasets present. Among recent developments in this area, we can note [3]. Along with the corpus, a novel annotation scheme and evaluation strategy specific for QA have been proposed. Another potentially useful dataset is CMIR, described in detail in [6]. This dataset consists of 1959 code-mixed tweets.

2.2 Dataset Collection and Analysis

A multilingual QA corpus dealing with above problems would have to satisfy the following requirements:

1. Not only questions and answers should align, but also the contexts. This alignment should be taken into account when working with existing multilingual collections such as Wikipedia, as the articles on the same topic might differ significantly across the languages. Otherwise, comparison of results for different languages might be affected.
2. Annotators should be bilingual. Proof of language knowledge needs to be provided to ensure quality translation. It should be noted that interrogative structures can sometimes present a bigger problem for non-native speakers. It is thus preferable to check how confident a crowd-source worker is with advanced grammar constructions.
3. The annotation scheme should include at least tokenisation and chunking to help researchers elicit a step in the preprocessing pipeline causing the most errors. In addition, question and answer type labels might be useful.

One issue that needs to be raised is which languages should be a priority? We can either choose according to the quality of machine translation or by the number of bilingual native speakers. Language pairs also ought to include languages with profoundly different grammar rules and preferably from several alphabets. Hence, we can separate four main types of parallel corpora (listed in increasing complexity): closely related languages with similar alphabets (Italian, Spanish), distant languages with similar alphabets (Danish, French), closely related languages with different alphabets (Polish, Russian) and distant languages with different alphabets (English, Chinese).

Possible sources of parallel data include Trivia and other worldwide question answering games, as well as multilingual countries' exam sheets. Nevertheless, current techniques to collect QA pairs are time-consuming. Another possibility is to generate question-answer pairs from existing parallel MT corpora. The recent success of deep learning question generation [10] is promising for doing so in an end-to-end (semi-) automated fashion, which is important for languages with scarce resources. A hybrid system can be considered when a neural network generates question-answer pairs, and a human annotator further refines them.

The properties of multilingual QA datasets have not been dealt with in depth. We argue that the following characteristics need to be considered: diversity and balance of answer and question types, reasoning type for questions along with the difficulty score. Whether the reasoning over multiple sentences or documents is required, the degree of syntactic and lexical divergence between the question and the answer.

We surmise that more attention should be paid to the properties of texts potentially useful for deep learning models. Among them is the perplexity of the dataset, which indicates how patterns are repeating in the dataset. The higher the perplexity, the more unlikely it is to see patterns repeating and hence the more difficult it is to learn a model. Besides, an appropriate metric should be chosen in a code-mixed scenario to evaluate the complexity of a corpus, such as Complexity Metric proposed in [14].

3   Methods

3.1   Related Work

In general, one can distinguish the following approaches:

- annotate data for each input language and then train separately
- use machine translation directly beforehand or as part of a QA system; and then to work in the monolingual setup of a target language
- use a universal cross-language representation (such as cross-lingual embeddings)
- map terms in several languages with a multilingual knowledge base or a semantic graph, such as Wikipedia or BabelNet [5]

An important question for MLQA is what can be seen as a universal baseline? It should satisfy the following conditions: applies to a wide variety of languages, easy to use, and freely available. The most widespread baseline at the moment is to translate texts to English with Google Translate [19]. A major drawback is an unequal quality of translation for different languages, which should be taken into account during a comparison.

Despite its extended use, machine translation remains a source of errors in multilingual text processing pipelines. A loss or corruption of named entities has frequently been observed during translation. Code-mixed texts are even more challenging in this regard [19]. Besides, in the traditional approach, the machine translation is performed independently of QA as a part of input preparation. Recently, there has been a trend to blend the two components. [36] draws our attention to the problem of joint training for machine translation and QA components. They propose an answer ranking model that learns the optimal translation according to how well it classifies the answer. This novel approach achieves 0.681 MAP (Mean Average Precision) on a collection of English, Arabic and Chinese forum posts, which outperforms the English translations baseline. Their findings also do not support the hypothesis that learning a custom classifier for each language would outperform the single classifier baseline. As a generalization of this idea, [15] reports on a novel method to incorporate response feedback to the machine translation system. The response is received based on performance in an extrinsic task. For instance, one might generate the translation of a question and define a successful response as receiving the same answer for both translation and the original question. Finally, [33] calls into question the correspondence between human assessment of translation, machine translation metrics and cross-lingual QA quality. They create a dataset and investigate the relationship between translation evaluation metrics and QA accuracy. The authors claim that the conversion of entities into logical forms, typical for methods utilising a knowledge base, can be heavily affected by a translation. Another potential issue is a change in the word order, which might harm the performance of predicate construction and merging. Overall, the authors conclude that QA system and humans do estimate the translation quality in a very different way. This effect is especially noticeable for named entities, but the correct translation of question words is also crucial.

Regarding the latest machine learning models, [17] considers the use of semantic parsing for multilingual QA over linked data. The authors propose a model that utilises DUDES (Dependency-based Underspecified Discourse Representation Structures) [9] universal dependencies. Experiments were carried out on the QALD-6 dataset covering English, German and Spanish language. Although the results are behind state-of-the-art, it is quite likely that semantic parsing might be helpful for fully exploiting information from several languages. [38] describes a combination of a Maximum Entropy model for keyword extraction and an SVM for answer type classification to find an answer in a knowledge base. One of the main advantages is language independence except for the use of a chunker. The paper reports an F1 score for Spanish data of 54.2 as compared to the 32.2 baseline score obtained by translating question into English with Google Translate.

Recent developments in deep learning have led to considerable interest from the natural language processing community. However, these models are just entering the field of multilingual QA. A promising direction is to use cross-lingual embeddings. The limitation is an assumption that a large parallel corpus is available for training cross-lingual embeddings. In [26], authors compare a tree-kernel-based system with a feed-forward neural network which uses cross-lingual embeddings for Arabic and English data. As a baseline, they translate questions into English and train a monolingual system. Another exciting result has been reported by [20], who developed a new method for community QA based on the Domain Adversarial Neural Network model [13]. They have adapted it to a cross-lingual task by coupling a detection network with a question-answering one. They achieve a MAP of 0.7589 on Arabic data and 0.7593 on English.

3.2 Benchmarks

As mentioned above, one of the most popular MLQA challenges is the CLEF campaigns. It includes 33 cross-language sub-tasks across 10 European languages. The corpus was combined out of ELRA/ELDA news and Wikipedia articles. During the challenge, the participating systems had to answer factoid, definition and list questions and provide supporting evidence in the form of text snippets. The performance metric was top-1 accuracy and, in most cases, MRR (mean reciprocal rank). More details on this topic can be found in [12].

Another notable shared task is NTCIR-6 [32]. The target languages are English, Chinese and Japanese. The corpus is based on newspaper articles. There can be only one or no answer, and its type is restricted to a named entity. The performance metric is top-1 accuracy and MRR. The organisers note that some questions can be answered correctly in CLQA but not in MLQA and that the named entity identification modules, as well as translation, significantly influence the performance.

Concerning code-mixed texts, there is a surge of interest from multilingual communities in India, specifically for Hindi, Telugu and Tamil. However, currently, the work is mainly limited to question type classification and information retrieval, encouraged by the recently shared tasks of MSIR and FIRE [2]. In the question classification task, [30] report an accuracy of 45.00%. [7] achieve an MRR of 0.37 and 0.32 for Hinglish and Tenglish respectively, using lexical translation and SVM-based question classification. In information retrieval, machine learning methods such as Naive Bayes and RF classifiers dominate, with the best MAP score being 0.0377.

4   Experiments

We have performed our experiments on two datasets: InsuranceQA (version 2) [11] and SemEval 2017 (subtask D) [28]. The approach involves training the same deep learning model on original texts and their translations to compare the performance. For both datasets, questions are non-factoid and can have multiple correct answers. The task is to rank the set of answers based on their relevance to the question. InsuranceQA texts are originally in English, while the SemEval ones are in Arabic. The texts were translated to German and English respectively. The Google Translate neural machine translation system for English - German language pair achieves a BLEU score of 24.60 [19]. For Arabic to English translation, the average precision is 0.449 [16].

Table 1. Statistics of the datasets

Dataset statistics	Train	Validation	Test	Train	Validation	Test
#Questions	12889	2000	2000	1031	250	1400
#Answers	21325	3354	3354	30411	7384	12600

The deep learning model we use is an attentional Siamese Bidirectional LSTM. The method is essentially the same as that introduced by [34] with some adjustments in hyper-parameters and loss function (see below). We chose this model because it performed the best over multiple runs for SemEval 2017 Subtask A in our previous experiments. There it has obtained a MAP of 0.8349 (the IR baseline is 0.7261, the best result is 0.8843, and the best only deep learning result is 0.8624 [28]). The model accepts a question, its correct answer and an incorrect answer from the pool as an input. The goal is to project them in such a way that correct answers are closer to their corresponding questions than the incorrect ones.

The motivation for using deep learning is a significant gap in parallel resources and advanced tools for many languages. Our current approach only requires a collection of texts to train monolingual word embeddings on, a translation system and a tokeniser.

We limit the word sequence length to 200 tokens during training. For all languages, we use FastText word embeddings pre-trained on Wikipedia [21]. We choose these embeddings because they are widely used in the community, are available for several languages and trained on the same dataset for each language, which reduces performance variation. For the English language for InsuranceQA, we also tried custom word2vec [27] embeddings pre-trained on Wikipedia[1] with similar results.

The number of units per two layers of Shared BiLSTM is 96 and 64 respectively. Parameters are randomly initialised, and the initial state is set to zero. The models are implemented in the Keras [8] for SemEval and PyTorch [29] for InsuranceQA. The optimiser is Adam [22] with a learning rate of 0.001 and batch normalization is used in Keras implementation. For PyTorch, optimiser is SGD with a learning rate of 1.1 (following the original implementation [34]). Training on a single GPU (NVIDIA TITAN Xp) takes approximately 30 and 15 min per epoch for PyTorch and Keras respectively.

4.1   InsuranceQA

Statistics. This dataset contains non-factoid questions and answers from the insurance domain. It consists of a training set, a validation set, and two test sets, which in practice can be combined. Table 1 presents the statistics of the dataset. There are two versions of the dataset available, the main difference between them being the construction of the wrong answers pool: it is either sampled randomly or retrieved with SOLR. We use the texts from the second version, as they are not lemmatised and as such are better suited for machine translation, but keep the pools random as in the first version, as such setup is better studied. Besides, the SOLR setup appears to be much more challenging. More specifically, the model trained on random pools achieves a validation accuracy score of 0.6241, and test scores of 0.6223 and 0.5987 respectively. In spite of this, it only obtains less than 0.1 accuracy when tested on SOLR pools. The pool size is 50 for the training set to make computations feasible and 500 for validation and test. The texts have been translated from English to German with Google Translate.

The preprocessing step for English is limited to lowercasing words. For German, we additionally apply compound nouns splitting and compare the performance of [31,35]. The tokenisation was already performed by the dataset authors, and we have also tried the SpaCy tokeniser [18]. The correct choice of splitter and tokenisation is crucial, as it reduces the number of out-of-vocabulary words from 40706 to 5304 and from 52596 to 22387 for FastText and Polyglot embeddings respectively. While there exist several strategies for handling such words, we chose to omit them completely. Studying the influence of alternative strategies is reserved for the future. We also opted to use fixed word vectors, as we empirically found that training the embeddings resulted in poorer performance.

---

[1] The parameters are as follows: skip-gram, window 5, negative-sampling rate −1/1000.

Performance. We compare the performance of the system on original English texts with that on translations to German. The loss function is margin ranking loss. The performance metric is top-1 accuracy. On English texts, we obtain the following scores: validation set - 0.6361, test set - 0.6448. On German texts the scores are significantly lower: respectively 0.5435 and 0.5654. Research into classifying errors is underway. Our first hypothesis is that the quality of machine translation might be the main source of errors. More specifically, translation changes the word order and might rephrase the salient content words. It is also known for omitting or incorrectly translating named entities and affecting the sentiment. Another possible error-introducing step is compound splitting, which affects the number of out-of-vocabulary words and can be crucial for a correct understanding of the question (Table 2).

Table 2. Performance on InsuranceQA v2 (accuracy) and SemEval 2017 (MAP). For InsuranceQA, texts are originally in English and translated into German. For SemEval, texts are originally in Arabic and translated into English.

Performance	InsuranceQA		SemEval	
	English	German	Arabic	English
Validation	0.6361	0.5435		
Test	0.6448	0.5654	0.4997	0.4939

4.2 SemEval

Statistics. The SemEval-2017 Task 3 [28] is concerned with community QA. Subtask D focuses on the Arabic language, and the task is to rank new answers for a given question. The dataset is divided into training, a validation and a test set. Their corresponding statistics are reported in Table 1. The set of 30 related questions retrieved by a search engine is given, and each is supported by one correct answer. The resulting set of answers should be ranked based on their relevance to the given question. There are three possible labels - "Direct", "Relevant" and "Irrelevant" - for an answer, but during the evaluation "Relevant" and "Direct" are grouped as a single label.

Arabic is believed to be one of the most challenging languages [1] for automated processing, because of its morphological richness, free word order, and the mix of dialect and standard spelling. One of the problems we encountered was a large number of out-of-vocabulary words, which can be connected to the informal nature of the texts (slang, code mixing, typing errors, etc.). We have created an additional dictionary mapping out-of-vocabulary (OOV) words to their synonyms. Synonyms were obtained by translating an Arabic word into English and back into Arabic with Google Translate. Theoretically, such procedure should return the most common meaning and form, thus allowing us to reduce the vocabulary gap. In practice, we first preprocessed 62 161 OOV words to exclude numbers and cases when a word was concatenated with a number. After this,

53 344 OOV were left. Next, we successfully extracted 23 445 synonyms. 29 899 words were still not present in the FastText vocabulary. The number of OOV words is still relatively large and might be critical for the performance if the important content words are not present in the vocabulary. As a possible solution, one can train custom word embeddings on a corpus with texts closer in spirit.

Performance. We compare the performance of the system trained and test on original Arabic texts with the one using translations to English. The loss function is cross-entropy, and the performance metric is a MAP. The evaluation is carried out with the official SemEval script. For the original Arabic texts, we obtain a test score of 0.4997. It is noticeably lower than the strong Google baseline of 0.6055, and we are now in the process of establishing the exact reasons for that. Contrary to expectations, for translated texts, the test MAP score is 0.4939, which is remarkably similar.

5   Discussion

Considering the challenges mentioned above, we suggest that further research should be undertaken in the following areas:

1. (Semi-) Automated collection of multilingual QA corpora. A procedure outlined in Sect. 2 of this paper might be adopted by other research groups in most widely spoken languages, such as Chinese, Arabic and Hindi.
2. Incorporation of response-based machine translation.
3. Interpretation and comparison of cross-lingual QA deep learning models with monolingual ones. It may be assumed that the features and the behaviour of the model will change with respect to the language, and thus it is of interest to find what aspects stay universal and what change, as well as why.
4. Code-mixed language detection and translation as a part of QA pipeline. Further investigation is required to assess whether including these components in joint training with QA model is beneficial.

More broadly, there are many research questions in need of further study. Some of them are:

- Do some classes of languages require fewer data and less time for deep learning models to reach a specified performance? What are the properties of the languages that might affect the performance? Is there a universal neural architecture for all languages? Are some languages more suitable for LSTM-based architectures and others for CNN-based ones?
- How does a translation to English affect performance? How far can a system go without machine translation? Can we efficiently transfer a QA model from one language to another just by machine-translating texts? Can it be done per some categories of questions better than for others? Are some machine translation metrics more suitable in this setting?
- How well do cross-lingual embeddings work in QA setup? Are some types of cross-lingual embeddings better suited for particular language pairs?

6   Conclusion

In conclusion, multilingual QA has attracted significant attention in the past. However, in the classical approach, techniques were mainly limited to machine translation of input texts and manual feature engineering. In the recent years, deep learning techniques for natural language processing have been developed which allow us to approach the problem in a new way. Nonetheless, it currently remains a challenging, yet neglected area. It is quite likely that the lack of research in the area may hinder the usage of more advanced dialogue systems and machine-human interfaces, if not addressed.

We have demonstrated that simply translating texts is not a sufficient solution, as it results in a significant drop in performance in some cases, and is not applicable to code-mixing or cross-script scenario. This paper also has highlighted existing problems with resources for multi- and cross-lingual applications. Moreover, it provides an agenda for collecting parallel QA corpora and gives an account of recent promising developments in the field.

Our future work will also concentrate on neural approaches. In particular, we are working on joint training of a machine translation and QA components, as well as experiments with cross-lingual embeddings for the code-mixed scenario.

Our work is still in progress. Nevertheless, we believe it could be a starting point, and we hope to attract more attention to the discussed area.

Acknowledgements. This work was partially supported by the German Federal Ministry of Education and Research (BMBF) through the project DEEPLEE (01IW17001).

References

1. Almarwani, N., Diab, M.: GW_QA at SemEval-2017 task 3: question answer re-ranking on Arabic Fora. In: Proceedings of the 11th International Workshop on Semantic Evaluation (SemEval-2017), pp. 344–348 (2017)
2. Banerjee, S., et al.: Overview of the mixed script information retrieval (MSIR) at FIRE-2016. In: Majumder, P., Mitra, M., Mehta, P., Sankhavara, J. (eds.) FIRE 2016. LNCS, vol. 10478, pp. 39–49. Springer, Cham (2018). https://doi.org/10.1007/978-3-319-73606-8_3
3. Banerjee, S., Naskar, S.K., Rosso, P., Bandyopadhyay, S.: The first cross-script code-mixed question answering corpus. In: MultiLingMine@ ECIR, pp. 56–65 (2016)
4. Boldrini, E., Ferrández, S., Izquierdo, R., Tomás, D., Vicedo, J.L.: A parallel corpus labeled using open and restricted domain ontologies. In: Gelbukh, A. (ed.) CICLing 2009. LNCS, vol. 5449, pp. 346–356. Springer, Heidelberg (2009). https://doi.org/10.1007/978-3-642-00382-0_28
5. Bouma, G., Kloosterman, G., Mur, J., van Noord, G., van der Plas, L., Tiedemann, J.: Question answering with Joost at CLEF 2007. In: Peters, C., et al. (eds.) CLEF 2007. LNCS, vol. 5152, pp. 257–260. Springer, Heidelberg (2008). https://doi.org/10.1007/978-3-540-85760-0_30
6. Chakma, K., Das, A.: CMIR: a corpus for evaluation of code mixed information retrieval of hindi-english tweets. Computación y Sistemas **20**(3), 425–434 (2016)

7. Chandu, K.R., Chinnakotla, M., Black, A.W., Shrivastava, M.: *WebShodh*: a code mixed factoid question answering system for web. In: Jones, G.J.F., et al. (eds.) CLEF 2017. LNCS, vol. 10456, pp. 104–111. Springer, Cham (2017). https://doi.org/10.1007/978-3-319-65813-1_9

8. Chollet, F., et al.: Keras (2015). https://github.com/fchollet/keras

9. Cimiano, P.: Flexible semantic composition with dudes. In: Proceedings of the Eighth International Conference on Computational Semantics, pp. 272–276. Association for Computational Linguistics (2009)

10. Du, X., Shao, J., Cardie, C.: Learning to ask: neural question generation for reading comprehension. arXiv preprint arXiv:1705.00106 (2017)

11. Feng, M., Xiang, B., Glass, M.R., Wang, L., Zhou, B.: Applying deep learning to answer selection: a study and an open task. In: 2015 IEEE Workshop on Automatic Speech Recognition and Understanding (ASRU), pp. 813–820. IEEE (2015)

12. Forner, P., et al.: Overview of the Clef 2008 multilingual question answering track. In: Peters, C., et al. (eds.) CLEF 2008. LNCS, vol. 5706, pp. 262–295. Springer, Heidelberg (2009). https://doi.org/10.1007/978-3-642-04447-2_34

13. Ganin, Y., et al.: Domain-adversarial training of neural networks. J. Mach. Learn. Res. **17**(1), 2096–2030 (2016)

14. Ghosh, S., Ghosh, S., Das, D.: Complexity metric for code-mixed social media text. arXiv preprint arXiv:1707.01183 (2017)

15. Haas, C., Riezler, S.: Response-based learning for machine translation of open-domain database queries. In: Proceedings of the 2015 Conference of the North American Chapter of the Association for Computational Linguistics: Human Language Technologies, pp. 1339–1344 (2015)

16. Hadla, L.S., Hailat, T.M., Al-Kabi, M.N.: Evaluating Arabic to English machine translation. Editorial Preface **5**(11) (2014)

17. Hakimov, S., Jebbara, S., Cimiano, P.: AMUSE: multilingual semantic parsing for question answering over linked data. In: d'Amato, C., et al. (eds.) ISWC 2017. LNCS, vol. 10587, pp. 329–346. Springer, Cham (2017). https://doi.org/10.1007/978-3-319-68288-4_20

18. Honnibal, M., Johnson, M.: An improved non-monotonic transition system for dependency parsing. In: Proceedings of the 2015 Conference on Empirical Methods in Natural Language Processing, pp. 1373–1378 (2015)

19. Johnson, M., et al.: Google's multilingual neural machine translation system: enabling zero-shot translation. arXiv preprint arXiv:1611.04558 (2016)

20. Joty, S., Nakov, P., Màrquez, L., Jaradat, I.: Cross-language learning with adversarial neural networks: application to community question answering. arXiv preprint arXiv:1706.06749 (2017)

21. Joulin, A., Grave, E., Bojanowski, P., Mikolov, T.: Bag of tricks for efficient text classification. arXiv preprint arXiv:1607.01759 (2016)

22. Kingma, D.P., Ba, J.: Adam: a method for stochastic optimization. arXiv preprint arXiv:1412.6980 (2014)

23. Magnini, B., et al.: Creating the DISEQuA corpus: a test set for multilingual question answering. In: Peters, C., Gonzalo, J., Braschler, M., Kluck, M. (eds.) CLEF 2003. LNCS, vol. 3237, pp. 487–500. Springer, Heidelberg (2004). https://doi.org/10.1007/978-3-540-30222-3_47

24. Magnini, B.: The multiple language question answering track at CLEF 2003. In: Peters, C., Gonzalo, J., Braschler, M., Kluck, M. (eds.) CLEF 2003. LNCS, vol. 3237, pp. 471–486. Springer, Heidelberg (2004). https://doi.org/10.1007/978-3-540-30222-3_46

25. Magnini, B., et al.: Overview of the CLEF 2004 multilingual question answering track. In: Peters, C., Clough, P., Gonzalo, J., Jones, G.J.F., Kluck, M., Magnini, B. (eds.) CLEF 2004. LNCS, vol. 3491, pp. 371–391. Springer, Heidelberg (2005). https://doi.org/10.1007/11519645_38
26. Martino, G.D.S., Romeo, S., Barrón-Cedeno, A., Joty, S., Marquez, L., Moschitti, A., Nakov, P.: Cross-language question re-ranking. arXiv preprint arXiv:1710.01487 (2017)
27. Mikolov, T., Sutskever, I., Chen, K., Corrado, G.S., Dean, J.: Distributed representations of words and phrases and their compositionality. In: Advances in Neural Information Processing Systems, pp. 3111–3119 (2013)
28. Nakov, P., et al.: SemEval-2017 task 3: community question answering. In: Proceedings of the 11th International Workshop on Semantic Evaluation (SemEval-2017), pp. 27–48 (2017)
29. Paszke, A., et al.: Automatic differentiation in pytorch (2017)
30. Raghavi, K.C., Chinnakotla, M.K., Shrivastava, M.: Answer ka type kya he?: Learning to classify questions in code-mixed language. In: Proceedings of the 24th International Conference on World Wide Web, pp. 853–858. ACM (2015)
31. Riedl, M., Biemann, C.: Unsupervised compound splitting with distributional semantics rivals supervised methods. In: Proceedings of the 2016 Conference of the North American Chapter of the Association for Computational Linguistics: Human Language Technologies, pp. 617–622 (2016)
32. Sasaki, Y., Lin, C.J., Chen, K.h., Chen, H.H.: Overview of the NTCIR-6 cross-lingual question answering task. In: Proceedings of the 6th NTCIR Workshop Meeting on Evaluation of Information Access Technologies: Information Retrieval, Question Answering and Cross-Lingual Information Access, 15–18 May 2007, pp. 153–163. Citeseer (2007)
33. Sugiyama, K., et al.: An investigation of machine translation evaluation metrics in cross-lingual question answering. In: Proceedings of the Tenth Workshop on Statistical Machine Translation, pp. 442–449 (2015)
34. Tan, M., dos Santos, C., Xiang, B., Zhou, B.: Improved representation learning for question answer matching. In: Proceedings of the 54th Annual Meeting of the Association for Computational Linguistics (Volume 1: Long Papers), vol. 1, pp. 464–473 (2016)
35. Tuggener, D.: Incremental coreference resolution for German. Ph.D. thesis, Universität Zürich (2016)
36. Ture, F., Boschee, E.: Learning to translate for multilingual question answering. arXiv preprint arXiv:1609.08210 (2016)
37. Vallin, A., et al.: Overview of the CLEF 2005 multilingual question answering track. In: Peters, C., et al. (eds.) CLEF 2005. LNCS, vol. 4022, pp. 307–331. Springer, Heidelberg (2006). https://doi.org/10.1007/11878773_36
38. Veyseh, A.P.B.: Cross-lingual question answering using common semantic space. In: Proceedings of TextGraphs-10: The Workshop on Graph-based Methods for Natural Language Processing, pp. 15–19 (2016)

Knowledge Base Relation Detection via Multi-View Matching

Yang Yu[1(✉)], Kazi Saidul Hasan[1], Mo Yu[2], Wei Zhang[2], and Zhiguo Wang[3]

[1] IBM Watson, Cambridge, USA
yangyuphd@gmail.com
[2] AI Foundations, IBM Research, Yorktown Heights, USA
[3] IBM Research, Yorktown Heights, USA

Abstract. Relation detection is a core component for Knowledge Base Question Answering (KBQA). In this paper, we propose a knowledge base (KB) relation detection model based on multi-view matching, which utilizes useful information extracted from questions and KB. The matching inside each view is through multiple perspectives to compare two input texts thoroughly. All these components are trained in an end-to-end neural network model. Experiments on SimpleQuestions and WebQSP yield state-of-the-art results on relation detection.

Keywords: Relation detection · Multi-view matching
Knowledge base

1 Introduction

Knowledge Base Question Answering (KBQA) systems query a knowledge base (KB) (e.g., Freebase, DBpedia) to answer questions [1–3, 14–16]. To map a natural language question to a KB query, a KBQA system needs to perform at least two sub-tasks: (1) detect KB entities appearing in a question and (2) detect a KB relation associated with a question. This paper focuses on the second sub-task, frequently referred to as **relation detection**, to identify which KB relation(s) are expressed by a given question. As discussed in Yu et al. [21], relation detection remains a bottleneck of KBQA systems owing to its inherent difficulty.

In this paper we propose to improve KB relation detection by exploiting multiple views i.e., by leveraging more information from KB to obtain better question-relation matching. Besides frequently used relation names, we propose to make use of entity type(s) a relation can logically have as tails (i.e., object in a KB triple <subject, predicate, object>). For instance, for a given question *"What country is located in the Balkan Peninsula?"*, the correct relation is *contains* and the best tail type for this relation in this question is *location*. We hypothesize that, in addition to relation names, it may also be useful to match this question against the tail entity type (i.e., *location*) since the question has the word "located", indicating that the answer to this question is a location.

© Springer Nature Switzerland AG 2018
A. Benczúr et al. (Eds.): ADBIS 2018, CCIS 909, pp. 286–294, 2018.
https://doi.org/10.1007/978-3-030-00063-9_27

Our contributions are two-fold. (1) We formulate relation detection as a multi-view matching task, where multiple views of information from both question and relation are extracted. We use an attention-based model to compare question and relation from multiple perspectives in each view. (2) We exploit tail entity types, automatically extracted from KB, in our multi-view matching model. These two contributions help us achieve state-of-the-art KB relation detection accuracies on both WebQSP and SimpleQuestions datasets.

2 Related Work

Relation Extraction. Relation extraction (RE) was researched originally as an sub-field of information extraction. The major research methods in the traditional RE has the knowledge of a (small) pre-defined relation set, then given a text sequence and two target entities, the goal of these methods is to choose a relation or none which means if this relation or no relation holds between the two target entities. Thus from another perspective, RE methods are usually described as a **classification task**. Most of these RE methods need a step to manually pick large amount of features [8,10,23]. Due to recent machine learning and especially deep learning advances, many recent proposed RE approaches begin to explore the benefits of deep learning instead of using hand-crafted features. The main benefits are ranging from pre-trained word embeddings [4,6] to deep neural networks like convolutional neural networks (CNN) and long-short term memories (LSTMs) [9,11,22] and attention models [12,24] which is the key for many NLP tasks, such as machine translation, NER, reading comprehension, etc.

One strong assumption mentioned above in the most RE methods is that a fixed (i.e., closed) set of relation types is given as an prior knowledge, thus no zero-shot learning capability (i.e. detecting new relations that did not occur during training) is required. Another commonality among these RE methods is that the relation set is usually not large. Here are some examples. The widely used ACE2005 has 11/32 coarse/fine-grained relations; SemEval2010 Task8 has 19 relations; TAC-KBP2015 has 74 relations although it considers open-domain Wikipedia relations. Compared to that, KBQA usually has thousands of relations. Thus most RE approaches may not work well by directly being adapted to large number of relations or unseen relations. The relation embeddings in a low-rank tensor method were used [20]. However it is still using a supervised way to train their relation embeddings and relation set used in the experiments is still not large.

3 Problem Overview

Problem Definition. Formally, for an input question q, the task is to identify the correct relation $r^{(gold)}$ from a set of candidate relations $\mathcal{R} = \{r\}$. The problem thus becomes learning a scoring function $s(r|q)$ for optimizing some ranking loss.

Both questions and relations have different views of input features. Each view can be written as a sequence of tokens (regular words or relation names). Therefore, for a view i of relation $\mathbf{r}$, we have $\mathbf{r}^{(i)} = \{r_1^{(i)}, \cdots, r_{M_i}^{(i)}\}$, where M_i is the length of relation $\mathbf{r}$'s word sequence for view i and $r_k^{(i)}$ is a token in the relation's word sequence. The same definition holds for the question side. Finally, we have the multi-view inputs for both a question $\mathbf{q} = \{\mathbf{q}^{(1)}, \cdots, \mathbf{q}^{(N_q)}\}$ and a relation $\mathbf{r} = \{\mathbf{r}^{(1)}, \cdots, \mathbf{r}^{(N_r)}\}$, where N_q and N_r denote the number of views for $\mathbf{q}$ and $\mathbf{r}$, respectively. Note that N_q and N_r may not be equal.

Views for KB Relation Detection. For an input question, we generate views from relation names and their corresponding tail entity types and use three pairs of inputs in the model (see Fig. 1).

1. <*entity name, entity mention*> pair captures entity information from question and KB.
2. <*relation name, modified question*> pair captures the interaction between an input question and a candidate relation. Following previous work [19, 21], we replace the entity mention in a question by a special token ("Balkan Peninsula" is replaced by <e> in Fig. 1), so that the model could focus better on matching a candidate relation name to the entity's context in a question.
3. <*relation tail entity types, modified question*> pair helps determine how well relation tail types match with a question. Section 4 describes how we extract and use tail entity types.

For an input question, the first pair of inputs remains the same for all candidate relations to help the model differentiate between the candidates.

For inputs to the 2nd and 3rd view, we generate two matching feature vectors, one for each of the directions of matching (i.e., for a pair <a, b>, the directions are $a{\rightarrow}b$ and $a{\leftarrow}b$). Finally, the model combines these two pairs of interaction information to have a high-level joint view. The joint view helps us detect the most promising relation given how the question matches with the candidate relation names and the corresponding tail entity types. We present more details in Sect. 5.

4   Relation Tail Entity Types Extraction

More often than not, KB relations can only have tail entities of specific types. For instance, for our example question "*What country is located in the Balkan Peninsula?*", the corresponding relation in Freebase is *contains* and the tail entity (i.e., the answer to the question) can only be of type *location*. This and other relations such as *adjoin_s*, *street_address*, *nearby_airports*, *people_born_here* can only have locations as tail entities, however the relations do not explicitly contain word(s) indicating the type of entities expected as answers. Motivated by this, we hypothesize that exploiting tail entity type information may improve relation detection performance. For our example, the learner may exploit the tail entity type (i.e., *location*) to learn that the relations are somewhat similar as they all share the same tail entity type and learn more generic representations for relations that have locations as tail types. Yin et al. [18] also exploit tail entity types as they predict answer entity type as an intermediate step before predicting an answer. In contrast, we describe next how we heuristically generate a short list of relevant tail entity types for each unique KB relation.

A tail entity in an instance of a relation may be associated with multiple types. Given the triple *<The_Audacity_of_Hope, author, Barack_Obama>*, *Barack_Obama* has types ranging from as generic as *person* to more specific ones such as *author*, *politician*, and *us_president*. Therefore, given the relation *author*, it is crucial to prune the unrelated entity types (*politician, us_president*) and retain the relevant ones (*person, author*). To achieve this, we first obtain at most 500 instances[1] for each unique relation from Freebase. Next, we query for the types for each of the tail entities obtained in the first step.[2] Finally, we retain only the types that at least 95% of the tail entities have. A default special token is used if we can not find any tail entity type for a relation in this approach. Once the tail types are obtained for a particular relation, we form one string by concatenating the words in each of the tail types and use the string as tail entity type string in the model described in Sect. 5.

5   Model Architecture

Figure 1 illustrates the architecture of our model. Apart from the entity alias and entity span pair (henceforth referred to as *entity pair*), each pair of inputs is

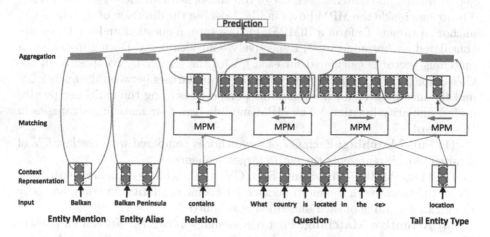

Fig. 1. Multiple view matching for detecting relation in "What country is located in the Balkan Peninsula?".

---

[1] We empirically found that 500 instances were sufficient for our entity type extraction experiment..

[2] In Freebase, the relation *type.object.type* lists the types for an entity.

matched from multiple perspectives, and then the matching representations of all pairs and the representations of entity pair are aggregated for final prediction. Next, we describe the three main components: inputs, matching module and aggregation module.

Inputs. The inputs to all views in the model are word sequences, and our model encodes each sequence in two steps. First, the model constructs a d-dimensional vector for each word with two components: a word and a character-based embedding. A word embedding is a fixed, pre-trained vector (e.g., GloVe [7], word2vec [5]). A character-based embedding is calculated by feeding each character (also represented by a vector) within a word into a LSTM. Second, the model leverages the same BiLSTM to encode all views of inputs. Then, the output *contextual vectors* (henceforth, CV) of each BiLSTM are used in the matching modules. The CVs for a question are fed into multiple matching modules to match with relation and tail types.

Matching Module. We design the matching module to match each view of a relation with a given question. We modify the bilateral multiple perspective matching (BiMPM) model [13], which performs comparably with state-of-the-art systems for several text matching tasks. We hypothesize that BiMPM could also be effective for relation detection since a unique view of a question may be required to match with either a relation or a tail entity type.

In Fig. 1, each box at the "Matching" layer is a single directional multi-perspective matching (MPM) module, therefore two such boxes together form a BiMPM module. Each MPM module takes two sequences, an anchor and a target, as inputs, and matches each CV of the anchor with all the CVs of the target. The arrows inside the MPM boxes in Fig. 1 denote the direction of matching i.e., anchor → target. To form a BiMPM, for instance, a question and a relation are considered anchor and target, respectively, and vice versa. During matching, a matching vector is calculated for each CV of the anchor by composing all the CVs of the target. Then, the model calculates similarities between the anchor CV and the matching vector from multiple perspectives using the multi-perspective cosine similarity function.[3] The MPM module uses four matching strategies in this regard.

(1) **Full-Matching:** Each CV of an anchor is compared with the last CV of a target, which represents the entire target sequence.

(2) **Max-Pooling-Matching:** Each CV of an anchor is compared with every CV of the target with the multi-perspective cosine similarity function, and only the maximum value of each dimension is retained.

(3) **Attentive-Matching:** First, the cosine similarities between all pairs of CVs in the two sequences are calculated. Then the matching vector is calculated by taking the weighted sum of all CVs of the target, where the weights are the cosine similarities computed above.

---

[3] See Wang et al. [13] for details.

(4) **Max-Attentive-Matching:** This strategy is similar to Attentive-Matching except that, instead of taking the weighted sum of all the CVs as the matching vector, it picks the CV with the maximum cosine similarity from the target.

Aggregation Module. The first step in this module is to apply another BiLSTM on the two sequences of matching vectors individually. Then, we construct a fixed-length matching vector by concatenating vectors from the last time-step of the BiLSTM models. This is the representation of the overall matching for one view.

For combining the matching results from different views of input pairs and entity pair, we have the aggregation layer at the end, which takes the matching representations or scores from different views and extracted feature representation for entity pair, then constructs a feature vector for relation prediction. In this work, we simply use the concatenation of different matching representations generated from all the views by the matching modules. The combined representation of all multiple views are transformed into a final prediction through a multiple perception layer.

6   Experiments

Datasets. We use two standard datasets - SimpleQuestions (SQ) [3] and WebQSP (WQ) [17]. Each question in these datasets is labeled with head entity and relation information. SQ has only single-relation questions i.e., there is one <*head, relation, tail*> triple per question. In contrast, WQ has both single and multiple-relation questions. For a multiple-relation question, there are multiple relations on the path connecting a head to a tail entity. We adopt the same approach as Yu et al. [21] to create positive and negative instances.

Experimental Setup. We used development sets to pick the following hyper-parameter values: (1) the size of hidden states for LSTMs (300); (2) learning rate (0.0001); and (3) the number of training epochs (30). All word vectors are initialized with 300-d GloVe embeddings [7]. During testing, we predict the candidate relation with the highest confidence score.

Results and Analysis. Table 1 shows that our model yields state-of-the-art relation detection scores for both WQ (Row 11) and SQ (Row 12) by beating the previous best system [21] by 3.42 and 0.45 points, respectively.

Rows 8–10 show that using relation and tail type as two separate inputs consistently outperforms the setting, where they are provided as a single input (Rows 6–7). Rows 8–9 also show that replacing entity mentions in question texts helps our model to focus more on the contextual parts of questions.

We found that using character embeddings on top of word embeddings does not have any significant impact. We hypothesize that this is due to the small number of KB relations and tail types. Although there are several thousands of

Table 1. Relation detection accuracies for WQ and SQ. The second column lists the pairs of inputs (enclosed in parentheses) matched in our model. Q and Q' denote original and modified (i.e., entity mention replaced) question text, respectively. "Relation" and "Type" denote candidate relation and tail entity types text, respectively. "Relation+Type" denotes a single input, where relation and tail entity types are concatenated by a special symbol. "Entity Pair" refers to entity alias and entity span pair. "Char" column shows if character embeddings are used besides word embeddings.

Row	Model	Char	WQ	SQ
1	BiCNN [16]	Y	77.74	90.0
2	AMPCNN [19]	N/A	-	91.3
3	Hier-Res-BiLSTM [21]	N/A	82.53	93.3
4	(Q', Relation)	Y	75.26	93.13
5	(Q', Relation)	N	75.63	93.25
6	(Q', Relation+Type)	Y	76.41	93.29
7	(Q', Relation+Type)	N	75.95	93.43
8	(Q, Relation)(Q, Type)	Y	83.71	93.13
9	(Q', Relation)(Q', Type)	Y	84.74	93.38
10	(Q', Relation)(Q', Type)	N	84.86	93.52
11	(Entity Pair)(Q', Relation)(Q', Type)	Y	**85.95**	93.69
12	(Entity Pair)(Q', Relation)(Q', Type)	N	85.41	**93.75**

these in Freebase, they are still much smaller in number compared to a vocabulary obtained from a large text corpus. Owing to this, there is little scope for character embeddings to capture prefix, suffix, or stem patterns that can otherwise be observed more frequently in a large corpus.

As the scores indicate, WQ is more difficult than SQ and several reasons may contribute to this trend. First, owing to multi-relations, the average number of candidate relations per question is more in WQ. Second, WQ has more questions that are close to real world questions asked by humans. In contrast, the questions in SQ are synthetic in nature as they are composed by looking at the true answer in KB. Third, WQ needs more complex reasoning on KB, as the path from head entity to answer often consists of multiple hops. As a result, scores for SQ are in the 90s whereas there is still room for improvement for WQ.

Last two rows show that our proposed model achieves the best performance on both WQ and SQ. While replacing entity mentions yields improvement, the model cannot use entity information in this process. However, our results confirmed that extracting features from entity pair inputs separately for final prediction was useful.

7   Conclusion

Relation detection, a crucial step in KBQA, is significantly different from general relation extraction. To accomplish this task, we propose a novel KB relation detection model that performs bilateral multiple perspective matching between multiple views of question and KB relation. Empirical results show that our model outperforms the previous methods significantly on KB relation detection task and is expected to enable a KBQA system perform better than state-of-the-art KBQA systems.

References

1. Bast, H., Haussmann, E.: More accurate question answering on freebase. In: Proceedings of the 24th ACM International on Conference on Information and Knowledge Management, pp. 1431–1440. ACM (2015)
2. Berant, J., Chou, A., Frostig, R., Liang, P.: Semantic parsing on Freebase from question-answer pairs. In: Proceedings of the 2013 Conference on Empirical Methods in Natural Language Processing, pp. 1533–1544. Association for Computational Linguistics, Seattle, Washington, USA, October 2013
3. Bordes, A., Usunier, N., Chopra, S., Weston, J.: Large-scale simple question answering with memory networks (2015). arXiv preprint arXiv:1506.02075
4. Gormley, M.R., Yu, M., Dredze, M.: Improved relation extraction with feature-rich compositional embedding models. In: Proceedings of the 2015 Conference on Empirical Methods in Natural Language Processing, pp. 1774–1784. Association for Computational Linguistics, Lisbon, Portugal, September 2015
5. Mikolov, T., Sutskever, I., Chen, K., Corrado, G.S., Dean, J.: Distributed representations of words and phrases and their compositionality. In: Advances in Neural Information Processing Systems, pp. 3111–3119 (2013)
6. Nguyen, T.H., Grishman, R.: Employing word representations and regularization for domain adaptation of relation extraction. In: Proceedings of the 52nd Annual Meeting of the Association for Computational Linguistics, vol. 2, pp. 68–74. Association for Computational Linguistics, Baltimore, Maryland, June 2014. Short Papers
7. Pennington, J., Socher, R., Manning, C.D.: Glove: global vectors for word representation. EMNLP **14**, 1532–43 (2014)
8. Rink, B., Harabagiu, S.: UTD: classifying semantic relations by combining lexical and semantic resources. In: Proceedings of the 5th International Workshop on Semantic Evaluation, pp. 256–259. Association for Computational Linguistics, Uppsala, Sweden, July 2010
9. dos Santos, C., Xiang, B., Zhou, B.: Classifying relations by ranking with convolutional neural networks. In: Proceedings of the 53rd Annual Meeting of the Association for Computational Linguistics and the 7th International Joint Conference on Natural Language Processing, vol. 1, pp. 626–634. Association for Computational Linguistics, Beijing, China, July 2015. Long Papers
10. Sun, A., Grishman, R., Sekine, S.: Semi-supervised relation extraction with large-scale word clustering. In: Proceedings of the 49th Annual Meeting of the Association for Computational Linguistics: Human Language Technologies, pp. 521–529. Association for Computational Linguistics, Portland, Oregon, USA, June 2011
11. Vu, N.T., Adel, H., Gupta, P., Schütze, H.: Combining recurrent and convolutional neural networks for relation classification. In: Proceedings of the 2016 Conference of the North American Chapter of the Association for Computational Linguistics: Human Language Technologies, pp. 534–539. Association for Computational Linguistics, San Diego, California, June 2016

12. Wang, L., Cao, Z., de Melo, G., Liu, Z.: Relation classification via multi-level attention CNNs. In: Proceedings of the 54th Annual Meeting of the Association for Computational Linguistics, vol. 1, pp. 1298–1307. Association for Computational Linguistics, Berlin, Germany, August 2016. Long Papers

13. Wang, Z., Hamza, W., Florian, R.: Bilateral multi-perspective matching for natural language sentences. In: IJCAI 2017 (2017)

14. Xu, K., Reddy, S., Feng, Y., Huang, S., Zhao, D.: Question answering on freebase via relation extraction and textual evidence. In: Proceedings of the 54th Annual Meeting of the Association for Computational Linguistics, vol. 1, pp. 2326–2336. Association for Computational Linguistics, Berlin, Germany, August 2016. Long Papers

15. Yao, X., Berant, J., Van Durme, B.: Freebase qa: Information extraction or semantic parsing? ACL **2014**, 82 (2014)

16. Yih, W.t., Chang, M.W., He, X., Gao, J.: Semantic parsing via staged query graph generation: question answering with knowledge base. In: Association for Computational Linguistics (ACL) (2015)

17. Yih, W.T., Richardson, M., Meek, C., Chang, M.W., Suh, J.: The value of semantic parse labeling for knowledge base question answering. In: Proceedings of the 54th Annual Meeting of the Association for Computational Linguistics, vol. 2, pp. 201–206. Association for Computational Linguistics, Berlin, Germany, August 2016. Short Papers

18. Yin, J., Zhao, W.X., Li, X.M.: Type-aware question answering over knowledge base with attention- based tree-structured neural networks. J. Comput. Sci. Technol. **32**(4), 805–813 (2017). https://doi.org/10.1007/s11390-017-1761-8

19. Yin, W., Yu, M., Xiang, B., Zhou, B., Schütze, H.: Simple question answering by attentive convolutional neural network. In: Proceedings of COLING 2016, the 26th International Conference on Computational Linguistics: Technical Papers, pp. 1746–1756. The COLING 2016 Organizing Committee, Osaka, Japan, December 2016

20. Yu, M., Dredze, M., Arora, R., Gormley, M.R.: Embedding lexical features via low-rank tensors. In: Proceedings of the 2016 Conference of the North American Chapter of the Association for Computational Linguistics: Human Language Technologies, pp. 1019–1029. Association for Computational Linguistics, San Diego, California, June 2016. http://www.aclweb.org/anthology/N16-1117

21. Yu, M., Yin, W., Hasan, K.S., dos Santos, C.N., Xiang, B., Zhou, B.: Improved neural relation detection for knowledge base question answering. In: Proceedings of the 55th Annual Meeting of the Association for Computational Linguistics, ACL 2017, Vancouver, Canada, 30 July–4 August, vol. 1, pp. 571–581 (2017). Long Papers

22. Zeng, D., Liu, K., Lai, S., Zhou, G., Zhao, J.: Relation classification via convolutional deep neural network. In: Proceedings of COLING 2014, the 25th International Conference on Computational Linguistics: Technical Papers, pp. 2335–2344. Dublin City University and Association for Computational Linguistics, Dublin, Ireland, August 2014

23. Zhou, G., Su, J., Zhang, J., Zhang, M.: Exploring various knowledge in relation extraction. In: Association for Computational Linguistics, pp. 427–434 (2005)

24. Zhou, P., Shi, W., Tian, J., Qi, Z., Li, B., Hao, H., Xu, B.: Attention-based bidirectional long short-term memory networks for relation classification. In: Proceedings of the 54th Annual Meeting of the Association for Computational Linguistics, vol. 2, pp. 207–212. Association for Computational Linguistics, Berlin, Germany, August 2016. Short Papers

First International Workshop on BIG Data Storage, Processing and Mining for Personalized MEDicine, BIGPMED

Software Tools for Medical Imaging
Extended Abstract

Luciano Caroprese[1]([⊠]), Pietro Lucio Cascini[2], Pietro Cinaglia[2],
Francesco Dattola[3], Pasquale Franco[3], Pasquale Iaquinta[3], Miriam Iusi[3],
Giuseppe Tradigo[2], Pierangelo Veltri[2], and Ester Zumpano[1]

[1] Department of Informatics, Modeling, Electronics and System Engineering,
University of Calabria, Rende, Italy
l.caroprese@dimes.unical.it
[2] Department of Surgical and Medical Sciences, University of Catanzaro,
Catanzaro, Italy
[3] e way Enterprise Business Solutions, Cosenza, Italy

Abstract. We are in the era of Big Data. Data are everywhere! They
are part of the information processing system of all sectors, from science to government, from healthcare to media, from university to real
time commerce. In healthcare, in particular, the increasing use of medical devices, such as the Computed Tomography (CT) and the Magnetic
Resonance Imaging (MRI) has led to the generation of large amounts
of data, including image data. Bioinformatics solutions provide an effective approach for image data processing techniques whose final aim is to
support scientists and physicians in diagnosis and therapies. This paper
surveys bioinformatics toolkits for medical imaging.

Keywords: Medical imaging · Decision support system
Medical information systems

1 Introduction

The use of sophisticated devices has greatly improved the acquisition of data at
very high resolution and faster rate. Bioinformatics tools allow to retrieve information able to support a scientist during a diagnosis in order to detect efficiently
abnormalities and to monitor their changes over time. In the last years, medical and biological images are quickly growing in terms of size and information
content. The term "bioimage" concerns all images related to biological samples
acquired using medical technologies such as the Computed Tomography (CT)
or the Magnetic Resonance Imaging (MRI).

The problem of defining diagnosis starting from images is an important task
and highly relevant in the medical domain. Emerging applications such as tele-
support to give advise from remote, increases the difficulties in giving advises
from image analysis. Similarly, during monitoring and ambient assisted living,
where the patient's condition is continually monitored and diagnosed for anomalies and therapy adherence, the image analysis and interpretation is a relevant

A. Benczúr et al. (Eds.): ADBIS 2018, CCIS 909, pp. 297–304, 2018.
https://doi.org/10.1007/978-3-030-00063-9_28

task. Also, for chronic diseases, a correct interpretation of images may be crucial for early disease detection.

To this end, the use of innovative technology instruments for supporting medical interdisciplinary collaboration among different teams (belonging to different departments, external structures and research institutes), geographically distributed in the network, is a crucial task. A collaborative tool allows to integrate skills, expertize, knowledge and more in general information. This facility helps in clinical case resolution as gives the opportunity to a specific structure to share a clinical case with external specialized structures so that obtaining what is called in the medical field, a "second opinion" (without physically moving neither the patient nor his documentation). This paper surveys bioinformatics solutions and toolkits for medical imaging with a particular emphasis on the eIMES 3D (Evolution Imaging System 3D) system. eIMES 3D supports clinicians for images studies, diagnostic and images reconstruction developed and it is a joint ongoing project that involves the DIMES Department of the University of Calabria and the e way Enterprise Solutions, a local software house. The system, in its basic features, has been designed and implemented following the requirements of the oncology department of an Italian Hospital and is currently used in many Italian Hospital. A further extension of the eIMES 3D system, that goes under the name of SIMPATICO 3D, has been selected for funding under the recently launched FESR 2014/2020. eIMES 3D has been developed within a project called ReCaTuR for RAre Cancer Network (i.e. Network of Rare Cancer), aiming to define a network for the management, organization and distribution of medical information. The software is proposed as a valuable technological support to the medical profession, without in any way reducing his role and expertise in the approach and in the clinical case resolution. eIMES 3D receives, stores, processes and transmits biomedical images through stereoscopic techniques; the high definition of the images allows remote diagnosis. The ability to build plug-in modules enables to easily implement new features in eIMES 3D, so that ensuring its further development and its sustainability.

2   Tools in Medical Imaging

Techniques and methods for image analysis are generally based on Machine Learning (ML) and Artificial Intelligence (AI). These allow to efficiently derive relevant information from heterogeneous data and are the most used for the developing of bioinformatics tools. A standard able to produce a comparison among toolkits are not defined, as each tool is often designed for determinate needs related to different problems, and its approach is therefore to be considered context-specific [1]. A list of useful toolkits is shown below; only objective criteria (e.g. programming-language, and features) are reported so that everyone may correlate a toolkit in reference to his needs.

ODTbrain. ODTbrain is a Python library that implements a back-propagation algorithm for dense diffraction tomography in 3D [2]. The three-dimensional (3D) refractive index distribution of a unique cell allows to describe its inner structure in a marker-free manner. The term dense, full-view tomographic data set denotes a set of images of a cell acquired for multiple rotational positions, densely distributed from 0 to 360°. The projection tomography, based on the inversion of the Radon transform, is generally used to perform the reconstruction and its quality is greatly improved when first order scattering is taken into account. This advanced reconstruction technique is called diffraction tomography. The first implementation of diffraction tomography has been proposed in ODTbrain [2]. The algorithm is an extension to optical projection tomography that takes into account diffraction of light due to the refractive index of the sample. In ODTbrain the reconstruction process in divided in three main steps: filtering, reconstruction, object data construction. ODTbrain is able to reconstruct 3D refractive index maps from projections of biological or artificial phase objects; the algorithm is validated performing the analysis on a simulated dataset and subsequently authors have compared results with the reconstruction qualities of Optical Diffraction Tomography (ODT) and Optical Projection Tomography (OPT).

OCP-CHARM. OCP-CHARM [3] is a user-friendly image-based classification algorithm. It is inspired by WND-CHARM. The latter is a multi-purpose image classification algorithm that can be applied without optimization or modifying the starting data; features are computed on the whole image, and no segmentation is required [4]. Using the CP-CHARM algorithm a user is able to extract several morphological features from an image without first being segmented; furthermore, in order to be suitable and accessible to all the biological research community, even with few expertise, CP-CHARM relies on CellProfiler an open source image analysis software for quantitative analysis of biological images [5]. The proposed method has been demonstrated to perform well on a wide range of bioimage classification problems. The proposed method has been validated firstly by showing that it could achieve performance similar to those of WND-CHARM. Then the algorithm has been used on several kinds of biological datasets, e.g. data freely available from the Broad Bioimage Benchmark Collection (BBBC, [12]) and tissue images from the Human Protein Atlas (HPA, [13]). CP-CHARM has been demonstrated to perform well on a wide range of bioimage classification problems.

SCIFIO. SCIFIO is a flexible framework for SCientific Image Format Input and Output. In other words, it is a library for reading and writing N-dimensional image data. SCIFIO is an open source plugin for the SciJava framework that offers support for handling of scientific images. SCIFIO defines a common pattern for image format construction and can be easily extended from custom formats to new metadata schema. It is developed by the ImageJ development team at the Laboratory for Optical and Computational Instrumentation (LOCI) at the University of Wisconsin-Madison. The Open Microscopy Environment's Bio-Formats library provides the ability to convert many proprietary image formats to a common OME-TIFF format, using the OME-XML schema. This allows scientists to freely share image data without being restricted by proprietary format barriers. It is part of the SciJavasoftware stack, and in use by several projects including ImageJ2, ImgLib2, and the Insight Toolkit (ITK). One of the main features of SCIFIO concerns the support of multiple domain-specific formats within a unified environment [6].

NIF. The Neuroscience Information Framework (NIF) is a framework that promotes the integrating access to Web-Based neuroscience resources [7]. It is supported from the Institutes and Centers forming the NIH Blueprint for Neuroscience Research. The framework is based on an Open Source design and offers dynamic and web-accessible resources focused on neuroscience that are described using an integrated terminology, also it is able to support concept-based queries as well as the integration of neuroscience information with complementary areas of biomedicine.

WHIDE. Web-based Hyperbolic Image Data Explorer (WHIDE) combines more features related to principles of machine learning, and scientific-information in order to analyze the aspects (space and collocation) of Toponome Imaging System (TIS) images. WHIDE uses Hierarchical Hyperbolic SOM (H2SOM) clustering to resolve non-linear features and dynamic interactive manipulation of the colors, as well as to organize the clusters in a hierarchical structure. Authors tested the tool for TIS analysis but is not excluded that it is applicable to other MBI data [8].

GALA. Graph-based Active Learning of Agglomeration (GALA) is an algorithm, implemented in python language, for image segmentation. GALA belongs a class of segmentation algorithms called agglomerative algorithms, in which segments are formed by merging smaller segments. It works by repeatedly consulting a gold standard segmentation (prepared by human annotators) as it agglomerates sub-segments according to its current best guess. More specifically, GALA accumulates a training dataset used to fit a classifier, that guides the subsequent agglomeration decisions. GALA includes several scientific Python libraries: numpy, scipy, and others, to perform segmentation analysis; also, it implements a solution based on machine-learning approach [9].

ACQ4. ACQ4 is a modular software for data acquisition and analysis in neurophysiology research. It is available for download at http://www.acq4.org. ACQ4 integrates the task of acquiring, managing and analyzing experimental data. It is developed as general-purpose tools with the main aim to combine traditional electrophysiology, photostimulation, and imaging for experiments automation. The system is highly modular, and therefore it is quite simple to add new functionalities. In [10] authors present several use-cases for ACQ4 to illustrate its functionalities reported as a set of experiments that are possible using this tool; below are briefly listed: (i) Multiphoton calcium imaging during whisker deflection; (ii) Laser scanning photostimulation; (iii) In vitro patch clamp with drug perfusion; (iv) In vivo recording during an operant conditioning task. ACQ4 uses free and open-source tools such as Python, NumPy/SciPy for numerical computation, PyQt for the user interface and PyQtGraph for scientific graphics.

jicbioimage. jicbioimage is a tool implemented in python language for automated and reproducible bioimage analysis; jicbioimage has been used on over fifteen internal projects at various stages of the publication pipeline [11]. Using jicbioimaget an user is able to: (i) read bioimage data in several format, for this aim the features of Python-BioFormat are imported by authors; (ii) transform and segment images using methods based on numpy, scipy, and scikit-image; (iii) examine the versions for an experiment: briefly, the versions for an initial image are stored by jicbioimage during all transformations to help a scientist to understands the steps performed by the tool and its sub-processes.

eIMES 3D. IMES 3D [14–16] has been implemented by using an enterprise development model which allows to design integrated software platforms suited for medical and technical specialists of the Complex Operative Unit of Medical Oncology, which ensures scalability and modularity. It allows the management, analysis and visualization of imaging data, which are processed and manipulated in 3D stereoscopic graphic environments [14]. It uses an advanced programming paradigm, called MVVM (Model-View-View-Model), that allow the direct binding of medical information with three-dimensional graphics objects. The structure of the eIMES 3D system is based on different information layers implemented with the latest generation of design patterns and directly interconnected through web services. Its main components are (Fig. 1):

- *DICOM Data Entry*, which populates the system with the 3D Imaging. The system allows to import and export 3D Imaging content. Data are in the standard DICOM format so that they can be easily exchanged within the Network in a non-destructive mode and displayed on different devices. eIMES

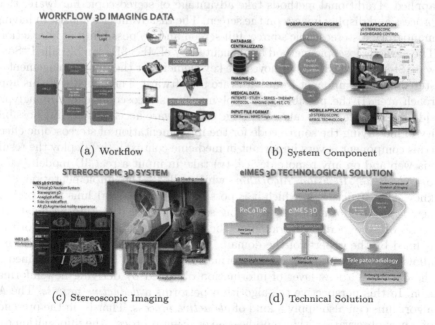

(a) Workflow

(b) System Component

(c) Stereoscopic Imaging

(d) Technical Solution

Fig. 1. eIMES 3D

3D manages different types of images: Monochrome (e.g.: CR, CT, MR) and color (e.g. US, 3D reconstruction); Static images (e.g.: CR, MG, CT) and dynamic sequences (e.g. XA, US); Tablets and uncompressed (RLE, JPEG Lossy, Lossless JPEG, JPEG 2000).

– *3D Navision Stereoscopic*, a 3D display system in a virtual environment that provides the possibility of applying stereoscopic effects in order to create the depth effect on the available data and to provide more information from a diagnostic point of view. In more details eIMES 3D uses an innovative technology for the representation of three-dimensional data called WebGL. The WebGL library provides an API (Application Programming Interface) for 3D graphics for all browsers that support this technology and implements advanced methods and algorithms for the representation of data in stereoscopic mode. One of the advantages of this technology is the ability to render images on different devices, from desktop workstation graphics to web browser, OLED Monitor and mobile device of latest generation. The stereoscopic effect is achieved by building a 3D stereogram. It is possible to construct the stereogram by selecting different mode. At the present, the system implements two different modes: (i) in the Anaglyph mode a 2D transformation is performed using filters of different (usually chromatically opposite) colors; (ii) in the Side-by-side mode, a 3D transformation is performed. In this case the transformation does not alter the image, but splits it into two different images each of them situated at a precise focal distance. The 3D effect can be visualized by using 3D glasses. The important thing that has to be evinced is that eIMES 3D introduces a new technology in the way stereoscopic 3D is applied. Traditional methods take advantage of stereoscopic hardware, that process and display images on the screen. The disadvantages consist in having mandatory a stereoscopic source, full-screen and no possibility of interaction. The new stereoscopic method implemented by eIMES 3D, can be called "Software Stereoscopic 3D" as it moves the key element for the right management of stereoscopic component from hardware to software. The benefits of this approach are: (i) the possibility of applying any stereoscopic effect (anaglyph, side-by-side, etc.), (ii) take advantage of hardware acceleration, (iii) possibility of modifying the source code for the implementation of stereoscopic effect (this component is very important in medicine context), (iv) deploy the result via web and on any remote device, (v) take in input a real 3D model.

– *Search Belief Revision Algorithm*, which allows the implementation of a knowledge structure in which it is possible to define algorithms that provide new layer of information by applying set of rules fixed by international protocols or by expert of the domain. The logical formalization of AI algorithm is fixed by the experts of the domain, that defines a set of logical rules that allow to extract from the basic information (data and imaging) contained in the database a new layer of information obtained by deriving new information. In this perspective the algorithm performs a *deductive process*. The AI algorithms can also apply a kind of *abductive process*. That is, in the presence of a new observation, that modifies the existing protocol, the information can be updated in order to be consistent with new specifications. This process can be performed on both stored data and imaging.

eIMES 3D realizes a 3D virtual laboratory in which different information from different diagnostic tests are combined to order to provide to the clinicians a powerful and comprehensive tool for diagnostic and case study analysis. eIMES 3D, by using the WebGL technology, allows the remote transfer of imaging dataset in non-destructive mode, that is without applying compression of images or other changes that would alter the nature of the image. Moreover, by using the innovative framework, called "Universal App Platform" (UAP), it allows to visualize data and image on different devices (Monitor stereoscopic, Laptop, WorkStation Graphics, tablets, smartphones, etc. ...) and on heterogeneous platforms (web, desktop, iOS, Android, WindowsPhone, blackberry and the mobile device legacy). The eIMES 3D GUI uses the WebGL 3D Controller library to allow the interactive 3D manipulation of three-dimensional datasets. In eIMES 3D, data and images can also be shared in videoconference sessions. To this aim the system contains a software module, Cisco System WebEx, that provides different and innovative functionalities for file sharing and team connectivity while guaranteeing high levels of security. Specifically, it allows to share multimedia content by activating cooperative sessions not only using PC Desktop and Workstations, but also using different app WebEx for iPhone, iPad, Android or BlackBerry.

3   Conclusions

The fast growth of medical imaging may be seen monitoring the increase of available solutions and the interest in its research field, as well as in clinical practice. The increasing adoption in the clinical practice of the 3D solutions, due also to the evolution of technologies in medical imaging, such as the Computed Tomography and the Magnetic Resonance Imaging, produces a large amount of data. In the last years, medical and biological images are quickly growing in terms of size and information content and this trend will increase in the next future. Knowledge extraction from medical images is still a complex task. This paper surveys bioinformatics toolkits for medical imaging.

References

1. Erickson, B.J., Korfiatis, P., Akkus, Z., Kline, T., Philbrick, K.: Toolkits and Libraries for Deep Learning. J. Digit. Imaging (2017)
2. Muller, P., Schurmann, M., Guck, J.: ODTbrain: a Python library for full-view, dense diffraction tomography. BMC Bioinf. (2015)
3. Uhlmann, V., Singh, S., Carpenter, A.E.: CP-CHARM: segmentation-free image classification made accessible. BMC Bioinf. (2016)
4. Orlov, N., Shamir, L., Macura, T., Johnston, J., Eckley, D.M., Goldberg, I.G.: WND-CHARM: multi-purpose image classification using compound image transforms. Pattern Recognit. Lett. (2008)

5. Dao, D., Fraser, A.N., Hung, J., Ljosa, V., Singh, S., Carpenter, A.E.: Cell Profiler-Analyst: interactive data exploration, analysis and classification of large biological image sets. Bioinf. (2016)
6. Hiner, M.C., Rueden, C.T., Eliceiri, K.W.: SCIFIO: an extensible framework to support scientific image formats. BMC Bioinf. (2016)
7. Gardner, D., et al.: The neuroscience information framework: a data and knowledge environment for neuroscience. Neuroinformatics (2008)
8. Kolling, J., Langenkamper, D., Abouna, S., Khan, M., Nattkemper, T.W.: WHIDE'a web tool for visual data mining colocation patterns in multivariate bioimages. Bioinf. (2012)
9. Nunez-Iglesias, J., Kennedy, R., Plaza, S.M., Chakraborty, A., Katz, W.T.: Graph-based active learning of agglomeration (GALA): a Python library to segment 2D and 3D neuroimages. Front Neuroinform. (2014)
10. Campagnola, L., Kratz, M.B., Manis, P.B.: ACQ4: an open-source software plat-form for data acquisition and analysis in neurophysiology research. Front Neuroin-form. (2014)
11. Olsson, T.S., Hartley, M.: jicbioimage: a tool for automated and reproducible bioimage analysis. PeerJ (2016)
12. Ljosa, V., Sokolnicki, K.L., Carpenter, A.E.: Annotated high-throughput microscopy image sets for validation. Nat. Methods 9(7), 637 (2012)
13. Uhlen, M., et al.: Towards a knowledge-based human protein atlas. Nat. Biotechnol. 28(12), 1248–50 (2010)
14. Turano, S., et al.: ReCaTuR - rare cancer network calabria - implementing a soft-ware system based on 3D stereoscopic imaging
15. Iaquinta, P., et al.: eIMES 3D mobile: A mobile application for diagnostic proce-dures. In: BIBM 2017, pp. 1634–1641
16. Iaquinta, P., et al.: eIMES 3D: an innovative medical images analysis tool to sup-port diagnostic and surgical intervention. Proc. Comput. Sci. 110, 459–464 (2017)

Humanity Is Overrated. or Not.
Automatic Diagnostic Suggestions
by Greg, ML
(Extended Abstract)

Paola Lapadula[1], Giansalvatore Mecca[1], Donatello Santoro[1(✉)],
Luisa Solimando[2], and Enzo Veltri[2]

[1] Università della Basilicata, Potenza, Italy
donatello.santoro@unibas.it
[2] Svelto! Big Data Cleaning and Analytics, Potenza, Italy

Abstract. This paper introduces Greg, ML, a machine-learning tool for
generating automatic diagnostic suggestions based on patient profiles.
We discuss the architecture that stands at the core of Greg, and some
experimental results based on the working prototype we have developed.
Finally, we discuss challenges and opportunities related to the use of this
kind of tools in medicine, and some important lessons learned developing
the tool. In this respect, despite the ironic title of this paper, we underline
that Greg should be conceived primarily as a support for expert doctors
in their diagnostic decisions, and can hardly replace humans in their
judgment.

1 Introduction

The larger availability of digital data related to all sectors of our everyday lives
has created opportunities for data-based applications that would not be con-
ceivable a few years ago. One example is medicine: the push for the widespread
adoption of electronic medical records [5,8] and digital medical reports is paving
the ground for new applications based on these data.

Greg, ML is one of these applications. It is a machine-learning tool for generating automatic diagnostic suggestions based on patient profiles. In essence, Greg
takes as input a digital profile of a patient, and suggests one or more diagnosis
that, according to its internal models, fit the profile with a given probability. We
assume that a doctor inspects these diagnostic suggestions, and takes informed
actions about the patients.

We notice that the idea of using machine learning for the purpose of examining medical data is not new [7,9,10]. In fact, several efforts that have been taken
in this direction [1,6]. To the best of our knowledge, however, all of the existing
tools concentrate on rather specific learning tasks, for example identifying a single pathology – like heart disease [11,13], or pneumonia [12], or cancer, where
results of remarkable quality have been reported [14]. On the contrary, Greg has

A. Benczúr et al. (Eds.): ADBIS 2018, CCIS 909, pp. 305–313, 2018.
https://doi.org/10.1007/978-3-030-00063-9_29

the distinguishing feature of being a broad-scope diagnostic-suggestion tool. In fact, at the core of the tool stands a generic learning model that allows to suggest large numbers of pathologies, currently several dozens, and in perspective several hundreds.

Greg is a research project developed by Svelto!, a spin-off of the data-management group at University of Basilicata. A crucial step in order to develop the system was to get access to large amounts of medical records. These were obtained based on a collaboration with GHS Srl, a company in Basilicata specialized in medical services, within a joint experimental trial with some hospitals.

The rest of the paper is devoted to introducing Greg, as follows. We discuss the internal architecture of the tool in Sect. 2. Then, we introduce the methodology and the additional tools in Sect. 3. We introduce some experimental results based on the current version of the tool in Sect. 4.

Finally, in Sect. 5 we conclude by discussing the possible applications we envision for Greg, and discuss a few crucial lessons learned with the tool, which, in turn, have inspired the title of this paper.

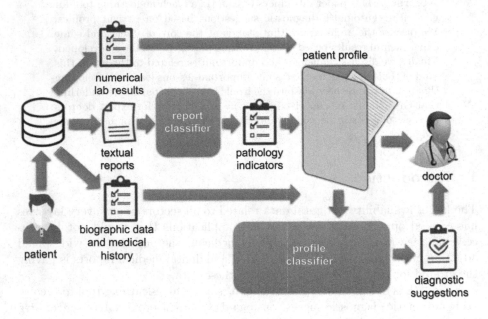

Fig. 1. Architecture of Greg.

2   Architecture of Greg

The architecture and the overall flow of Greg is depicted in Fig. 1.

As we have already discussed, at the core of Greg stands a classifier for patient profiles that provides doctors with diagnostic suggestions. Profiles are entirely anonymous, i.e., Greg does not store nor requires any sensitive data about patients, and are composed of three main blocks:

- anonymous biographical data, mainly age and gender, and medical history of the patient, i.e., past medical events and pathologies, especially the chronic ones;
- result of lab exams, in numerical format;
- textual reports from instrumental exams, like RX, ultrasounds etc.

These items compose the patient profile that is fed to the profile classifier in order to propose diagnostic suggestions to doctors. Notice that, while biographic data, medical history and lab exam results are essentially structured data, and therefore can be easily integrated into the profile, reports of instrumental exams are essentially unstructured. As a consequence, Greg relies on a second learning module to extract what we call *pathology indicators*, i.e., structured labels indicating anomalies in the report that may suggest the presence of a pathology.

The report classifier is essentially a natural-language processing module. It takes the text of the report in natural language and identifies pathology indicators that are then integrated within the patient profile.

The report classifier is, in a way, the crucial module for the construction of the patient profile. In fact, reports of instrumental exams often carry crucial information for the purpose of identifying the correct diagnostic suggestions. At the same time, their treatment is language-dependent, and learning is labor-intensive, since it requires to label large set of reports in order to train the classifier.

Once the profile for a new patient has been built, it is fed to the profile classifier that outputs diagnostic suggestions to the doctor. There are a few important aspects to be noticed here.

- First, Greg is trained to predict only a finite set of diagnoses. This means that it is intended primarily as a tool to gain positive evidence about pathologies that might be present, rather than as a tool to exclude pathologies that are not present. In other terms, the fact that Greg does not suggest a specific diagnosis does not mean that can be excluded, since it might only be the case that Greg has not be trained for that particular pathology. It can be seen that handling a large number of diagnoses is crucial, in this respect.
- Second, Greg associated a degree of probability with each diagnostic suggestion, i.e., it ranks them with a confidence measure. This is important, since the tool may provide several different suggestions for a given profile, and not all of them are to be considered as equally relevant.

It can be seen that a tool like Greg is as effective as seamless its integration with the everyday procedures of a medical institution is. To foster this kind of adoption, Greg can be used as a stand-alone tool, with its own user-interface, but it has been developed primarily as an engine-backed API, that can be easily integrated with any medical information system that is already deployed in medical units and wards. Ideally, with this kind of integration, accessing medical suggestions provided by Greg should cost no more than clicking a button, in addition of the standard procedure for patient-data gathering and medical-record compilation.

3   The Greg Workflow and Ecosystem

As we have discussed in the previous sections, the effectiveness of a system like Greg is strongly related to the number of pathologies which it can provide suggestions for. We therefore put quite a lot of effort in structuring the learning workflow in order to make it lean and easily reproducible. In this section we summarize a few key findings in this respect, that led us to the development of a number of additional tools, which compose the Greg ecosystem.

A first important observation we make is that a system like Greg needs to make reference to a standardized set of diagnosis. As it is common, we rely on the international classification of diseases, *ICD-10 (DRG)*[1]. This, however, poses a challenge when dealing with large and heterogeneous collections of medical records coming from disparate sources, which do not necessarily are associated with a DRG. This poses a standardization problem for diagnosis labels. In fact, standardizing the vocabulary of pathologies and pathology indicators is crucial in the early stages of data preparation. To this end, we leveraged the consolidated suite of data-cleaning tools developed by our research group over the years [2–4].

A second important observation is that we need to handle large and complex amounts of data gathered from medical information systems, including biographical data, admissions and patient medical history, medical records, multiple lab exams, and multiple reports. These data need to be explored, selected and prepared for the purpose of training the learning models. In order to streamline the data-preparation process, we decided to develop a tool to explore the available data. The tool is called Caddy and is essentially a data warehouse build on top of the transactional medical databases. This allowed us to adopt a structured approach to data exploration and data selection, that proved essential in the development of the tool.

However, the tool that proved to be the most crucial in the development of Greg is DAIMO, our instance labeler. DAIMO stands for *Digital Annotation of Instances and Markup of Objects*. It is a tool explicitly conceived to support the labeling phase of machine learning projects. A snapshot of the system is shown in Fig. 2.

DAIMO is a semi-automated tool for data labeling. It provides a simple and effective interface to explore pre-defined collections of samples to label. Samples may be either textual, or even structured – for example, in tabular format– or even of mixed type. Users that are tasked with labeling can cooperatively explore the samples, pick them, explore existing labels and add more. Figure 2 shows the process of labeling one report. Labels associated with the report are on the right. Each corresponds to a colored portion of the text.

We believe that even only the availability of an intuitive tool to support cooperative labeling-work significantly increases productivity. In addition to this, DAIMO provides additional functionalities that further improve the process.

First, it allows to define *label vocabularies*, in order to standardize the way in which labels are assigned to samples. Users usually search labels within the

---

[1] http://www.who.int/classifications/icd/icdonlineversions/en/.

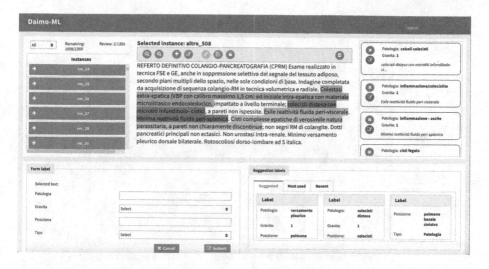

Fig. 2. DAIMO, the ML Labeling Tool.

vocabulary, and add new ones only when the ones they need are not present. When dealing with complex labeling tasks with many different labels, such a systematic approach is crucial in order to get good-quality results.

Second, DAIMO is able to *learn* labeling strategies from examples. After some initial training, it does not only collects new labels from users, but actually suggests them, so that users need only to accept or refuse DAIMO's suggestions. This approach really transforms the labeling process from the inside out, since after a while it is DAIMO, not the user to do most of the work.

In fact, in our experience, working with DAIMO may lower text-labeling times up to one order of magnitude with respect to manual, unassisted labeling.

4   Experimental Results

Greg is an ongoing effort. We plan to have a first release by mid 2018, but an advanced prototype is already available at URL http://demo.svelto-spinoff.it/greg. We have used the prototype to conduct a number of experiments to assess the feasibility of the overall approach.

In particular, we conducted some first experiments based on a handful of medical records – a total of 300 – that were made available to us for an early trial. Figure 3 shows some results from these preliminary tests, with reference to 4 diagnosis. In order to train the classifier, 70% of the records were used to train the classifier, the remaining 30% to test predictions. The chart shows the values of precision, recall, and accuracy over the test set. As a ground truth for medical records we used the diagnoses reported in the associated discharge letters.

Given such a small number of samples, the classifier was trained in order to favor precision over recall. In fact, one of our priorities was to understand what

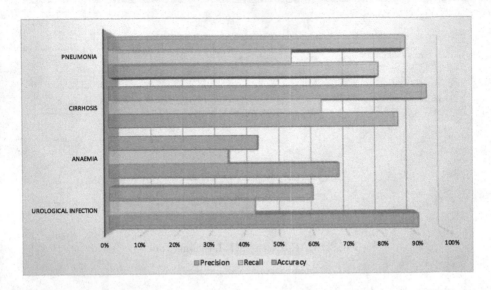

Fig. 3. Experimental results prior to diagnosis review

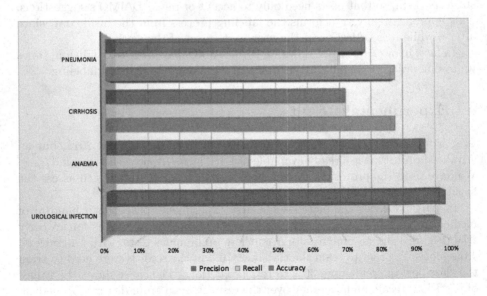

Fig. 4. Experimental results after diagnosis review

levels of precision could be obtained, even when a small number of samples were available.

Results shown in Fig. 3 are not as good as we would have expected, especially for anaemia and urological infection. Our investigation of the data, however, showed us that Greg performs better than that. In essence, in several cases Greg suggested a more thorough set of diagnoses than the one indicated by the doctor. As an example, this happened frequently with patients suffering from anaemia, which is often associated with cirrhosis, even though doctors had not explicitly mentioned that specific diagnosis in the discharge letter.

We therefore conducted a second experiment. We asked our team of doctors to review the set of diagnoses associated with patient profiles used for the test. In essence, our doctors made sure that all relevant diagnoses were appropriately mentioned, including those that the hospital doctors had omitted in the discharge letter.

Figure 4 reports Greg's results over this revised dataset. As it can be seen, precision is quite high for all diagnoses, consistently over 70%, in two cases well over 90%. Not surprisingly, recall is generally lower than precision.

To summarize, our preliminary tests show that Greg can effectively achieve high accuracy in its predictions. In addition, it may effectively assist doctors in formulating their diagnoses, by providing systematic suggestions.

5 Conclusions: Opportunities and Lessons Learned

We believe that Greg can be a valid and useful tool to assist doctors in the diagnostic process. Given its ability to learn diagnostic suggestions at scale, we envision several main scenarios of use for the system in a medical facility:

- We believe Greg can be of particular help in ER, during the triage and first diagnostic phase; in particular, based on first evidences about the patient, it may help the ER operator to identify a few pathologies to it is worth exploring, perhaps with the help of specialized colleague.
- Then, we envision interesting opportunities related to the use of Greg in the diagnosis of rare pathologies; these are especially difficult to capture by a learning algorithm, because, by definition, there are only a few training examples to use, and therefore a special treatment is required. Still, we believe that supporting doctors – especially younger ones, that might have less experience in diagnosing these pathologies – in this respect is an important field of application.
- In medical institutions that rely on standardized clinical pathways or *integrated care pathways (ICPs)* – PDTAs in Italy – Greg may be used to quickly suggest which parts of a pathway need to be explored, and which ones can be excluded based on the available evidence.
- Finally, Greg may be used as a second-opinion tool, i.e., after the doctor has formulated her/his diagnosis, for the purpose of double checking that all possibilities have been considered.

While in our opinion all of these represent areas in which Greg can be a valid support tool for the doctor, we would like to put them in context by discussing what we believe to be the most important lessons we have learned so far.

On the one side, the development of Greg has taught us a basic and important lesson: in many cases, probably the majority, the basic workings of the diagnostic process employed by human doctors is indeed reproducible by an automatic algorithm.

In fact, it is well known that doctors tend to follow a decision process that looks for specific indicators within the patient profile – e.g., values of laboratory tests, or specific symptoms – and decides to consider or excludes pathologies based on them. As fuzzy as this process may be, as any other human-thinking process, to our surprise we learned that for a large number of pathologies this process provides a perfect opportunity for the employment of a machine learning algorithm, which, in turn, may achieve very good accuracy in mimicking the human decision process, with the additional advantage of scale – Greg can be trained to learn very high numbers of diagnostic suggestions. In this respect, ironically quoting Gregory House, we might be tempted to state that "Humanity is overrated", indeed.

However, our experiences also led us to find that there are facets of the diagnostic process that are inherently related to intuition, experience, and human factors. These are, by nature, impossible to capture by an automatic algorithm. Therefore, our ultimate conclusion is that humanity is not overrated, and that Greg can indeed provide useful support in the diagnostic process, but it cannot and should not be considered as a replacement of an expert human doctor.

References

1. Deo, R.C.: Machine learning in medicine. Circulation **132**(20), 1920–1930 (2015)
2. Geerts, F., Mecca, G., Papotti, P., Santoro, D.: Mapping and cleaning. In: Proceedings of the IEEE International Conference on Data Engineering - ICDE (2014)
3. Geerts, F., Mecca, G., Papotti, P., Santoro, D.: That's All Folks! LLUNATIC goes open source. In: Proceedings of the International Conference on Very Large Databases - VLDB (2014)
4. He, J., Veltri, E., Santoro, D., Li, G., Mecca, G., Papotti, P., Tang, N.: Interactive and deterministic data cleaning. In: Proceedings of the 2016 International Conference on Management of Data, SIGMOD Conference 2016, pp. 893–907 (2016)
5. Heinis, T., Ailamaki, A.: Data infrastructure for medical research. Found. Trends Databases **8**(3), 131–238 (2017)
6. Holzinger, A.: Machine learning for health informatics. In: Holzinger, A. (ed.) Machine Learning for Health Informatics. LNCS (LNAI), vol. 9605, pp. 1–24. Springer, Cham (2016). https://doi.org/10.1007/978-3-319-50478-0_1
7. Kononenko, I.: Machine learning for medical diagnosis: history, state of the art and perspective. Artif. Intell. Med. **23**(1), 89–109 (2001)
8. Miller, R.H., Sim, I.: Physicians' use of electronic medical records: barriers and solutions. Health Aff. **23**(2), 116–126 (2004)
9. Mohammed, O., Benlamri, R.: Developing a semantic web model for medical differential diagnosis recommendation. J. Med. Syst. **38**(10), 79 (2014)

10. Peek, N., Combi, C., Marin, R., Bellazzi, R.: Thirty years of artificial intelligence in medicine (aime) conferences: a review of research themes. Artif. Intell. Med. **65**(1), 61–73 (2015)
11. Rajpurkar, P., Hannun, A.Y., Haghpanahi, M., Bourn, C., Ng, A.Y.: Cardiologist-level arrhythmia detection with convolutional neural networks (2017). arXiv preprint arXiv:1707.01836
12. Rajpurkar, P., et al.: Chexnet: radiologist-level pneumonia detection on chest x-rays with deep learning (2017). arXiv preprint arXiv:1711.05225
13. Soni, J., Ansari, U., Sharma, D., Soni, S.: Predictive data mining for medical diagnosis: an overview of heart disease prediction. Int. J. Comput. Appl. **17**(8), 43–48 (2011)
14. Steadman, I.: IBM's Watson is better at diagnosing cancer than human doctors. In: WIRED (2013)

Variable Ranking Feature Selection for the Identification of Nucleosome Related Sequences

Giosué Lo Bosco[1,2(✉)], Riccardo Rizzo[3], Antonino Fiannaca[3],
Massimo La Rosa[3], and Alfonso Urso[3]

[1] Dipartimento di Matematica e Informatica,
UNIPA, Universitá degli Studi di Palermo, Palermo, Italy
`giosue.lobosco@unipa.it`
[2] Dipartimento di Scienze per l'Innovazione Tecnologica,
IEMEST, Istituto Euro-Mediterraneo di Scienze e Tecnologia, Palermo, Italy
[3] ICAR-CNR- National Research Council of Italy, Palermo, Italy
`{riccardo.rizzo,antonino.fiannaca,`
`massimo.larosa,alfonso.urso}@icar.cnr.it`

Abstract. Several recent works have shown that K-mer sequence representation of a DNA sequence can be used for classification or identification of nucleosome positioning related sequences. This representation can be computationally expensive when k grows, making the complexity in spaces of exponential dimension. This issue affects significantly the classification task computed by a general machine learning algorithm used for the purpose of sequence classification. In this paper, we investigate the advantage offered by the so-called *Variable Ranking Feature Selection method* to select the most informative $k - mers$ associated to a set of DNA sequences, for the final purpose of nucleosome/linker classification by a deep learning network. Results computed on three public datasets show the effectiveness of the adopted feature selection method.

Keywords: Deep learning models · Feature selection
DNA sequences · Epigenomic · Nucleosomes

1 Scientific Background

In eucaryotes cells, the DNA is packed in a very complex hierarchical structure. At a lower level, a 150 bp (base pairs) long DNA segment is wrapped around a core constituted by eight histone proteins, and this structure is called *nucleosome*. Nucleosomes are connected by DNA segment called *linkers*, and these are packed forming more complex structures that finally bring to chromosomes. Nucleosome positioning plays an important role in gene regulation [1], and their binding can sometimes enhance transcription by bringing distant DNA regulated elements together.

© Springer Nature Switzerland AG 2018
A. Benczúr et al. (Eds.): ADBIS 2018, CCIS 909, pp. 314–324, 2018.
https://doi.org/10.1007/978-3-030-00063-9_30

Genome-wide studies have found that transcription activity is inversely proportional to nucleosome depletion in promoter regions in general. Recent studies show that distinct DNA sequence features have been identified to be associated with nucleosome positioning [2], and methods have been developed to predict genome-wide patterns, sometimes with great accuracy.

The alignment-free methods [3] have emerged as a promising approach to investigate the feature frequency in a sequence. Some of these methods are based on substring counting of a sequence, and they are named as *spectral*, *k-mers* or *L-tuples* representations [4–8]. Informally, such representation associates a string sequence to a feature vector of fixed length, whose components count the frequency of each substrings belonging to a finite set of words (the so-called $k - mer$). The main advantage of these representations is that the sequence is embedded into a numerical space making possible the application of several practical machine learning methods. The interested reader can find some applications of such ideas in the following review [3].

$K - mers$ representation was used for sequence classification in many works [9,10]. Several studies on nucleosome identification have shown that nucleosome seems to be related to the presence of particular $k - mers$ and their specific arrangements [2,11], this leads to the suggestion that a feature selection method could be particularly useful in such classification task.

Machine learning methods used in supervised classification tasks are strongly based on the features that represent the objects to classify. Recently neural deep learning architectures or deep learning models were proved to be able to solve successfully very complex artificial intelligence tasks. The term *deep* refers intuitively to the number of layers that are used in these networks, and, more precisely, is related to the path from an input node to the output node in the network (considering the network as a directed graph) [12]. Among the deep learning architecture, it is usually comprised the LeNet-5 network, or convolutional neural network (CNN), a neural network inspired by the visual system's structure that has shown its efficacy on several complex classification problems [13].

The main contribution of deep learning methods in bioinformatics has been in genomic medicine and medical imaging research field. To the best of our knowledge, very few contributions have been provided for the sequence classification problem [14–19].

Among them, the CNN has been already applied in the specific problem of nucleosome identification [16]. For sure, a disadvantage of a neural network is the huge computational cost of the training phase, especially when the input vector is represented in a high dimensional space. This is the case of the k-mer representation of DNA sequences for k = 5, which brings to a vector $x \in \Re^{1024}$. In the paper, [16] it can be noticed that the performances of the CNN classifier have a plateau or even worst performances for sequence representations with $k = 4$ or $k = 5$. This is surprising because in [20] it is reported that $k - mers$ with high k can be more effective in metagenomes representation. It is possible that the noise in $k - mers$ representation increase while k increases so that the performances of the CNN network can be improved by selecting a subset of meaningful $k - mers$, and this is the hypothesis investigated in this paper.

2   Materials and Methods

2.1   Convolutional Neural Network

Convolutional neural networks (CNN) are made by many processing layers, and are classified as feedforward networks because the information is processed through the network from the lower layers (the ones near the input), that are used to capture local patterns in input data, to the higher layers (the ones close to the output).

If we consider the classical application of these networks to the problem of objects recognition on digital images, the first layers are devoted to learning the identification of simple patterns such as small edges or colour and gradients patterns. The higher layers learn to recognize more complex patterns resulting from the combination of the simple patterns identified by the lower layers. We think that this is an example of the main paradigm that the CNN uses to process the input data.

The CNN used in this work is a modified version of the LeNet-5 network introduced by LeCun et al. in [13] and is implemented using the Python Tensorflow package for deep learning. The LeNet-5 is a network made by two lower layers of convolutional and max-pooling processing elements, followed by two - traditional' fully connected Multi-Layer Perceptron (MLP) processing layers, so that there are a total number of 6 processing layers, as represented in Fig. 1.

Figure 1 shows a simple block of processing layers repeated two times: a convolutional layer followed by a rectified linear layer (ReLU in Fig. 1) and a max–pooling layer. The convolutional layer is used to extract simple features in the input vector. It is followed by a non-linear ReLU layer that simply processes a transfer function defined as $g(x) = max\{0, x\}$ on its input. The following max–pooling layer implements a non-linear down-sampling operation. More in detail, the input vector is partitioned into a set of non-overlapping subregions, and, for each subregion, the maximum value is used as the output value. The max-pooling layer operates as a sub-sampling layer and implements a sort of translational invariance. Adding more of these processing blocks (convolutional layer, ReLU layer and max-pooling) usually improves the accuracy but always increments the training time.

In the proposed architecture the first convolutional layer has $L_1 = 32$ filters of $m_1 = 5$ elements, followed by a max-pooling layer of dimension 2, while the second layer has $L_2 = 64$ filters of the same dimension, and the same max-pooling layer. The dimension of the filters in the first layer L_1 is a compromise between the computational load and the need to obtain meaningful features from the input vectors, which have exponentially increasing dimensions. The number of the filters $L - 1$ is limited by the number of different configurations with 5 bits (see Sect. 3.1). The kernel dimension of the second layer is limited by the computational load, but using a max-pooling layer of dimension 2 the interesting features will be denser. The two upper-level layers correspond to a traditional fully-connected MLP: the first layer of the MLP operates on the total number of output from the lower level (the output is flattened to a 1-D vector) and the total number hidden units is 1024 to reduce the number of connections towards the output layer. The connections between the first layer and the hidden layer are randomized by using the function dropout that activates only 50% of the connections during learning. The output layer has one unit for each class.

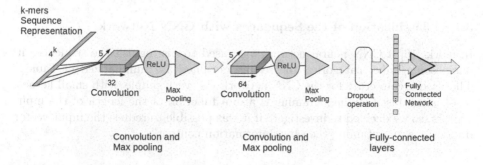

Fig. 1. A representation of the architecture of the network.

2.2   K-Mer Sequence Representation

$K - mer$ representation of a DNA sequence s of length M is based on the counting of occurrences of words of length k $(k - mer)$ in the sequence. The $k - mer$ representation generate a vector of fixed length $l = 4^k$ that can be used for sequence comparison. In this case, each sequence s is mapped to a vector $\mathbf{x}_s \in R^l$ with $l = 4^k$, such that the component $x_{s,i}$ counts the occurrence of the $i - th$ tuple k into the string s. The counting process uses a window of length k that runs by step of 1 through the sequence, from string position 1 to $M - k + 1$.

The length of the $k - mer$ k is an important parameter of the representation, for example, values of $k = 15 - 30$ generate representations with a high computational cost. As reported in [20], one of the possible approaches to this problem is to select a fraction of the set of $k - mers$ that describes the desired properties of the sequences set.

2.3   Dataset

In this study we have considered three datasets of DNA sequences underlying nucleosomes from the following three species: *Homo sapiens (HM or "Sapiens")*; *Caenorhabditis elegans (CE or "Elegans")* and *Drosophila melanogaster (DM or "Melanogaster")*. Details about all the step of data extraction and filtering of the three datasets can be found in the work by Guo et al. [21] and in the references therein. Each of the three datasets is composed of two classes of samples: the nucleosome-forming sequence samples (positive data) and the linkers or nucleosome-inhibiting sequence samples (negative data). The HM dataset contains 2, 273 positives and 2, 300 negatives, the CE 2, 567 positives and 2, 608 negatives and the DM 2, 900 positives and 2, 850 negatives. The length of a generic sequence is 147 bp.

3   Results

3.1   Classification of the Sequences with CNN Network

In work [16] a CNN neural network was used to distinguish the sequences in nucleosome/linker categories. the results obtained are summarized in Table 1. The used architecture for the CNN network was very simple, with small kernels to obtain a fast training. Training is also a function of the length of the input vectors, so we decided to investigate if it was possible to reduce the input vector dimensions, maintaining the same information content.

Table 1. In column, for each k in the range $\{3,.,5\}$ the mean (μ) values of the deep learning classifier accuracy (A), Precision (Pr) and Recall (Re) computed on 10 folds in the cases of the Caenorhabditis elegans (CE), Drosophila melanogaster (DM) and Homo sapiens (HM) dataset.

	K = 3			K = 4			K = 5		
	A	Pr	Re	A	Pr	Re	A	Pr	Re
CE	88.7	86.7	80.0	84.7	82.2	82.2	84.9	86.7	82.6
DM	78.1	76.7	80.3	78.6	78.0	79.3	77.0	76.9	77.0
HM	80.3	83.3	76.2	85.2	86.8	83.4	87.3	87.3	82.4

The CNN network mechanism can be used for our kind of input vectors, of course, due to the absence of ordering in the $k - mers$ frequency values, the feature extracted by the first convolutional layers will look like random pixels sequences if compared to the one obtained from an image, but the mechanism still holds. In the proposed system the first stage of the CNN network is trained to select useful k-mers patterns, the ones that will constitute a distinguishing feature. These features are filtered by the first CNN layer, and then the second layer will combine them to build a representation of the input vector. The goal of this work is to select the meaningful $k - mers$ and to discard the ones that carry less information, for example, the most common or rare, to have a faster training session and a more effective classifier.

Due to the mechanism of the CNN a first idea could be to analyse the kernels of the first layer of the network, this is done for the best trained CNN networks in the work [16], these are 9 networks, one for each dataset, and for each representation ($k = 3$, $k = 4$, and $k = 5$). From these kernels, it is hard to extract useful information because they are "shifted over" the input vector during the convolution operation so that the kernel values cannot be translated into $k - mers$ frequency information. Figure 2 reports an example of these kernels for the classifier of the dataset *elegans* with $k = 4$.

Fig. 2. A depiction of the kernel values in the first layer of the CNN classifier trained for C. Elegans dataset with $k - mer$ representation with $k = 4$.

3.2 Variable Ranking

Variable ranking is a simple method for variable selection. Considering a set of examples $\{x_l, y_l\}$ $l = 1, 2, \ldots L$ where $x_l \in \Re^{4^k}$ is the input variable, in our case the sequence representation and $x_{l,i}$ is the count of the $k - mer$ i in the sequence s_l, and y_l in an output variable, in our case the label nucleosome/linker. Variable ranking uses a scoring function $S(i)$ computed from the values $x_{l,i}$. We assume that a high value of $S(i)$ indicates a "good" variable. This is a "greedy" selection criterion because we are selecting variables, considering their predictive power without the interaction with the other variables.

We want to select the variables by using their predictive power, for example by using as criterion the performances of a classifier with a single variable as input. The simplest classifier can be obtained by using a simple threshold θ on the variable value; assuming that $y_l = 1$ indicates a nucleosome and $y_l = 0$ a linker, the classifier is implemented using this simple algorithm:

```
if  x > theta then        yl_pred = 1

else      yl_pred = 0
```

Comparing y_l^{pred} with y_l we can obtain an error rate for this classifier. By varying the value of the threshold θ we can build a ROC curve for each variable, and the AUC value associated to the ROC curve can be used as a scoring function $S(i)$ [22].

By using this method it is possible to obtain a set of 4^k AUC values, one for each component of the $k - mer$ representation, for each representation and each dataset, and the distribution of these values is plotted as boxplot in Figs. 3. It is possible to notice that the predictive power is decreasing with the increasing values of k and this is because $k - mers$ with $k = 5$ or $k = 6$ are much rarer than k-mer with $k = 4$.

The AUC value is used as scoring function for the $k - mers$ and these values are calculated for $k = 3, 4, 5, 6$. The value k = 3 is considered because it is the minimum value that generates high contrast representing vectors, with $k = 2$ (16 elements vectors) the frequency values are almost similar for all the components and all the sequences. The value $k = 6$ is considered even if not used in the work [16] because it generates very large representing vectors. Given a classifier architecture it is possible to select the variables by using two criteria: (i) we can use a threshold on the AUC values for the three datasets, obtaining a different number of variables for each value of k and each dataset; in this case we fixed the minimum level of the "quality" of the variable, and we have to modify the number of input variable of the classifier; (ii) we can decide the number of variables and set the AUC threshold accordingly. In this second case, we can use the same number of input variables because the dimension of input vectors is the same across the datasets. We decided to fix the number of variables to 4^3 and select the 64 variables that have the highest predictive value. The classifier has the same architecture, and it is shown in Fig. 1. This classifier is also very easy to train, with a training time of about 500 s as reported in [16]. The obtained values of accuracy, precision and recall are plotted in Fig. 4. The results with $k = 3$ are not reported because all the variables are used, and the results are the same as in Table 1. In these figures we can notice that all the values are still decreasing with k, this effect is not as strong as the one in paper [16], but it is still present. Given that the classifier architecture is the same, this means that the representation with increasing k is still less effective for this kind of sequences. We also notice that the *Melanogaster* dataset still gives the worst results. That is probably due to the peculiar dataset and needs more investigations. The advantage of this representation is that to train a classifier that processes the full sequence representation using $k = 5$ we need about 6800 s [16] (more than one and half hours), and only 500 if we select the 64 variables with the highest predictive value. There is a final consideration to make. Variable selection should be one of the purposes of this first convolutional layers of the CNN network. It should be interesting to check if the variables selected using the AUC ranking are the same used in the features extracted by the CNN trained using the complete representation, this is left for future investigations.

All the results shown are obtained by using a ten-fold cross-validation procedure. Variance of the classification results is very low [16] and varies from 0.01% to 0.12%, and this was also noticed by Hinton et al. in [23], in that paper authors claim that deep networks rarely get stuck in local minima and give the same performances even starting from random initializations as we did in these experiments.

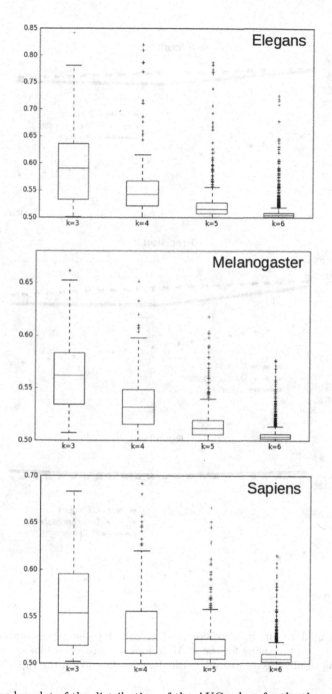

Fig. 3. The boxplot of the distribution of the AUC values for the three datasets.

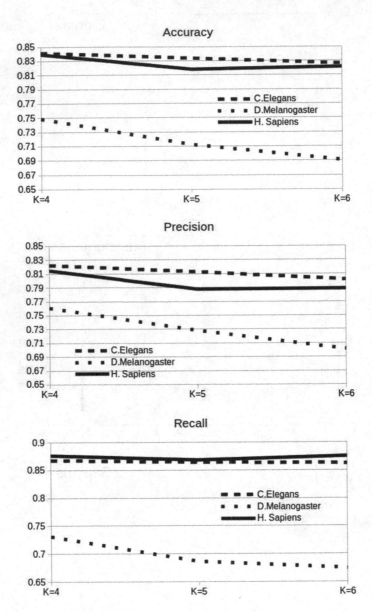

Fig. 4. Averaged Accuracy, Precision and Recall, for the representations with 64 selected $k - mers$; the values for the $D.Melanogaster$ are always lower that the other datasets. The results are comparable with the one obtained in the experiments of the paper [16]

4 Conclusion

$K - mers$ representation of genomic sequences is used for classification and similarity measure. The value of k is an important parameter, and an increasing value of k is usually associated with an increased accuracy [20]. The results obtained in [16] seems to contrast with this observation. In this work, we filtered the $k - mer$ representation to obtain, from $k = 4, 5, 6$ representations a shorter and more effective representation. The obtained results indicate that the classifier performances are more stable using the reduced representation and the training is one order of magnitude faster than the one using the complete representation presented in [16], but regarding accuracy, precision and recall the classifier is less effective than the one in [16]. Future investigation will be in the adoption of a k-mers vector representation that incorporates in the same vector the frequency values of all the k-mers ranging from a minimum k_{min} to a maximum k_{max} of k-mer length. We think that these will improve the final classification accuracy paying the price of a significant increase on the size of the input. Conversely, this will motivate better the adoption of the feature selection approach presented in this work.

References

1. Luger, K., Mader, A.W., Richmond, R.K., Sargent, D.F., Richmond, T.J.: Crystal structure of the nucleosome core particle at 2.8 A resolution. Nature **389**(6648), 251–260 (1997)
2. Struhl, K., Segal, E.: Determinants of nucleosome positioning. Nat StructMol Biol **20**(3), 267–273 (2013)
3. Pinello, L., Lo Bosco, G., Yuan, G.-C.: Applications of alignment-free methods in epigenomics. Briefings Bioinf. **15**(3), 419–430 (2013)
4. Pinello, L., Lo Bosco, G., Hanlon, B., Yuan, G.-C.: A motif-independent metric for DNA sequence specificity. BMC Bioinf. **12**(408) (2011)
5. Giosué, L.B., Luca, P.: A new feature selection methodology for K-mers representation of DNA sequences. In: di Serio, C., Liò, P., Nonis, A., Tagliaferri, R. (eds.) CIBB 2014. LNCS, vol. 8623, pp. 99–108. Springer, Cham (2015). https://doi.org/10.1007/978-3-319-24462-4_9
6. Lo Bosco, G.: Alignment free dissimilarities for nucleosome classification. In: Angelini, C., Rancoita, P.M.V., Rovetta, S. (eds.) CIBB 2015. LNCS, vol. 9874, pp. 114–128. Springer, Cham (2016). https://doi.org/10.1007/978-3-319-44332-4_9
7. Ferraro, P.U., Roscigno, G., Cattaneo, G., Giancarlo, R.: Informational and linguistic analysis of large genomic sequence collections via efficient Hadoop cluster algorithms. Bioinformatics **34**(11), 1826–1833 (2018)
8. Pandey, P., Bender, M.A., Johnson, R., Patro, R.: Squeakr: an exact and approximate k-mer counting system. Bioinformatics **34**(4), 568–575 (2018)
9. Kuksa, P., Pavlovic, V.: Efficient alignment-free DNA barcode analytics. BMC Bioinf. **10**(S14) (2009)
10. Rizzo, R., Fiannaca, A., La Rosa, M., Urso, A.: The general regression neural network to classify barcode and mini-barcode DNA. In: di Serio, C., Liò, P., Nonis, A., Tagliaferri, R. (eds.) CIBB 2014. LNCS, vol. 8623, pp. 142–155. Springer, Cham (2015). https://doi.org/10.1007/978-3-319-24462-4_13

11. Yuan, G.C.: Linking genome to epigenome. Wiley Interdisc. Rev. Syst. Biol. Med. **4**(3), 297–309 (2012)
12. Bengio, Y.: Learning deep architectures for AI. Found. Trends Mach. Learn. **2**(1), 1–127 (2009)
13. LeCun, Y., Bottou, L., Bengio, Y., Haffner, P.: Gradient-based learning applied to document recognition. Proc. IEEE **86**(11), 2278–2324 (1998)
14. Rizzo, R., Fiannaca, A., La Rosa, M., Urso, A.: A deep learning approach to DNA sequence classification. In: Angelini, C., Rancoita, P.M.V., Rovetta, S. (eds.) CIBB 2015. LNCS, vol. 9874, pp. 129–140. Springer, Cham (2016). https://doi.org/10. 1007/978-3-319-44332-4_10
15. Lo Bosco, G., Di Gangi, M.A.: Deep learning architectures for DNA sequence classification. In: Petrosino, A., Loia, V., Pedrycz, W. (eds.) WILF 2016. LNCS (LNAI), vol. 10147, pp. 162–171. Springer, Cham (2017). https://doi.org/10.1007/ 978-3-319-52962-2_14
16. Lo Bosco, G., Rizzo, R., Fiannaca, A., La Rosa, M., Urso, A.: A deep learning model for epigenomic studies. In: Proceedings of SITIS 2016 Conference, Naples, Italy (2016)
17. Di Gangi, M.A., Gaglio, S., La Bua, C., Lo Bosco, G., Rizzo, R.: A deep learning network for exploiting positional information in nucleosome related sequences. In: Rojas, I., Ortuño, F. (eds.) IWBBIO 2017. LNCS, vol. 10209, pp. 524–533. Springer, Cham (2017). https://doi.org/10.1007/978-3-319-56154-7_47
18. Fiannaca, A. et al.: Deep learning models for bacteria taxonomic classication of metagenomic data. BMC Bioinform. **19**(S7:198) (2018)
19. Di Gangi, M.A., Lo Bosco, G., Rizzo, R.: Deep learning architectures for prediction of nucleosome positioning from sequences data. BMC Bioinf. (2018, to appear)
20. Dubinkina, V.B., Ischenko, D.S., Ulyantsev, V.I., Tyakht, A.V., Alexeev, D.G.: Assessment of k-mer spectrum applicability for metagenomic dissimilarity analysis. BMC Bioinf. **17**(1) (2016)
21. Guo, S.-H., et al.: iNuc-PseKNC: a sequence-based predictor for predicting nucleosome positioning in genomes with pseudo k-tuple nucleotide composition. Bioinformatics **30**(11), 1522–1529 (2014)
22. Fawcett, T.: An introduction to ROC analysis. Pattern Recogn. Lett. **27**(8), 861–874 (2006)
23. LeCun, Y., Bengio, Y., Hinton, G.: Deep learning. Nature **521**(7553), 436–444 (2015)

First Workshop on Current Trends in Contemporary Information Systems and Their Architectures, ISTREND 2018

Towards an Integrated Method
for the Engineering of Digital Innovation
and Design Science Research

Udo Bub[(⊠)] [iD]

Faculty of Informatics, Eötvös Loránd University (ELTE), Budapest, Hungary
udobub@inf.elte.hu

Abstract. This paper presents steps towards the construction of a method for the engineering of innovation ensuring both scientific rigor and practical relevance. The resulting new method artifact shall describe the design activities, design outcomes, and the necessary roles for organizations that deliver innovation. An important construct as part of the method is the process model to describe the sequence of the design activities. This paper focusses on the design of this integrated process model to ensure both practice-driven innovation as well as design science research. Its scientific construction is introduced by a reverse engineered Action Design Research approach based on a successful implementation in a university-industry co-innovation lab.

Keywords: Digital innovation engineering · Design science research
Action design research · Method engineering

1 Introduction

Sourcing innovation is a key task for future oriented enterprises. However, little attention has been given to the systematic engineering of innovation in Information Systems (IS) and its neighboring disciplines such as computer science [2]. We consider this a shortcoming given that the main drivers of digital transformation (digitalization) are related to these disciplines.

The contribution of this paper to science is to introduce a new method for the operations of innovation labs delivering innovative IT-artifacts and integrating them into existing businesses. With "innovation lab" we consider stand-alone organizations that interact with stakeholders which are the consumers of the innovation and which are located outside of the innovation lab itself. The presented method addresses above requirements and features a central process model for the engineering of digital innovation by combination of a practitioner's innovation process with a scientist's design science research (DSR) processes producing output with both practical relevance and scientific rigor at the same time as inherently required by design science research (e.g. [11]). The constructed method can serve as starting model for further improvement in future work.

The paper is structured as follows: in Sect. 2 the scientific approach is presented including the literature review together with the used research methodology along with

© Springer Nature Switzerland AG 2018
A. Benczúr et al. (Eds.): ADBIS 2018, CCIS 909, pp. 327–338, 2018.
https://doi.org/10.1007/978-3-030-00063-9_31

a closer view on the central artifact "situational method." Section 3 features the construction of the integrated process model and Sect. 4 the construction of the method itself as an emergent artifact. Section 5 presents the generalized method artifact whereas Sect. 6 discusses the results and refers to further implementations, the result and presents future work and concludes the paper.

2 Scientific Approach

Central contribution of this paper is the construction of the process model of the method by Action Design Research (ADR) [19] by applying situational method engineering [3].

2.1 Literature Review

Considerable research on innovation processes and their organizational management has been carried out in the related field of innovation management of which [4, 6, 22] give an overview and examples of project oriented innovation processes. These findings are integrated into the method as state-of-the-art into this approach. However, none of them integrate the design of IT-artifacts by scientific standards from the field of information systems. [2] acknowledges these shortcomings and provides a framework for strategic positioning of intra-company research organizations, but do not focus on methods or engineering to be applied by these. [17] has described scientifically an approach where multiple industry partners find consensus in a moderated academic platform about joint research projects that are then carried out in a consortium. However, the created artifacts are not linked inherently into innovations processes of the respective companies. None of the above listed approaches presents a contribution design theory for the engineering of innovation in the information systems domain.

2.2 Research Methodology

The design of information systems and its related artifacts is generally accepted as research [9, 11]. Our paper aims at contributing to the knowledge base of design science with a focus on method design theory. We build on the definition of [7] where under "theory" we understand a generalized body of knowledge together with conjectures, models and frameworks. This definition itself builds on earlier work by [21] that states "that the purpose of a theory is prediction and/or explanation of a phenomenon". [20] supports a broad view on a design theory stating that an appropriate form of a design theory is a so-called utility theory that makes an assertion that a "particular type or class of technology has utility in solving or improving a problematic situation", which is applied in our research. The presented design work aims at the fulfillment of utility statements when answering to the requirements formulated in the upcoming Sect. 3.

Among the possible design theory types, more specifically, Information Systems design theories are theories for design and action [7]. Based on this, [8] identified eight components of a design theory for IS research. A detailing of these eight components for the artifact "method" in a proposal for components of method design theories has been achieved in [14] which is applied in this paper.

The design of our method for the Engineering of Innovation itself is grounded in Action Design Research (ADR) as presented in [19] with integrated evaluation during its emergence. On the other hand, the scientific IT-artifacts that are created by the method itself are based on a more conventional class of stage-gate-oriented design research processes with a separate stages for evaluation as described in [12]. The main components of the method have been designed within 50 projects run through the observed innovation lab [18]. The requirements and design decision are presented using the SOAM project as exemplar [13] and using the Action Design Research (ADR) [19] paradigm. ADR was formalized only after the SOAM was developed. However, we found that the foreseen steps of ADR structure very well the steps that have actually taken place during the development steps. As a matter of fact our approach has to be treated as a reverse engineering approach including design recovery in the sense described by [5]. With the accomplishment of this work the method shall be continuously refined and furtherly developed based on this first version of method artifact in the future.

2.3 Closer View on the Artifact Type: Situational Method

A method consists of design activities that are executed by roles in a certain order using techniques, and deliver a defined design output. Process models are part of a method and they order the design activities and their output in a dedicated sequence. Situational methods are an expansion of the concept of method artifacts. [3] introduces an enhanced meta model for situational method engineering on the basis of [10] which has identified as the five constituent elements of a method: "design activities", "design results", "roles, techniques", and the "information model" of the method. This meta model of [10] is expanded by the elements "context type" and "project type" that aggregate to a "development situation" which influence the applicability of "method fragments" [3]. The to be constructed method is a situational method, where the project type can be changed through the method application following context types as given for example in [1]. The context type is invariant during the method application and is given e.g. by specifics of the industry (e.g. telecommunications with an approach to modularization, what part of the value chain the innovation should focus on).

3 Integrated Process Model: Innovation and Design Science Research

The underlying idea for the integrated process model is a combination of an innovation process and a design science research (DSR) process. In interviews with the lab management, that have been partially pre-published in [18] with a different focus, the main requirements were sorted out and the design decisions taken accordingly. As a result, it is found necessary that the seamless transfer of the results of the process is ensured by stakeholders that are coming from the absorbing business units (which are responsible for the productization). As a consequence the opinion of these stakeholders is necessary to be prominently integrated which leads to the requirement R1. It was considered crucial that all activities of the lab take place in the form of projects with both well defined starting and ending points in order to ensure controllability and transparent resource allocation (requirement R2). At the same time the lab is realized as a university-industry-collaboration where it is necessary that scientific staff like PhD students can pursue their research accompanying the innovation projects, which leads to the requirement R3. At the same time the process should give room for agile elements to combine the need for control with the necessity to introduce agile elements which results in requirement R4. Finally, the practical relevance of the resulting process should fulfill and document the achievement of commercial KPIs for productization in business units in order to secure the market impact that are inherent to innovations. This results in requirement R5. The summary of these main requirements is exhibited in Table 1.

Table 1. Main requirements for the integrated method.

R1	Rigid synchronization points with stakeholders
R2	All activities take place in the form of projects
R3	Pursuit of research accompanying innovation projects (e.g. PhD students)
R4	Support of agile elements
R5	Fulfill commercial KPIs jointly with business units

Practice-Driven Innovation Process

Evidence of success has been documented specifically when innovation in enterprises can be brought forward in a project format, i.e. as innovation projects, following a dedicated idea-to-launch process with roles and responsibilities that systematically involve key experts in the domain and decision makers in the firm at so-called "gates" (e.g. [6]). We use the initial dimensioning in context of a setting at a telecommunication company's innovation center with an experience of more than 50 innovation projects previously piped through at the time of initiating the method. The innovation process is intended to act as an innovation proposal funnel as described e.g. by [4]: the gates act as filters, sorting out ideas that are not considered to be viable to make it to production, whereas the stages serve as phases of refinement and detailing of the proposal including feedback from the stakeholder groups present at the gates. The underlying concept is "to fail often and to fail early" at little costs, whereas admission to further progress of the proposal at the gates is carried out with higher probability of success and as such also higher preparation costs during the higher stages are better justifiable. The gates are also used for filtering and transformation based on stakeholder input as required by R1. The stakeholders are generalized to the role "decision maker" further on.

In the used version there are three gates after which the innovation project is formally kicked off. Then the project is executed and if the milestones are met as planned it will finish at a fourth gate after which the created artifacts are handed over for productization by product units acting on the market or to technology- and IT-organizations outside of the innovation lab. It is common to start a joint transfer project carrying out the necessary transition from a prototype to a full product. Generalized and aggregated remarks about the implementation of an innovation funnel can be found e.g. in [22]. The roles necessary for the innovation research process are "innovation project manager", "expert" (for passable simplicity the expert will also be the product manager with domain specific expertise whom the artifact is handed over to), and "decision maker". Thus, the innovation process ensures practical relevance to a high degree, fulfilling also R5. However, it does not enforce scientific rigor and the systematic creation of design knowledge and contribution to design theories. Hence, R3 is not yet fulfilled. This will be overcome by means of an embedded DSR process.

Design Science Research (DSR) Process
In the past a number of DSR processes were introduced, among which [16] can be arguably named as one of the most widely used ones. [12] has compared five processes including [16] and mapped them into the common three stages "Problem Identification", "Solution Design", and "Evaluation". Furthermore, [12] has also introduced an own process as a sixth one with comparable features, but with a focus on method design. These processes have in common that they are as well stage-gate oriented, with the notable features of separate design and evaluation phases (as opposed to Action Design Research where the evaluation is an integrated part of the design [19]). Both [16, 12] foresee iterative cycles of these three phases with subsequent refinements of the design. For the following reasoning we leave it open for the tailoring of the method which design research process is applied provided it belongs to the described class of processes that is defined by the mapping into the three distinct stages Problem Identification, Solution Design, and Evaluation and that these stages can be passed iteratively. The necessary additional role for the DSR process is "design science researcher". Applying the DSR process in the combined model fulfills requirement R3.

Initial Method Design: Combination to an Integrated Process Model
Because of the comparable modeling these stage-gate oriented processes can be easily integrated into the presented innovation stage-gate process category. Although the DSR process goes through iterations more frequently, the gates act as synchronization points as depicted in Table 2. Immediate advantage of the integration for researchers is that the experts and decision makers in every gate can be sourced for the expert interviews to ensure practical relevance and the testing of hypotheses. Agile elements can be integrated into the process between the gates (R4). Thus, the integrated process fulfills all main requirements from Table 1.

4   The Approach as an Emergent Method Artifact Itself

The context from which to generalize during the ADR stages is defined by a telecommunications industry setting in an intra-company innovation center that was institutionalized as a university-industry cooperation (e.g. [18]). This context specific implementation is considered as an instantiation of the class of problems for innovation organizations as described in the introduction section (innovation labs). The class of problems itself does not account for domain or industry specificity, which shall be

Table 2. Summary of synchronization points between innovation process and design science research (DSR) process.

Synchronization point	Role in innovation processes	Role in design science research process
Gate 1	First innovation idea stable, filter for "go" vs. "no go" decision	Research problem formulation stable, utility statement stable
Gate 2	Project scheme available, filter for "go" vs. "no go" decision	Design strategy stable, design outputs named
Gate 3	Full project plan with business case available, filter for "go" vs. "no go" decision	Preliminary evaluation of research hypotheses, practical relevance ensured in alignment with innovation process
Milestone	Project fulfillment is actualized and compared to project plan	Progressing status of individual design components presented, pre-evaluated, and commented
Gate 4	Fully functional prototype ready, transfer project kicked off	Suggestion regarding behavior in a Summary of research, publication

achieved by the respective situational tailoring through the context type during the instantiation of the generalized artifact.

The artifact design of the method follows the stages "ADR Stage 1: Problem Formulation", "ADR Stage 2: Building, Intervention, Evaluation (BIE)", "ADR Stage 3: Reflection Learning", and "ADR Stage 4: Formalization of Learning" as proposed by [19]. The stages are passed based on the innovation project "Service Oriented Architecture Method and Tool (SOAM)" whose output are the IT-artifacts "method" and "system design" along with their fully functional prototypes as instantiation that have been published in [13] with further related reflections about its emergence from a class of problems for innovation project engineering in [12, 15]. This means, however, that the IT-artifacts related to SOAM have been created before the formalization of ADR was published in [19]. But both the SOAM method and tool have been developed by DSR and action research applying the process from Sect. 3 in settings that are equivalent to ADR Stage 1 and ADR Stage 2 with building, intervention, and evaluation that can be reinterpreted in the context of ADR accordingly. Given that SOAM has been excellently analyzed and published under the references given above it provides fully suitable material to be exhibited as ADR. ADR Stage 3 (Reflection and Learning) was started in parallel, among which individual reflections were published in [12, 15], but unfinished so far. Together, both ADR Stage 3 and ADR Stage 4 (Formalization and Learning) were finished along with reflections from further projects and settings at the time of the finalization of this paper. Altogether, this work is a reverse engineering and design recovery approach in the sense of [5].

ADR Stage 1: Problem Formulation
The problem identification for the method came from the lab center management by formulating the requirements from Table 1. Consequently, the artifact itself shall provide a conscious approach toward re-use and generation of design science

knowledge. Roles and Responsibilities for ADR Stage 2: Building, Intervention, and Evaluation (BIE):

- Building: Artifact Designer, Process Architect.
- Evaluation: Innovation Project Manager.
- Intervention: Management Team (Innovation Center Management, Product Unit Management, Technology Unit Management, Sponsors).

The ADR Team consists of design science researchers (action design researchers) and process architects. Parallel work that requires separate roles that can be combined in one person. But typically the research process is conducted by a PhD student whereas the innovation process is carried out by an industrial project manager.

ADR Stage 2: Building, Intervention, and Evaluation (BIE)

ADR Stage 2 follows the principle of reciprocal shaping between method and organization and mutually influential roles. Researchers, process architects, as well as innovation project managers learn from each other.

The combined process model as described in Sect. 3 is used as initial design from which to start the BIE iterations. The sequence of the creation of SOAM is published in the case study of [12], however without naming the synchronization with the innovation process gates which is added here complementarily.

The impulse and requirements for building SOAM method & tool came from the business units of the enterprise (the absorbing organization). A Gate 1 proposal was prepared using an extensive literature research by the building team. Additionally the market of SOA tools was presented that included intensive interaction with the (domain) experts to pre-evaluate the relevance. A preliminary solution design was sketched to substantiate the ambition of the innovation project. As such the Gate 1 was passed and the relevance successfully pre-evaluated. Based on the results of the problem identification phase, a method and a tool were chosen as the design artefacts. The building team looked at existing methods to design systems according to the service-oriented architecture (SOA). Based on the existing methods, they then proposed a new method to design SOA-systems that overcomes the weaknesses. A sketch of the design strategy was presented at Gate 2 along with the further non-functional project design. A preliminary evaluation based on hypotheses and mock-up designs was carried out before Gate 3. This way the first iteration of the three phases of the design research was already finished, however only the problem identification and the design strategy was stable. The final project plan was presented and passed Gate 3. After kick off the full functional design of the SOAM was carried out and progress was monitored according to the milestones. A fully functional SOAM method and tool prototype was designed. Subsequently a full evaluation of the method were carried out. The research process was passed through several iterations with specific focus during some stages. A summary of the results took place as part of Gate 4 clean up and the transfer for productization. The transfer was carried out with the absorbing product department (absorbing organization). The SOAM project was finished as an innovation project with the completion of this transfer. The organization (service systems) finally decided to adopt the integrated method artifact which ends the BIE stage of ADR according to [19].

ADR Stage 3: Reflection and Learning.
The generalization (ADR Stage 3) for industry independent setting was initiated in parallel to the Stages 1 and 2 by thinking of a class of problems leading to the generalization of the DSR process [12] and the identification of the research strategies in [15] based on situation independent analyses. The learnings with respect to the precise alignment guidelines between the combined processes at the gates:

Before Gate 1: Focus on Problem Identification. On DSR side at Gate 1 the utility statement has to be already stable and the knowledge of the state of the art assessed e.g. by literature research. The utility has to be pre-evaluated. It is possible that some artifact fragment such as mock-ups as first design output are already being designed and to be presented and tested at Gate 1, however the focus is on the formulation of the utility statement including positive novelty analysis e.g. based on literature research.

Before Gate 2: First iteration of Solution design. On way to Gate 2 the utility statement should be clear and the first design outputs in form of functional and non-functional statements formulated, the feasibility assessed and evaluated.

Before Gate 3: further planning of solution design, preliminary evaluation. At Gate 3 problem identification should be finished and only in exceptional cases be refined. The Gate 3 approval can be considered as a first positive evaluation of the utility, otherwise the Gate will not be passed and a new project to be set up.

Kick off and Milestones: focus on solution design, partial evaluations possible. At the kick off, the problem identification is finished and the core of the design activity takes place, the progress of the design output is evaluated.

Gate 4: focus on evaluation and transfer. At Gate 4 the concrete implementation of the artifact in form of a prototype should be evaluated.

Based on the transfer BIE at ADR Stage 2 the generalization to a class of problems was carried out resulting in the design of the situational method fragment for the facilitation of the transfer and published in [1] as a generalization. It became evident that the method has built-in consensus finding among all necessary stakeholders in a company by means of the Gates. This highly necessary feature for the introduction of innovation in large organizations however works against disruptive innovation, which risks to be eliminated during the process through censorship by some concerned decision makers as it cannibalizes the existing business. As a matter of fact it was decided to tackle such innovation in a separate process with possible commercialization outside the company. At the same time it was found that highly creative and non-linear, agile tools such as presented in [18] can be easily integrated during the stages in order to solve partial wicked problems in the big setting.

ADR Stage 4: Formalization of Learning
In this stage we generalize the outcomes and derive the design principles from the previous stages into the method in a way that it can contribute to method design theories. The formalization of the learnings as a solution concept is summarized in Sect. 5.

5   A Method for the Engineering of Innovation

The formalization of the learning for the combined innovation and research process is exhibited in Fig. 1, where the dark shaded phases is in the focus of the DSR process during each stage.

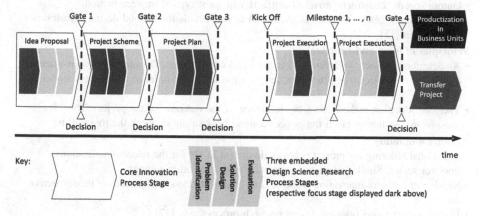

Fig. 1. Combined innovation and design research process model.

As design is considered a search process, usually several iterations of the DSR process are necessary involving optionally all other phases in a less pronounced way.

In order to add knowledge to method design theories, we present the designed method guided by the components of design theories as proposed by [8] with the method specific refinements as proposed by [14] and answers to the related evaluation criteria in Table 3:

Table 3. Contribution to method design theories through the new integrated method for the engineering of digital innovation and design science research following the structure as proposed in [15].

Purpose and scope

- Project type: situational method to carry out innovation projects that create novel IT artifacts and their prototypical implementation. The projects shall ensure novelty, economic impact and systematically contribute to the design science body of knowledge. Necessity to cover R1 to R5 from Table 1
- Project context: innovation center (innovation service system) that delivers innovation for transfer into to enterprises with an existing business
- Lifecycle coverage: from sourcing of idea, via start of project to delivery of prototype and transfer for further productization by the absorbing service system
- Role coverage: innovation project manager, design science researcher, domain expert, decision maker
- Activity coverage: Project Identification, Solution Design, Evaluation, Idea Proposal, Project Scheme, Project Plan, Project Execution, Project Transfer as depicted in Fig. 1

(*continued*)

Table 3. (*continued*)

Constructs
- Enhanced meta-model for situational method engineering from [3]
- Stage-gate-oriented DSR process model as e.g. [13] or [17]
- Stage-gate-oriented idea-to-launch process model as in e.g. [6]
- Combined process model as in Fig. 1
- Output specific constructs: novel IT-artifacts with prototypical implementation. Components of design theories as structured in [8], details for method design theories as described in [15]

Principles of form and function
- As described in Sect. 4. Define project type and context type. Do situational adjustments depending on project type. Carry out design activities in the order or the process model in Fig. 1
- The role "decision maker" has a big influence of the outcome of the project. Thus, it remains to fine tuning given the project context how strong or weak the role will be

Artifact mutability
- Situational tailoring for project types as described in [1] for the telecommunications operator sector. Similar adaptations are encouraged for other settings
- Number of gates for innovation processes can be adjusted to specific needs of the respective enterprise
- Use other stage-gate oriented design research process, e.g. [17]
- Modular approach is encouraged when applicable to the domain, but not mandatory
- Disruptive projects should be carried out outside the formal process (out-of-scope)

Testable propositions
- Utility statement for method output: does the method deliver artefacts that are novel and come with a positive business case to deliver economic impact (innovation) and contribute to the body of knowledge in design science?
- Truth statement for method output: does the delivered artefact at gate 4 match its specification from previous gates? Is the new business case viable? Does the utility statement fulfil criteria of the gate process and contributes to DSR? Further Gate-criteria according to context type can be introduced and checked

Justificatory knowledge
- Method design theories as in [15]
- Theories about the application context including innovation management, examples are [4, 19]
- Theories about DSR as summarized in [13]
- To be used in innovation systems such as University-Industry-Collaborations
- Other aspects of interest: Innovation Process applied in 50 and more innovation projects

Principles of implementation
- Tailoring as proposed in [1]
- Requires already implemented idea-to-launch process or willingness to implement at enterprise

Expository instantiation
- See Case Study from emergent artefact in Sect. 4 around the SOAM project including further documentations from SOAM in [13, 14, 16]

6 Discussion, Future Work, and Conclusion

The integrated process model is particularly useful for complex innovation projects, especially for digitalization projects where an established business has to be incrementally innovated. Agile elements can be integrated between the gates. However, due to the required rigid synchronization with stakeholders the support for disruptive innovation risks censorship by stakeholders during the gates. Further optimization and tailoring for disruptive innovation and agility will be the subject of upcoming research (possibly using ADR).

The presented work has laid the basics for an integrated method for the engineering of innovation including research. The proposed method presents a combination of Design Science Research processes with innovation processes that are characterized by stage-gate-orientation. Consequently, it supports practitioners and researchers at the same time, securing practical relevance and scientific rigor at the same time. The method provides a solution to be applied to a class of problems that is domain independent and that can be adjusted during the implementation given a class of project contexts.

References

1. Aier, S., Riege, C., Schönherr, M., Bub, U.: Situative Methodenkonstruktion für die Projektbewertung aus Unternehmensarchitekturperspektive. In: Proceedings of the 9th International Conference on Wirtschaftsinformatik, Vienna (2009)
2. Aier, S., Fischer, C., Schönherr, M.: A framework for the positioning of intra-company ICT research organizations. In: Proceedings of the 19th European Conference on Information Systems, Helsinki (2011)
3. Bucher, T., Winter, R.: Dissemination and importance of the "Method" artifact in the context of design research for information systems. In: Proceedings of the Third International Conference on Design Science Research in Information Systems and Technology (DESRIST), Atlanta, GA (2008)
4. Chesbrough, H., Vanhaverbeke, W., West, J. (eds.): Open Innovation – Researching a New Paradigm. Oxford University Press (2006)
5. Chikofsky, E., Cross, J.: Reverse Engineering and Design Recovery – A Taxonomy. IEEE Softw. 7(1) (1990)
6. Cooper, R.G.: Stage-gate systems - a new tool for managing new products. Bus. Horiz. 33(3), 44–54 (1990)
7. Gregor, S.: The Nature of Theory in Information Systems. MIS Q. 30(3), 611–642 (2006)
8. Gregor, S., Jones, D.: The anatomy of a design theory. J. Assoc. Inf. Syst. 8(5), 312–335 (2007)
9. Gregor, S., Hevner, A.: Positioning and Presenting Design Science Research for Maximum Impact. MIS Q. 37(2), 337–356 (2013)
10. Gutzwiller, T.: Das CC RIM-Referenzmodell für den Entwurf von betrieblichen transaktionsorientierten Informationssystemen. Physica, Heidelberg (1994)
11. Hevner, A., March, S., Park, J., Ram, S.: Design science in information systems research. MIS Q. 28(1), 75–105 (2004)

12. Offermann, P., Levina, O., Schönherr, M., Bub, U.: Outline of a design science research process. In: Proceedings of the 4th International Conference on Design Science Research in Information Systems and Technology (DESRIST), Malvern, PA (2009)
13. Offermann, P., Bub, U.: A method for information systems development according to SOA. In: Proceedings Americas Conference on Information Systems (AMCIS 2009), San Francisco, CA (2009)
14. Offermann, P., Blom, S., Levina, O., Bub, U.: Proposal for components of a method design theory. Bus. Inf. Syst. Eng. 2(5), 295–304 (2010)
15. Offermann, P., Blom, S., Bub, U.: Strategies for creating, generalising and transferring design science knowledge – a methodological discussion and case analysis. In: Proceedings International Conference on Wirtschaftsinformatik, Zurich (2011)
16. Peffers, K., Tuunanen, T., Rothenberger, M., Chaterjee, S.: A design science research methodology for information systems research. J. Manage. Inf. Syst. 24(3), 45–77 (2008)
17. Österle, H., Otto, B.: Consortium research. Bus. Inf. Syst. Eng. 52(5) (2010)
18. Rohrbeck, R., Hölzle, K., Gemünden, H.G.: Opening up for competitive advantage – how deutsche telekom creates an open innovation ecosystem. R&D Manage. 39(4), 420–430 (2009)
19. Sein, M., Henfridsson, O., Purao, S., Rossi, M., Lindgren, R.: Action design research. MIS Q. 35(1), 37–56 (2011)
20. Venable, J.R.: The role of theroy and theorising in design science research. In: Proceedings of the 1st International Conference on Design Science Research in Information Systems and Technology (DESRIST), Claremont, CA (2006)
21. Walls, J.G., Widmeyer, G.R., El Sawy, O.A.: Building an information system design theory for vigilant EIS. Inf. Syst. Res. 3(1), 36–59 (1992)
22. Von Zedtwitz, M., Friesike, S., Gassmann, O.: Managing R&D and new product development. In: Dodgson, M., Gann, D., Phillips, N. (eds.) The Oxford Handbook of Innovation Management. Oxford University Press (2014)

A Data-Driven Framework for Business Analytics in the Context of Big Data

Jing Lu[✉]

University of Winchester, Winchester SO22 5HT, UK
Jing.Lu@winchester.ac.uk

Abstract. A vast amount of complex data has been generated in every aspect of business and this enables support for decision making through information processing and knowledge extraction. The growing amount of data challenges traditional methods of data analysis and this has led to the increasing use of emerging technologies. A data-driven framework is therefore proposed in this paper as a process to look at data and derive insights in a procedural manner. Key components within the framework are data pre-processing and integration together with data modelling and business intelligence – the corresponding methods and technology are discussed and evaluated in the context of big data. Real-world examples in health informatics and marketing have been used to illustrate the application of contemporary tools – in particular using data mining and statistical techniques, machine learning algorithms and visual analytics.

Keywords: Business analytics · Conceptual modelling · Data pre-processing
Information visualisation · Data mining · Business intelligence
Analytical tools · Big data applications · Decision support

1 Introduction

The digital economy has facilitated an explosion in the data available to the world. This has affected businesses, jobs, education and healthcare. The term 'Big Data' refers to datasets so large and complex that it would be impossible to analyse them using traditional methods. Big data has been defined by Gartner in 2001 as "high-volume, high-velocity and/or high-variety information assets that demand cost-effective, innovative forms of information processing for enhanced insight and decision making" [3]. *Volume* is the amount of data that's created; *Velocity* refers to the speed at which new data is generated and the speed it moves around – this can help to appreciate the difference between large datasets and big data; *Variety* is the number of types of data and places that are creating it. The 3 Vs can be used to set up common ground and also point out where big data challenges and opportunities arise.

Contributing significantly to the explosive growth in volume is the Internet of Things (IoT), which is now driving big data to the next level with regards to the enabling technologies and also the future possibilities. With many forms of big data, quality and accuracy are less controllable. IBM data scientists break big data down into four dimensions by adding a 4th V as *Veracity*, referring to the trustworthiness of the data. However all this volume of fast-moving data of different variety and veracity has

© Springer Nature Switzerland AG 2018
A. Benczúr et al. (Eds.): ADBIS 2018, CCIS 909, pp. 339–351, 2018.
https://doi.org/10.1007/978-3-030-00063-9_32

to be turned into *Value*, which leads to the 5th V for big data [15]. Some analysis must be applied to the data as the value is not in raw bits and bytes, but rather the insights gathered from them. Big data analytics technology is generally available today, stretching from simple statistical tools to more sophisticated machine learning approaches, with deep learning among the latest trends.

Big data can deliver value in almost any area of business or society: to better understand and serve customers; to optimise their processes; to improve healthcare and security etc. The term big data remains difficult to understand because it can mean so many different things to different people. The understanding will be different depending on the perspectives from technology, business or industry [14]. Analysts at Gartner estimate that upwards of 80% of enterprise data today is unstructured. Most of it is irrelevant noise so, unless non-technical business people are clear about the kinds of data being gathered and how to make practical use of it, they will be overwhelmed. Despite the huge volume of data generated, only 0.5% of all data is currently analysed. Organisations are aware that there are growing opportunities to use big data to make better decisions, but there is a significant gap between collecting the data and making the decisions.

This paper will focus on approaches to extracting value and generating insights from complex data by using advanced data analytics techniques, e.g. predictive analytics or customer behaviour analytics. In particular, it will include details of a corresponding methodology highlighting relevant tools and technologies while illustrating sample real-world applications in health informatics and marketing.

2 Methodology

2.1 (Big) Data-Driven Framework

A data-driven framework is shown in Fig. 1 which covers aspects of the business analytics life cycle from data management, data pre-processing and integration through to data modelling and business intelligence, culminating in the essential tasks of insight management – indicated on the right-hand side of the framework. The 5 Vs of big data are linked within the framework and labelled on the left-hand side of Fig. 1. A 6th V also features across the main stages of the framework, i.e. *Visualisation*.

Data-driven means that algorithms derive key characteristics of the models from the data itself rather than from the hypotheses/assumptions of the analyst. The process starts with business knowledge and market understanding – growing business without understanding the market and competitors is risky. Domain expertise is needed to frame business goals in a way that provides value to the organisation.

Data management is the data layer of the framework, which may include the internal data environment within an organisation and the external data sources as necessary. Data exists in different formats and has various types – data or database experts are needed to identify what data is available for modelling and how that data can be accessed and normalised. Data analysts are needed later to build the model that achieves the business objectives [17]. The Computing Research "Big Data & IoT Review 2017" shows that currently *structured* data from internal and external sources

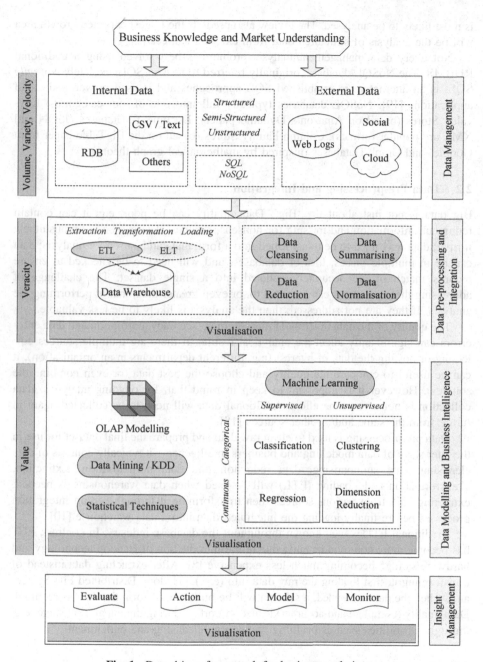

Fig. 1. Data-driven framework for business analytics.

is most likely to be analysed. The review also predicts the largest expected growth area will be the analysis of structured data from external sources [2].

Not every data management/analysis problem is best solved using a traditional RDBMS. The NoSQL database, originally referred to as *Non*-SQL and lately *Not only* SQL, is an alternative to established SQL approaches and is used in web and cloud applications [19]. NoSQL databases typically fall into one of four categories: Key-value Stores (based on Amazon's Dynamo paper), Document Databases (JSON and XML are popular formats), Column Family Stores (based on the BigTable paper from Google) and Graph Databases (inspired by mathematical graph theory).

2.2 Data Pre-processing and Integration

Big data is not just about the 'Big'. Data quality can be poor, e.g. it can contain redundant information and missing (or nonsense) values; data can be in an unsuitable format; data may need to be transformed into a form that can be used for analysis; data can be in multiple pieces, files or databases, and will need to be checked to ensure records match or are accurately collated into a single dataset. The challenge of addressing these problems can be equal to, or even greater than, that of performing the analysis. If they are not addressed, then the analysis is likely to be less valuable.

The quality of the data in terms of measurement accuracy, corruption and data entry errors can significantly affect the analytical results. If there are multiple sources collecting or hosting the data of interest (e.g. different departments in an organisation), it can be useful to compare the quality and choose the best data (or even combine the sources). However it is important to keep in mind that, for ongoing analytics, data collection is not a one-time effort. Additional data will need to be collected again in future from the same and/or other sources [18].

Data pre-processing is used to clean raw data and prepare the final dataset for use in the later stage of data modelling and business intelligence – it typically consists of data cleansing, data summarising, data reduction and data normalisation. Extraction, Transformation and Loading (ETL) will be used when data warehousing is needed: extracting data from various sources then transforming it through certain integration processes before finally loading the integrated data into a data warehouse [10].

Traditional ETL is well known throughout the database industry. In contrast, ELT has become more common recently due to the introduction of Hadoop technology and hardware/storage becoming much less expensive [8]. After extracting data instead of transforming it, first loading the raw data into (e.g.) a Hadoop Distributed File System and, when the data is needed, a schema will be built to transform the data as required. Data quality (complete and accurate) is also important during the integration stage, e.g. through capabilities such as profiling, validation, cleansing and enrichment.

2.3 Data Modelling and Business Intelligence

The success of most organisations is highly dependent on the quality of their decision making and Business Intelligence (BI) focuses on supporting and improving the decision-making process. BI can be defined as "a set of methodologies, processes, architectures and technologies that transforms raw data into meaningful and useful information which enables effective strategic, tactical and operational insights and decision making" [11]. OLAP (On-Line Analytical Processing) is a term used to describe a technology that takes a *multi-dimensional* view of aggregate data and provides quick access to information for the purpose of advanced analysis. OLAP and SQL searches on databases are descriptive in nature and based on business rules set by the user, but don't involve statistical modelling or automated algorithmic methods.

Data mining is the essential part of *knowledge discovery in databases* (KDD) – the overall process of converting raw data into useful information and derived knowledge – one definition being "the science of extracting useful information from large datasets or databases" [6]. After data preparation, some data mining methods can be applied, e.g. considering examples in the market basket analysis area: (1) Association rules – which items are commonly bought together? (2) Sequential patterns mining – what are common purchase sequences in which customers buy products across time? (3) Classification – how likely is a customer to respond to a marketing campaign? (4) Clusters and outliers – what cohesive groups of customers do we have?

Both machine learning and statistical inference are fundamentally involved with extracting information from a dataset and for this reason there is a significant overlap between the fields. Analytics problems can be broadly segregated by whether the output is continuous or categorical (classes) and whether it is supervised (includes desired outputs) or unsupervised. Data-driven decision making is becoming the norm for analytics and business intelligence, with research showcasing to what extent supervised and unsupervised learning are underlying this.

2.4 Insight Management

Insight is information that can make a difference – insight management is about understanding information needs and then managing the way that information flows through so that it has a positive effect. Once a model is built from a data analysis perspective, it is important to evaluate the results and take action, reviewing the steps executed to construct the model.

Data is the most valuable asset of many organisations today, but only if its interpretation and impact delivers competitive advantage. Arguably the key difference between data and insight is that the latter resonates with senior stakeholders within the client business, enabling them to make decisions. The process of trying to generate insight from information is not just a matter of using algorithms to analyse data. Customers and other stakeholders increasingly participate in improving existing products and services – without customers engaging with organisations it will continue to be a struggle to develop insight. Consumers are expecting ever-increasing degrees of personalisation of goods and services they purchase – both driving the creation of data and the requirement to be able to draw actionable insights from it.

3 Tools and Technology

3.1 Overview

Technologies related to collecting, cleansing, storing, processing, analysing and visualising big data are evolving at a fast pace. Table 1 provides an outline description of some analytical tools in the broad technology categories associated with pre-processing, data mining, statistics and visualisation.

Table 1. Analytical tools and technologies.

Tools	Technologies		
	Pre-processing	Data mining and statistics	Visualisation
Excel - electronic spreadsheet program	Show missing data in pivot table	Analysis ToolPak, XLCubed, PowerPivot	Graphs/charts, PivotCharts
Alteryx - data preparation, blending and analysis	Drag and drop tools to eliminate SQL coding/formulae	Pre-packaged tools and procedures for predictive analytics	Workflow for self-service data analytics
SPSS - statistical analysis software package	Validate data, unusual cases and optimal binning	Descriptive statistics, inferential analysis, prediction	Chart builder, Graphboard Template Chooser
R - statistical computing and graphics environment	Raw => correct => consistent data	Statistics, time series, classification, clustering	Base, grid, lattice and ggplot2
iNZight - data exploration and insight generation	Quick explore => missing values	Relationships, estimation, time series	Visual Inferential Tools (VIT)
Weka - machine learning and data mining software	Discretisation, normalisation, attribute selection	Classification, clustering, association rules and sequential patterns mining	Plot, ROC, tree/graph/boundary visualiser
Tableau - data visualisation and analytics	Joins, unions, splits and pivots	Segmentation and cohort analysis, predictive analysis	Interactive and visual analytics

3.2   Data Extraction and Preparation

A study of European decision-makers' attitudes to data and analytics in modern business was conducted in 2016 (Alteryx) – 500 organisations were surveyed in all. Surprisingly this research found that while more data sources, systems and applications were being deployed, Excel spreadsheets were still used for analysis across 58% of businesses [1]. Excel can be used for data entry, manipulation and presentation, but it also offers a suite of statistical analysis functions and other tools that can be used to run descriptive statistics and to perform inferential statistical tests. Even if using alternative analytical software, Excel is often helpful when preparing data for processing by those packages.

Alteryx is a tool especially made to extract, transform and load data. Its key capabilities for data preparation include: connecting to and cleansing data; improving data quality; offering repeatable workflow design to assist with data integrity. Alteryx will be used in the health informatics application below to illustrate the extraction of data from a relational database into a dimensional data warehousing model.

3.3   Statistical Techniques

IBM SPSS was originally a widely used program for statistical analysis in the social sciences. It is now used by market researchers, health researchers, survey companies, government, education researchers, marketing organisations, data miners and others. An SPSS Python plug-in has been developed which connects SPSS with Python and thus makes everything in it available to SPSS and conversely. IBM SPSS Modeler is a data mining and text analytics software application used to build predictive models and conduct other analytical tasks. It has a visual interface which allows users to leverage statistical and data mining algorithms without programming [7]. The IBM SPSS Direct Marketing option enables advanced analysis of customers or contacts, potentially improving marketing campaigns and maximising return on investment.

R is a language and environment for statistical computing and graphics, with RStudio providing a user-friendly interface to analyse and manipulate data (https://www.r-project.org). R is commonly used for big data management and analysis – it is widely accepted by the data science area and has a very active support community. Developed using R, iNZight can generate insights into real-world data by producing graphs and summaries through statistical analysis. The iNZight desktop software and iNZight Lite web-based version are comparatively simple menu-driven (point and click) systems which are gaining popularity.

3.4   Machine Learning and Visual Analytics

Weka (Waikato Environment for Knowledge and Analysis) is open source software which offers a wide range of statistical inference and machine learning algorithms [5], primarily for data pre-processing, classification, regression, clustering, association rules, sequential patterns mining and visualisation. It can be applied to real-world problems and also used to analyse big data. Weka's main user interface is Knowledge Explorer, which features several panels giving access to key components of the workbench – e.g. the Classify panel can apply classification and regression algorithms to estimate the accuracy of predictions and visualise models through decision trees.

As shown in Fig. 1, visualisation is an important aspect of data pre-processing and integration, data modelling and business intelligence as well as insight management. Tableau Software (https://www.tableau.com) supports an integrated iterative approach that combines data analysis with data visualisation and human interaction. It provides a collection of interactive visualisation products designed for business intelligence. Advanced functionalities include cohort analysis via drag-and-drop segmentation, what-if analysis of scenarios and predictive analytics using (e.g.) forecasting models – an R plug-in allows integration with other platforms and handles statistical needs.

4   Applications

4.1   Health Informatics

A case study from breast cancer research considered one of the electronic patient records systems within a University Hospital which contained over sixteen thousand patient records [12]. The objectives defined for this case study and the follow-on investigation [13] were as follows: (1) evaluate emerging database technologies and analytical tools, especially the application of data mining and visual analytics within the healthcare domain, (2) test the ability of selected analytical software to derive useful information from the extracted and anonymised cancer patient records, and (3) show-case the utilisation of tools and technologies to visualise the analytical results in order to maximise insight, evaluating outcomes in conjunction with domain experts.

Data cleansing was carried out through SQL, Alteryx and Weka. When patient records with errors or missing information are excluded, associated records from other workflows would be removed from corresponding data tables. For instance, where patient details were incomplete and excluded from the patients dataset, records for these patients could then also be excluded from the diagnosis events dataset. The Alteryx workflow in Fig. 2 removes duplicate records relating to the same diagnosis so that the event table only contains one record per event. It also shows the filtering of records to remove diagnosis events prior to 1960.

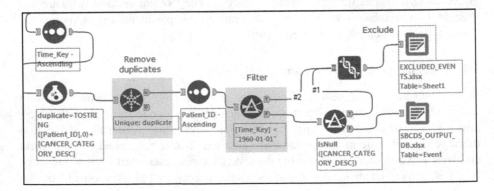

Fig. 2. Integration tool filtering records – Alteryx.

The software selected for visual analytics was Tableau, which presents information using a variety of chart types – its ability to support the analysis and visualisation of multi-dimensional models made Tableau an appropriate choice. Dashboards are typically used as a means of displaying live data where each dashboard is a collection of individual indicators, designed in such a way that their significance can be understood intuitively. Figure 3 gives an example of a diagnosis dashboard from Tableau which contains five charts each demonstrating a different situation [13].

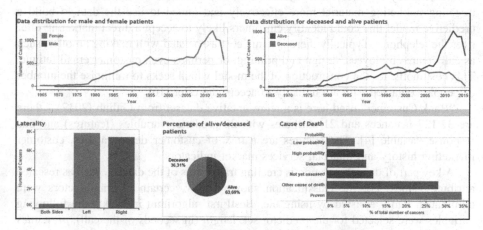

Fig. 3. Visual analytics dashboard – Tableau.

Several data mining techniques were implemented for the case study by using Weka with the cancer patient records. In particular, Generalized Sequential Patterns mining has been used to discover frequent patterns from disease event sequence profiles based on separate groups of living and deceased patients. A directed acyclic

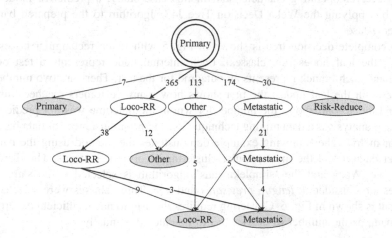

Fig. 4. SPG for maximal sequential patterns when *minsup* = 0.5% (alive patients).

Sequential Patterns Graph (SPG) represented the maximal sequential patterns found from subsets of the breast cancer data [12]. Figure 4 shows the SPG for alive patients only, when the minimum support threshold is 0.5%, where it can be seen that nodes of SPG correspond to elements (or disease events) in a sequential pattern and directed edges are used to denote the sequence relation between two elements.

4.2   Direct Marketing in Banking

This case study is based on a common business scenario: a bank was interested in targeting marketing material more effectively and aimed to use the data to build a predictive model that could identify customers likely to accept a direct marketing offer over the telephone. Typically there is some cost associated with making an offer, such as call centre employees, design and printing, or perhaps even customer email fatigue. This cost motivates the construction of the model which seeks to minimise the number of people contacted who are unlikely to accept the offer [16].

"Bank Customer" used here is a representative dataset from Github (2017) – there are 32,127 instances and 21 attributes with 20 predictor variables (features) and one response variable [4]. The features are a mix of customer demographics, customer marketing history and financial services market indicators.

A key part of data preparation is creating transforms of the dataset, such as rescaled attribute values. For the classification shown below, certain external factors were eliminated. Partly assisted by using the 'BestFirst' algorithm in Weka, the following variables were selected for the predictor set: *length* (in seconds of the call), *prev.sales* (number of sales to this customer in the past) and *age* (age of customer). The outcome status is either 'Yes', i.e. a sale was made during the call, or 'No'.

During the pre-processing stage, the *length* variable has been divided into 5 groups: <0.5 h, 0.5–1 h, >1–1.5 h, >1.5–2 h, >2 h. And customer age has been divided into 3 groups of <42 years, 42–67 years and >67 years. Several of the classification algorithms have been evaluated using Weka and compared according to a number of measures: (1) accuracy, sensitivity and specificity, (2) n-fold cross validation and (3) receiver operating characteristic. In this case study, a predictive model was created by applying the Weka Decision Tree J48 algorithm to the prepared banking customer dataset.

The complete decision tree is shown in Fig. 5 with seven rectangular boxes representing the leaf nodes (i.e. classes). Each internal node represents a test on the variable and each branch represents an outcome for the test. There are two numbers in parentheses in the leaf nodes: the first shows how many customers reached this outcome and the second shows the number for whom the outcome was not predicted.

Cluster analysis is a data mining technique used to group instances of data based on a similar metric. The following example demonstrates the method using the banking customer dataset and the most popular clustering algorithm, k-means. The dataset is loaded into Weka and the 'simplekmeans' algorithm is selected – the same three variables are considered: *length*, *prev.sales* and *age*. Three classes were selected and the output is shown in Fig. 6. Clustering requires the user to have sufficient expertise in the domain, as the number of classes has to be entered manually.

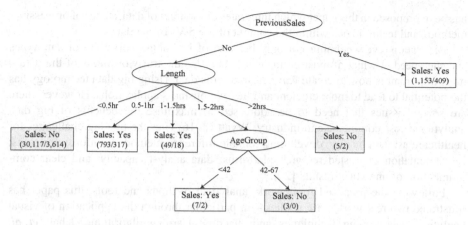

Fig. 5. Decision tree example for banking/marketing analysis.

```
Cluster centroids:
                            Cluster#
Attribute    Full Data       0           1           2
             (32127)        (4872)      (9962)      (17293)
==================================================================
prev.sales    0.0701        0.2943      0.0304      0.0298
length      516.6318      932.5649    447.0528    439.5324
age          40.0164       40.6232     50.9184     33.5651
y                no           yes          no          no
```

Fig. 6. Clustering example for banking/marketing analysis.

Cluster 0 – these are the 15% of customers who purchased the products. It shows the average previous sales for this group was the highest at ~0.3, compared with the other two clusters which were ~0.03. In terms of the length of phone call, this cluster is also the highest, ~15 min – twice as long as the other two groups. Finally, the average age within this group is about 40 years.

Cluster 1 – the number of customers in this group is more than twice that of Cluster 0, although they didn't accept the sales offer – average age is around 50 years.

Cluster 2 – the final cluster is the largest (54%) – this youngest group with average age about 33 years did not purchase any products from the bank.

5 Conclusion

Businesses have generated and developed a vast amount of complex data over the years. This data is a precious resource and could play a vital role enabling support for decision making through insight generation and knowledge extraction. The growing amount of data exceeds the ability of traditional methods for data analysis and this has led to the increasing use of emerging technologies. A data-driven framework for business analytics has been proposed in this paper which integrates the sources of data, stages of processing, methods and technologies within the context of the 5 Vs of big data.

Big data is overwhelming not only because of its volume, diversity of data types and the speed at which it must be managed, but also the trustworthiness of the data – most important is how to create *value* from all this data. Using big data technology has the potential to lead to more efficient and flexible business applications. However, there are several issues that need to be addressed to maximise the benefits of big data analytics across commerce and industry. Wyatt (2016) cites the five big challenges for healthcare as: data quality; developing reliable inference methods to inform decisions; implementation of trusted research platforms; data analyst capacity; and clear communication of analytical results [20].

Following the proposed framework, analytical methods and tools, this paper has illustrated two real-world case studies – in particular through the application of visual analytics, data mining techniques and machine learning algorithms. Khan *et al.* (2016) suggested that, while many organisations still build market value and advantage over their rivals through traditional means, algorithms have emerged as a better way to change the business and gain a more competitive edge [9]. If algorithms are applied correctly they can provide insights that make a business process more profitable and highlight new ways of doing business as well as new opportunities for growth.

Data analytics algorithms vary significantly in capability and scope. Consequently there are algorithms which aim to find the '*known* knowns' – e.g. OLAP analysis; then there are algorithms which are able to discover 'known *unknowns*' – e.g. through data mining and machine learning; and recently there are algorithms which are even able to extract the '*unknown* unknowns' from datasets – e.g. deep-learning algorithms. By applying such digital innovation, the ultimate goal is improving decision making in the business environment harnessing the full potential of big data.

References

1. Alteryx: The business grammar report: a study of european decision-makers' attitudes to data and analytics in modern business (2016). https://www.alteryx.com/resources/the-business-grammar-report-a-study-of-european-decision-makers-attitudes-to-data
2. Computing Research: Big Data & IoT Review 2017 (2017). https://www.computing.co.uk/ctg/news/3010002/computing-big-data-iot-review-2017
3. Gartner IT Glossary (2001). https://www.gartner.com/it-glossary/big-data
4. GitHub (2017). https://github.com/QUT-BDA-MOOC/FLbigdataStats
5. Hall, M., Frank, E., Holmes, G., Pfahringer, B., Reutemann, P., Witten, I.H.: The WEKA data mining software: An update. SIGKDD Explor. **11**(1), 10–18 (2009)
6. Hand, D.J., Smyth, P., Mannila, H.: Principles of Data Mining. MIT Press Cambridge, USA (2001)
7. IBM: IBM SPSS Statistics for Windows, Version 22.0. IBM Corporation, Armonk, NY (2013)
8. IBM developerWorks: Hive as a tool for ETL or ELT (2015). http://www.ibm.com/developerworks/library/bd-hivetool

9. Khan, I., Gadalla, C., Mitchell-Keller, L., Goldberg, M.S.: Algorithms: The new means of production. Digitalist Magazine (2016). www.digitalistmag.com/executive-research/algorithms-the-new-means-of-production
10. Kimball, R., Ross, M.: The Data Warehouse Toolkit – The Definitive Guide to Dimensional Modeling. Wiley, New York (2013)
11. Lans, R.: Data Virtualization for Business Intelligence Systems: Revolutionizing Data Integration for Data Warehouses, Morgan Kaufmann Publishers Inc. (2012)
12. Lu, J., et al.: Data mining techniques in health informatics: a case study from breast cancer research. In: Renda, M.E., Bursa, M., Holzinger, A., Khuri, S. (eds.) ITBAM 2015. LNCS, vol. 9267, pp. 56–70. Springer, Cham (2015). https://doi.org/10.1007/978-3-319-22741-2_6
13. Lu, J., Hales, A., Rew, D.: Modelling of cancer patient records: a structured approach to data mining and visual analytics. In: Bursa, M., Holzinger, A., Renda, M.E., Khuri, S. (eds.) ITBAM 2017. LNCS, vol. 10443, pp. 30–51. Springer, Cham (2017). https://doi.org/10.1007/978-3-319-64265-9_4
14. Marr, B.: Big Data: Using Smart Big Data, Analytics and Metrics to Make Better Decisions and Improve Performance. Wiley, Chichester (2015)
15. Marr, B.: Big Data In Practice: How 45 Successful Companies Used Big Data Analytics to Deliver Extraordinary Results. Wiley, Oxford (2016)
16. Moro, S., Cortez, P., Rita, P.: A data-driven approach to predict the success of bank telemarketing. Decis. Support Syst. 62, 22–31 (2014)
17. Shearer, C.: The CRISP-DM model: the new blueprint for data mining. J. Data Warehouse 5 (4), 13–22 (2000)
18. Shmueli, G.: Practical Time Series Forecasting with R: A Hands-on Guide. Axelrod Schnall (2016)
19. Wiese, L.: Advanced Data Management: For SQL, NoSQL, Cloud and Distributed Databases. De Gruyter Textbook (2015)
20. Wyatt, J.: Plenary Talk: Five big challenges for big health data. In: 8th IMA Conference on Quantitative Modelling in the Management of Health and Social Care, London (2016)

An Industrial Application Using Process Mining to Reduce the Number of Faulty Products

Zsuzsanna Nagy$^{(\boxtimes)}$, Ágnes Werner-Stark, and Tibor Dulai

Department of Electrical Engineering and Information Systems,
University of Pannonia, Egyetem str. 10, Veszprém 8200, Hungary
nagyzsuzsi25@gmail.com,
{werner,dulai.tibor}@virt.uni-pannon.hu

Abstract. Process mining is a field of research that provides mining of more and more useful hidden information to the industry. The core of effective information retrieval lies in the application of process mining tools that best fits the task and the data. The current problem is that there is no universal solution available to track the formation of faulty products in time and space to make it possible to be reduced. To solve this problem, methods have been developed that can be used to analyze a production process from multiple perspectives. The methods were also implemented in software and tested on real production data. The methods created are based on time and space distribution and grouping of faulty products. The methods were applied to the processing and measurement data of an automated coil production and assembly line. The data is originally stored in different files, so before they were used, they had to be transformed and sorted into database. Using the software which use the methods, a comprehensive view of the production process can be obtained, and conclusions can be drawn from the generated statements about the state of the production tools and the possible source of the errors. The results make it possible to design more efficient maintenance, reduce outage time, and increase production time, thus reducing the number of faulty products.

Keywords: Process mining · Production log data analysis · Fault detection

1 Introduction

The desire for continuous performance improvement of manufacturing processes is as old as manufacturing itself. To ensure this, the analysis of data from manufacturing processes can be used. Process mining tools help to effectively analyze process data. Process mining is a field of research that provides mining of more and more useful hidden information to industry [1], health [2, 3], education, and other areas. Process mining is well recognized as a valuable tool for observing and diagnosing inefficiencies in processes based on event data. Process mining can be used in many industrial applications. Hong suggests a framework for performance analysis in manufacturing processes based on process mining [4]. Aals et al. described the application of process mining for the construction and maintenance of the road and water infrastructure [5].

© Springer Nature Switzerland AG 2018
A. Benczúr et al. (Eds.): ADBIS 2018, CCIS 909, pp. 352–363, 2018.
https://doi.org/10.1007/978-3-030-00063-9_33

In study of Unal et al. acoustic analysis with classification is used for fault diagnosis of rolling bearings [6]. It has been recognized that effective fault detection techniques can help semiconductor manufacturers reduce scrap, increase equipment uptime, and reduce the usage of test wafers. He et al. developed a fault detection method using the k-nearest neighbor rule (FD-kNN) [7]. Son et al. developed a manufacturing execution system that is analyzed with several process mining techniques. This system keeps track of manufacturing process events and takes process-oriented information automatically. It helps operation managers to make a better decision in manufacturing [8]. Jansen processed the transaction log data for web searches [9]. In the related case, important information from this article was how to prepare log data for testing and what tools to use to look at data. Most of the log data which had to be processed, were generated by machine vision. Machine vision is the name of a combination of technologies and procedures that allow the use of digital picture-based automated tests in an industrial environment. The results of the tests are used for production process control, quality control and robot coordination tasks [10]. Topics related to this subject include articles such as object classification and supervised learning [11], robust main component analysis [12], but no more in-depth analysis of output values. The authors see whether the values indicate a deviation, or even what degree of deviation is, but the data is no longer used for further analysis. The purpose of this study was to create process mining methods that can be used to track faulty product formation in time and space. Traceability allows the faster and more accurate detection and elimination of the source of error, thus reducing the number of errors and the outage time. In this study, errors are identified and characterized, so no classification algorithm is required. By applying the methods, a production process can be studied from a variety of perspectives. Multi-view analyses are needed because some hidden information can be extracted only that way. The methods were implemented in a software and were tested with real production data.

In Sect. 2, the production process is presented along with the log files (that were available for the task) and then the process for creating the database for the production data is explained. In Sect. 3, the methods for examining the data are described and then in Sect. 4 the result of using the implemented methods on real production data is shown.

2 Preparing the Data

Understanding the manufacturing process is an indispensable first step for selecting the most efficient data processing and process mining analysis methods for data. In addition, to better understand the purpose of the work to be performed, the critical points of the process were highlighted, which later provided assistance in selecting the most appropriate analyses. The studied production process is executed by two production lines: one coil producer and one assembly line. The assembly machine has a total of 8 stations and is connected to the coil production line at Station 4. The product is assembled from Station 1 to Station 6. At the last two stations, only quality checks are done. The finished product is subjected to electrical inspection at Station 7 and to optical inspection at Station 8. During the examination of the log files and their content, all the important information about the data, their role, their possible values and the meaning of the values were collected. There are 5 different types of log files for the two production lines which contain data about the main products, electrical measurement values of the products, commodities (PCB) and manufactured commodities (coil). Exploring the relationship between the production process and the log files was needed to find out where the data is generated and recorded in the process. This task was performed in parallel with examining the production process and the log files. After that, special data was searched for, that could be used to connect the files. To bring data into processable state, the following steps were necessary: 1. Creating the database schema; 2. Shaping the data into an understandable form for the database management software; 3. Importing the data into the database; 4. Creating a connecting table.

3 Methods

New methods were needed to properly analyze the process data. Methods were developed that can be used for other manufacturing processes with similarly structured data. In this chapter, the criteria and the operation of these methods is presented.

Several methods can be used to analyze production data, depending on the aspects in which those needed to be analyzed. The methods hereinafter are marked with letters A, B, C and so on. Execution of method A is necessary for all of the other methods. Method B observes the production only in space, methods C, D and E only in time and method F both in space and time.

3.1 Criteria for Applying the Methods

The production process involves a total of n types of production machines. The i-th production machine uses a total of k tools, all of which are involved in the production. The utilization rate of the tools of the i-th production machine (normally) is the same. Thus, all the k tools used by the i-th production machine participate in the production of almost the same quantity of products. Only 1 tool can be used to manufacture 1 product per production machine. For each product, it is recorded exactly which tools have been used. There are a total of w error classifications, and for each product there is exactly 1 of them. For the sake of completeness, good products are also labelled, indicating a lack of error. Error classifications can be divided into s groups according to their occurrence place, and each error classification belongs to exactly one group.

3.2 The Mathematical Notations Used to Illustrate the Methods

- $M := \{M_i | 1 \leq i \leq n\}$ where M is the set of examinable production machines, M_i is the set of tools of the i-th production machine and n is the number of machines
- $M_i := \{m_{i_j} | 1 \leq j \leq k_i\}$ where m_{i_j} is the j-th tool from the set of tools of the i-th production machine and k_i is the number of tools of the i-th production machine
- $P := \{p_i | 1 \leq i \leq q\}$ where P is the set of manufactured products, p_i is the i-th product and q is the number of manufactured products

- $F := \{f_i | 1 \leq i \leq w\}$ where F is the set of error classifications, f_i is the i-th error classification and w is the number of error classifications
- $H := \{H_i | 1 \leq i \leq s\}$ where H is the set of error classifications grouped by place of occurrence, H_i is the set of error classifications which occurs at the i-th place and s is the number of places
- $H_i := \{f_l | f_l \in F\}$ where f_l is the l-th error classification (from the set of error classifications). Each error classification is included in a group ($\bigcup_{i=1}^{s} H_i = F$) and all error classifications are included only in one group ($\forall H_i \cap H_j = \emptyset, where\ i \neq j$).
- $q = q_g + q_f$ where q is the number of manufactured products, q_g is the number of products which were marked good by the system and q_f is the number of products which were marked faulty by the system
- $q_f = q_{f_1} + q_{f_2} + \ldots + q_{f_w} = \sum_{i=1}^{w} q_{f_i}$ where q_{f_i} the number of faulty products that have been tagged with the i-th error classification

3.3   Method A - Common Feature in the Methods

The common feature of the methods is to specify the time horizon within which the examination of the production process will be realized.

Algorithm:

1. Determine the time period of the examination: giving values to *start time point* and *finishing time point* variables AND/OR giving value to the variable which contains the identifying code of the *special time interval*.

3.4   Method B - Determination of the Distribution of Faulty Products Among the Tools of a Production Machine

The purpose of this method is to support the detection process of sources of errors that are causing large number of malfunctions. The method examines only one production machine at a time. In order to increase the probability of detecting the source of error, it is recommended to carry out the method defined in this point for all production machines. For example, any tool in any production machine may get defective, misadjusted, or dirty during production, so it is important to examine all the data on each production machine. For multiple types of examinations, it is important to use the same time interval for compatibility. If the error distribution between the tools is the same or nearly the same, then the source of the error is presumably the tool of another production machine or the material itself. If the error distribution is of very different proportions, the source of the error is presumably the highest-rate tool. In this case, it is recommended to carry out maintenance on the tool. The weakness of the method is that it can only help with error source detection in case of many errors. If there are many tools and error classifications, and a few faulty products, the errors will probably not be concentrated to a single location, so the exact location of the error source cannot be found. In such cases more examinations are required.

Algorithm:
1. Perform the step described in method A.
2. Select the production machine to be included in the examination (i).
3. Load the data required for the examination:
   a. the list of tools of the given production machine (M_i)
   b. the list of possible error classifications (F)
   c. the list of manufactured products (P)
4. Create the result table. The result table will show the number of errors summed by the tools of the given production machine and the possible error classifications. The row headers of the table contain the identifier number of the tools (the k elements of the set M_i), and the column headers contain the type of errors (the w elements of the set F). The cells contain the total number of products manufactured by the given tool and marked with the given error classification.
5. Fill the result table. The algorithm examines products made during the specified time interval one by one. For each tool, you can see how many different types of errors have occurred in the products that were made by that tool. The algorithm also displays the number of good products per tool, which can be used to compare the number of good and defective products when representing the result.
6. The final result can be displayed both in tabular and graphical form.

3.5 Method C - Evolution of the Number and Composition of Manufactured Products During Production

The purpose of this method is to facilitate the examination of the production process by filtering and preprocessing the data. This method is the starting step for the methods D and E. During production, a large quantity of products is manufactured during short time, from which a great deal of data is recorded. In order to comprehensively examine this process, not all data is required and the process does not need to be monitored in every millisecond. It is desirable to optimize the amount and composition of the data and to make the data appropriate for further processing.

Algorithm:
1. Perform the step described in method A.
2. Create measurement time points with a given (equal) distance between them.
3. Load the list of manufactured products (P). For the algorithm, the products should be sorted in ascending order based on the time of their production.
4. Create the result table. The result table will show the number of good and faulty products manufactured between the measurement time points. So in the row of the x-th measurement there will be the number of products manufactured between the $x-1$-th and x-th measurement divided into two groups based on their classification.
5. Fill the result table. The algorithm investigates the manufactured products one by one and classifies them in the right place according to their production time point. If the production time point of the current product (which is under investigation) is greater than the current measurement time point (i.e.: the product was finished after the current measurement) then the algorithm proceeds to the next measurement time point and then compares it to the production time point of the product.

The algorithm steps ahead in time until the current measurement time point is greater than or equal to the production time point of the product (i.e.: the product was finished before or at exactly the same time as the current measurement happens). The product is then assigned to the current measurement time point. The algorithm also divides the product set into two groups based on their error classification: good and faulty products.

3.6   Method D – Highlighting of Outages During Production

The purpose of this method is to make longer breaks visible so that the production process can be improved by improving its efficiency. The outage time is a time period where the production line did not produce any new products (either good or faulty), the production stopped. Longer stoppages aren't beneficial for the company so it is important to detect and eliminate them as soon as possible. The starting step of the method is the method C, i.e. the algorithm is the continuation of that.

Algorithm:

1. Perform the steps described in method C.
2. Create a table to store the outage times. The number of rows must be the same as in the table which is used to store the results of method C and the distance between the measurement time points should also be unchanged.
3. Fill the table. The algorithm detects the total number of outgoing products at each time interval delimited by the measurement time points. If the number of products is 0, then there was an outage: the time interval between the current and the previous measurement time point is recorded as outage time (e.g.: "1" value is recorded). If the number of products is greater than 0, then there was production: the time interval between the current and the previous measurement time point is recorded as production time (e.g.: "0" value is recorded).
4. The final result is recommended to display graphically.

3.7   Method E - Investigation of Rejection Rate Change During Production

The purpose of this method is to track changes in the rejection ratio within the given time interval to help improve the efficiency of the manufacturing process. The starting point of the method is method C, so the algorithm is a continuation of that.

Algorithm:

1. Perform the steps described in method C.
2. Create a table to store the rejection rate change.

3. Fill the table. The algorithm calculates the current rejection rate at each measurement time point. The current rejection rate is calculated according to the formula 1 below:

$$RR_k = \frac{\sum_{i=1}^{k} q_{f_i}}{\sum_{i=1}^{k} q_i} \cdot 100 = \frac{\sum_{i=1}^{k} q_{f_i}}{\sum_{i=1}^{k} q_{f_i} + \sum_{i=1}^{k} q_{g_i}} \cdot 100 \tag{1}$$

$$1 \leq k \leq n, \qquad RR_0 = 0, \qquad q_0 = q_{f_0} = q_{g_0} = 0$$

Where

n	– the number of measurements,
k	– the identifying index for the current measurement time point,
i	– the running index identifying the measurement time point,
RR_k	– the rejection rate at the k-th measurement,
q_{f_i}	– the number of new faulty products between the i-1-th and i-th measurement,
q_{g_i}	– the number of new good products between the i-1-th and i-th measurement,
q_i	– the number of new products between the i-1-th and i-th measurement.

Time 0 indicates the beginning of the manufacturing process. At this time, there are no products at all (neither good nor faulty) so the number of the products and the rejection rate is 0. The algorithm calculates the rejection rate for the current measurement time point only if there can be a change in it compared to the previous measurement time point. There may be a change when the production was ongoing and there were new product(s). If the production (was) stopped, then there are no new products, so the rejection rate is unchanged.

4. The final result is recommended to display graphically.

3.8   Method F - Determination of the Distribution of Faulty Products During the Production

The purpose of this method is to support the detection process of such sources of errors that are causing a large number of faulty products. With this method, the number of possible sources of errors can be decreased using the resulting time and place distribution of the faulty products that were manufactured during the production process.

Algorithm:

1. Perform the step described in method A.
2. Create measurement time points with a given (equal) distance between them.
3. Load the data required for the examination:
   a. the list of manufactured products (P)
   b. the list of possible error classifications (F) grouped by place of occurrence (H)
4. Create the result table. The row headers of the table contain the measurement time points, and the column headers contain the places (the unique identifier name of each s element of the set H). The result table will display the number of faulty

products produced between the start and the measurement time points, grouped by place of error. So, in the row of the *x*-th measurement there will be the number of faulty products manufactured since the beginning of the production, until the *x*-th measurement.

5. Create an array (e.g. *sum_products*) to store the current cumulative number of faulty products in different places.

6. Fill the result table. The algorithm iterates the manufactured products one by one and sorts them to the right place according to their production time point and error code. Since the goal is the error source detection, it only deals with faulty products. If the production time point of the investigated product is greater than the current measurement time point, then the algorithm records all the values from the array *sum_products* for the current measurement time point in the result table, and proceeds to the next measurement time point. The algorithm steps ahead in time until the current measurement time point is greater than or equal to the manufacturing time point of the product. If this condition is met, then the value at the error occurrence place of the product in the array *sum_products* will be increased by one.

7. The final result is recommended to display graphically.

4   Implementation of Methods and Application to Real Data

To test the methods and to reveal hidden information, a computer application was created. The application allows users to examine output data for completed production processes that are already stored in the database, and provides the ability to upload new data from files to the database. The process analytical analysis and the uploading of data files are realized by two separate components. In this paper, the analytical component (hereinafter simply "application") implementing the methods below is presented.

Using this application, hidden information from the data can be revealed, which can be presented in a tabular and a graphical display format for the process engineer. The data displayed makes the production process transparent, the process becomes comparable with the process model. Conclusions may be drawn about the possible source of errors during the process and about the state of resources.

Instead of specifying date and time in the app, order identifiers can be chosen as they all unambiguously identify a production cycle. Order identifiers define non-overlapping intervals with a maximum length of about 23 h. There are pages on the graphical interface of the application, which include the results of various tests.

4.1   Examples of the Results of the Application of the Methods, Result Analysis

"The number of good and faulty products per hour during production" is a bar chart showing the number of good and faulty products manufactured by hours. The information required for the chart is obtained by using method C. The interval between the measurements was set to 1 h. An example diagram is shown on Fig. 1.

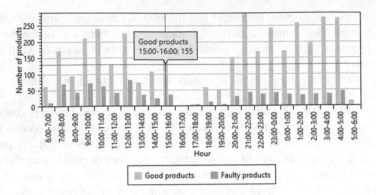

Fig. 1. "The number of good and faulty products per hour during production" diagram

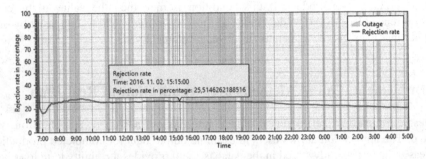

Fig. 2. "Evolution of the rejection rate during the production process" diagram

The "Evolution of the rejection rate during the production process" line diagram shows the rejection rate and the outages during production. The information required for the diagram is obtained by using methods E and D. The interval between the measurements was set to 1 min. An example diagram is shown in Fig. 2. The gray background marks the minutes where no new product came out of the production line. If the gray background is wider (the downtime lasted for more than a few minutes), there was probably an outage in the production process.

Figures 1 and 2 both show that there was no production between 16 h and 17 h and only a very small amount of products were manufactured between 17 h and 18 h (with more faulty products than good products). Longer downtimes can mean a serious loss of resources for the company, so it is important to remedy them as soon as possible.

The error classifications have been divided into 8 groups according to the stations, because there are 8 stations in total. The stations are a physical part of the assembly line, each of which carries out a special task in the production process. If a station has a lot of faulty products, it does not necessarily mean that the source of the error is at that particular station. There are three possible cases: 1. the station controller device is defective, 2. the operating device of the station is defective, 3. the product is defective. Only in the first two cases locates the actual source of the error at that station. It is difficult to detect errors caused by machines at the station. To get better conclusions, it is recommended to perform other kind of analyses first. If it is not possible to clearly deduce the possible source of errors from the results of the other analyses, then there is a high possibility that the source of the errors is at that station.

"The cumulative number of faulty products per station during production" line diagram shows the cumulative number of faulty products per station as a function of time. The information required for the diagram is obtained by applying methods F and D. The interval between the measurements was set to 1 min. An example diagram is shown in Fig. 3.

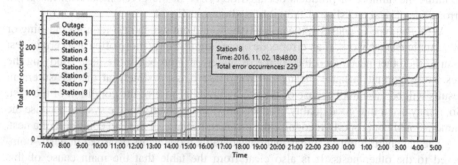

Fig. 3. "The cumulative number of faulty products per station during production" diagram

The assembly line has 8 nests for holding and moving the product. A nest is a "seat" for a product that travels from station to station until it is taken out of the process. In the application both a table and a graph show the status of the nests. The information required for the diagrams is obtained by applying method B.

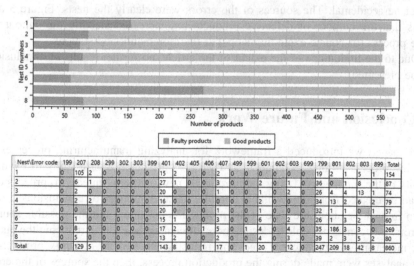

Nest\Error code	199	207	208	299	302	303	399	401	402	405	406	407	499	599	601	602	603	699	799	801	802	803	899	Total
1	0	105	2	0	0	0	0	15	2	0	0	2	0	0	0	0	0	0	19	2	1	5	1	154
2	0	6	1	0	0	0	0	27	1	0	0	3	0	0	2	0	1	0	36	0	1	8	1	87
3	0	2	0	0	0	0	0	20	0	0	0	1	0	0	1	0	2	0	26	4	4	13	1	74
4	0	2	2	0	0	0	0	16	0	0	0	0	0	0	2	0	0	0	34	13	2	6	2	79
5	0	0	0	0	0	0	0	20	0	0	0	1	0	0	1	0	0	0	32	1	1	0	1	57
6	0	1	0	0	0	0	0	15	1	0	0	3	0	0	6	0	2	0	26	1	3	2	0	60
7	0	8	0	0	0	0	0	17	2	0	1	5	0	1	4	0	4	0	35	186	3	3	0	269
8	0	5	0	0	0	0	0	13	2	0	0	2	0	0	4	0	3	0	39	2	3	5	2	80
Total	0	129	5	0	0	0	0	143	8	0	1	17	0	1	20	0	12	0	247	209	18	42	8	860

Fig. 4. "The cumulative number of faulty and good products per nest at the end of production" diagram and "The total number of faulty products per nest and per error code at the end of production" table (Color figure online)

"The cumulative number of faulty and good products per nest at the end of production" bar chart shows the number of good and faulty products per nests at the end of the production. Green bars indicate the number of good products that have reached the last station. Red bars indicate the number of faulty products that were in the nest when it was declared faulty by the system. An example diagram is shown in Fig. 4.

"The total number of faulty products per nest and per error code at the end of production" table shows the total number of faulty products manufactured by the end of production classified by nests and error codes. The faulty products are grouped by nest in the rows and by error code in the columns. The intersection of a column and a row contains the number of products declared defective in the given nest, with the given error code. The screenshot of the table is shown in Fig. 4.

With this type of analysis, it can easily be found out which nest requires cleaning or other maintenance work. If an error code occurs significantly more often at a certain nest than at the other nests, then the source of the error is probably the nest. Studying the nests is important because in any control phase it is possible that the measurement results will be false not because of the product but because of the condition of the nest. So, it may occur that good quality products are declared faulty by the system because the camera could not properly recognize the product, because of the bad condition of a nest.

The bar chart in Fig. 4 shows that considerable more errors occurred in nest 7 compared to the other nests. It is also clear from the table that the main cause of this spectacular difference is the 801 error code (on station 8, camera 2 reported a measurement error). This error occurred 209 times during the production process, of which 186 were in nest 7. So the system detected 89% of the errors in nest 7. The bar diagram presented on the Fig. 4 shows that nest 1 also has a greater difference from the other six nests. From the table, it can be seen that error code 207 (on station 2 the PCB measurement was wrong) occurred significantly more in nest 1. The error code occurred 129 times during the production process, of which 105 were in nest 1. So the system detected 81% of the errors in nest 1. In both cases, the ratio is so high that it cannot be accidental. The sources of the errors were clearly the nests. Figure 3 also shows that the number of defective products has increased steadily throughout the entire process (of course excluding stops) at the aforementioned stations.

Due to the limitations of the extent of the article, no further results or conclusions can be presented.

5 Conclusion and Future Work

In this paper, we introduced a framework for analyzing manufacturing processes by applying process mining techniques, and we also presented a case study to examine validity of the framework. Using the introduced new methods, an easy to process data set can be created from the available complex data. A number of conclusions can be drawn from these about the state of the production machines and the possible sources of errors. It becomes possible to design more efficient maintenance, reducing the outage time, increasing the production time, and reducing the number of faulty products. If these analyses were made during the production process, then the sources of the errors could be detected in time. The error could be remedied sooner and the rejection rate would also be lower. Only the most important analyses have been made on the data, but there is still a number of additional examinations that can be done. It was kept in mind when the database used by the software was designed and implemented. All data from the log files are stored in the database.

In the future, we are going to focus on online processing, which will further reduce the number of faulty occurrences.

Acknowledgements. We acknowledge the financial support of Széchenyi 2020 under the **EFOP-3.6.1-16-2016-00015**.

References

1. Feau, B., Schaller, C., Moliner, M.: A method to build a production process model prior to a process mining approach. In: The Fifth International Conference on Intelligent Systems and Applications, pp. 129–132 (2016). ISBN: 978-1-61208-518-0
2. Mans, R.S., Schonenberg, M.H., Song, M., van der Aalst, W.M.P., Bakker, P.J.M.: Application of process mining in healthcare – a case study in a Dutch hospital. In: Fred, A., Filipe, J., Gamboa, H. (eds.) BIOSTEC 2008. CCIS, vol. 25, pp. 425–438. Springer, Heidelberg (2008). https://doi.org/10.1007/978-3-540-92219-3_32
3. Tóth, K., Machalik, K, Fogarassy, Gy. Vathy-Fogarassy, Á.: Applicability of process mining in the exploration of healthcare sequences. In: Szakál, A. (ed.) IEEE 30th Jubilee Neumann Colloquium, Neumann Colloquium 2017, Budapest, Magyarország, pp. 151–155 (2017). ISBN: 978-1-5386-4635-9
4. Hong, T.T.B.: Process mining-driven performance analysis in manufacturing process: cost and quality perspective (2016)
5. van der Aalst, W.M.P., et al.: Business process mining: an industrial application. Inf. Syst. **32**, 713–732 (2007)
6. Unal, M., Sahin, Y., Onat, M., Demetgul, M., Kucuk, H.: Fault diagnosis of rolling bearings using data mining techniques and boosting. J. Dyn. Syst. Meas. Contr. **139**(2), 021003 (2017)
7. He, Q.P., Wang, J.: Fault detection using the k-nearest neighbor rule for semiconductor manufacturing processes. IEEE Trans. Semicond. Manuf. **20**(4), 345–354 (2007)
8. Son, S., et al.: Process mining for manufacturing process analysis: a case study. In: Proceeding of 2nd Asia Pacific Conference on Business Process Management, Brisbane, Australia (2014)
9. Jansen, B.J.: Search log analysis: what it is, what's been done, how to do it. Libr. Inf. Sci. Res. **28**(3), 407–432 (2006)
10. Beyerer, J., León, F.P., Frese, C.: Machine Vision: Automated Visual Inspection: Theory, Practice and Applications. Springer, Heidelberg (2015)
11. Barbu, A., She, Y., Ding, L., Gramajo, G.: Feature selection with annealing for computer vision and big data learning. IEEE Trans. Pattern Anal. Mach. Intell. **39**(2), 272–286 (2017)
12. De la Torre, F., Black, M.J.: Robust principal component analysis for computer vision. In: 2001 Proceedings of the Eighth IEEE International Conference on Computer Vision, ICCV 2001, vol. 1, pp. 362–369. IEEE (2001)

Towards a Hypergraph-Based Formalism for Enterprise Architecture Representation to Lead Digital Transformation

Bálint Molnár[1] and Dóra Őri[2(✉)]

[1] Information Systems Department, Eötvös Loránd University, ELTE,
Pázmány Péter Sétány 1/C, Budapest, Hungary
molnarba@inf.elte.hu
[2] Department of Information Systems, Corvinus University of Budapest,
Fővám tér 8., Budapest, Hungary
DOri@informatika.uni-corvinus.hu

Abstract. In this paper a concept will be proposed about a hypergraph-based formalism for representing enterprise architecture. The paper presents a formal model using TOGAF and hypergraph theory. Hypergraphs provide a flexible mathematical structure to describe complex relationships in an enterprise architecture, mirroring the dependencies among components, and exploring integrity and consistency issues. The proposed approach extends the analytical potential for discrepancy checking in complex enterprise architecture structures. The approach can be utilized for EAM-based analysis of information systems.

Keywords: Enterprise architecture · TOGAF · Artifact · Formal modeling
Hypergraph

1 Introduction

Information strategy planning is a complex and utterly important activity in organizations, an exercise through which an organization utilizes its technological resources [17]. Information strategy is a major tool to integrate information technology (opportunities and concerns) into business planning, harmonizing the business and IT domains. The overall goal of IT planning, as part of the broader concept of IT governance is the alignment of information systems (IS) and business plans. In the era of digitalization, the growing organizational complexity, emerging disruptive technologies, and rapid technological changes make strategic planning of IS extremely challenging. Whereas classic planning approaches [16] are still in use, enterprise architecture management (EAM) based approaches became the major facilitators of the planning initiatives [10]. The planning cycle, integrated with implementation and monitoring activities requires the support of EAM. Strategic harmonization of business and IT domains is more relevant than ever before, and EAM can be a major facilitator of strategic alignment by discovering, analysing and avoiding misalignment problems and achieving competitiveness [18]. EAM provides methods to ease organizational complexity, promotes agility, and controls uncertainties [8]. EAM helps the alignment

© Springer Nature Switzerland AG 2018
A. Benczúr et al. (Eds.): ADBIS 2018, CCIS 909, pp. 364–376, 2018.
https://doi.org/10.1007/978-3-030-00063-9_34

of the organisation with strategic goals, the control of interdependencies in business and IT, and it enables organisations to agility and fast reaction.

The complexity of IT and IS infrastructures coerces the exercise of modeling of Enterprise Architecture (EA) within companies. There are several approaches of Enterprise Modeling [1, 19] that provide opportunities for semi-formal modeling through exploiting visual representations and specifications of various pre- and post-conditions. The central concept of Enterprise Architecture Modeling is the artifact that is the outcome of some modeling, designing and analysis activities. The artifacts can be considered as documents that describe architectures through complex relationships among the elements of artifacts. As the documents allow for depicting multifaceted relations among components that reflect the intricate relationships among the building blocks of architecture, the representation by a formal approach requires a flexible descripting method in which there are no restrictions on enhancing and extending the representation with new type of relationships, concepts, hierarchies, and networks. The hypergraph theory provides a very elastic mathematical structure that has the capability, on the one hand, to mirror the multifarious dependencies among constituents, and on the other hand, to exploit the graph structure for analysis utilizing the tool set of mathematics. This paper is intended to discuss the topic of EAM-based analysis of misalignment problems, introducing an existing method. The EAM-oriented analysis model is extended with our proposition for a hypergraph-based EA representation, and the foundations of the extended conceptual framework are described.

The rest of the paper is structured as follows: Sect. 2 summarizes the role of EA in leading digital transformation. Section 3 presents the connection between digital transformation and the modeling of enterprise. Section 4 introduces the mathematical background to hypergraphs. The hypergraph-based approach is presented in Sect. 5. Section 6 presents an illustrative example for the proposed formalism. At the end of the paper conclusions are drawn.

2   The Role of EA in Leading Digital Transformation

Digital innovation - the use of digital technologies in the process of innovation - results in new products, services, business processes and business models. Digital transformation handles the effects of digital innovations: the emergence of new actors, new network, new structures, practices [11]. Organisations in the digital era face the changing role of digitality in their business models, organisational design, compliance, regulation and economic environment [4]. This changing role concerns business strategies as well: Digital technologies transform traditional business strategies into digital business strategies [2]. Digital transformation strategies are plans that govern organisations in transforming products, processes, organisation design due to the emerging digital technologies in the organisation. As it is becoming more and more difficult to disunite digital products and services from their underlying IT infrastructures, corporate IT plays an important role in leading digital transformation [2]. IT-enabled processes made digital product and service architecture more complex. It is necessary to revisit the present enterprise architectures and IT governance practices to successfully manage this digital transformation. Goerzig and Bauernhansl [9] collected several aspects to compare enterprise architecture and digital transformation. According their comparison, EA and digital transformation evolve from different drivers, consist of different target groups, differ in subject, development approach, value stream and lifecycle phases. These aspects facilitate the search for new methods, models and tools of EAM in its changing role.

3   Digital Transformation and Modeling of Enterprises

The digital transformation of enterprises affects the business model and business architecture including the business process models. As the overall EA contains the process chains for value creation, the actors and roles related to processes thereby each single element of EA is impacted by digital transformation. The

> *"Digital transformation (DT) – the use of technology to radically improve performance or reach of enterprises –is becoming a hot topic for companies across the globe. Executives in all industries are using digital advances such as analytics, mobility, social media and smart embedded devices – and improving their use of traditional technologies such as ERP – to change customer relationships, internal processes, and value propositions."* [7]

As it can be seen from the quotation, the business level *meta-process* is the Digital Business Transformation [5], i.e. the profound re-structuring and engineering of enterprises or organizations. This procedure can be perceived as a total redefinition of EA. The requirements for the business can be formulated as the exploitation of the full potential of IT (Information Technology) along the entire process chain dedicated to value creation. Thus, the Digital Transformation means the application of the most recent technologies to increase the performance and enhance the scope of business services. The application of IT and other modern technologies touches several perspectives of EA, namely business processes, users and human roles, the networks of communication within and outside of the cyberspace, the operation through the business model.

As the business model is the foundation logic of enterprises, it describes the benefits for partners that can be provided and the way of access to the business services. The dimensions and elements of business models strongly correlates to EA:

- Customer/consumer dimension related to the human and user roles perspective;
- The benefits dimension for partners (services and value for money) connected to the motivation, "why" perspective;
- The value creation dimension strongly coupled to resources (data asset, business and IT networks, human actors, and roles) and business processes;
- The partner dimension linked to the (business) networks and human roles;
- The finance dimension encompasses the costs and revenues that depends on the business processes, business rules.

The goal of Digital Transformation at enterprises is to re-engineer the business model, and the business processes, the functions of the organizations, the information interchange between organizational functions. It is anticipated that enterprises will build intelligent business models that will re-shape the customer relationship models profoundly that can be seen in phenomena as the interaction between customers and enterprises will take place through on-line, e-commerce and m-commerce channels, digitalized manner. On describing the preceding and sub-sequential states of the operating business, the Enterprise Architecture framework is an apt solution. The Zachman ontology provides the theoretical background for comprehension of the actual and future situation. However, the Digital Transformation requires lots of architectural building blocks that belong to the realm of Information Technology, and software systems.

The Open Group's TOGAF method [1] is a suitable approach for putting order in a chaotic environment, for defining a strategic, project process chain for transformation. The fundamental steps of any project dedicated to Digital Transformation is as follows scope analysis, business process modeling, gap analysis, evaluation of the architectural continuum on the specific business sector of enterprises. The TOGAF method for analysis, design and phased transition architecture yields a generic set of processes, steps, tasks, and work packages for programme and project management. The process chain at project and engineering level, which is customized and tailored to the actual situation, is good starting point to realize Digital Transformation at a single enterprise as it is an overarching approach that includes the organizational and information technology perspectives. The transition of enterprise architecture from the recent position to an enterprise architecture of a digitalized company can be perceived as Business Process Innovation involving the whole firm.

The alignment requirements between business model and technology to be applied can be examined in a systematic approach. A simplistic version of IT strategy formulation and alignment can be utilized (illustrated in Fig. 1):

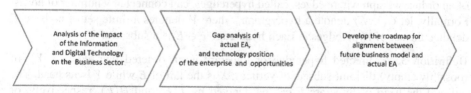

Fig. 1. The method elements for aligning EA and opportunities for digital transformation

Analysis of the Impact of the Information and Digital Technology on the Business Sector. Several scenarios are elaborated for investigation of possible amendment of value creation whereby the technologies to be applied and the market niche scrutinized. The deliverable is a proposal for changes.

Gap Analysis of Actual EA, and Technology Position of the Enterprise, and Opportunities. The second stage comprises the analysis of products, services, customers/consumers, and geographical distribution including cyberspace, thus, an IT and digital strategy for business will be developed. The deliverable will enclose the description of gaps on the competencies and enterprise engineering.

Develop the Roadmap for Alignment Between Future Business Model and Actual EA.
The alternatives of future scenarios will be developed. The various aspects of Digital
Transformation are conceptualized in detail. Several perspectives of EA will be affected
as e.g. Business Process for Value Creation, Collaboration and Workflow Model, the
Functioning Enterprise. In this way, the future EA is articulated, then the layer for
technology, physical and operational architecture is worked out. The alignment
between the operation model and business and IT services will be carried out.

4   Mathematical Background for Hypergraph Formalism

The hypergraphs, especially the generalized hypergraphs provide a flexible structure to
describe complex relationships that can be explored among models during analysis and
design of IS [6].

Definition 1. The concept of the directed hypergraphs is an ordered pair of vertices
and hyperarcs that are directed hyperedges, i.e. each hyperarc is an ordered pair that
contains a tail and a head.

Definition 2. The generalized or extended hypergraph. The notion of hypergraph may
be extended so that the hyperedges can be represented – in certain cases – as vertices,
i.e. a hyperedge e may consist of both vertices and hyperedges as well. The hyperedges
that are contained within the hyperedge e should be different from e [12].

The hypergraphs as a tool for describing Information Systems from various viewpoints yields a formal method to analyze the system, and to check the conformance,
compliance, and consistency of the set of models [13]. A hypergraph is a generalization
of an ordinary graph where edges, called hyperedges, can connect any number of nodes.
Formally, let $G(V, E)$ denote a hypergraph, where V denotes a finite set of nodes v, E
denotes the set of hyperedges e. Each hyperedge $e \in E$ is a subset of V.

Definition 3. A directed hyperedge or hyperarc is an ordered pair, $E = (X, Y)$, of
(possibly empty) disjoint subsets of vertices; X is the tail of E while Y is its head. The
tail and the head of hyperarc E can be denoted by $T(E)$ and $H(E)$, respectively, or
alternatively a hyperarc $\vec{e}_i \in \vec{H} = \left(V; \vec{E} = \{\vec{e}_i | i \in I\}\right)$ can be perceived as an ordered
pair $\vec{e}_i = \left(\overrightarrow{e_i^+} = (e_i^+; i); \overrightarrow{e_i^-} = (e_i^-; i)\right)$, where $e_i^+ \subseteq V$ is the set of vertices of $\overrightarrow{e_i^+}$
and $e_i^- \subseteq V$ is the set of vertices $\overrightarrow{e_i^-}$. The elements of $\overrightarrow{e_i^+}$ (hyperedges and/or vertices)
are called *tail* of $\vec{e}_i$, while elements of $\overrightarrow{e_i^-}$ are called *head* [6].

Definition 4. Limb is either the head or the tail of a hyperarc and designated by $\vec{e}_i^{\mp}$.

Definition 5. *Architecture Describing Hypergraph* is a generalized hypergraph that
can be extended by some functions and operations [12]. It can be designated as a tuple
$\langle V, A, E, E_U, E_D, Attr \rangle$:
   V is the set of *vertices*;
   A is the set of arcs, i.e. directed edges, an arc is an ordered pair $\langle i, j \rangle$, where $i, j \in V$
(in the sense of traditional graph theory);

E is the set of hyperedges;

E_U is the set of the *undirected* hyperedges, because of the properties of generalized hypergraphs, a hyperedge e is

- either $e_i \neq \emptyset$, $e \subseteq V$, (*basic hyperedge*),
- or a *bag* of hyperedges;

E_U is divided up at a meta-level into partitions:

- E_C consists of the *configuration hyperedges*. Each $h_i \in E_C$ is a simple hyperedge, i.e. containing only vertices, not complex structures and other hyperedges. All $h_i \in E_C$ can be labeled unambiguously. The configuration hyperedges manifests the structure of "things", the vertices within a hyperedge are the properties of the specific "thing". The properties can be perceived as variables or attributes (depending on the context) that can be valuated thereby they linked to an individual value (vertex in D (see Definition 5.)) or a set of values, e.g. to a grouping hyperedge.

- E_E is composed of the *extensional hyperedges*. The extensional hyperedges can represent collections of data, the instances of *generic artifacts*. For example, the collections of data can be built up by tuples of data items, the instances of artifacts can be composed of certain bags of free variables that are contained in the particular artifacts' object/element structure. In these examples, the distinct elements, the vertices of these hyperedges can be considered as constituents of extensional hyperedges.

- E_I comprises the *intensional hyperedges*. The intensional hyperedges show the logical and rule-based interrelationships among the vertices (models within the architecture), moreover configuration hyperedges.

- E_G is made up of *grouping hyperedges* that embody various structuring principles on components, as e.g. view, viewpoint and perspectives etc. in architecture describing approaches; they symbolize interrelationships between certain models and pieces or parts of documents as e.g. business activity models, business process models, catalogues of architecture building blocks and responsibilities of roles within an organization unit. The hyperedge $h \in E_G$ can be utilized for sorting out the vertices (representing either artifacts, viewpoints, or models) into organizational-related, artifact-related and activity related relationships.

E_D is a set of *hyperarcs*, i.e. *directed hyperedges;* the hyperarc $\vec{e}_i \in E_D$ can be as it follows (see Definition 2.):

$$\vec{e}_i = \langle v_j, \vec{h} \rangle = (\vec{e}_i^{\,+} = (e_i^{\,+} = \langle v_j, i \rangle); \vec{e}_i^{\,-} = (\langle i, e_i^{\,-} = h \rangle))$$

where $v_j \in V$, and $\vec{h} \in E_G$;

$$\vec{e}_i = \langle v_j, \vec{h} \rangle = (\vec{e}_i^{\,+} = (e_i^{\,+} = \langle v_j, i \rangle); \vec{e}_i^{\,-} = (\langle i, e_i^{\,-} = h \rangle)), v_j \in V, \text{ and } \vec{h} \in E_C;$$

$$\vec{e}_i = \left\langle v_j, \vec{h} \right\rangle = (\vec{e}_i^+ = (e_i^+ = \langle v_j, i \rangle); \vec{e}_i^- = (\langle i, e_i^- = h \rangle)) \quad \text{where} \quad v_j \in V, \text{ and}$$

$\vec{h} \in E_E$; there does not exist two hyperarcs $\vec{e}_i = \left\langle v_j, \vec{h} \right\rangle$ and $\vec{e}_k = \left\langle v_l, \vec{h'} \right\rangle$ that either

$\vec{h}, \vec{h'} \in E_C$ or $\vec{h}, \vec{h'} \in E_E$, i.e. every vertex $v_j \in V$ is linked, at most, to one configuration hyperedge (E_C) and at most to one extensional hyperedge (E_E). These conditions can be interpreted the following way: a vertex may belong to a configuration structure (either artifact or model), or it may belong to an extension that represents the instantiation of either an artifact or a model.

> $label_{node} : V \to L_{node}$; where L is a set of labels, it is a vertex labeling function;
> $label_{edge} : V \to L_{edge}$; where L is a set of labels, it is an edge labeling function;
> $source_E : E \to V$, $target_E : E \to V$ these functions return the source and target vertices of an edge E;
> $attr : Attr \to V$ attribute assignment function;
> $source_{Attr} : Attr \to V$; he vertex that owns the attribute is returned;
> $target_{Attr} : Attr \to D$. The *data values* of attributes are yielded; D represents the set of data;

D can be grasped again as vertices within the hypergraph and it can be interpreted as *variables*. Over D as a set of variables, set of operations (OP) can be defined that can be used to describe constraints and rules within formulas.

5   Enterprise Architecture Representation with Hypergraph Formalism

In this section our high-level description will be presented about the hypergraph-based structure of an enterprise architecture. The Enterprise Architecture at a given organization can be perceived as an overarching artifact that contains all potential artifacts and represents the architecture in a comprehensive way. This overarching conceptual artifact consist of generic artifact types that comprise artifact types. The hierarchical relationships can be described by *configuration hyperedges* (E_C); the instances of a member of a hierarchy that is made of either generic artifact types or artifact types can be perceived as extensions and can be represented by extensional hyperedges. Thereby, this way of representation makes possible for a recursive definition of artifact types and grouping them into a generic artifact type. A *generic artifact type* **GAT** is a *hierarchy of artifact types* **ATH**. The elements of **ATH** can belong to a configuration hyperedge $e_{Ci} \in E_C$ as vertices. The generalized hypergraphs allow that the vertices may appear as complex structures, as hyperedges. Therefore, a node can be a hyperedge that itself a configuration hyperedge that contains a hierarchy of document types. Thereby, the representation makes possible for a recursive definition of document types and gathering them into a generic document type [12].

Definition 6. The elements of a Metamodel Entity in an Enterprise Architecture are represented in hypergraph by hyperedge m_i where $m_i \in E_{mm\_ent} \subseteq E$ the set of hyperedges. The elements of m_i are the vertices that represent metamodel entities that will describe an artifact. In the Metamodel Entity hyperedge metamodel relationships enmesh the set of metamodel entities by using directed hyperedges.

According to our model, an artifact is composed of a set of metamodel entities and the related overarching metamodel relationships.

Definition 7. The elements of an Artifact in an Enterprise Architecture are represented in hypergraph by hyperedge a_i where $a_i \in E_{art} \subseteq E$ the set of hyperedges. The elements of a_i are the vertices that represent a set of metamodel entities that describe the artifact in the TOGAF Metamodel. Overarching metamodel relationships that enmesh the set of metamodel entities are also connected to an artifact hyperedge by using directed hyperedges.

After defining the concept of artifacts, we now turn to build the different grouping options for dimensioning, structuring and categorizing the artifacts, using viewpoints, architecture layers and artifact types. We start the description of grouping options with defining Viewpoints, which serve as a container of artifacts to create a specific perspective of the architecture for a specific stakeholder group.

Definition 8. The elements of a Viewpoint in an Enterprise Architecture are represented in hypergraph by hyperedge h_i where $h_i \in E_{viewp} \subseteq E$ the set of hyperedges. The elements of h_i are the vertices that represent artifacts that each of them describes a single model.

Artifacts can be parts of several Viewpoints at the same time. After defining Viewpoints, we now turn to the dimensioning option of EA by describing the concept of Architecture Layer in hypergraph-based manner.

Definition 9. The elements of an Architecture Layer in an Enterprise Architecture are represented in hypergraph by hyperedge l_i where $l_i \in E_{layer} \subseteq E$ the set of hyperedges. The elements of l_i are the vertices that represent artifacts that each of them describes a single model.

Like viewpoints, architecture layers provide similar multi-containing possibilities. To complete the definition of grouping options, we now specify Artifact Type, which provides categorization for the different kind of artifacts.

Definition 10. The elements of an Artifact Type in an Enterprise Architecture are represented in hypergraph by hyperedge at_i where $at_i \in E_{art\_type} \subseteq E$ the set of hyperedges. The elements of at_i are the vertices that represent artifacts. An artifact has a single artifact type: at_c stands for *catalog* artifact type, at_m stands for *matrix* artifact type, while at_d stands for *diagram* artifact type.

Unlike viewpoints and architecture layers, the sets artifact types are disjoint, i.e. every artifact has only one artifact type: catalog or matrix or diagram. Figure 2 presents our concept for describing enterprise architecture in a hypergraph-based structure, using the above introduced definitions.

Constraints for defining an enterprise architecture by using this hypergraph-based approach include: (1) An artifact covers a set of metamodel entities. This set is enmeshed by metamodel relationships. (2) An artifact can be part of several viewpoints. (3) An artifact can be part of more architecture layers. (4) An artifact can be part of both viewpoints and architecture layers. (5) Hyperedges of artifact types are disjoint.

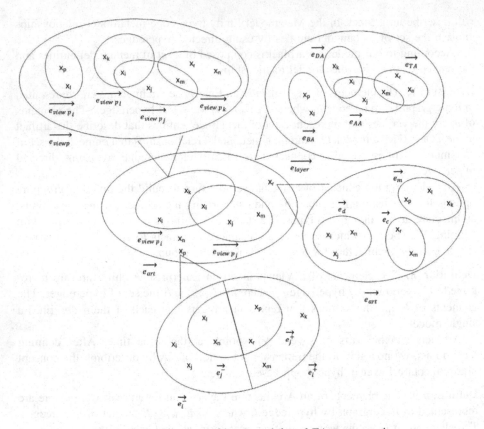

Fig. 2. Schematic view of hypergraph-based EA representation.

Finally, we define relationships between the components of an EA. In the proposed concept has-a and is-a relationships cover the whole architecture.

Definition 11. We refer to relationships as a hyperedge $r_i \in E_{rel} \subseteq E$ that contains directed hyperedges r_{is-a} and r_{has-a}. These hyperedges contain hyperedges (the components that we will connect to each other) on both the head and the tail parts. The relationship is composed by defining edges between the head and the tail. Figure 3 presents our view for defining is-a and has-a relationships.

6   Motivating Example and Preliminary Results

This part of the paper presents a motivating example for utilizing the hypergraph-based approach to describe an enterprise architecture and analyse strategic misalignment. The problem of revealing the typical symptoms of misalignment will be addressed in order to assess the state of alignment in an organization [17]. The illustrative example focuses on a public sector organisation. The analysis was performed in a fragment of the organisations's EA model structure. The initiative is a pilot project for setting up the

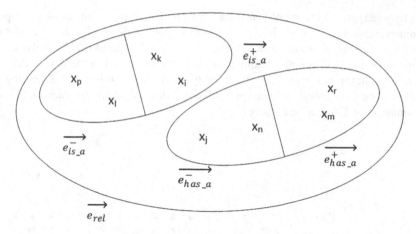

Fig. 3. Schematic view of relationship types.

EA practice in the organisation. It was set off to outline the process of road control with EA methods over 2 set of changes. To-be phases deal with the changes in process execution, supportive applications and underlying technological infrastructure. We use the organization to utilize the proposed hypergraph-based approach for analysing strategic and structural misalignment problems in an enterprise architecture structure.

In a former approach [14, 15] an XML-based analysis tool was created, which detected the symptoms of misalignment with rule assessment techniques. The applied research methodology used an alignment perspective-driven approach. In the first step, traditional alignment perspectives were connected with typical misalignment symptoms. In the second step, relevant artifacts were provided with the misalignment symptoms, i.e. the models which may contain the symptom in question. In the third step, suitable EA analysis types were suggested to the misalignment symptoms. These EA analysis types were able to detect the symptoms in the recommended containing artifacts [17]. To translate the above introduced methodology into the hypergraph-based approach, we need the following concepts: (1) Alignment perspectives: This list contains the corresponding alignment perspective for symptom detection. (2) Misalignment symptom catalog: This list comprises the perceived misalignment symptoms. (3) Artifact catalog: This list encompasses the possible containing EA models. (4) EA analysis catalog: This list includes the possible EA analysis types to recommend. (5) Presence in the artifact: This concept describes the sign of the symptom in the EA models. (6) Occurrence on model entity level: This concept defines how the symptom is manifested on model entity level. (7) Occurrence in XML model export: This item describes how the symptom is manifested in the XML export of the EA model. (8) XML-based query. We provide some examples of artifact representation in the proposed hypergraph structure. Figure 4 presents an incidence directed hypergraph (dirhypergraph). This illustration shows how Artifact hyperedges exist in the Metamodel Entity hyperedge. The figure consists of two further representations for the incidence dirhypergraph: an incidence digraph of the dirhypergraph, and a line directed graph for the dirhypergraph. Figure 5 illustrates an Architecture

Layer hyperedges and the related incidence graph. The hypergraph-based description and representation of EA models provides extended analysis potential based on a formalized conceptual framework. While the original rule-based framework was appropriate to discover the misalignment problems represented in the EA models, the results were highly constrained by the quality of the EA models. By extending the approach using the hypergraph concept a more detailed and formalized description and representation of EA can be achieved.

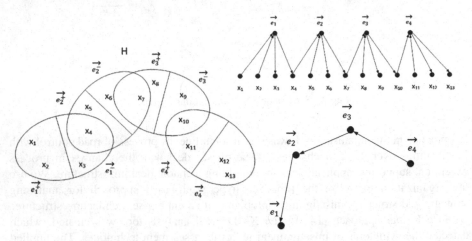

Fig. 4. (a) Example of an incidence directed hypergraph: artifact hyperarchs in the metamodel entity directed hypergraph, (b) Incidence digraph of the directed hypergraph and (c) Line directed graph of the directed hypergraph.

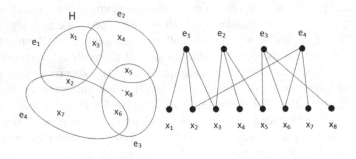

Fig. 5. (a) Example of viewpoint hyperedges within artifact hyperedge, (b) example of architecture layer hyperedges with incidence graph.

7 Conclusion

The proposed approach provides the opportunity to make use of formal and mathematical analytic methods for discovering misalignment among IT strategies, information systems and information architecture. The hypergraph modeling and representation offers the chance to check and control the discrepancies in complex enterprise architecture structures. Our proposed model gives way to automatized and algorithmic analysis as well. The approach enables organizations to explore and analyse misalignment symptoms, but workflow patterns, implementation phases-related issues, dynamic changes, broader business and management concepts can also be involved (e.g. "case management" [3]). Based on our conceptual model for EA description, future work needs to be done to formulate restrictions when building an enterprise architecture. These constrains will later be built into the hypergraph-based representation of EA.

Acknowledgement. This work was partially supported by EFOP-3.6.3-VEKOP-16. Supported by the ÚNKP-17-4 New National Excellence Program of the Ministry of Human Capacities.

References

1. Bent, H.V.D., Sante, T.V., Kerssens, D., Kemmeren, J.: TOGAF, the open group architecture framework. Van Haren Publishing, Zaltbommel (2008). http://www.opengroup.org/togaf/
2. Bharadwaj, A., El Sawy, O.A., Pavlou, P.A., Venkatraman, N.: Digital business strategy: toward a next generation of insights. MIS Q. **37**(2), 471–482 (2013)
3. Bouafia, K., Molnár, B., Khebizi, A.: A functional approach for transformation to abstract specifications for Web services from BPEL Programs Characteristics of the approach, winter school, at Pecs – Hungary, February 2017
4. Bounfour, A.: Digital Futures. Digital Transformation, Springer, Cham (2016)
5. Bowersox, D.J., Closs, D.J., Drayer, R.W.: The digital transformation: technology and beyond. Supply Chain Manag. Rev. **9**(1), 22–29 (2005)
6. Bretto, A.: Hypergraph Theory: An Introduction, pp. 111–116. Springer, Berlin (2013)
7. Capgemini: digital transformation: a roadmap for billion dollar organizations. MIT Center for Digital Business and Capgemini Consulting, Cambridge (2011)
8. Choi, J., Nazareth, D.L., Jain, H.K.: The impact of SOA implementation on IT-business alignment: a system dynamics approach. ACM Trans. Manage. Inf. Syst. (TMIS) **4**(1) (2013)
9. Goerzig, D., Bauernhansl, T.: Enterprise architectures for the digital transformation in small and medium-sized enterprises. Procedia CIRP **67**, 540–545 (2018)
10. Hanschke, I.: Strategic IT management: a toolkit for enterprise architecture management. Springer Science & Business Media, Heidelberg (2009)
11. Matt, C., Hess, T., Benlian, A.: Digital transformation strategies. Bus. Inf. Syst. Eng. **57**(5), 339–343 (2015)
12. Molnár, B., Benczúr, A., Béleczki, A.: A model for analysis and design of information systems based on a document centric approach. In: Nguyen, N.T., Trawiński, B., Fujita, H., Hong, T.-P. (eds.) ACIIDS 2016. LNCS (LNAI), vol. 9621, pp. 290–299. Springer, Heidelberg (2016). https://doi.org/10.1007/978-3-662-49381-6_28

13. Molnár, B., Béleczki, A., Benczúr, A.: Information systems modelling based on graph-theoretic background. J. Inf. Telecommun. 1–23 (2017)
14. Őri, D., Szabó, Z.: Pattern-based analysis of business-IT mismatches in EA models: insights from a case study. In: Proceedings of the IEEE EDOCW 2017, pp. 92–99 (2017)
15. Őri, D.: On exposing strategic and structural mismatches between business and information systems: misalignment symptom detection based on enterprise architecture model analysis, Ph.D. thesis, May 2017
16. Peppard, J., Ward, J.: Strategic Planning for Information Systems, 4th edn. Wiley, Chichester (2016)
17. Szabó, Z., Őri, D.: Information strategy challenges in the digital era. How enterprise architecture management can support strategic IS planning. In: 2017 11th International Conference on Software, Knowledge, Information Management and Applications (SKIMA), pp. 1–8 (2017)
18. Versteeg, G., Bouwman, H.: Business architecture: a new paradigm to relate business strategy to ICT. Inf. Syst. Front. 8(2), 91–102 (2006)
19. Zachman, J.A.: A framework for information systems architecture. IBM Syst. J. 26(3), 276–292 (1987)

EAM Based Approach to Support IT Planning for Digital Transformation in Public Organizations

Dóra Őri[✉] and Zoltán Szabó

Department of Information Systems, Corvinus University of Budapest,
Budapest, Hungary
{DOri,Szabo}@informatika.uni-corvinus.hu

Abstract. Organisations in the digital era face a changing role of digitality in several areas, e.g. in their business models, organisational design, compliance, regulation and economic environment. In this transformation, the role of IT is changing as well. As it is becoming more and more difficult to disunite digital products and services from their underlying IT infrastructures, corporate IT plays an important role in digital transformation. Moreover, IT-enabled processes increase the complexity of digital product and service architecture. These aspects point out the need for revisiting the present enterprise architectures and IT governance practices to successfully manage digital transformation. This paper discusses IT-based opportunities for digital transformation initiatives based on an Enterprise Architecture Management (EAM)-related method for assessing strategic alignment problems. The paper presents an analysis using the proposed framework to indicate areas for digital transformation initiatives, to facilitate the harmonisation of business and IT as well as to promote digital transformation implementation and post-implementation.

Keywords: Digital transformation · Digital strategy · Strategic alignment
Misalignment · Enterprise Architecture Management

1 Introduction

The increasing awareness for the disruptive innovations and integrating digital technologies (social media, mobile applications, business analytics and cloud-based services) and the emerging new business models emphasize the importance of agile and effective approaches in IT planning. Digitally matured organizations develop digital strategies to transform the business [9]. Maturity in Strategic Alignment has positive effect on digital transformation planning and initiatives, but neither planning, nor implementation is an evident activity. In this article we would like to contribute to this emerging issue, by discussing opportunities based on Enterprise Architecture Management (EAM) related analysis.

The rest of the paper is organised as follows: Sect. 2 describes basics of digitalization, digital transformation and digital strategy in the light of strategic information systems planning and strategic enterprise architecture management. Section 3 proposes an overview about EAM-induced digital transformation planning and implementation.

© Springer Nature Switzerland AG 2018
A. Benczúr et al. (Eds.): ADBIS 2018, CCIS 909, pp. 377–387, 2018.
https://doi.org/10.1007/978-3-030-00063-9_35

Section 4 presents an EA-based analysis method for misalignment assessment and a case organisation in which the subsequent analysis will be conducted. Section 5 summarizes the results of the analysis, including different areas where the method can support Digital Transformation (DT) planning and implementation.

2 Digitalization and Strategy

Digital innovation refers to the use of digital technologies in the process of innovation, it enables new products, new services, new processes and new business models. The phenomenon of digital transformation covers the effects of digital innovations in terms of the emergence of new actors, new network, new structures and practices [11]. Digital transformation creates digital organizational forms, digital institutional infrastructures and digital institutional building blocks [8]. It means that organisations in the digital era face the changing role of digitality in their business models, organisational design, compliance, regulation and economic environment. This changing role concerns business strategies as well. Digital technologies transform traditional business strategies into digital business strategies. Digital transformation affects the business strategy on four areas: on its scope (extension beyond traditional borders), on its scale (including network effects caused by increased amount of data), on its speed (including the acceleration in decision making, network building, etc.) and on the source of value creation and value capture in digital business strategy [3]. Digital transformation strategies are plans that govern organisations in transforming products, processes, organisation design due to the emerging digital technologies in the companies. Digital transformation strategies differ from business and IT strategies in perspective and in goals [11]. Sia et al. [16] defined key success factors for designing and executing digital business strategy: (1) It requires strong leadership. (2) Agile and scalable digital operations are needed. (3) Via digital business strategy information abundance needs to be exploited to design new digitally enabled customer experience. (4) It continually needs to monitor digital landscape to incubate and accelerate emerging digital innovations. Whereas, challenges with digitalization include (1) the high cost of digital business platforms development and (2) operation and the technical interoperability of service providers when connecting to digital business platforms [4].

Bharadwaj et al. [3] states, that a digital strategy should be different of traditional IT strategy. Information strategy is a managerial responsibility to integrate information technology and concerns into business planning, establishing a direct relationship between them [17]. Aron [2] from Gartner stated, that IT Strategy is a technical answer to a business question, while Digital Strategy is a business answer to a digital question. So, digital strategy is usually a corporate level, cross-functional strategy that address all functions and processes of an organization. From this aspect the role of IT strategy is to fulfil the requirements of the digital strategy that is interpreted as a special form of business strategy.

Traditionally, information strategy plays crucial role in enterprises to gain and sustain competitive advantage through IT investments. The primary objective of Information Systems (IS) planning is to align IS plans with the business plans. Although the alignment of IS operations with business operations, matching organizational characteristics with IS operations, and matching IS plans with business plans have been emphasized, only a few studies have addressed the fit among these variables in a formal sense [17]. Digital strategies are more business oriented, than the formal IS planning, more agile and usually business driven initiatives, while traditional planning is a robust, bilateral procedure that is anchored to IT architecture.

Considering the traditional Strategic Information Systems Planning (SISP), the influential grouping of Earl [5] (IS strategy, Information Management (IM) strategy, Information Technology (IT) strategy as the major components of Information Strategy) is still relevant. These three main components of the information strategy are the focal points of planning. Information System Strategy focuses on business needs and demand, aligns IT developments with business goals, seeks beneficial IT opportunities [17]. The IS strategy is based on a combination of basic short-term tactical applications, medium-term business needs and long-term investment in business vision [17]. It has three main pillars too: the top-down IS portfolio planning based on the business needs, the bottom-up evaluation of current IT portfolio, and seeking for innovations. IT Strategy addresses technology policies, principles, clarifies the issues of architecture, supplier policies, technology standards [17]. This strategy gives the framework for development and operations. IM strategy considers management issues, it deals with the role and structure of IT, the relationships between IT and business, and defines a framework for management control, responsibility and management of IT processes [17].

Digital strategies focus only on the Information Systems component. Planning of digitalization is mainly the innovation pillar of the traditional IS strategy component, leaving behind the waterfall life-cycle based planning approaches that are necessary to translate business strategy to IS needs (traditional IS portfolio planning). An agile, innovation-oriented process to prepare the digitalization strategy neglect the technical details of the evaluation of the actual IS and IT portfolio. Business orientation and agility in planning let only very limited consideration of IT and IM strategies. But all these aspects should be aligned to the digitalization-related plans to avoid any problems of misalignment: brilliant innovative ideas cannot be implemented without a solid background of IT. So, consolidation of digital strategy with the traditional IS, IT and IM strategies is a key success factor. We argue, that in the era of digitalization, strategic business planning and IT planning becomes a challenging task, and enterprise architecture management can be a major facilitator of the planning initiatives, by providing many opportunities for harmonization of plans, IT and business domains, business and IT alignment and organizational engineering.

3 EAM-Induced Digital Transformation Planning and Implementation

As it is becoming more and more difficult to disunite digital products and services from their underlying IT infrastructures, corporate IT plays an important role in leading digital transformation [3]. IT-enabled processes made digital product and service architecture more complex. Digitalization changes the role of IT in organisation from several perspectives. Changing role can be perceived on business level (e.g. networked, dynamic business processes, distributed process management practice), on application level (e.g. SaaS, SOA), on information level (e.g. open data, Big Data and analytics, Information Architecture) as well as on technology level (e.g. open platforms, virtualized environment). IT services will be an accentual part of digital business strategies and therefore future customer experience. It is needed to revisit the present enterprise architectures and IT governance practices to successfully manage this digital transformation. IS governance is an effective tool in coordinating and achieving digital transformation [4]. Several authors (e.g. [6]) claim the application of EA for implementation of business transformation. Nowadays the role of EA in implementing digital transformation is examined.

Architecture is regarded as the fundamental structure of a system, including its components and their relationships. It is a formal description which also shows the main architectural principles and guidelines that facilitate the construction and operation of the system. In this respect, enterprise architecture is the construction of an enterprise, described by its entities and their relationships. EA is an organising logic for business processes and IT infrastructure in order to review, maintain and control the whole operation of an enterprise. This organising logic acts as an integrating force between business planning, business operations and enabling technological infrastructure. Enterprise architecture integrates information systems and business processes into a coherent map. Enterprise architecture supports IT strategy, IT governance and business-IT alignment [18]. It also helps to capture a vision of the entire system in all its dimensions and complexity. Enterprise architecture is a structure which helps, (1) coordinate the many facets that make up the fundamental essence of an enterprise and (2) provide a structure for business processes and supportive information systems [12, 17].

In order to cope with architecture complexity, different frameworks, methods, and tools have been developed. An enterprise architecture framework is a collection of descriptions and methods to create and manage enterprise architecture. The most recognised ones are the Zachman Framework (for rather theoretical purposes) and the TOGAF framework (for rather practical usage).

TOGAF (The Open Group Architecture Framework) is a holistic approach which describes a metamodel for enterprise architecture and proposes different methods for building and maintaining enterprise architectures. The core of the TOGAF approach is the Architecture Development Method (ADM), which proposes an iterative method for developing and managing enterprise architecture. TOGAF provides 4 architecture domains: (1) Business Architecture, (2) Data Architecture, (3) Application Architecture and (4) Technology Architecture. TOGAF provides a minimum set of necessary EA models, called artefacts. There are both descriptive and composite artefacts in the recommended artefact list. These artefacts are attached to certain ADM phases.

Enterprise architecture management is a management philosophy concerned with corporate change. Factors leading to the need for strategic EAM can be summarised as follows [1, 10, 14, 15]: (1) The fact that adaptation to the changing environment means a competitive factor. (2) The observation that poorly coordinated changes generate risks and paralyze business. (3) The perception that complex enterprise architecture increases costs and risks and decreases flexibility and transparency [17].

Goerzig and Bauernhansl [7] collected several aspects to compare enterprise architecture and digital transformation. According their comparison, EA and digital transformation evolve from different drivers, consist of different target groups, differ in subject, development approach, vertical hierarchy levels, value stream and lifecycle phases. As for drivers, whereas EA has an IT focus, digital transformation has a business focus. Similarly, target groups differ as IT architects, IT experts versus management specialized staff, respectively. While EA builds on stable information systems, digital transformation operates with fast changing serving systems. Likewise, development approach from waterfall to agile approaches. In case of EA, the focused vertical hierarchy levels are the regular architecture domains: business, data, application, technology and their integration. In case of digital transformation, the focused vertical hierarchy levels differ by using the strategic, business model, organisational and integration levels. As for value streams, EA concentrates on ISs for stable value chains and customer needs, whereas digital transformation works with ecosystems and context-sensitive value creation. Finally, the lifecycle phases include development-maintenance-documentation   versus   agile   development-usage-maintenance-documentation, respectively. The above introduced aspects indicate the search for new methods, models and tools to support EAM in this changing role. Further research needs to be conducted to reveal how to support digital transformation by utilizing and enhancing IT-enabled organizational capabilities.

The management of enterprise architecture results in increased transparency, documented architecture vision and clear architecture principles and guidelines. These factors contribute to efficient resource allocation, the creation of synergies, better alignment, and reduced complexity. In the end, better business performance can be achieved by using the EAM concept. EAM promotes the vertical integration between strategic directions and tactical concepts, design decisions, and operations. Additionally, it provides horizontal alignment between business change and technology. In addition, EAM improves the capability of an enterprise for perceiving, analysing and responding to organisational changes. It helps (1) to align the organisation with strategic goals, (2) to coordinate interdependencies in business and IT, (3) to prepare an organisation for an agile reaction. EAM plays a role in strategy formulation as well. Strategic EAM helps (1) to analyse the current situation, (2) assess strategic options, (3) formulate strategic initiatives, (4) develop an architectural vision, (5) roadmap migration activities, (6) assess and prioritise project portfolio and (7) monitor architecture evolution [1, 10, 17].

This paper attempts to investigate how a company can use EAM-based analysis methods to:

- discover digital transformation opportunities by exploring uncovered IT needs, underserved business activities, fragmented processes, etc.,
- support the harmonization with IS and business planning by facilitating and integrating detailed planning,
- facilitate implementation of digital transformation by avoiding technical and organizational design related divergences, unrecognized interdependencies,
- promote post-implementation of digital transformation by identifying organizational or technical misalignments.

EAM facilitates strategic management of IT [1], and it is a valuable tool for the planning and implementation of digitalization. [13] proposed an EAM based method to analyse strategic alignment problems – misalignment symptoms - in organizations.

That approach can be extended to a valuable tool that is appropriate for the support of digitalization initiatives.

The process of digital transformation and the definition of a digital strategy broadens the roles and responsibilities of EA and IS governance. This extended role includes the definition and modelling of a digital architecture as well as its integration with connecting architecture domains.

4   EA-Based Analysis Method for Misalignment Assessment

In the proposed methodology, that was developed according to the Design Science Research approach [13], the concepts of TOGAF will be used for EA-based misalignment symptom analysis. In particular, the partition of architecture domains will be utilised. The proposed framework aims to analyse the symptoms of misalignment in enterprise architecture models. The structure of the framework is based on four main parts (illustrated in Fig. 1): (1) Alignment perspectives are used to structure the approach of misalignment symptom detection. (2) A misalignment symptom catalogue is composed from symptom collections found in the recent literature on misalignment. (3) An artefact catalogue is introduced, which summarises potential containing EA models. (4) EA analysis catalogue describes potential EA analysis types that are suitable for revealing misalignment symptoms in containing EA models [14, 17].

The proposed research methodology uses an alignment perspective-driven approach. In the first step, traditional alignment perspectives are provided with typical misalignment symptoms. In the second step, relevant artefacts are connected to the misalignment symptoms, which may contain the symptom in question. In the third step, suitable EA analysis types are recommended to the misalignment symptoms. These EA analysis types can detect the symptoms in the recommended containing artefacts [14, 17]. Misalignment symptoms are translated into analysable rules, and finally into queries for detection. Symptoms are detected in the XML exports of the EA models. The XML-based query originates from the analysis results of the framework.

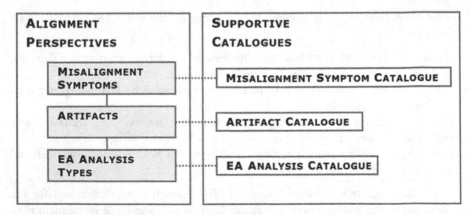

Fig. 1. The structure of EA-based misalignment assessment framework (based on [13])

To demonstrate the applicability of the proposed framework, a case study has been conducted [13]. The case study clarified the operation of the framework by applying it in the context of a real EA model structure [14, 17]. The empirical investigation focused on a public service company. The case organisation is a non-profit government corporation that handles matters relating to road safety, road traffic management, and transportation for around 32,000 km of a national public road network [14]. The initiative under review was a pilot project for setting up EA practice in the organisation. The study was carried out on a fragment of the organisation's EA model structure.

5 Analysis of Relevant EA Models for Digital Transformation Planning and Implementation Using the Proposed Research Framework

This subsection describes how EA models play a role in Digital Transformation planning and implementation using the proposed framework. Table 1 introduces the EA model structure at the case organisation. The general model structure consists of several layers. As we can see, there are some modeling resources available concerning the Business Architecture (Layer 0–2, 5), Data Architecture (Layer 3) and Application Architecture (Layer 4), but there is no modeling instance for technological/infrastructural projection of the organisation [14]. The model structure in the organisation offers an in-depth analytical potential for Digital Transformation planning and implementation using the proposed framework.

Table 1. General model structure for discovering DT-facilitating misalignment symptoms (based on [13])

Layer	Category	Organisational models
0	Strategy	Business Function – IT System Matrix, Business Process Map, Architectural Principles Catalogue
1	Organisational Structure	Organigram
2	Business Processes	Value Chain Diagram, Business Process Models, Primary Activities, Support Activities, Governance Activities
3	Data	Regulations, Data Components, Document Model
4	Applications	Application Portfolio, Application Type - Application Component Matrix, Data Flow Diagram, Application Cooperation Diagrams, Interface Diagram
5	Products and Services	Service Map

As discussed before, digital strategy provides the digital positioning of an organisation, including the operation model, the competitors and the customer needs. A digital architecture describes the to-be architecture domain states through which the digital strategy objectives can be achieved. At the case organisation EA models in the Business Architecture domain (the strategic level, the organisational level, the business process level and the products and services level) set the context for a digital strategy.

They contribute to describe (1) the digital vision, mission and statements, (2) the business services and functions necessary to digital services, (3) the digital organisation. Data-related EA models (data level) described in a Data Architecture provide the data model and document model for a digital architecture and therefore, for the digital strategy. EA models in the Application Architecture domain (application level) deliver the details about applications and their interconnectedness into a digital architecture together with their connections to business and data levels. Business-to-Application models describe a mapping of business functions-business services and the delivering application components for digital initiatives. Data-to-Application models describe a mapping of communication relationships between applications and the related data flows. EA models in the Technology Architecture - not represented in this case – deliver the infrastructural details for a digital platform including technological components and their interrelatedness with business, data and application levels.

In the following we provide sample symptoms of misalignment in the architecture domains, using the proposed framework. Misalignment symptoms indicate several insights about the progression and performance of digital strategy and the process of digital transformation. On the one hand, misalignment symptoms show the signs of alignment problems between digital strategy and traditional business strategy, i.e. digital initiatives anticipate the business strategy and structure causing misalignment in several organisational areas and levels. On the other hand, symptoms of misalignment can be considered as drivers for digital initiatives. Misalignment symptom analysis helps the organisation in detecting the organisational areas where disruptive changes should be initiated. Following the above introduced directions, we provide some sample symptoms of misalignment that promote digital transformation phases. Symptoms stem from the misalignment symptom catalogue presented by [13].

Misalignment symptoms that help to discover digital transformation opportunities, include e.g.: unsupported processes, many supporting systems for a single business process, undefined or multiple hierarchy or lines of reporting, lack of data ownership, lack of application interfaces, non-automatic data migration among applications, incompatible platforms or technologies, critical business process does not depend on scalable and available applications, inappropriate application functionality, multiple applications managing the same information.

Misalignment symptoms that support the harmonization with IS and business planning, include e.g.: no formal architectural integration at functional organisation level, information consistency or integrity problems, undefined business process goals and business process owners, undefined organisational mission, strategy, and goals, lack of relation between process goals and organisational goals, lack or minority of changes in business (organisation, processes, goals) induced by IT (over time).

Misalignment symptoms that facilitate implementation of digital transformation (by breakdown of plans for projects, harmonization, etc.) include e.g.: sporadically existing or too technical Service Level Agreements, undefined business service levels, undefined business information requirements, insufficient involvement of business users in systems developments, undefined criteria to prioritise IT projects, lack of translation from business service levels to IT service levels, frequent IT reorganisations.

Misalignment symptoms that promote post-implementation of digital transformation (i.e. the harmonization of digitalized and pre-digitalized areas) include e.g.: incoherent replicas of the same data, because they are updated by multiple applications, lack of or incomplete coherency from multiple transactions, because a single business process crosses multiple applications, systems integration difficulties, technological heterogeneity, incompatible platforms or technologies, information consistency or integrity problems.

To illustrate the usage of the proposed framework in supporting digital transformation planning and implementation, we provide analysis results of 1–1 sample symptom for each of the above introduced digital transformation support areas. Table 2 mirrors the structure of the framework, presenting misalignment symptom detection utilizing for digital transformation.

Table 2. Sample matching results of operating the framework for DT planning and implementation (based on [13])

Area of DT support	Perspective & component	Misalignment symptom	Containing EA model	EA analysis
To discover DT opportunities	Strategy Execution: Business Strategy & Business Structure matching	Undefined or multiple hierarchy or lines of reporting	Organigram Business Process Models Regulations	Dependency analysis Enterprise interoperability assessment
To support the harmonization with IS and business planning	Strategy Execution: Business Strategy & Business Structure matching	Undefined organisational mission, strategy, and goals	Business Function – IT System Matrix Application Type – Application Component Matrix	Coverage analysis
To facilitate implementation of DT	Service Level: IT Structure & Business Structure matching	Undefined business service levels	Service Map Value Chain Diagram Application Portfolio	Coverage analysis Enterprise coherence assessment
To promote post-implementation of DT	Service Level: IT Structure & Business Structure matching	Information consistency or integrity problems	Data Components Data Flow Diagram	Enterprise interoperability assessment

Misalignment symptom detection provided valuable feedback about the progression and performance of digital transformation initiatives. The use of the proposed framework was appropriate to indicate areas for digital transformation initiatives, to facilitate the harmonisation between business and IT as well as to promote digital transformation implementation and post-implementation.

6 Conclusion and Further Research

Digitalization changes business models, organisational design and technology, collaboration within and between organizations. While IT was a major facilitator of business innovations in the last few decades, recently the concept of digital strategy has been emerged among companies. Although the primary objective of traditional Information Systems planning is to align IT and business plans, digitalization is more about revolutional, sometimes disruptive innovations, so the risks and the chance of failures are higher. Planning and implementation of a digital strategy is very challenging task that can be supported by Enterprise Architecture Management.

The EAM based model we introduced in the paper was originally developed and tested to discover and analyse misalignment symptoms related to IT initiatives, built on the strategic alignment concept. Considering the potential aspects of digital planning and implementation we found that EAM-based analysis approach can be used in many activities: (1) to discover digital transformation opportunities, (2) to support the harmonization with IS and business planning, (3) to facilitate implementation of digital transformation, and (4) to promote post-implementation of digital transformation by identifying organizational or technical misalignments.

The proposed method is based essentially on the concepts of enterprise engineering and enterprise architecture. EA models and the analysis of the relevant models can be valuable inputs for planning and implementation. The quality and coverage of the available models limit the usability of the method, but companies with matured competencies in planning and EAM can use the proposed approach to facilitate digitalization. Many of the testable rules developed for misalignment analysis can be used directly, but new, more digitalization-specific symptoms and analysing perspectives can be developed, based on the digital architecture concept.

Acknowledgement.   Supported by the ÚNKP-17-4 New National Excellence Program of the Ministry of Human Capacities.

References

1. Ahlemann, F., Stettiner, E., Messerschmidt, M., Legner, C.: Strategic Enterprise Architecture Management: Challenges, Best Practices, and Future Developments. Springer, Heidelberg (2012). https://doi.org/10.1007/978-3-642-24223-6
2. Aron, D.: The Difference Between IT Strategy and Digital Strategy (2013). http://blogs.gartner.com/dave-aron/2013/11/12/the-difference-between-it-strategy-and-digital-strategy/

3. Bharadwaj, A., El Sawy, O.A., Pavlou, P., Venkatraman, N.: Digital business strategy: towards a next generation of insights. MIS Q. **37**(2), 471–482 (2013)
4. Collin, J., Hiekkanen, K., Korhonen, J.J., Halén, M., Itälä, T., Helenius, M.: IT Leadership in Transition - The Impact of Digitalization on Finnish Organizations. Aalto University Publication Series SCIENCE + TECHNOLOGY, 7/2015 (2015)
5. Earl, M.J.: Management Strategies for Information Technology. Prentice-Hall, London (1989)
6. Gardner, D., Fehskens, L., Naidu, M., Rouse, W.B., Ross, J.W.: Point-counterpoint: enterprise architecture and enterprise transformation as related but distinct concepts. J. Enterp. Transf. **2**, 283–294 (2012)
7. Goerzig, D., Bauernhansl, T.: Enterprise architectures for the digital transformation in small and medium-sized enterprises. Procedia CIRP **67**, 540–545 (2018)
8. Hinings, B., Gegenhuber, T., Greenwood, R.: Digital innovation and transformation: an institutional perspective. Inf. Organ. **28**(1), 52–61 (2018)
9. Kane, G., Palmer, D., Nguye, P.A., Kiron, D., Buckley, N.: Strategy, Not Technology, Drives Digital Transformation. MIT Sloan Management Review (2015). http://sloanreview.mit.edu/projects/strategy-drives-digital-transformation/. Accessed 18 Jan 2016
10. Lankhorst, M.: Enterprise Architecture at Work: Modelling, Communication and Analysis. Springer, Heidelberg (2013). https://doi.org/10.1007/978-3-642-29651-2
11. Matt, C., Hess, T., Benlian, A.: Digital transformation strategies. Bus. Inf. Syst. Eng. **57**, 339–343 (2015)
12. OMG: The Open Group: TOGAF Version 9. The Open Group Architecture Framework (TOGAF) (2015). http://theopengroup.org/
13. Őri, D.: On exposing strategic and structural mismatches between business and information systems: misalignment symptom detection based on enterprise architecture model analysis. Corvinus University of Budapest, Ph.D. thesis, May 2017
14. Őri, D.: Pattern-based misalignment symptom detection with XML validation: a case study. In: Pergl, R., Lock, R., Babkin, E., Molhanec, M. (eds.) EOMAS 2017. LNBIP, vol. 298, pp. 151–158. Springer, Cham (2017). https://doi.org/10.1007/978-3-319-68185-6_11
15. Schekkerman, J.: How to Survive in the Jungle of Enterprise Architecture Frameworks: Creating or Choosing an Enterprise Architecture Framework. Trafford Publishing, Victoria (2004)
16. Sia, S.K., Soh, C., Weill, P.: How DBS bank pursued a digital business strategy. MIS Q. Executive **15**(2), (2016)
17. Szabó, Z., Őri, D.: Information strategy challenges in the digital era. How enterprise architecture management can support strategic IS planning. In: 2017 11th International Conference on Software, Knowledge, Information Management and Applications (SKIMA), pp. 1–8 (2017)
18. Zachman, J.A.: A framework for information systems architecture. IBM Syst. J. **26**(3), 276–292 (1987)

Doctoral Consortium

Similarity Queries on Script Image Databases

Shruti Daggumati[✉][iD]

University of Nebraska-Lincoln, Lincoln, NE 68588, USA
sdagguma@cse.unl.edu

Abstract. For a long time, researchers and archaeologists have studied evolution and similarity among ancient scripts. The vast image libraries which have recently become available allow for data mining to enable the study of evolution of these ancient scripts. In particular, the origin of the Indus Valley script is highly debated and is considered an undeciphered script. In this paper, we use convolutional neural networks to test which alphabets/symbols from various languages may be related to the Indus Valley script. The languages focused on include the Proto-Elamite script and Sumerian.

Keywords: Indus Valley script · Proto-Elamite script
Sumerian · Convolutional neural networks

1 Introduction

The Indus Valley Civilization thrived primarily in northwest South Asia (present-day Afghanistan, India, and Pakistan) from 3300 to 1300 BCE [9]. Indus Valley civilization was one of three early civilizations of the Old World, other than Ancient Egypt and Mesopotamia. The Indus Valley civilization had a writing system which remains undeciphered; examples can be found on pottery, seals, tablets, jewelry, and weights. Due to the brevity of the inscriptions and a nonexistent "Rosetta Stone" the script of over 400 unique symbols (Fig. 1) and the true meaning behind these inscriptions remains a mystery.

2 Objectives and Problem Definition

Decipherment attempts are often aided by bilingual inscriptions, however, it is nonexistent for the Indus Valley script as of yet. Another clue to script decipherment could possibly be attained by finding a similar script where the symbols could be mapped. That matching can give the unknown script symbols a tentative phonetic value. Usually, the known scripts occur later in time than the unknown script. In this paper, we use convolutional neural networks and two scripts to find tentative phonetic assignments to the Indus Valley script symbols. These two scripts are the following:

© Springer Nature Switzerland AG 2018
A. Benczúr et al. (Eds.): ADBIS 2018, CCIS 909, pp. 391–401, 2018.
https://doi.org/10.1007/978-3-030-00063-9_36

Proto-Elamite: The Proto-Elamite script was briefly used around 3000 BCE in present-day Iran and southern Iraq. The script uses around 1900 non-numerical signs, although 1700 of those signs only appear a maximum of nine times in the 1600 Proto-Elamite texts [6]. Proto-Elamite is said to be logographic or ideographic. Similar to the Indus Valley script, the Proto-Elamite script is considered undeciphered.

Sumerian: The Sumerian script is primarily a syllabic writing system, written from left to right. It was used between 3100 BCE to 1st century AD in southern Mesopotamia to convey the Sumerian language.

In this paper, we aim to answer which script, Proto-Elamite or Sumerian, is more visually closely related to the Indus Valley script? In addition to this, we discuss implemented work which compares the Indus Valley, the Phoenician, and the Brahmi scripts.

3   Approach

3.1   Data

For this work, three different ancient scripts were used: (1) Indus Valley script, (2) Proto-Elamite script, and (3) Sumerian. For the Indus Valley script, we use 25 of the symbols (Fig. 1). Given that the Indus Valley script has over 400 symbols we chose to use the symbols with the most common frequency as shown in [27]. For the Proto-Elamite script we use 11 of the most frequent symbols (Fig. 2). Finally, for the Sumerian script 12 of the symbols were used (Fig. 3).

The MNIST Database [14] is the main inspiration for the construction of the dataset. The MNIST database contains 60,000 training images of handwritten black and white digits, where they use 10,000 images for validation images. In comparison to the MNIST Database, our training and validation datasets contain far fewer images, as we use transformations and distortions on the images to create a bigger dataset.

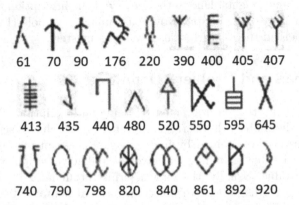

Fig. 1. Twenty-Five of most frequent Indus Valley script symbols [27].

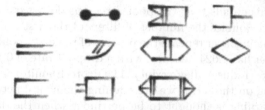

Fig. 2. Eleven of most frequent Proto-Elamite script symbols.

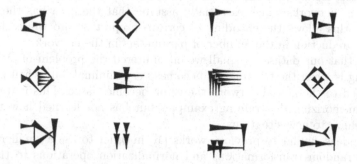

Fig. 3. Twelve of the unique Sumerian script symbols, using the consonants with the vowel quality /a/.

Each symbol has 100 images associated with it: 80 training images and 20 validation images. Each image is 25 × 25 pixels and is black and white. In total, we have 4800 images.

3.2 Software

The created neural networks use Python and TensorFlow and a Keras wrapper. Python has a large number of existing libraries which allows the ease of building a neural network. TensorFlow is an open source software library that is used for high-performance numerical computation which uses data flow graphs. Keras provides an API for high-level neural networks, and it is a wrapper that allows the use of the TensorFlow back end, providing modularity and Python-nativeness. Keras also allows out-of-the-box implementations of common network structures.

3.3 Neural Network Setup

The constructed neural networks have various levels of accuracy dependent on the alphabet/script. They use three main layers; 2D convolutional layer, 2D pooling layer, and a dense layer [1]. The first convolutional layer applies 32, 3 × 3 filters, which extracts 3 × 3-pixel subregions, using the ReLU activation function. The first pooling layer performs maximum pooling with a 2 × 2 filter and stride of 2; this entails that the pooled regions do not overlap. The second convolutional layer doubles the number of filters of the first convolutional layer, and the second pooling layer repeats the process of the first pooling layer. Finally, the first dense layer has 1,024 neurons, with a dropout rate of 0.4 and the second dense layer has 25 (Indus Valley script), 11 (Proto-Elamite), or 12 (Sumerian) neurons depending on the script we are training the neural network on.

Often deep learning is thought to be pertinent when the data set available is large. The use of convolutional neural networks(CNNs) allows the use of a small dataset from which the neural network can learn from. CNNs are multi-layer neural networks which essentially assume that the data has the form of an image, this allows the encoding of certain properties into the architecture entailing a reduction in the number of parameters in the network.

Given that our dataset is small we encountered the problem of overfitting. Overfitting is when the training set becomes very minimal, but when new data is presented to the neural network the error becomes large. This is due to the network memorizing the training examples but has not learned how to adapt and generalize to new situations.

Using ideas similar to previous works [4], in order to use a smaller dataset we apply random transformations and normalization operations to the training image dataset. The image is transformed in the following ways: rotation, shearing, scaling, zooming, and flipping. These augmentations are solely applied when creating the weight files for each language, not when cross comparing for prediction purposes.

3.4 Script Recognition

For each of the datasets, a neural network was created and given an appropriate amount of epochs to run, given that it had a fairly high accuracy rating and overfitting did not occur. Tables 1 and 2 show how the accuracy varies as the number of epochs increases.

Table 1 shows how accurate each neural network is at predicting validation data, which it has not encountered before. Table 2 shows how accurate the neural network is with training and validation data supplied to it. We see from Table 1 that as the number of epochs increases, the validation accuracy of the neural network recognizing the correct symbols increases for all three scripts.

Table 1. Validation accuracy

	25	50	75	100
Proto-Elamite	91.93	94.55	97.05	99.09
Sumerian	89.79	95.21	95.94	97.40
Indus	93.50	95.50	96.80	98.00

Table 2. Training and validation accuracy

	25	50	75	100
Proto-Elamite	87.73	89.09	89.55	90.00
Sumerian		91.25	97.92	98.33	98.33
Indus		83.82	91.98	94.02	96.22

3.5 Data Analysis

From Table 1, we see that the Proto-Elamite neural network has the highest accuracy overall for 75 epochs and 100 epochs, even though the Indus Valley script has a higher accuracy at the beginning. Sumerian has the lowest validation accuracy regardless of the number of epochs amongst the three scripts.

From Table 2 we see that Proto-Elamite has the lowest accuracy rating among the three scripts regardless of the number of epochs. This is fairly different from the pattern of the validation accuracy table. Similarly, Sumerian is also different from the pattern shown in Table 1. Even at the lowest epoch, it has the highest accuracy rating among the three scripts. The Indus Valley script has a consistent pattern among the two tables.

Among the three scripts Proto-Elamite and the Indus Valley Script have a few symbols with a similar structure and shape. This could be a source of a lower accuracy rating for the Proto-Elamite script in Table 2 and a lower accuracy

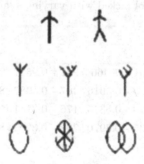

Fig. 4. Indus Valley script symbols - each row contains symbols with similar shape/structure

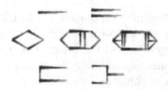

Fig. 5. Proto-Elamite script symbols - each row contains symbols with similar shape/structure

when dealing with fewer epochs for the two scripts. Figures 4 and 5 show some rows of symbols where confusion could occur.

4   Experiments

Given that the neural networks perform well at recognizing and classifying each symbol set to its respective value, we sought to look at how the Proto-Elamite and Sumerian datasets would be classified as input to the Indus Valley script neural network. These predictive measures were done using one hundred sample images for symbols. The use of neural networks to visually compare the languages removes human bias.

The Indus Valley script neural network was run a total of five times, due to neural networks running differently on each trial. From each of the trials, we stored the weights according to the classification to determine how the Proto-Elamite and Sumerian symbols would be classified according to the Indus Valley script. Among the five trials, there are times where the symbol classified has an overall consensus regarding the only symbol which can be mapped (Rows 1 and 2 - Fig. 3). However, there are other times where there is an equal mapping to two symbols, in this case, we decide to use the symbol with a high strength match (Row 3 - Fig. 3). In the case of a few symbols that have a random mapping for all five trials, we choose the mapping with the highest strength (Row 4 - Fig. 3). The similarity measures are based on visual proximity of two symbol sets (Table 3).

Table 3. Symbol picked with varying symbol consensus.

Trials (Symbol - Strength)					Symbol picked
1	2	3	4	5	
861 - 0.7268	861 - 0.4819	861 - 09466	861 - 0.9621	861-0.9111	861
820 - 0.4395	407 - 0.4170	820 - 0.5616	407 - 0.4087	820 - 0.3254	820
520 - 0.7017	176 - 0.2973	520 - 0.5345	176 - 0.3131	550 - 0.7619	520
595 - 0.3446	740 - 0.4497	435 - 0.3970	798 - 0.3292	840 - 0.4957	840

5   Results

Figures 6 and 7 show the classification of each Proto-Elamite and Sumerian symbol passed to the Indus Valley neural network. The tables are ordered from the strongest match amongst symbols to the least. The average strength among all the symbols for Proto-Elamite (0.595300899) is much stronger than Sumerian (0.525458755). In addition to this, the Proto-Elamite symbol set has less double mappings to the Indus Valley script symbol set in comparison to Sumerian.

Visually, we can see that the symbols which the neural network picked are more reasonable for the Proto-Elamite versus the Sumerian symbol sets. The shape structure as to why a neural network may pick a selected symbol is quite clear for the majority of the symbols.

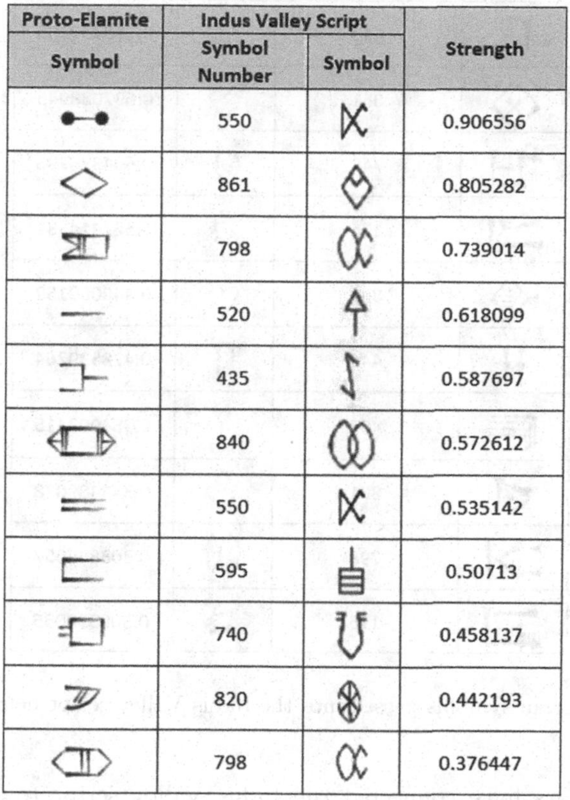

Proto-Elamite	Indus Valley Script		Strength
Symbol	Symbol Number	Symbol	
●—●	550	Ⱪ	0.906556
◇	861	◇	0.805282
⊒⊐	798	∝	0.739014
—	520	⇧	0.618099
⊐⊢	435	∫	0.587697
◁□▷	840	⊗	0.572612
≡	550	Ⱪ	0.535142
⊏	595	⊟	0.50713
⊐□	740	∪	0.458137
⟋	820	✿	0.442193
◁⊐▷	798	∝	0.376447

Fig. 6. Proto-Elamite symbols passed into the Indus Valley script neural network.

6 Related Work

6.1 Indus Valley Script Decipherment

Scholars debate the decipherment of the Indus Valley script. One of the first to encounter the Indus Valley script, Sir Alexander Cunningham assumed the seals to be of foreign import. He later stated that Brahmi might be a descendant of the Indus Valley script. To date, many other scholars have connected Indus Valley script to Brahmi [19–21].

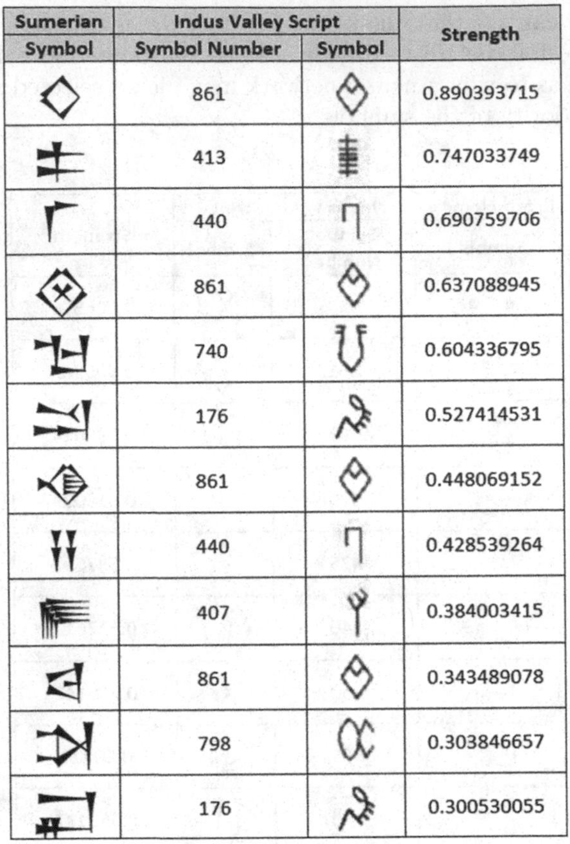

Sumerian	Indus Valley Script		Strength
Symbol	Symbol Number	Symbol	
◇	861	◈	0.890393715
ǂ	413	𝍶	0.747033749
⌐	440	⌐	0.690759706
◈	861	◈	0.637088945
𒀷	740	∪	0.604336795
𒈾	176	⤳	0.527414531
◁	861	◈	0.448069152
‖	440	⌐	0.428539264
⊯	407	ⵢ	0.384003415
⊿	861	◈	0.343489078
𒀭	798	∝	0.303846657
𒀯	176	⤳	0.300530055

Fig. 7. Sumerian symbols passed into the Indus Valley script neural network.

Other scholars have connected the Indus Valley script to Dravidian [16–18, 26, 28–30], where the work from [30] was one of the first publications in regards to using computer aid to decipher the Indus Valley scripts.

The majority of scholars and publications tie the Indus Valley script to indigenous roots. Although, a few scholars exist who believe that the Indus Valley script isn't warranted to be referred to as a language [10]. In their belief, it is comparable to nonlinguistic signs which symbolize family or clan names/symbols and religious figures/ concepts.

Various scholars have proposed that the Indus Valley script is a descendant of other ancient languages; i.e. Elamite. Linguist David McAlpin is the primary supporter for the Elamo-Dravidian hypothesis [15], which links the Indian Dravidian languages to the Elamite language. He believes that the Indus Valley script is could be part of the Dravidian family, and thus be linked to Elamite. Evidence exists of extensive trade between Elam and Indus Valley civilization suggesting a connection between the two regions.

6.2   Database

Bryan Wells and Adreas Fuls have created a database with the Indus Valley script and other ancient scripts [27]. The Indus Valley script sign list according to Wells contains 695 distinct signs [28]. The database shows for each symbol the statistics in regards to its frequency, location, and the texts or items that contain the symbol. The database contains an analysis of the distribution of the symbol. We use this database sign list and frequency statistics, to determine the Indus Valley script symbols which are the most apt.

6.3   Indus Valley Script Vs Phoenician and Brahmi

We have conducted research on comparing the Indus Valley script to the Phoenician alphabet and the Brahmi script [5]. In this work, we show that there is a closer similarity between the Indus Valley script and Phoenician, and less similarity to Brahmi. This is surprising as many scholars perceive the closest relative to be between an indigenous script/language, and our visual unbiased analysis states a different path.

7   Conclusion

Recently the decipherment of ancient scripts has become a multi-disciplinary effort between linguists and computer scientists [22, 23]. The computer science methods in this paper identified a strong connection between the Proto-Elamite alphabet and the Indus Valley Script symbols and that can lead to some interesting scientific deductions. In particular, the neural networks-based matchings between the Proto-Elamite and the Indus Valley symbols suggest some similarity among the two undeciphered scripts.

8   Future Work - Ph.D. Thesis

The data generated is user-created for training purposes. Therefore the open question is *"How would a neural network behave on actual samples of the ancient scripts?"* That is yet to be explored and will require the image datasets for these ancient scripts to be available. For the next phase of this research, we plan to add images from the scripts themselves.

Adding other ancient scripts to this study would benefit in narrowing down the visually most proximal scripts and languages. We plan to research all possible script/alphabet connections to the Indus Valley script without human bias. The use of Neural networks provides us this, however, refinements are needed, as well as a larger sample set.

We plan to extend not only the current datasets but to expand the number of scripts which can be mapped visually to the Indus Valley script. The current datasets are small, and different methods i.e. SVMs or decision trees could be used to see if their conclusions are better. Finally, adding geographic and historical components might lead to a breakthrough in regarding the decipherment of the Indus Valley script.

References

1. A guide to tf layers: Building a convolutional neural network, April 2018. https://www.tensorflow.org/tutorials/layers
2. Bhattacharya, U., Chaudhuri, B.: Databases for research on recognition of handwritten characters of Indian scripts. In: Eighth International Conference on Document Analysis and Recognition, Proceedings, pp. 789–793. IEEE (2005)
3. Blazek, V.: Elam: a bridge between ancient near east and dravidian india. Archaeology and Language IV. Language Change and Cultural Transformation. Routledge, London, New York, pp. 48–78 (1999)
4. Chollet, F.: Building powerful image classification models using very little data, June 2016. https://blog.keras.io/building-powerful-image-classification-models-using-very-little-data.html
5. Daggumati, S., Revesz, P.Z.: Data mining ancient script image data using convolutional neural networks. In: Proceedings of the 22nd International Database Engineering & Applications Symposium. ACM (2018)
6. Dahl, J.L.: Proto-elamite sign frequencies. Cuneiform Digit. Libr. J. **2002**(1) (2002)
7. Devi, H.: Thresholding: A Pixel-Level image processing methodology preprocessing technique for an OCR system for the Brahmi script. Ancient Asia 1 (2006)
8. Englund, R.K.: The proto-elamite script. The World's Writing Systems, pp. 160–164 (1996)
9. Fairservis, W.A.: The Harappan civilization and its writing: a model for the decipherment of the Indus script. Brill (1992)
10. Farmer, S., Sproat, R., Witzel, M.: The collapse of the Indus-script thesis: the myth of a literate Harappan civilization. Electron. J. Vedic Stud. **11**(2), 19–57 (2016)
11. Gupta, S.P., Ramachandran, K.S.: The origin of Brahmi script, vol. 2. DK Publications (1979)
12. Kak, S.C.: A frequency analysis of the Indus script. Cryptologia **12**(3), 129–143 (1988)
13. Kelley, D.H., Wells, B.: Recent developments in understanding the Indus script. Q. Rev. Archaeol. **16**(1), 15–23 (1995)
14. LeCun, Y., Cortes, C., Burges, C.: Mnist handwritten digit database (1998). http://yann.lecun.com/exdb/mnist/
15. McAlpin, D.W.: Proto-elamo-dravidian: the evidence and its implications. Trans. Am. Philos. Soc. **71**(3), 1–155 (1981)
16. Parpola, A.: The Indus script: a challenging puzzle. World Archaeol. **17**(3), 399–419 (1986)
17. Parpola, A.: Study of the Indus script. In: Proceedings of the International Conference of Eastern Studies, vol. 50, pp. 28–66 (2005)
18. Parpola, A.: Deciphering the Indus Script. Cambridge University Press, Cambridge (2009)
19. Rao, R.P., Yadav, N., Vahia, M.N., Joglekar, H., Adhikari, R., Mahadevan, I.: Entropic evidence for linguistic structure in the Indus script. Science **324**(5931), 1165–1165 (2009)
20. Rao, R.P., Yadav, N., Vahia, M.N., Joglekar, H., Adhikari, R., Mahadevan, I.: A Markov model of the Indus script. Proc. Nat. Acad. Sci. **106**(33), 13685–13690 (2009)
21. Rao, S.R.: The Decipherment of the Indus Script. Asia Publishing House, Mumbai (1982)

22. Revesz, P.Z.: Bioinformatics evolutionary tree algorithms reveal the history of the Cretan Script Family. Int. J. Appl. Math. Inf. **10**, 67–76 (2016)
23. Revesz, P.Z.: A computer-aided translation of the Cretan Hieroglyph script. Int. J. Sig. Proces. **1**, 127–133 (2016)
24. Salomon, R.: Deciphering the Indus Script. JSTOR (1996)
25. Salomon, R.: Indian Epigraphy: A Guide to the Study of Inscriptions in Sanskrit, Prakrit, and the Other Indo-Aryan Languages. Oxford University Press, Oxford (1998)
26. Wells, B.: An Introduction to Indus Writing. University of Calgary, Calgary (1998)
27. Wells, B., Fuls, A.: Online Indus Writing Database (2017). http://caddy.igg.tu-berlin.de/indus/welcome.htm
28. Wells, B.K.: Epigraphic approaches to Indus writing. Oxbow Books (2011)
29. Wells, B.K., Fuls, A.: The Archaeology and Epigraphy of Indus Writing. Archaeopress, Oxford (2015)
30. Zide, A.R., Zvelebil, K.V.: The Soviet Decipherment of the Indus Valley Script: Translation and Critique, vol. 156. Walter de Gruyter (1976)

Payload-Based Packet Classification and Its Applications in Packet Forwarding Pipeline

Mohammed Fekhreddine Seridi[✉]

Eötvös Loránd University, Pázmány Péter stny. 1/C, Budapest 1117, Hungary
seridi@inf.elte.hu

Abstract. As the number of protocols and applications is increasing, the need for accurate and dynamic identification methods becomes crucial for many applications such as security and QoS. The SDN and programable data plane architectures changed the way of designing the network and how to implement networking functions. In our work we will use that advance in the architecture to solve the challenge of packet classification. Although there are other payload-based techniques that tackle this problem, but each method has some limitations and it is used in specific scenarios and usually compromise some advantages over some others. The main approaches are either using regular expressions, statistical properties, or some app signature extracted by complex natural language processing techniques. Our approach is aimed to be fast, simple, easy to be implemented, accurate and learn new protocols. To achieve this, we introduced a new approach of keyword generation based on (position, byte) model which insures the uniqueness, in which a protocol is not defined by the statistical properties of the first few bytes of the packets and not all the first few bytes are used. Our work currently is in its mid-stage and it is promising technique that will reduce the complexity and processing time and achieve higher order of accuracy.

Keywords: Protocol identification · Application identification
Packet classification · Payload-based · SDN · P4 · Programable data plane

1 Introduction

Software Defined Networking (SDN) architecture provides a useful way of processing and transmitting data through the network. Since the separation of Control and Data planes provides modularity and allow innovation at each level. The control plane gained a lot of research interest since SDN was invented; and even other layers were added to the model such as Network Virtualization layers. Recently, a revolutionary idea comes to exist, concerning the Data Plane Programmability (DPP). In [1] the Programable Protocol Independent Packet Processing (P4) language which is a convenient tool was introduced. This tool allows the network administrator and researchers to develop and create data-plane-based tailored solutions for specific problems. Large efforts and a growing community are supporting the Portable Switch Architecture (PSA) [2]. In another side by taking a look at the network traffic nowadays, it is clear that the applications and Layer seven (L7) protocols are growing rapidly. These applications and

© Springer Nature Switzerland AG 2018
A. Benczúr et al. (Eds.): ADBIS 2018, CCIS 909, pp. 402–412, 2018.
https://doi.org/10.1007/978-3-030-00063-9_37

protocols have different behavior and they should be treated in different ways. The previously mentioned advances in DPP allow an efficient implementation of forwarding schemes based on L7 protocol.

1.1 Motivation

Processing packets based on their generating applications and the L7 protocols needs, as a first step, to detect these apps and protocols. Standard encapsulation doesn't include explicitly information about the L7 protocols, this fact makes researcher to induce the protocol by looking at other indicators such as the port numbers in the header. Also, the applications, in most of the times, include some signatures (or keywords) in the data. These keywords are usually unique to each application, and some applications also provide many other useful information that could be extracted and used in specific problems. In Fig. 1, we can see the hexadecimal representation of an image file using a file-editor. The underlined worlds represent the file format (3AExif) Exchangeable Image File Format, the brand and the model of the phone (OPPO X9009) and the name of the application (MediaTek Camera Application). In addition to the date and time of taking the picture (don't appear in the figure). Another example is the Bittorrent protocol which always starts with "0x/03bittorrent" keyword. Since the application layer contains some important information, it can be used to classify traffic and make decisions in packet processing and forwarding. Payload based packet classification could be used in large areas in computer networks, such as designing a network architecture, routing and forwarding, queuing, Quality of Service QoS, load balancing and even security check. For example, a Programable data plane architecture could be designed where tables and actions process packets based on the L7 protocol and have the possibility to egress flows through specified ports. Also, the insurance of a high QoS through giving the priority to apps that need less processing time. An example of the security issue is that it could be used to drop or keep flows of given applications. These are just examples to show the importance of the topic.

1.2 Problem Statement

The payload-based packet classification is of high importance and benefits. There exist other techniques such as the port based and deep packet inspection. The problem with the former is that most protocols use dynamic port allocation, and with latter is that it is costly and time consuming and not optimum in many cases. In the previous works [3–5], it was shown that payload-based provide better results with some limitations, in this work we will address some of these challenges. Given a stream of bytes of data how to detect the generating application and specifically how to extract the most representative keywords of each application? In such a way the detection is accurate, and the approach is fast, simple and easy to be implemented, given that the application fingerprint in payload in most of the time is explicitly written, but generally these keywords follow a pattern.

```
            00 01 02 03 04 05 06 07 08 09 0a 0b 0c 0d 0e 0f
0000000000  ff d8 ff e1 33 41 45 78 69 66 00 00 49 49 2a 00   ...3AExif..II*.
0000000010  08 00 00 00 12 00 0e 01 02 00 20 00 00 00 e6 00   .......... .....
0000000020  00 00 0f 01 02 00 20 00 00 00 06 01 00 00 10 01   ...... .........
0000000030  02 00 20 00 00 00 26 01 00 00 12 01 03 00 01 00   .. ...&.........
0000000040  00 00 01 00 00 00 1a 01 05 00 01 00 00 00 46 01   ..............F.
0000000050  00 00 1b 01 05 00 01 00 00 00 4e 01 00 00 28 01   ..........N...(.
0000000060  03 00 01 00 00 00 02 00 00 00 31 01 02 00 20 00   ..........1... .
0000000070  00 00 56 01 00 00 32 01 02 00 14 00 00 00 76 01   ..V...2.......v.
0000000080  00 00 13 02 03 00 01 00 00 00 02 00 00 00 20 02   .............. .
0000000090  04 00 01 00 00 00 00 00 00 00 21 02 04 00 01 00   ..........!.....
00000000a0  00 00 00 00 00 00 22 02 04 00 01 00 00 00 00 00   ......".........
00000000b0  00 00 23 02 04 00 01 00 00 00 00 00 00 00 24 02   ..#...........$.
00000000c0  04 00 01 00 00 00 01 00 00 00 25 02 02 00 20 00   ..........%... .
00000000d0  00 00 8a 01 00 00 69 87 04 00 01 00 00 00 aa 01   ......i.........
00000000e0  00 00 25 88 04 00 01 00 00 00 2c 03 00 00 45 04   ..%.......,...E.
00000000f0  00 00 00 00 00 00 00 00 00 00 00 00 00 00 00 00   ................
0000000100  00 00 00 00 00 00 00 00 00 00 00 00 00 00 00 00   ................
0000000110  00 00 4f 50 50 4f 00 00 00 00 00 00 00 00 00 00   ..OPPO..........
0000000120  00 00 00 00 00 00 00 00 00 00 00 00 00 00 00 00   ................
0000000130  00 00 58 39 30 30 39 00 00 00 00 00 00 00 00 00   ..X9009.........
0000000140  00 00 00 00 00 00 00 00 00 00 00 00 00 00 00 00   ................
0000000150  00 00 48 00 00 00 01 00 00 00 48 00 00 00 01 00   ..H.......H.....
0000000160  00 00 4d 65 64 69 61 54 65 6b 20 43 61 6d 65 72   ..MediaTek Camer
0000000170  61 20 41 70 70 6c 69 63 61 74 69 6f 6e 0a 00 00   a Application...
```

Fig. 1. Hexadecimal representation of an image file

1.3 Structure of the Paper

We have seen that the payload-based classification is promising technique. In this paper wee will show our work on how to optimize the detection of keywords and to make accurate classification. In next section we will summarize the previous approaches and point out their limitations, in Sect. 3 we will describe our idea and show the novelty in it. We will describe our methodology and experiments in Sect. 4. In Sect. 5 we will discuss our future planed work and directions. In Sect. 6 we talk about the applications of our work and Sect. 7 conclude this paper.

2   Previous Works

To understand the challenges in this topic we will look to the pervious works and analyze their results and limitations. In the literature there are mainly three outstanding approaches: Regular expressions based, statistical and machine learning based and using natural language processing techniques. The references [3–5] give good description of these approaches respectively. All these approaches tend to increase the accuracy of the classification using the payload data. These three approaches are detailed bellow.

2.1   Using Regular Expressions

This technique uses previously defined Regular expressions (RegExp) that are obtained from analyzing how apps and protocols create their data. These RegExp are usually predefined. After having these regular expressions for each application and protocol and while classifying the flows, the payload data are matched against these Regular expressions; and if there is a match the flow is considered to belong to the L7 protocol having the matching RegExp. In this case increasing the number of protocols used (i.e. more RegExp) the throughput decreases exponentially even if the processing capacity is increased. Another limitation with is, is that it could not resolve for previously unseen applications. So only the applications with saved RegExp can be detected. In case of a new version of an application or a protocol updates in which the saved RegExps are no more used the classification would be useless. This technique has better performance when checking only the few first packets (practically no more than only one packet per flow) otherwise it will slow down the forwarding system. This approach is best for traffics and networks in which few protocols are used, and the updates are not too frequent

2.2 Statistical Approach

In this case, there is no need to know any expression distinguishing a specific L7 protocol. There are two main stages: Offline stage where the system is trained and an online stage. In the former, the statistical properties of a labeled traffic payloads are analyzed and using different algorithms a classification scheme will be developed. Some popular classification algorithms are Random Forest (RF), Context Tree Weighting (CTW) and Markov models. After training the classifier the statistical probabilities of the model are stored in terms of the distribution of the first byte and transaction probabilities between bytes, this is in the case of zero or first order models. In higher order some techniques to reduce the memory and time complexity are used in [4] an example is to cut the branches that doesn't split anymore in a decision tree. and in the online stage a decision is made based on analyzing the sequence of bytes in the first few bytes of the first few packets for each flow. The experiments show that the system reaches its perfect state in terms of the True Positives and False Positives ratios at 16 bytes of the first packet, any increase in either the number of packets or bytes results in a very moderate improvement. The problem with this approach is that it has a high chance of confusion between protocols with the same statistical properties, also, it detects only the upper L7 protocols in case where two L7 protocols are used for example in case HTML over HTTP only the HTTP is obtained.

In addition, in most of the cases it should be a supervised training since the number of used applications enforces the classes. This approach is best for pre-classification due to its light weight and speed.

2.3 Natural Language Processing Techniques

Since the payload data is a sequence of bytes with a limited alphabet set (the 256 possible bytes) it could be perceived as a structure similar to a natural language where there are some rules that govern the creation of words, their order and their occurrence; and hence natural language processing is applicable to it. This approach was described in [5]. The technique was based on three main offline stage processing steps. After collecting the data, it is used to get protocol language model for the different protocols, this model is created using an approximated Pitman-Yor process and n-gram techniques. Both the data and the model are fed into a protocol keyword inference unit, this unit decides about the most probable keywords that are more representative. And then these keywords are used in learning module to train different weak classifiers using a semi-supervised training algorithm. The online stage consists of keyword interference module that use the language models as a first step, the obtained keywords are used as an input of a protocol classifier that rely on the learning module output. The decision will be made per packet. The advantage of this approach is to apply n-gram in an efficient way in which the computational complexity is overcame. Also, it could learn new protocols and resolve unseen ones, it was shown to be more accurate compared to existing solution. But, the disadvantage of this approach is that it slows down the system in a nutshell due to the two consecutive stages of online processing. This method could be used in situations where the transmission time is of less importance and more accuracy is needed.

2.4   Limitations and Challenges

Each of the previous works comprises between some desired objectives. These techniques either needs predefined regular expressions, and sometimes confuses between similar protocols and even slow down the system and increase complexity. Some solutions enhance the accuracy over the throughput, others allow dynamic classification. These facts create a challenge between the simplicity of the system and how far is it easy to be implemented and ensure that it maintain the general throughput of the system with a high accurate classification and detection.

3   Proposed Solution

Knowing the important of that topic, we tackle this by proposing an approach that will achieve the maximum of the classification objectives. The above-mentioned limitations lead us to think about a solution that will solve the challenge and satisfy some criteria. So, we set the objectives described in the next sub section.

3.1   Objectives of the Solution

Our work focus on creating a solution that benefit from the advance in the field and be more practical. Our main objectives are:

- Fast approach: The online stage processing steps should be minimized as much as possible and make more parallel units rather subsequent ones.
- Simple: The complexity of the core function of the system should be reduced so that only simple operations and less memory are used.
- Implemented easily: As we aim our solution to be practical, implementation is a very important aspect. Also, the two previous objectives make the implementation possible. The advances in programable data plane will help the realization of the solution.

- Accuracy: This is the most important goal in any classification problem. Our solution should detect the exact protocol and don't confuse between protocols with the same properties, and able to resolve multi-protocols available.
- Learn new protocols: This is also important because the number of protocols is augmenting, and updates become too frequent. So, our solution should adopt itself to a fast-changing environment.

Our work doesn't target encrypted traffic for the moment.

3.2 Main Idea and Novelty

Our solution responds the set objectives and exploit the advances in technology in the following way:

- To achieve accuracy, we introduced a new (position, byte) relationship.
- To make the implementation easy an SDN architecture is considered for implementation, where the data plane will perform the online classification.
- To allow innovation and classify previously unseen flows; these flows, for which the data plane is unable to resolve, are sent to the control plane which will use this flow to create a new class in the classifier.

The novelty of our work lies in increasing the perspective of the problem by adding a new dimension to the classification task. All the previous works restrict themselves to the use of a fixed set of bytes [7] (say the first N bytes) of the packets. These bytes are use either to be matched against regular expressions, used to mine keywords or their statistical properties used to build a model. Instead of using all the N bytes in the online stage, specific bytes will be used. The used bytes are set during the offline stage. These elements are chosen to form (location, bytes) pairs. Since the occurrence of given bytes usually in a given protocol is the same location, or at least there exists unique (position, byte) pairs that distinguish each protocol from another. Although the position was used explicitly in the previous works, it is always related to previous and next byte. Also, the first byte of the data is generally follow a random distribution. Even though a relative relation between successive byte position was used to extract keywords, it was not used during the online stage and the matching or keyword lookup is performed over the all N bytes. This suggested approach gives a new way to ensure accuracy and reduce the online processing time. Also, the most informative positions could be after a given number of packets, for example in TCP flows the few first packets doesn't contain any useful data because they are used for establishing connection. Our idea is to find a pattern that governs the distribution of (position, byte) pairs, the positions could be either fixed or dynamic. A protocol will be defined by a set of $(P_i; B_i)$ where P_i's and B_i's are the positions and their corresponding byte content respectively. In fixed byte location pattern, Pi is a number representing the order of the byte starting from the beginning of the data; whereas in dynamic the Pi is a function of other parameters.

In this work we will develop, design and test the classification system. The implementation will be done in our upcoming works.

4 Procedure and Methodology

To achieve the idea described above, we set the following procedure of work.

4.1 Offline Stage Procedure

The task in the offline training of our classifier is to find the model that describe the distribution of the (position, byte) pairs that will distinguish each single protocol from another and ensure the ability to figure out new unseen protocols.

The steps of our work are the following:

1. Collect packet traces: in our work we used Packet Capture (PCAP) files. The data was a real traffic generated manually and captured using Wireshark [6] software. The data generated was enough to test and guarantee the well functionality of our work through the different stages. The data mainly consists of Skype traffic (chatting and 5–10 min video calls), bittorent traffic and other applications. The data collected was for the aim to test the functionality of our algorithms.
   A wide range of data will be used to assess our system and get the final results.
2. Label the flows with their applications: To label the flows, we saved the logs of flows using "netstat" command. The flows and there generating executable files (applications). In case of TCP the netstat command provides the IP source and destination addresses, source and destination TCP port numbers. Incase of UDP flows only a port number is always provided but only in some cases an IP address is provided. In our used data we checked that applications don't share some common port numbers, i.e. each port number is used only in a unique application.
3. Extract the payload: Using packet captures, the payload data was extracted from the packet in the PCAP file. The transport layer protocols are restricted to TCP and UDP protocols only, because they are the most widely used in real network traffic. Also, to reduce complexity with dealing with many layer 4 protocols. Also, IPv6 packets are filtered out so that only IPv4 flows are analyzed, since our goal is analyzing and creating a payload-based classification, the version of the IP protocol is limited to IPv4 for simplicity purposes and to target the most used version. For TCP flows, only packets containing payload data are taken into consideration, since some packet doesn't take any L7 data. In UDP all packets are taken. The payloads are saved in the form of a dictionally (in python), where the keys are the flows' identifiers and the value of the dictionary is a list of the L7 data, where each element in the list is a data contained in one packet. For TCP flows, the flow ID is defined by the IP source address, the TCP source port, the IP destination address and the TCP destination port. For UDP the flow ID is defined by the source and destination ports as far as only one flow uses these ports.
4. Group the payload of each application: After having the flows with their L7 data and the applications with the list of flows belonging to it. These two data are combined to give us a dictionary with keys refer to the different applications used and the value of each key is a list of payloads. Each element in a list represent a data of a packet. For more convenience the data is written in text files, each

application has a text file and each line in a file refer to one packet data. Bytes are separated by a colon ":" and represented in hexadecimal.

5. Take the first N bytes of each packet for each application. All the first N bytes are used in the offline stage. The reason why the few first bytes are chosen, is because the information about the application usually written at the beginning of the data stream and the data in the middle is about the content for example (a message, a video, a website page ...) also, there are some applications that add information at the end and this will be considered in upcoming work. Another problem that will be faced in this case is that the packets are not of the same size. There are small packets with length less than N and other that are too long. There is no problem with long packets. For short packets, our solution was to consider the empty position as a byte with no value (XX) and in the later computations it will be represented by a decimal value (256), remember that "0x/00 and 0x/ff" are represented by the decimal values (0 and 255) respectively.

6. Compute the frequencies of and the Histogram of bytes per position for each protocol. Having N positions and M packets we compute the number of occurrence of each byte at each position. These numbers are normalized over the total number of packets used M. We have 257 possible options, this is 256 the number of possible byte combinations plus the empty position. This will result in 257*N matrix for each protocol analyzed.

7. Compute the entropy with respect to all the protocols for (position, byte) combinations.

8. Create a model that describe the relationship between the positions and bytes. The positions are selected based on their entropy, the ones which contain more information are selected so that their content will distinguish between the analyzed protocols. The selection will be done using some deep learning and Artificial intelligence techniques.

9. Design a classification algorithm: Based on the model obtained in the previous step, we create a classifier that uses the data of the model. This classifier will be used in the online stage.

10. Asses the performance of the system in terms of accuracy (true positives and false negatives) and in terms of the processing speed.

11. Change N the number of positions used and redo the steps from 5 to 10. Create a new model edit the classifier based on the new model. Compare the different results.

4.2 Online Stage Procedure

In the online classification, the bytes in given positions, specified by the (position, byte) model in a given packet are extracted. These bytes form a keyword that will be used in the classifier. The classifier will decide about the application, and the appropriate actions will be performed on that flow.

The general model of our procedure, taking into consideration an SDN architecture, is shown in Fig. 2.

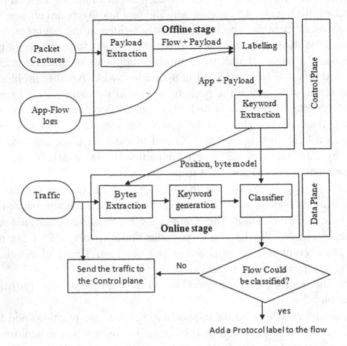

Fig. 2. Architecture of suggested procedure

4.3 Current Status

So far, we have collected the data, label the flows, extract the payload and get the frequencies matrices for each of the protocols. The next step is to obtain the (position, byte) model that will distinguish each protocol from the others. Many decisions, concerning the selection of the classification algorithm and the settings of the model, need to be done.

5 Future Work

In our next research project, we are planning to continue and extend the work described in the previous section. Knowing the need in research, we have some promising research planes and directions. The main planes to extend this work are:

5.1 Implementation on Programmable Switch

Our goal after creating and assessing the classification system is to have an implementation of it. The advantage of this is that we had an experience with P4 programming and it is able to implement any system, architecture and network function in an easy way. Another advantage is that the old-fashioned switches and routers have fixed function and if an extra feature is to be implemented another hardware is usually needed, the flexibility that P4 offers will permit an efficient implementation of our payload classification system.

5.2 Security Checking

Our approach could be slightly edited to fit the detection of malwares, viruses, unwanted applications and any threats that could affect a network. It is also planed to design based on what we have achieved a payload-based firewall.

5.3 Resolve New Protocols

To make our system up to date and able to deal with new protocols, we will add in the implementation an extra function to the control plane. The control plane will update the models based on the new unresolved data. It will provide the data plane with the new updated (position, byte) relationships.

5.4 Bit Level Detection

To reduce the size of keywords and to make the lookup faster, we plane to go to the bit level and define a (position, bit) models that distinguish each protocol from another, instead of the using the whole byte.

5.5 Others

Another way to make an efficient classification is to use hybrid methods where both data from the payload and the header information are combined to get more useful, accurate and practical solutions. The packet position also could be included, for example in case of TCP flows the first few packets could be skipped. Another important thing, which is a different approach of solving the protocol classification challenge, is to solve the roots of the problem by creating an encapsulation method in which the information about the protocol and the application are written in an explicit way.

6 Applications of Packet Classification

The packet classification could be applied to many network functions to improve their performance and provide significant increase in their efficiency. One of the most important things is to create a routing and packet forwarding approach based on the L7 protocol or application, managing the traffic and prioritize flows based on their application and this will result in a good QoS management approach. Also, the congestion control could be improved in some network environments where the most important applications are processed and the less important are either discarded or queued. Another crucial application is the security checking and packet content verification, if some applications are considered harmful or there is a prohibition to use it in a given network, it could be an enterprise network environment.

The way how this could be used and applied is always dependent on the system to be designed in general and the user specific needs.

7 Conclusion

In this paper we presented our research approach, methodology and its actual status. We explained our ideas and showed the significance of our research and the importance of the payload-based packet classification. The novelty of our work is the introduction of a new classification parameter which is the (position, byte) model. Our approach could be implemented on a programable switch architecture which is a promising future of computer networks. SDN is a good architecture to implement our approach. Packet classification is applied widely and one important aspect that it improves in the security of the networking system.

Acknowledgment. The project was supported by the European Union, co-financed by the European Social Fund (EFOP-3.6.3-VEKOP-16-2017-00002).

References

1. Bosshart, P., et al.: P4: programming protocol-independent packet processors. SIGCOMM CCR **44**(3), 87–95 (2014)
2. P4 Consortium. www.p4.org
3. Ando, S., Nakao, A.: L7 packet switch: packet switch applying regular expression to packet payload. In: 2014 IEEE International Workshop Technical Committee on Communications Quality and Reliability (CQR)
4. Hullár, B., Laki, S., György, A.: Efficient methods for early protocol identification. IEEE J. Sel. Areas Commun. **32**(10), 1907–1918 (2014)
5. Wang, Y., Yun, X., Zhang, Y., Chen, L., Zang, T.: Rethinking robust and accurate application protocol identification. Comput. Netw. **129**, 64–78 (2017)
6. Wireshark. https://www.wireshark.org/
7. Sija, B.D., Goo, Y.-H., Shim, K.-S., Hasanova, H., Kim, M.-S.: A survey of automatic protocol reverse engineering approaches, methods, and tools on the inputs and outputs view. Secur. Commun. Netw. **2018**, 17 pages (2018). Article ID 8370341. https://doi.org/10.1155/2018/8370341

Consistency Maintenance in Distributed Analytical Stream Processing

Artem Trofimov[1,2(✉)]

[1] JetBrains Research, St. Petersburg, Russia
trofimov9artem@gmail.com
[2] Saint Petersburg State University, St. Petersburg, Russia

Abstract. State-of-the-art industrial and research projects in the area of distributed stream processing mainly consider only a limited set of delivery-level consistency models, which do not guarantee consistency regarding business requirements. However, such guarantees are able to make stream analytics more reliable. In this paper we define a problem of designing mechanisms, which can detect and possibly fix semantic-based inconsistencies. The results which have been already obtained and a detailed plan of further research are discussed.

1 Introduction

In recent years large-scale data analytics has become a hot area of research and a crucial task for industrial applications [25]. The main reasons behind this fact are the continuous growth of the amount of the data available for analysis and the lack of the appropriate tools. Distributed batch processing systems, e.g., Google MapReduce [9] and Apache Hadoop [1], address some issues of large-scale data analytics. They can provide high throughput while being fault-tolerant and strong consistent in some sense. However, several issues still remain. In particular, MapReduce model suffers from high latency between event arrival and its processing, the lack of iterative processing, the lack of early termination [10], etc. Nevertheless, there are scenarios which require one more of the mentioned properties. These tasks include news processing, fraud detection, short-term personalization, etc.

Distributed stream processing systems were designed to address the mentioned issues with prevention of some consistency guarantees. The central concept of stream processing is a stream. The stream is a potentially unlimited sequence of input items. Typically, stream processing system is a shared-nothing distributed runtime, that handles input items and processes them one-by-one according to user-provided logic. A computational pipeline is usually specified by *execution graph*, where vertices define operations and edges determine the order between them. Operations within the pipeline can be stateless and stateful. The typical system manages the state of operations, e.g., periodically takes snapshots. Flink [7], Samza [21], and Storm [4] are the examples of modern stream processing engines. There are three main types of consistency guarantees

© Springer Nature Switzerland AG 2018
A. Benczúr et al. (Eds.): ADBIS 2018, CCIS 909, pp. 413–422, 2018.
https://doi.org/10.1007/978-3-030-00063-9_38

regarding stream processing, which is considered in the literature [3,6,16]. *At most once* semantics guarantees that each input event is processed once or not processed at all. *At least once* states that each input item is processed, but possibly multiple times. *Exactly once* semantics guarantee that each input event is processed exactly one time. In this work we will call these guarantees *low-level.*

Generally, the main purpose of the users of stream processing systems is to retrieve valuable insights from input data. However, the processing result can be consistent in terms of low-level consistency, but at the same time be entirely incorrect from the business perspective. As an example, we can note the scenario of migration to the new version of data processing pipeline that computes some metrics on a stream. In this case the latest version of the algorithm for metrics can contain bugs. However, only low-level consistency guarantees do not allow to detect this kind of faults.

Therefore, it would be extremely useful for users of stream processing systems to have a mechanism that allows defining a custom consistency semantics. The system should maintain such user-defined consistency or alarm if it is not possible. We will call this kind of consistency *high-level.* As examples of high-level consistency semantics, we can mention requirements for the particular statistical test, suitability of data for making reasonable decisions, and the presence of some structure in data. Although such semantics-based consistency is not a new area of research [12], this task is not seemed to be solved. Some papers on this topic are pure theoretical [13,22], while others propose only some predefined higher-level guarantees [11,20].

Keeping in mind all the mentioned above, a lot of theoretical and practical questions are arising, e.g., How does low-level consistency correspond with high-level? How can it be implemented without high overhead? What is the most appropriate and convenient way to declare custom consistency for users? How to make preserving of high-level consistency suitable for applying in performance-sensitive scenarios? The main purpose of our research work is to try to answer these questions. We aim at designing and evaluating effective mechanisms for high-level consistency within distributed stream processing in order to make large-scale stream analytics more stable and reliable. We believe that this concept can influence the overall efficiency of the process of stream analytics. The following list demonstrates the plan of our research:

1. Analyze modern approaches for achieving low-level consistency and design a new one if needed
2. Investigate existing models and implementations of high-level consistency
3. Understand how low-level and high-level consistency levels are correlated
4. Implement high-level consistency on the top of an efficient implementation of low-level guarantees
5. Design convenient, possibly declarative mechanisms for setting up high-level guarantees
6. Make proposed approaches compatible with state-of-the-art stream processing engines in terms of performance.

Currently, we have been working on the first three steps. It has been realized that some high-level guarantees require low-level consistency, while current methods for achieving exactly-once are too ineffective. In [17] we introduced a novel stream processing model and approach for handling out-of-order items. We briefly showed how these concepts can provide for exactly-once semantics with significantly lower overhead compared to state-of-the-art industrial solutions in [18].

In this paper we discuss the obtained results and share our initial ideas about the rest of our plan. We introduce an idea of *semantic types* concept for declaring computational pipelines within stream processing systems and show how this model can be applied for high-level consistency mechanisms. We demonstrate main problems, which we expect to face, and an initial plan of the implementation.

The rest of the paper is organized as follows: in Sect. 2 we discuss existing approaches for low-level and high-level consistency and analyze their applicability, the results that have been already obtained are detailed in Sect. 3, our plans and prospects regarding high-level consistency are mentioned in Sect. 4, and we summarize the full research in Sect. 5.

2   State of the Art

Currently, low-level and high-level consistency are mainly considered separately from each other. Modern industrial stream processing engines desire to achieve low-level consistency, especially exactly-once semantics. The area of high-level consistency is primarily discussed in research papers. In this section we review some relevant results in both directions.

2.1   Low-Level Consistency

As it was mentioned above, there are several basic low-level guarantees: at most once, at least once, and exactly-once. At most once is the weakest guarantee, so most projects are focused on at least once and exactly-once semantics.

In most approaches, input data is replayed in case of system failures. In this case, to output only valid results, the system must recover some previously snapshotted consistent state before starting the replay. The variations of this method are implemented in Storm [4], Heron [16], Flink [6], and Samza [21]. The common method to take the consistent snapshot is to periodically inject the special items into a stream. These items go along the stream as ordinary elements, but trigger taking snapshots in stateful operations. On recovery, each operation can retrieve previously snapshotted state. However, even if the recovered state of the system is consistent, duplicates can be generated. It can be explained by the fact that most stream processing models are non-deterministic, so it is hard to figure out which data elements have been already released at the moment of failure. Therefore, such approach can only guarantee at least once semantics.

The methods for achieving exactly-once semantics vary more. One way is to atomically take state snapshot and output items that affect the state. This technique is applied in Flink and IBM Streams [15]. The atomicity is obtained using the slight modifications of the 2PC protocol, which provide high-overhead in terms of latency [18].

Another way is to apply so-called *strong productions*, which are introduced in Google MillWheel [3]. The main idea behind this method is to persistently save each input item before each operation in order to filter out duplicates. This approach makes the system idempotent, and, hence, provides for exactly-once semantics. However, accessing persistent storage before each stateful operation can negatively influence latency and throughput.

Exactly-once can also be achieved using strong ordering on data items. Strong ordering requirements lead to deterministic processing, that can be easily converted into idempotence. Currently, this approach is adopted only by so-called *micro-batching* technique, that is used in Spark Streaming [24] and Storm Trident [2]. The main disadvantage of micro-batching is high latency due to extra buffering on input [8].

2.2   High-Level Consistency

The idea that business semantics can be used efficiently in data management is not a new, e.g., in [12] the methods to speed up transactions by providing only guarantees required for the particular problem are proposed. In [13] the model for semantic consistency in communication between collaborators is motivated and discussed. The method to obtain a consistent result in a distributed database even if some nodes are inconsistent is introduced in [22]. In spite of the fact that all these papers provide valuable ideas for the topic, they are rather theoretical than practical. Therefore, it is hard to evaluate the performance of the proposed approaches.

There are several tries to adopt the ideas of semantic consistency for stream processing. In [20] several higher-level consistency models are proposed and evaluated. The mechanisms to dynamically check static semantical criteria are discussed in [11]. Nevertheless, these solutions provide for only a limited set of predefined consistency guarantees, while we aim at entirely custom user-defined consistency semantics.

3   Optimistic Low-Level Consistency

In some cases high-level consistency cannot be implemented without low-level guarantees. For example, if user-defined consistency is based on some metric, the system must ensure that the values of this metric are reliable, not lost, and do not contain duplicates. Therefore, there is a need for exactly-once semantics. However, as it was mentioned above, all existing methods for achieving exactly-once provide high overhead that makes them not suitable for performance-sensitive scenarios.

We propose a novel technique for achieving exactly-once. We introduce a deterministic model that is based on a low-overhead optimistic approach for handling out-of-order items [17]. Determinism implies that if we assign monotonic logical timestamps to input data items at system's entry, the order of output items will be monotonic regarding the timestamps, too. The property of determinism is converted to idempotence by simple deduplication mechanism that maintains the timestamp of the last released item and filters out all items with less timestamp. In [18] we show that such approach is able to significantly outperform alternative solutions in terms of latency.

The central idea behind our extremely low-overhead method for achieving exactly-once is the optimistic model that guarantees that the order between input and output items is preserved in spite of non-deterministic nature of the distributed systems. There are several existing techniques for ordering, but they require extra buffering before each stateful operation [19]. Our speculative approach requires single buffer per computational pipeline. It is based on the following idea: we can assume that all items are ordered and try to fix the data within the stream if out-of-order items exist. This technique can be efficiently implemented because any stateful operation can be expressed in the form of the sequence of a stateless map and windowed grouping operation, while windowed grouping can be easily implemented in an optimistic manner.

4   Providing Reliable Analytics

Our primary goal is to provide high-level user-defined guarantees on data. We start with a discussion about the desired way to define and work with such guarantees from a user perspective. After that, the key problems, which we expect to address, are mentioned. Eventually, we touch on the initial thoughts about the implementation plan.

4.1   Concepts

The key purpose of the high-level consistency mechanisms within stream processing is to validate data in terms of business logic. High-level validation is not a novel approach, e.g., *acceptance tests* have been successfully applying in software engineering for a long time [14]. Acceptance testing is also applied in data processing. As an example, we can mention uniformity checking in test and baseline samples within a popular A/B testing task. Besides, data validation is a key task regarding machine learning model deployment in TFX [5]. However, usage of acceptance testing for stream processing pipelines requires complex technical implementation, because modern engines do not provide native mechanisms for this feature.

In general, acceptance tests validate some statistical or structural constraints on data. Let *semantic type* be a set of high-level consistency constraints with a label. Our goal is to build a system that maps semantic type to the part of the streaming computational pipeline. In this case, a user can define the full pipeline as a sequence of semantic type conversions. The key motivation behind this model is that it is declarative, but unlike common declarative approaches provides for defining high-level constraints by design.

Regarding the A/B test example, we can define "uniform users" semantic type with corresponding constraints. Users data in the stream of this type is guaranteed to be uniform. If it is not, stream processing system alerts and stops processing or tries to fix the issue. A user can also define derivative streams, e.g., "uniform mobile users" or "uniform desktop users". Now, we assume that constraints are statistical or structural, but formulating the complete list of constraint types that we plan to support is an area for further research.

Therefore, we aim at migration from the conservative low-level graph or SQL-based declaration of a computational pipeline to semantic types. It allows users to reason in terms of what to implement from the business perspective, not how to implement it. Hence, users can concentrate on business tasks, while concrete procedures for data transformation are hidden.

4.2   Challenges

Conversions between types can be expressed in the form of ordinary execution graphs. Basic conversions can be defined manually by administrators or defined natively, but the system must automatically infer some defined semantic types from existing ones if it is possible. However, there are several open problems regarding this feature, e.g., it is not clear how to implement type inference subsystem that generates low-level execution plans, which are optimal regarding CPU and network usage, and at the same time provide minimal time for detecting inconsistencies in a stream. Besides, there is a need to design a mechanism that allows determining which type of low-level consistency is needed for the particular high-level requirements. In the most cases, high-level consistency is hard to achieve without strong low-level guarantees. Therefore, our model for low-overhead exactly-once, that is discussed in the previous section, can be successfully applied here.

If a pipeline is defined in terms of semantic types, consistency requirements must be checked after each type conversion. On the execution level type conversion is a sequence of low-level operations, so consistency requirements must be checked after some physical operations. However, operations can be partitioned into multiple computational units. Merging data from all partitions after each operation for consistency checking may provide high overhead on network and serialization. The only way to implement effective consistency maintenance mechanisms is to check requirements independently on each partition. In order to have a strong statistical grounds for this approach, we need to ensure that the distribution of data samples has the same properties on all partitions.

We suppose that user can define distinct consistency requirements on distinct types. Therefore, different parts of the computational pipeline can require different consistency guarantees. Moreover, these requirements can depend on each other. Thus, consistency checking mechanisms can generate additional streams which can go along the execution graph and transfer meta-information about the consistency of some parts of the pipeline. An idea of such additional stream is not new, e.g., the concept of punctuations [23] is similar. Nevertheless, we plan to make these streams more complex and suitable for providing custom high-level guarantees.

Our model of meta-streams for high-level consistency faces a lot of complicated statistical problems. For instance, even perfectly uniform hash functions guarantee only the uniformity of samples, but not the uniformity of the load. For example, the first partition can receive 90% of the data for the first operation and 10% of the data for the second operation, while the proportion of the data for the second partition can be the opposite. Hence, there is a need for statistical corrections for meta-information to achieve statistically significant results. Another example of the problem that we address is to statistically compensate the imperfectness of the hash functions if we know the probability of the collision.

4.3   Implementation Plan

We plan to start the implementation with migration from typical API for manual configuration of execution graph to semantic types-based API within FlameStream stream processing engine [18]. At this point, we consider semantic type just as a label without constraints on data. As it was mentioned above, the complex technical task here is to implement efficient types inference mechanisms, which utilize CPU and network usage.

After that, it is planned to design a suitable approach to declare custom high-level consistency guarantees for particular types. This mechanism should be easy to use for analysts, but flexible enough in order to allow declaring a wide range of constraints, e.g., constraints on data distribution, on a schema, on particular values, etc. We wonder if it is possible to automatically determine required low-level consistency requirements from the high-level definition. If it is not, we plan to allow users to manually set up required low-level guarantees for custom high-level ones.

The next step is to build a subsystem for checking high-level consistency semantics within the whole computational pipeline. Initially, we plan to implement a proof-of-concept without deep performance optimization. Merging data from all partitions after each operation for consistency checking is also acceptable for us on this level. The main goal of the step is to demonstrate that maintenance of high-level consistency semantics is possible within distributed stream processing.

The last step in our list is an accurate performance optimization. We aim at achieving minimal overhead on the proposed functionality. The key problem regarding this step is to design statistical methods for checking high-level consistency independently on each physical partition.

5   Summary

Currently, state-of-the-art stream processing systems concentrate only on proving low-level consistency guarantees. However, it was realized that providing high-level guarantees on the top of low-level can significantly improve the efficiency of stream analytics. Therefore, our objective is to fill this gap and to provide reliable, efficient, and convenient mechanisms for high-level consistency maintenance within distributes stream processing.

We recognized the following main problems on the way to achieving our goal:

- Design low-overhead approach for achieving low-level consistency in order to use it as a building block for high-level guarantees
- Invent convenient and reliable mechanisms to declaratively define high-level guarantees in terms of semantic types
- Realize the correspondence between distinct high-level and low-level consistency requirements
- Efficiently implement meta-stream processing for handling complex high-level guarantees
- Bind data management and statistics in order to obtain reliable and valuable results.

The model of semantic types is a basic concept behind high-level consistency mechanisms. Unlike typical approaches for defining computational pipelines, such model combines declarative approach and custom constraints on data. It allows concentrating on high-level aspects of the data processing task, mitigating implementation details.

Our current contribution is a novel stream processing model that provides for exactly once with extremely low overhead [17,18]. Although this result is a desired part of the full project, there is a lot of an ongoing theoretical and practical work on our track.

References

1. Apache Hadoop, October 2017. http://hadoop.apache.org/
2. Trident, March 2018. http://storm.apache.org/releases/current/Trident-tutorial.html
3. Akidau, T., et al.: Millwheel: fault-tolerant stream processing at internet scale. Proc. VLDB **6**(11), 1033–1044 (2013)
4. Apache Storm, Octoner 2017. http://storm.apache.org/
5. Baylor, D., et al.: Tfx: a tensorflow-based production-scale machine learning platform. In: Proceedings of the 23rd ACM SIGKDD International Conference on Knowledge Discovery and Data Mining, KDD 2017, pp. 1387–1395. ACM, New York (2017). https://doi.org/10.1145/3097983.3098021
6. Carbone, P., Ewen, S., Fóra, G., Haridi, S., Richter, S., Tzoumas, K.: State management in Apache Flink®: consistent stateful distributed stream processing. Proc. VLDB **10**(12), 1718–1729 (2017)

7. Carbone, P., Katsifodimos, A., Ewen, S., Markl, V., Haridi, S., Tzoumas, K.: Apache Flink: stream and batch processing in a single engine. Bull. IEEE Comput. Soc. Tech. Comm. Data Eng. **36**(4), 28–38 (2015)
8. Chintapalli, S., et al.: Benchmarking streaming computation engines: storm, flink and spark streaming. In: 2016 IEEE International Parallel and Distributed Processing Symposium Workshops (IPDPSW), pp. 1789–1792, May 2016. https://doi.org/10.1109/IPDPSW.2016.138
9. Dean, J., Ghemawat, S.: Mapreduce: simplified data processing on large clusters. Commun. ACM **51**(1), 107–113 (2008). https://doi.org/10.1145/1327452.1327492
10. Doulkeridis, C., Norvaag, K.: A survey of large-scale analytical query processing in mapreduce. VLDB J. **23**(3), 355–380 (2014)
11. Fischer, P.M., Esmaili, K.S., Miller, R.J.: Stream schema: providing and exploiting static metadata for data stream processing. In: Proceedings of the 13th International Conference on Extending Database Technology, EDBT 2010, pp. 207–218. ACM, New York (2010). https://doi.org/10.1145/1739041.1739068
12. Garcia-Molina, H.: Using semantic knowledge for transaction processing in a distributed database. ACM Trans. Database Syst. **8**(2), 186–213 (1983). https://doi.org/10.1145/319983.319985
13. Guo, J., Lam, I.H., Chan, C., Xiao, G.: Collaboratively maintaining semantic consistency of heterogeneous concepts towards a common concept set. In: Proceedings of the 2nd ACM SIGCHI Symposium on Engineering Interactive Computing Systems, EICS 2010, pp. 213–218. ACM, New York (2010). https://doi.org/10.1145/1822018.1822052
14. Hambling, B., Van Goethem, P.: User acceptance testing: a step-by-step guide. BCS Learning & Development (2013)
15. Jacques-Silva, G., et al.: Consistent regions: guaranteed tuple processing in IBM streams. Proc. VLDB Endow. **9**(13), 1341–1352 (2016)
16. Kulkarni, S., et al.: Twitter heron: stream processing at scale. In: Proceedings of the 2015 ACM SIGMOD International Conference on Management of Data, SIGMOD 2015, pp. 239–250. ACM, New York (2015). https://doi.org/10.1145/2723372.2742788
17. Kuralenok, I.E., Marshalkin, N., Trofimov, A., Novikov, B.: An optimistic approach to handle out-of-order events within analytical stream processing. Accepted at SEIM (2018). http://seim-conf.org/en/about/accepted-papers/
18. Kuralenok, I.E., Trofimov, A., Marshalkin, N., Novikov, B.: Flamestream: model and runtime for distributed stream processing. In: Proceedings of the 5th ACM SIGMOD Workshop on Algorithms and Systems for MapReduce and Beyond, BeyondMR 2018, pp. 8:1–8:2. ACM, New York (2018). https://doi.org/10.1145/3206333.3209273
19. Li, J., Tufte, K., Shkapenyuk, V., Papadimos, V., Johnson, T., Maier, D.: Out-of-order processing: a new architecture for high-performance stream systems. Proc. VLDB Endow. **1**(1), 274–288 (2008)
20. Mihaila, G.A., Stanoi, I., Lang, C.A.: Anomaly-free incremental output in stream processing. In: Proceedings of the 17th ACM Conference on Information and Knowledge Management, CIKM 2008, pp. 359–368. ACM, New York (2008). https://doi.org/10.1145/1458082.1458132
21. Noghabi, S.A., et al.: Samza: stateful scalable stream processing at Linkedin. Proc. VLDB Endow. **10**(12), 1634–1645 (2017)

22. Rodríguez, M.A., Bertossi, L., Caniupán, M.: An inconsistency tolerant approach to querying spatial databases. In: Proceedings of the 16th ACM SIGSPATIAL International Conference on Advances in Geographic Information Systems, GIS 2008, pp. 36:1–36:10. ACM, New York (2008). https://doi.org/10.1145/1463434.1463480

23. Tucker, P.A., Maier, D., Sheard, T., Fegaras, L.: Exploiting punctuation semantics in continuous data streams. IEEE Trans. Knowl. Data Eng. **15**(3), 555–568 (2003). https://doi.org/10.1109/TKDE.2003.1198390

24. Zaharia, M., Das, T., Li, H., Shenker, S., Stoica, I.: Discretized streams: an efficient and fault-tolerant model for stream processing on large clusters. In: Proceedings of the 4th USENIX Conference on Hot Topics in Cloud Ccomputing, HotCloud 2012, p. 10. USENIX Association, Berkeley (2012)

25. Zou, Q., et al.: From a stream of relational queries to distributed stream processing. Proc. VLDB Endow. **3**(1–2), 1394–1405 (2010)

Author Index

Abid, Younes 105
Azuan, Nurzety A. 3

Bellatreche, Ladjel 45
Belyaev, Kirill 12
Benndorf, Dirk 80
Bielikova, Maria 63
Braslavski, Pavel 71
Breja, Manvi 265
Broneske, David 80
Bub, Udo 91, 327

Campero Durand, Gabriel 80
Caroprese, Luciano 297
Cascini, Pietro Lucio 297
Cauteruccio, Francesco 153
Cerquitelli, Tania 138, 205
Chiusano, Silvia 205
Cimini, Giampiero 191
Cinaglia, Pietro 297

Daggumati, Shruti 391
Dahanayake, Ajantha 91, 218, 231, 242
Daraio, Elena 205
Darmont, Jérôme 91
Dattola, Francesco 297
De Matteis, Andrea 178
Di Cerbo, Francesco 118
Di Corso, Evelina 205
Diamantini, Claudia 91, 165
Dulai, Tibor 352

Embury, Suzanne M. 3
Endres, Markus 20

Fassetti, Fabio 91
Fazekas, Bálint 29
Fenske, Wolfram 80
Fermé, Eduardo 91
Fiannaca, Antonino 314
Franco, Pasquale 297

Giacalone, Francesco 138
Giudice, Paolo Lo 165

Gorbulin, Andrei 218
Gusev, Vladimir 71

Hao, Wei 54
Hasan, Kazi Saidul 286
Helmer, Sven 37
Heyer, Robert 80

Iaquinta, Pasquale 297
Imine, Abdessamad 105
Ioini, Nabil El 37
Iusi, Miriam 297

Jain, Sanjay Kumar 265
Janki, Atin 80

Kabachi, Nadia 91
Khouri, Selma 45
Kiss, Attila 29

La Rosa, Massimo 314
Lapadula, Paola 305
Lewis, Dave 127
Lo Bosco, Giosué 314
Loginova, Ekaterina 274
Longo, Antonella 178
Lu, Jing 339

Matsuzaki, Kiminori 54
Matteucci, Ilaria 91
Mecca, Giansalvatore 305
Mircoli, Alex 191
Molnár, Bálint 91, 364
Moro, Robert 63
Musarella, Lorenzo 165
Musto, Jiri 231

Nagy, Zsuzsanna 352
Navathe, Sham 91
Neumann, Günter 274

O'Sullivan, Declan 127
Öri, Dóra 364, 377
Oro, Ermelinda 91

Pahl, Claus 37
Pandit, Harshvardhan Jitendra 127
Paton, Norman W. 3
Petrocchi, Marinella 91
Potena, Domenico 165, 178

Ravindran, Rohith 80
Ray, Indrakshi 12
Rizzo, Riccardo 314
Roggia, Matteo 37
Rombo, Simona E. 91
Rudenko, Lena 20
Ruffolo, Massimo 91
Rusinowitch, Michaël 105

Saake, Gunter 80
Santoro, Donatello 305
Sato, Shigeyuki 54
Schallert, Kay 80
Seridi, Mohammed Fekhreddine 402
Solimando, Luisa 305
Spognardi, Angelo 91
Stefancova, Elena 63
Storti, Emanuele 165, 178
Szabó, Zoltán 377

Terracina, Giorgio 153
Thalheim, Bernhard 91

Tiufiakov, Nikita 242
Trabelsi, Slim 118
Tradigo, Giuseppe 297
Trofimov, Artem 413
Tropmann-Frick, Marina 254

Ursino, Domenico 91, 165
Urso, Alfonso 314

Varanasi, Stalin 274
Veltri, Enzo 305
Veltri, Pierangelo 297
Ventura, Francesco 138

Wang, Zhiguo 286
Werner-Stark, Ágnes 352

Yu, Mo 286
Yu, Yang 286

Zappatore, Marco 178
Zhagorina, Ksenia 71
Zhang, Wei 286
Zoun, Roman 80
Zudilova, Tatiana 218, 242
Zumpano, Ester 297

Printed in the United States
by Bookmasters

Printed in the United States
By Bookmasters